RENEWALS 458-4574

DATE DUE

GAYLORD   PRINTED IN U.S.A.

THE ROUTLEDGE COMPANION
TO PHILOSOPHY OF SCIENCE

The Routledge Companion to Philosophy of Science is an outstanding guide to the major themes, movements, debates and topics in philosophy of science. Fifty-five entries by a team of renowned international contributors are organized into four parts:

- Historical and Philosophical Context
- Debates
- Concepts
- Individual Sciences

The *Companion* begins with a critical examination of how philosophy of science has been involved in a mutually fruitful interaction with philosophical theories in areas such as metaphysics, epistemology, and the philosophy of language, and reassesses the major schools of philosophy of science in the twentieth century.

The second part explores the development of current debates among philosophers and scientists on issues such as confirmation, explanation, realism, scientific method, and the ethics of science. Part three discusses controversial concepts such as causation, prediction, unification, observation, and probability that lie at the heart of many disputes about science and scientific theories. The final part addresses some of the main philosophical problems that arise within eight branches of science: biology, chemistry, cognitive science, economics, mathematics, physics, psychology, and the social sciences.

The Routledge Companion to Philosophy of Science is essential reading for anyone interested in philosophy of science and the connections between philosophy and the natural and social sciences.

Stathis Psillos is an Associate Professor of Philosophy of Science at the University of Athens, Greece. He is the author of *Scientific Realism: How Science Tracks Truth* (Routledge), *Causation and Explanation* and *Philosophy of Science A–Z*.

Martin Curd is an Associate Professor of Philosophy at Purdue University, USA. He is co-editor (with Jan Cover) of *Philosophy of Science: The Central Issues*.

Routledge Philosophy Companions

Routledge Philosophy Companions offer thorough, high quality surveys and assessments of the major topics and periods in philosophy. Covering key problems, themes and thinkers, all entries are specially commissioned for each volume and written by leading scholars in the field. Clear, accessible and carefully edited and organised, *Routledge Philosophy Companions* are indispensable for anyone coming to a major topic or period in philosophy, as well as for the more advanced reader.

The Routledge Companion to Aesthetics, Second Edition
Edited by Berys Gaut and Dominic Lopes

The Routledge Companion to Philosophy of Religion
Edited by Chad Meister and Paul Copan

The Routledge Companion to Philosophy of Science
Edited by Stathis Psillos and Martin Curd

The Routledge Companion to Twentieth Century Philosophy
Edited by Dermot Moran

Forthcoming:
The Routledge Companion to Nineteenth Century Philosophy
Edited by Dean Moyar

The Routledge Companion to Philosophy of Psychology
Edited by John Symons and Paco Calvo

The Routledge Companion to Philosophy of Film
Edited by Paisley Livingston and Carl Plantinga

The Routledge Companion to Ethics
Edited by John Skorupski

The Routledge Companion to Metaphysics
Edited by Robin Le Poidevin, Peter Simons, Andrew McGonigal, and Ross Cameron

The Routledge Companion to Epistemology
Edited by Sven Bernecker and Duncan Pritchard

The Routledge Companion to Seventeenth Century Philosophy
Edited by Dan Kaufman

The Routledge Companion to Eighteenth Century Philosophy
Edited by Aaron Garrett

THE
ROUTLEDGE COMPANION
TO PHILOSOPHY OF
SCIENCE

Edited by
Stathis Psillos and
Martin Curd

Routledge
Taylor & Francis Group

LONDON AND NEW YORK

First published 2008
by Routledge
2 Park Square, Milton Park, Abingdon, OX14 4RN

Simultaneously published in the USA and Canada
by Routledge
270 Madison Ave, New York, NY 10016

Routledge is an imprint of the Taylor & Francis Group, an informa business

Typeset in 10.5/13pt Goudy Oldstyle Std by Fakenham Photosetting, Fakenham, Norfolk
Printed and bound in Great Britain by TJ International Ltd, Padstow, Cornwall

British Library Cataloguing in Publication Data
A catalogue record for this book is available from the British Library

Library of Congress Cataloging in Publication Data
The Routledge companion to philosophy of science / edited by Stathis Psillos and Martin Curd.
p. cm. -- (Routledge philosophy companions)
Includes bibliographical references and index.
1. Science--Philosophy. I. Psillos, Stathis, 1965- II. Curd, Martin.
Q175.R68 2008
501--dc22
2007020000

ISBN10: 0-415-35403-X (hbk)
ISBN10: 0-203-00050-1 (ebk)
ISBN13: 978-0-415-35403-5 (hbk)
ISBN13: 978-0-203-00050-2 (ebk)

CONTENTS

CONTENTS

PART III

ILLUSTRATIONS

FIGURES

TABLE

CONTRIBUTORS

Peter Achinstein is Professor of Philosophy at Johns Hopkins University, and author of many works in the philosophy of science, including *The Book of Evidence* (2001) and *Particles and Waves* (which received the Lakatos Award in 1993).

Robert Almeder is the recent Alan McCullough Distinguished Professor of Philosophy at Hamilton College in Clinton, New York. He has published several essays on American Philosophy, and his books include *The Philosophy of Charles Peirce: A Critical Introduction* (1980), *Blind Realism: An Essay on Human Knowledge and Natural Science* (1991), and *Harmless Naturalism: The Limits of Science and the Nature of Philosophy* (1998).

Theodore Arabatzis is an Assistant Professor in the Department of Philosophy and History of Science at the University of Athens. He is the author of *Representing Electrons: A Biographical Approach to Theoretical Entities* (2006).

Roger Ariew is Professor and Chair, Department of Philosophy, University of South Florida, author of *Descartes and the Last Scholastics* (1999) and editor of *Perspectives on Science: Historical, Philosophical, Social*. His primary area of research is early modern philosophy and science, especially that of Descartes and Leibniz, and he has an abiding interest in historicist philosophy of science.

Maria Baghramian is Associate Professor of Philosophy in the School of Philosophy, University College Dublin. She is the author of *Relativism* (2004) and editor of the *International Journal of Philosophical Studies*.

Diderik Batens is Professor of Logic and Philosophy of Science and director of the Center for Logic and Philosophy of Science at Ghent University, Belgium. Currently, he is completing a book on adaptive logics.

Rod Bertolet is Professor of Philosophy at Purdue University. He is the author of *What Is Said: A Theory of Indirect Speech Reports* (1990) and numerous articles in the philosophy of language, as well as a few in philosophy of mind, metaphysics, and epistemology.

Alexander Bird is Professor of Philosophy at the University of Bristol. He is the author of *Philosophy of Science* (2nd edn, 2005), *Thomas Kuhn* (2000), and *Nature's Metaphysics* (2007). His research interests include Kuhn, naturalism, epistemology, and the metaphysics of science.

Nancy Cartwright is Professor of Philosophy at the London School of Economics and at the University of California at San Diego, and Director of the Centre for

Philosophy of Natural and Social Science at LSE. Her original area of research was philosophy of physics but her primary research interests now are in philosophy of the social and economic sciences, especially in questions that matter for putting science to use, such as modeling, causation, objectivity, and evidence.

Hasok Chang is Reader in Philosophy of Science at University College London. His primary research area is the history and philosophy of physics and chemistry from the eighteenth century onward. He is the author of *Inventing Temperature: Measurement and Scientific Progress* (2004), which was a co-winner of the 2006 Lakatos Award.

Peter Clark is Professor of Philosophy and Head of the School of Philosophical, Anthropological, and Film Studies in the University of St Andrews. He works primarily in the philosophy of physical sciences and mathematics, and was editor of the *British Journal for the Philosophy of Science* (1999–2005). He is co-editor (with Katherine Hawley) of *Philosophy of Science Today* (2003).

Michael Devitt is a Distinguished Professor of Philosophy at the Graduate Center of the City University of New York. He is the author of *Designation* (1981), *Coming to Our Senses: A Naturalistic Defense of Semantic Localism* (1996), *Ignorance of Language, Realism and Truth* (1997), and (with Kim Sterelny) *Language and Reality: An Introduction to the Philosophy of Language* (1999).

Gerald Doppelt is Professor of Philosophy at the University of California, San Diego, and is a UCSD Academic Senate Distinguished Teacher. He has published widely in philosophy of science and political philosophy.

Igor Douven is Professor of Philosophy at the University of Leuven. He has published mainly on topics in the philosophy of science and epistemology, such as the realism debate, confirmation theory, and formal theories of coherence.

Brian Ellis is Emeritus Professor at La Trobe University and Professorial Fellow in Philosophy at the University of Melbourne, Australia. He is the author of *Scientific Essentialism* (2001) and *The Philosophy of Nature* (2002), and other books on philosophy of science or metaphysics.

Malcolm Forster is Professor of Philosophy at the University of Wisconsin–Madison. His published research has focused mainly on the foundations of statistical inference and general philosophy of science, even though most of his time is spent pondering the mysteries of the quantum world.

Steven French is Professor of Philosophy of Science at the University of Leeds. He is the editor of *Metascience* and co-author (with Newton da Costa) of *Science and Partial Truth* (with Newton da Costa; 2003) and (with Décio Krause) *Identity in Physics* (2006).

Maria Carla Galavotti is Professor of Philosophy of Science at the University of Bologna. Her main research topics are explanation, causality, and the foundations of probability. She recently published *A Philosophical Introduction to Probability* (2005) and edited *Cambridge and Vienna: Frank P. Ramsey and the Vienna Circle* (2006).

Ronald N. Giere is Professor of Philosophy Emeritus, and a member and former Director of the Center for Philosophy of Science, at the University of Minnesota. A past President of the Philosophy of Science Association, he is the author of *Understanding Scientific Reasoning* (5th edn, 2006), *Explaining Science: A Cognitive Approach* (1988), *Science Without Laws* (1999), and *Scientific Perspectivism* (2006).

Stuart Glennan is Professor of Philosophy at Butler University in Indianapolis. His main areas of research are causation, explanation, and the nature of mechanisms.

Alan Hájek is Professor of Philosophy at the Research School of Social Sciences at the Australian National University. His primary areas of research are the philosophical foundations of probability and decision theory.

Robin Findlay Hendry is Senior Lecturer in Philosophy at Durham University. He has published on the history and philosophy of chemistry, and has recently completed a book on chemical kinds and the relationship between physics and chemistry.

Christopher Hitchcock is Professor of Philosophy at the California Institute of Technology. He has published numerous articles in the philosophy of science, especially on the topic of causation.

Colin Howson is Professor of Philosophy at the London School of Economics and Political Science, and the author of *Logic With Trees* (1997), *Hume's Problem: Induction and the Justification of Belief* (2001), and (with Peter Urbach) *Scientific Reasoning: the Bayesian Approach* (3rd edn, 2006).

Gürol Irzik is Professor of Philosophy at Bogazici University, Istanbul. He has published on causal modeling, Carnap, Popper, Kuhn, and science education. Recently, he co-authored (with Robert Nola) *Philosophy, Science, Education and Culture* (2005).

Todd Jones is the Chair of the Philosophy Department at the University of Nevada, Las Vegas. He has degrees in philosophy, cognitive science, and anthropology. His research centers around explanation in the social sciences.

James M. Joyce is a Professor of Philosophy at the University of Michigan. His research concerns epistemology, rational choice, and philosophical aspects of probability theory. His better-known works include *The Foundations of Causal Decision Theory*

(1999), "A Nonpragmatic Vindication of Probabilism," *Philosophy of Science* (1998), and "How Degrees of Belief Reflect Evidence," *Philosophical Perspectives* (2005).

Harold Kincaid is Professor of Philosophy at the University of Alabama in Birmingham and is the author of *Philosophical Foundation of the Social Sciences* (1996) and co-editor of *Value-Free Science: Ideals and Illusions* (2007) and *The Oxford Handbook of the Philosophy of Economics* (forthcoming).

André Kukla is Professor Emeritus at the University of Toronto. His books include *Studies in Scientific Realism* (1998), *Ineffability and Philosophy* (2005), and *Mental Traps* (forthcoming).

James Ladyman is Professor of Philosophy at the University of Bristol and co-editor of the *British Journal for the Philosophy of Science*. He is the author of *Understanding Philosophy of Science* (2002), and (with Don Ross, Don Spurrett, and John Collier) of *Every Thing Must Go: Metaphysics Naturalised* (2007).

Marc Lange is Professor of Philosophy at the University of North Carolina, Chapel Hill. His books include: *Natural Laws in Scientific Practice* (2000), *An Introduction to the Philosophy of Physics: Locality, Fields, Energy, and Mass* (2002), and *Laws and Lawmakers* (forthcoming).

Peter Lipton (1954–2007) was the Hans Rausing Professor of the History and Philosophy of Science at Cambridge University and a Fellow of King's College. He was the author of *Inference to the Best Explanation* (2nd edn, 2004).

Barry Loewer is Professor of Philosophy and Director of the Rutgers Center for Philosophy and the Sciences. He has published papers in philosophy of science, philosophy of mind, and philosophy of language. He is currently finishing a book on laws, chances, and causation.

Uskali Mäki is an Academy Professor at the Academy of Finland. Previously, he was Professor of Philosophy at the Erasmus Institute for Philosophy and Economics, Rotterdam, and an editor of the *Journal of Economic Methodology*.

Ernan McMullin is O'Hara Professor Emeritus of Philosophy at the University of Notre Dame. Much of his writing has been directed at the historical dimension of the philosophy of science.

Margaret Morrison is Professor of Philosophy at the University of Toronto. Her main research interests are in the history and philosophy of physics and she is the author of *Unifying Scientific Theories: Physical Concepts and Mathematical Structures* (2000).

Stephen Mumford is Professor of Metaphysics at the University of Nottingham. Author of *Dispositions* (1998) and *Laws in Nature* (2004), he is currently working on the metaphysics of causation.

Thomas Nickles is Professor of Philosophy and Adjunct Professor of Psychology at the University of Nevada, Reno. Among his interests are problem-solving, heuristics, and frontier epistemology. He recently edited *Thomas Kuhn* (2003).

Robert Nola is Professor of Philosophy at the University of Auckland, New Zealand. His more recent books are *Rescuing Reason* (2003) and (with Gürol Irzik) *Philosophy, Science, Education and Culture* (2006).

Graham Oddie is Professor of Philosophy at the University of Colorado, in Boulder. His main philosophical focus has been the nature of realism, and he has published on philosophy of science, metaphysics, and value theory, including *Likeness to Truth* (1986) and *Value, Reality, and Desire* (2005).

Cassandra L. Pinnick teaches philosophy at Western Kentucky University.

Oliver Pooley is Lecturer in Philosophy at Oxford University and Fellow and Tutor in Philosophy at Oriel College, Oxford. He is writing a book on the reality of spacetime.

Demetris Portides is Assistant Professor of Philosophy of Science at the University of Cyprus. He has published on the nature and function of models, the nature of the processes of idealization, and abstraction in scientific modeling. His current research focuses primarily on the nature and structure of scientific theories and models.

David B. Resnik is a bioethicist at the National Institute of Environmental Health Sciences, National Institutes of Health. He is the author of six books, including *Responsible Conduct of Research* (2003), *Owning the Genome* (2004), and *The Price of Truth* (2006).

Alexander Rosenberg is R. Taylor Cole Professor of Philosophy and Biology at Duke University. He won the Lakatos Award in 1993 and was the Phi Beta Kappa Romanell Lecturer in 2007. His most recent book is *Darwinian Reductionism or How to Stop Worrying and Love Molecular Biology* (2006).

Paul A. Roth is Professor and Chair of the Philosophy Department at the University of California, Santa Cruz. His primary areas of research and publication are naturalism in epistemology and explanation in science and social science (particularly history).

Richard Samuels is Professor of Philosophy at Ohio State University, USA. His primary areas of research are in the philosophy of psychology and foundations of cognitive science. He is writing a book on cognitive architecture.

Howard Sankey is Associate Professor in the School of Philosophy at the University of Melbourne, Australia, with teaching responsibilities in the Program in History and Philosophy of Science. His areas of research and publication include semantic incommensurability, relativism and rational theory-choice, methodology, epistemic naturalism, and scientific realism.

Sahotra Sarkar is Professor in the Section of Integrative Biology and the Departments of Geography and Environment and Philosophy at the University of Texas, Austin. He is author of *Genetics and Reductionism* (1998), *Molecular Models of Life* (2004), *Biodiversity and Environmental Philosophy* (2005), *Doubting Darwin? Creationist Designs on Evolution* (2007), and (with Chris Margules) *Systematic Conservation Planning* (2007).

Simon Saunders is Reader in the Philosophy of Physics and a Fellow of Linacre College at Oxford University. He has recently been working on symmetries, discrete and continuous.

Elliott Sober is Hans Reichenbach Professor of Philosophy at University of Wisconsin, Madison. He wrote *The Nature of Selection* (1984), *Reconstructing the Past* (1988), *Philosophy of Biology* (1994), and (with David Sloan Wilson) *Unto Others – the Evolution and Psychology of Unselfish Behavior* (1998). His book *Evidence and Evolution* is forthcoming (2008).

Paul Teller is Professor of Philosophy at the University of California, in Davis. He has published extensively on interpretive problems in quantum theories and many other topics in the philosophy of science. Currently his particular interest is in the repercussions of seeing science as a model-building enterprise.

Paul Thagard is Professor of Philosophy and Director of the Cognitive Science Program at the University of Waterloo, Canada. His recent books are *Mind: Introduction to Cognitive Science* (2nd edn, 2005) and *Hot Thought: Mechanisms and Applications of Emotional Cognition* (2006).

Thomas Uebel is Professor of Philosophy at the University of Manchester. Most of his research concerns the history of philosophy of science. His most recent publication (co-edited with Alan Richardson) is the *Cambridge Companion to Logical Empiricism* (2007).

Denis Walsh holds the Canada Research Chair in Philosophy of Biology in the Department of Philosophy and the Institute for the History and Philosophy of Science and Technology at the University of Toronto. His primary research interest is in the relations between statistical, teleological, and causal explanations in evolutionary biology.

Joanne Waugh is Associate Chair and Director of Graduate Studies in the Department of Philosophy, University of South Florida. Her areas of research include ancient

Greek philosophy and aesthetics, but she is interested in the history of philosophy, in general, and the historiography of philosophy, in particular. She also works in feminist philosophy and is co-editor of *Feminists Doing Ethics* (2001).

James Woodward is J. O. and Juliette Koepfli Professor of the Humanities at the California Institute of Technology. He is the author of *Making Things Happen* (2003), which won the 2005 Lakatos Award.

John Worrall is Professor of Philosophy of Science at the London School of Economics. He is the author of numerous articles on confirmation theory, the rationality of theory-change in science, and scientific realism, and is currently completing *Reason in 'Revolution': A Study of Theory-Change in Science*. He is also now researching issues concerning evidence in medicine.

INTRODUCTION
Stathis Psillos and Martin Curd

Philosophy of science deals with philosophical and foundational problems that arise within science. It can be divided into two major strands: general philosophy of science and the philosophies of the individual sciences. General philosophy of science strives to understand science as a cognitive activity that is uniquely capable of yielding justified beliefs about the world; the philosophy of the individual sciences focuses on more specialized issues within physics, biology, psychology, economics, etc. Some of the questions raised by general philosophy of science are:

- What is the aim (or aims) of science and what is its method (or methods)? More generally: What *is* science, in the first place, and how does it differ from non-science and pseudo-science?
- What is a scientific theory and how do scientific theories relate to (and thus represent) the world? How do theoretical concepts get their meaning and how are they related to observation?
- What is the structure and content of concepts such as causation, explanation, confirmation, theory, experiment, model, reduction, and probability?
- What rules, if any, govern theory-change in science? What is the function of experiment? What role do values (both epistemic and pragmatic) play in scientific decisions and how are they related to social, cultural, and gender factors?

Some of the questions raised by philosophers of the individual sciences concern the basic conceptual structure of particular sciences (e.g., the problem of measurement in quantum mechanics, the ontology of space and time, the concepts of biological function and adaptation, the nature of psychological and sociological explanation, and the status of economic models). Others relate to the commitments that flow from the individual sciences (What is the right interpretation of quantum mechanics? Are there laws in the special sciences? What is the status of causal mechanisms?). The philosophies of the individual sciences have acquired an unprecedented maturity and independence over the last few decades. This seems to have been due to, among other things, the collapse of simple-minded reductive and hierarchical accounts of how science is ordered. Shifting attention from the macro-structure of science towards the micro-structure of the individual sciences promises answers even to the most general philosophical questions about science. Still, there is a sense in which the science we build is one, and looking for a unified and broad understanding of this science is bound to remain among the central concerns of philosophers of science.

General philosophy of science is as old as philosophy itself, especially if we take into account that science has long been regarded as a paradigm of privileged knowledge (Greek: *episteme*; Latin: *scientia*); that is, systematic and reliable knowledge of the world as opposed to mere opinion or ungrounded belief. From the ancient Greeks onwards, philosophers have taken science as an exemplar and sought to understand its nature and methods. Aristotle's view – which prevailed until the seventeenth century – saw science as a stable, deductive structure based on first principles. These first principles (about forms and essences) are arrived at from the world as it appears to us by a process that Aristotle called "induction" (that is, for Aristotle, by observation and intellectual reflection, not by experiment) and provide understanding of observed patterns ("knowledge of the reasoned fact" – why things have to be the way they are) via their role as premises in causal explanations. For Aristotelians, the first principles of science are necessary truths about the natures of things expressed in qualitative, universal generalizations. Thus, Aristotelian science is both realist and empiricist. Science is a deductive, axiomatic structure whose aim is causal explanation (not prediction) based on first principles about the essences of things. Those first principles are derived from experience and known with certainty. Aristotle's formal, deductive model of science was Euclidean geometry; his best empirical example was biology.

In two areas, Aristotelian science failed miserably: terrestrial and planetary motion. Qualitative generalizations such as "earthy bodies tend to move towards the center of the universe" and "Planets tend to move in circles with uniform speed about the center of the universe" were incapable of accounting for the trajectory of projectiles, the acceleration of falling bodies, or the details of the apparent retrograde motion of the planets against the backdrop of the stars. Beginning with Ptolemy, astronomers abandoned the official Aristotelian account of science as they developed increasingly sophisticated, quantitatively accurate models of planetary motion. Some astronomers remained frustrated Aristotelian realists; others became more or less openly instrumentalists (at least about astronomy). After the Copernican revolution and the new science of motion pioneered by Galileo and Descartes – a theory that applied to all bodies, whether terrestrial or celestial – the time was ripe for a reassessment of the nature of science and its method.

For Galileo, Francis Bacon, and René Descartes, post-Aristotelian science required a new method; but the nature of that method remained a matter of dispute. Was it, ultimately, inductive or hypothetico-deductive; or was it based on some *a priori* insight into first principles? The Copernican revolution turned on a sharp distinction between appearance and reality, but the reality that post-Aristotelian science sought to understand was covered by a network of idealizations and abstractions. The book of nature, Galileo famously said, is written in the language of mathematics; but describing the mathematical structure of the world does not *ipso facto* disclose its underlying physical structure. In hypothesizing (and then testing by experiment) his law of falling bodies, Galileo explicitly avoided any inquiry into what *causes* falling bodies to accelerate. Similarly, Isaac Newton disparaged all hypotheses (recall his dictum *hypotheses non fingo* – concerning the causes of gravitational attraction, Newton would "feign no hypotheses"), thereby placing a constraint on legitimate science: all metaphysical, speculative, and non-mathematical hypotheses that aim to explain phenomena or to provide their ultimate ground – whether from Aristotle or from Descartes – were disparaged as unscientific. Newton's inductivist philosophy seemed to limit science to the discovery of testable laws about observable phenomena (*horizontal* induction), thus ruling out inquiry into the micro-structure of bodies (*vertical* induction).

Newton's friend John Locke shared his pessimism about *vertical* induction. Though Locke allowed that knowledge of real essences (basically, truths about the underlying micro-structure of things) might be possible in principle, he strongly doubted that we would ever come to know them because of the limitations of our perceptual faculties. Since real essences cannot be known through intuition or demonstration (the other two sources of knowledge for Locke) he concluded that natural philosophy of the unobservable realm would never become genuine *science* (that is a body of certain knowledge, as opposed to probable belief or mere opinion). David Hume went much further in this skeptical direction. He argued that all factual beliefs (hence all beliefs, however probable, about what causes what) are derived, not from reason, but solely from experience by inductive inference. Induction (even of the *horizontal* kind about observable objects) does not wear its justification on its sleeve, and Hume argued that any attempt to show that it is justified, based on experience, would be circular and hence question-begging. Although Newton was Hume's scientific model, Hume denied that Newtonian science could be given any rational or justified foundation of the sort demanded by Aristotle, Descartes, or Locke. The best we can do is to codify and describe patterns of inference (such as induction) that form part of human nature and scientific practice. Thus Hume is seen by some as the first *naturalistic* philosopher of science.

Immanuel Kant found Hume's radical empiricism unable to do justice to the magnificent edifice of Newtonian mechanics. Kant was struck by the complete confidence with which scientists apply Newton's laws of motion and gravitation to all bodies, no matter how small or how distant. It seemed that Newton's laws *had* to be true in order to justify such confidence; their unrestricted universality and apparent necessity outstripped anything that can be derived from experience by inductive generalization. Kant undertook to show that although all knowledge starts with experience it does not *arise* from it: it is actively shaped by the *a priori* categories of the understanding (concepts such as causation and substance) and the forms of pure intuition (space and time). Kant thought, in effect, that there are unchanging, universal, and *a priori* principles of knowledge (synthetic *a priori* truths) that lie at the heart of empirical science and that they can be revealed by philosophical investigation. Kant's rationalist interpretation of science was eventually challenged by developments in geometry and arithmetic (especially the discovery in the nineteenth century of non-Euclidean geometries) and was shaken by the emergence of relativity theory and quantum mechanics that formed the new, post-classical, framework for science in the twentieth century.

It was during the twentieth century that philosophy of science emerged as a distinct yet central part of philosophy and acquired its own professional structure, departments, and journals. By and large, modern philosophy of science has been the product of philosophically informed scientists who, in the midst of fierce theoretical battles over the credentials of emerging scientific theories (e.g., atomism and quantum mechanics), felt the need to understand better the aim and structure of scientific theories, the role of hypotheses and experiment in science, the origins and justification of central scientific concepts, and the nature and limits of explanation. The likes of Pierre Duhem, Henri Poincaré, Ludwig Boltzmann, Heinrich Hertz, Albert Einstein, Ernst Mach, and Max Planck (to name but some of the best known) produced well-articulated methodological, and philosophical works concerning the status of scientific theorizing and the nature of scientific method.

Most of the "-isms" that have become prominent in twentieth-century philosophy of science (realism, instrumentalism, conventionalism, positivism, etc.) were advanced as responses to the crisis in the sciences: not only new theories were needed, but also new ways to understand what science is and how it works. Quantum mechanics and the theory of relativity cast into doubt the philosophical foundations on which not only classical physics, but also science as a whole and its claim to knowledge, had rested. On the one hand, Hermann von Helmholtz's rallying cry "Back to Kant!" encapsulated one distinctive tendency among scientists to look to philosophy for conceptual help – at least when it came to securing a place for *a priori* principles in our understanding of the world. On the other hand, John Stuart Mill's controversy with Auguste Comte over the role of induction and of particular facts in knowledge highlighted that, even among those who gave experience the first and last word in knowledge, there was substantial disagreement as to what exactly should be counted as the scope and limits of experience. The relationship between the "factual" and the "rational" (to use one of Ernst Cassirer's happy phrases) in doing, and thinking about, science was being renegotiated and redrawn.

The new logic of Gottlob Frege and Bertrand Russell, and the development of David Hilbert's formalistic program in mathematics, presented a first-rate opportunity to the young philosophers and scientists who gathered around Moritz Schlick in Vienna in the early 1920s to employ formal methods in an attempt to clarify, analyze, and solve (or dissolve) traditional philosophical disputes. It was thought that philosophy itself would become a rigorous enterprise – scientific philosophy – and would be set apart, once and for all, from empirical science as well as (meaningless) metaphysics. Armed with a criterion of meaningfulness (in slogan form: non-analytic statements are meaningful – "cognitively significant" – if and only if they can be verified), the logical positivists thought they could secure a distinction between the *rational* and the *factual* within the scientific theories, while at the same time distinguishing sharply between science and metaphysics. In the 1930s, philosophy of science became the logic of science: the logical–syntactic structure of the basic concepts of science should be laid bare so that their conditions of application would be transparent and intersubjectively valid. The dominant view separated sharply between the *context of discovery* and the *context of justification*. This project of the logic of science culminated, in the 1950s, in Rudolf Carnap's attempt to devise a formal system of inductive logic and in Carl Hempel's deductive–nomological model of explanation. Though Karl Popper put forward a different conception of scientific method, based on the falsifiability of scientific hypotheses and the rejection of inductivism, Popper's critical rationalism shared with logical positivism the hostility to psychologism and the view that philosophy of science is, by and large, a normative enterprise. Before the 1960s, philosophy of science had become synonymous with anti-psychologism, anti-historicism, and anti-naturalism.

This conception of philosophy of science was strongly challenged by three important and influential thinkers. First, W. V. Quine rejected the analytic–synthetic distinction that lay at the heart of the logical positivist approach. He argued that no *a priori* principles were necessary for science, based mostly on the claim that no principle is immune from revision. In line with this, the factual and the rational were *not* as sharply separated as had been thought by Quine's predecessors – empiricists and rationalists alike. Quine rehabilitated naturalism, viz., the view that philosophy is continuous with science and that there is no special philosophical method (by means of *a priori* conceptual analysis) in virtue of which philosophical knowledge is distinct from, or superior to, the empirical knowledge afforded by the sciences. Despite Quine's commitment to naturalism, he showed little interest in the rationale for the non-deductive principles that scientists employ in choosing between rival theories or in deciding which components of scientific theories to modify or retain in the face of experiment and observation. Similarly, though it is not inconsistent with his holist view of theories, Quine largely ignored the insight (emphasized by several of the logical positivists; often under the guise of conventionalism) that some components of theories (especially those in physics), play a special role: they provide a constitutive framework that the rest of the theory presupposes and without which its key terms cannot be defined. (Think, for example, of the role of space and time in Newtonian mechanics.) These framework components are not immutable or unrevisable; but they have a special status that has been aptly described as "relativized *a priori*." Insulated from the possibility of any direct confrontation with experiment, they are usually revised or abandoned only when the entire edifice constructed around them is replaced.

Second, Wilfrid Sellars attacked instrumentalism (the view that scientific theories are merely instruments for classifying, summarizing, and predicting observable phenomena) and defended scientific realism. He argued for the explanatory indispensability of unobservable entities: unobservables posited by a theory explain *directly* why observable entities behave the way they do and obey empirical laws to the extent that they do. Thus Sellars rejected the so-called "levels" or "layer-cake" picture of science – the view that there is a strict hierarchy of explanation, first from theories to empirical laws, and then from laws to individual observable objects – that had been a core presupposition of the reductionist program of the logical positivists and empiricists. Sellars also attacked foundationalism in epistemology by revealing and rejecting "the myth of the given," viz., the view that experiential episodes ("the given") directly justify some elite subset of one's beliefs. In its place, Sellars articulated a form of Kantian empiricism that distinguishes between two sorts of empirical generalizations in science: those connected fairly directly to observation by inductive inferences (broadly construed); and those constitutive principles, expressed using theoretical terms, that connect with experience indirectly through their explanatory power.

Finally, Thomas Kuhn argued that any adequate understanding of science should pay serious attention to the actual history of science (as opposed to the "rational reconstructions" concocted by philosophers of science as an idealized substitute). This historical turn repudiated the view of the philosophy of science as a purely conceptual activity. Kuhn denied that theory-change in science is governed by rules, and – taking a cue from Duhem – he stressed the role of values (both epistemic and pragmatic) in scientists' decisions about which theories to pursue and accept. Interestingly, all three thinkers were influenced, in differing degrees, by American pragmatism. Pragmatism's disdain for drawing artificially sharp distinctions and its emphasis on fallible experience (not reason or philosophical analysis) as the sole arbiter of scientific practice helped to undermine the rationale for the logical positivist way of doing philosophy of science.

By the 1960s, philosophy of science saw the rise of psychologism, naturalism, and historical studies. From then on, the findings of the empirical sciences were allowed to have a bearing on, perhaps even to determine, the answers to standard philosophical questions about science. One particularly interesting strand in the naturalist turn favored the use of findings in cognitive science in an attempt to understand how theories represent the world, how theories relate to experience, and how scientific concepts are formed. Another development was the growth of sociological studies intent on understanding science as a social practice amenable to the same empirical study as any other human activity. But the real bite of the naturalist turn was that it made available a totally different view of how scientific methods (and inductive methods in particular) are justified. Naturalists regard methodology as an empirical discipline that is part and parcel of natural science: methodological norms are *hypothetical imperatives* that link methods and aims; their justification is a function of their (empirically certified) effectiveness in bringing about those aims.

Until the early 1980s, philosophy of science was preoccupied with grand theories of how science grows and how theories change. Kuhn himself offered such a theory, based on the claim that long periods of normal science, governed by a dominant paradigm, are punctuated by short but turbulent periods of scientific revolution which engender new and competing paradigms. Imre Lakatos devised his *methodology of scientific research programmes* in an attempt to combine some of the insights of the Popperian view of science – most notably that theories should be abandoned when they conflict with experience – with the Kuhnian view that there are no algorithmic rules that govern theory-change. The historical turn showed that the received rational reconstructions of science were often caricatures, self-serving distortions of the historical record produced by philosophers in the grip of normative theories. Yet, the historicists' grand models of science turned out to be equally unsatisfactory, if only because the individual sciences are too diverse to be lumped under grand macro-models.

In the 1930s and 1940s, the dominant dogma was the unity of science, favored by the logical empiricists. Driven by epistemological motives (and more specifically, by the empiricist doctrine that all meaning derives from experience), the logical positivists aimed, in effect, at a double reduction: the reduction of the language of the special sciences to the language of physics and the reduction of the language of physics to the intersubjective thing-language. By the 1980s, the current had shifted towards the disunity of science. Physicalism was widely accepted because of the wide cosmological role ascribed to physics: physical entities are the ultimate constituents of everything there is (at least everything in space and time), and so all truths about the world should be reducible to truths about those entities. But the advances in the special sciences, their explanatory and predictive strengths and their empirical successes made it all the more difficult to argue against their autonomy from physics. Jerry Fodor (among others) made a strong case for non-reductive physicalism by arguing that the ontic priority and generality of physics does not imply reductionism. The special sciences formulate proper laws connecting natural kinds; those laws and kinds play an ineliminable explanatory and predictive role. What else should we require to regard psychology, biology, and chemistry as genuine (and autonomous) sciences?

The renaissance of scientific realism in the 1960s resulted in an epistemic optimism with regard to science's claim to truth, though new forms of empiricism emerged in the 1980s. In the 1950s, Humean views of causation and laws of nature ruled: there is no necessity in nature; laws, *qua* cosmic regularities, are contingent; causation is (more or less) regular succession. By the 1980s, non-Humean accounts of causation and laws had taken center-stage. It was generally accepted that an appeal to causation could cast light on a number of important philosophical issues, such as the justification of beliefs, the reference and meaning of theoretical terms, and the nature of scientific explanation. Along with it came a resurgence of Aristotelianism in the philosophy of science. Essentialism acquired new currency and the belief in the existence of necessity in nature (which is knowable *a posteriori*) again became popular. Prior to the Second World War, most philosophers of science had considered metaphysics meaningless because it transgressed the bounds of meaningful (verifiable or analytic) discourse captured by mathematics and science. But as the century was drawing to a close, philosophers of science had to swim in deep metaphysical waters in order to address a number of key issues.

Though the application of formal methods in the philosophy of science seemed to be under attack in the 1970s, a fresh, over-arching, formal approach to many problems in the philosophy of science has become very influential: Bayesianism. Based on the probability calculus, Bayesianism aims to provide a general framework in which key concepts, such as rationality, scientific method, confirmation, evidential support, and inductive inference, are cast and analyzed. Though there is no systematic and well-worked out alternative to Bayesianism, many of its critics regard it as simply part of the legend that has animated most philosophy of science, at least in the first half of the twentieth century, viz., that there is a topic-neutral characterization of scientific method and a formal explication of the central scientific concepts.

Philosophy of science continues to be a vibrant field: terrain has shifted; fresh ground has been broken; old ideas have resurfaced and been given new life. More importantly, philosophy of science has cast light both on science as a whole and on individual sciences (including established sciences, such as chemistry, that had previously drawn little systematic attention, and new sciences, such as cognitive science). Recently, philosophy of science has also started looking at its own past with an eye to gaining a better understanding of its development and what was at stake in past intellectual battles.

This volume is a state-of-the-art collection of essays on some of the most central and perennial issues in the philosophy of science. The *Companion* is divided into four parts:

I   Historical and philosophical context
II   Debates
III Concepts
IV   Individual sciences.

The chapters of Part I place philosophy of science within a broader context, by showing how the main issues that philosophers of science think about are related to issues, themes, and problems in other philosophical areas, most notably in logic, epistemology, metaphysics, philosophy of language, and the history of philosophy. Several of the chapters discuss the main schools in twentieth-century philosophy of science and contribute to the growing trend to reappraise and re-examine the basic tenets and views of those schools and their place within the broader philosophical enterprise.

Understanding the main debates in the philosophy of science is the central theme of Part II. The chapters present in a careful and lively fashion the development of the important debates, the basic stances, conceptions and theses, as well as the main arguments and lines of defense. The authors are major participants in those debates and hence they make no secret of their own commitments and point of view. After all, there is hardly any neutrality in philosophy.

The aim of Part III is to explain the structure and content (if you like, the *debate* about the content) of controversial concepts that are involved in many disputes in the philosophy of science. The chapters analyze the concepts in some detail, show their development, refinement or change, unravel their role in a number of philosophical problems, and present the authors' own views as to how they ought to be understood.

Finally, Part IV surveys some of the main issues that arise within eight individual sciences (or clusters of sciences, such as social science and cognitive science). These chapters discuss foundational issues within particular disciplines as well as their connections with broader problems in the philosophy of science.

We have been fortunate to have had fifty-eight outstanding philosophers working with us to produce this volume. Their chapters display some of the best work currently being done in the philosophy of science, while offering a balance between explaining standard views and advancing new ideas and criticism. We thank them wholeheartedly. Their contributions demonstrate the pluralism and richness of current philosophical thinking about science.

The chapters in this *Companion* range widely over the philosophy of science at the beginning of the twenty-first century. There are some inevitable overlaps, but we believe they make the volume livelier by offering different and competing points of view on related topics. At the end of each chapter there are cross-references to other chapters and suggestions for further reading. These are intended to help readers to follow up points of interest and to plunge into some of the exciting work that is not directly referred to in the chapters.

Work for this *Companion* has taken nearly four years to complete as we persevered through some setbacks and delays. Many thanks are due: to Tony Bruce of Routledge (who had the idea of the *Companion*) and his team who showed us unfailing support and encouragement; to Ron Price for his deft copyediting and to Andrew Watts for his efficient production of this volume; to two anonymous readers for Routledge for useful suggestions about possible chapters (though we did not always follow their advice); to all the contributors, thanks (again) for all your hard work; and an especial thanks to two contributors (Cassandra and Rod) who came to our rescue by joining the project during its final year. At the moment these lines were written the two editors had not yet met (though they have come to know each other extremely well!). The *Companion* was edited somewhere in the cyberspace that links Athens and West Lafayette and was written in Australia, Belgium, Bermuda, Canada, Cyprus, Finland, Greece, Ireland, Italy, New Zealand, Turkey, the UK, and the USA.

Part I

HISTORICAL AND PHILOSOPHICAL CONTEXT

1

THE EPISTEMOLOGY OF SCIENCE AFTER QUINE

Paul A. Roth

> My present suggestion is that it is nonsense, and the root of much nonsense, to speak of a linguistic component and a factual component in the truth of any individual statement. Taken collectively, science has its double dependence upon language and experience; but this duality is not significantly traceable into the statements of science taken one by one... The unit of empirical significance is the whole of science. (Quine 1961 [1953]: 42)

Few epistemological doctrines seem to fit the sciences more readily than do empiricism, taken as a philosophical doctrine about evidence, and naturalism, understood as a philosophical account of scientific method. Empiricism explains how scientific theories connect to the world; naturalism proposes optimal procedures for learning about the world. But a fundamental problem appears to attach to these doctrines. For the very type of knowledge these philosophical doctrines purport to support and clarify turns out to be implicated in supporting and clarifying empiricism and naturalism themselves. Examining this threat of circularity and its consequences leads, I suggest, to reconceptualizing the status and role of philosophical inquiry vis-à-vis scientific inquiry and empirical knowledge.

"Epistemology," Quine declares in "Epistemology Naturalized," "is concerned with the foundations of science" (1969: 69). Yet, (in)famously, Quine also maintains in the same essay that the relation between epistemology and science is one of "reciprocal containment" (*ibid.*: 83). Because Quine's writings have decisively influenced two lines of debate within epistemology generally and the relation between epistemology and science in particular – holism and naturalism, respectively – his account provides a convenient basis for surveying how these debates have evolved. My particular concern will be, in line with the Quinean perspective adopted herein, determining in what respects empiricism remains epistemologically fundamental as an account of scientific knowledge.

In what follows, I offer a sketch of a movement in twentieth-century epistemology from what I term a "bottom–up" to a "top–down" approach regarding the relation of epistemology and the sciences. This will follow lines of argument found in

"Epistemology Naturalized" by tracing the development of the arguments that systematically strip away attempts to justify science independently of science. This engenders key problems in specifying what to count as empirical, and so as evidence for and against individual scientific claims. This turns out to be the crucial step in Quine's naturalism, i.e., elimination of philosophy as a form of inquiry independent of science. Yet against those who maintain that Quine's blurring of the lines between speculative metaphysics and science represents a politically (if not philosophically) retrograde move, I indicate how Quine's holism and naturalism helped motivate and make possible a proliferation of alternative approaches to the study and understanding of science. Making explicit this connection allows a somewhat different perspective on the current disputes between philosophers of science and science studies researchers.

Towards that end, consider reference to "the whole of natural science" from "Epistemology Naturalized" (written *circa* 1968) in light of the context of an earlier use of that phrase in "Two Dogmas of Empiricism" (*circa* 1950–51). In the latter case, Quine urges a vast enlargement of the unit assessed as having (or lacking) empirical significance. In the former, he declares for naturalism, i.e., treating epistemological questions as questions within science, and so using science to account for how humans manage to acquire such knowledge. By implication, the notion of *empirical significance* must itself be subject to naturalistic scrutiny along with all other aspects of scientific method and theorizing.

By unpacking just why Quine makes use of so vague a phrase reveals just how radically Quine's critique of empiricism forces a reconception of the relation between epistemology and the philosophy of science. In particular, I suggest, terms such as "empiricism" no longer hold promise of epistemological insight regarding the basis for scientific knowledge. Empiricism simply ceases to have standing as an epistemological doctrine *apart* from science. It becomes, rather, a *consequence* of naturalism (and pragmatism), a thesis about the nature of scientific evidence maintained on the basis of scientific investigation (see Nelson and Nelson 2000).

Empiricism, epistemology, and science in "Two Dogmas"

With regard to knowledge of the external world – empirical knowledge – Quine takes "empiricism" to name a theory of evidence – sense impressions – that provides the fundamental basis for legitimating all beliefs about what there is. In "Two Dogmas," Quine challenges a traditional empiricist view that one can discriminate by semantic criteria alone exactly which statements evidence supports (or not) and which need no evidential support because they are true "come what may." This challenges the positivist claim to be able to distinguish between statements that are meaningful and those that are not, and so, as Quine states, blurs the boundary that positivism attempted to put in place "between speculative metaphysics and natural science."

Quine's two key lines of argument go as follows. First, he gives reasons to doubt that we can classify sentences in a way that would permit us to identify just some but not others as expressions of empirical knowledge. Second, he extends this doubt about distinguishing between what stands in need of empirical confirmation and what does not to include finding "equivalences of meaning" between linguistic items such as sentences and non-linguistic ones such as sense impressions. For if the notion of "equivalence of meaning" cannot be cashed out in terms of the constituent elements of so-called analytic statements, the notion cannot be made to work for alleged equivalences between linguistic and non-linguistic items. In this respect, at least, the "two dogmas are, indeed, at root identical" (see Quine 1961 [1953]: 41; see also Ben-Menahem 2005).

Quine's "countersuggestion" that the measure of epistemic goodness be taken as the "whole of science," in sum, raises two key questions regarding how to construe the relationship between epistemology and philosophy of science. For his phrase "the unit of empirical significance," the term "empirical significance" should be understood as "meaningful in terms of experience." But the problematic terms – the questions invoked by the phrase – involve the terms "unit" and "empirical." For a unit to be a unit, it must be bounded. So, the first question to be answered would be: What bounds or determines the unit tested for empirical significance? The second question concerns the epistemic work to be done by an appeal to a notion of the empirical. Presumably, the job of the empirical should be to provide some evidential basis independent of the science being evaluated for the assessment of scientific claims. For otherwise the unit under test certifies as appropriate the elements used to test it. And this renders unclear the nature of any claimed epistemic advantage.

The allusion to the "whole of science" suggests that any attempted epistemic assessment of a single belief implicates *all* those beliefs comprising that theory to which a sentence belongs. For how what go by the label "beliefs" (sentences held true) and how what goes by the label of "experience" (perception) *fit* together can be logically accommodated in any number of ways. Attempts to differentiate structurally among types of linguistic items and to identify a tight logical and evidentiary fit between the linguistic and the non-linguistic ultimately reveal that there exists no such logically neat interrelationship between how the world works on us and what we think about it. In this regard, attempts to distinguish between, e.g., some type of limited holism and a more global form presuppose an ability to mark off one type of theory (e.g., those in physics) from other types (those in economics). But our beliefs do not come so neatly packaged, and their areas of possible interdependence or independence so clearly marked. The problem involves just the inability to logically specify which beliefs might be revised should experience disappoint expectations (see Nelson and Nelson 2000, esp. Ch. 5).

Reflections on the logic of science, the history of science, and the sociology of science all confirm this point, each in its own way. (Let me be clear here that what I take to be called into question involves a notion of *the empirical* or *experience* that can be made sense of as epistemically basic independently of appeal to science.) But why then believe that there exists any epistemic leverage in appeals to *the empirical*?

The two questions – the unit of empirical significance and the content of the notion of the empirical – moreover, prove deeply interrelated. For a variety of scientific theories (broadly construed, so as to include the social sciences) serve to determine just which experiences count and under what conditions they count as relevant for assessment purposes. Science ultimately delimits, e.g., how many senses there are, how they function, and so what even the senses properly so-called *could* provide *qua* evidence. Both questions give rise to worries about how diffuse the notion of the empirical becomes once it cannot be restricted to terms or simple statements.

One of the most philosophically unsettling consequences of epistemic assessments so conceived involves the many ways of accommodating experience to theory. Conceiving of the theory–evidence relation as interrelated and logically diffuse receives further reinforcement from significant pre-Quinean historical and philosophical work by Duhem as well as the powerful influence of work in the history and philosophy of science by Kuhn and others who came later. In addition, as Ian Hacking (1989) insists, questions of how to sort experiences into kinds remain vexed and unanswered.

Science without foundations

If notions of sense and sensing themselves require scientific investigation in order to articulate the respects in which they support science, then the very empirical base to which science appeals becomes one best understood through science. Thus, in charting how the "unit question" and the corresponding "experience question" evolved to something like their present forms, an understanding emerges regarding how these notions in turn affect what the terms "epistemology" and "science" connote. Unlike empiricists of old, Quine does *not* look to the notion of experience to clarify those of thought or belief: all three, he maintains, stand in need of clarification. Quine links the notions of meaning, thought, belief, and experience as kindred concepts in the sense that "they are in equal measure very ill suited for use as instruments of philosophical and scientific clarification and analysis. If some one accepts these notions outright for such use, I am at a loss to imagine what he can have deemed more in need of clarification and analysis than the things he has thus accepted" (Quine 1981: 184). In particular, by conceiving of the notion of empirical knowledge as of a piece with the articulated theorizing of experience that sciences provide, the suggestion regarding the unit of empirical significance made in "Two Dogmas" turns out to imply the "reciprocal containment" of science and epistemology proposed in "Epistemology Naturalized." (How Quine's declaration for pragmatism in "Two Dogmas" fits with his later declared naturalism poses an interesting but, to the best of my knowledge, presently unanswered question.)

In understanding how to disentangle this relationship of reciprocal containment, it helps to appreciate the deep link between Quine's critique of the notion of analyticity and his critique of positivist, and particularly Carnapian, conceptions of mathematics. For example, although Quine uses remarks about foundational studies in mathematics to frame the challenges to epistemology as he understands them in "Epistemology Naturalized," this framing remains almost universally ignored in subsequent discussions of Quine's essay and his account of naturalism (see Roth 1999).

On my telling of the tale, the epistemological program Quine advocates – and, *inter alia*, what he means by "naturalism," "epistemology," and "science" – involves assessing the fate of empirical knowledge once attempts to *ground* such knowledge meet a fate that parallels attempts to ground mathematical knowledge. The primary argument of "Epistemology Naturalized" elaborates the parallel types of problems or failings that plagued both mathematical and empirical knowledge, and how those problems transform or otherwise alter what such knowledge comes to in each case.

Quine develops the parallelism in two respects, which he terms the "conceptual" and the "doctrinal." Conceptual matters are semantic, concerning definition or explication. Doctrinal issues involve justification and formal priority. Ideally the definitions would generate all the concepts from clear and distinct ideas, and the proofs would generate all the theorems from these self-evident truths. The intended parallel would then be to the logicist program for having a consistent, fully axiomatized, and complete set of rules adequate to all of mathematics. This approach, had it succeeded, would have provided an analysis, in the best understood sense of the term, of the entire range of truths about the world.

Yet, Quine argues, the project for providing foundation for science (i.e., for empirical knowledge) parallels the fate of the logicist project in mathematics. On the doctrinal side, the project falls because of Hume's problem – generalizations from experience outrun evidence for them. Hence, derivation of scientific laws proves impossible.

The problem on the conceptual side is not quite as neat or as venerable. For here the principal difficulty resides in the relation of the theoretical sentences and the evidence adduced in their support, i.e., holism. For holism (of the Quine–Duhem sort) forecloses the possibility of the sort of term-by-term explication that the foundational project presupposes and requires. There are, then, two irremediable failings in the case of empirical knowledge. Neither laws nor concepts can be accounted for as hoped, i.e., in terms of sensory impressions and logic alone. This dashes any hope of finding within empiricism a philosophical foundation for science. As a result, empiricism becomes itself an hypothesis within accepted science, one that helps explain why science provides the engineering success that it does. It also leaves us without a justificatory standard better than those that the sciences (broadly and collectively understood) themselves provide, since that "better standard" – deductive justification from a specified base – is not to be had. The incompleteness results for empirical knowledge, in short, redefine what can be hoped for or expected by way of justification of empirical knowledge.

In this regard, Quine's use of the term "naturalism" must be treated circumspectly, since a definition of "naturalism" typically makes reference to the "methods of science," yet what to count as science cannot be readily taken for granted in Quine. There is no small irony in the complaint that Quine's notion of naturalism is vague. For it typically emanates from those who assume that they know exactly what science is or what epistemology is, and this despite lacking a demarcation criterion for the former or settled explications of belief, justification, and truth for the latter.

Science fully naturalized

Ironically, this relocation of empiricism within science breaks down whatever divides may be thought to remain between philosophy of science and science studies. Philosophy of science and science studies were distinguished primarily by the elements that were cited in the *explanans* for a given *explandandum* event (e.g., theory change, theoretical commitment, confirmation). Typically, philosophers downplay and science studies' practitioners emphasize how the practice of science stands implicated in the customs and mores of those societies in which the science takes place.

I suggest that those problems that led, in the first place, to the expansion of the unit of empirical significance and the *theorizing* of the empirical make moot those disputes. What counts as experiences and how to assess their effect (e.g., social psychology v. neurology) will depend in part on the science at issue. For while socially mediated experiences cannot, in principle, be excluded from epistemological consideration, attempts to map those experiences to individual beliefs remain subject to all the usual indeterminacies. In this respect, the key problems inherent in the epistemological project on the philosophical side – bounding the unit of experience and theorizing the empirical – emerge, like the return of the repressed, in science studies' efforts to provide a "social epistemology."

Indeed, many debates regarding the epistemology of science – the rationality of theory choice, accounting for theory change, hypothesis acceptance – that divide philosophical and sociological accounts of scientific claims actually split on the question of which experiences prove relevant to explaining scientific claims. Sociologists claim to favor causal explanations of beliefs and philosophers prefer reason-based justifications. Put another way, one means by which to understand disputes in the area of science studies, at least with regard to the explanation or assessment of scientific knowledge claims, would be to take them as disagreements regarding what tests test, and even which aspects within the experience of individuals bear on the assessments of epistemic claims.

Consider, for example, how accounts offered by Galison (1987) differ from what one finds in Pickering (1986). Both of these accounts, moreover, appear to be relatively *internal* histories – they do not look much beyond the scientific communities. But Galison emphasizes how debate in a scientific community becomes settled by citing the reasons which prevailed, while Pickering emphasizes unacknowledged concerns – for instance, the need to be able to *recycle expertise* and yet have a more viable theory – as leading scientists to favor one view over another. These approaches can be contrasted in turn with, for example, Shapin and Schaffer (1985), who take a yet wider view of the factors determining one's theoretical preferences. Background beliefs regarding social status or religious affiliation might influence which individual beliefs count or how they count. In addition, which beliefs might be open to revision will be determined by perceptions regarding how those beliefs connect to religious or political views deemed important. Consideration such as these makes the "unit of empirical significance" culture sized.

In saying this, I acknowledge some discomfort in moving from theories conceived of as linguistic entities to cultures so conceived. As I indicate in what follows, the question of the relevant "unit" being assessed has become increasingly diffuse and problematic. I find no general answer to the question of how to bound or otherwise specify the unit in which to embed the epistemic evaluation of a specific scientific claim. Debates need to proceed on a case-by-case basis in this regard. From this perspective, the label "naturalism" only obscures uncertainties regarding the scope and content of the present notions of science and experience.

Questions concerning the unit assessed and which experiences serve to assess also affect questions of how to distinguish between epistemic norms and the methods of epistemology and scientific norms and the methods of science. For first philosophy regards (as it must) epistemic norms and methods as *independent* of natural science. Scientific knowledge, properly so-called, would then be a consequence of the units (typically, sentence sized) certified by the right epistemic processes, whatever those may be taken to be. This leads to a *bottom–up* strategy. The sort of esoteric and non-observational claims to know made within particular natural sciences count as knowledge provided that they can be legitimized by iteration of those methods and norms – whatever they are – for certifying, for example, basic perceptual statements or clear and distinct ideas.

By contrast, if epistemology can claim no norms or methods certified by procedures that stand aloof from all other modes of inquiry, then epistemology proceeds from within science. First philosophy requires an account of epistemic assessment that can be independent of science. But Quine argues that we cannot successfully isolate the preferred empiricist standards – analyticity, experience – and that this failure turns on irremediable problems concerning the character of word–world connection. He offers as an alternative account one in which science should be understood as ranging over just the panoply of norms and methods deemed legitimate for purposes of inquiry. Epistemology, so conceived, becomes a *top–down* investigation, at least in the following sense. Evaluation assumes a certain theoretical stance, and from within that stance proceeds to make what sense it can of our putative sense-making procedures and claims.

Thus, I take there to be a type of affinity between, on the one hand, the alleged independence of epistemology and a bottom–up strategy as opposed to, on the other hand, conceiving of epistemology as pursued from within a scientific account of the world. Epistemology-within-science proceeds top–down, that is, by asking how, given an explanatory theory and its justificatory norms provisionally accepted, to encompass within it a justificatory account of their acquisition and justification. Naturalizing epistemology by making it part of science exemplifies this top–down strategy. Bottom–up strategies take an ultimately dogmatic stance (knowledge begins *here*), while top–down strategies allow for a pragmatic approach to judging a theory's merit.

From the standpoint of examining the relationship between philosophy of science and epistemology, those strategies yield very different results. Viewed bottom–up, justification consists only of inferential links. Traditional puzzles here concern justifying generalizations – typically, laws; related epistemic problems involve articulating the logic that connects evidence to experimental tests, experimental tests to theories, and the logical connections that exist among those statements comprising a scientific theory. Epistemic evaluation involves justified inference and nothing else.

Hans Reichenbach offers a straightforward and representative formulation of this view: "The essence of knowledge," he declares, "is *generalization*." Moreover: "Generalization … is the origin of science" (Reichenbach 1951: 5). Although the strategy for assessing laws must be bottom–up – from evidence of experiment to laws – once the laws are in hand, epistemology becomes top–down.

Reichenbach's core philosophical question asks how knowledge of the world manages to transcend what observation alone provides. His answer echoes themes repeated frequently during the first half of the twentieth century, viz., that the philosophical study of science can clarify the inferential processes that lead from experience to theory. For science trumps claims of common sense because of its superiority in explaining how things, in general, hang together. Science can explain what passes for common sense; common sense cannot account for scientific understanding. The study of inference, moreover, marks the special, albeit limited, place for philosophy.

Quine takes science to be about trying to construct a "systematization of our sensory intake" (Quine 1995). The initial systematization comes with learning the language one first learns to speak, and of the objects and events about which we communicate with others. The "reciprocal containment" of epistemology and natural science takes epistemology to be a part of an attempt to systematize experience. But, though only an aspect of the scientific enterprise, epistemology so conceived contains the scientific enterprise, since all of it results in the end from shared stimulations. Quine's reconceptualization of knowledge still takes knowledge to be the best systematic account for beliefs held, but takes science to constitute this.

Quine's very liberal view of what to count as science can be adopted here without epistemological loss. For by taking science to be just the extensional equivalent of those empirically oriented disciplines and their collective methods, one does not assume the burden of discerning deep relations between, for example, physics and history, on the one hand, while, on the other hand, one can criticize freely those forms of inquiry, for instance, astrology, that might assume some of the techniques of science (measurement, prediction) but without the desired results. The appeal to the empirical remains one that the sciences themselves endorse, but it may be jettisoned if results warrant that conclusion. As Quine somewhere remarks, should a ouija board prove a better predictor than physics, it would be pragmatically rational to abandon physics and go with the ouija board.

Those favoring philosophy of science as epistemology most characteristically insist on the virtues of systematicity and explanatory power. Those favoring the ordinary (i.e., those who take as the work of epistemology an analysis of the great many truths already known prior to science) most typically appeal to truths known as truths *prior* to any investigation and which any plausible theory of knowledge must yield as a result. In this regard, circular reasoning might be thought to undercut the above characterization. For Reichenbach's assertion that science "requires a reinterpretation of everyday life" already decides what for many epistemologists remains the fundamental question at issue: What does a theory of knowledge need to be a theory of?

Naturalism and normativity/politics and epistemology

Indeed, debates regarding the role of natural science in and as epistemology proceed under the rubric, in the current philosophical climate, as debates about the role of naturalism. I take these debates, that is, to be just disputes as to whether and how an empirical theory can play a role as an epistemological theory. The nub of this debate centers on the claim that epistemology provides a normative theory and that no scientific theory can provide an account of norms since such theories simply account for (describe) the world and so cannot determine what the standards of knowledge ought to be.

Scientific theories presumably might employ such standards, but it falls to philosophy to discover and account for the norms determinative of knowledge. In this regard, disputes about naturalized epistemology focus less on what it is for epistemology to be naturalized than on what qualifies a naturalistic/scientific approach as epistemology.

Some recent work illustrates problems connected to the "unit question" and the "theorizing of the empirical" by exploring debate about these issues within American philosophy of science and pragmatism, and various European imports (from logical empiricism to Marxism). In their Introduction, Hardcastle and Richardson (2003) correctly acknowledge that "the best current tool for understanding 'analytic philosophy' must surely be sociology of knowledge, especially the notion of 'boundary work'." Alan Richardson stresses an intellectual evolution within naturalism and pragmatism from Dewey and Morris, on the one hand, to Quine, on the other. On Richardson's account, Morris and Dewey view science as a tool for progressive politics, while Quine decouples naturalism from any progressive view of science. For Quine, science neither progresses (if "progress" means "comes closer to the truth"), nor does it provide a basis either for enlightened politics (which would be another form of progress).

Richardson, in particular, emphasizes that in the debate between Quine and Carnap, the "semantic, pragmatic, logical, epistemological, scientific, 'natural,' formal, and metaphysical are at stake all at once". On Richardson's account, the Morris and Carnap conception of scientific philosophy was structured so as to exclude traditional metaphysics or epistemology. Precisely by limiting the scope of the intelligible, philosophy of science was to clarify *philosophical* disputes. Since inferential relations (including inductive inference) could be explicated without appeal to values, the clarificatory role of logic allowed real progress (both intellectual and political) in debate to be achieved. Critiques of, for instance, Heidegger by positivists attempted to show just how this was to go. By making precise the notion of inference, philosophy could be of social utility by debunking efforts to rationalize certain types of claim.

Yet the political utility of philosophy of science and logic to debunk requires – in the view Richardson finds in Morris and Carnap – the separation of the logic of inquiry from explicitly normative concerns. But in order to maintain their concept of a neutral "logic of science," Morris and Carnap needed the notion of analyticity. Hence, Quine's critique reverberates across a very broad intellectual and cultural front.

On this reading, it comes as no surprise that Richardson situates Quine's naturalism as "conservative." For Quine famously declares at the close of "Two Dogmas" that the rejection of the analytic–synthetic distinction blurs the "supposed boundary between speculative metaphysics and natural science." Yet it was the drawing of this boundary that underwrote the political utility which Carnap and others conceived the philosophy of science to have. Quine's skepticism also muddies ethical waters. For Carnap stresses the element of choice in the selection of frameworks in order to indicate that our way of understanding the world involves an element of free choice, and so an action for which one bears responsibility. Blurring the boundaries between theory and experience blurs questions of responsibility because how beliefs map on to experience, and so rationalizations of what one believes, loses just the sharpness and clarity that gave it some political purchase. No one adaptation of experience to belief necessarily counts as more rational than some other.

Richardson thus terms Quine's pragmatism "thin" because Quine does not address questions of policy or action. For Quine, pragmatic considerations enter in with respect to how the web of belief gets warped in order to incorporate recalcitrant experiences. No sentence stands aloof from revision, including the putatively analytic ones. Choice of frameworks, in this regard, does not insulate from revision statements assumed to constitute the framework of inquiry. Construing all statements as potentially revisable, however, scotches the hope that philosophy of science could serve the cause of political demystification by appealing to the independence of logic and purely inferential connections between evidence and beliefs. What counts as "pragmatic" turns out only to be how from within the framework one adjudicates questions of confirmation and so the *adjustment* of beliefs. Likewise, without a purely logical criterion for which beliefs *ought* to be revised in light of the experience, philosophy provides no objective guide to action. In one important sense of "pragmatic," philosophy loses its pragmatic value.

But Richardson surely takes a misstep when he then goes on to claim that "Quine's naturalism is intellectually conservative" inasmuch as it "opens up a way back into metaphysics and epistemology and changes the revolutionary, forward-looking rhetoric of logical empiricism and American pragmatism into a story of continuity going back all the way to Locke and Hume" (Hardcastle and Richardson 2003). For here Richardson seems strangely blind to the radical upheavals that did in fact follow from the changes rung by Quine on "the unit of empirical significance." While Quine's critique does not allow the critique of metaphysics to serve the political purposes some positivists had hoped, it does serve (unwittingly, I suspect) to broaden (and so, in one sense, liberalize) discussion of the factors that play into scientific decision-making.

Richardson bemoans Quine's version of pragmatism since it does not dictate how to revise beliefs in the face of experience. Yet that very feature of Quine's thought becomes a license for insisting on the relevance of the sociology of science. Relatedly, Richardson's linking of Quine's project to the empiricist tradition of Locke and Hume misses precisely what makes Quine a philosophical radical because of his thorough and substantive reconceptualization of empiricism, science, and epistemology.

Keep in mind that for Quine the social aspect of the story remains key: "Language is a social art. In acquiring it we have to depend entirely on intersubjectively available cues as to what to say and when" (Quine 1960). Additionally, and even more importantly, this change shifts accounting for beliefs from inference alone (as Reichenbach thought) to inference or explanation. This *mixing* of inferential and causal accounts leaves some beliefs *unrationalized*. But which? For reasons alluded to above and now well known, inferential considerations alone do not mandate how to adjust beliefs in the face of recalcitrant experience. While this frustrates those who would like to see each individual belief assessed by its rational merits, it also allows seeing change in belief as a function of change in circumstance. As noted below, each conception of belief change carries with it its form of political critique.

Richardson worries that Quine's turn away from the analytic–synthetic distinction was a turn toward "conservative" thought, at least insofar as the *failure* of scientific prediction did not necessarily direct one to which associated belief to revise. Hence his concern that Quine's "thin" pragmatism is no pragmatism worthy of the name, since it fails to direct action. But this only brings into a focus a part of the epistemological story, and ignores much of what has actually transpired in the wake of Quine's work. For the practical upshot of those reflections has not been the sort of intellectual paralysis or ennui about which Richardson appears to worry, but a proliferation of non-philosophic accounts of what scientific theories just are theories about. The effect has been the creation of an unruly but not-to-be-denied *social* approach to epistemology. The hallmark of this approach, or at least the aspect of greatest interest to those concerned with the relation of science and epistemology, involves the inclusion of various factors – race, gender, class – said to influence the imputed "logic" shaping theories and the criteria for judging them adequate.

While the sociology of science has flourished in the wake of philosophic work criticizing the supposed epistemic foundations of science, too much of this sociological work simply seeks to redo by means of a social logic what could not be done by more austere formalisms. The results prove correspondingly (and unsurprisingly) unsatisfying. The obsession with theoretical formulation brings out the worst in both philosophical and social–cultural analyses of science. More interesting than the now well-rehearsed shortcomings of understanding science in purely inferentialist or theory-centric terms are laboratory-centered studies of how science succeeds when it does. For the account of *knowledge production* that emerges in these contexts provides a much better sense of how theory connects to the world, and what it takes to make this connection succeed.

Quine's conceptualization of the relation of epistemology and science proves deeply ironic. Empiricism requires science to explicate that notion – experience – on which, in turn, to base confidence in science. A further irony involves the fact that the proposed unit of empirical significance – "the whole of science" – cannot itself be tested *qua* unit. So confidence in the whole of science cannot be licensed in this way – the way in which science supposedly issues such license. What then guides changes rung on scientific theories? Quine appears to endorse a "pragmatic" basis for such change (Quine 1961 [1953]). And while Richardson protests that Quine's blurring of boundaries fails to be pragmatic because it provides no neutral guide to change, that blurring helps underwrite Quine's view that there exists no point of cosmic exile (Quine 1969), and so makes adjustment a pragmatic rather than purely logical matter. A final, albeit surely unintended, irony then situates Quine with Heidegger and against Carnap in seeing humans as having a choice at every level of their understanding of the world (see Stone forthcoming).

Acknowledgements

I thank David Hoy, Kaija Mortensen, Abraham Stone, and Stephen Turner for helpful comments on an earlier draft of this essay.

See also Empiricism; The historical turn in the philosophy of science; Naturalism; Scientific method; Social studies of science; Underdetermination.

References

Ben-Menahem, Yemima (2005) "Black, White, and Gray: Quine on Convention," *Synthese* 146: 245–82.
Galison, Peter (1987) *How Experiments End*, Chicago: University of Chicago Press.
Hacking, Ian (1989) "Quine's Natural Kinds," in R. Gibson (ed.) *Perspectives on Quine*, Oxford: Blackwell, pp. 129–42.
Hardcastle, Gary L. and Richardson, Alan (eds) (2003) "Introduction," *Logical Empiricism in North America*, Minneapolis: University of Minnesota Press.
Nelson, Lynn Hankinson and Nelson, Jack (2000) *On Quine*, Belmont, CA: Wadsworth.
Pickering, Andrew (1986) *Constructing Quarks*, Chicago: University of Chicago Press.
Quine, W. V. (1960) *Word and Object*, Cambridge, MA: MIT Press.
—— (1961 [1953]) *From a Logical Point of View*, 2nd edn, rev., Cambridge, MA: Harvard University Press.
—— (1969) *Ontological Relativity and Other Essays*, New York: Columbia University Press.
—— (1981) *Theories and Things*, Cambridge, MA: Harvard University Press.
—— (1995) *From Stimulus to Science*, Cambridge, MA: Harvard University Press.
Reichenbach, Hans (1951) *The Rise of Scientific Philosophy*, Berkeley: University of California Press.
Roth, Paul A. (1999) "The Epistemology of 'Epistemology Naturalized'," *Dialectica* 53: 87–109.
Shapin, Steve and Schaffer, Simon (1985) *Leviathan and the Air Pump*, Princeton, NJ: Princeton University Press.
Stone, Abraham (forthcoming) "Heidegger and Carnap on the Overcoming of Metaphysics," in Stephen Mulhall (ed.) *Martin Heidegger*, Burlington, VT: Ashgate Publishing.

Further reading

An excellent overview of the consequence of Quine's "liberalization" of the notion of empirical significance is John Zammito, *A Nice Derangement of Epistemes* (Chicago: University of Chicago Press, 2004). Some sense of the diversity of issues here and the numerous perspectives from which these are explored can be found in Paul A. Roth "Will the Real Scientists Please Stand Up? Dead Ends and Live Issues in the Explanation of Scientific Knowledge," *Studies in the History and Philosophy of Science* 27 (1996): 813–38. A philosophically conservative account is Larry Laudan, *Beyond Positivism and Relativism* (Boulder, CO: Westview Press, 1996); a more radical and polemical introduction is Steve Fuller's *The Philosophy of Science and Technology Studies* (New York: Routledge, 2006). Interesting and challenging approaches to the set of issues scouted in this essay include: Joseph Rouse's "What Are Cultural Studies of Scientific Knowledge?" *Configurations* 1 (1993): 57–94; Donna Haraway's "A Game of Cat's Cradle: Science Studies, Feminist Theory, Culture Studies," *Configurations* 2 (1994): 59–71; and Steve Fuller's *Thomas Kuhn: A Philosophical History for Our Times* (Chicago: University of Chicago Press, 2000). For a range of critical reactions to Fuller's book (including my own), see *Social Epistemology* 17 (2003): 2–3. The *locus classicus* for the science studies approach remains B. Latour and S. Woolgar, *Laboratory Life* (Beverly Hills, CA: Sage, 1979).

2

THE HISTORY OF PHILOSOPHY AND THE PHILOSOPHY OF SCIENCE

Joanne Waugh and Roger Ariew

Philosophy and science, as well as their respective histories, are not recognized as distinct genres until relatively late in Western philosophy. Even when they are thought to be distinct genres, neither can be written independently of the other, occasional protestations to the contrary notwithstanding. Philosophy and science were seen as almost one and the same activity for most of Western intellectual history, and the description of the relations between the history of philosophy and the philosophy of science not only forms a very large part of any account of philosophy and its history, but must include discussion of the history of science as well. Still, the terms "philosophy," "history of philosophy," "history of science," and "philosophy of science" are not interchangeable because the networks of associated concepts and practices constituting each activity change over the long history of their relations.

One could argue that Aristotle's criticism of the pre-Socratics in *Metaphysics* is at one and the same time the first history of philosophy, the first history of science, and the first attempt at a philosophy of science. Aristotle does not distinguish *philosophia* from *episteme*, that is, scientific knowledge; indeed, these terms appear side by side in *Metaphysics* at 993b20: "It is right also that philosophy should be called knowledge of the truth." This knowledge of the truth comes from studying *sophia*, or first philosophy, together with physics and mathematics, but not only from the study of these theoretical sciences. *Philosophia* includes also the pursuit of *phronesis*, or practical wisdom, as well as the knowledge of the "productive sciences" such as poetics and rhetoric. For Aristotle, *episteme* encompasses all of what now goes under the name "philosophy" but it is not the same as what contemporary philosophers of science would count as science. There is, however, at least one respect in which Aristotle's *Metaphysics* indulges in a practice that seems to be characteristic of the history of philosophy as written by philosophers: Aristotle criticizes his predecessors for not grasping the nature of philosophy and science, that is, *episteme*, but in doing so he fails to characterize their work accurately.

The tradition of identifying science with *episteme* in its ancient sense, and *episteme* with philosophy, as encompassing all of what Aristotle would call the theoretical, practical, and productive sciences, persists well into the early modern period. René Descartes's *Principia Philosophiae* progresses from Part I: The principles of human knowledge, and II: The principles of material things, to Part III: The visible world, and IV: The earth. Descartes had envisaged a Part V, on living things, that is, on animals and plants, and VI, on man. Indeed, he extends this broad scope for philosophy even further when, in the Preface to the French translation of the work, he talks about philosophy being "like a tree whose roots are metaphysics, whose trunk is physics, and whose branches, which issue from this trunk, are all the other sciences. These reduce themselves to three principal ones, namely, medicine, mechanics, and morals."

In the same work, Descartes, who does not typically indulge in history, engages in some reconstructive history of philosophy in the service of his philosophy of science. In this instance, however, he both attenuates the contrast between his philosophy and that of Aristotle, and accentuates his differences with atomists such as Democritus, presumably in the hope of bringing his Aristotelian readers into his camp. The title to Principles IV, article 200, announces that "there are no principles in this treatise that are not accepted by everyone, so that this philosophy is not new, but is the most ancient and most common of all." As part of that argument, Descartes claims that he "made use of no principle which has not been approved by Aristotle and by all the other philosophers of every time." Descartes asserts that he has considered only the figure, motion, and magnitude of each body, and what must follow from their collisions according to the laws of mechanics, as they are confirmed by certain and daily experience. He thus turns Aristotle into a fellow mechanist. Two articles later, he reinforces this revisionist history through a comparison of his principles and those of both Democritus and Aristotle: "That the philosophy of Democritus is not less different from ours than from the vulgar [or Aristotelian philosophy]" (IV, art. 202). Democritus's atomism is for Descartes very distant from his own philosophy, since he rejects both atoms and the void as absurd or impossible. He shares with Democritus only the endorsement of mechanism, what he calls "the consideration of figure, magnitude and motion." Therefore, he concludes,

> inasmuch as because the consideration of figure, magnitude and motion has been admitted by Aristotle and all others, as well as by Democritus, and as I reject all that the latter has supposed with this one exception, while I reject practically all that has been supposed by the others, it is clear that this method of philosophizing has no more affinity with that of Democritus than with any of the other particular sects.

Aristotle and Descartes are not atypical in their "rational reconstructions" of the philosophical tenets of their predecessors; this activity is repeated many times in the history of Western philosophy. From such philosophers of nature as G. W.

Leibniz and Isaac Newton in the seventeenth century to the nineteenth century scientists–philosophers of science William Whewell and Pierre Duhem, one finds not only remnants of the identification of philosophy and science, but also histories of philosophy constructed to support or reject some particular philosophy. Certainly much more can be said about the views of these and other thinkers forming the background that shapes our present views on the relations between the philosophy of science and history of philosophy. In particular, the debate between the neo-Kantians and the positivists seems to loom large. Immanuel Kant's Copernican turn, coupled with his division of philosophy into different spheres in accordance with the mental activities involved, preserved the identification of philosophy with science, but only with respect to the grounds of empirical knowledge. The history of science and the history of philosophy were irrelevant to transcendental philosophy and the scientific knowledge it made possible.

An alternative to the ahistoricity of Kant's transcendental philosophy was provided by the historicism of G. W. F. Hegel and Karl Marx. In both cases, the study of the history of philosophy – and of the history of science – was necessary in order to understand either or both activities. The point of difference was whether ultimately the history of philosophy should be seen as comprised of episodes in the history of mind or the history of matter. The neo-Kantians attempted to capture those aspects of Kant's philosophy that provided a non-empirical ground for empirical knowledge, by positing a set of logically coherent structures that must govern scientific knowledge, and between which sense experience provided no basis for choice. An alternative conception of history was offered by the positivists, notably Auguste Comte, in which scientific philosophy was the end result of philosophy's being purified of metaphysics. On the positivist view of history, however, studying the history of philosophy and the history of science was no longer necessary once scientific philosophy emerged.

The end of history

What is, perhaps, most distinctive about the project of modernism in the early part of the twentieth century, at least initially, is its desire not to re-write history, but to repudiate it altogether. The dominant philosophical presence in early twentieth-century philosophy of science – logical positivism – is in its initial formulation explicitly aligned with the modernist project in rejecting the past, reconstructing society, and the transforming not just science, art, and philosophy, but culture in all of its manifestations, including education, and architecture. Thus Rudolf Carnap writes in the Preface to his *Aufbau* (1967 [1928]: xvii–xviii) that he and his comrades feel

> an inner kinship between the attitude on which our philosophical work is founded and the intellectual attitude which presently manifests itself in entirely different walks of life; we feel this orientation in artistic movements, especially in architecture, in movements that strive for meaningful forms of personal and collective life, of education and of external organization in general. We feel all around us the same basic orientation, the same style of

thinking and doing... Our work is carried on by the faith that this attitude
will win the future.

The explicit goal of the logical positivists is to make philosophy rigorous and scientific in a way that it had never been, not even in the neo-Kantianism in which they
were educated, a philosophical movement itself dedicated to rescuing science from the
excesses of German Idealism. They announce their arrival at "an altogether decisive
turning point in philosophy," from which point onward there would be "no questions
which are in principle unanswerable, no problems which are in principle insoluble"
(Schlick, in Ayer 1959: 56). This "new, scientific method of philosophizing" consists
in the "logical analysis of the statements and concepts of empirical science" (Carnap,
in Ayer 1959: 133); hence, the name logical positivism. During the same period that
the Vienna Circle (*Der Wiener Kreis*, another name given to the group) met, Hans
Reichenbach led a group of philosophers in Berlin who subscribed to the same ideas,
the Berlin Society for Empirical Philosophy. The Berlin group apparently preferred to
be known as the "logical empiricists," but Reichenbach's name appears among the list
of members and sympathizers in an Appendix to *Wissenschaftliche Weltauffassung*, the
manifesto published in 1929 by the Vienna Circle.

Like their philosophical predecessors, the logical positivists see themselves as
outstripping previous philosophy in being rigorous and scientific. And like the
positivists after whom they take part of their name, the logical positivists do not regard
studying the history of philosophy (or the history of science) as necessary for progress
in science or philosophy, not even in the interest of showing how logical positivism
is superior to previous philosophy (of science), or in locating the origins of their
opposition to history. Schlick explicitly contrasts the historian's and philosopher's
ways of studying the history of philosophy (in Ayer 1959: 43), and Reichenbach states
that those "who work in the new philosophy [scientific philosophy] do not look back;
their work would not profit for historical considerations" (1951: 325). Not wishing
to "belittle the history of philosophy," he insists, nonetheless, "it is history, and not
philosophy" (*ibid.*). Scientific philosophy "attempts to get away from historicism and
to arrive by logical analysis at truths as precise, as elaborate, and as reliable as the
results of the science of our time" (*ibid.*). Its practitioners are "a new class of philosophers" who are "trained in the techniques of the sciences, including mathematics" and
are able to concentrate on philosophical analysis (123).

Much of what past philosophers have deemed philosophical – metaphysics, ethics,
aesthetics – is, in Carnap's words, only an "expression of the general attitude of a
person towards life (*Lebenseinstellung, Lebensgefühl*)" (in Ayer 1959: 78). Metaphysics,
ethics, and aesthetics appear to make meaningful assertions, but these are, in truth,
meaningless, for they either cannot be translated into a logically correct form or there
are no empirical conditions by which one could determine their truth or falsity. Carnap
also lodges this charge at contemporaries in the German philosophical landscape,
notably Martin Heidegger. Heidegger, too, saw himself as revolutionary, engaged also
in an *aufbau* of society, but one opposed to the socialist, internationalist, technological, and scientific project of modernism. It is Heidegger's metaphysical philosophy

that is specifically cited as "eliminable through the logical use of language," although Carnap sometimes speaks also of the "meaningless of all metaphysics" (73). He finds the origins of metaphysics in mythology that bequeaths its heritage partly to poetry, and partly to "theology, which develops mythology into a system" (78). Metaphysics substitutes for theology on the level of systematic conceptual thinking, but further investigation reveals that metaphysics has the same content as mythology, and arises from the need to give expression to a man's attitude to life, to the environment, to society, to the tasks that he must undertake and to the misfortunes which befall him. Art is an adequate means of expression for such an attitude, but metaphysics is not: "the form of its works it pretends to be something that it is not ... a system of statements which are apparently related as premises and conclusion ... of a theory" (79). The metaphysician deludes himself not because he "selects language as the medium of expression and declarative sentences as the form of expression; for lyrical poets do the same without succumbing to self-delusion" (ibid.). But lyrical poets know their domain is art and not theory, and the metaphysician thinks he has asserted something when he has "only expressed something, like an artist" (ibid.).

Carnap's criticisms of the traditional conceptions of the history of philosophy, metaphysics, aesthetics, and ethics, and of the phenomenological tradition of continental European philosophy became standard in the Anglicized, de-politicized, and de-historicized version of logical positivism that emerged after Carnap and other logical positivists left continental Europe for Britain and the United States in the face of impending war. The successful repatriation of logical positivism entailed a deracinating of sorts; the Anglicized version of logical positivism embraced the technological and scientific successes of modernism and disowned its socialist and internationalist ambitions, the meaning of which had changed in the post-war political atmosphere. Post-war logical empiricism neither required nor encouraged any study of the history of philosophy or the history of science; what was required was a sharp distinction between studying philosophy and studying the history of philosophy, including, if not especially, the history of logical positivism. When genealogies of logical positivism do appear, they do not include the philosophy of Kant and the post-Kantians of continental Europe, nor the political and cultural context of German-speaking Europe in which logical positivism was initially formulated. The standard view of logical positivism in the English-language countries is epitomized by A. J. Ayer's remarks in the editor's Introduction to Logical Positivism. "It is indeed remarkable," Ayer wrote, "how much of the doctrine that is now thought to be characteristic of logical positivism was already stated, or at least foreshadowed, by Hume" (1959: 4). It is significant that Reichenbach wrote The Rise of Scientific Philosophy in English, in 1951 after he and many other Viennese or Berlin positivists achieved a high profile in the philosophical landscape of the English-speaking countries. Reichenbach's words meant something different in the American philosophical landscape of the 1950s from what they would have meant in Vienna during the days of the Vienna Circle. Ayer's view was more or less the standard and largely undisputed view of logical positivism until the closing decade or two of the twentieth century when a different and far more interesting story has emerged.

Reichenbach insists that philosophy (of science) be distinguished not only from the history of philosophy but also from science itself. The "professional philosopher of science," to use Reichenbach's phrase, is the product of a new and indispensable distribution of work between scientific research and logical analysis. Indeed, logical analysis aims at "clarification rather than discovery" and may even "impede scientific productivity" (1951: 123). Thus does Reichenbach distinguish between the context of discovery and the context of justification, which, in turn, allows for a clear demarcation to be drawn between philosophers, who are concerned with *justification*, and historians, who, in one way or another, are concerned with *discovery*. Philosophers and historians can then go on their separate ways without having to consider the other – which they did until the 1960s. Before 1960, there are at least three recognizable and distinct domains – history of science, history of philosophy, and philosophy of science – each with its own perspectives, but in relative harmony with one another. Historians of science and historians of philosophy, although separated by training and professional societies, could still subscribe to a similar intellectualist historiography; Alexandre Koyré, for example, was one of the dominant post-war historians of science who espoused a methodology for the history of science that looked very much like the one practiced by historians of philosophy. At the time a rather unproductive debate was being waged between *internal* and *external* history of science.

An anecdote that may provide insight into this debate comes from the 1999 History of Science Society meetings in Pittsburgh. I. B. Cohen gave a paper there entitled, "Context and Construction: Allies of the History of Science Old and New," in which he related the excitement created by Koyré's work in the late 1950s and early 1960s, work whose liberating influence was characterized by Cohen as Koyré's externalism, although Koyré was widely considered to be the arch internalist. However, Cohen's perspective is informed by the work that preceded Koyré, that is, an inductivism in which philosophical world-views, such as the purported Platonism of Archimedes, are regarded as metaphysical programs external to science and therefore can play no role. From this perspective, what Koyré was advocating was external history. But Koyré, in contrast to historians who would make use of social factors, restricted his historical accounts to intellectual factors, and thus could be seen as advocating only internal history.

Koyré's approach complemented that of the dominant sociology of science, of Robert Merton and others, which was institutional and large in scale, that is, *externalist*. While historians of philosophy, like historians of science, usually treated their subject as an intellectual matter divorced from social and cultural considerations – philosophy or science *sub specie aeternitatis* – historians of philosophy also thought it advisable, if not mandatory, to proceed in a reconstructivist mode. For example, John Austin and Gilbert Ryle argued that the history of philosophy would be of greater use philosophically if it were divorced from its historical contingencies, or detours, a claim Edwin Curley (1986) easily and justly criticizes. As late as 1984, at the founding of the new *History of Philosophy Quarterly*, the editorial statement could request essays that "cultivate philosophical history in the spirit of *philosophia perennis*," historical material that "should be exploited to deal with matters on the agenda of current discussion."

Such "history" has closer filiations with pre-Koyréan history of science than with the history of science being done at the time of the founding of that journal.

History recalled

In the 1960s and 1970s the notion that the history of science, the history of philosophy, and the philosophy of science occupied distinct and independent intellectual realms was subject to a serious challenge, instigated by the publication, in 1962, of Thomas Kuhn's *The Structure of Scientific Revolutions* (SSR). In its very first sentence Kuhn questions the assumption that the history of philosophy and the history of science are an expendable part of philosophy and science: "History, if viewed as a repository for more than anecdote or chronology, could produce a decisive transformation in the image of science by which we are now possessed." After Kuhn, philosophers are required once again to study the history of philosophy and the history of science, but the point is not to show that a particular philosophy (of science) is superior to previous ones. Rather, philosophers are required to study the history of philosophy and science in order to understand the very concept of philosophy (of science). History of science, it seems, could be seen as *evidence* for philosophy of science. In his Preface, Kuhn in fact apologizes for his inability to produce sufficiently broad evidence or suitably wide-ranging historical accounts: "Far more historical evidence is available than I have had space to exploit below… In addition, the view of science to be developed here suggests the potential fruitfulness of a number of new sorts of research, both historical and sociological" (1962: ix).

Kuhn also overtly rejects the distinction between the context of justification and the context of discovery, making room for closer integration – again – between philosophy of science and history of science:

> Undoubtedly, some readers will already have wondered whether historical study can possibly effect the sort of conceptual transformation aimed at here. An entire arsenal of dichotomies is available to suggest that it cannot properly do so. History, we too often say, is a purely descriptive discipline. The theses suggested above are, however, often interpretive and sometimes normative … I may even seem to have violated the very influential contemporary distinction between "the context of discovery" and the "context of justification." (*Ibid.*: 8–9).

But these distinctions, he asserts, are neither elementary logical nor methodological dicta that are prior to the analysis of scientific knowledge. Rather, they seem to Kuhn to be integral parts of a traditional set of substantive answers to the very questions on which they have been deployed:

> If they are to have more than pure abstraction as their content, then that content must be discovered by observing them in application to the data they are meant to elucidate. How could the history of science fail to be a source

of phenomena to which theories about knowledge may legitimately be asked to apply?

Kuhn also lays the seeds of a larger debate about the desirability, if not necessity, of an external and social history of science in contrast to an internal and intellectual one. Kuhn sees *SSR* as extending the positions he wrote about in 1957 in *The Copernican Revolution* (*CR*), a study of the transformation of the Aristotelian geocentric image of the world to the heliocentric one in the style of Koyré. In *SSR* Kuhn writes:

> Gradually, and often without entirely realizing that they are doing so, historians of science have begun to ask new sorts of questions and to trace different, and often less than cumulative, developmental lines for the sciences... They ask, for example, not about the relation of Galileo's views to those of modern science, but rather about the relationship between his views and those of his group, i.e., his teachers, contemporaries, and immediate successors in the sciences. (1962: 3)

The movement in *SSR* toward social history is accentuated in its 1969 Postscript in which Kuhn declares that a different kind of history might have been more appropriate for the work: "If this book were being rewritten, it would therefore open with a discussion of the community structure of science, a topic that has recently become a significant subject of sociological research and that historians of science are beginning to take seriously" (*ibid.*: 176). Indeed, he ends by repeating the call for a wider social history: "Having opened this postscript by emphasizing the need to study the community structure of science, I shall close by underscoring the need for similar, and above all, comparative study of the corresponding communities in other fields" (209).

Imre Lakatos puts Kuhn's conclusions in *SSR* in stark perspective: "Kuhn's position concerning the Copernican Revolution changed radically from the essentially internalist simplicism of his [*CR*] to his radically sociologistic [*SSR*]" (Lakatos and Zahar, in Lakatos 1978: 177). While Lakatos endorses neither of these historiographical positions, the latter to his mind is clearly the worse: he characterizes it as a view that sees only "irrational change" in the historical details (118, 133). For Lakatos, historical details are neither so simple nor immune from analysis; indeed, he is famous for a "problem shift" with regard to the internal–external distinction (102). The distinction changes depending on the particular relevant historiography: what is external for the inductivist may be internal for the conventionalist (for Lakatos "internalist simplicism" is a genre of conventionalism, in the mode of Pierre Duhem). What is external for the conventionalist may be internal for the methodological falsificationist, and so on. Doubtless, Lakatos is right about the degree of complexity involved, but for the purposes of the present discussion we can restrict the meaning of 'internal' and 'external' to those Kuhn uses in his 1968 article, cited by Lakatos, "Science: The History of Science." For Kuhn, "'internal history' is usually defined as intellectual history; 'external history' as social history" (1978: 102).

Although there is merit in Lakatos's criticism, things are even more complex than he allowed. Kuhn's historiographical stance is not one-dimensional in either of his primary works, and thus neither of Lakatos's descriptions fit just right. There are sufficient non-internalist–simplicist accounts in *CR* for Kuhn to be able to refer back to them in *SSR*. For example, in its Preface Kuhn apologizes also for having said "nothing about the role of technological advances or of external social, economic, and intellectual conditions in the development of the sciences," adding that, "one needs, however, to look no further than Copernicus and the calendar to discover that external conditions may help transform a mere anomaly into a source of acute crisis" (1962: x). The footnote to this statement states, "these factors are discussed in [*CR*], 122–32, 270–1." Indeed, Kuhn proceeds to use *CR* as a source for non-internalist historical detail in the body of *SSR*: when he refers to Copernicus's Preface to *De Revolutionibus* as "one of the classic descriptions of a crisis state," Kuhn cites *CR*, pp. 135–43 (1962: 69; see also 83). Even when Kuhn argues that Copernicus achieved a scientific revolution in substituting for the old paradigm a new and incommensurable one, he refers to his previous work. In *SSR* Kuhn claims: "Copernicus' innovation was not simply to move the earth. Rather, it was a whole new way of regarding the problems of physics and astronomy, one that necessarily changed the meaning of both 'earth' and 'motion.'" The footnote to that statement refers to *CR*, Chapters 3, 4, and 7, and states that "the extent to which heliocentrism was more than a strictly astronomical issue is a major theme of the entire book" (*ibid.*: 149–50). Although it is likely that Kuhn here is reading back his later views into his earlier work, there had to be enough materials in *CR* to allow him to read it in the fashion of *SSR*.

While *CR* is not the internalist–simplicist manifesto that Lakatos alleges, neither is *SSR* a radically sociologistic tract. What may be overlooked in Kuhn's apology for not having said anything about the role of technological advances or external social, economic, and intellectual conditions in the development of the sciences is that he also asserts that "explicit consideration of effects like these would not," he thinks, "modify the main theses developed in [*SSR*]." Later in *SSR* (*ibid.*: 69), when discussing the Copernican crisis, he repeats that

> breakdown of the normal puzzle-solving activity is not, of course, the only ingredient of the astronomical crisis that faced Copernicus. An extended treatment would also discuss the social pressure for calendar reform, a pressure that made the puzzle of precession particularly urgent. In addition, a fuller account would consider the medieval criticism of Aristotle, the rise of Neo-Platonism, and other historical elements besides. But technical breakdown would still remain at the core of the crisis.

Thus, even in the seemingly most psychological–sociological element of *SSR* – that is, in crisis and the emergence of scientific theories – Kuhn is sure that external elements would not modify his conclusions and internal technical matters would be key to grasping the issues.

Yet the issue raised by Lakatos resonates, for Kuhn does seem to invite research in the social history of science and even sociology of science, research that includes traditional methods as well as more novel approaches such as qualitative or internal sociology. Social history of science develops, as does sociology of science; one can find an excellent exposition of the historical stance of such work, in the Introduction to Steve Shapin and Simon Shaffer's *Leviathan and the Air-Pump* (1985). There had been other significant developments, of course: Joseph Agassi (1963) argued that the accounts given by historians of science were influenced by their philosophies of science, with inductivists constructing inductivist history of science, conventionalists constructing conventionalist history, and Popperians, Popperian history. Lakatos extended Agassi's point: "philosophy of science without history of science is empty; history of science without the philosophy of science is blind" (1978: 102). Thus the issue of the relation between history (of science) and philosophy (of science) is raised anew. This can be seen in Larry Laudan's reflective equilibrium model of history of science with philosophy of science and his attempts at demarcating various kinds of histories (1978: Ch. 5), all of which he rejects in subsequent work. More importantly, history of philosophy finally learned from history of science. As Daniel Garber recounts:

> What my generation of historians of philosophy was reacting against was a bundle of practices that characterized the writing of the history of philosophy in the period: the tendency to substitute rational reconstructions of a philosopher's views for the views themselves ... the tendency to treat the philosophical positions as if they were those presented by contemporaries.

The antidote was to adopt the stance previously accepted by history of science; Garber continues: "My own particular heresies in the history of philosophy derived from my acquaintance with the history of science... I began reading more and more in the history of science, trying to link the history of science to the history of philosophy." And since "[o]ne of the important trends of history of science in the 1980s and 1990s was its interests in the social background to science," he confesses, "I made some stabs at trying to integrate aspects of these more sociological approaches to my work in the history of philosophy" (2004: 2–4).

At this stage in the 1990s there might have been a different marriage envisioned between social history of science, contextualist history of philosophy, historicist philosophy of science, and *internalist* sociology of science. But the image of science painted by the sociologists was in the end unacceptable to Kuhn, who had brought history from the exile to which the logical positivists had condemned it. Kuhn's strongly cognitivist, anti-relativist approach led him to disassociate himself from the conclusions advanced by social studies of science, which had the further consequence that Kuhn, in one stroke, had also distanced himself from much of recent history of science and history of philosophy (1992). Kuhn's reinterpretation of himself has had defenders, such as Vasso Kindi (2005), who argue that Kuhn was consistent all along in seeking first principles of philosophy of science apart from the history of science: the history of science provides only illustration, not evidence, for the philosophy of science. It remains to be seen whether Kuhn's last words on the subject will have the same effect on the philosophy of science and the history of philosophy, and their once-ancient and then-recent companion, the history of science, that *SSR* had in the four decades after its publication.

See also The historical turn in the philosophy of science; Logical empiricism; Scientific method.

References

Agassi, Joseph (1963) "Towards an Historiography of Science," *History and Theory: Studies in the Philosophy of History*, Supplement 2.

Ayer, A. J. (ed.) (1959) *Logical Positivism*, Glencoe, IL: Free Press.

Carnap, Rudolf (1967 [1928]) *The Logical Structure of the World and Pseudo-Problems in Philosophy* (English translation by R. A. George of *Der Logische Aufbau der Welt*, Leipzig: Felix Meiner Verlag, 1928), Berkeley: University of California Press.

Curley, Edwin (1986) "Dialogues with the Dead," *Synthese* 67: 33–49.

Garber, Daniel (2004) "Philosophy and the Scientific Revolution," in J. B. Schneewind (ed.) *Teaching New Histories of Philosophy: Proceedings of a Conference*, Princeton, NJ: University Center for Human Values, pp. 1–17.

Kindi, Vasso (2005) "The Relation of History of Science to Philosophy of Science in *The Structure of Scientific Revolutions* and Kuhn's Later Philosophical Work," *Perspectives on Science* 13: 495–530.

Kuhn, Thomas S. (1957) *The Copernican Revolution*, Cambridge, MA: Harvard University Press.

—— (1962) *The Structure of Scientific Revolutions*, Chicago: University of Chicago Press.

—— (1992) *The Trouble with the Historical Philosophy of Science*, Cambridge, MA: Harvard University Press.

Lakatos, Imre (1978) *Philosophical Papers*, Cambridge: Cambridge University Press, Volume 1.

Laudan, Larry (1977) *Progress and its Problems*, Berkeley: University of California Press.

Reichenbach, Hans (1951) *The Rise of Scientific Philosophy*, Berkeley: University of California Press.

Shapin, Steve, and Simon Shaffer (1985) *Leviathan and the Air-Pump*, Princeton, NJ: Princeton University Press.

Further reading

Every paragraph of our essay could be expanded to form an essay on its own. There are many works we could suggest as further reading; we cite here only a few. Harold Cherniss' *Aristotle's Criticism of Pre-Socratic Philosophy* (Baltimore, MD: Johns Hopkins University Press, 1935) examines Aristotle's treatment of his predecessors and Andrea Falcon's *Aristotle and the Science of Nature: Unity without Uniformity* (Cambridge: Cambridge University Press, 2005) the relation of Aristotle's philosophy and science. Similarly, for Descartes, Roger Ariew's *Descartes and the Last Scholastics* (Ithaca, NY: Cornell University Press, 1999) discusses Descartes's dealings with his predecessors and Daniel Garber's *Descartes Embodied: Reading Cartesian Philosophy through Cartesian Science* (Cambridge: Cambridge University Press, 2000), the interactions between Descartes's philosophy and science. Studies devoted to later episodes in the philosophy of science and history of philosophy include such exemplars as J. Albert Coffa, *The Semantic Tradition from Kant to Carnap* (Cambridge: Cambridge University Press, 1993), and Michael Friedman, *A Parting of the Ways: Carnap, Cassirer, and Heidegger* (Chicago: Open Court, 2000). See also the various essays in Ronald N. Giere and Alan W. Richardson (eds), *Origins of Logical Empiricism* (Minneapolis: University of Minnesota Press, 1996).

3
METAPHYSICS
Stephen Mumford

Introduction

Both science and metaphysics are concerned with the question of what there is and, to that extent, they have the same subject matter. Historically, some of the most significant debates in metaphysics have concerned the nature of universals (properties and relations), substance, causation, laws of nature, modality, identity, time, and truth. This list is not exhaustive, however, and there can be metaphysical issues in all other areas of philosophy. The mind–body problem is a metaphysical debate in the philosophy of mind, for instance, and in philosophical logic we may consider the nature and existence of propositions and logical forms, which is to consider metaphysical issues.

Given that metaphysics and science seem to seek the same thing – a description of the nature and workings of the world – we can well ask the question how, if at all, they differ. Assuming that we can find some difference between them, we can then ask how they relate. Is one discipline above the other in any respect? Is either of them logically or epistemologically prior to the other? We will see that philosophers of science and metaphysicians have had views on these questions and that there has been substantial disagreement. In the spectrum of views that are available, we find at one extreme the view that metaphysics is meaningless nonsense and at the other the view that all empirical and scientific knowledge is dependent on prior metaphysical understanding.

The chief concern of this essay will be with the demarcation of science and non-science: what it is, if anything, that makes them different subjects or ways of investigating, despite having seemingly the same subject matter. Given that the rest of this book is concerned with the nature of science, the focus here will be on the contrasting nature of metaphysics. Some philosophers have wondered how metaphysics is possible, given its abstract and non-experiential character. I will consider, therefore, how metaphysics relates, if at all, to empirical knowledge. It should be conceded, however, that there is very little agreement over the precise nature of metaphysics, even among the metaphysicians themselves. The nature of metaphysics is one among the number of problems considered by metaphysicians.

Early attempts at demarcation

The term "metaphysics" comes from Aristotle's book of that name in which he discusses various problems that are of this general nature. Aristotle did not call it metaphysics but, rather, the study of Being *qua* Being (*Metaphysics*, Book IV.1). To have Being is to exist, and Aristotle's concern was with what it was in general to exist and what it was for different categories of thing to exist. He also wanted to map out relations between the different categories of existence and thus produce the most general inventory of Being. Being *qua* Being covered everything: it would be an account of all that existed, not just what exists in the natural or empirical world, though that would be included as well. The *Metaphysics* was so named by later scholars just because the book appeared in their edition after *The Physics*, and metaphysics is often translated literally as "after physics." But, coincidentally (or not, as the case may be), metaphysics is after physics in another sense, namely in being above or beyond physics in its subject matter. Aristotle considered Being in such a general and abstract manner that the study went beyond the empirical and thus we have the earliest case of metaphysics being distinguished from science as a distinct subject. There were, however, metaphysicians before Aristotle, as Plato's theory of the Forms in the *Republic* is recognizably a metaphysical thesis and even the concerns of pre-Socratic philosophers were primarily metaphysical. A misnomer has been common since Aristotle in that the practitioners of metaphysics are standardly referred to as "metaphysicians." If their discipline is after or beyond physics, however, then clearly they should be named "metaphysicists." Practitioners of physics are known as "physicists," whereas physicians practice medicine. I shall not here try to replace standard usage, however.

Aristotle's metaphysics had a distinctly more abstract content than empirical science. Philosophers of science have tended to seek other distinguishing features with which to demarcate science and metaphysics. The concern has been largely to vindicate the position and legitimacy of science and in so doing distinguish it from various non-sciences: superstition, prejudice, pseudo-science, and metaphysics. Bacon famously concentrated on the context of discovery as the mark of science, proposing in the *Novum Organum* a new inductive method that could generate scientific truths as if by machinery. Knowledge was *scientific* if and only if it was derived in the right way, moving from observation of particular facts, through the tabular method, to a general theory, such as that heat is motion or that all swans are white.

The need for empirical evidence is even stronger in the empiricist tradition because of its view that all knowledge comes from experience (see Locke's *Essay Concerning Human Understanding*, 2.1.2). This generates the principle that for any human idea or concept to be legitimate, we must be able to show from what original experience(s) it is derived. If we are unable to do so, then such an idea is illegitimate. This led, some centuries later, to an overall condemnation of metaphysics in logical positivism, particularly as described by Ayer (1936: Ch. 1). Ayer's view employs Hume's fork to savage effect. In order for a statement or judgment to be meaningful it must be, at least in principle, empirically verifiable. Hence, if I claim that there is a cat in my room, the statement has meaning if and only if there are some experiences it would be possible to have – cat-like experiences in my room – that could verify it. But metaphysics seems to be non-empirical. When I claim that God exists, I do not claim this to be an empirical truth because God stands outside space and time and so cannot be seen or heard. But if verifiability is taken as a criterion of meaningfulness, then such a claim is deemed not just false – strictly speaking not false at all – but meaningless. The words are just empty sounds because we have literally no idea at all of what we are speaking when we use the word "God." Non-science is therefore nonsense, according to this form of empiricism, though, like Hume, logical positivists allow truths of logic and mathematics, which are just relations between ideas and utterly trivial. The problem of metaphysics is that it purports to be both substantial – non-trivial – but also non-empirical. This is not a permissible combination, so Ayer advocates, provoca-tively, the "elimination" of metaphysics. The argument is, however, just the modern version of that famously offered by Hume:

> When we run over libraries, persuaded by these principles, what havoc must we make? If we take in our hand any volume; of divinity or school metaphysics for instance; let us ask, *Does it contain any abstract reasoning concerning quantity or number?* No. *Does it contain any experimental reasoning concerning matter of fact and existence?* No. Commit it then to the flames: for it can contain nothing but sophistry and illusion. (Hume 1748: 165)

Karl Popper (1959) was a critic of both Baconian induction and logical positivism. The inductive method, no matter how refined it may be, is logically invalid. And because scientific theories are general, they are not verifiable, even in principle. Logical positivism would have to pronounce them meaningless. It was clear to Popper, therefore, that verifiability is not the criterion by which we can distinguish science and non-science. In its place, Popper offered *falsifiability*. While no particular observation can verify a general theory, there are many observations that could falsify it. Popper then saw that a theory of science, and a demarcation between science and non-science, could be based on this. Any theory that was unfalsifiable was non-scientific. But here, too, Popper departed from logical positivism. Both Popper and the logical positivists had read Wittgenstein's *Tractatus* (1921), but left it with differing views of metaphysics. Non-science need not be nonsense, according to Popper, as metaphysical claims may be among the most important to us. That is not to say that all non-science is important or good. Popper went to lengths to discredit Marxism and psychoanalysis for being pseudo-sciences: unfalsifiable theories claiming scientific credentials. But in allowing that metaphysics can be important, Popper scores an interesting victory over logical positivism. The logical positivist claim that statements must be verifiable to be meaningful is not itself verifiable, because, among other reasons, it is a modal claim. Hence it is self-undermining. In contrast, that a statement must be falsifiable to be scientific is not a self-undermining statement even if it is not itself falsifiable. That would just mean that it was not a scien-tific claim, but it may, instead, be legitimate as a philosophical one.

Popper's account does not, however, tell us much about the nature of metaphysics, how it is possible and how it is meaningful if it is not falsifiable. It has also been questioned whether the criterion of science that Popper offers is tenable. Science is likely to involve existential claims as well as general claims. Hence, it may be claimed that "There is a fifth basic force" or "There is a seventh kind of quark." Such statements have the logical form $\exists x F x$: that something is F. While I can in principle verify statements of this form, for example by finding a seventh kind of quark, I can never falsify such a claim. No matter how many unsuccessful searches I conduct for a fifth basic force, I do not falsify the claim that there is one. Perhaps, then, falsificationism gains credence only by concentrating on a limited domain of scientific statements. Furthermore, it is clear that falsification of theories can be resisted. The Duhem–Quine thesis states that a general theory can still be held in the light of any apparently countervailing evidence, simply by rejecting the evidence rather than the theory. Hence, while I see a black swan I may nevertheless decide to retain my theory that all swans are white, by accepting some supplementary claim such as that my observation is unreliable.

Since Popper, more holistic accounts of scientific theories have been given, though these weaken the division between science and metaphysics. Theories are equated with paradigms (Kuhn 1962), research programmes (Lakatos 1970) or ideologies (Feyerabend 1975) which come in whole packages that can determine observations. Observation is depicted as theory-dependent such that if one accepts a theory then one will be unable to find empirical refutations of it. But then the theory as a whole seems as empirically unaccountable as metaphysics and we are left wondering again what, if anything, distinguishes the two.

Rethinking the divide

We have seen that neither the logical positivists nor Popper can be said to have succeeded in drawing a substantial divide between science and metaphysics. This suggests that we might want to rethink the assumption that there is such a clear distinction between the two disciplines. In this section I look more closely at the basis of the assumption and then, in the next section, consider some of the options we now have before us.

Traditionally, metaphysics has been thought to be substantive and synthetic but also *a priori*. Science was understood to be entirely empirical and metaphysics entirely non-empirical, so the only real distinction was thought to be that truth in science was discovered *a posteriori* while truth in metaphysics was *a priori*. Hence, the world will look the same to an observer no matter which metaphysical theory is true. There is a division in metaphysics, for instance, between bundle and substratum theorists over the nature of substance (Loux 2002: Ch. 3). Bundle theorists think that particular substances are nothing more than bundles of qualities or properties, while substratum theorists think that there has to be an underlying, property-less substratum that collects together and individuates those bundles. Bundle theorists and substratum theorists can agree on all the empirical data, however, so the difference between the two theories cannot be an observable difference. If we are to decide between the two, therefore, it seems that we must use reason alone, unaided by the senses. Our choice between competing theories of metaphysics can only, it seems, be rational and *a priori*, hence the classification of such a practice as rationalist metaphysics. Spinoza's *Ethics* is perhaps the *opus classicus* of this approach, as an entire world system is built up from rational first principles through *a priori* deduction.

However, what has made such an approach to metaphysics difficult to defend is the additional claimed features that it is also substantive and its truths are synthetic. Other forms of *a priori* knowledge, such as logic and mathematics, are insubstantive in that they do not purport to say anything about what is. To argue that if A then B, and if B then C, *then* if A then C, says nothing about whether A, C, or anything else exists. Following Hume, we may think of such truths as nothing more than expressing relations between ideas. But metaphysics clearly does make existential claims that are not simply relations between ideas, as when we say, for instance, that universals exist. This is not an analytic or conceptual truth: it is not true simply in virtue of the meaning of the terms employed; so it is synthetic. The combination of being substantive but non-empirical can now be seen as very deeply puzzling. In the case of substantive empirical truths, we have a grasp of how to confirm one such truth, perhaps by observing whether something in the world corresponds to the state of affairs reported in the statement (assuming we accept some version of the correspondence theory of truth). In saying that metaphysics is substantive, the metaphysician is wanting to say that "There are universals" is true if and only if there are indeed universals, regardless of the fact that realists and nominalists agree over all the empirical data and so we cannot discover its truth or falsehood empirically.

This worried, among others, Kant (1781), who asked how synthetic *a priori* knowledge was possible. His solution was ingenious though it is not one that matches the ambitions of many metaphysicians. Kant made metaphysics a more modest exercise by claiming that synthetic *a priori* knowledge was possible only because it is knowledge about the nature and limits of our own *thinking*. Instead of claiming, for instance, that causation is a real feature of the world, a Kantian account would say something along the lines of human beings, in virtue of what they are and the way they think, having to conceptualize the world around them in causal terms. Similarly, I cannot say that the world in itself is spatio-temporal but I can say that spatio-temporality is a necessary condition of human perception and apprehension.

Such an approach to metaphysics can be considered deflationary. Instead of saying something substantial about the world, metaphysics would be saying something substantial only about the nature of human thought: a far more modest ambition. And it is also worth noting that this issue is not simply a problem for metaphysics but is arguably a general feature of all philosophy. In ethics, for example, whether utilitarianism is the correct moral theory cannot be decided empirically; nevertheless a moral realist may claim that it is true or false – that it is a substantive thesis. Similarly, whether knowledge is justified true belief cannot be empirically known. So this is a very general problem for the whole of philosophy (including the philosophy of science). It can be argued that philosophy in general has the appearance of being synthetic *a priori*, so a Kantian deflationary view of metaphysics would have to apply to other areas of philosophy. To say that these were also just about the nature of human thought would clearly be controversial. Although some philosophers may think that moral theories are just about the way we think, that itself is a philosophical position, one with which moral realists disagree. Similarly, metaphysical realists will disagree with the philosophical position that metaphysics is not about the world itself.

Another approach, which is also in a sense deflationary, is to deny that metaphysics, and any other part of philosophy, is correctly characterized as synthetic and *a priori*. Such an approach would seek to maintain that metaphysics is about the world but deny that metaphysical thinking has the kind of features that we have found so puzzling. One could claim that metaphysical thinking was not synthetic after all, but that metaphysicians were largely in the business of collecting conceptual truths; or one could claim that metaphysics was not after all *a priori*, despite appearances and centuries of philosophical opinion to the contrary. I consider those options in more detail in the final section, but I wish to consider first an implication of this kind of response. It has been assumed that philosophers, and metaphysicians *par excellence*, have a distinctive way of thinking about the world that is sharply divided from the way scientists think about the world. Philosophers are able to find substantial non-empirical truths while scientists find empirical truths. But this may just be a philosopher's confidence trick, attempting to carve out some distinctive, esoteric domain that justifies philosophy as a separate discipline. In which case, there may not be a distinctly metaphysical way of thinking at all. Indeed, why should we think there might be? How would it have evolved? What use to humans would it be to think metaphysically? It is hard to see how thought that has no empirical consequences could bestow any evolutionary advantage on its thinker. Whether one believes realism about universals or resemblance nominalism, one is just as likely to survive and reproduce, so why should any such ability be selected and developed over the course of human evolution?

Contemporary responses: getting our priorities right

In these final sections I look at some contemporary responses to the problems outlined above. In doing so, I bring back into focus the two issues with which I began: How, if at all, does metaphysics differ from science? And what are the relations between the two? I will consider three different live options. These are not exhaustive, but represent the range of options that are still in the running as explanations of how metaphysics can be a substantive discipline. They differ on the nature of metaphysics and the degree to which it is empirically informed. This comes down to a disagreement over the order of priority between metaphysics and science. One view says that metaphysics is rationally prior to science and all empirical knowledge. Opposed to this is a view that metaphysics is a branch or extension of empirical knowledge, and the way that it differs from science is not in virtue of being *a priori* but in virtue of being more abstract. Another position is a halfway house, claiming that metaphysics and science are equal partners in the endeavor for knowledge. I do not side with any of these three views, partly because I see both merit and problems in all. I call the three positions, in the order I discuss them, *realism*, *the Canberra plan* (the equal partner view), and *a posteriorism*. I end with consideration of a more widespread conciliatory view of the correct method in metaphysics.

Realism

E. J. Lowe advocates metaphysics as a substantial and primary discipline. He says that his aim is "to restore metaphysics to a central position in philosophy as the most fundamental form of rational enquiry, with its own distinctive methods and criteria of validation" (1998: 1). Metaphysics does not tell us what there is, but it does tell us what is possible. It is then up to science to tell us which of the possibilities is actual (or which of the many possible worlds is ours). Science unaided cannot tell us what is possible, unless it becomes itself metaphysical. Science tells us what is actual, though that will rest on metaphysical and ontological assumptions about the possible. Metaphysics thus provides the modal background against which we set our empirical discoveries. For example, we can discover empirically that the morning star is identical with the evening star only if we accept the modal claim that two distinct material objects cannot occupy the same place at the same time. This cannot itself be an empirical claim as only *a priori* metaphysics may deliver it through its investigation of what is, and what is not, possible. Similarly, physics will often assume an ontology based on metaphysical rather than empirical commitments. Whether objects are just bundles of sensation or are mind-independent, continuing to exist unperceived, cannot by its very nature be decided empirically. Such considerations prompt Lowe to claim: "We are all metaphysicians whether we know it or not, and whether we like it or not" (2002: 4).

The biggest problem for such an account to overcome is how such modal knowledge can be acquired, which of course harks back to Kant's question. Lowe continues to depict metaphysics as substantial: it is about the world (or at least what is possible for the world) rather than human thought. Yet it is *a priori*. It is also funda-mental and primary, returning to the Aristotelian priority of metaphysics as First Philosophy. Lowe does make some concession to the empirical, however. Empirical and metaphysical considerations can interact so that we may choose to develop an empirically informed metaphysics. Science may tell us, for instance, that it is plausible that the world contains atomistic elements, and this could inform and justify atomism in metaphysics. Such a theory would no longer then be purely *a priori*, so would no longer have the certainty of the pure *a priori*; but certainty, says Lowe, is something we should be prepared to sacrifice in metaphysics.

The Canberra plan

Lewis (1970) proposes a way of doing philosophy, and metaphysics in particular, that has proved influential in recent years. It has been developed by Canberra philos-opher Frank Jackson (1998). The metaphysician's job is to gather the platitudes: all the *a priori* truths that tell us what some phenomenon is; for example, what it is that causation is supposed to be, or a law of nature. We form these into a "Ramsey sentence" that describes a complete role of something. $\exists x \, (Fx \,\&\, Gx \,\&\, Hx \,\&\, \ldots)$ says that there is something of which it is true that F, G, H, and so on. In the Ramsey sentence for causation we might say that there is something that relates events, creates constant conjunctions among types of event, supports counterfactuals, and so on. But this is only the first step. Next we look at the world and discover what, as a matter of empirical fact, fills such a role: modal relations between particulars, energy transference, causal powers or whatever. Scientists perform this second step.

The advantage of such an account is that it explains, even vindicates, the philosophical process. Philosophers doing conceptual analysis from the comfort of their living-rooms play a crucial organizational role in the acquisition of knowledge. They are concerned only with the *a priori* portion, but provide an ineliminable and vital contribution. The metaphysician uncovers the constraints on a theory. Anything offered as a theory of causation, for example, would have to satisfy the relevant Ramsey sentence.

There are two problems with this account, however. First, it is contentious that metaphysics is concerned only with the first of the two steps. Gathering the platitudes seems a relatively mundane and uninteresting task, which for the most part is merely assumed to have been completed. In the case of causation, for example, disputes are rarely about the platitudes themselves. Rather, there is a host of theories that claim to be able to satisfy the Ramsey sentence just as easily as any other theory, and that is more commonly the area of dispute among metaphysicians. They have proved reluctant to leave the second step to the empirical scientists. A second problem is that it offers no challenge to supposedly natural ways of thinking. Metaphysics is slave to the platitudes, which are just a collection of common sense. Philosophy in the Socratic tradition is depicted more as an antidote or challenge to common sense. Why should a pre-philosophical way of thinking about the world be right? It has proved enough for us to survive as a species but it might not have got right the more subtle points about the nature of our world (Lowe 1998: 6–7). Metaphysics might be able to improve, revise, and regiment our ways of thinking, and the Canberra plan does not seem to make room for this.

A posteriorism

Quine challenged the analytic–synthetic distinction and Putnam (1962) has argued that seeming knowledge of *a priori* necessities could turn out to be wrong. Cats may turn out, on empirical investigation, to be not animals but robots. That cats *are* animals ought, therefore, to be understood as an *a posteriori* truth after all. Putnam challenges in general the view that there are necessary, immutable truths. If this is correct, what would be left of metaphysics, which until now has been presented as a self-professed *a priori* enterprise?

Metaphysics might still be possible, though now understood as a kind of *a posteriori* study only. The division between science and metaphysics would not be that one is empirical and one is *a priori*, but then what would the division be? An option is to think of types of study falling on a spectrum of more-or-less concrete or abstract. Metaphysics would be continuous with physics but more abstract. We will sometimes reflect on our empirical knowledge and want to bring it together to form a global view, looking at what there is in the abstract. We may note, for instance, that scientists invoke various specific laws of nature, such as the law of gravitational attraction and Coulomb's law. The metaphysician will then consider laws of nature in general, deciding what features something must have to qualify as a law, what role laws generally have in the functioning of our world, whether they relate events or properties, and so on. Metaphysics is, then, as *a posteriori* as anything else, but is distinguished by being at the more abstract end of the *a posteriori*.

Such a view would still have to answer Lowe's claim that metaphysical knowledge is a precondition for empirical knowledge. This last view reverses the order of priority claimed by realism: science, as empirical study, is prior to metaphysics. Presumably, the knowledge that distinct material objects cannot occupy the same space at the same time would be an empirical generalization from the cases of particular distinct objects. It is nevertheless difficult to explain how this knowledge can be modal and can support counterfactuals. If one is more of an empiricist philosopher, however, one may well deny that knowledge has any such modal value and be attracted to some such form of *a posteriorism*.

Non-alignment

Rather than adopt one of these three positions, many metaphysicians take a non-aligned, conciliatory view of their task. Metaphysics is for the most part judged to be non-empirical, so we are left to reason carefully about the truth of the matter. David Armstrong (1989: 135), for instance, who is one of the most important and influential contemporary metaphysicians, says:

> Metaphysicians should not expect any certainties in their inquiries. One day, perhaps, the subject will be transformed, but for the present the philosopher can do no more than survey the field as conscientiously as he or she can, taking note of the opinions and arguments of predecessors and contemporaries, and then make a fallible judgment arrived at and backed up as rationally as he or she knows how.

Also like many other current metaphysicians, Armstrong accepts a cost–benefit approach:

> We have to accept, I think, that straight refutation (or proof) of a view in philosophy is rarely possible. What has to be done is to build a case against, or to build a case for, a position. One does this usually, by examining many different arguments and considerations against and for a position and comparing them with what can be said against and for alternative views. What one should hope to arrive at … is something like an intellectual cost–benefit analysis of the view considered… One important way in which different philosophical and scientific theories about the same topic may be compared is in respect of intellectual economy. In general, the theory that explains the phenomena by means of the least number of entities and principles (in particular, by the least number of sorts of entities and principles) is to be preferred. (*Ibid.*: 19–20).

Whether this is sufficient to generate truth in metaphysics is another matter. The factors mentioned are pragmatic, suggesting that the truth delivered by the cost–benefit analysis is truth as coherence only. If one generally favors a view of truth as correspondence, one may feel that the cost–benefit analysis in metaphysics cannot quite attain the substantial metaphysical truths that are being sought.

See also Critical rationalism; Essentialism and natural kinds; The history of philosophy and the philosophy of science; Logical empiricism; Scientific method; Underdetermination.

References

Armstrong, D. (1989) *Universals: An Opinionated Introduction*, Boulder, CO: Westview Press.

Ayer, A. J. (1936) *Language, Truth and Logic*, 2nd edn repr., London: Penguin, 1971.

Feyerabend, P. (1975) *Against Method*, London: New Left Books.

Hume, D. (1975 [1748]) *An Enquiry Concerning Human Understanding*, Selby-Bigge edition, Oxford: Clarendon Press.

Jackson, Frank (1998) *From Metaphysics to Ethics: A Defence of Conceptual Analysis*, Oxford: Oxford University Press.

Kuhn, T. (1962) *The Structure of Scientific Revolutions*, Chicago: University of Chicago Press.

Lakatos, I. (1970) "Falsification and the Methodology of Scientific Research Programmes," in I. Lakatos and A. Musgrave (eds) *Criticism and the Growth of Knowledge*, Cambridge: Cambridge University Press, pp. 91–196.

Lewis, D. (1970) "How to Define Theoretical Terms," in *Philosophical Papers*, Oxford: Oxford University Press, 1983, Volume I, pp. 78–95.

Loux, M. J. (2002) *Metaphysics: A Contemporary Introduction*, 2nd edn, London: Routledge.

Lowe, E. J. (1998) *The Possibility of Metaphysics: Substance, Identity and Time*, Oxford: Oxford University Press.

Popper, K. (1959) *Logic of Scientific Discovery*, London: Hutchinson.

Putnam, H. (1962) "It Ain't Necessarily So," in *Mathematics, Matter and Method*, Cambridge: Cambridge University Press, 1979, pp. 237–49.

Wittgenstein, L. (1921) *Tractatus Logico-Philosophicus*, trans. 1961, London: Routledge.

Further reading

There are many introductory books on metaphysics. M. J. Loux's *Metaphysics: A Contemporary Introduction*, 2nd edn (London: Routledge, 2002) is excellent and up to date. E. J. Lowe has two useful books both of which could be starting points: *A Survey of Metaphysics* (Oxford: Oxford University Press, 2002) is slightly more technical than Loux, as is *The Possibility of Metaphysics*, which asks Kant's question anew. For a development of the Canberra plan, Frank Jackson's *From Metaphysics to Ethics: A Defence of Conceptual Analysis* (Oxford: Oxford University Press, 1998) is the best source. For thorough treatment of individual topics there is Le Poidevin, Simons, McGonigal and Cameron (eds) *The Routledge Companion to Metaphysics* (London: Routledge, forthcoming). The classics remain rewarding, however. Metaphysics as a distinct subject begins with Aristotle in the *Metaphysics* (London: Penguin 1998) and the classic examination of how metaphysics is possible is to be found in Kant's 1781 *Critique of Pure Reason*, Kemp-Smith edition (London: Macmillan). For the attack on metaphysics, the most readable source is A. J. Ayer's *Language, Truth and Logic*, 2nd edn (London: Penguin, 1936).

4
PHILOSOPHY OF LANGUAGE

Rod Bertolet

The central topic in the philosophy of language that impinges on work in philosophy of science is the theory of meaning, particularly the distinction between meaning and reference. Disputes about the relation among language, truth, and reality, the connection between what is necessary and what is *a priori*, the prospects of a commitment to various sorts of natural kinds and viable forms of essentialism, and the incommensurability of theories are all tied to views about meaning and reference. What determines that expressions mean what they do also figures in the section on holism and incommensurability, below.

The meaning–reference distinction has been marked with other terminology, when philosophers have distinguished connotation and denotation, sense and reference, or intension and extension. Motivating the distinction involves appeals to obvious ways in which terms can be different even if they apply to the same things. Let "renate" be shorthand for "creature with a kidney" and "cordate" be shorthand for "creature with a heart." Facts about the world make it the case that "renate" and "cordate" refer to or denote the same things, or have the same extension. But clearly they ascribe different properties to the same set of things, and that difference is among those we capture by saying they differ in meaning. Time-worn and artificial as it is, the example makes the point nicely. Differences in description provide the clearest examples of intuitive difference in meaning: for instance, "the first heavenly body visible in the morning" and "the first heavenly body visible in the evening" differ in meaning, although as it happens both expressions (or expansions of them) pick out the planet Venus. But whether all referring expressions work the same way is another question.

One view is that all such expressions are alike in having both meaning and reference. The clearest instance of this is probably Rudolf Carnap's *Meaning and Necessity* (1956 [1947]), in which *every* expression up to and including a full sentence was assigned an intension that determines its extension. However, one can hold, and many have held, different sorts of theories about different sorts of expressions. Mill, for example, famously said in *A System of Logic* that proper names have denotation but no connotation, that they do not connote or express properties, whereas common nouns have both connotation and denotation. Or one might claim, as some contemporary writers do, that common nouns fall into different sub-species, some of them being natural-kind terms whose reference is not determined by any properties associated with them, perhaps "cat" or "oxygen," for instance, while others, such as "veterinarian" or "chemist," do have reference-determining properties associated with them.

Proper names: the description view

While few philosophers of science are interested in proper names, they provide a useful point of departure because the issues and arguments surrounding them are similar to those regarding natural-kind terms. Mill's account of proper names as connotationless tags did not enjoy much support through most of the twentieth century. Aside from providing no account at all of why proper names refer to the individuals that they do, the account seemed susceptible to a powerful argument that Frege gave in 1892 in "Über Sinn und Bedeutung." The argument proceeds from the premise that sentences such as "Hesperus is Hesperus" and "Hesperus is Phosphorus" are significantly different to the conclusion that the terms "Hesperus" and "Phosphorus" must differ in sense, or the mode of presentation of their shared referent, which is the planet Venus. Frege locates the difference in the two statements in a difference in cognitive significance, claiming that "Hesperus is Hesperus" is analytic and *a priori*, whereas statements such as "Hesperus is Phosphorus" are neither of those but instead can provide "very valuable extensions of our knowledge." He appears to locate the difference in the sense or meaning of the names in different concepts expressed by descriptions such as "the evening star" and "the morning star." It is debatable whether Fregean senses are not considerably richer than this, but Frege was usually taken to hold the single-description view, as was Russell. However one wants to specify such details, the argument takes the difference in the significance of different statements such as these to be due to the meaning, or semantic properties, of the only things about them that differ, viz., the names that occur in them.

When one adds Frege's doctrine that sense determines reference and the claim that understanding a term is a matter of grasping its sense or meaning, the result is an attractive account of how words refer to what they do and how speakers know that they refer to what they do. To grasp the sense of a name is to associate the appropriate description with it, and the referent is the thing satisfying that description, and known to be the thing satisfying the description. When one pairs this with a similar account of how common nouns work, one has in sight a unified account of how singular and general terms work. The meaning of a term is given by some description expressing a concept grasped by any competent speaker (this being just what linguistic competence is), and the term refers to whatever thing or class or set of things which that concept applies to. Questions arise about which descriptions count, and possible answers range from a single defining property to the extreme holism that has all associated properties count. While holism has had some defenders, the progression of mainstream thought in the second half of the twentieth century was from a single-description view to what is often known as a cluster theory.

A cluster theory seems implicit in some of Wittgenstein's remarks and was explicitly advocated by Searle and Strawson. The theory attributed to Frege and Russell, according to which, for example, the name "Aristotle" had as its sense the conceptual content expressed by "the pupil of Plato and teacher of Alexander the Great," had the following consequences. First, one could not be wrong about whether Aristotle taught Alexander the Great, since "teacher of Alexander the Great" is included in the meaning of the name "Aristotle." Second, again because of that meaning connection, it is a necessary truth that Aristotle taught Alexander the Great. The connection would be just like the meaning connection between "Smith is a bachelor" and "Smith is unmarried." But it seems as though we could readily enough be mistaken in some of the things we believe about historical figures, and it certainly seems as though it is at best a contingent truth and not a matter of necessity that Aristotle taught Alexander the Great. There were also some doubts about whether proper names have definitions at all, in the way that many common nouns do. It seemed more plausible to suppose that "Aristotle" has its reference fixed by some of the cluster of descriptions that speakers might offer when asked for Aristotle's important properties. The approach left room for counting some descriptions as more important than others and suggesting that the cluster determines reference without being the meaning or definition of a name. It was usually left unspecified how many descriptions had to apply to something for it to be the referent of the name. The vagueness of the story was cited as a virtue by its proponents, a proper reflection of the imprecision of ordinary language.

The new theory of reference

The origins of what is sometimes called the new theory of reference are a matter of dispute, but Donnellan and especially Kripke have generally been credited with overturning cluster as well as earlier versions of the description theory starting in the early 1970s. Kripke gave modal arguments against cluster theories, urging that it is not only not necessary that Aristotle taught Alexander, but not necessary that Aristotle did any of the things we regard as his most important achievements. Both Donnellan and Kripke offered examples to show that speakers need not be able to provide the individuating descriptions the theory requires, and need not be able to provide descriptions that correctly pick out the person or thing to which they refer. One might, for example, have little to offer for the name "Cicero" or something as wrongheaded as "inventor of the atomic bomb" for Einstein and yet refer to Cicero and Einstein by using their names. Kripke argued that intuition tells us that names are rigid designators, ones that designate the same object in every possible world in which it exists. This provided an additional argument against description theories: since empirical descriptions such as "the discoverer of oxygen" vary in reference across worlds, those descriptions cannot determine the reference of names.

These arguments greatly diminished the popularity of description theories. The new rival view, sometimes known as a "causal" or "historical explanation theory of reference," held that the factor determining reference was not descriptive fit, but a causal–historical connection between the item originally named and our uses of a name: the chain of communication from us back to the referent. An important if controversial outcome of all this was that there were necessary but *a posteriori* truths, such as the truth that Hesperus is Phosphorus. Since both names refer to the planet Venus, there is no possible world in which it is false that Hesperus is Phosphorus; but it was an empirical discovery that Hesperus is Phosphorus, not a suitable matter for *a priori* astronomical speculation. (There also emerged the possibility of contingent *a priori* truths, although the examples were more controversial and the idea was less shocking to standard views.) "Hesperus" refers to a planet, while count or mass nouns such as "cat" or "water" have multiple mammals or puddles in their extensions, but the question naturally arises of whether the mechanism for reference fixing is the same for these terms.

Parallel considerations were brought to bear against the traditional view of some common nouns, the view that (as Mill put it) they connoted properties, indeed have as their meaning a set of predicates (or the properties they pick out) that provide necessary and sufficient conditions for the applicability of the term they define. Kripke and Putnam were in the forefront of a repudiation of the traditional view for natural-kind terms, among which they numbered "lemon," "water," "tiger," and "gold." Considerations of necessity took the discussion in two different directions. The necessity of the properties typically found in dictionary entries – that lemons are yellow or tigers are striped for instance – was called into question. Putnam had argued earlier that it is not a matter of meaning, or an analytic truth, that cats are animals (if they are), since the things we call "cats" might have turned out to be cleverly designed robots left by the Martians to spy on us. On the other hand, both Kripke and Putnam endorsed varieties of essentialism, for instance, that tigers have some biological property such as a certain kind of DNA that it is the proper business of biologists to specify, that gold having the atomic number 79, and that water being H_2O are essential properties of tigers, gold, and water respectively. These are empirically discovered essences, so they provide further examples of truths that are necessary, but *a posteriori*. Such claims are more controversial for biological than for chemical or physical kinds.

Putnam's "Twin Earth" examples

Putnam's so-called "Twin Earth" examples have figured prominently in discussions of essentialism and natural kind terms. Putnam asks us to imagine a planet Twin Earth, which is very much like earth, including the use of what is known there as "English," but the language called "English" on Twin Earth differs from English as spoken on earth because the liquid in the rivers, lakes, and reservoirs on Twin Earth is not water. On Twin Earth, the liquid called "water" is not H_2O; it is indistinguishable from our water at the macro level, looking and tasting, and quenching thirst in the same way, but it is a physically different compound, with a chemical formula that Putnam abbreviates as XYZ. Empirical investigation would eventually reveal this to sufficiently curious travellers from one planet to the other, but it would not have done so in 1750, and Putnam asks us to compare the typical speakers of earthian English and Twin Earthian English at that time, particularly their beliefs or psychological states concerning their terms "water." These were the same, and so they were in the same psychological state. If they were in the same psychological states and hence "meant the same thing" by "water," and if meaning determines reference or extension, then the extension of "water" should have been the same on earth and Twin Earth. But it was not. For dramatic purposes, Putnam invites us to think that Oscar₁ on earth and Oscar₂ on Twin Earth are exact duplicates with exactly the same psychological states, but who nonetheless refer to collections of H_2O in one case and XYZ in the other. A more humdrum example offered to those who are not so fond of science-fiction cases involves "elm" and "beech," for which, Putnam assures us, he has exactly the same concept, although he refers to elm and beech trees as successfully as the more botanically sophisticated among us. Putnam thinks that just as he need not be able to distinguish gold from fool's gold to be able to refer to gold with "gold" (as long as experts can tell them apart), he need not be able to distinguish elms from beeches to be able to refer to elms with "elms." Twin Earth examples are widely taken to have established that meaning or intension conceived as a set of predicates expressing the properties we take to define the term does not suffice to determine reference or extension.

Such examples are designed to show that what is in the physical environment matters to reference: it is this point, that factors external to individuals are involved in the determination of the reference of our terms, that Putnam's famous slogan "Meanings ain't in the head" is designed to capture. The point is not that nothing pertinent to meaning is in the head. Putnam says that the reference of such terms is fixed by appeal to the notion of something being the *same liquid as* or the *same kind as* something in a sample glass of water or a sample tiger wandering by, where the presence of the perceived sample is crucially involved. He says that this reveals an indexical component in our terms previously unnoticed, since the extension includes things that are determined by scientific investigation to be of the same kind as *this* liquid or tiger, the one that is the sample. In fact, he claims that his point about there being an indexical component to natural-kind terms is the same as Kripke's claim about rigid designation, provided we extend the terminology to names for such things as substances. The role of the sample also highlights the importance of some sort of causal contact with the sample involved in the reference-fixing.

Other examples, primarily due to Burge, were designed to take the anti-individualistic arguments one step further, suggesting that the social as well as the physical environment matters to reference determination. Many of Burge's examples are terms for artefacts such as "sofa" which are perhaps irrelevant here (although artefacts include lab equipment). But another involving a term for a medical condition presumably is pertinent. Burge considers someone who thinks that arthritis is a condition that can affect muscles and not merely joints, and utters along with complaints about various arthritic joints "I have arthritis in my thigh." Burge claims that this person is using *our* term in *our* way and hence has a false belief about the medical condition arthritis, not just a false belief about the medical term "arthritis." Were he in a linguistic community in which the term was applied to rheumatoid conditions not in joints, then, with no difference in him, he would be using *their* term *their* way and have a true belief about arthritis. (That there would be no difference in him is the way in which the argument is anti-individualistic.) The conclusion is that social as well as physical environment matters.

Some have taken one lesson of these examples to be that we need to distinguish *narrow* meaning, roughly what we get by considering just the mental states of individuals, and *wide* meaning, generally treated as narrow meaning together with the extra-cranial states of affairs that make it the case that our terms refer to or have in their extensions what they do. Thus, Putnam's Oscars could be said to share narrow meaning but differ in wide meaning or, as it is sometimes put, share narrow content but differ in wide content. This is important to debates in philosophy of mind and philosophy of psychology over the adequacy of psychological explanations that appeal only to the narrow versions.

It is worth noting one thing that accepting these arguments does *not* require, and indeed that was no part of Putnam's program in the 1970s. It is again instructive to start with proper names, and note that one prominent account of these, usually called direct reference, assigns no role at all to any sort of descriptive content. On this view, the only semantic properties names have is referring to their bearers, which they do directly, rather than through the intermediation of any descriptive content.

While Kripke did not address such matters, Putnam offered a multi-faceted picture of what the meaning of a natural kind term involves, suggesting that a type of "normal form for the description of meaning" for the term "water" would include at least syntactic markers (*mass noun, concrete*), semantic markers (*natural kind, liquid*), stereotype (*colorless, transparent, tasteless, thirst–quenching* . . .), and extension (H_2O – give or take impurities). Moreover, he conjectured that these components, *except for the extension*, are part of the competence of the individual speaker. So competent speakers need to know that "water" picks out a natural kind in liquid form that is transparent, colorless, odorless, and so forth, though they do not need to know that what it picks out is H_2O (as we did not in 1750). The Twin Earth examples do their work of assigning a crucial role to external circumstances in the determination of reference without denying that we have in our heads fairly rich meaning-relevant mental states. But they do support what is sometimes called semantic externalism by assigning to those external states an important role in reference determination. Putnam appealed to semantic externalism in defense of scientific realism, which he then favored. His idea was that if reference is a significant part of meaning, and reference is determined by causal connections with the world (rather than by descriptions that can vary across theories), then we can explain how, for example, the expression "electric charge" has referred to the same magnitude in quite different theories of electric charge. For "we can identify that magnitude in a way that is independent of all but the most violent theory change by, for example, singling it out as the magnitude which is causally responsible for certain effects" (Putnam 1975: ix).

The two-dimensionalist backlash

In this section I consider two problems that are prominent in the literature, and then a complete rejection of the Kripke–Putnam position. Earlier I noted Putnam's claim that the reference of "tiger" might be fixed by appeal to something being of the same biological kind as a passing tiger. But a passing tiger is a passing cat and a passing mammal and a passing animal: which *level* counts? This is the *qua* problem: if a term is bestowed, *qua* what – tiger, mammal – is that thing construed? This looks to be a matter of how it is classified by the person introducing the term, and this classification may require that descriptions be reintroduced into the theory. (These would not necessarily be ones rich enough to determine extension, so it might be that they could be part of what Putnam called the stereotype: but re-admitting descriptions is unwelcome to those hoping that we could show that these terms refer directly.) A separate issue is how to understand the idea that a natural-kind term is a rigid designator. Since names pick out individuals, the claim that a name picks out the same individual in every possible world in which it exists is easy to grasp. However, "tiger" has different extensions in different possible worlds, so we don't seem to have the *same* notion here. Some suggest that natural kind terms pick out kinds that are invariant across worlds although their members differ, but this has its own problems. This second problem is to clarify the view of natural-kind terms as rigid designators by explaining what they rigidly designate.

The view Kripke and Putnam develop has an important consequence for the view that philosophy is solely a matter of conceptual analysis: it seems false. Quineans, of course, dispute the idea that there is a sharp line between philosophy and empirical science, but many resist this idea and take a central task – perhaps the sole task – of philosophy to be the *a priori* pursuit of necessary conceptual truths. The arguments against descriptive theories of names and natural-kind terms and the widespread acceptance of the alternative new theory provide no comfort for those who hold this view. It is no part of the assault on description theories that names and natural-kind terms *could not* have worked as description theories indicate. (Indeed some concede that there are so-called attributive names that do function just as the theory requires, offering "Jack the Ripper" as a plausible example, and few deny that there are common nouns such as "ornithologist" or "bachelor" that have descriptive meanings that determine reference.) Rather, the *a priori* work in these areas consisted of clearing away unconvincing arguments for the description theory that assured us that Mill's view *could not* be right, so that we could then see that it is just an empirical fact that names and natural-kind terms in natural languages such as English function as rigid designators or their cousins.

This rejection of the classical view of philosophy might have been expected to provoke resistance. The claims that there are necessary *a posteriori* truths and contingent *a priori* truths might also have been expected to provoke resistance. They did. A new version of descriptivism designed to avoid those objections and rescue the more traditional picture of philosophical inquiry emerged. The new approach, usually known as two-dimensionalism, posits two aspects or dimensions of meaning and two propositions expressed by a sentence such as "Water is H_2O." One is necessary and the other is *a posteriori*, but neither is necessary and *a posteriori*. There are some (legitimate) understandings of two-dimensionalism on which direct-reference theorists endorse a version of it, but here we understand two-dimensionalism more narrowly as involving a revival of description theories of reference determination. Here is an oversimplified presentation of Frank Jackson's version (with many technical details suppressed).

The two dimensions of meaning posited are both intensions, a primary and a secondary intension. The primary intension of "water" is taken to be "the watery stuff of our acquaintance." (On this view, there must be some description that fixes the reference of "water" and we let this do duty for it until we learn what it is.) Due to the indexical component, the primary intension picks out whatever the watery stuff at a given world is: H_2O here; XYZ on Twin Earth. The secondary intension of "water" is given by a description that is converted into a rigid designator by the addition of the term "actual" or a technical device, so that the reference is determined to be what "water" picks out in the actual world, viz., H_2O. The intensions of the sentences are then as follows. The secondary intension of "Water is H_2O" is the necessary proposition *that $H_2O = H_2O$*, one that (uninterestingly) says that the compound H_2O stands in the identity relation to itself. The primary intension of "Water is H_2O" (the *other* proposition it expresses) is *that the watery stuff of "our" acquaintance = the chemical compound whose molecules consists of two hydrogen atoms and one oxygen atom.* This proposition is contingent, since the watery stuff of our acquaintance might have been XYZ, as it indeed is for those who inhabit Twin Earth. But it is also *a posteriori*. One may take "Water is H_2O" to be a necessary *a posteriori* sentence, but the necessity attaches to one proposition, while the need for experience to be known attaches to another proposition. Proponents of two-dimensionalism appear to hold that what is expressed by utterances of "Water is H_2O" is the primary proposition. Discussion of this ingenious proposal is ongoing.

Holism and incommensurability

There are also significant consequences of different accounts of what is part of or relevant to meaning. The most ontologically parsimonious approach is Mill's view that the meaning of a term is nothing but its referent or, as it is sometimes put, that the semantic role of a term is exhausted by its role of referring to its bearer. At the opposite end of the spectrum are extreme forms of holism that take every belief one has to matter to every term one uses, or in the case of a theory take every statement in it to contribute to the meaning of all of its terms, observational and theoretical alike (if these can be distinguished). Quine appears to have endorsed such views in some of his writings. There are many alternatives one might adopt between reference-only-minimalism and everything-matters-holism, from atomistic views that allow one description to serve as the meaning of a term and sanction a notion of analyticity or truth by virtue of meaning alone to a wide range of those that take more than one but fewer than all of the beliefs or theoretical claims one has to count toward meaning. Let us look at the consequences of such views for theory change and incommensurability.

Assume extreme holism, so that every statement in our theory of electrons contributes to the meaning of the term "electron" and every other term in the theory. Then without a reason for thinking otherwise, any change in the theory will involve a change in the meaning of "electron" and "pointer" and every other term in the theory. It appears to follow that what might have been taken to be an improved theory of electrons is instead an entirely new theory whose terms differ in meaning from the original, and that this holds for "pointer" just as much as "electron." It also appears to follow that theories that differ in this way – not just drastically different theories of the sort on which Kuhn focused such as Ptolemaic and Copernican accounts of the solar system but ones that differ in what might have seemed to be a small way – are not theories of the same things and so cannot be compared with one another. After all, each and every one of the terms of the two theories differ in meaning. Thus we seem to get very quick *semantic* arguments for the impossibility of improved successor theories and the incommensurability of any two theories. The argument begins not with any claim about the theory-ladenness of observation, but simply with the nature of the meaning of terms.

There are many ways of resisting such apparent consequences. An obvious move is to retreat from extreme holism, restricting the number and nature of statements we take to be relevant to what "electron" and "pointer" and other terms mean. But this may prove neither necessary nor sufficient for avoiding the results. It may not be sufficient, because one would need a reason for discounting changes in theoretical claims specifically about electrons from changing the meaning of "electron," and the claim or assumption that whatever a theory specifically says about electrons does matter to what "electron" means in that theory is not implausible (though my own view is that this is nonetheless false). It may not be necessary because attention to the distinction between meaning and reference seems to provide a different reason for resisting the conclusion. This discussion has presumed that being about the same thing is a matter of meaning the same thing, but the renate–cordate example is one of many demonstrating that this presumption is naïve. Being about the same thing might just be a matter of referring to the same thing, with differences in meaning reflecting different ways of thinking (theorizing) about the same thing. The basic idea is that what we think often happens at the level of our individual sets of beliefs could happen at the level of scientific theories as well. Just as you and I could have different beliefs that are nonetheless about the very same thing, whether that is the cognitive capacities of canines or the reason that gasoline prices seem to decline just before American presidential elections, different theories could give different accounts of the very same substance, force, physical quantity, etc.

An alternative involving attention to scientific theories merits special mention. This is Hartry Field's notion of partial reference, which does not require denying that meaning is relative to one's theory. Field claims that scientific terms can be referentially indeterminate. The example Field discussed at length is outdated, and pursuing it would not be helpful. (It involved Newton's term "mass" and the use of two concepts of mass in twentieth-century physics texts – "relativistic mass" and "rest mass" – that contemporary physicists have largely abandoned. Physicists now recognize just one notion of mass – invariant mass – which, like Newton's, does not vary with velocity.) Genetics and molecular biology can provide more suitable examples. As David Hull notes, nothing in molecular biology has all the features genes were assumed to have in Mendelian genetics, for example no single entity is the unit of crossover, mutation, and function. Cistrons are units of function while recons are units of recombination, and mutons are the smallest DNA segments that can undergo mutation. If we have no reason to prefer one or the other of these as the denotation of the Mendelian term "gene," Field would argue that there is no fact of the matter about which it denotes. But we presumably want to hold that "gene" in Mendelian genetics does denote, partly because we want to say that many earlier claims about genes have truth values. Further, Field would reject the suggestion that it denotes some "Mendelian gene" with the features Mendelian genetics requires (since there is no such thing). How can all that be reconciled with the claim that "gene" in Mendelian genetics does not denote, for instance, cistrons or recons? The solution Field offers is that the term *partially* denotes these and perhaps other things, but doesn't *fully* denote any of them, enabling us to say, as Field thinks we should, that some earlier claims about genes were true while others were false. It also enables us to say that some were neither true nor false, or more precisely, partially true and partially false, in that they would have been true with one denotation but false with the other. Whatever one makes of Field's theory, the apparent facts about theoretical terms which his view is designed to accommodate are worthy of attention.

Acknowledgements

I am grateful to my colleague Chris Pincock as well as the editors for very helpful comments and suggestions.

See also Chemistry; Essentialism; Logical empiricism; Natural kinds, Psychology; Realism/anti–realism; Relativism; Theory-change in science.

References

Burge, Tyler (1979) "Individualism and the Mental," in P. A. French, T. E. Uehling, and H. K. Wettstein (eds) *Midwest Studies in Philosophy*, No. 4, Minneapolis: University of Minnesota Press, pp. 73–122.

Carnap, Rudolf (1956 [1947]) *Meaning and Necessity*, Chicago and London: University of Chicago Press.

Donnellan, Keith (1972 [1970]) "Proper Names and Identifying Descriptions," *Synthese* 21: 335–58, reprinted in D. Davidson and G. Harman (eds) *Semantics of Natural Language*, Dordrecht: D. Reidel Publishing Company, pp. 356–79.

Field, Hartry (1974) "Theory Change and the Indeterminacy of Reference," *Journal of Philosophy* 70: 462–81.

Frege, Gottlob (1960 [1892]), "Über Sinn und Bedeutung," originally published in *Zeitschrift für Philosophie und philosophische Kritik* 100: 25–50; trans. M. Black as "On Sense and Reference," in M. Black and P. Geach (eds) *Translations from the Philosophical Writings of Gottlob Frege*, 2nd edn, Oxford: Basil Blackwell (1960), pp. 56–78.

Hull, David (1974) *Philosophy of Biological Science*, Englewood Cliffs, NJ: Prentice-Hall.

Jackson, Frank (1998) *From Metaphysics to Ethics*, Oxford: Oxford University Press.

Kripke, Saul A. (1980) *Naming and Necessity*, originally in D. Davidson and G. Harman (eds) *Semantics of Natural Language*, Dordrecht: Reidel (1972), pp. 253–355, with addenda pp. 763–9, issued as a monograph with the same title 1980, Cambridge, MA: Harvard University Press.

Mill, John Stuart (1843) *A System of Logic*, London: Longmans.

Putnam, Hilary (1973) "Meaning and Reference," *Journal of Philosophy* 73: 699–711.

—— (1975), *Mind, Language and Reality, Philosophical Papers*, Volume 2, Cambridge: Cambridge University Press.

Quine, W. V. (1953) "Two Dogmas of Empiricism," in *From a Logical Point of View*, Cambridge, MA: Harvard University Press.

Russell, Bertrand (1912) *The Problems of Philosophy*, London: Home University Library, issued by Oxford University Press 1959.

Searle, John (1958) "Proper Names," *Mind* 67: 166–73.

Strawson, Peter (1959) *Individuals*, London: Methuen.

Wittgenstein, Ludwig (1953) *Philosophical Investigations*, trans. G. E. M. Anscombe, London: Macmillan; 2nd edn, London: Basil Blackwell & Mott Ltd., 1958.

Further reading

For proper names, there are sympathetic criticisms and suggestions for revision in Gareth Evans, "The Causal Theory of Names," *Aristotelian Society Supplementary Volume* 47 (1973): 187–208, and unsympathetic criticisms in John Searle, *Intentionality: An Essay in the Philosophy of Mind* (Cambridge: Cambridge University Press, 1983), Ch. 9. Michael Devitt's *Designation* (New York: Columbia University Press, 1981) was the first detailed version of a causal theory of reference focused on names. William G. Lycan summarizes the state of the discussion in "Names" in Michael Devitt and Richard Hanley (eds) *The Blackwell Guide to the Philosophy of Language* (Oxford: Blackwell, 2006), pp. 255–73. Two useful collections of papers treating natural kind terms and Putnam's arguments are Stephen P. Schwartz (ed.) *Naming, Necessity, and Natural Kinds* (Ithaca, NY: Cornell University Press, 1977), and Andrew Pessin and Sanford Goldberg (eds), *The Twin Earth Chronicles: Twenty Years of Reflection on Hilary Putnam's "The Meaning of 'Meaning'"* (New York: M. E. Sharpe, 1996). Schwartz's "General Terms and Mass Terms," also in *The Blackwell Guide* (pp. 274–87), provides a fine overview of the discussion and more suggestions for further reading. Chapter 5 of Michael Devitt and Kim Sterelny's *Language and Reality: An Introduction to the Philosophy of Language*, 2nd edn (Cambridge, MA: MIT Press, 1999) is an excellent place to start. The second main proponent of two-dimensionalism, along with Jackson, is David J. Chalmers, most famously in *The Conscious Mind* (Oxford: Oxford University Press, 1996); see particularly pp. 56–89, which make it clear that the point is to defend the use of *a priori* arguments about necessity against the challenge arising from Kripke's work. Earlier relevant work includes Robert Stalnaker's "Assertion," in Peter Cole (ed.) *Syntax and Semantics 9: Pragmatics* (New York: Academic Press, 1978), pp. 315–32, and Martin Davies and Lloyd Humberstone, "Two Notions of Necessity," *Philosophical Studies* 38 (1980): 1–30. The most detailed criticism of the approach to date is Scott Soames, *Reference and Description: The Case Against Two-Dimensionalism* (Princeton, NJ: Princeton University Press, 2005). An early defense of meaning holism concerning scientific theories is in Paul Feyerabend, "Explanation, Reduction, and Empiricism," in Herbert Feigl and Grover Maxwell (eds) *Minnesota Studies in the Philosophy of Science, 3* (Minneapolis: University of Minnesota Press, 1962), pp. 28–97. An early paper of Putnam's criticizes the view expressed in this paper, and as reported in an (as far as I know) unpublished paper by J. J. C. Smart, and also anticipates in some ways Putnam's later views: "How Not to Talk About Meaning," originally in Robert Cohen and Marx Wartofsky (eds) *Boston Studies in the Philosophy of Science* (New York: Humanities Press, 1965), Volume 2, pp. 205–22, and reprinted in Putnam's *Mind, Language and Reality*, pp. 117–31. Thomas Kuhn's *The Structure of Scientific Revolutions*, 2nd edn (Chicago: University of Chicago Press, 1970) is probably the best-known source of holism and incommensurability in philosophy of science. W. V. Quine offered a version of holism based on consideration of the notions of meaning and analyticity, in reaction to logical positivism generally and Carnap's work in particular, in "Two Dogmas of Empiricism," in Quine, *From a Logical Point of View* (Harvard University Press, 1951). There is a good discussion of both the general view and its applicability to scientific theories in the editors' commentary to Ch. 3 of Martin Curd and J. A. Cover (eds) *Philosophy of Science: The Central Issues* (New York: W. W. Norton & Company, 1998), pp. 365–408. For a comprehensive discussion of the philosophy of language issues see Jerry Fodor and Ernie Lepore, *Holism: A Shopper's Guide* (Oxford: Blackwell, 1992).

5

THE ROLE OF LOGIC IN PHILOSOPHY OF SCIENCE

Diderik Batens

Introduction

For logical empiricists, logic was the clue to separating sound reasoning from unsound reasoning, and this separation was fundamental, first for understanding science, and next for demarcating science. So logic, formal logic that is, was central for the philosophy of science. The situation changed with the advent of the historicist movement. Science was seen by this movement as content-driven, as contextual. The role of formal logic was reduced to checking deductive inferences. Logic had nothing interesting to contribute to the mechanisms that are responsible for scientific change.

Shapere (2004) offers an interesting analysis of the reasons why both movements were bound to fail, of the roots of the difficulties, and of their solution. A crucial statement is that "the content of the science that is accepted at any given epoch provides the reasons guiding, and sometimes driving, further inquiry" (*ibid.*: 50). So science is *content-guided*: the basis for scientific reasoning is "what we have learned, including what we have learned about how to learn" (52). Viewing science in this way will enable philosophers to avoid regarding the scientific method, or possible scientific methods, as identifiable *a priori* without, at the same time, embracing the relativism of the historicist movement. This view has been gaining wide adherence in the late twentieth and early twenty-first centuries.

One might conclude that this view still heavily restricts the role of logic, viz., to avoiding mistaken deductive inferences, but here I try to show that this conclusion is mistaken. Precisely because science is content-guided, articulating a precise philosophy of science requires a heavy dose of logic. It requires, moreover, intense creative work in logic.

In this chapter, I deal mainly with methodological issues. Before getting there, however, it is useful to briefly discuss the issue of the standard logic.

The standard logic

We need logic for avoiding mistaken deductive inferences, but which logic? First-order classical logic (henceforth CL) is clearly best established and most widely promoted by logicians. However, many logicians do not accept CL as "the true logic." Intuitionists and (mathematical) constructivists see intuitionistic logic as the standard in mathematics, and sometimes as the general standard. Relevance logicians have argued that CL is mistaken in several respects and that the true logic is a relevant one. Dialetheists argue that there are true contradictions and hence the true logic should be paraconsistent, i.e., that it should not validate the inference from a contradiction to arbitrary statements (from A and not-A to derive B). And a number of logics, actually too many to mention the most representative ones, have been presented for specific purposes. The sciences played hardly any role in most of these proposals – quantum logic is an exception. The driving arguments came from insights into everyday language, from metaphysics, and from the history of logic.

So the logic community is not much help in identifying the true logic. But is there a true logic? A logic determines the meaning of *logical words* such as "and," "not," "for all," etc. These words are part of languages by which humans try to get a grasp on the world. But choosing a language does not warrant that it is suitable for correctly describing the world. The transition from Newton and Maxwell to relativity requires that the language is modified ("conceptual change"). The same apparently holds for every scientific revolution and even for less drastic scientific changes. The point is hardly contentious: a half-century ago Hempel (1958) acknowledged that conceptual change is just as legitimate a move as a replacement of accepted statements within the current conceptual system. If the meaning of logical words does not form an exception in this respect, then only the future history of science can determine which is the true logic.

Every logic contains certain presuppositions about the world. Thus CL presupposes, among many other things, that the world is consistent (that no A is true together with not-A). Note, however, that scientific reasoning should enable us to derive conclusions from, among other things, statements that we have reasons to accept on the basis of our best scientific insights. Clearly, *stipulating* that inconsistencies are false cannot exclude that the available data together with the accepted theories might provide reasons to accept A as well as reasons to accept not-A. Moreover, there are historical cases, from both mathematics and the empirical sciences, in which reasons to accept a statement as well as its negation were present – for references to case studies see Meheus (2002).

Some will argue that, if we have a reason to accept A as well as a reason to accept not-A, then at least one of the reasons is bound to be a bad one. This means that, if a scientific discipline is in an inconsistent state, then one should try to reform it and bring it to a consistent state. I largely agree with this (Batens 2002). It is crucial, however, to understand that, in order to transform the inconsistent state to a consistent state, one needs to *reason from* the inconsistent state. Only by doing so can one locate the inconsistencies and delineate the statements that are consistently affirmed by the theory. Given this still inconsistent state, one has to search for ways to remove the inconsistencies while retaining most of the *consistent part* of the theory. To do so by means of CL is impossible.

Analogous arguments apply to the other presuppositions of CL and, more generally, to the presuppositions of every logic, L. The world might resist being grasped by a language of which the logical words are governed by L. In this sense, the true logic is at best the logic that would underlie a complete and correct science, and hence cannot be known at this moment. Meanwhile, however, even were we to know this true logic, it would be of little use to us, because we have to reason from present-day science in order to improve it.

Methodological concepts

Philosophers of science aim to define their concepts in a precise way, and logic is often a good means for doing so. Definitions become more transparent when phrased in terms of a formalized language. Next, the metatheory of logic provides a set of clear tools: the consequence relation, logical relations between statements, model, contradiction, and so on. Where required, logic is extended with the use of set theory, probability theory, and similar mathematical structures. Good illustrations of all this are found in Kuipers (2000). Note that logic not only enables one to attain a high level of precision; it functions also as a heuristic tool: it suggests ways of looking at the problems and of categorizing them; it provides possible relations between statements, sets of statements, and the like; it facilitates seeing the consequences of proposed solutions; etc. The most technically elaborated proposal of the sort considered is probably the belief-revision approach as applied, for example, by Gärdenfors (1988); because the elaboration leaves little room for varying the three central operations (expansion, contraction, and revision) and requires severe idealization, it seems not to agree with a content-guided understanding of scientific change. Set-theoretic tools were heavily used by the structuralists (Balzer, Moulines and Sneed 1987) and probabilistic tools – Markov chains – are used in Pearl's theory of causality (2000).

The examples just cited proceed in terms of CL and extensions thereof. Sometimes alternative logics are more suitable for clarifying certain methodological concepts. Among the more popular examples, I refer especially to van Fraassen's supervaluations and to the partial structures of da Costa and associates.

A different use is made of logic when the aim is not to define a concept, but rather to describe, in more or less detail, the stages of a reasoning process. Note that, for example, defining an explanation of a certain kind is a very different thing from describing the process by which this kind of explanation is obtained. A typical example is presented in Kuipers and Wiśniewski (1994). Wiśniewski's erotetic logic is invoked to characterize the "train of thought" in searching for an explanation by specification. The central tool here is erotetic implication: how questions together with declarative statements imply other questions.

The most elaborate unified approach of this kind is Hintikka's work on interrogative logic (see e.g. Hintikka 1999). This logic uses a variant of Beth tableaux for book-keeping. Beth intended these two-sided tableaux as a device for testing inference: the premises are written on the left-hand side, the conclusion on the right, and then the tableau rules are applied, which sometimes results in a sub-tableau being started; a tableau may close, remain open, or not stop. Hintikka interprets the tableaux in a game-theoretic way, for example, as a game against nature.

Consider an application to the search for an explanation of a singular statement, E, in terms of a theory, T. The axioms of T are introduced on the left-hand side and E on the right. An explanation of E in terms of T requires that E is not a CL-consequence of T. So, in order for the tableau to close, new information has to be introduced. This is obtained by introducing questions on the left, which requires that their presupposition occurs on the same side. The answers that nature gives are represented by a fixed set, S; if the answer to a question is in S, the answer is added on the left. Apart from the rules of the game, there is also a deductive heuristic as well as an interrogative heuristic (I avoid Hintikka's "strategy" for reasons that become clear below). Where the rules determine which moves are permitted, a heuristic is directed towards applying the rules in such a way that the game is won. In our example the game is won when the tableau closes, because this means that one has obtained a set of answers (singular statements) that jointly form an explanation of E in terms of T.

Hintikka has applied his interrogative logic to many problems from the philosophy of science, among them induction. He sees this logic as central to the logic of inquiry and to the logic of discovery, and even as a general theory of reasoning. The advantage of the distinction between rules and heuristics is that the latter allow for a context-guided understanding of inquiry. The disadvantage, however, is that it is difficult to say much about heuristics in the present framework, as is apparent from Hintikka's work on the topic. Moreover, there are clearly two kinds of considerations that determine a heuristic. One of them is determined by the logical structure of the problem one tries to solve, which is here represented by the tableau one tries to close. A very different kind of consideration, however, is determined by the historical situation: that the problem one tries to solve is similar to problems solved in the past and that we know which set of moves was successful in solving the latter. Considerations of the first kind can clearly be described in a systematic way – they are a matter of logic. Considerations of the second kind depend on the historical situation. On the basis of historical case studies, one may try to spell out the parameters of possible problem-solving situations as well as their possible values. Any such general theory, however, is bound to be provisional because it depicts at best the present and past situations.

Logics for methodological concepts

Methodological concepts give rise to forms of reasoning that are not deductive. Think about inductive generalization, abduction, interpreting an inconsistent theory as consistently as possible, handling background generalizations in the presence of exceptions, invoking theories or hypotheses that are ordered by priorities, etc. – more examples are discussed in Batens (2004). Clearly such reasoning forms are not guided by deductive logic alone, which is why one needs the proposals presented in the previous section. One may try to approach the reasoning in terms of a definition, which settles whether the result of the reasoning is an object of the suitable kind. Alternatively one may try to say more about the reasoning itself, by characterizing the "train of thought" that underlies it or by setting it up as a specific application of interrogative logic.

Different and more radical approaches attempt a characterization by a logic. Indeed, the reasoning forms are, in a clear sense, logics: they assign a set of correct consequences to every set of premises. In some respects they differ from usual logics. Let us consider the most striking feature. Most of those forms of reasoning are dynamic in that statements that are seen as consequences at some point in the reasoning are rejected at a later point, when the reasoning has led to a better understanding of the premises. At a still later point they may be reinstated as consequences in view of the continuation of the reasoning.

The dynamics are related to the fact that many of those reasoning forms are non-monotonic: what follows from part of the premises need not follow from all of them. Inductive generalization, which obviously relies on background knowledge, is non-monotonic because the derived generalizations need to be compatible with the data. As new data are taken into consideration, formerly derived conclusions may have to be withdrawn. The opposite move may also be justified: the data may prevent us from accepting either that all P are Q or that all R are not-Q (because, although some P are known to be Q and some R are known to be not-Q, some P are known to be R while their Q-hood is unknown). If the further data reveal that some R are Q, and hence falsify that all R are not-Q, this may (in some circumstances) make it sound to conclude that all P are Q.

Even monotonic reasoning processes may display the dynamics described in the next to last paragraph. Indeed, the cause of the dynamics is not non-monotonicity, but the absence of a *positive test* for the consequence relation – in other words, the consequence relation is not even partially recursive. This requires a brief digression. If a logic, L, is decidable, there is a mechanical procedure that tells us (after finitely many steps) whether, for an arbitrary set of premises, Γ, and an arbitrary statement, A, A is a L-consequence of Γ or not. CL is undecidable. However, there still is a positive test for CL-derivability: there is a mechanical procedure that informs us so after finitely many steps that A is a CL-consequence of Γ if and only if this is the case (but may never answer if it is not the case).

For the aforementioned reasoning processes there is not even a positive test. No mechanical procedure will, for an arbitrary Γ and an arbitrary A that is a consequence of Γ, tell us after finitely many steps that A is a consequence of Γ. The absence of a positive test may be a serious handicap from a computational point of view, but it is very familiar to philosophers of science. Much sound reasoning is not *conclusive*; it may require revision in view of further consideration.

Approaching methodological concepts by means of logics has some advantages (see below), which makes further discussion of the matter worthwhile. I do so in terms of the approach with which I am most familiar, the adaptive logics approach. Let us look first at the logics themselves and in the next section consider their application in a problem-solving context. My description will be informal and slightly inaccurate at some points – an accessible and up-to-date description is available in Batens (2007: §§2–5) and in Batens (forthcoming).

An adaptive logic (in standard format) is characterized by a triad: a lower limit logic, a set of abnormalities, and a strategy. The lower limit logic is a logic of the usual type (reflexive, transitive, monotonic, and compact) that has a characteristic semantics. The set of abnormalities is a set of formulae characterized by a logical form. Abnormalities are taken to be false, until and unless the premises prevent this. Strategies need not worry us here: they are a technical device to handle cases where the premises require that at least one of a finite set of abnormalities is true, but fail to specify which one.

Let us consider an example that extends CL, the logic of inductive generalization. Which statements of the form "All A are B" can be jointly and justifiedly upheld in view of a given set of empirical data (which need not be primitive formulae)? Realistic applications require that one takes background theories into account. Moreover, some background theories are rejected when falsified by the data, whereas others are retained except for the falsified generalizations or even except for the falsified instances of generalizations. This is realized by combining a diversity of adaptive logics for handling background generalizations with the adaptive logic for inductive gener-alization – space limitations force me to restrict the discussion to the latter.

The lower limit logic is CL. The set of abnormalities is the set of formulae of the form something-is-A-and-something-is-not-A. This is obviously inspired by Carnap's idea of uniformity (1952). Inductive generalization (which, incidentally, Carnap was unable to obtain in terms of his probabilistic approach) is made possible by inter-preting the world as uniformly as the data permit. So abnormalities are taken to be false until and unless the data force us to consider them as true.

Adaptive logics of inductive generalization assign to every set of data, phrased in a given language, a unique set of inductive generalizations that are jointly consistent with the data – they do the same when the data are first extended in terms of background theories. Non-derivable generalizations are either falsified or jointly conflict with the data. In the latter case (see the third paragraph of this section for an example) their disjunction is typically derivable. Just as with the connected set of abnormalities, this guides research, as we shall see in the next section. If no instance of a generalization, G, is derivable from the data, there always is a generalization, H, that is equally justified from the data and for which G and H jointly conflict with the data.

The derivable set of generalizations is arguably the best set of generalizations to act on, given that the predicates are well entrenched. Moreover, Reichenbach's "pragmatic justification of induction" applies: if a set of generalizations holds in a list of singular data, the logic of inductive generalization will reveal them in the long run.

Handling inconsistency requires weakening CL, but proceeds according to the same structure. If a theory, T, that was intended as consistent turns out to be incon-sistent, we will wish to replace it by a consistent theory that retains the *good parts* of T. In order to do so, we first have to interpret T *as consistently as possible* in order to retain whatever can be retained of T as originally intended. This is precisely what inconsistency-adaptive logics do, whereas monotonic paraconsistent logics offer too weak an interpretation in this respect. An inconsistency-adaptive logic, AL, is characterized as expected: the lower limit logic is a paraconsistent logic and the set of abnormalities is the (existential closure of) formulas of the form A-and-not-A. By taking these as false in so far as the premises permit, the AL interprets the premises as consistently as possible: the AL-consequences of the premises contain all desired CL-consequences and do not contain the undesired ones (viz., do not contain all statements).

There is obviously a large set of inconsistency-adaptive logics. They are obtained by varying (mainly) the paraconsistent lower limit logic. So the bad news is that inconsistency-adaptive logics require a justification: are they suitably applicable to the present situation? The good news is that the available multiplicity of paraconsistent logics makes it likely that the suitable inconsistency-adaptive logic for many specific contexts is readily available – for the multiplicity see Béziau and Carnielli (2006), the references therein, etc. The situation is different for the adaptive logic of inductive generalization: few sensible alternatives for the lower limit logic CL are at present available (and the strategy offers not much variation). This is largely compensated for by the multiplicity of adaptive logics for handling background knowledge.

Many more adaptive logics have been studied, most of them relating to problems in the philosophy of science. Characterizing a methodological concept in terms of an adaptive logic (in standard format) has a number of attractive consequences. First, it provides an exact definition of the concept in terms of the lower limit logic and the set of abnormalities. Next, it defines the proof theory as well as the semantics of the logic. The semantics are essential for clarifying the underlying idea of the logic: they select the lower limit models of the premises that verify only the abnormalities that are required by the premises to be true (the precise meaning of this depends on the strategy). Whatever is true in all those models is a consequence of the premises. The proof theory – basically three generic rules and a marking definition – is equally important: if offers an explication of the informal reasoning by which we try to find out whether the methodological concept applies. In this respect, the availability of dynamic proofs is one of the strengths of adaptive logics. The basic idea is that statements that are derivable only by relying on the falsehood of certain abnormalities, are derived on a *condition*, viz., the set of those abnormalities. Next, it depends on the (disjunctions of) abnormalities that are derived at a certain stage of the proof whether a line is marked (and hence OUT) or unmarked (and hence IN).

The standard format itself takes care of the metatheory. It warrants that the proof theory and the semantics are equivalent, and it warrants that a set of desirable metatheoretic properties is present (Batens 2006; Batens forthcoming) – in other words that the logics do the required job required of them. So, as soon as one is able to characterize a methodological concept in terms of an adaptive logic in standard format, all the logician's hard work is provided for free. The standard format even provides one with a set of criteria for determining, for some premise sets, Γ, and conclusions, A, whether A is or is not an adaptive consequence of Γ. Although no algorithm is available, the criteria may apply. Where they do not, the proof theory (together with the prospective dynamics which I describe below) explicates sensible reasoning *towards* establishing a conclusion.

Formal problem-solving processes

If a methodological concept is characterized by a logic, much of the connected reasoning is explicated by that logic. For example, whether a statement, A, is compatible with a theory, T, is reduced to the problem of whether A is a CO-consequence of T, where CO is the adaptive logic of compatibility. So part of Hintikka's heuristics is taken over by the logic, whereas the rest of Hintikka's heuristics should now be phrased as a heuristics with respect to the adaptive logic – CO in the example.

Part of the remaining heuristics *still* depends on the logical structure of the problem one is trying to solve. As this is a matter of formal reasoning itself, it is sensible to attempt to push it into the proofs. There is indeed an easy way to do so, viz., in terms of a prospective dynamics. Let us consider the situation for CL, which will be the most transparent for the reader. Suppose that one is trying to derive A and that "If B, then A" is one of the premises. Then one obviously can obtain A by obtaining B and next applying *Modus Ponens*. Instead of remembering this, or writing it down on a separate piece of paper, one writes [B]A in the proof. On the one hand [B]A expresses that A can be obtained by obtaining B; on the other hand it is a book-keeping device to remind one that one is trying to obtain B. If B can be obtained directly from one of the premises, one will introduce that premise and start analyzing it. If B itself cannot be obtained from the premises, it is analyzed. Thus if B is C-and-D, then one derives [C,D]A from [B]A. The prospective dynamics can be usefully combined with marking definitions. Thus, if [C,D]A occurs in the proof and D turns out to be a dead-end (not derivable from the premises), then it is useless to try to derive C in order to obtain A. So [C,D]A is a dead-end itself. Similarly, if both [C,D]A and [C]A occur in the proof, then the former should be marked as redundant: C is sufficient to derive A. The prospective dynamics may be spelled out for other logics than CL, including adaptive logics. The advantage is, as noted above, that those parts of the heuristics that depend on the logical structure of the problem can be written into the proof and can thus be made transparent.

A formal problem-solving process is composed of a number of elements, among them a combination of logics, the prospective dynamics for those logics, an erotetic logic (resembling the logics of Wiśniewski (1996)), and a heuristic, which is actually a kind of procedure (a set of instructions to extend a given proof in a certain way in view of the lines of the proof). One starts from a problem (a set of questions of a certain type) together with the premises. The problem gives rise to a prospective statement that determines a target. This is usually followed by deductive steps. Where these come to an end, unsolved problems together with declarative statements may give rise to further problem derivation, which then again starts the prospective machinery.

The above schema may easily be extended. Consider one example. In line with Hintikka's work, the schema can be extended with a question-answering device, which leads to the introduction of new premises. The interesting point is that adaptive logics may be used for guiding research, viz., for deciding which questions should be asked. Typically, new consequences may be derived if one succeeds in *narrowing down* a derived disjunction of abnormalities to (a shorter disjunction or) a single abnormality. So this is one important source of *derived* problems that may be built into the procedure. At any point in time, scientists have a fairly good idea of the problems that can be solved by empirical means. Formal problem-solving processes will guide one in deciding to make certain observations. If an experiment is required, a related problem-solving (sub)process will be started (to make the experiment easy to perform, plausibly conclusive ...).

The plot behind the above should be clear by now. On the one hand one tries to fix (in the logic, the prospective dynamics, and the procedure) all aspects that can be mastered by formal means. On the other hand one tries to leave room for a content-guided heuristics wherever that is possible. The final section deals with the latter.

Content-guided reasoning

At any given point in time, the language of a scientific discipline has been molded by that discipline's history. This obviously applies generally and is not typical for the proposals discussed in the previous section.

All adaptive logics have rules that are not validated by the lower limit logic, but would be valid if all abnormalities are false. Such rules are neither validated nor invalidated by an adaptive logic. The logic validates certain *applications* of the rule, viz., those that are permitted by the premises. Put more precisely, it depends on the disjunctions of abnormalities derivable from the premises by the lower limit logic whether an application of such a rule is valid or invalid. In this sense, adaptive logics are a means by which to formally characterize a specific (but restricted) form of content guidance.

We have seen that the multiplicity of adaptive logics allows one to select the variant that is suitable in a specific situation and forces one to justify the choice. The same applies to the choice of an erotetic logic and to the choice of the procedure that governs the prospective dynamics.

The above plot enables one to take background theories seriously, while still allowing for several forms of defeasibility in view of the data (rejecting a theory, rejecting only some generalizations that follow from a theory, rejecting only instances of such generalizations).

An equally fascinating aspect is that the plot leaves ample room for the introduction of guesses, which may either be wild or rely on worldviews and similar personal constraints. Which guesses are useful is determined by the derived disjunctions of abnormalities. The origin of the guesses is (and should be) extra-logical, but the logic (or combination of logics) guides the guess in handling it as defeasible.

The most important content-guided aspect obviously lies in the heuristic that is not determined by the formal problem-solving process itself. Let me mention just a few aspects. It will depend on this heuristic whether one tries to derive a conclusion along one road rather than the other. It will depend on the heuristic whether one recurs to an observational question, to an experimental question, or rather tries to obtain a theoretical derivation first. (The use of models is another alternative, which should, as soon as possible, be built into the plot.) How one should proceed cannot be spelled out beforehand, but should be decided in view of the case under consideration, in view of what one has learned about "the world" and about learning. So the basic demand on a plot for formal problem-solving processes it that it leaves sufficient freedom for the heuristic. In order to do that, and to situate the heuristic, the logical framework has to be spelled out. This framework should be malleable. It should consist of a set of related slots that can be filled in agreement with the demands of the case under consideration. But even then the framework, just as much as the standard deductive logic, can at best be a provisional hypothesis based on what we have learned about problem-solving. A good hypothesis is one that takes into account the insights of our own day. But more days are to come.

See also Confirmation; Inference to the best explanation; Logical empiricism; Scientific discovery; Scientific method.

References

Balzer, W., Moulines, C. U., and Sneed, J. D. (1987) *An Architectonic for Science: The Structuralist Program*, Dordrecht: Reidel.

Batens, D. (2002) "In Defense of a Programme for Handling Inconsistencies," in J. Meheus (ed.) *Inconsistency in Science*, Dordrecht: Kluwer, pp. 129–50.

—— (2004) "The Need for Adaptive Logics in Epistemology," in D. Gabbay, S. Rahman, J. Symons, and J. P. V. Bendegem (eds) *Logic, Epistemology and the Unity of Science*, Dordrecht: Kluwer, pp. 459–85.

—— (2007) "A Universal Logic Approach to Adaptive Logics," *Logica Universalis* 1: 221–42.

—— (forthcoming) *Adaptive Logics and Dynamic Proofs: A Study in the Dynamics of Reasoning*.

Béziau, J.-Y. and Carnielli, W. A. (eds) (2006) *Paraconsistent Logic with no Frontiers*, Studies in Logic and Practical Reasoning, Amsterdam: North-Holland–Elsevier.

Carnap, R. (1952) *The Continuum of Inductive Methods*, Chicago: University of Chicago Press.

Gärdenfors, P. (1988) *Knowledge in Flux: Modeling the Dynamics of Epistemic States*, Cambridge, MA: MIT Press.

Hempel, C. G. (1958) "The Theoretician's Dilemma: A Study in the Logic of Theory Construction," in H. Feigl, M. Scriven, and G. Maxwell (eds) *Minnesota Studies in the Philosophy of Science*, Volume 2, Minneapolis: University of Minnesota Press.

Hintikka, J. (1999) *Inquiry as Inquiry: A Logic of Scientific Discovery*, Dordrecht: Kluwer.

Kuipers, T. A. F. (2000) *From Instrumentalism to Constructive Realism: On some Relations Between Confirmation, Empirical Progress, and Truth Approximation*, Volume 287 of Synthese Library, Dordrecht: Kluwer.

Kuipers, T. A. F. and Wiśniewski, A. (1994) "An Erotetic Approach to Explanation by Specification," *Erkenntnis* 40: 377–402.

Meheus, J. (ed.) (2002) *Inconsistency in Science*, Dordrecht: Kluwer.

Pearl, J. (2000) *Causality: Models, Reasoning, and Inference*, Cambridge: Cambridge University Press.

Shapere, D. (2004) "Logic and the Philosophical Interpretation of Science," in P. Weingartner (ed.) *Alternative Logics: Do Sciences Need Them?*, Berlin and Heidelberg: Springer, pp. 41–54.

Wiśniewski, A. (1996) "The Logic of Questions as a Theory of Erotetic Arguments," *Synthese* 109: 1–25.

Further reading

Most of the relevant papers are spread over journals. Hintikka (1999) and Kuipers (2000) present approaches based on classical logic. So does Gärdenfors (1988), concentrating on applications within the reach of the belief-revision mechanism. Batens (forthcoming) and the other cited papers by Batens concern an approach in terms of adaptive logics.

6
CRITICAL RATIONALISM
Gürol Irzik

What is critical rationalism?

Critical rationalism is a school of thought whose major exponent is Karl Popper. Joseph Agassi, Hans Albert, William W. Bartley, Ian Jarvie, Noretta Koertge, Alan Musgrave, David Miller, and John Watkins are other philosophers who have contributed to it. Here I follow mainly Popper's version of critical rationalism. In a nutshell, it can be characterized as "an attitude of readiness to listen to critical arguments and to learn from experience; it is fundamentally an attitude of admitting that 'I may be wrong and you may be right, and by an effort, we may get nearer to the truth'" (Popper 1971: 225).

Critical rationalism differs radically from the traditional rationalism of Plato, Descartes, and the like, in a number of ways. First, traditional rationalism puts reason above experience in knowledge acquisition. Second, it claims that reason can justify our beliefs, claims, and theories. Third, it asserts that it is possible to obtain certain, indubitable, foundational knowledge by reason. Critical rationalism rejects all of these. Neither reason nor experience has any priority in acquiring knowledge. Nor does critical rationalism try to do justice to reason and experience by taking them as equally primordial. Critical rationalism is, above all, a matter of willingness to correct one's mistakes by appealing to both. "Reason" in this context refers not to a faculty possessed by all people but to clear, critical thinking which is essentially social and grows in interaction with others.

Critical rationalism is modeled on the Socratic method of critical inquiry. The sole function of critical argumentation and experience is to check whether our beliefs, claims, or theories are true or false. If we are lucky, we can show them to be false and eliminate them. But neither reason nor experience can ever justify a belief, a claim, or a theory to be true or even probably true. Critical rationalism is thoroughly anti-justificationist. In that respect, it is an extremely radical approach which diverges from the entire tradition of epistemology, whether rationalist or empiricist. Traditionally, a belief is said to be held rationally if it is justified by reason or experience. Justification appears as a necessary condition also of (propositional) knowledge. More explicitly, according to the traditional account of knowledge, a person, S, knows that p (where p is a proposition) if and only if (i) S believes that p, (ii) S has justification (evidence, good reasons) for p, and (iii) p is true. But that account is threatened by an infinite regress. For one can always demand further justification for the evidence or the reasons one has. If one does not want to be a dogmatist or a skeptic, one must stop this regress somewhere. It is at this point that traditional epistemologists appeal to foundational beliefs which are epistemologically basic. Whereas rationalists such as Descartes resort to clear and distinct ideas or intuitions, empiricists like Locke turn to sense experience or observation. Both camps take refuge in some form of foundationalism.

Critical rationalism denies that there can ever be justification (experiential or otherwise) for our beliefs. It gives an account of "knowledge" that is antithetical to the one widely accepted by rationalists and empiricists alike. Moreover, for the critical rationalist there are no truths about the world that can be known beyond any doubt, either through reason or experience. Certainty is unattainable, and the search for it is futile. Even the simplest empirical claim might be wrong, no matter how strongly it is believed. Critical rationalism is fallibilist as well as being anti-justificationist and anti-foundationalist. Nevertheless, rationality and objectivity are possible. Rationality has nothing to do with justification, but has everything to do with openness to criticism. Similarly, objectivity is a matter not just of impartiality or open-mindedness of the believer, but of collaborative efforts of relentless criticism of our views that are inter-subjectively criticizable.

Critical rationalism and science

According to its advocates, critical rationalism is best exemplified by (empirical) science. To see this, let us to turn to Popper's analysis of the nature of science. Popper claims that science can be distinguished from non-science. The problem of distinguishing between science and non-science is called "the demarcation problem," and is not to be confused with the problem of empirical meaningfulness. This latter problem of distinguishing meaningful statements from meaningless ones was the concern of logical positivists who suggested the criterion of verifiability by possible experience as a solution to it. Popper rejects both the criterion, on the grounds that it renders the laws of science meaningless, and the problem itself as merely verbal and thus insignificant.

Popper's solution to the demarcation problem has two components. First, at the formal logical level, scientific statements must satisfy *the criterion of falsifiability* (or, equivalently, of refutability, testability); that is, they "must be capable of conflicting with possible, or conceivable, observations" (Popper 1968a: 39). This point can be made more clearly in terms of Popper's *falsificationism*, according to which the deductive method of testing constitutes the scientific method. A scientific theory is tested by deducing from it observational consequences. Those consequences can be compared with *basic statements* that express the results of observations. More specifically, basic statements are singular, existential statements asserting the occurrence of an observable event localized in space and time. If *the potential falsifiers* of a theory, T, are defined as the class of basic statements with which it is inconsistent, then the following definition can be given (see Popper 1968b: 86):

A theory is *falsifiable* (*testable, refutable*) if and only if the class of its potential falsifiers is non-empty.

Falsifiability is necessary but not sufficient for solving the demarcation problem. To see why, suppose a theory, T, has an observational consequence which conflicts with some accepted basic statement. Then it is always open to a supporter of T to add auxiliary assumptions to protect T against possible falsification. Therefore, the formal logical condition must be supplemented by a (meta-)methodological rule that says that "the other rules of scientific procedure must be designed in such a way that they do not protect any statement in science from falsification" (Popper *ibid.*: 54). Thus, the scientific status of a theory depends not just on its being falsifiable, but also on our attitude toward it; we must not be uncritical and attempt to save the theory from refutation using conventionalist stratagems such as appealing to ad hoc auxiliary hypotheses. If some theory, T, has a false observational consequence, then adding auxiliary hypothesis A is permissible only if the degree of testability of T and A taken together is increased. "Avoid making ad hoc auxiliary assumptions," "Formulate bold theories," and "Test them as severely as possible" are some of the methodological rules that must be adopted as a result of the critical attitude essential to scientific activity. Let us look at them more closely.

A bold theory is one that has high empirical content; it can be tested more easily than a cautious one. This is because a bold theory prohibits more, so it has a larger class of potential falsifiers. Testing severely means deducing the most improbable observational consequences of a theory relative to background knowledge and checking them against observation. More precisely, consider a new theory T to be tested. Call B the background theory and let E be some test evidence which is a logical consequence of T and B. Then the following definition can be given (Popper 1968a: 390):

The severity of the test relative to the background theory B, $S(E,B)$, is $1/P(E\,|\,B)$, where $P(E\,|\,B)$ means the probability of E given B.

Hence, the smaller the probability of E given B (i.e., the more surprising the test evidence is against the background knowledge we have), the severer a test it constitutes. Finally, consider the rule that says that ad hoc auxiliary assumptions must be avoided. This is because ad hoc assumptions are not independently testable; they result in an overall reduction in empirical content and hence in the degree of falsifiability.

Note that all these methodological rules are related to testing or testability. This is no surprise since testing is arguably the most effective organon of criticism in science. Theories can be criticized by testing them against observations or experiments. The bolder a theory, the more testable it is; it "sticks its neck out," so to speak. The more severely tested a theory, the easier it is to see its falsity if it is false, so that it can be discarded and replaced by something better. But even if a theory passes all the severe tests it has been subjected to, it does not mean that it has been thereby shown to be verified (i.e., true) or confirmed. Popper says that such successful theories have been *corroborated.* Corroboration is not another term for confirmation since it does not involve any notion of inductive support for a theory. Theories remain as unsupported hypotheses or conjectures forever. Popper's falsificationism is therefore antithetical to all forms of confirmationism.

Popper's anti-confirmationist approach to science results from his anti-inductivism. Broadly speaking, inductivism takes induction both as a method of discovering generalizations (or laws) on the basis of neutral observations and as a method of justifying the former on the basis of the latter. Popper objects to both. Without a viewpoint, prior expectation, interest, problem, or something like a theory, observations are pointless. What science needs is relevant facts, and relevance is always relative to a problem, interest, or perspective, often a theoretical one. Furthermore, every observation (basic) statement (as simple as "This liquid is water") is theory-laden in the sense that terms occurring in it (like "liquid" and "water") are universals and have a dispositional character: they refer to physical objects which exhibit a law-like behavior. Hence, there can be no theory-neutral description of observational facts. As Anthony O'Hear puts it, "asserting a singular statement about the world commits one just as much as asserting a universal statement to an open-ended predictive set of implications because of the dispositional character of the descriptive term" (1980: 70). That is why observation statements or, equivalently, basic statements are also fallible: no amount of observation can ever justify or establish their truth. They remain as conjectural as universal statements or theories. As for induction as a method of justification, Popper endorses David Hume's negative arguments to the effect that no inductive inference from observed facts to generalizations can ever be justified.

Nevertheless, science does grow by eliminating false theories, if we are lucky enough to refute them, and by replacing them by others that have higher empirical content. The aim of science is truth (or more precisely, explanatory truth) in the realist sense (i.e., correspondence between theories and mind-independent facts), but we can never be sure that we have hit on it even when our theories have been highly corroborated. In later years Popper came to believe that truthlikeness, or verisimilitude, is a more realistic aim for science than truth *simpliciter*. Providing a successful definition of verisimilitude is important because it enables the critical rationalist to argue that science not only grows but actually progresses by producing theories that have increasing verisimilitude. Given two theories, even if both are false, it may be possible to determine that one is closer to truth than the other. Verisimilitude, therefore, is a comparative notion which Popper has attempted to define as follows (see Popper 1968a: 233):

> Let *F* and *G* be two theories with comparable content. Then G has greater verisimilitude than *F* if and only if (a) the truth-content but not the falsity-content of G exceeds that of *F* and (b) the falsity-content of *F*, but not its truth-content, exceeds that of G.

Unfortunately, not only Popper's attempt but all similar attempts to define verisimilitude thus far have failed. Even if they were successful, the relationship between verisimilitude and corroboration would remain conjectural because corroboration is not a measure of verisimilitude. To put it differently, saying that the better-corroborated theory is also the one that is closer to truth would be no more than a guess even if a successful definition of verisimilitude were available.

Finally, it should be noted that both the methodological rules and the basic statements have the status of conventions. The former are accepted as a result of a decision to increase the falsifiability of theories; the latter are motivated (but not dictated) by observations and are required for testing. Both can be criticized and revised if necessary; they can also be used to refute theories that contain falsifiable generalizations or laws. Because of this, Popper does not consider his philosophy a form of conventionalism.

Some criticisms of critical rationalism

Most critical rationalists claim that while evidence can corroborate a theory, it cannot confirm or inductively support it. To say that a theory is corroborated implies no more than that it has to date withstood testing, that we have so far failed to refute it. Corroboration is a mere summary of the theory's past performance. If that is the case, then why is it rational to act on the basis of a decision informed by the best (i.e., best tested and corroborated) theory, to apply it to new situations – in other words, to decide to use it as basis for practical action? After all, as Popper himself admits, corroboration says absolutely nothing about the *future* performance of a theory. In what sense, therefore, is the decision to act a rational one? The reply of Popper and other critical rationalists is that since it is the best theory, what could be more rational than acting on such a theory, than holding a "pragmatic belief in the results of science" (Popper 1975: 27; see also Popper 1974: 1074; and Miller 1994: 38–45)? This reply is not entirely satisfactory. For if Popper and his followers are right, then, under the circumstances, the rational thing to do is not to act at all. For human actions are goal-directed, and if our best theory provides us with no clue as to the prospect of achieving our goals, then it cannot sufficiently motivate us to act. Obversely, for our best theory to guide us in our actions, its past success should give us some reason (no matter how inconclusive) for its future success. In short, Popper must allow for at least a "whiff of inductivism," as he himself seems to do in a similar context (see Popper 1974: 1192–3, fn 165b).

Let us now turn to falsificationism as the critical rationalist's scientific methodology. As we have seen, the rule against ad hoc moves is part-and-parcel of that methodology. But as Popper himself later admitted, science does benefit from such moves, even if only occasionally. Pauli's hypothesis that introduced the existence of neutrinos is a good example (see Popper 1974: 986). What are we to make of such cases? Popper's response is to point out that Pauli's hypothesis eventually did become an independently testable hypothesis. But that response is unsatisfactory because it ignores the fact that even ad hoc hypotheses can be fruitful, can pave the way for scientific progress. This issue is a symptom of a more general problem with falsificationism. Falsificationism does not have the conceptual resources to deal adequately with the complexity of scientific activity, especially of the history of science. This is a point brought home variously by historically minded philosophers of science like Thomas Kuhn, Imre Lakatos, and Paul Feyerabend. If we value scientific progress above all else, then we should allow even ad hoc hypotheses, as Feyerabend has urged. If we wish to make sense of the actual practice of science, then we need a more nuanced framework, such as Kuhn's or Lakatos's, that is sensitive to the historical development of science. As their works show, falsification of theories is a historical process, and no scientific theory is abandoned, even when it gets falsified, unless there is a better alternative.

Finally, Popper's (and, e.g., Miller's and Bartley's) categorical denial of "good reasons" – of any form of justification – for our beliefs and theories verges on skepticism. As we saw earlier, knowledge can no longer be defined in terms of justified true belief. (I ignore the famous Gettier problem in this context as it does not affect this discussion.) What, then, is the alternative? Here critical rationalists disagree. Surprisingly, Popper nowhere defines knowledge. In *Objective Knowledge* he tells us that *knowledge in the objective sense* (as opposed to knowledge in the subjective sense as a state of mind) has no knowers, and that it consists of problems, theories, and arguments (Popper 1975: 108–9). But, clearly, it does not make sense to predicate truth of a problem or an argument; only propositions can be true or false. More sensibly, Popper can define propositional knowledge as consisting of theories that are highly corroborated. However, since this characterization leaves out truth as a condition, and since even corroborated theories can be false, it allows for the possibility of "false knowledge," which is a contradiction in terms, since, as Gilbert Ryle has pointed out, "to know" is a success or achievement verb, whatever else it might be.

Miller defines knowledge as mere true belief, leaving out the justification condition from the justified-true-belief account altogether (Miller 1994: 63–6). The problem with this, of course, is that there is now no way of distinguishing between knowing and guessing rightly by sheer luck. Musgrave (1999: 331–2), on the other hand, suggests, on Popper's behalf, replacing the justification condition with the following: S can justify *his believing* that p. In this way, he distinguishes between S's *justifying that p* and S's *justifying his belief that p* and argues that the definition of knowledge should include the latter, not the former. He then introduces the hitherto unnoticed *justificationist principle*, according to which S's believing that p is justified (reasonable) if and only if S can justify (or give good reasons for) p. The amended condition and the newly added principle then yield the traditional account given in the first section. According to Musgrave, Popper's anti-justificationism is tantamount to his rejection of the justificationist principle. Musgrave's suggestion is an ingenious move, but it is not welcomed by many critical rationalists on the grounds that by allowing in justification, as well as belief in the subjective sense, it diverges too much from the spirit of *critical* (as opposed to justificationist) rationalism.

Critical rationalism and its limits

Scientific theories, metaphysical doctrines, and philosophical arguments can all be criticized rationally in various ways. Does the theory have wide explanatory scope? Does it withstand tests? Is it consistent and simple? Does it solve the problems it set for itself? Even though metaphysical doctrines are not testable, they too can be criticized to see if they have heuristic power, if they are fruitful and free of contradictions. Arguments, too, can be subjected to criticism on the grounds of validity, as logic teaches us. Is everything criticizable or are there some limits to the things to which critical rationalism can be applied? Popper has recognized two kinds of limits.

The first kind arises from the application of critical rationalism to social phenomena. According to Popper, while natural events are explained by subsuming them under laws, human actions are explained by what he calls "situational analysis," that is, by appealing to the problem situation of the agent, his or her perception of it, and *the rationality principle* according to which agents always act appropriately to the situation in which they find themselves. Now, Popper advises us *not* to criticize this principle under any circumstances. If our explanation of an action fails, he says, nothing can be gained by criticizing the rationality principle, as opposed to criticizing the description of the agent's problem and problem situation. In a similar vein, Popper advocates piecemeal social engineering for social reform, arguing for conservative conjecturing and cautious testing instead of bold conjecturing and severe testing. This is because the aim of social engineering is not just to acquire knowledge but to lessen human suffering. Since human actions always have unintended consequences, some of which can be undesired, we might end up doing more harm than good. Thus, despite his rhetoric of the unity of method, Popper restrains his falsificationism in the case of the social sciences.

Once the limits of falsificationism are recognized for the social sciences, however, it is easy to see that the same considerations apply to the physical and biological sciences as well. Where there are serious risks of harming people or damaging the environment, we should again refrain from bold conjecturing and severe testing. This is a further limit to the applicability of critical rationalism, often not recognized by its advocates.

Finally, critical rationalism seems to limit itself. Can there be any non-circular, rational argument for adopting critical rationalism in the first place? Popper thinks not. A person will not be moved by critical argumentation unless he or she is already willing to listen to it. Thus, concludes Popper, critical rationalism can be adopted only through an irrational leap of faith in reason (Popper 1971: 231). In this way an element of *fideism* is smuggled into critical rationalism. Can this unwelcome consequence be avoided? Bartley argued that his pancritical (or comprehensively critical) rationalism avoids it. This is the position that "[any] position may be held rationally without needing any justification at all – provided that it can be and is held open to criticism and survives severe examination" (Bartley 1984: 119). The idea is that because the essence of rationality lies in criticism and not in justification, pancritical rationalism, which is a position and a practice of critical argument, can be applied to itself rationally, without an irrational commitment to its own principles. Pancritical rationalism can be criticized by its own standard and, depending on the outcome of criticism, can be adopted or rejected rationally. Pancritical rationalism does not limit itself in the way that critical rationalism does, hence its comprehensiveness. In this way, fideism is avoided.

Both John Watkins (1993) and John Post (1993) argued that Bartley's pancritical rationalism leads to something like a paradox. To see this, consider the following statement, A, which presumably represents pancritical rationalism or an essential component of it:

A: Every rational statement is criticizable.

Furthermore, pancritical rationalism conjectures that

B: A is itself criticizable.

Now, we can argue for the following pair of statements (here, I simplify Post's argument for reasons of scope):

1　Every criticism of B is a criticism of A; (this is because, since pancritical rationalism is comprehensive, in so far as A is itself rational, B follows from A).
2　No criticism of A is a criticism of B. (The argument in a nutshell is this: a criticism of A would entail that A is criticizable. But that is precisely what B says. Hence, a criticism of A ends up confirming B.)

From this pair, it follows that there is no criticism of B. Thus, B is not criticizable after all. But since B is not criticizable, not all rational statements are criticizable, assuming B to be rational. Hence, A is false as well.

Now, what does this argument show? Does it refute pancritical rationalism? Is criticizability a necessary or a sufficient condition of rationality? What exactly does criticism involve? Bartley's work and responses to it have generated a considerable literature attempting to answer such questions. Bartley himself argued that Watkins's and Post's arguments do not affect his pancritical rationalism because his *position* is not adequately characterized by *the statement* that all rational statements can be criticized. Miller too defended pancritical rationalism by pointing out that deriving an uncriticizable statement from it is no refutation of it, much less a concession to irrationalism. For pancritical rationalists are not committed to the claim that *all* consequences of their position must be criticizable; what matters is that they merely conjecturally hold the position that opens all positions, including itself, to criticism, and that is all pancritical rationalism requires.

Acknowledgements

I thank Ilhan Inan and the editors of this volume for helpful comments. I also gratefully acknowledge the support of the Turkish Academy of Sciences.

See also Confirmation; Epistemology of science after Quine; The historical turn in the philosophy of science; Logical empiricism; Metaphysics; Scientific method; Truthlikeness.

References

Bartley, W. W. (1984) *The Retreat to Commitment*, Chicago: Open Court.

Miller, D. (1994) *Critical Rationalism*, Chicago: Open Court.

Musgrave, A. (1999) *Essays on Realism and Rationalism*, Amsterdam: Rodopi.

O'Hear, A. (1980) *Karl Popper*, London: Routledge & Kegan Paul.

Popper, K. (1968a) *Conjectures and Refutations*, New York: Harper Torchbooks.

—— (1968b) *The Logic of Scientific Discovery*, New York: Harper Torchbooks.

—— (1971) *The Open Society and its Enemies*, Volume 2, Princeton, NJ: Princeton University Press.

—— (1974) "Replies to My Critics," in P. A. Schilpp (ed.) *The Philosophy of Karl Popper*, La Salle, IL: Open Court.

—— (1975) *Objective Knowledge*, Oxford: Clarendon Press.

Post, J. (1993) "A Gödelian Theorem for Theories of Rationality," in G. Radnitzky and W. W. Bartley (eds) *Evolutionary Epistemology, Rationality, and the Sociology of Knowledge*, Chicago: Open Court.

Watkins, J. (1993) "Comprehensively Critical Rationalism: A Retrospect," in G. Radnitzky and W. W. Bartley (eds) *Evolutionary Epistemology, Rationality, and the Sociology of Knowledge*, Chicago: Open Court.

Further reading

Popper's major works are listed above. To these may be added his *Realism and the Aim of Science*, which is volume 1 of *The Postscript to The Logic of Scientific Discovery*, ed. W. W. Bartley (London: Hutchinson, 1983). Miller (1994) is arguably the best defense of critical rationalism. John Wettersten's *The Roots of Critical Rationalism* (Amsterdam: Rodopi, 1992) uncovers the historical background to critical rationalism. O'Hear (1980) provides an overall critical exposition of Popper's philosophy. Adolf Grünbaum's "Is Falsifiability the Touchstone of Scientific Rationality? Karl Popper versus Inductivism," in R. S. Cohen, P. K. Feyerabend, and M. W. Wartofsky (eds) *Essays in Memory of Imre Lakatos* (Dordrecht: Reidel, 1976) is an incisive criticism of Popper's view that the rationality of science can be characterized in terms of falsifiability, to the exclusion of inductive supportability. For the application of Popper's falsificationism to the social sciences see Noretta Koertge's "Popper's Metaphysical Research Program for the Human Sciences," *Inquiry* 18 (1975): 437–62. Radnitzky and Bartley's *Evolutionary Epistemology, Rationality, and the Sociology of Science* contains, among other things, a number of important articles on the limits of rationality and critical rationalism, including Watkins's and Post's criticisms of Bartley's pancritical rationalism and his reply to them.

7

THE HISTORICAL TURN IN THE PHILOSOPHY OF SCIENCE

Alexander Bird

Introduction

The history of science itself has a long history, often found as an introductory part of a scientist's scientific writings (from Aristotle to Priestley). But only in the nineteenth century, with William Whewell, did the history of science begin to find its own place in academic life, a place not properly secured until the twentieth century, thanks largely to the pioneering efforts of George Sarton. Although Whewell intended history of science to furnish the materials against which a satisfactory philosophy of science could be constructed, philosophers of science in the first half of the twentieth century largely ignored the growing historical discipline.

The principal reason for this failure of philosophers to engage with the history of science was the widespread acceptance of a distinction between a context of discovery and a context of justification. The former concerns the circumstances and causes of a scientific development while the latter concerns its justification. The former may refer to historical and psychological data, but these are not relevant to the epistemic assessment of a hypothesis, which will refer, for example, to an *a priori* standard, such as Carnap's inductive logic. Given this distinction, the normative function of philosophy of science, concerned with the context of justification, could ignore the factual historical domain of the context of discovery. This perspective was shared even by those, such as Popper, who rejected many of the assumptions of logical positivism.

Thomas Kuhn

Mounting problems with logical positivism (e.g. Quine's attack on the analytic–synthetic distinction and Goodman's new riddle of induction) opened up the opportunity for a rapprochement between history of science and a post-positivist philosophy of science. Leading the way was Thomas Kuhn, whose second book, *The Structure of*

Scientific Revolutions (Kuhn 1962) dominated much of philosophy of science in the last third of the twentieth century.

The Structure of Scientific Revolutions may be called "theoretical history," by which I mean that it does two things that have an analogue in natural science:

(i)   a *descriptive* element – it identifies a general pattern in the development of science: science is a puzzle-solving enterprise which shows a cyclical pattern of normal science, crisis, revolution, normal science;

(ii) an *explanatory* element – it proposes an explanation of the pattern identified in (i): puzzle-solving is driven by adherence to a *paradigm* (an exemplary puzzle solution).

In Kuhn's description of scientific puzzle-solving, the history of a scientific field is dominated by periods of *normal science*. Normal science, superficially at least, resembles scientific progress as traditionally described and of the kind one might expect from a standard positivist viewpoint. Scientific success is cumulative; it is by and large steady; it does not encounter significant obstacles or anomalies; scientists of all levels of skill are able to make worthwhile contributions. According to Kuhn normal science is highly conservative, contrasting with Popper's description of science as attempting to refute its own best theories. During periods of normal science scientists share a great deal by way of accepted theory, methodology, experimental equipment and techniques, and values. These are not questioned during normal science; indeed an acceptance of these things is a prerequisite for entering the profession as a scientist in the relevant field. These provide the background that makes normal science, the process of puzzle-solving, possible. Kuhn describes various kinds of puzzle-solving, including determining the value of constants in equations, perfecting experimental techniques, and extending the application of an existing theory to new instances. In so doing, scientists are not challenging or attempting to refute basic theory, which, on the contrary, forms an essential assumption of their work.

In the course of basic science observations may be made that seem to conflict with the underlying accepted theory. These are *anomalies*. But even these do not count as Popperian refutations. Anomalies may themselves be regarded as just further fodder for puzzle-solving. The puzzle is to reconcile the observations and the theory. A good example of this is the anomalous orbit of Uranus, which although in apparent conflict with Newton's law, was shown in fact to be in full conformity by the discovery of Neptune by Leverrier and Adams.

Other unsolved anomalies may be shelved for later consideration. They become troubling only when they arise in sufficient numbers or, more importantly, when they arise in an area that is particularly significant for the underlying theory or its applications (or which is central to the employment of some important technique or piece of apparatus) and continue to defy solution. Under such circumstances it is difficult for normal science to continue in its previously settled vein, and the field is on the verge of *crisis*. A crisis arises when the accumulation of significant solution-resistant anomalies is such that a sizable proportion of practitioners come to doubt the efficacy of the underlying theory (technique, equipment) to continue to support a puzzle-solving tradition. This in turn means that the field is ripe for *revolution*, which is the proposal of a new and rival theory to replace the old one.

Kuhn notes that revolutions are typically not smooth affairs. There may be considerable resistance to change. For reasons we will come to, Kuhn does not regard the decision to change as one that is rationally forced. However, an important factor may be noted immediately. This is the phenomenon known as "Kuhn-loss." According to Kuhn a new theory never solves all the puzzles that were regarded as solved by the old theory. It must solve a respectable proportion of the worrying anomalies, but this will be at the cost of leaving unsolved some of the puzzles that had previously be solved successfully. Thus there is a trade-off which may not have a rationally obvious balance of benefits over costs.

Kuhn not only describes this cyclical pattern in the history of science, but gives an explanation for it. Kuhn's key idea is that of a "paradigm." Since that term has become something of a cliché, it is important to understand exactly what Kuhn meant by it. While its use in *The Structure of Scientific Revolutions* was somewhat varied, Kuhn later clarified that usage into two related meanings. The broader meaning is that of a consensus around a variety of components of scientific activity: key theories and equations, a terminology, accepted mathematical techniques and experimental procedures. A constellation of such things around which there is a consensus in normal science Kuhn called a "disciplinary matrix." For the narrower sense of "paradigm" Kuhn used the term "exemplar." Exemplars are one element of the disciplinary matrix. But they are the most important element, that which explains the remainder. An exemplar is a particularly significant scientific achievement, a puzzle solution (or set of related puzzle solutions) which is so effective that it can crystallize support around it, and which serves as a model for future research.

When the paradigm-as-exemplar functions as a model for future research, the resulting proposed puzzle solutions are evaluated according to their similarity to the exemplar. Making judgments of similarity is not a matter that can be settled by the application of rules. When students learn to become scientists they do not learn facts and methodological rules for making discoveries or for evaluating potential discoveries. Rather they are trained in the use of exemplary techniques. This training is a matter of familiarization through repeated exposure and practice.

This explains the conservatism of normal science. Training with shared exemplars induces a shared mindset that constrains and directs the thinking of scientists. It enables them to see certain new puzzle solutions and to come to a shared judgment concerning proposed puzzle solutions. So long as the exemplar is fruitful, this process is efficient and effective. Kuhn, conservative in Mannheim's sense, emphasizes the importance of tradition in shaping what people think and do. There is a normative element, since Kuhn thinks that science cannot function without some degree of respect for the tradition, without which we would be permanently in a state of pre-paradigm foundational dispute, failing to add to our knowledge. At the same time, scientists must be able to innovate and to discard paradigms that have outlived their usefulness. This conflict between tradition and innovation Kuhn describes in his essay "The Essential Tension."

The functioning of paradigms-as-exemplars also explains the nature of crisis and revolution. A single anomaly does not refute a theory in the simple logical fashion that Popper claimed. Equally there is no logically clear and decisive refutation of a theory by an accumulation of significant anomalies. Hence there is room for rational disagreement about whether and to what degree a paradigm is in trouble when anomalies arise. Similarly there is room for rational disagreement over whether a new paradigm should supersede an older one.

The Structure of Scientific Revolutions had an enormous influence on the philosophy of science; its portrayal of science and its history, and more importantly, the explanation in terms of paradigms-as-exemplars, was in deep tension with the conceptions of scientific reasoning provided by the logical empiricists. Philosophers as divergent as Carnap and Popper agreed that the inferential relationship (whether inductive confirmation or falsification) between evidence and theory should be a formal, logical matter. The proposed confirmation or falsification of a hypothesis is rule-governed, where the notion of a rule is of something that can be explicitly written down and followed algorithmically. That inference should be so understood was held to be a criterion of its rationality.

Consequently, that Kuhn should be suggesting that acceptance of a hypothesis is governed not by explicit, formal rules, but instead by a non-formal, imprecise condition of similarity to an exemplar was taken by his critics to be suggesting that science is irrational. To many, critics and supporters alike, Kuhn's proposal seemed to be a version of relativism, on the grounds that scientific acceptability is defined relative to a paradigm, rather than by reference to some fixed standard (such as a sempiternal logic). Since paradigms both explain the decisions of scientists and act as a standard of evaluation, Kuhn also rejects a sharp distinction between the contexts of discovery and justification.

Kuhn did not intend to promote relativism or irrationalism. Rather he was arguing, in effect, that scientific rationality is not as the logical empiricists took it to be. Learning from exemplars is a ubiquitous feature of human learning, especially, but not only, in language learning; it is not irrational elsewhere, nor is it in science.

Kuhn's work consequently shows how history of science could be highly influential in philosophy of science. Philosophers of science held two theses: (i) if science is to be rational, scientific inference must take form X (viz., the following of logical rules); (ii) science is in fact rational. Since (ii) is a factual claim, the combination of these two had empirically testable results. Much of science, and the best science in particular, should show that it takes form X. The empirical tests here are a matter of looking at episodes from the history of science. Kuhn's historical work shows that science did not have form X at all. As we have seen, that could be taken as having only an empirical conclusion concerning science, that it is irrational. But if we agree that science is the best example of rationality we have (or at least an example), then we are forced instead to draw the philosophically more significant conclusion that the logical positivists and other logical empiricists were wrong about what constitutes rationality in science. Thus, even if one thinks of history of science as descriptive and philosophy of science as normative, the former can be relevant to the latter in that, given certain assumptions about science in fact satisfying the norms (e.g., science is largely rational), it had better be that the historian's description meshes with the philosopher's prescription.

The interrelationship between history of science and philosophy of science that became so prominent in the 1960s and 1970s led to the founding of programs and departments of history and philosophy of science. Kuhn (1977) himself denied that the two disciplines could merge. In his view quite different mindsets were required to practice each and there could not be a common objective to be achieved in carrying out both simultaneously – one might do both, but separately. Nonetheless, history of science could be a useful source of data in the manner described above. Very frequently, Kuhn complained, the picture of science, even as an idealized picture, provided by philosophers was unrecognizable to the historians of science and indeed to scientists themselves. (Kuhn felt that this relationship is asymmetrical. Historians would often need to know about the philosophical schools of thought prevalent in the periods they were studying. But they did not need to know any contemporary philosophy of science.)

Imre Lakatos

Kuhn's conception of science contrasts not only with positivism but also with Popper's methodological falsificationism (viz., critical rationalism applied to scientific change). In Popper's view scientific progress occurs only as a result of the rejection of a hypothesis, whereas in Kuhn's account the latter occurs only during *extraordinary* science, which is to say as the result of a scientific revolution. Thus Popper ignores normal science and regards all progressive science as revolutionary. Furthermore Popper regards refutation as a logical matter whereas Kuhn holds that the rejection of an old paradigm is not logically compelling and may be a matter over which rational disagreement is possible, as a consequence of which a scientific revolution may be a drawn-out affair. Normal science violates the requirements of critical rationalism. Rather than criticize accepted theories, Kuhnian normal scientists unquestioningly take them as given and seek to fill in any remaining gaps in those theories or to apply them to new phenomena. During normal science anomalies are typically shelved rather than taken as grounds for rejecting the theory. Only the accumulation of particularly problematic anomalies – those that present difficulties for the very practice of normal science – leads to doubt concerning the paradigm theories. According to Popper, Kuhnian normal science shows pernicious conservatism. According to Kuhn, Popperian methodological falsificationism fails to match the facts of the history of science.

Kuhn's apparent paradigm-relativism and his rejection of the idea that rules of rationality play a significant role in science (plus a brief passage in which Kuhn mentions the possible significance of extra-scientific factors in scientific revolutions), led Lakatos to regard Kuhn as taking scientific change to be a matter of "mob psychology" (Lakatos 1970: 178). Lakatos, a student then colleague of Popper's, did recognize the force of Kuhn's historical criticism of Popper – important theories are often surrounded by an "ocean of anomalies", which on a falsificationist view would require the rejection of the theory outright. In his "Falsification and the Methodology of Scientific Research Programmes" (1970) Lakatos sought to reconcile the rationalism of Popperian falsificationism with what seemed to be its own refutation by history.

Popper's conception of a theory and its relationship to the evidence is essentially a static one, driven by the logical relation between a universal generalization and the singular existential statements that may contradict it. Lakatos instead took the object of research to be a dynamic entity that may change over time – the *research program* – not a theory understood as a static set of propositions. At its heart is the *hard core*, the leading theoretical idea. Lakatos noted, following Duhem, that theoretical claims do not get tested against observation directly, but only via intermediary, or *auxiliary*, propositions. In Lakatos's central example, the Newtonian research program, the hard core consists of the laws of motion and gravitation. But these imply nothing about what we should observe when looking at the moon, sun, and the planets, unless we add various claims about their masses, positions at particular times, even their shapes and orientations. To advance the research program, Newtonians sought to add to the body of auxiliary propositions in such a way that the application of the combined theory and auxiliary belt grows in scope and accuracy. Anomalies are to be expected in a young research program whose auxiliary hypotheses may be over-simplified, inaccurate, or incomplete. In the Newtonian case, the application of the hard core to the sun and each of the planets individually will produce anomalous results, since such applications ignore the gravitational force of the other planets. In such a case the program itself shows clearly how one is to develop the auxiliary belt in order to eliminate those anomalies, for it tells us that the other planets will have a gravitational attraction which, though small, will need to be considered for the program to grow in accuracy. The steer that the program gives to its own development Lakatos called the "positive heuristic." This complements the "negative heuristic," which is the injunction not to change the hard core in the face of an anomaly. For, following Quine's development of Duhem, Lakatos noted that any proposition may be saved from falsification if one is willing to make sufficient changes to other propositions with which it is connected. The negative heuristic directs change away from the hard core to the auxiliary belt, while the positive heuristic tells us which changes to make.

Thus far Lakatos's account seems to be little more than a redescription of Kuhn's, the hard core replacing the paradigm theory, the development of the auxiliary belt being the practice of normal science, the positive heuristic being the model provided by the exemplary applications of the paradigm theory, and the negative heuristic being the fact that paradigms are unquestioned during normal science. There are nonetheless important differences. While Kuhn regards the operation of a paradigm as largely tacit, Lakatos condemns this as an anti-rationalistic elitism. More significant still was the difference in view concerning revolutions or the refutation of a research program. Lakatos did accept against Popper that scientists do not reject a hitherto successful theory in the face of even serious anomalies, unless some alternative is available. Thus the question is not "When is a theory refuted?" but "When is one theory shown to be superior to another?" But unlike Kuhn, Lakatos thought that this question may be given a definite rational answer. Just as a research program is progressing when it increases in content and has independent corroboration for its growing content, a research program is *degenerating* when, in order to obey the negative heuristic ("protect the hard core"), the program reduces its scope (e.g., by building in exceptions) or adds uncorroborated ad hoc hypotheses. A research program will be degenerating during the period that Kuhn would identify as a crisis. A revolution occurs when a rival, progressive research program supersedes the degenerating one, as occurred, argues Lakatos's student Elie Zahar, when Einstein's program superseded Lorentz's in the early years of the twentieth century. According to Lakatos it is acceptable for a scientist to continue working on a degenerating research program. Nonetheless, such a scientist should keep a score of the relative merits of that program and is rivals. Rational scientists, whichever program they happen to be working on, should be able to agree on the score at any given time.

Kuhn accused Lakatos of rewriting history when it came to showing how history vindicated his position. The relationship between history of science and philosophy of science is a difficult one. One could take the view that philosophy of science is normative, articulating what inferences scientists *should* make, while history is descriptive, telling us what scientists in fact did. These could be independent – we do not think that normative ethics is answerable to history, since we all know that people do not do what they (morally) ought to do. Science is different, since most philosophers of science think that scientists are by and large rational or at least that "science" is rational. In which case what a good philosophical theory says ought to happen in science should not diverge too far from what history tells us actually does happen. In this way a philosophical methodology turns into a historical research program. For example, Popperian methodology becomes the historical claim that revolutions are frequent and are accompanied by decisive crucial experiments. Consequently history can help in arbitrating methodological disputes between inductivism, falsificationism, conventionalism, and, of course, Lakatos's methodology of scientific research programs.

In the light of this, Kuhn's accusation that Lakatos falsifies history ought to be a serious charge – perhaps history does not vindicate Lakatos as strongly as he thought it did? Lakatos did not think that the *historical* research program of scientific methodology is just a matter of writing history as accurately as possible, independently of any conception of rationality, to give a result that may be compared with the various philosophical methodologies. Instead Lakatos conceived of the appropriate kind of history as a rational *reconstruction* of history.

To understand Lakatos's rational reconstructions of history it is important to recognize the Hegelian element in Lakatos's thought. According to Hegel history has an underlying "logic." While that logic is inevitable, particular events may be mere chance occurrences of no lasting significance, that merely obscure the underlying logic. A perfect chronology might record such facts, but such a chronology would fail to reveal the deeper structure of history (rather as a mere record of experimental outcomes would fail to show the underlying laws of nature). A philosophical history should demonstrate the working of that structure and may thus ignore the distracting details that may on occasion deviate from it. The "logic" referred to is well known. An idea or *thesis*, which may govern some historical epoch, has within itself certain "contradictions" (internal tensions) which in due course give rise to an opposing idea, the *antithesis*. The creative friction between thesis and antithesis brings about a third idea, the *synthesis* which is a resolution of that struggle. In Lakatos's work the Hegelian triad first appears in the description of how "counter-examples" to a mathematical proof lead to conceptual improvement and a more generalized proof.

In the methodology of scientific research programs, a similar idea is at work. The thesis is the current state of the research program, and an anomaly plays the role of the antithesis, so that the synthesis is the later stage of the research program, with the auxiliary belt amended and improved so as to expand its scope and accuracy. In both the mathematical and the scientific cases, the Hegelian element comes not simply in the application of the triad but also in the fact that its application matches a progressive and rational underlying logic. The history of mathematics and science ought to lay bare the operation of that logic and thus should display and clarify the *rationality* of the process; but as mentioned, that logic may be obscured, especially by individual chance occurrences. Consequently what is required is not a description of the events but a reconstruction of them so that they display the rational and progressive nature of the unfolding of history. (In this respect, rationally reconstructed history is rather like the report of an experiment in a scientific paper whose organization reflects the logic of the argument, not the experiment's actual chronology.)

Kuhn and Lakatos thus had widely differing conceptions of the relationship between philosophy of science and history of science. Kuhn held that the relationship was asymmetrical. Philosophy of science needed history of science to ensure that its implicit descriptions of science indeed do apply to some actual practice. On the other hand, history of science might get along fine without any philosophy of science. Lakatos, on the other hand, saw a rather more subtle relationship between the two. Appropriating Kant, Lakatos (1971: 91) remarked: "Philosophy of science without history of science is empty; history of science without philosophy of science is blind." He thus agrees with Kuhn that philosophy of science needs history of science in order to have a subject matter – indeed he goes further since the very point of philosophy of science is to reveal the Hegelian logic underlying the surface history of events. At the same time, the aim of the history of science should be to demonstrate the working out of the logic in particular cases, which it can hardly do in ignorance of philosophy, without which history will be the blind collection of miscellaneous facts.

Paul Feyerabend

Paul Feyerabend, also a student of Popper (and a one-time colleague of Kuhn), initially stressed the normative character of the philosophy of science. But as the 1960s progressed the emphasis shifted towards a more descriptive, historical approach to understanding science. In 1970 Feyerabend published a long article (later to become the book *Against Method*, 1975) in which he argued that no methodological rule would promote scientific progress under all circumstances – any proposed rule would inhibit progress under some circumstance or other. Feyerabend's approach was to consider historical episodes that we pre-theoretically regard as progressive and then to show that those episodes violate the methodological prescriptions that one might expect to apply.

Feyerabend's much-discussed case study concerns Galileo's arguments for Copernicanism. According to Feyerabend, had Galileo been either a naive empiricist or a Popperian falsificationist, then Galileo would have had to abandon his endorsement of Copernicanism. For example, Galileo defended Copernicanism against the *tower argument*. Were the earth moving, the argument proceeds, we would expect a rock dropped from a tower not to fall at its base but rather at some distance, the distance that part of the earth has moved during the fall of the rock. Galileo counters by describing the case of throwing a ball within the cabin of a moving ship. The force with which the ball should be thrown and its direction are independent of the ship's (uniform) motion, which is shared by the throwers. Galileo's argument shows that the rock falling at the tower's base is predicted by his theory also. In which case his moving-earth theory and the Aristotelian static-earth theory are observationally equivalent. If that were the only ground for choice the naive empiricist should refuse to prefer one theory to the other. Thus Galileo's endorsement of one over the other is inconsistent with naive empiricism. Assuming that Galileo did assist science in progressing, then naive empiricism is a methodological prescription that would have been anti-progressive in that context.

Galileo's behavior does not respect the requirements of naive falsificationism, since Copernicanism is refuted by the observed brightness of Mars and Venus. There ought to be much greater perceived variation in brightness of the planets, depending on whether Venus and Mars are at their greatest or least distance from earth. Feyerabend also considered sophisticated falsificationism, according to which we should prefer theories with greater empirical content, including additional falsifiable predictions. Feyerabend claims that the Copernican system had no additional empirical content. It is true that Galileo asserted that the telescopic observations of the phases of Venus are direct confirmation of a novel prediction of the theory. (The observations of the moons of Jupiter are indirect supporting evidence. Note also that the phases of Venus also undermine the objection based on the smaller than predicted variation in observed brightness of Venus, since the phases compensate for the distances from earth – Venus is full when most distant but new when close.) Feyerabend argued that Galileo was not entitled to rely upon such observations because the telescope could not be held to be reliable for celestial observations, and indeed the competing Aristotelian theory justified not inferring from the telescope's terrestrial reliability to celestial reliability, because it held the laws to differ in the two regions. Furthermore, Galileo's new physics represented a reduction in content in that it concerned only locomotion as compared with the wider range of phenomena of change encompassed by Aristotelian physics – which in addition to locomotion included qualitative change, and generation and corruption.

When it comes to Lakatos's methodology of scientific research programs, matters are a little different. For Lakatos accepts that early in the development of a new theory it will encounter apparently falsifying instances and may need to reduce its scope, and hence empirical content, relative to a well-established rival. Hence the evidence Feyerabend presents does no damage to that view. Instead Feyerabend claims that Lakatos's account fails to provide any methodological prescriptions worth the name. Indeed Feyerband regards Lakatos's view as being closet anarchism disguised as methodological rationalism. It should be noted that Feyerabend's claim was not that standard methodological rules should never be obeyed, but rather that sometimes progress is made by abandoning them. In the absence of a generally accepted rule, there is a need for alternative methods of persuasion. According to Feyerabend, Galileo employed stylistic and rhetorical techniques to convince his reader, while he also wrote in Italian rather than Latin and directed his arguments to those already temperamentally inclined to accept them.

Recent developments

Feyerabend's work caused considerable debate, principally over the historical accuracy of his interpretation of Galileo. Moreover, the focus on conceptions of rationality and method then prominent leaves room for other conceptions that may be consistent with Galileo's behavior.

Nonetheless, Feyerabend's work, along with Kuhn's, did have the effect of persuading philosophers of science and others that their accounts of science, even if intended normatively, should be tested against the history of science. The legacy of this historical philosophy of science may be regarded as having bifurcated, with radical historians and sociologists of science on the one side and the majority of philosophers of science on the other. On the former side the tacit assumption that scientific rationality, were there such a thing, would be a matter of following rules of method, is accepted. This, along with Kuhn's and Feyerabend's demonstration that scientists do not follow such rules, leads to the conclusion that science is not the rational enterprise it is often held to be. Feyerabend's emphasis on rhetoric and other non-rational forms of persuasion meshes with versions of the Hessen thesis, that scientific change is explained by social and political forces rather than new evidence. Consequently much effort has been put into historico-sociological work, much of it under the heading "Sociology of Scientific Knowledge," intended to show such forces at work in key episodes in the history of science.

Among philosophers of science a typical response has been to disassociate rationality from the idea of a scientific method. Science might be rational even without fixed rules of method. For example, it might be rational for a scientist to infer the likely truth of the hypothesis that is the best explanation of the evidence; but there may be no methodical rule for determining which hypothesis is the best explanation. Furthermore, many philosophers of science have taken on board the lessons of naturalized epistemology. According to one version of that view, the methods of inquiry that lead to progress or truth cannot be uncovered *a priori*, as the logical empiricists including Popper thought, but need themselves to be discovered *a posteriori* by scientific and other means. Consequently, prescriptive philosophy of science has largely been abandoned. Descriptive philosophy of science remains, in that one may wish to describe the general features of rational science, and in such cases philosophers recognize the importance of showing that historical episodes do exemplify these generalized descriptions.

See also Critical rationalism; Discovery; Logical empiricism; Scientific method; Relativism; Social studies of science; History of philosophy and the philosophy of science; Values in science.

References

Feyerabend, P. (1975) *Against Method*, London: Verso.

Kuhn, T. S. (1962) *The Structure of Scientific Revolutions*, Chicago: University of Chicago Press.

—— (1977) *The Essential Tension: Selected Studies in Scientific Tradition and Change*, Chicago: University of Chicago Press. (See especially "The Essential Tension: Tradition and Innovation in Scientific Research," pp. 225–39; and "The History and the Philosophy of Science," pp. 3–20).

Lakatos, I. (1970) "Falsification and the Methodology of Scientific Research Programmes" in I. Lakatos and A. Musgrave (eds) *Criticism and the Growth of Knowledge*, Cambridge: Cambridge University Press, pp. 91–195.

—— (1971) "History of Science and its Rational Reconstructions," in R. C. Buck and R. S. Cohen (eds) *PSA 1970, Boston Studies in the Philosophy of Science VIII*, Dordrecht: Reidel, pp. 91–108.

Further reading

Comprehensive works on Thomas Kuhn include P. Hoyningen-Huene, *Reconstructing Scientific Revolutions: Thomas S. Kuhn's Philosophy of Science* (Chicago: University of Chicago Press, 1993); A. J. Bird, *Thomas Kuhn* (Chesham: Acumen, 2000); and A. J. Bird, "Thomas Kuhn," in Edward N. Zalta (ed.) *The Stanford Encyclopedia of Philosophy* (spring 2005 edition), available: http://plato.stanford.edu/archives/spr2005/entries/thomas-kuhn. Lakatos is discussed in B. Larvor, *Lakatos: An Introduction* (London: Routledge, 1988). For Feyerabend, see J. M. Preston, *Feyerabend: Philosophy, Science and Society* (Cambridge: Polity Press, 1997); E. Oberheim, *Feyerabend's Philosophy* (Berlin: De Gruyter, 2007); and J. M. Preston, "Paul Feyerabend," in Edward N. Zalta (ed.) *The Stanford Encyclopedia of Philosophy* (spring 2006 edition), available: http://plato.stanford.edu/archives/spr2006/entries/feyerabend.

8

LOGICAL EMPIRICISM

Thomas Uebel

There can be little doubt that analytical philosophy of science would not be what it is today had there not been the philosophical movement called "logical empiricism" (also called "logical positivism" or "neo-positivism"). Its most influential figures were Rudolf Carnap, Hans Reichenbach, Herbert Feigl, and C. G. Hempel, European émigrés who had developed their philosophies in the context of the Vienna Circle and the Berlin Society for Scientific Philosophy. Though not entirely so (given the support they were given by pragmatists like Ernest Nagel and sympathetic critics like W. V. Quine and Wilfrid Sellars), it was largely under their aegis that around the middle of the twentieth century philosophy of science became a recognized sub-discipline in its own right with its distinct methodology. Notably, it was the logical empiricists' formalist approach to philosophy, not their material concerns with science, that for a while even appeared to have set the agenda and standard for analytical philosophy as a whole. It is only in retrospect, and in step with the rediscovery of the great variety of doctrines promoted under its name, that the pragmatic and holistic elements in logical empiricism have been discerned that were introduced by Otto Neurath and Philipp Frank. After a period of wholesale rejection, logical empiricism has regained a measure of respect, as careful historical and philosophical studies have replaced hostile caricatures.

The analytic and the synthetic

Logical empiricist philosophy of science was informed by the fundamental assumption – shared, before them, by philosophers as different as Occam, Leibniz, Kant, Peirce and Mach – that only those propositions are *cognitively* meaningful whose truth or falsity makes a difference that is discernible, at least in principle and however fallibly, by scientific means. (Cognitive meaning, unlike non-cognitive meanings, always concerns a factuality of sorts.) What distinguishes logical empiricist philosophy of science is the sharp division it draws between the empirical sciences (physics, biology, the social sciences, etc.) and the formal sciences (logic, mathematics). This division reflects the logical empiricist strategy of attempting to renew empiricism by freeing it from the impossible task of grounding logical and mathematical knowledge. (Their factuality was evidenced not in empirical but formal reasoning.) This strategy was codified in the basic axiom all logical empiricists accepted, whatever their further positions. This was that either propositions were of a synthetic nature and their assertion justifiable only *a posteriori*, or they were analytic in nature and justifiable by *a priori* reasoning – *tertium non datur*.

The claim contained in this axiom is neither without appeal nor without problems. The knowledge-claims of logic and mathematics gained their justification on purely formal grounds, by proof of their derivability by stated rules from stated axioms and premises. Depending on the standing of these axioms and premises, justification was conditional or unconditional; axioms and principles of derivation in turn were considered linguistic rules and determined by convention. Thus logic and mathematics were thought easily integrated into the empiricist framework. Gödel's incompleteness results complicated matters, but Carnap proposed to accommodate these by separating analyticity from effective provability and by postulating arithmetic to consist of an infinite series of ever richer arithmetical languages (Carnap 1934/37: §§60a–d).

The synthetic statements of the empirical sciences, meanwhile, were held to be cognitively meaningful if and only if they were empirically testable in some sense (and their justification as knowledge claims derived from such successful tests). Roughly, if synthetic statements failed to be testable in principle they were considered to be cognitively meaningless, giving rise in philosophy only to pseudo-problems. (Their non-cognitive meaning provided ample material for analysis in biology, psychology, sociology, and history.) Here logical empiricists appealed to a meaning criterion the correct formulation of which proved controversial and elusive (Hempel 1965: Ch. 4). While some construals of logical empiricism are affected, it is not clear whether the entire logical empiricist project is derailed by this. To begin with, if the status of the criterion itself was that of a metalinguistic proposal (such that it was neither straightforwardly descriptive and empirical nor analytical such that its negation was self-contradictory), then nothing much follows from the meaning criterion not applying to itself. Moreover, if the proposal is limited to formal languages, a late proposal of Carnap's can be successfully defended (Creath 1976), while the more pragmatic form of logical empiricism represented by Neurath and Frank sidesteps the need for a precise formal criterion of significance by its exemplar-oriented under-standing of the criterion of making a discernible difference.

What kind of empiricism?

In logical empiricism, empiricism itself underwent change, sometimes even radically so. Logical empiricists dealt harshly with opponents, denying the very meaningfulness of their theses: Kant's synthetic *a priori* was declared empty, having been refuted twice over by the progress of science itself (once by the discovery of non-Euclidean geometries and once by the general theory of relativity's showing that Euclidean geometry was false of physical space), while knowledge-claims for any deliverances of so-called metaphysical intuition were rejected as unintelligible. But logical empiricism also came to shed traditional philosophical ambitions of earlier empiricisms: to give an account of logical and mathematical knowledge, as well as account for the very possibility of knowledge. For the logical empiricists, philosophy of science became an entirely second-order inquiry, reflecting on the methodology of the first-order sciences. Unlike traditional empiricist epistemology, it did not manage to reserve for itself even a very last domain of its own, by disputing radical skepticism. Skeptical doubts that were not themselves scientific doubts, in principle allayable by scientific means, lay beyond its brief.

A further restriction came in the form of the distinction between contexts of inquiry. Philosophy was postulated to concentrate entirely on the context of justification, the normative dimension of scientific knowledge claims, not the context of discovery and the descriptive inquiries into scientific practices appropriate there. Orthodox logical empiricist philosophy of science took the discovery–justification distinction to require abstaining from all empirical reasoning: the normative was itself understood atemporally and analyzed in terms of propositional structures ordered by formal relations of logical entailment. Heterodox logical empiricism, by contrast, happily accepted input from biology, psychology, sociology, and history for its study of scientific reason. Naturally, a formalist understanding of the logical empiricist project favored an *apriorist* interpretation of the context postulate, while a pragmatist understanding favored an interdisciplinary approach for a partly empirical meta-theory.

Historically, the formalist understanding dominated the logical empiricist project, as is shown by the effort spent on the elaboration of its so-called two-languages model of scientific theories (for a critical overview see Suppe 1977). Logical empiricist philosophy of science separates sharply propositions concerning observable data and their regularities from propositions that are purely theoretical. Its understanding of the concept of a scientific theory as a finitely axiomatized set of propositions applies primarily to the latter (and extends only derivatively to the former). Here the prominent role of Schlick must be mentioned, whose 1918 *General Theory of Knowledge* was one of the first publications by (future) logical empiricists to introduce it. (Schlick took Hilbert's axiomatization of geometry as his model, but other precursors can be found in the work of the French conventionalists Poincaré, Duhem, and Rey, as Frank noted early on.) According to the two-languages model, scientific theories comprise an observational part formulated with observational predicates as customarily interpreted, in which observations and experiential laws were stated, and a theoretical part which consisted of theoretical laws or law-like statements the terms of which merely implicitly defined, namely, in terms of the roles they played in the laws in which they figured. Both parts were connected in virtue of a correlation that could be established between selected terms of the theoretical part and observational terms. In the later 1920s Schlick's model was challenged by a more streamlined conception of scientific theories with just one system of concepts along the lines suggested by Carnap's *Aufbau* (1928). The well-known difficulties of defining dispositional terms (let alone fully theoretical terms) explicitly in observational terminology led to a return to the two-languages model, this time with the conception of scientific theories as uninterpreted calculi connected to observation by potentially complicated correspondence rules (Carnap 1939) that became standard in the *received view* (some of the problems of which will be further discussed below).

The formalist understanding of the logical empiricist project is evidenced also by its rich literature in confirmation theory and the theory of probability. Hempel's career is symptomatic for this, its long middle period closely associated with the pursuit of formal confirmation theory, but spectacularly ended with his own late pragmatic turn (1988). But by opting for formalist methodology as the key to its disciplinary professionalization, orthodox post-Second World War logical empiricism did not only discount (often unknowingly) the socio-cultural dimension its project had possessed in the inter-war years, but also (again mostly unknowingly) the post-Kantian dimension its project had possessed in Central Europe. As a result, it rendered itself liable in part to traditional concerns again – with the result that both the point of Carnap's deflationist formal explicationism and of Neurath's and Frank's pragmatic–naturalistic explorations were lost sight of. Instead, with Feigl in the lead, mainstream logical empiricism drifted into discussions of scientific realism and lost its anti-metaphysical edge.

The language of theory

Throughout its career, mainly due to the example of Schlick and Reichenbach, logical empiricism claimed Einstein's theory of relativity as its inspiration and the two-languages model of a theory did sterling service. (Later, Reichenbach, and to some extent Frank, also turned their attention to quantum theory.) What has been questioned recently is whether logical empiricism possessed the resources to comprehend correctly the complexities of the theoretical language of advanced mathematical physics, especially when it comes to the theory of general relativity. Three issues dominate here:

- the applicability of the analytic–synthetic distinction to the theoretical language;
- the nature of the empirical basis; and
- the reference of theoretical terms.

The analytic–synthetic distinction and theoretical language

Around 1920, Schlick persuaded Reichenbach that the creative interventions that helped theory to cope with the data – for instance, the geometries that are presupposed for the description of physical space, or other mathematical apparatus required to represent physical phenomena – should be considered not as new forms of a relativized synthetic *a priori*, but as conventions. This understanding presupposes precisely the sharp distinction between analytic and synthetic statements for which logical empiricism is well known. However, it has been argued that especially the theoretical language of general relativity is more holistic than this, blending physics and geometry and putting pressure on the traditional distinction central to the Schlick–Reichenbach understanding of relativity theory (Ryckman 1992).

Carnap found that his 1956 criterion of significance for theoretical terms made it impossible to uphold the analytic–synthetic distinction for theoretical language, and for a while he even contemplated acquiescing in this result (1966: Ch. 28). Carnap's later efforts to reinstate this distinction by reconstructing a scientific theory by means of so-called Ramsey sentences were not successful. Roughly, Carnap's so-called "ramseyfication" of theories consisted in the replacement of the theoretical terms of a finitely axiomatized theory by bound higher-order variables, leaving a theory in a descriptively purely observational but mathematically very rich language. This led to Carnap inheriting Russell's "Newman problem" that, due to the logical machinations involved, the supposedly synthetic theory became trivially true whenever its observational consequences obtained (see Demopoulos 2003 and Psillos 1999: Ch. 3). What is significant, however, is that Carnap still found a way to deal with the difference between the languages of special and general relativity. To do so, he needed to assume only the distinction between logical and descriptive terms; then he could show that the fundamental tensor determining the metrical structure of physical space is a logical–mathematical concept in special relativity, but a descriptive concept in general relativity (1934/37: §50). Despite the fact that logical empiricism thus appears to possess the resources to account for the difference in the status of the concept of the fundamental metric tensor in special and general relativity, Carnap and Reichenbach never discussed their apparently divergent responses on this issue. (Perhaps Reichenbach preferred to overlook Carnap's generalization of a view that he himself once abandoned under pressure from Schlick when in the early 1920s he dropped talk of the "relative a priori" for talk of "conventions" (see Friedman 1999: 66–70) and Carnap chose not to make too much of it.) In any case, it seems that Reichenbach's should not be considered the last logical empiricist word on the matter.

The nature of the empirical basis

Once the analytic–synthetic distinction was deployed only with regard to the observational language, what falls under *analytic* (beyond the logical and mathematical truths recognized as such also in the theoretical language) are meaning postulates, definitional conventions that have no testable consequences for what can be said. Turning to the other side of the distinction, we can ask how we should conceive of the class of *synthetic* statements of the observational language. Clearly, they typically speak of middle-sized objects and events and their properties, but was there no more basic class of statements from which they derived? Traditionally, empiricism had provided a foundationalist answer here, and against this as well as against Carnap's methodological phenomenalism in the *Aufbau* Reichenbach set his own realist answer (1938). But this was also the issue discussed in the Vienna Circle's so-called "protocol sentence debate" between Schlick, Carnap, and Neurath: how to conceive of the content, form and status of scientific evidence statements. Differently expressed, the debate concerned the reach of the physicalistic language of science: Did its assertions need to be backed up by something epistemically more primary?

A brief summary of the positions taken here helps to make evident that the collective characterization of the epistemology of logical empiricism, especially of its early phase, as phenomenalist foundationalism is very wide of the mark. Which is not to say that there were no such tendencies to be discerned at all. Schlick, for instance, came close when he seemed to locate the "foundation of knowledge" in the elusive "affirmations" of immediate experience (e.g., 1934), yet there are serious doubts as to whether these could serve as epistemic foundations for science. Schlick's affirmations concern phenomenal matters, are unrevisable and not expressible in the physicalistic language of science itself. Relying on ostension to aspects of private experience, they cannot function as scientific evidence statements, which Schlick correctly took to be fallible. Neurath, by contrast, thought of protocol statements as concerned with inter-subjectively accessible matters, formulated in the physicalistic language of science and, of course, revisable, expressly so from 1930 onwards. In addition he made very concrete proposals (1932) for the form of the protocol statements, naming in them not only the intersubjectively accessible state of affairs at issue, but also the observer and the sense modality of the observation – in short, Neurath's protocols expressed subject–object relations whereas Schlick's constatations described subjective states of mind.

Carnap was located very roughly between the two, and unlike them changed his views on the matter not only in points of detail but also in overall conception. Between his *Aufbau* and his more or less final position (1935), one can distinguish two major intermediate shifts. The first, around 1929–30, concerned his recognition of the indispensability of the physicalist language for intersubjectivity (e.g., 1932a), the second concerned dropping his insistence on the need for the phenomenalist language for epistemological purposes (e.g., 1932b). The final shift, around 1935–36, concerned the recognition that only statements about intersubjectively observable states of affairs should be recognized as protocol statements (1936–37).

Given the differences between Carnap's and Neurath's physicalisms – Carnap never accepted Neurath's conception of protocols and retained the option for a methodologically phenomenalist protocol language – it is clear that at least three different positions were defended in the Viennese debate which, like Reichenbach's variant, reflected different conceptions of the new philosophy of science. Roughly, in competition were Schlick's Wittgenstein-inspired non-formal activity of deter-mining the meaning of scientific discourse, Carnap's reconstructive formalist logic of science, and Neurath's naturalist–pragmatist interdisciplinary metatheory of science, as well as Reichenbach's early form of scientific realism. Given, moreover, that even Carnap's *Aufbau* was pursued without the foundationalist ambitions often attributed to it (Friedman 1999; Richardson 1998), it must be recognized that already in Vienna empiricist foundationalism was under attack from early on.

The reference of theoretical terms

Yet what of the reductionism of which logical empiricism is often accused and that is said to turn up in a number of different guises? One of these is the apparent behaviorism that Carnap sported in "Psychologie in physikalischer Sprache" (1932c). Here one must ask whether its intent was eliminative. That it was not is readily seen when it is compared with the psychological doctrine of behaviorism; Carnap sought only to provide individuation conditions for mental phenomena via behavioral and nervous system states. Of course, that reduction failed, but once it was noted that the reduction of disposition terms to observational terminology was impossible, Carnap, for instance, did not hesitate to accept much looser conceptions of *reduction* than definitional ones as legitimating conditions for scientific discourse, ultimately recognizing psychological terms as fully fledged theoretical terms (1956). Here, of course, we come upon another difficulty concerning logical empiricism's two-language model. Talk of correspondence rules between theoretical and observational terms only masks the problem that is raised by theoretical terms by their so-called "surplus meaning" over and above their observational consequences. This issue is closely related to the problem of scientific realism: are there truth-evaluatable matters of fact for scientific theories beyond their empirical, observational adequacy?

Everyone in the Vienna Circle followed Carnap's and Schlick's contentions that questions like that of the reality of the external world are not well-formed but are merely pseudo-questions. While this left the observables of empirical reality clearly in place, theoretical entities remained a problem: were they really only computational fictions introduced for the ease with which they allowed complex predictive reasoning? This hardly seems to do justice to the surplus meaning of theoretical terms over and above their computational utility: theories employing them seem to tell us about non-observable features of the world. This indeed was Feigl's complaint (1950) in what must count as the first of very few forays into *empirical realism* (scientific realism by another name) by a former member of the Vienna Circle – and one that was quickly opposed by Frank's instrumentalist rejoinder (1950). Carnap sought to remain aloof on this as on other ontological questions. So while in the heyday of the Vienna Circle itself the issue had not yet come into clear focus, by 1950 one could distinguish among its surviving members both realists (Feigl), anti-realists (Frank), and ontological deflationists (Carnap). Reichenbach, of course, had been realist in approach all along.

Carnap's general recipe for avoiding undue commitments (while pursuing his investigations of various language forms, including the intensional forms Quine frowned on) was given in terms of the distinction between *internal* and *external* questions (1950). Given the adoption of a logico-linguistic framework, we can state the facts in accordance with what that framework allows us to say. Given any of the languages of arithmetic, say, we can state as arithmetical fact whatever we can prove in them; to say that accordingly there are numbers, however, is at best to express the fact that numbers are a basic category of that framework (irrespective of whether they are logically derived from a still more basic category). As to whether certain special types of number exist, that depends on the expressive power of the framework at hand and on whether the relevant facts can be proven. Analogous considerations apply to the existence of physical things (the external world) given the logico-linguistic frameworks of everyday discourse and empirical science. For Carnap, it is an empirical question whether the scientists who adopt the logico-linguistic framework of microphysics come to the conclusion that statements attributing certain properties to electrons, say, are true. Such existence questions and answers, categorical or specific, are meaningful and legitimate once they are seen as relative to a certain framework.

Unlike such so-called internal questions, so-called external questions, such as whether electrons or unobservable entities generally *really exist* irrespective of any framework, are ruled out as illegitimate; at best, they could be reformulated as pragmatic questions concerned with the utility of talk about such entities, of adopting a certain framework. As existence questions they are idle.

Carnap's neutralism has been challenged repeatedly as collapsing into anti-realism (e.g., Psillos 1999: Ch. 3) and, as noted above, his later attempt to marshal Ramsey sentences for his purposes cannot be considered successful. Yet it should be noted that it is not yet entirely clear whether Carnap was independently committed to the virtual anti-realism *vis-à-vis* theoretical terms to which his ramseyfication of scientific theories condemned him. (The ramseyfication of theoretical terms brought on the Newman problem which in turn spelt out that, on this conception, theoretical terms had only formal but no empirical significance.) There is, of course, the stark fact that the received view considers theoretical terms in their own domain as initially uninterpreted and as given only partial interpretations by correspondence rules, etc. This difference in interpretability is easily read as signaling a diminished commitment to the truth-evaluability of the theoretical discourse on the part of the received view, rather than as indicating that we have only a much less direct evidential handle on it. Some logical empiricists clearly understood it this way (prompting Feigl's foray into scientific realism). The question is whether Carnap did so as well.

Two considerations counsel caution. First, to be anti-realist *vis-à-vis* theoretical terms would seem to require being a realist with regard to observational terms. But Carnap's discussion of internal questions makes clear that he draws no such distinction. Whether there really are trees is to him as nonsensical a question as whether there really are electrons. (As he once responded to Feigl's discussion of his own contributions to the development of the mind–body identity theory, instead of affirming ontological existence claims, he himself preferred to speak of different languages being equally useful.) Second, there is the remarkable fact that, as a language constructor, Carnap was fully aware that the distinction between logical and descriptive terms was not one that was objectively given, but one that could be drawn only language by language. Just as, given Carnap's logical pluralism, there is no sense in asking whether a term is a logical term independently of the logico-linguistic specification of the language to which the term belongs, so also there is no sense in asking what are empirical matters independently of specifying a language in which to talk about them (Ricketts 1994). This consideration again militates against Carnap drawing a sharp distinction in ontological standing between observational and theoretical propositions. If this is correct, the possibility cannot yet be ruled out that Carnapian deflationism (like his criterion of empirical significance) could yet be saved from the ravages of Carnap's own misadventure into ramseyfication.

The unity of science

One other general doctrine that looms large in logical empiricist philosophy of science is that of the unity of science. Originally the doctrine emerged in opposition to the categorical distinction drawn primarily in idealist German-language philosophy between the natural and the human sciences (*Natur-* versus *Geisteswissenschaften*). Often over-interpreted as denying all differences between the natural and the social sciences, say, the doctrine of the unity of science rather claims that there are no fundamental epistemological or ontological discontinuities – like Rickert's between the realm of being (*Sein*) and the realm of normative validity (*Gelten*) – that would prevent the results of different sciences being combined for purposes of prediction or explanation. What is also often forgotten is that back in the 1920s and 1930s in Central Europe, social scientific separatism was often allied to authoritarian (if not fascist) politics, and that therefore opposition against a separate *Geisteswissenschaft* carried with it a practical urgency that the doctrine of the unity of science did not possess in North America or Britain.

Despite general agreement among logical empiricists, different views of how precisely one was to think of the unification of the sciences obtained. Here we must note the differences between Carnap's and Neurath's conceptions of unified science: where the formalist Carnap once preferred a hierarchical, reductive ordering of the languages of the different disciplines that allowed cross-language definitions and derivations – these requirements were liberalized over the years – the pragmatist Neurath opted from early on to demand only the interconnectability of predictions made in the different individual sciences. (Meteorology, botany, and sociology must be combinable to predict the consequences of a forest fire, say, even though each may have its own autonomous theoretical vocabulary.) Whether this difference directly reflects the different scientific backgrounds as between Carnap and Neurath – together with Zilsel, the latter was the only representative of the social sciences in the Vienna Circle – is hard to say, but it clearly shows how their different interpretations of the logical empiricist project had concrete consequences for their joint project. (These tensions often were palpable in the grand publication project undertaken by Carnap and Neurath in conjunction with Morris, the *International Encyclopedia of the Unity of Science*.) What is notable, however, is that Neurath's approach to the unity of science, like much of the pragmatic version of logical empiricism which he shared with Frank, disappeared from view shortly after his early death, in 1945, with Frank unable to keep interest in it alive amid the ever more entrenched formalist orthodoxy. What is notable as well is that an even more strictly hierarchical approach to the unity of science than Carnap's was promoted by the young Hilary Putnam, nowadays a sharp critic of logical empiricism's alleged reductionisms, still in the late 1950s (Oppenheim and Putnam 1958).

Lastly there is the issue of the ahistoricity of logical empiricist philosophy of science. Again its different versions must be distinguished. But even Carnap, whose own formalist logic of science paid no attention to it, welcomed the contribution made by Thomas Kuhn to the *International Encyclopedia* with his *Structure of Scientific Revolutions* (Reisch 1991). (Neurath had planned a volume on history and sociology of science all along.) Far from feeling his philosophy undermined, Carnap found much to agree with in Kuhn and explained their different foci on science as instances of the division of labor. (A recent commentator agreed: see Friedman 2001.) As with

Duhem's thesis of the underdetermination of scientific theories by observational data, a thesis that was widely perceived to undermine logical empiricism once it gained currency in the 1960s, some of the older logical empiricists had long incorporated into their thinking what post-positivists thought detrimental to their entire creed. Frank, Hahn, and Neurath were virtually brought up on Poincaré and Duhem, and Carnap too had long recognized the phenomenon of underdetermination as pervasive in scientific reasoning (1934/37: §82).

Conclusion

In conclusion, it may be noted again that it is not easy to separate sharply the logical empiricist philosophy of science from all approaches that dissent in some way or other or, indeed, to state without any ambiguity who was/is and who wasn't/isn't a logical empiricist. Thus much of Reichenbach's own differentiation of his physicalist verificationism (1938) from the methodologically phenomenalist verificationism of Carnap's earlier *Aufbau* – which has occasionally been styled into a categorical difference between logical empiricism and logical positivism – merely marked a temporary difference that already was redundant at the time of Reichenbach's writing. For many present-day readers, meanwhile, the later differences between the logical empiricist Hempel (1965) and the more pragmatist Nagel (1961), for example, would signify but internal variations in terms of their relative emphases on formalization and the absolute sharpness of the distinctions employed. But already in their day, such sharp differences as obtained between Feigl and Frank over the issue of what came to be called "scientific realism" and instrumentalism also did not merit excommunication. Similarly, despite pronounced differences over the analytic–synthetic distinction and the probity of other intensional notions, Quine's explorations of the canonical notation of scientific discourse stand squarely in the tradition of logical empiricism. Once we add to the picture of pre-Second World War logical empiricism the distinctively naturalistic initiatives of Neurath and Frank, note Hempel's post-war siding with Quine's holism and take account of Hempel's own later pragmatic turn, we are even prompted to discern within logical empiricism a number of dialectics in different areas: between instrumentalism and realism in ontology, atomism and holism in epistemology, and formalist explicationism and pragmatist naturalism in metaphilosophy, to name but three where, in addition, an elusive middle way was often sought. That these dialectics continue to be played out in the philosophy of science still today need hardly be stressed. If logical empiricism continues to be associated more or less exclusively with a type of orthodox version that no leading individual theorist propounded in that very combination – typically, ontologically instrumentalist, epistemologically atomist and formalist in orientation – then this says more about the historical consciousness of self-conscious *post-empiricism* than the highly varied legacy that logical empiricism has actually left us.

See also Confirmation; Empiricism; Epistemology of science after Quine; The historical turn in the philosophy of science; Probability; Realism/anti-realism; Reduction; Space and time; The structure of theories; Underdetermination; Unification.

References

Carnap, Rudolf (1928) *Der logische Aufbau der Welt*, Berlin: Bernary; trans. R. A. George as *The Logical Structure of the World*, Berkeley: University of California Press, 1967, repr. Chicago: Open Court, 2003.

—— (1932a) "Die physikalische Sprache als Unversalsprache der Wissenschaft," *Erkenntnis* 2: 432–65, trans. M. Black, with author's Introduction, as *The Unity of Science*, London: Kegan, Paul, Trench, Teubner, & Co., 1934.

—— (1932b) "Über Protokollsätze," *Erkenntnis* 3: 215–28; trans. R. Creath and R. Nollan as "On Protocol Sentences," *Noûs* 21 (1987): 457–70.

—— (1932c) "Psychologie in physikalischer Sprache," *Erkenntnis* 3: 107–42, trans. G. Schick as "Psychology in Physicalist Language," in A. J. Ayer (ed.) *Logical Positivism*, New York: Free Press, 1959, pp. 165–98.

—— (1934/37) *Logische Syntax der Sprache*, Vienna: Springer, 1934, rev. edn trans. A. Smeaton, *The Logical Syntax of Language*, London: Kegan, Paul, Trench Teubner & Cie, 1937, Chicago: Open Court, 2002.

—— (1936–37) "Testability and Meaning," *Philosophy of Science* 3: 419–71, and 4: 1–40, repr. with corrigenda and additions, New Haven: Yale Graduate Philosophy Club, 1954.

—— (1939) *Foundations of Logic and Mathematics*, Chicago: University of Chicago Press.

—— (1950) "Empiricism, Semantics and Ontology," *Revue International de Philosophie* 4: 20–40, repr. in Carnap, *Meaning and Necessity*, 2nd edn with supplementary essays, Chicago: University of Chicago Press, 1956, pp. 205–21.

—— (1956) "The Methodological Character of Theoretical Concepts," in Herbert Feigl and Michael Scriven (eds) *The Foundations of Science and the Concepts of Science and Psychology*, Minnesota: University of Minneapolis Press, pp. 38–76.

—— (1966) *Philosophical Foundations of Science*, New York: Basic Books; repr. as *An Introduction to the Philosophy of Science*, 1972.

Creath, Richard (1976) "Kaplan on Carnap on Significance," *Philosophical Studies* 30: 393–400.

Demopoulos, William (2003) "On the Rational Reconstruction of Our Theoretical Knowledge," *British Journal for the Philosophy of Science* 54: 371–403.

Feigl, Herbert (1950) "Existential Hypotheses: Realistic versus Phenomenalistic Interpretations," *Philosophy of Science* 17: 32–62.

Frank, Philipp (1950) "Comments on Realistic versus Phenomenalistic Interpretations," *Philosophy of Science* 17: 166–9.

Friedman, Michael (1999) *Reconsidering Logical Positivism*, Cambridge: Cambridge University Press.

—— (2001) *The Dynamics of Reason*, Stanford, CA: CSLI Publications.

Hempel, Carl Gustav (1965) *Aspects of Scientific Explanation*, New York: Free Press.

—— (1988) "Provisoes: A Problem Concerning the Inferential Function of Scientific Theories," *Erkenntnis* 28: 147–64, repr. in Hempel, *Selected Philosophical Essays*, ed. R. Jeffrey, Cambridge: Cambridge University Press, 2000, pp. 229–49.

Nagel, Ernest (1961) *The Structure of Science*, New York: Routledge & Kegan Paul, repr. Indianpolis: Hackett, 1979.

Neurath, Otto (1932) "Protokollsätze," *Erkenntnis* 3: 204–14, trans. as "Protocol Statements," in Neurath, *Philosophical Papers 1913–1946*, ed. and trans. Robert S. Cohen and Marie Neurath, Dordrecht: Reidel, 1983, pp. 91–9.

Oppenheim, Paul, and Putnam, Hilary (1958) "The Unity of Science as a Working Hypothesis," in Herbert Feigl, Grover Maxwell, and Max Scriven (eds) *Minnesota Studies in the Philosophy of Science*, 2, Minneapolis: University of Minnesota Press, pp. 3–36.

Psillos, Stathis (1999) *Scientific Realism: How Science Tracks the Truth*, London: Routledge.

Reichenbach, Hans (1938) *Experience and Prediction: An Analysis of the Foundations and the Structure of Knowledge*, Chicago: University of Chicago Press, repr. Notre Dame: University of Notre Dame Press, 2006.

Reisch, George (1991) "Did Kuhn Kill Logical Empiricism?" *Philosophy of Science* 58: 264–77.

Richardson, Alan W. (1998) *Carnap's Construction of the World*, Cambridge: Cambridge University Press.

Ricketts, Thomas (1994) "Carnap's Principle of Tolerance, Empiricism and Conventionalism," in P. Clark (ed.) *Reading Putnam*, Oxford: Blackwell.

Ryckman, Thomas (1992) "P(oint)-C(oincidence)-Thinking," *Studies in History and Philosophy of Science* 23: 471–97.

Schlick, Moritz (1918) *Allgemeine Erkenntnislehre*, 2nd rev. edn, Berlin: Springer, 1925, transl. by H. Feigl and A. Blumberg as *General Theory of Knowledge*, La Salle, IL: Open Court, 1974.

—— (1934) "Über das Fundament der Erkenntnis," *Erkenntnis* 4: 79–99, trans. P. Heath as "The Foundation of Knowledge," in Schlick, *Philosophical Papers, Volume 2 (1925–1936)*, ed. Henk L. Mulder and Barbara van de Velde-Schlick, Dordrecht: Reidel, 1979, pp. 370–87.

Suppe, Frederic (1977) "The Search for a Philosophical Understanding of Theories," in Suppe (ed.) *The Structure of Scientific Theories*, 2nd edn, Urbana: University of Illinois Press, pp. 3–241.

Further reading

For bibliographies of logical empiricism, see O. Neurath, R. Carnap, C. Morris (eds) *Foundations of the Unity of Science: Toward an International Encyclopedia of Unified Science*, 2 vols (Chicago: University of Chicago Press, 1970); A. J. Ayer (ed.) *Logical Positivism* (New York: Free Press, 1959); R. M. Rorty (ed.) *The Linguistic Turn*, 3rd edn (Chicago: University of Chicago Press, 1992); and Friedrich Stadler (listed below). From the standard secondary literature, two publications remain pertinent. An analysis of the *received view* of scientific theories and standard treatments of logical empiricism are given, respectively, in Frederic Suppe (ed.), *The Structure of Scientific Theories*, 2nd edn (Urbana: University of Illinois Press 1977), pp. 3–41, and Peter Achinstein and Steven Barker (eds) *The Legacy of Logical Positivism* (Baltimore, MD: Johns Hopkins University Press, 1969). A good place to start on the new scholarship would be the synoptic investigations by the late Alberto Coffa in *The Semantic Tradition from Kant to Carnap: To the Vienna Station*, ed. L. Wessels (Cambridge: Cambridge University Press, 1991), or the equally ground-breaking essays by Michael Friedman collected in *Reconsidering Logical Positivism* (Cambridge: Cambridge University Press, 1999). Complex historical and excellent bibliographical resources are provided by Friedrich Stadler in *The Vienna Circle: Studies in the Origins, Development, and Influence of Logical Empiricism* (Vienna and New York: Springer, 2001). Up-to-date assessments of many of the great variety of topics raised by logical empiricism are given in Richard Creath and Michael Friedman (eds) *The Cambridge Companion to Carnap* (Cambridge: Cambridge University Press, 2007), and Alan Richardson and Thomas E. Uebel (eds) *The Cambridge Companion to Logical Empiricism* (Cambridge: Cambridge University Press, 2007). A critical look at the dynamics of logical empiricism's American enculturation is taken by George Reisch in *How the Cold War Transformed Philosophy of Science: To the Icy Slopes of Logic* (Cambridge: Cambridge University Press, 2005). Carnap's encounter with Cassirer and Heidegger is discussed in Michael Friedman, *A Parting of the Ways* (Chicago: Open Court, 2000). Much interest centers particularly on the work of Carnap and Reichenbach, the leaders of logical empiricism in its American exile. For a benchmark monograph on the early Carnap, see Alan Richardson, *Carnap's Construction of the World* (Cambridge: Cambridge University Press, 1998); on the later Carnap, see Bryan Norton, *Linguistic Frameworks and Ontology: A Reexamination of Carnap's Metaphilosophy* (The Hague: Mouton, 1977); see also Ramon Cirera, *Carnap and the Vienna Circle* (Amsterdam: Rodopi, 1994). For excellent collections of essays with this focus see Wolfgang Spohn (ed.) *Hans Reichenbach, Rudolf Carnap: A Centenary*, *Erkenntnis* 35 (1991), special edition; Sahotra Sarkar (ed.) *Rudolf Carnap Centenary*, *Synthese* 93:1–2 (1992), special edition; Wesley Salmon and Gereon Wolters (eds) *Logic, Language, and the Structure of Scientific Theories* (Pittsburgh, PA: Pittsburgh University Press, 1994); Thomas Bonk (ed.) *Language, Truth and Knowledge: Contributions to the Philosophy of Rudolf Carnap* (Dordrecht: Kluwer, 2003); Steve Awodey and Carsten Klein (eds) *Carnap Brought Home: The View from Jena* (Chicago: Open Court, 2004). Another figure attracting much attention has been the heterodox Otto Neurath, in which connection see: Danilo Zolo, *Reflexive Epistemology* (Dordrecht: Kluwer, 1989); Thomas Uebel (ed.) *Rediscovering the Forgotten Vienna Circle: Austrian Studies on Otto Neurath and the Vienna Circle* (Dordrecht: Kluwer, 1991); Nancy Cartwright, Jordi Cat, Lola Fleck, and Thomas Uebel, *Otto Neurath: Philosophy Between Science and Politics* (Cambridge: Cambridge University Press, 1996); Elisabeth Nemeth and Friedrich Stadler (eds) *Encyclopedia and Utopia* (Dordrecht: Kluwer, 1996). Other specialist interests are served by the collections by B. McGuinnes (ed.) *Moritz Schlick, Synthese* 64:3 (1985), special edition; Jan Wolenski and Eckehart Kohler (eds) *Alfred Tarski and the Vienna Circle* (Dordrecht: Kluwer, 1999); J. Fetzer (ed.) *Science, Explanation and Rationality: Aspects of the Philosophy of C. G. Hempel* (Oxford: Oxford University Press, 2000); Maria Carla Galavotti (ed.) *Cambridge and Vienna: Frank P. Ramsey and the Vienna Circle* (Dordrecht: Springer, 2006); Veronika Hofer and Michael Stöltzner (eds) *Philipp Frank: Vienna–Prague–Boston* (Chicago: Open Court, 2007). Monographs about the protocol sentence debate include: Thomas Oberdan, *Protocols, Truth and Convention* (Amsterdam: Rodopi, 1993); and Thomas Uebel, *Overcoming Logical Positivism from Within* (Amsterdam: Rodopi, 1992), rev. and enlarged as *Empiricism at the Crossroads* (Chicago: Open Court, 2007). Significant collections looking at logical empiricism as whole are: Nicholas Rescher (ed.) *The Heritage of Logical Positivism* (Lanham, MD: University Press of America, 1985); Barry Gower (ed.) *Logical Positivism in Perspective* (London: Croom Helm, 1987); Friedrich Stadler (ed.) *Scientific Philosophy: Origins and Developments* (Dordrecht: Kluwer, 1993); Ron Giere and Alan Richardson (eds) *The Origins of Logical Empiricism* (Minneapolis: University of Minnesota Press, 1996); Paolo Parrini, Wesley Salmon, and Merrilee Salmon (eds) *Logical Empiricism: Historical and Contemporary Perspectives* (Pittsburgh, PA: University of Pittsburgh Press, 2003); Gary Hardcastle and Alan Richardson (eds) *Logical Empiricism in North America* (Minneapolis: University of Minnesota Press, 2003); Friedrich Stadler (ed.) *The Vienna Circle and Logical Empiricism* (Dordrecht: Kluwer, 2003).

9

PRAGMATISM AND SCIENCE

Robert Almeder

Pragmatism

Originating with C. S. Peirce and William James, pragmatism is a philosophical movement embracing different proposed solutions to problems in the epistemology and logic of natural science. Pragmatists believe that the rational justification of scientific beliefs ultimately depends on whether the method generating the beliefs is the best available for advancing our cognitive goals of explanation and precise prediction. So characterized, scientists can be, and have been, pragmatists simply for believing that the fruits of good scientific method generally produce, better than any other method, explanations and precise predictions, thereby allowing for successful human adaptation relative to various interests. Such success, they say, justifies the method and indicates the basic purpose of science. One way to express more succinctly the pragmatic principle (PP) implied by all this is as follows: Assuming that P is a proposition about the world,

PP. A person is justified in accepting P as true
(a) if P is either soundly inferred directly by inductive or deductive inference from other known or justified beliefs; or
(b) if when P is not so soundly inferred, there is some real possibility that accepting P as true will tend to be more productive of explanations and precise predictions than would be the case if one had accepted instead either the denial of P or nothing at all.

Applying (b) of PP, for example, pragmatists are sympathetic to accepting the inductive method itself as the most reliable way of providing justified beliefs about the world simply because, while there is no deductive nor inductive justification for induction within science, nevertheless there is no good reason not to accept it either, and accepting it tends to produce explanations generating reasonably precise predictions of sensory experiences, and thereby other beliefs whose adoption and applications allow navigating our world more successfully. Those who deny PP are not pragmatists.

Pragmatists are also *fallibilists*. However well-confirmed one's beliefs, and however confident one may be in their truth, they are always subject to revision pending their adequacy as predictive and adaptive instruments in the face of new and changing bodies of evidence. Finally, implicit in PP, pragmatists generally agree that the truth or justification of a belief is less a function of how the belief originates than it is of whether the belief, however it originates, leads to successful predictions. This particular feature of pragmatism is what James christened 'radical empiricism,' in contradistinction to Humean empiricism, when he asserted that it is in the fruits of our beliefs, and not the roots, that the truth resides (James 1907). These then are the core features of pragmatism.

A persistent objection to pragmatism is that knowledge requires truth, just as epistemic justification requires truth-conduciveness, but neither is reducible to utilities associated with successful prediction. There is, anti-pragmatists say, a difference between believing what best serves the goal of predictive success and believing the truth; and the goal of inquiry is to find the truth rather than what it is best for us to believe. Two pragmatic responses to this objection permit distinguishing two types of pragmatist.

The first response, advanced by Richard Rorty and others, consists in affirming that the objection assumes that truth is certifiably attainable, that we can sometimes decisively show which of our beliefs are true rather than simply justified by appeal to currently acceptable standards of rational justification. But that, says Rorty, we cannot do, and so truth is a myth, no less than knowledge that would require either truth, or the strong likelihood of truth (2000: 2–4, 4–14). This is *radical pragmatism*, often called cultural relativism in epistemology.

The second response, advocated by John Worrall (1989: 99–124) and myself (1992: Ch. 4), asserts that pragmatism is free to emphasize the utility of beliefs as the criterion for their acceptance as true without abandoning the idea that some of them are in fact true. That a system of beliefs may allow successful adaptations is consistent with thinking plausibly that the reason it has such consequences is because at least some of those beliefs, or beliefs implied by them, succeed in correctly describing the world, even if fallibly and incompletely. So even if we cannot determine *which* of our beliefs are true, we can avoid making a mystery or a miracle of scientific progress by urging that the success we so often find in our theories and predictive hypotheses is there simply because some of them, at least in part, are true. This we can call *non-radical pragmatism*.

Let us turn now to pragmatic solutions to the problem of induction, the problem of theoretical entities, and the problem of scientific explanation.

Pragmatism and induction

We reason inductively when we infer that all Xs are Ys because all past observed Xs were also Ys. Such an inference assumes that the future will be like the past, or that the unexamined members of a class will be like the members already examined. Hume claimed that we have neither an inductive nor a deductive justification for believing that the future will be like the past. Any inductive justification of induction based on the fact that past futures were like past pasts would be circular. Also, sometimes, past futures were not like past pasts. Moreover, there can be no deductive proof that the future will be like the past, because it is logically possible that the future will not be like the past. Nor should we argue that there is a principle of uniformity in the world that can both explain our past success in predicting the future and guarantee that success in predicting that the future will be like the past. At best, that argument shows only that a principle of uniformity held in the past; the question is whether such a principle of uniformity will continue to hold in the future. Pragmatists agree with Hume's conclusion that there can be no inductive or deductive justification of induction. Nonetheless, pragmatists have offered at least three distinct solutions to Hume's problem.

Peirce offered the first. He granted that while inductive inference can yield false conclusions, the method of induction is justified as the only reliable method for establishing reliable beliefs about the world because repeated application of inductive reasoning will eventually lead to the true answer to any answerable question. Peirce argued that all inquiry assumes that there is a correct objective answer to any answerable question and that inquiry pursued indefinitely long under inductive reasoning *will* reach this one true irreversible answer (cf. Almeder 1980). Without that assumption no inquiry will proceed. Thus believing in the *general* reliability of induction to lead sooner or later to the truth was, for Peirce, something we have to do. Without a method to predict accurately our sensory experiences, our beliefs would not satisfy the proximate end of scientific inquiry, which is not, according to Peirce, to find the truth but rather those beliefs *we sincerely think to be true* by applying a method that guarantees objectivity. For Peirce, evolutionary forces drive us to the method that best enables us to establish beliefs relieving the discomfort of not knowing what to believe, and only inductive reasoning can do that trick. Is Peirce's defense persuasive?

Hume could accept that all inquiry proceeds on the assumption that there is a final objective answer to any answerable question, and then note that the assumption itself is an inductive conclusion based on an examination of all past cases of inquiry. That leads us back into the vicious circle of trying to justify induction inductively. Either that or Peirce was avoiding the necessity of an infinite regress of justification by implicitly asserting that all reasoning begins with certain assumptions that cannot be justified except by their practical consequences for promoting cognitive success. But then, Hume would reply that unjustified assumptions are unjustified assertions, and however intuitively acceptable they may seem, any conclusion based on them will be unsound.

To this Humean reply, contemporary pragmatists often respond, and this is the second pragmatic defense of induction, that unless we start with assumptions we are unable to justify, except to say there is no good reason to doubt them as reliable sources of belief, not only will we end up with no justified belief or knowledge, but we are also implicitly faulting inductive inference for not being infallible. This, for example, is the justification proposed by Nicholas Rescher (2000). Nor, for these pragmatists, can we establish the validity of induction *a priori*. Rather induction can, and should, be justified pragmatically by directly seeing whether, when simply adopted, the fruits of induction facilitate the attainment of the primary goal of science in generating good explanations and accurate predictions. If the skeptic demands more than this, then Rescher, like Peirce, locates the demand, in a Cartesianism that mistakenly regards every empirical belief as doubtful until justified as infallible.

The third pragmatic response to Hume came initially from Reichenbach (1938), and is more recently defended by Brian Skyrms (1999) and Wesley Salmon (1967). According to Skyrms, this proposal affirms that if any method succeeds in forming reliable beliefs about the world, the inductive method will (1999: 43). The reason, frequently noted, why we should accept this view is simply because of the self-correcting nature of induction. If we find any method other than induction successful in producing generally reliable beliefs, then induction will sanction it.

Hume could respond to this pragmatic defense by agreeing that *if* any method succeeds, the inductive method will succeed; but then Hume could ask how we could be justified in accepting the antecedent. Showing that any method *will* provide reliable empirical beliefs will presuppose, and not show, that the future will be like the past. Here pragmatists will again reply that Hume is blaming induction for not being deduction.

Scientific realism

Scientific realists believe that

(a)   there is an external world;
(b)   some of our beliefs about that world are, even if somewhat incomplete at any time, correct descriptions; and
(c)   we can justifiably determine and say *which* of those beliefs, including our theoretical beliefs, are in fact the correct descriptions.

Scientific realism shares with classical realism (a) through (c). What distinguishes scientific realism from classical realism is that scientific realists extend classical realism to include explicitly the existence of unobservable theoretical entities postulated to exist by empirically adequate theories.

The main alternatives to scientific realism are scientific non-realism and scientific anti-realism. Scientific non-realists are agnostic about theoretical entities. They allow that the world may or may not satisfy conditions (a) through (c), but they insist that we cannot know that all three of these conditions hold. Moreover, scientific non-realists argue that the success of scientific theories does not require acceptance of (a) through (c) as true of theoretical entities. The only interesting question, for scientists, is whether scientific theories work by allowing us to make reliable predictions of phenomenal experience; and for that, all we need is confirmation theory. Anything more is philosophically debatable.

Scientific anti-realists are atheists about theoretical entities. Often their position stems from a broader rejection of realism, even in its classical form. For example, some anti-realists contend that (a) is false because all properties are linguistic in nature, and so go on to dismiss (b) and (c) as indefensible (cf. Rorty 2000). Whereas scientific non-realists willingly concede that our best scientific theories may, for all we know, correctly describe the external world and theoretical entities, scientific anti-realists reject that concession. Classical anti-realists are phenomenalists, restricting reality to the contents of experience; scientific anti-realists may allow that observable physical objects exist in addition to our experience of them, but deny that theoretical entities exist.

Historically, it seems doubtful that there is a distinctively pragmatic position on the question of scientific realism or on the ontological status of theoretical entities. Well-known pragmatists have defended different versions of classical scientific realism, while others have defended different species of scientific non-realism, and others have defended scientific anti-realism. All claim to be pragmatists. Peirce endorsed (a) through (c), and believed that the scientific community will come eventually to answer every answerable question about that world. This destined irreversible opinion of the scientific community will be the truth about the extra-mental world. Thus Peirce was both a classical realist and a scientific realist (cf. Almeder 1992).

We can find other classical scientific realists among pragmatists who have argued for (a) through (c). Unlike Peirce, however, some recent pragmatists think we should postulate or posit, rather than profess to prove, the existence of the external world. Quine, Rescher, Sellars, Putnam, and Carnap fall into this group. More recently, Rescher (2000), for example, rejects both Peirce's attempt to prove the existence of the external world and his view that the truth will be seen only in some final irreversible theory. On the contrary, Rescher – like Quine and Carnap – argues that asserting the existence of the external world is licensed by PP as a posit and insists that we now know many irrefutable truths about that world and that there will never be any final irreversible theory.

Although classical pragmatists are scientific realists, pragmatism is widely perceived as dismissive of realism, both classical and scientific. Indeed, leaving aside such anti-realists as Rorty, pragmatists often embrace non-realism, simply by urging that whether there is an external world or theoretical entities are questions of whether the physicalistic language countenancing such entities is more successful than any proposed phenomenalist language when it comes to describing experience. Some said that it is equally successful; some said that it is more successful. For this second group what is real is what the theory asserts to be the case when the theory is adequate. The former are non-realists, or agnostics about the external existence of theoretical entities as well as the existence of an external world. The latter are not so agnostic, and qualify as realists – but only as long as the preferred language of science is physicalist and requires quantification over abstract or theoretical entities. Thus many pragmatists have taken the linguistic turn and argued that if phenomenalism and classical realism are equally acceptable for constructing theories that reliably predict our sensory experience, then there is no reason (on pragmatic grounds) to choose between them. If we can do science equally well in either language, then non-realism seems to be the conclusion. But the crucial conditional assumption here is often thought false for the alleged reason that we cannot do science successfully without quantifying over theoretical terms and sentences asserting the existence of theoretical entities (cf. Hempel 1965).

Several pragmatists urge caution here. We should not, they say, see ontological questions as a set of conflicts over what would be a preferred language ultimately justified by the pragmatic value of that language for constructing more adequate theories. According to them, we should not regard theories as descriptions of reality that are literally true or false in some preferred language for some time. Theories are simply tools or instruments, no better and no worse than the power they provide for predicting observational experience. This too is a non-realist story.

Perhaps the most engaging non-realist version of pragmatism in contemporary philosophy of science is Bas van Fraassen's *constructive empiricism*. According to van Fraassen (1980), we should interpret scientific theories at face value, construe their assertions literally, and abandon any instrumentalist attempt to reduce talk about theoretical entities to talk about observables. However, along with Werner Heisenberg and others, van Fraassen asserts that the basic goal of science is to find theories that are empirically adequate, not theories that are true. As soon as we attain to the former, we may accept the proposed hypothesis as true, but of course, it may not be; and it is risky to infer the truth from corroborated or confirmed theoretical claims (1980: 151–2). To assert anything more, according to van Fraassen, is epistemologically unwarranted and scientifically unnecessary; we should remain agnostic about the truth of theoretical claims about unobservables.

Realists invariably insist that theoretical explanations must be true: false theories explain nothing. Thus it is incumbent on van Fraassen, and the other pragmatic non-realists (or instrumentalists), to articulate a pragmatic model of explanation that does justice to scientific practice without embracing scientific realism. Let us turn to that issue now.

Explanation

Many philosophers of science insist that if we wish to explain why something occurs at some time we must appeal to true law-like generalizations. They implicitly assume that there is a way the world is, and its being what it is is causally and logically independent of the existence and cognitive activities of minds. On this view, explanations are truth-seeking instruments, or attempts at *understanding* how things really are and why they are what they are. Hence the premises of explanatory arguments must be true. In advancing their classic deductive–nomological (D–N) model of explanation, Hempel and Oppenheim argued that in order to explain why something occurs in the way it does, we must appeal to true law-like generalizations, followed by a true statement of the current initial conditions under which the law designated by the statement of law applies. The event to be explained is then explained as the deductive conclusion of the statement of law and the conditions under which it applies. It is also a feature of this model that a good explanation is one we could have used to predict the *explanandum event* prior to its occurrence. If a proposed explanation does not do as much, then it fails to be explanatorily relevant (cf. Hempel 1965).

There are well-known criticisms of the D–N model on the grounds of scope and relevance (cf. Salmon 1984). Invariably, critics of the D–N model do not question that the goal of an explanation is to find the truth, and that explanations are adequate only if they provide a true understanding of the causes of the phenomena to be explained. But there are pragmatists who, as instrumentalists, have challenged the received view.

For example, van Fraassen, in advancing constructive empiricism, has argued that the goal of science, and hence of scientific explanation, is not truth, but rather empirical adequacy, meaning thereby that theoretical science is not necessarily concerned with finding the truth as much as in confirming proposed hypotheses. As soon as we attain to the latter, we may accept the hypothesis as true, but, of course, it may not be true (1980: 151–2).

For pragmatists such as van Fraassen explanation is less a matter of seeking truth than it is of satisfying cognitive and non-cognitive needs for adaptation via precise predictions of sensory experience. Explanation is also regarded as context-sensitive: depending on one's purposes or goals, different explanations of the same event may be adequate, and the adequacy or completeness of an explanation should be judged relative to different goals and purposes (*ibid.*: 125; Salmon 1984: 127ff).

The difference between what Salmon and van Fraassen regard as the goal of an explanation has its roots, as Salmon himself acknowledged (1984), in what each regards as the purpose of an explanation. Van Fraassen's view is that if we ask practicing scientists what they seek, the answer will be *empirical adequacy* first and foremost. Classical pragmatists generally agree.

Other radical pragmatists will take issue with van Fraassen's pragmatic instrumentalism for countenancing even the possibility that one's theories and explanations might be true in the usual sense of "true," or with van Fraassen's claim that knowledge or true beliefs about observed phenomena are necessary if we are to confirm theories or explanations.

Conclusion

If there is a defensible pragmatic position on the problem of induction, it is that induction is justified because it generally leads to beliefs reliable for allowing successful adaptation, even though there is strictly no inductive or deductive proof of the validity of induction as a source of knowledge. But that proposal requires defending the view that the primary purpose of inquiry is to establish beliefs that allow us to adapt successfully to our environment. That goal seems more defensible to most pragmatists than having the goal of attaining the truth as the end of belief-formation. Moreover, there is the claim of several pragmatists that denying that induction leads to knowledge is to condemn induction for failing to be deduction.

On the question of theoretical entities, although there is no distinctively pragmatic position, the most attractive pragmatic proposal may well be the non-realist instrumentalism of van Fraassen and others on the question of the external world and the existence of theoretical entities. Doubtless, if we think pragmatists typically adopt some form of warranted assertibility theory of truth, or abandon truth wholesale for some form of verificationism as adequate, but fallible, for the purposes of science, that would tend to render van Fraassen's position problematic for countenancing true statements at the common-sense level and then too the possibility that some theoretical claims are true.

Finally, turning to scientific explanation, there is a distinctively pragmatic position countering all variations on, and emendations of, the D–N model. Insofar as we can see all pragmatists holding to some warranted assertibility theory of truth, combined with a deep fallibilism, we can view them as abandoning truth traditionally understood as a necessary condition for adequate statements of law. Truth, platitudinally understood, may well be abandoned as necessary for statements of law if so doing still allows for successful prediction under warranted but fallible generalizations. This last point may turn out to be the core pragmatic proposal along with a van Fraassen-like instrumentalism regarding the existence and nature of an external world and theoretical entities.

See also The epistemology of science after Quine; Logical empiricism; Naturalism; Scientific method.

References

Almeder, R. (1992) *Blind Realism: An Essay on Human Knowledge and Natural Science*, Lanham, MD: Rowman & Littlefield.

Almeder, R. (1980) *The Philosophy of C. S. Peirce: A Critical Introduction*, Oxford: Blackwell.

Brandom, R. (ed.) (2000) *Rorty and His Critics*, Oxford: Blackwell.

Hempel, C. (1965) *Aspects of Scientific Explanation*, New York: Free Press.

James, W. (1907) *Pragmatism*, ed. B. Kuklick, Indianapolis, IN: Hackett.

Kitcher, P. and Salmon, W. (1987) "Van Fraassen on Explanation," *Journal of Philosophy* 84: 315–30.

Nagel, E. (1961) *The Structure of Science*, London: Routledge & Kegan Paul.

Reichenbach, H. (1938) *Experience and Prediction*, Chicago: University of Chicago Press.

Rescher, N. (2000) *Realistic Pragmatism: An Introduction to Pragmatic Philosophy*, Albany and New York: SUNY Press.

Rorty, R. (2000) "Is Truth the Goal of Inquiry: Davidson vs. Wright?" in R. Brandom (ed.) (2000), *Rorty and His Critics*, Oxford: Blackwell.

Salmon, W. (1967) *The Foundations of Scientific Inference*, Pittsburgh, PA: University of Pittsburgh Press.

Salmon, W. (1984) *Scientific Explanation and the Causal Structure of the World*, Princeton, NJ: Princeton University Press.

Skyrms, B. (1999) *Choice and Chance: An Introduction to Inductive Logic*, Belmont, CA: Wadsworth Press.

Van Fraassen, B. C. (1980) *The Scientific Image*, Oxford: Clarendon Press.

Worrall, J. (1989) "Structural Realism: The Best of Both Possible Worlds?" *Dialectica* 43: 99–124.

Further reading

Interpretations of C. S. Peirce differ widely. See A. J.Ayer *The Origins of Pragmatism* (London: Macmillan, 1968) and C. J. Misak (ed.) *The Cambridge Companion to Peirce* (Cambridge: Cambridge University Press, 2004). For differing evaluations of Peirce's solution to the problem of induction, and his thesis that science is self-correcting, see I. Levi, "Induction as Self-Correcting According to Peirce," in D. H. Mellor (ed.) *Science, Belief and Behaviour: Essays in Honour of R. B. Braithwaite* (Cambridge: Cambridge University

Press, 1980), pp. 127–40; L. Laudan, "Peirce and the Trivialization of the Self-Correcting Thesis," in R. Giere and R. Westfall (eds) *Foundations of Scientific Method: The 19th Century* (Bloomington, IN: Indiana University Press, 1973), pp. 275–306; F. F. Schmitt, *Truth: A Primer* (Boulder, CO: Westview Press, 1995), Ch. 3 reviews objections to the pragmatic theory of truth. C. G. Hempel, "A Logical Appraisal of Operationalism," reprinted in *Aspects of Scientific Explanation* (New York: Free Press, 1965), exposes problems with Percy Bridgman's pragmatically inspired attempt to define the meaning of scientific concepts via experimental and observational tests. The merits of pragmatism as an account of scientific methodology (the grounds on which scientists choose between competing theories) is explored in J. Worrall, "Pragmatic Factors in Theory Acceptance," in W. H. Newton-Smith (ed.) *A Companion to the Philosophy of Science* (Oxford: Blackwell, 2000) and L. Laudan, *Science and Relativism* (Chicago: University of Chicago Press, 1990).

Part II
DEBATES

10
BAYESIANISM
Colin Howson

Its probability of being correct with respect to the standard model [of dark matter and energy] is one part in a million. (Cosmologist David Spergel in a TV interview talking about Mordehai Milgrom's theory of variable gravity)

The betting among physicists, however, was that there was an even chance that the SSC [superconducting supercollider] would find exotic particles beyond the Standard Model. (Michio Kaku 1995: 183)

In my opinion, [Abraham's and Bucherer's] theories should be ascribed a rather small probability... (Albert Einstein 1907: 493)

Introduction

Informal evaluations of probabilities like those above are the unofficial currency in which theoretical scientists evaluate the theories they consider, and which correspondingly guide the flow of research activity. An interesting, and important, question is whether the formal theory of probability can be used to underwrite such evaluations. That it can is an increasingly influential doctrine, called *Bayesianism* after the eighteenth-century English clergyman–mathematician Thomas Bayes, who was the first to give a reasonably rigorous proof that the newly developed mathematical theory of probability could be given an epistemic interpretation, and the first to use it to calculate the probability of a nontrivial scientific hypothesis from the experimental data (he found what is called the "posterior distribution of a binomial probability parameter").

The rules of epistemic probability

In a way that anticipates recent work, Bayes chose to measure the probability of a proposition, A, in terms of the degree to which a payment of a sum conditional on A's truth was discounted by the uncertainty attaching to A. Thus, he defined *probability* as "the ratio between the value at which an expectation depending on the happening of the event ought to be computed, and the value of the thing expected upon its happening" (1763: Definition 5).

Bayes then showed that natural criteria of consistency in the pricing of uncertain options require that all probabilities lie between 0 and 1 inclusive, that the probability of two mutually exclusive propositions is equal to the sum of their probabilities, and that the probability of A given B is equal to the ratio $P(A\&B)/P(B)$, where $P(B)>0$.

What people have regarded subsequently as a major theoretical defect in this account is the assumption, implicit in Bayes's definition, that the value of the expectation of a reward is proportional to the value of the reward. This is certainly false if value is measured in money, because of the related phenomena of risk-aversion and the diminishing marginal utility of money. On the other hand, if rewards and prices are measured in terms of pure value, or utility, then some systematic theory of this is clearly needed.

Such a theory was provided by Ramsey (1926), and then Savage (1954) and others, who used the techniques of measurement theory to show that there is a probability/utility representation of personal preferences satisfying axioms of consistency (the probability is unique, and the utility function is unique up to determining what is called an *interval scale*, i.e. ratios of utility-differences are the same for all admissible utility functions). Though this approach became dominant in the second half of the twentieth century, there are also significant non-utility-based approaches. De Finetti (1937) showed that the finitely additive probability axioms characterize the *coherence* of betting odds, i.e., their invulnerability to a so-called "Dutch Book" (a Dutch Book is a set of stakes that ensures a positive net loss independently of the truth-values of the propositions bet on).

A quite different approach, completely divorced from considerations of choice among valued options, is that of R. T. Cox (1961). Approaching the subject from a physicist's point of view, he imposed conditions that he believed a numerical measure $M(A|B)$ of the probability of A given B should satisfy, *independently of any choice of scale or specific rules of combination*, and showed that M is representable in the unit interval by a finitely additive conditional probability function $P(A|B)$, from which we get an unconditional function by defining $P(A) = P(A|T)$, where T is a tautology. By suitably enriching the algebra of propositions, P can be determined uniquely. I personally find Cox's method the most satisfactory and least question-begging of all the approaches mentioned.

"Logical omniscience"

Many Bayesians regard epistemic probability as a measure of the belief of an ideally rational agent. But a well-known result, due to Turing and Church, states that *for logical reasons* not even an idealized digital computer with infinitely large memory can decide all deductive relationships for non-trivial systems; yet it is a consequence of the probability calculus that probability respects these relationships. This has led some to charge Bayesianism with assuming "logically omniscient" agents, and hence being inadequate to the task of modeling the real world of *boundedly rational* reasoners, i.e., agents who cannot decide all deductive relationships, and do not have the time or ability to decide all but a rather limited set (everyone, in other words).

The charge is potentially a serious one against those who see probability as one of the twin foundations, with utility, of rational choice theory; as noted above, this is the preferred option of many if not most Bayesians. In response, some recommend weakening the probability axioms. For example, the axiom stating that the probability of a tautology is 1 would be replaced by one stating that if the agent *believes* that A is a tautology then $P(A) = 1$, etc. An obvious objection to this strategy is that as a theory of *rationality* the result loses a good deal of its normative status. However, the logical omniscience charge does not impugn those who, like the great co-founder of the modern Bayesian theory Bruno de Finetti (1937: 103), see the axioms merely as *defining* what it means to have a consistent belief distribution (see "Subjective Bayesianism" below): nothing here is explicit or implicit about what rational agents should do.

Bayesian confirmation theory

Though Bayes applied the theory of epistemic probability to a statistical problem, its applicability is quite general, and based largely on a simple consequence of the probability axioms known as "Bayes's Theorem," which is most revealingly expressed in the following form:

$$P(H \mid E) = P(H) / [P(H) + B(1 - P(H))] \qquad (1)$$

$B = P(E \mid \neg H)/P(E \mid H)$, and is called "the Bayes factor" (sometimes also "the likelihood ratio") "in favor of $\neg H$ against H." Here H is a hypothesis and E observational evidence, and $P(H \mid E)$ is called the "posterior probability" of H relative to E. It is easy to see from (1) that the posterior probability is a decreasing function of the Bayes factor and an increasing function of the *prior probability* $P(H)$. For any given value of $P(E \mid H)$, the smaller $P(E \mid \neg H)$ is the larger the value of $P(H \mid E)$ and the higher the confirmation of H by E, in the sense of the greater the difference between the posterior and prior probabilities of H. But making $P(E \mid \neg H)$ small is to ensure that every possible factor that might cause E to be true other than H is eliminated in advance by the experimental design. This dependence on the Bayes factor means that $P(H \mid E)$ is sensitive to the degree to which plausible alternative explanations of the data exist: other things being equal, the fewer these are, the greater the confirmation of H by E. The importance of this is dramatically illustrated by "Lindley's Paradox" (Lindley 1957): in ignoring the effect of alternative explanations, a standard significance test will declare suitable sample data significant to an arbitrarily high degree which, under almost any prior distribution, can be shown using (1) to confirm the null hypothesis (i.e., the hypothesis that typically says some treatment or other has no causal effect) to an arbitrarily great extent.

A very important range of applications of (1) is where E records the possible values x of a data-generating experiment X, and H is one of a class of possible explanatory hypotheses. In statistics, these hypotheses are often the possible values θ of a parameter or set of parameters Θ, and the pair (X, Θ) is called a statistical model. Such models usually specify an explicit functional form for $P(x|\theta)$ which, considered as a function of θ for fixed x, is called the "likelihood function." For the great majority of models it can be shown that the posterior probability that θ will lie in a small interval around the maximum value, call it θ-*max*, of the likelihood function will be close to 1, *almost independently of the prior probability distribution*. For example, suppose that X specifies tossing a coin n times and observing the number x of heads. Let θ signify the chance of the coin landing heads at any toss, where the chance is regarded as a physical property of the coin, whose possible values lie between 0 and 1 inclusive. Assuming a further condition of the *probabilistic independence* of the tosses, the likelihood is shown in elementary textbooks to be proportional to $\theta^x(1-\theta)^{n-x}$. Here θ-*max* is x/n and the posterior probability of a value of θ close to x/n tends to 1 almost independently of the prior distribution $P(\theta)$ (a probability *density* distribution because θ has continuum-many possible values). I return to the discussion of results in "Convergence of opinion" below.

Bayesians generally regard E as *confirming* H if the inequality $P(H|E)>P(H)$ holds, and many also adopt the difference $S(H,E) = P(H|E)-P(H)$ as the accompanying measure of *degree of confirmation*. Some prefer the measure $logP(H|E) - logP(H)$ (basis arbitrary), but this has the defect that it is equal to $logP(E|H) - logP(E)$, since $P(H|E)/P(H) = P(E|H)/P(E)$, which is independent of $P(H)$: a defect because it has the obvious consequence that all hypotheses predicting E are equally supported by E, even though some may have been engineered ad hoc to agree with E. Even the qualitative definition itself has been subject to objections, principal among which is that it is vulnerable to the so-called "tacking paradox," and to the *old-evidence problem*.

I describe both these objections briefly, the former very briefly because it has the simpler resolution. It proceeds as follows. It is easy to show that if H entails E and $0<P(H)$, $P(E)<1$, then $P(H|E)>P(H)$; i.e., H is confirmed by E according to the definition above. But this implies that any hypothesis entailing E is confirmed by E, and in particular any conjunction of H with an arbitrary statement A. This might sound counterintuitive, but an easy exercise shows that $S(H\&A|E) = P(A|H)$ $S(H|E)$. Hence the degree of confirmation, according to the measure S, of $H\&A$ will be small if the probability of A given H is small, as it will be the less plausible A is, a fact which goes a long way to dispelling the "paradoxical" nature of the tacking problem.

The old-evidence problem

A good deal of inductive reasoning in science involves evaluating hypotheses on data already available when they were proposed. A much-discussed example in the philosophical literature is the precession of Mercury's perihelion, discovered halfway through the nineteenth century and widely regarded as supporting Einstein's general theory of relativity (GTR) after Einstein discovered, in 1915, that GTR predicted the value of the precession to within observational error. Indeed, that discovery arguably did more to displace the classical theory of gravitation than either of GTR's other two dramatic contemporary predictions, the bending of light by massive bodies and the gravitational red-shift. But, as Clark Glymour was the first to point out, since E is known then $P(E) = 1$ and it is a simple calculation that $P(H|E) = P(H)$; i.e., E does not confirm H according to the Bayesian definition of confirmation.

Several solutions have been offered to this problem. One is that it was the *logical* discovery that the perihelion precession is a deductive consequence of GTR that was the true causal factor in the increase in confidence felt to be due to GTR. There are two problems with this. The first is that it implies that the holding or not of a deductive relation can be treated as a random variable. But random variables are things whose values are dependent on what happens in a relevant class of possible worlds, and it is difficult to see what different possible *logical* worlds could be like. Second, the solution does not work in general. For example, suppose I am virtually certain that the relation between X and Y is linear, and I have two joint readings of (X, Y). On the basis of this information, call it E, and disregarding experimental uncertainty, I will regard the data as maximally confirming the hypothesis L that the relation is the linear function uniquely determined by E. Here is a case where I used the existing data to generate a hypothesis which I regard as very highly confirmed by it; yet clearly the confirmation was not induced by my recognition of a deductive relationship, but by the facts described in E.

The other most-widely canvassed solution to the old-evidence problem is to define the relation of confirmation not in terms of the agent's *actual* probability function, but in terms of that function relativized to the agent's information *minus E*, so that on the relativized function P', we no longer have $P'(E) = 1$. It might be argued that this is what is done in any estimate of probabilistic support, since even if E was obtained after H was proposed, $P(E)$ is still equal to 1 once E is known, thus again reducing $S(H,E)$ to 0. Granted this, it might be claimed that evaluating S in terms of current information is actually a misuse of the Bayesian formalism. Some have objected that there is no canonically uniform way of defining current information minus E, especially if E is sufficiently "entangled" with current beliefs. However it is not clear that, to "subjective Bayesians," at any rate (see next section), the lack of an algorithm is problematic. Moreover, it is possible to define such a relativized function in many cases of interest, of which the anomalous precession example is plausibly one (Howson and Urbach 2006: 298–301).

Conditionalization

The philosophical Bayesian literature contains much discussion of whether and under what circumstances the conditional probability $P(H|E)$ can be identified with an unconditional probability $P_E(H)$, interpreted as your probability of H once you have learned E and nothing else. This identification, or "updating rule" as it is referred to, is called "conditionalization," and there are various justifications of it in the literature. Principal among these are proofs that if you bet at your probability evaluations and your betting strategy violates conditionalization then you can be Dutch-Booked. The force of this result depends on how one views Dutch-Book theorems generally, which remains a matter of controversy. Nevertheless the vast majority of Bayesians adopt conditionalization, and a generalization of it called "Jeffrey Conditionalization," for which a Dutch-Book result also holds. (For further discussion see Howson and Urbach 2006: 80–5.)

The problem of priors

How to evaluate prior probabilities is the crucial issue between Bayesian and non-Bayesian methodologies. Much of contemporary statistical inference, and many contemporary philosophical discussions of confirmation, are broadly hypothetico-deductive in character (which I take to subsume Popper's and Fisher's very similar testing methodologies): they deliberately avoid appeal to epistemic probability, largely because of what are widely seen as problems with the use of prior probabilities.

Why should priors be a problem? There are plausibly objective principles, agreed by Bayesians and non-Bayesians alike, which determine the likelihoods $P(E|H)$ in standard methodological contexts:

(a) if E is predicted by a deterministic H then $P(E|H)=1$ by the probability calculus, and if the negation of E is predicted then $P(E|H)=0$;
(b) if H describes a statistical model of the data E then $P(E|H)$ is equal to the probability of E given by that model (this is traditionally called the "principle of direct probability," the rule was later redubbed the "principal principle" by David Lewis, and the name has stuck).

For over two centuries it was also thought that a comparably objective method of determining priors existed, at any rate if the space of alternatives is either finite or can be represented by a closed interval in Euclidean space. If that were the case (as it is in many important applications), then the procedure in question was to assume prior neutrality over the alternatives, expressed in the form of a uniform distribution; indeed, this was Bayes's justification for his adoption of a uniform prior density over the interval [0,1]. The strategy was called the "principle of insufficient reason" by James Bernoulli, and the "principle of indifference" by Keynes over two centuries later. It is Keynes's nomenclature which is more commonly used today.

The principle of indifference

The problem with the principle of indifference is that the choice of a fundamental partition is rather dependent on the choice of descriptive categories, or *language*. This is especially true in continuous spaces where there is usually a large class of invertible parameter transformations. For example, the mapping $t(p) = p^2$ continuously transforms [0,1] into [0,1]. But if p is uniformly distributed t is not: by elementary calculus the probability density function $f(t)$ of t is related to the constant density $g(p) = 1$ by $f(t) = (dp/dt)g(p) = (1/2)t^{-1/2}$: t and p cannot both be uniformly distributed. The situation is worse if the random variable is some physical magnitude, since any transformation like the one above amounts to no more than a conventional change of units.

A solution to the problem was suggested by the physicist E. T. Jaynes (1973). His idea was that in any "well-posed" problem of finding a prior there are implicit constraints determining which transformations of the possibility-space should be counted as equivalent, and these may in many typical cases determine a unique solution. Suppose, for example, that the sampling distribution of a variable is known except for a parameter σ which is known to be a scale parameter (a familiar example of a scale parameter is the standard deviation of a normal distribution). According to Jaynes, the distribution of σ should be invariant under arbitrary choices of scale, i.e. under the transformation group $\varphi = a\sigma$, $a>0$. Using elementary calculus it is not difficult to show that the prior must be proportional to σ^{-1}. This is an *improper* distribution, however (i.e., one whose integral is infinite, and therefore inconsistent with the probability calculus), as are many of the priors elicited by this method.

Improper priors can often be accommodated as approximations of an ordinary distribution over reasonable ranges of values of the parameter. But there is a deeper, conceptual, problem with Jaynes's idea, which is that identifying the implicit constraints in a problem relies on a good deal of subjective judgment. For example, in an application to Bertrand's celebrated "geometrical" paradox, where the principle of indifference appears to generate three different *a priori* probabilities that a randomly selected chord in a circle has a length less than that of a side of the inscribed equilateral triangle, Jaynes argued that invariance under rotation, translation, and scale transformations is implicit in the idea of a randomly selected chord, and shows that this uniquely determines Bertrand's own favored solution, ½. To make it more plausible that the problem demanded invariance with respect to just those transformations Jaynes redefined it in terms of an actual physical experiment, though there is arguably some degree of subjective judgment in determining exactly which groups of transformations the problem is supposed to specify. (For a more extended discussion, see Howson and Urbach 2006: 284–5.)

The geophysicist Harold Jeffreys proposed a rather different criterion of invariance for selecting priors. An expert on the mathematics of tensors, he advocated those which could be expressed by a *covariant* (i.e., form-invariant) rule. One such, called the "Jeffreys prior" (though because it depends on the statistical model used to define the likelihoods it generates a class of sometimes very different prior densities), is to define the prior density as the square root of the so-called "Fisher information." There are independent merits to this rule, but also problems with it: it also generates improper priors, it disobeys what is called the "likelihood principle" (that all the information from an observation is carried in the likelihood function), and it gives intuitively a wrong joint (improper) prior for the mean and standard deviation of a normal distribution (it is not the product of the priors for each separately).

Other Bayesian authors, familiar with the transformational problems afflicting the principle of indifference, but reluctant to abandon it completely, resort to a weak form of it which merely recommends prior distributions, so-called "reference priors," which are dominated by the likelihood function in the region of maximum likelihood; such a prior allegedly expresses an attitude of neutrality among the competing alternative explanations. There is a certain amount of ad hocness in this strategy, however, and many feel that the posterior distributions so derived are to that extent question-begging (though the convergence result mentioned earlier implies that most priors will be reference priors for large enough samples).

Without any principle for determining prior probabilities, however, they remain undetermined parameters in the posterior distribution. Some Bayesians, like Jeffreys and Jaynes himself, have worried that leaving things like this makes the theory irredeemably subjective. Others, like de Finetti, Ramsey, and Savage, regard it as irrelevant whether the priors are objectively justified or not. I briefly examine these positions in turn: the former has come to be called "objective Bayesianism" and the latter, "subjective Bayesianism."

Objective Bayesianism

Objective Bayesians differ on detailed proposals but all agree that some principles must be introduced to constrain in some objective way the admissible prior distributions. Jaynes's invariance theory above was one such proposal. Another was his theory of *maximum entropy*. I shall discuss this briefly and then consider a quite different type of proposal, of long pedigree: *simplicity*.

The *entropy* of a probability distribution p taking finitely many values is the functional $H(p) = -\Sigma p_i log p_i$, where the base of the logarithm is arbitrary. Jaynes argued that an objective prior distribution should contain the least information beyond our prior data, and claimed that this demand is satisfied by selecting the prior distribution, p, which maximizes the entropy subject to whatever prior informational constraints exist. Maximizing H subject to constraints obviously means that those constraints must impose conditions on p, and that they do so in a way that guarantees the existence of a maximum. In Jaynes's examples the constraints usually take the form of expectation values obtained from very large sets of observations, relative to which there is always a unique maximizing solution.

A problem is that background information will offer up such well-defined constraints only in exceptional and artificial cases. But a deeper, conceptual, problem arises where there is *no* non-trivial background information, where it is straightforward to show that the entropy-maximizing distribution exists and is the uniform (discrete) distribution. Unfortunately, this bequeaths to maximum entropy all the transformational problems of the principle of indifference. And there is at least potential conflict between maximum entropy and conditionalization, since both are in effect methods of generating distributions from empirical data. In fact, as Seidenfeld (1979) showed, the conflict is actual.

A quite different attack on the problem of objectively constraining prior distributions, *simplicity*, was proposed by Jeffreys. The idea that special merit attaches to simple hypotheses goes back to antiquity, and was famously enunciated in Newton's remark: "Nature is pleased with simplicity, and affects not the pomp of superfluous causes." This expresses an Occam's razor sense of simplicity, and it was this that Jeffreys himself exploited in his *simplicity postulate*, which states that the simpler hypothesis is that with the fewer independent adjustable parameters (1961: 246). This formulation avoids the problem associated with expressing simplicity in terms of linguistic complexity, that of *language-dependence*: for example, the equation of a circle with radius k centered at the origin has the equation $x^2 + y^2 = k^2$ in Cartesian coordinates, and the apparently simpler $r = k$ in polar coordinates.

Simplicity in Jeffreys's sense certainly seems important to scientists: as we saw, it was to Newton, and for many particle physicists a major defect of the *standard model* is that it has no fewer than twenty such parameters. Jeffreys's postulate is merely a Bayesian reflection of this widespread view. However, as such it has been strongly criticized, with Popper (1959: 383–4) and more recently Forster and Sober (1994), claiming that as a constraint on prior probabilities it is *inconsistent* since a polynomial of degree n is also one of every higher degree $m>n$, with the coefficents of all terms of degree $>n$ set equal to 0; and the lower-degree hypothesis cannot have a larger probability since probability respects deductive entailment. The force of the objection is diminished, however, by noting that the interest is typically in testing against each other not compatible but incompatible hypotheses, for example, whether the data are better explained by an existing hypothesis or by adding a new parameter in the form of a non-zero coefficient to a higher-degree term; and if the simplicity postulate is regarded as applying only to such incompatible hypotheses, then it is certainly consistent.

The question remains of what *methodological* justification there is for such a rule. Jeffreys pointed out that there is an obvious penalty for adding parameters simply to fit existing data: the result will almost certainly be *overfit*: "we should change our law with every observation. Thus the principle that laws have some validity beyond the original data would be abandoned" (1961: 245).

A result of Akaike shows that under certain regularity conditions a statistic called the "Akaike information criterion" (AIC in the literature), determined by the observations, is an unbiased estimate of a type of distance in function-space between the hypothesis H and the true distribution, which decreases with the number k of parameters in H. In their 1994 paper Forster and Sober attempt to use this to give a formal proof of the claim, implicit in Jeffreys's remarks, that simpler hypotheses will be more predictively accurate on the average. A Bayesian analogue of AIC due to Gideon Schwarz, often called the "Bayesian information criterion" (BIC), shows that, for an extensive family of distributions, a formally similar statistic to AIC is asymptotically equal to the corresponding posterior probability. To what extent, if any, this justifies choosing the simpler hypothesis at any given finite stage is, however, unclear (a more extended discussion is in Howson and Urbach, 2006, Ch. 13).

Subjective Bayesianism

In the light of the difficulties attending attempts to formulate uncontroversial criteria for objective prior distributions, some Bayesians regard the quest as too question-begging to be worth considering. Their response to the charge of subjectivism is to regard the Bayesian theory as merely a theory of quasi-logical *consistency* in the agent's distributions of their probabilities and to point to an analogous situation in deductive logic, where objectivity resides in the criteria for what is a valid inference and not in the premises. Ramsey saw the program of epistemic probability as "simply bringing probability into line with ordinary formal logic, which does not criticize premises but merely declares that certain conclusions are the only ones consistent with them" (1926: 91). And de Finetti took the same view: "As with the logic of certainty, the logic of the probable adds nothing of its own: it merely helps one to see the implications contained in what has gone before" (1974: 215).

There is no doubt that at a stroke this overcomes all the difficulties with criteria for objective priors, as Ramsey himself pointed out, and while it appears to introduce a degree of arbitrariness in any evaluation of posterior probabilities, some Bayesians hold that this is present, in a suitably concealed form, in all allegedly objective methodological theories, and because of the underdetermination phenomenon is an inevitable component in evaluation of theories. These Bayesians also have an answer to why we appear to see scientific opinion converge as more data are gathered, a fact which many take by itself to embody the idea of scientific objectivity. The answer is a group of theorems, known as "Bayesian convergence-of-opinion theorems," which show that under surprisingly general circumstances the posterior probability will converge to within a small interval, *independently of the prior distribution*, as the sample size increases.

Convergence of opinion

We have already seen that convergence of this type occurs if the likelihood function peaks around the maximum likelihood value with increasing data, and in fact this will generally be the case if the sample is independent given the model (Jeffreys 1961: 193–4). There are much stronger results, however, the strongest of which states that, subject to some standard regularity conditions (non-vanishing of the prior, etc.), with increasing sample data the posterior probability will with probability 1 converge to 1 on the true hypothesis and 0 on its complement *independently of both any assumed data model and the prior distribution*.

Though they may look like a precise mathematical solution to the venerable problem of induction, these "with probability 1" theorems depend on the use of a powerful axiom, the *axiom of countable additivity*, extending the property of additivity over finite partitions to countably infinite ones (i.e., partitions that can be indexed by the positive integers). The status of this axiom is controversial. Some see its justification precisely in the extent to which it generates a powerful mathematical theory (it is equivalent to a principle of continuity), and it was as such that it was first introduced by Kolmogorov (it is his "axiom V"), uniting probability with measure theory. There is a Dutch-Book argument for it, as de Finetti knew, but he nevertheless rejected it as a general principle, principally because any distribution over a countably infinite partition (A_i) must converge fairly quickly to 0 as i tends to infinity. In forbidding *a priori* a uniform distribution over (A_i), while permitting them over finite and uncountable partitions, the axiom in his view was an arbitrary principle adopted simply for mathematical convenience. It is precisely this skewedness that underlies the strong convergence-of-opinion results, ensuring that if a predictive hypothesis is false the probability that a falsification will occur within the first n observations tends to 1. These results might be seen, not implausibly, as an artifact of a purely mathematical assumption for which, if de Finetti is right, there is little independent justification (there is an extended discussion in Kelly 1996: 321–30).

New directions

More recent work has introduced the new techniques of so-called "Bayesian networks" to attack problems thought previously to be beyond its scope. Principal among these are the problem of finding an adequate theory of causation (Williamson 2005), and that of showing that coherent bodies of belief should command more confidence than incoherent ones (Bovens and Hartmann 2004). There is not space to discuss these here, and I shall simply refer the reader to the principal sources. But this new work shows that the seminal ideas of the Reverend Bayes are finding new worlds, if not to conquer, then at the very least to explore and illuminate.

See also Confirmation; Evidence; Prediction; Probability, Scientific method; Underdetermination.

References

Bayes, T. (1763) "An Essay Towards Solving a Problem in the Doctrine of Chances," *Philosophical Transactions of the Royal Society of London*.

Bovens, L. and Hartmann, S. (2004) *Bayesian Epistemology*, Oxford: Oxford University Press.

Cox, R. T. (1961) *The Algebra of Probable Inference*, Baltimore, MD: Johns Hopkins University Press.

De Finetti, B. (1937) "La prévision; ses lois logiques, ses sources subjectives," *Annales de l'Institut Henri Poincaré* 7: 1–68; repr. 1964 in English translation as "Foresight: Its Logical Laws, its Subjective Sources," in H. E. Kyburg, Jr. and H. E. Smokler (eds) *Studies in Subjective Probability*, New York: John Wiley & Sons.

—— (1974) *Theory of Probability*, Volume 1, New York: Wiley.

Einstein, Albert (1907) "Über das Relativitätsprinzip und die aus demselbem gezogenen Folgerungen," *Jahrbuch der Radioaktivität und Elektronik* 4: 411–62.

Forster, M. and Sober, E. (1994) "How to Tell When Simpler, More Unified, or Less *ad hoc* Theories Will Provide More Accurate Predictions," *British Journal for the Philosophy of Science* 45: 1–37.

Howson, C. and Urbach, P. (2006) *Scientific Reasoning: The Bayesian Approach*, 3rd edn, Chicago: Open Court.

Jaynes, E. T. (1973) "The Well-Posed Problem," *Foundations of Physics* 3: 413–500.

Jeffreys, H. (1961) *Theory of Probability*, 3rd edn, Oxford: Clarendon Press.

Kaku, Michio (1995) *Hyperspace: A Scientific Odyssey Through Parallel Universes, Time Warps, and the 10th Dimension*, New York: Anchor.

Kelly, K. (1996) *The Logic of Reliable Inquiry*, Oxford: Oxford University Press.

Lindley, D. V. (1957) "A Statistical Paradox," *Biometrika* 44: 187–92.

Popper, K. R. (1959) *The Logic of Scientific Discovery*, London: Hutchinson.

Ramsey, F. P. (1926) "Truth and Probability," in *The Foundations of Mathematics and Other Logical Essays*, London: Routledge & Kegan Paul (1931).

Savage, L. J. (1954) *The Foundations of Statistics*, New York: John Wiley & Sons.

Seidenfeld, T. (1979) "Why I Am Not an Objective Bayesian: Some Reflections Prompted by Rosenkrantz," *Theory and Decision* 11: 413–40.

Williamson, J. (2005) *Bayesian Nets and Causality: Philosophical and Computational Foundations*, Oxford: Oxford University Press.

Further reading

Most of the seminal contributions to the Bayesian theory are by working scientists, and tend to be somewhat technical. John Earman's book *Bayes or Bust? A Critical Examination of Bayesian Confirmation Theory* (Cambridge, MA: MIT Press, 1991) is written by a well-known philosopher of science and is a fairly thorough philosophical survey, particularly of the convergence-of-opinion theorems. Kelly's book (1996), already referred to, is an excellent discussion of those same results, plus a lot of other fascinating material, also written by a philosopher. For the working physicist, Jaynes's posthumously published *Probability Theory: The Logic of Science* (Cambridge: Cambridge University Press, 2003) is a monumental work presenting Jaynes's own, sometimes idiosyncratic but always illuminating, development of the Bayesian theory from first principles (supplied by R. T. Cox's axioms), with a host of applications to physical problems.

11
CONFIRMATION
Alan Hájek and James M. Joyce

Introduction, motivation, central concepts

Introduction

Confirmation theory is intended to codify the evidential bearing of observations on hypotheses, characterizing relations of inductive *support* and *counter-support* in full generality. The central task is to understand what it means to say that datum E confirms or supports a hypothesis H when E does not logically entail H.

While there were important investigations into confirmation theory by Bacon, Whewell, Mill, and Duhem, the modern study of confirmation was pioneered by Hempel (1945) and Carnap (1962). Given its importance to the philosophy of science and to epistemology, it is surprising that philosophy had to wait so long for well-developed theories of confirmation. This may have been due to a general skepticism about the possibility of inductive support stemming from Hume's *problem of induction*. Hume famously questioned our entitlement to infer things about the future from our experience of the past, and his skeptical arguments can be generalized to cover all non-deductive inferences. More recently, Popper's deductivist philosophy of science has been equally unfriendly to confirmation theory.

Yet the denial of non-deductive confirmation relations is tantamount to skepticism. Without such relations, you have no right to infer the existence of an external world from your perceptions, nor the existence of other minds from the existence of your own, nor anything about your past from your apparent memories of it. Whatever its philosophical credentials, confirmation theory is deeply rooted in common sense, and rational decision and science would be impossible without it.

Concepts of confirmation

Confirmation theorists countenance two relations of confirmation, characterized by the following schemata:

Absolute: H is highly supported given evidence E.
Incremental: E increases the evidential support for H.

Both notions assume a background of total evidence. "E is absolute evidence for H" means that given E, the total evidence for H lies above some salient threshold. "E incrementally confirms H" means that adding E to the background data increases the total evidence for H. It is important to recognize that E can be incremental evidence for H without being absolute evidence for H, and conversely. For example, testing positive for AIDS provides incremental evidence that you have AIDS, but it may not provide absolute evidence: it may be more likely that the test has produced a false positive than it is that you have AIDS.

The ordinary notion of *confirmation* seems to involve both incremental and absolute elements, neither fully accounting on its own for our speech or our practices. Even so, we will focus largely on incremental confirmation, taking the notion of absolute confirmation as understood.

Theories of confirmation

Qualitative confirmation

Hempel thought that the development of the "logic" of confirmation should proceed in stages: qualitative, comparative, and quantitative. He encountered problems at the first stage. In keeping with his logical empiricism, he sought to characterize confirmation in largely deductive terms. His 1945 article presents the following conditions as *prima facie* plausible:

1 *Entailment condition*: If E implies H, then E confirms H.
2 *Special consequence condition*: If E confirms H, and H implies H', then E also confirms H'.
3 *Special consistency condition*: If E confirms H, and H is incompatible with H', then E does not confirm H'.
4 *Converse consequence condition*: If E confirms H, and if H is implied by H', then E also confirms H'.

But, as Hempel recognized, any relation satisfying 1–4 will hold between *every* pair of propositions, clearly an unacceptable result. (Actually, 1 and 4 jointly suffice for the unacceptable result, as Moretti (2003) observes.) Hoping to preserve as much of 1–4 as possible within a unitary account of confirmation, Hempel restricted 4 to cases where H is obtained from H' by instantiation, while maintaining 1–3.

Carnap (1962, new Preface) argues that Hempel conflated incremental and absolute confirmation. In any case, while 1–3 are plausible for absolute confirmation, 4 is not – e.g., the fact that H is well supported given E does not imply that the conjunction of H with some highly unlikely proposition is also well supported given E. The situation regarding incremental confirmation is more nuanced. 3, a squarely *absolutist* principle, clearly fails. 1, 2 and 4, which mix absolute and incrementalist intuitions, hold only in special cases, albeit important ones: 1 fails when H is already known, but otherwise holds. 2 breaks down when E increases the evidence for H while more strongly decreasing the evidence for H'&¬H, but it holds when E either supports or is irrelevant to H'&~H. 4 fails when E increases the evidence for H'&~H

while decreasing the evidence for H' by a smaller amount, but it holds when $H' = H$ & X for X an "irrelevant conjunct" that is not evidentially germane to either H or E (Fitelson 2002).

Instance confirmation and the ravens paradox

Hempel also endorses a famous condition that is *prima facie* plausible for incremental confirmation, but completely implausible for absolute confirmation:

> *Nicod's condition*: All universal generalizations of the form "All Fs are G" are confirmed by all statements of the form "*a* is both F and G."

For example, it seems plausible that the report of a particular black raven incrementally confirms the generalization "All ravens are black," but implausible that the report absolutely confirms the generalization.

A special case of 2 (and of 4), and compelling in its own right, is the *equivalence condition*:

> If H is logically equivalent to H', and E confirms H, then E also confirms H'.

Nicod's condition and the equivalence condition yield Hempel's notorious *ravens paradox*. Since "All ravens are black" is equivalent to "All non-black things are non-ravens," Nicod's condition apparently entails that the latter generalization is confirmed by the report of the observation of any non-black non-raven, e.g., a white shoe. But by the equivalence condition, "All ravens are black" is likewise confirmed by any such report. This seems paradoxical: white shoes seem to have no evidential bearing whatsoever on ornithological hypotheses.

Hempel embraces the paradox, arguing that our intuitions recoil only because we know that there are far more non-black things than ravens. Confirmation relations, on Hempel's view, should presuppose no such background knowledge. Good (1967) replies that a confirmation theory that ignores knowledge is of little interest to science. But once we make confirmation a three-place relation, with background knowledge as the third relatum, Nicod's criterion plainly fails – see sub-section "Probability theory and probabilistic measures of support."

Quine (1969) argues that Nicod's criterion is false insofar as it quantifies over *all* predicates F and G. He insists that confirmation relations must be restricted to *natural kind* predicates, those whose instances are objectively similar to each other. While "raven" and "black" are plausibly natural kind predicates, "non-raven" and "non-black" are not (their miscellaneous instances including electrons and quasars). Alternatively, one might regard Quine as casting doubt on the Equivalence condition: while "All ravens are black" is apt for confirmation, "All non-black things are non-ravens" is not.

As we shall see, such extreme remedies seem like overkill on probabilistic approaches to confirmation. But first we must consider their best-known rival.

H-D confirmation

Hypothetico-deductivism is perhaps the most familiar and historically influential confirmation theory. Its more sophisticated forms, e.g., Ayer (1936), are motivated by the thought that a hypothesis is confirmed by data it entails, but are tempered by the recognition that entailments between hypotheses and data are almost always mediated by background knowledge.

> *H-D confirmation*: E incrementally confirms H iff there are true "auxiliary hypotheses" $A_1, A_2, \ldots, A_n$ such that (a) A_1 & A_2 & $\ldots$ & A_n does not entail E, while (b) H & A_1 & A_2 & $\ldots$ & A_n entails E but not $\sim E$.

Unfortunately, as Duhem (1905) already recognized, auxiliary hypotheses that figure in confirmation relations are, like the hypothesis under test, fallible conjectures based on inconclusive evidence. This led Quine (1951) to insist that confirmation is *holistic*, i.e., that evidence never confirms or disconfirms any hypothesis in isolation. H-D confirmation is thus restricted to "total theories" with enough content to entail observations on their own. While such total theories are confirmed by their empirical consequences, their individual hypotheses are not. This has the unpalatable result that there is no principled way to differentially distribute praise or blame over hypotheses.

Another serious challenge to hypothetico-deductivism, in either its holistic or atomistic form, is the *underdetermination of theory by evidence*. Moreover, the model does not address *statistical hypotheses*, since these have no empirical consequences (e.g., any pattern of "heads" and "tails" is compatible with a coin's being fair). As these problems illustrate, H-D confirmation is not sufficiently nuanced to isolate the evidential relationships we care about. For those we need to invoke probabilities.

Probabilistic theories of confirmation

Probability theory and probabilistic measures of support

Probabilistic theories of confirmation assume that claims of confirmation and disconfirmation must be evaluated relative to some probability function (or set of such functions), which encodes all the background information relevant in a context of inquiry. A probability function P is an assignment of real numbers to elements of some set S of propositions, closed under negation and countable disjunction, obeying the following axioms (for all $A, B \in S$):

1 $P(A) \geqslant 0$.
2 $P(A \vee \sim A) = 1$.
3 $P(A \vee B) = P(A) + P(B)$ when A and B are contraries.
4 The probability of A conditional on B is given by

$$P(A|B) = \frac{P(A \& B)}{P(B)}, \text{ provided } P(B) > 0.$$

If P encapsulates all of an agent's opinions and background knowledge, then $P(H)$ reflects the total evidence for H based on her prior knowledge alone, while $P(H|E)$ reflects the evidence for H when E (and nothing else) is added to that knowledge. In contrast, $P(E)$ and $P(E|H)$ convey information about E's predictability: $P(E)$ reflects E's predictability based on what is known; $P(E|H)$ reflects its predictability when H (and nothing else) is added to this knowledge. Conditional probabilities can thus be used to reflect either the epistemic status of a hypothesis in light of potential data or the predictive power of the hypothesis with respect to that data.

Probabilistic theories represent increases in evidential support using relations of probabilistic relevance and independence. At the qualitative level, the idea is that confirming evidence raises the probability of a hypothesis, disconfirming evidence lowers it, and irrelevant evidence leaves it unchanged:

> *Probabilistic theory of incremental evidence (qualitative)*: Relative to probability function P,
> - E incrementally confirms H iff $P(H|E) > P(H)$.
> - E incrementally disconfirms H iff $P(H|E) < P(H)$.
> - E is evidentially irrelevant to H iff $P(H|E) = P(H)$.

This simple theory has some appealing consequences:

- Evidence for a hypothesis is always evidence against its negation.
- Most H-D confirmation is probabilistic confirmation since $P(H|E)$ exceeds $P(H)$ when H entails E unless $P(H)$ or $P(E)$ equal 0 or 1.
- E increases the evidence for H iff H increases E's predictability.

The probabilistic approach also provides a useful framework for understanding the effect of background information on confirmation. To see how, let's revisit the raven paradox. On a probabilistic picture, instance confirmation is straightforward:

> *Probabilistic IC*: $\forall x(Fx \supset Gx)$ is incrementally confirmed by any learning experience in which (a) one of its *logical* instances $\sim Fa \vee Ga$ becomes certain, (b) there was some positive prior probability that a is both F and $\sim G$, and (c) nothing else of relevance is learned.

Let H be $\forall x(Fx \supset Gx)$. Intuitively, $\sim Fa \vee Ga$ confirms H by ruling out a "live" counterexample in which $P(Fa \ \& \sim Ga) > 0$. Because it relies on a logically weaker notion of an instance, probabilistic-IC has significant advantages over Nicod's condition. Here are two:

- Given (a)–(c), $\sim Fa \vee Ga$ always confirms both $\forall x(Fx \supset Gx)$ and $\forall x(\sim Gx \supset \sim Fx)$.
- $\sim Fa \vee Ga$ increases the evidential support for H only if there is a non-zero probability that a is both F and $\sim G$.

(c) deserves special attention since much of the raven paradox's *paradoxicality* can be traced directly to it. Probabilistic IC implies that learning that some object is either a non-raven or black, *and nothing more*, always raises the probability of H. But experience often delivers *additional* information, whose effect on H's probability can vary greatly depending on the information encoded in P. Suppose we are sampling birds, at random and with replacement, from a fixed population of 1,000, and consider the following states of prior knowledge:

(i)   Either 950 birds are ravens but only 949 of these are black, or 10 birds are ravens and all are black (Good 1967).

(ii) 998 birds are black ravens. At least one of the other two is white, but it is unknown whether either is a raven.

(iii) 900 birds are black ravens. All the others are white, but it is unknown whether any are ravens.

(iv) There are 990 ravens, 980 already known to be black. Of the 20 remaining birds either 10 are black ravens and 10 are white doves, or all are ravens, each equally likely to be white or black.

(v)   There are at most 50 ravens. Ten ravens have been found to be black. The rest of the population is heterogeneous with respect to color.

Suppose that probabilities equal the corresponding proportions. In (i), observing a black raven *lowers* H's probability, whereas observing a non-black non-raven raises H's probability. In (ii), a non-black non-raven *raises* H's probability. A black raven also raises H's probability, but less so. In (iii), a black raven does not alter H's probability at all, but something known only to be a non-black non-raven increases it. In (iv), a black raven raises H's probability slightly. Something known only to be neither black nor a raven lowers H's probability. But a white non-raven raises $P(H)$ to 1! Case (v) is most like the one in which we find ourselves. Observing either a black raven or a non-black non-raven raises H's probability, but since there are vastly more non-black things than ravens, the increase is much greater for the first observation than for the second.

In all these cases, information beyond that found in $\sim Ra \lor Ba$ has a significant effect on confirmation relations. Depending on the background information, such extra information can alter the probability of the hypothesis in almost any way. Moreover, this information can be about white shoes, red herrings, or anything else. For instance, if we know that all ravens are black iff white shoes exist, then observing a white shoe verifies the hypothesis. This does not, however, conflict with the intuition that "All ravens are black" can only be confirmed by evidence about ravens. Information about non-ravens can, given the right background knowledge, also be evidence about ravens. The raven paradox seems paradoxical only when we fail to appreciate this point.

The dependence of prior probability on background information also offers some relief from the Duhem–Quine problem. Suppose that the conjunction of H and auxiliary hypothesis A entails $\sim E$, and that E is observed. Depending on P, E may:

- decrease H's probability but not A's (or vice versa);
- increase H's probability but decrease A's (or vice versa);
- decrease both H's and A's probability.

The question of which of these occurs depends on the prior probabilities of the four conjunctions of $H/\sim H$ and $A/\sim A$, and on the predictability of E when these combinations are assumed. See Earman (1992) for discussion.

Probabilistic approaches also facilitate discussion of confirmation in comparative and quantitative terms through *Bayes's theorem*:

$$\frac{P(H|E)}{P(H)} = \frac{P(E|H)}{P(E)}, \text{ when } P(E), P(H) > 0.$$

The equation's left side tracks the increase in H's probability brought about by conditioning on E. This is one way (among many) to measure the incremental confirmation that E provides for H. The equation's right side is a way of measuring the marginal change in E's predictability afforded by the supposition of H. The theorem thus formalizes the intuition that hypotheses are incrementally confirmed to the extent that their predictions are borne out in experience.

Bayes's theorem reveals many facets of this *evidence–prediction duality*. For example, it relates *odds ratios* to *likelihood ratios*. The *odds* of one hypothesis H relative to another H^* is the ratio of their probabilities $O(H, H^*) = P(H)/P(H^*)$. Odds conditional on E are defined as

$$O_E(H, H^*) = P(H|E)/P(H^*|E).$$

When P encodes the total background evidence, the odds ratio $O_E(H, H^*)/O(H, H^*)$ measures the incremental change that E makes to the disparity between the total evidence for H and the total evidence for H^*. The likelihood ratio $P(E|H)/P(E|H^*)$ is a way of expressing the relative disparity between H and H^* in incremental predictive power with respect to E. Bayes's Theorem requires the likelihood and odds ratios to coincide:

$$O_E(H, H^*)/O(H, H^*) = P(E|H)/P(E|H^*).$$

So, the degree to which E increases the disparity between the evidence for H and for H^* always coincides with the disparity between H and H^*'s incremental predictive power *vis-à-vis* E.

Probability theory provides many ways to say that conditioning on E increases H's probability. Here are four, where $O(H) = O(H, \sim H)$:

	Probability	*Odds*
Incremental	$P(H|E) > P(H)$	$O_E(H) > O(H)$
Probative	$P(H|E) > P(H|\sim E)$	$O_E(H) > O_{\sim E}(H)$

The columns correspond to two (intertranslatable) ways of quantifying uncertainty. The rows represent two ways of thinking about confirmation. *Incremental* relations, which compare unconditional and conditional quantities, concern the degree to which acquiring datum E will perturb the balance of total evidence for H above or below its current value. *Probative* relations compare the *posterior* evidence for H when E is added to the *posterior* evidence for H when ~E is added. Here the issue is the extent to which the total evidence for H varies with changes in E's probability. When $P(H \mid E)$ and $P(H \mid {\sim}E)$ are close together, changes in $P(E)$ have little effect on $P(H)$, but when they are far apart such changes have a significant impact.

Depending on whether we express disparities in probabilities using ratios or differences, each of these relations gives rise to two confirmation measures:

	Probability	Odds
Incremental	$P(H \mid E)/P(H)$	$O(H \mid E)/O(H)$
	$P_E(H) - P(H)$	$O(H \mid E) - O(H)$
Probative	$P(H \mid E)/P(H \mid {\sim}E)$	$O(H \mid E)/O(H \mid {\sim}E)$
	$P_E(H) - P_{\sim E}(H)$	$O(H \mid E) - O(H \mid {\sim}E)$

This is but a small sampling of the measures of evidential relevance that can be defined. They have different formal properties and can seem to deliver incompatible verdicts on particular cases. Consider, for example, the following constraints on confirmation:

> *Law of likelihood:* E supports H more strongly than E supports H^* iff $P(E \mid H) > P(E \mid H^*)$.
> *Law of conditional probability:* E supports H more strongly than E^* supports H iff $P(H \mid E) > P(H \mid E^*)$.

The first says that the comparative evidentiary import of a single datum for distinct hypotheses is exclusively a matter of the degree to which the datum is predictable on the basis of the hypotheses. The second says that the relative evidential impact of two items of data for a single hypothesis is entirely a matter of the final probabilities of the hypothesis given the data. Some measures satisfy the law of likelihood (e.g., both probability ratio measures), but others violate it (e.g., both odds ratios). Some measures obey the law of conditional probability (e.g., both incremental ratio measures), but others do not (e.g., both probative ratios).

In addition to satisfying different formal properties, measures can seem to disagree about cases. Suppose that Ellen is a randomly chosen citizen of a town inhabited by 990 Baptists, 2 Catholics, and 8 Buddhists. Let H say that Ellen is not a Buddhist. According to all incremental measures, the datum E that Ellen is a Baptist provides exactly the same amount of evidence for H as does the datum E^* that she is a Catholic. The probative measures disagree, saying Ellen's being a Baptist provides a great deal of evidence for H whereas the datum that she is Catholic provides hardly any.

Probabilists draw different morals at this point. Some, e.g. Eells and Fitelson (2002), see the plethora of measures as posing a dilemma. Since the measures are not equivalent, it seems that an adequate quantitative confirmation theory must either choose among them or restrict its scope to cases where all reasonable confirmation measures agree. One might then seek to identify some apparently necessary formal conditions that adequate measures of confirmation must satisfy, and go on to prove that one particular measure satisfies them. Milne (1996) argues for $P(H|E)/P(H)$ in this fashion. Likewise, Eells and Fitelson (2000, 2002) appeal to formal considerations, including the law of conditional probability, to rule out measures other than (log of) the incremental odds ratio. Alternatively, one might despair of finding any one correct measure and adhere only to claims about confirmation that are invariant under all reasonable measures.

A third approach, advocated by Joyce (1999, 2004), denies that there is any problem. Rather than being competitors, the various measures capture distinct, complementary notions of evidential support. Recall Ellen. When the incremental measures say that E and E^* provide equal evidence for H, this means only that both items of data increase the total evidence for H by the same increment, $1 - P(H)$. When the probative measures say that E is better evidence than E^* is for H, this means that the total evidence for H, as it currently stands, depends much more on information about E's truth-value than on information about E^*'s truth-value. (The disparity between $P(H|E) = 1$ and $P(H|{\sim}E) = 0.2$ far exceeds the disparity between $P(H|E^*) = 1$ and $P(H|{\sim}E^*) = 0.99198$.) When understood this way, these claims clearly do not conflict.

The distinction between incremental and probative evidence dissolves other issues in probabilistic confirmation theory. Take the *problem of old evidence* (Glymour 1980): explaining how someone who is certain or nearly certain of E, and who knows that H entails E, can see E as evidence for H. Highly probable evidence often seems to have great evidentiary value even when the values of $P(E)$, $P(E|H)$ and $P(E|{\sim}H)$ are nearly identical, thus preventing any of the incremental measures of evidence from being large. For example, when Einstein recognized that his new hypothesis of General Relativity entailed the well-known anomalous advance of Mercury's perihelion, he saw this "old evidence" as strongly supporting his theory. As Christensen (1999) and Joyce (1999) suggest, the problem evaporates once we countenance more than one probabilistic notion of evidential support. Antecedently probable data cannot have much *incremental* effect since they are already incorporated into the total evidence. They can, however, still have great probative value: the total evidence for a hypothesis can vary greatly depending on the data's probability.

The contrast between incremental and probative evidence can be made more vivid by the following principle:

Surprisingness: For fixed values of $P(E|H)$ and $P(H)$ with $P(E|H) > P(E)$, the degree to which E confirms H decreases with increases in $P(E)$.

This is a precise formulation of the oft-heard idea that, *ceteris paribus*, hypotheses are better confirmed by unlikely data than by likely data. Surprisingness is not, however, an incontestable fact about confirmation: many philosophers have held that the prior probability of data is irrelevant to their confirming power – see Hempel (1966: 38). And people with disparate opinions about the probability of data often agree about central aspects of their evidential significance. For example, on the basis of preliminary examinations, one clinician might be almost certain that Josh has strep throat, while another might deny this. The clinicians will also disagree about the probability of a strep test on Josh yielding a positive result. But, even though the incremental effect of the test data will be different for each clinician (in virtue of its different surprisingness for them), they can still agree about the data's probative value: both recognize that a positive result, expected or not, will leave the hypothesis well supported, while a negative result will leave it poorly supported.

How is P to be interpreted?

Any assessment of probabilistic confirmation theory must depend on the nature of the probability functions that underlie the enterprise. Various interpretations might be given to P. On a subjectivist "Bayesian" reading, P captures the strengths of somebody's opinions: probabilistic confirmation theory concerns the doxastic states of individuals. Many object to the use of subjective probabilities in confirmation theory on the grounds that an individual's credences have no place in science, since they are a function both of her prior personal judgments and biases and the particular sequence of evidence she happens to receive (see, e.g., Sober 2002).

In response, Bayesians often observe that the subjectivity of a probability does not render it inaccurate or ill-founded. Credences of competent scientists are excellent guides to the truth in most areas of inquiry. Bayesians sometimes seek to buttress these remarks with "convergence theorems" which show that, under certain conditions, idiosyncratic differences in priors will tend to "wash out" as the evidence increases, thus making the probabilities more "objective"

But some probabilists want more, and aim to provide P with an objective interpretation that does not depend on what anyone happens to believe. The most influential attempt to do this, in philosophical circles, is Carnap's.

Logical probability: Carnap's program

The *logical interpretation* of probability seeks to determine universally the degree of confirmation that evidence E confers on hypothesis H. Pioneered by Johnson and Keynes, and developed most fully by Carnap, the goal is to provide an *inductive logic* that generalizes entailment to *partial entailment*.

Carnap's early (1950) systems begin with a first-order language containing a finite number of monadic predicates and countably many individual constants. The most detailed descriptions in the language – *state descriptions* – affirm or deny the attribution of each predicate to each individual. For example, in a language containing the predicate "F" and the constants "a," "b," and "c," the state descriptions are:

1 Fa & Fb & Fc	2 Fa & Fb & $\neg Fc$
3 Fa & $\neg Fb$ & Fc	4 $\neg Fa$ & Fb & Fc
5 Fa & $\neg Fb$ & $\neg Fc$	6 $\neg Fa$ & Fb & $\neg Fc$
7 $\neg Fa$ & $\neg Fb$ & Fc	8 $\neg Fa$ & $\neg Fb$ & $\neg Fc$

The choice of a probability measure m for state descriptions induces a *confirmation function*:

$$c(H, E) = \frac{m(H \ \& \ E)}{m(E)} \ (m(E) > 0).$$

A *structure description* is a disjunction of state descriptions that agree on how many individuals instantiate each predicate. For example, the disjunction of state descriptions 2, 3, and 4 yields the structure description characterized as "two F's, one $\neg$F." Carnap's preferred measure, m^*, gives equal weight to each structure description, these weights in turn shared equally among the constituent state descriptions. In our example, there are four structure descriptions, corresponding to

"three F's,"
"two F's, one $\neg$F,"
"one F, two $\neg$F's,"
"three $\neg$F's."

They each receive 1/4 of the probability, subdividing it equally internally. Thus, m^* assigns 1/4 to state descriptions 1 and 8, and 1/12 to the rest. In contrast to c, the resulting confirmation function c^* allows inductive learning: evidence of some individuals' having a property confirms other individuals' having that property. For instance, the *a priori* probability of Fa is $m^* (Fa) = 1/2$. However,

$$c^*(Fa, Fb) = \frac{c^*(Fa \ \& \ Fb)}{c^*(Fb)}$$

$$= \frac{1/3}{1/2}$$

$$= 2/3.$$

So, the evidence that Fb confirms the hypothesis that Fa.

While the early Carnap favored c^* for its simplicity and salience, it is not obvious that it is the unique confirmation function he sought, since infinitely many candidates have this "inductive learning" property. He later (1962) generalizes his confirmation function to a continuum of functions c_λ. He considers languages containing sets of one-place predicates such that, for each individual, exactly one member of each set applies. He lays down a host of axioms of symmetry and inductive learning. They imply that, for the set of predicates $\{P_i\}$, $i = 1,2,\ldots,k$, $k > 2$,

c_λ (individual $n+1$ is P_j, n_j of the first n individuals are P_j)

$$= \frac{n}{n + \lambda} \left(\frac{n_j}{n}\right) + \frac{\lambda}{n + \lambda} \left(\frac{1}{k}\right), \text{ where } 0 < \lambda < \infty.$$

The bracketed fractions are respectively the proportion of observed "successes," and the symmetrically assigned *a priori* probability; their unbracketed weights sum to 1. λ is an index of "caution": the higher it is, the less responsive is c_λ to evidence. At $\lambda = 0$, we have the inductively incautious "straight rule" that simply equates the conditional probabilities to the corresponding relative frequencies. At $\lambda = \infty$, we have the rigid method that never learns from experience. In between we have the range of all admissible inductive rules. Carnap regards the choice of λ as a pragmatic matter, something to be decided in a particular context.

Several problems for Carnap concern the languages over which his confirmation functions are defined. These languages are clearly too impoverished to do justice to much scientific theorizing; yet as they are enriched with further expressive power, the confirmation relations change. Still more seriously, these relations are determined solely by the *syntax* of the sentences – their *meanings* play no role.

The fact that meanings should play a role is one lesson of Goodman's *new riddle of induction*. Our evidence of observing many green emeralds surely confirms that emeralds observed at any future time will be green. Now consider the predicate "grue," which applies to objects that are green and observed before some future time t, or blue and not observed before t. Our evidence can be equivalently described as the observation of many *grue* emeralds; but it does *not* confirm that emeralds observed after t will be grue – for that would mean that they are blue. The challenge for any confirmation theory is to account for the differing confirmation relations that our evidence bears to the "green" and the "grue" hypotheses. Any such theory must apparently be sensitive to features beside syntactical form, since syntactically "green" and "grue" are on a par.

One might protest that "grue" is somehow syntactically more complex than "green" – after all, "grue"'s definition above involves a somewhat complicated disjunction. But now define "bleen," which applies to objects that are observed before t and blue, or not observed before t and green. Then there is an alarming interdefinability of the "green/blue" and the "grue/bleen" vocabulary. In particular, an emerald is green iff it is grue and observed before t, or bleen and not observed before t. So what counts as a "complicated disjunction" depends on which predicates we start with. Nor will it help to claim that "grue" is in some sense "gerrymandered," or "positional" (referring as it does to a particular time, t). For whatever these pejoratives may mean, the interdefinability point will underwrite the same claims about "green."

So Carnap's languages apparently have to privilege certain predicates over others – presumably outlawing monstrosities such as "grue." It is hard to see how this can have any basis in *logic*, and how this privileging can be done in a principled way. Goodman, for example, appeals to the somewhat nebulous notion of *entrenchment*: a predicate is entrenched iff we have used it in successful inductive inferences in the past. But our commonsense predicates are often better entrenched than those of science; that is hardly a reason to favor the former when making predictions.

Finally, return to the dependence of Carnap's confirmation functions on the parameter λ. Nothing in logic determines, or even constrains, its value. Carnap thought that it might be determined empirically, but the bearing of empirical data on its value is itself a problem of confirmation, and an infinite regress threatens. This problem is only exacerbated for the late Carnap (1971), when he generalizes his system further to include analogical considerations. This involves a further parameter over whose setting there is again much freedom, and certainly no constraint from logic. We have thus come a long way from his initial hope for a unique confirmation function.

Conclusions

We began by noting how little of our reasoning is captured by deductive logic, and how there is an apparent need for confirmation theory. Carnap's *inductive logic* was intended to assimilate confirmation theory to deductive logic. To be sure, confirmation theory does bear some interesting analogies to deductive logic: it is not a matter of the truth of some piece of evidence E, nor of some hypothesis H, but rather of the bearing that E has on H. But we have learned that there are apparently some important disanalogies. Unlike deductive entailment,

- Confirmation relations come in varying degrees.
- The relations cannot be captured purely syntactically: meanings of terms are important.
- The relations may not be uniquely constrained.
- They apparently involve at least a three-place relation, between an evidence sentence E, a hypothesis H, and background knowledge K (which may be captured in a probability function P).

That said, we side with Carnap, and against Hume and Popper, in insisting that relations of confirmation may be non-trivial, of importance to science, philosophy, and daily life, and susceptible to genuine illumination.

Acknowledgements

We thank Martin Curd, Franz Huber, and Stathis Psillos for very helpful comments on earlier drafts.

See also Bayesianism; Evidence; Prediction; Probability; Scientific method; Underdetermination.

References

Ayer, A. J. (1936) *Language, Truth and Logic*, London: Penguin.

Carnap, R. (1962) *Logical Foundations of Probability*, 2nd edn, Chicago: University of Chicago Press.

Christensen, D. (1999) "Measuring Confirmation," *Journal of Philosophy* 96: 437–61.

Duhem, Pierre (1905) *La Théorie physique: son objet, sa structure*, 2nd edn, Paris: Marcel Rivière, 1914; trans. P. P. Wiener as *The Aim and Structure of Physical Theory*, Princeton, NJ: Princeton University Press, 1954.

Earman, J. (1992) *Bayes or Bust? A Critical Examination of Bayesian Confirmation Theory*, Cambridge, MA: MIT Press.

Eells, Ellery and Fitelson, Branden (2000) "Measuring Confirmation and Evidence," *Journal of Philosophy* 97: 663–72.

—— (2002) "Symmetries and Asymmetries in Evidential Support," *Philosophical Studies* 107: 129–42.

Fitelson, Branden (2002) "Putting the Irrelevance Back into the Problem of Irrelevant Conjunction," *Philosophy of Science* 69: 611–22.

Glymour, Clark (1980) *Theory and Evidence*, Princeton, NJ: Princeton University Press.

Good, I. J. (1967) "The White Shoe Is a Red Herring," *British Journal for the Philosophy of Science* 17: 322.

Hempel, Carl (1945) "Studies in the Logic of Confirmation," *Mind* 54: 1–26, 97–121.

—— (1966) *Philosophy of Natural Science*, New York: Prentice-Hall.

Joyce, James M. (1999) *The Foundations of Causal Decision Theory*, Cambridge: Cambridge University Press.

—— (2004) "Bayesianism," in A. Mele and P. Rawling (eds) *The Oxford Handbook of Rationality*, Oxford: Oxford University Press, pp. 132–55.

Milne, Peter (1996) "Log[$p(h/eb)/p(h/b)$] is the One True Measure of Confirmation," *British Journal for the Philosophy of Science* 20: 21–6.

Moretti, Luca (2003) "Why the Converse Consequence Condition Cannot Be Accepted," *Analysis* 63: 297–300.

Quine, W. V. (1951) "Two Dogmas of Empiricism," *Philosophical Review* 60: 20–43.

—— (1969) "Natural Kinds," in W. V. Quine, *Ontological Relativity and Other Essays*, New York: Columbia University Press, pp. 114–38.

Further reading

Two excellent overviews of Bayesian confirmation theory are: Colin Howson and Peter Urbach, *Scientific Reasoning: The Bayesian Approach*, 3rd edn (La Salle, IL: Open Court, 2005); and John Earman, *Bayes or Bust?* (Cambridge, MA: MIT Press, 1992). Clark Glymour (1980) advocates his "bootstrap" theory of confirmation. John Earman (ed.) *Testing Scientific Theories* (Minneapolis: University of Minnesota Press, 1983) is a volume of responses. Useful discussions of the problem of old evidence can be found in: Lyle Zynda, "Old Evidence and New Theories," *Philosophical Studies* 77 (1995): 67–95; David Christensen, "Measuring Confirmation," *Journal of Philosophy* 96 (1999): 437–61; and Jim Joyce, *The Foundations of Causal Decision Theory* (Cambridge: Cambridge University Press, 1999). The problem of measuring confirmation is discussed in many of Branden Fitelson's papers, available at http://fitelson.org/research. htm. Recent defenses of the law of likelihood can be found in Richard M. Royall, *Statistical Evidence: A Likelihood Paradigm* (New York: Chapman & Hall, 1997) and papers by Elliott Sober available at http:// philosophy.wisc.edu/sober. A detailed discussion of the interpretations of probability, including the logical interpretation, can be found in Alan Hájek, "Interpretations of Probability," in Edward N. Zalta (ed.) *The Stanford Encyclopedia of Philosophy* (summer 2003 edition); available online: http://plato.stanford.edu/ archives/sum2003/entries/probability-interpret.

12

EMPIRICISM

Elliott Sober

Empiricism is an *ism* with many meanings. In accounts of the history of philosophy, empiricism is often contrasted with *rationalism*, though serious historians frequently look with jaundiced eye at this way of telling the story (van Fraassen 2002). According to this formula, empiricists emphasize the role of sense experience, rationalists the role of reason. Each position can be given extreme formulations, as in the clashing claims that sense experience is the *only* source of knowledge *or* that reason is, and each position can be moderated, with the attendant possibility that they no longer conflict. The debate was usually framed in terms of the existence of "innate ideas" and often blurred the distinction between psychological and epistemological questions.

A different kind of empiricism has been central to philosophy of science. Here empiricism contrasts with *scientific realism*, not with rationalism. When Galileo found himself in conflict with the Church, the philosophical issue concerned how heliocentrism should be interpreted. Galileo's interrogator, Cardinal Bellarmine, did not object to Galileo's using the hypothesis that the earth goes round the sun as a device for making predictions. His objection was to Galileo's assertion that heliocentrism is *true*. As a first approximation, realism maintains that well-confirmed scientific theories should be regarded as true, while empiricism maintains that they should be regarded as empirically adequate – as capturing what is true about observable phenomena. Empiricists deny that it is ever rationally obligatory to believe that theories provide true descriptions of an unobservable reality. It isn't that empiricists *deny* that quarks or genes exist; rather, they regard such realist affirmations as going beyond what the evidence demands. Empiricism is to realism as agnosticism is to theism. A third option corresponds to atheism. This is *fictionalism*, the thesis that scientific theories are always false. A closely related fourth option is *instrumentalism*, which is often interpreted as claiming that theories do not have truth-values and are merely useful tools for making predictions.

In the contest between empiricism and scientific realism, the empiricist's preoccupation with sense experience takes the form of a thesis about the role of *observation* in science and the rationalist's emphasis on reason is transformed into a claim about the indispensable role of the *super-empirical virtues* (Churchland 1985). For an empiricist, if a theory is logically consistent, observations are the only source of information about whether the theory is empirically adequate. For a realist, the observations provide information about whether the theory is true, but there are other relevant considerations as well: if one theory is more explanatory, or simpler, or more unified than another, that counts too. Empiricists often dismiss these considerations as merely pragmatic or aesthetic – theories with those virtues are easier to use or more beautiful to behold, and that is all.

Observation

The verb "observes" has a double meaning, and that requires empiricists to choose between two ways of developing their philosophical position. We observe that various propositions are true and we also observe objects; we say that S sees that there is a linear accelerator in the valley and we also say that S sees the linear accelerator (Dretske 1969); call these the *objectual* and the *propositional* notions of observation. The important logical feature of the objectual notion is that it involves an extensional context. If S sees o_1, and o_1 is one and the same object as o_2, then it also is true that S sees o_2. Children and dogs can see linear accelerators, even though they are unable to think of what they see in those terms. The propositional notion of observation, on the other hand, involves an opaque context. If S sees that there is a linear accelerator in the valley, and linear accelerators are the things that Joe loathes, it does not follow that S sees that there is an object in the valley that Joe loathes. Propositional observation requires conceptual competence; the observer must have mastery of the concepts that figure in the proposition seen to be true.

Van Fraassen (1980) maintains that empiricism needs the distinction between observable and unobservable *entities*, not the distinction between observation and theoretical *statements*. He says that for an object to be observable "by us" (i.e., by human beings) is for there to be circumstances such that, if we were in those circumstances, we would observe the object. Dinosaurs are observable entities even though they existed long ago, and so are Jupiter's moons, even though they are far away. If we were at the right place at the right time, we would see them both with the naked eye. Van Fraassen (1980: 58) also says that people sometimes observe electrons and molecules. The circumstances do not involve looking through a microscope; rather, a crystal sometimes consists of a single molecule that is big enough for us to see without the aid of instruments, and there are flashes seen by astronauts that turn out to be high-energy electrons.

Observability is a modal notion; for objects that are unobserved but observable, it is counterfactual. The counterfactuals that van Fraassen thinks are relevant involve changing our spatio-temporal location, not our sensory endowment. He thinks it irrelevant that we would see objects that presently are invisible to us if we had more powerful eyes. He also thinks it does not matter that other organisms sometimes observe what we can not, and that the human perceptual apparatus might evolve. Van Fraassen does not discuss the fact that there is variation among human beings with respect to what can be observed. If observability means observability-by-us, why is it the entire human race that constitutes the relevant epistemic community, rather than a group that is larger or smaller?

For van Fraassen, if x is an observable object, then the evidence can demand that we believe that x exists. However, if y is not observable, the evidence can never oblige us to believe that y exists; the most we can be required to believe is that the claim that y exists is empirically adequate. Many of van Fraassen's critics have argued that if this is what observability means, then the concept lacks epistemological significance – our evidence for the existence of y can be stronger than our evidence for the existence of x (Maxwell 1962; Churchland 1985; Sober 1993).

Since the distinction between observable and unobservable entities is central to van Fraassen's empiricism (which he terms "constructive" empiricism), one might expect him to have provided an account of what is involved in observing an object. He does not; he thinks that science, not armchair philosophy, has the task of explaining why human beings can observe some objects but not others (van Fraassen 1980: 57). Van Fraassen is right that it is an empirical question what the observational capacities are that human beings have, but that does not relieve empiricists of the obligation to say what observing an object involves. By the same token, "Which events cause others?" is an empirical question, but that does not mean that philosophers of causation need not clarify what *causation* is.

Empiricists need to address problems in the philosophy of perception. The most obvious first stab at saying what seeing an object involves is to describe the passage of light from the object into the eye, with the result that a visual experience occurs. However, the invisibility of white cats in snowstorms and the fact that we see silhouettes (like the moon during an eclipse) shows that this is neither sufficient nor necessary (Dretske 1967; Sorensen 1999). Consider, also, van Fraassen's comment that astronauts see electrons but that scientists do not see electrons when they look at the screen of a cloud chamber. Why is an electron the object of perception in the first case but not the second? If electrons lead this double life, should we conclude that *all* electrons are visible or that only *some* are?

The reason van Fraassen (1980: 81) uses the distinction between observable and unobservable entities to formulate his brand of empiricism, and not the distinction between observational and theoretical statements, is his conviction that every term in our language is theory-laden; he takes this to entail that there are no observation statements. Van Fraassen does not explain what he means by "theory-laden," perhaps because this position is so familiar from the work of Kuhn (1962) and others. The thought may simply be that each term in our language requires knowledge if we are to apply it. We can't tell whether the term "apple" applies to something by just looking at it; we need to have beliefs about what an apple is. If these beliefs comprise a "theory of apples," then van Fraassen's claim that all empirical statements are "theoretical" is correct.

If all statements are theory-laden in this sense, how can there be observation statements? The answer is to relativize the notion of an observation statement to a testing problem. The difference this makes can be understood by considering the following two claims, which differ in terms of the order of the quantifiers used:

(EA) There exists a set of observation statements that presuppose no theories whatever, and these can be used to evaluate any theories we wish to consider.

(AE) For any set of competing theories, there exists a set of observation statements that presuppose none of the theories under test, and these can be used
to evaluate those theories.

The statement (EA) characterizes *absolute* theory-neutrality, while (AE) defines
relative theory-neutrality. The claim that all statements are theory-laden impugns
(EA), but leaves (AE) untouched. (AE) expresses the important point that observation statements need to be *epistemically independent* of the hypotheses they are used
to test (Sober 1990, 1993).

Not only is a suitably relativized concept of observation statement intelligible: it is a
concept that empiricism needs. The distinction between observable and unobservable
objects is not enough. According to constructive empiricism, the goal of science is to
find theories that are empirically adequate. Van Fraassen (1980: 44–7) illustrates this
idea with an example from Newtonian mechanics. He says that the observables in
Newtonian mechanics (the "appearances") are "relative motions;" different versions
of Newtonian mechanics may accurately represent these relative motions even though
they disagree with each other about the location of *absolute space*. One version of the
theory says the center of mass of the solar system is at rest with respect to absolute
space; others say that it is moving with constant velocity v_1, v_2, v_3, etc. These different
theories – $NT(0)$, $NT(v_1)$, $NT(v_2)$, and so on – are empirically equivalent, though
incompatible. They disagree with each other, but they say exactly the same thing
about observables; either all these theories are empirically adequate or none of them
is.

In this example, the observables are "relative motions," but what does that
mean? We know well enough what it means for a billiard ball to be observable,
but relative motions are not physical objects. You can bounce light off a billiard
ball, but what would it mean to bounce light off the relative motion that one
object has with respect to another? What is needed is the idea that there is a set of
propositions that describe the relative motions of objects. These propositions have
the form "Object x is moving with velocity v at time t with respect to object y";
"Object x is moving with acceleration a at time t with respect to object y"; and so
on. Empiricists may disagree about how the objects x and y should be restricted,
but that is not the point of importance here. Rather, the point is that these statements are the *observation statements* on which the different theories just mentioned
agree. Van Fraassen thinks that these observation statements are theory-laden. He
is right: the idea of instantaneous velocity is highly theoretical – it is defined as
the limit of velocities over temporal intervals as those intervals are made smaller
and smaller. However, there is no need for observation statements to be *absolutely*
atheoretical. The point is that we can tell by observation which statements about
relative motions are true *without assuming any of the versions of Newtonian physics
that we wish to compare*.

If empiricism requires the concept of an observation statement, how should that
concept be defined? I suggest the following explication of "S sees that p" (where p is
some proposition):

S sees that p if and only if (1) S knows that p, (2) S sees objects $o_1 \ldots o_n$, and (3) condition (1) is true because (2) is.

Propositional seeing is knowledge mediated by seeing objects. The definition allows that you can see that the gas tank in your car is empty by seeing the gas gauge on the dashboard. You don't need to see the gas tank to see that it is empty. We sometimes use the word "see" to means "realize," with no implication that vision is involved; this is not a usage that the definition of propositional seeing is intended to capture. The definition of propositional seeing is an example; similar definitions apply to the concept of hearing that p, and similarly for the other senses. Observing that p is the genus of which propositional seeing is a species.

The concept of observing that p can be used to define the relevant notion of an observational statement:

> Proposition p is an observational statement for S in the context of testing hypothesis H_1 against hypothesis H_2 if and only if (1) S observes that p and (2) S's reason for believing p does not depend on S's believing that H_1 is true or that H_2 is true.

Observation statements are a subset of the non-question begging considerations that may be able to adjudicate between the competing hypotheses under test.

It is an important consequence of this definition that a proposition can be an observation statement in one testing problem while not having that status in another. For example, even if van Fraassen is right that we do not see electrons in cloud chambers, this does not rule out the possibility that there are testing problems in which reports about electrons in cloud chambers count as observation statements. Not, of course, if we are trying to test the hypothesis that electrons exist. However, if the testing problem concerns some other matter, and the electron theory is already well established, there is nothing wrong with describing what one observes in this way.

Another feature of the definition is that *whether p is an observation statement depends on the individual S*. The usefulness of the measuring devices found in laboratories depends on our ability to perceive those devices and to tell with ease what states they occupy. Sighted people can see what a thermometer says, but blind people can not. It is a contingent biological fact that people share, to the extent they do, the ability to make various perceptual discriminations. There is no reason why individuals with different observational abilities cannot form an *epistemic community*, sharing information with each other and conducting their inquiries together. But this does not undercut the fact that blind people do not see that this or that proposition is true (in the sense of using vision to obtain this knowledge). Even so, blind people can *hear* that a proposition is true, and this can make the proposition an observational report for them. The individuals in an epistemic community experience perceptual inputs and share information with each other by sending and receiving information, which involves further acts of perception. We tend to think of epistemic communities as groups of people, but pet-owners and primatologists have formed such communities with non-human animals, and our descendants may do the same with extraterrestrials, should such beings ever present themselves. The range of *objects* you can perceive is limited by your perceptual faculties, but the range of *propositions* you can observe to be true can be expanded by making contacts.

Acceptance

If the concept of an observation statement should be understood along the lines just described, what becomes of empiricism? It is relevant here to consider another feature of van Fraassen's constructive empiricism. After saying that realists hold that the goal of science is to find true theories while empiricists maintain that the goal is to find theories that are empirically adequate, van Fraassen (1980: 8, 12) adds a comment about *acceptance*. For realism, acceptance means regarding theories as true; for empiricism, acceptance means regarding them as empirically adequate. I suggest that these comments about acceptance burden empiricism and realism with extraneous commitments. How much evidence in favor of a proposition does it take for one to be entitled (or required) to believe it? I suspect that there is no uniquely correct answer to this question. In addition, the lottery paradox (Kyburg 1970) lurks in the background as a further warning against embracing the concept of acceptance. It is well to think here of Jeffrey's *radical probabilism* (2002), which is an epistemology that abandons the dichotomous concept of acceptance and restricts itself to using the concept of *degree of belief*. You do not need to be a Bayesian to see the merits of this approach. Realists do not need to *accept* theories as true, and empiricists don't need to *accept* theories as empirically adequate.

If we drop the concept of acceptance, new questions arise concerning what remains of van Fraassen's description of the difference between realism and empiricism. Since "T is true" entails "T is empirically adequate," evidence confirming the latter will often confirm the former, at least when confirmation is understood on the Bayesian model:

Observation O confirms hypothesis H if and only if $Pr(H|O) > Pr(H)$.

To identify a sufficient condition for confirmation of a logically weaker statement W to imply confirmation of a stronger statement S, let A be the additional content that the stronger statement has; this means that $S \equiv W\&A$, where W does not entail A. Now consider the following:

$Pr(S) = Pr(W\&A) = Pr(W)Pr(A|W)$.
$Pr(S|O) = Pr(W\&A|O) = Pr(W|O)Pr(A|W\&O)$.

This entails that if $Pr(W|O) > Pr(W)$ and $Pr(A|W\&O) = Pr(A|W)$, then $Pr(S|O) > Pr(S)$. The confirmation of the weaker proposition entails the confirmation of the stronger proposition if W screens off A from O. Van Fraassen's example about Newtonian mechanics fits this pattern. Let W be Newtonian mechanics with no mention of absolute space, and let A assert that the center of mass of the solar system is at rest relative to absolute space. The observations that confirm W, such as the observation that the tides and the phases of the moon are correlated, do not affect how probable A is given W. Because of this, all the empirically equivalent theories $NT(0)$, $NT(v_1)$, etc. are confirmed when the claim that NT is empirically adequate is itself confirmed.

Van Fraassen grants that the $NT(0)$, $NT(v_1)$, and so on can each be *disconfirmed* by observations. According to Bayesianism, this means that they also can be *confirmed*. Given this, what would it mean to say that confirming and disconfirming "T is empirically adequate" is the goal, and that the confirmation or disconfirmation that accrues to "T is true" is a mere by-product, not the goal of science at all? Both "T is true" and "T is empirically adequate" have their probabilities rise and fall. A purely Bayesian approach to evidence thus throws doubt on van Fraassen's definitions of empiricism and realism, once "acceptance" is deleted.

A similar conclusion concerning how empiricism should be formulated follows if we use other conceptions of evidence. Consider, for example, the law of likelihood (Hacking 1965):

Observation O favors hypothesis H_1 over hypothesis H_2 if and only if $Pr(O|H_1) > Pr(O|H_2)$.

If an observational result favors "T_1 is empirically adequate" over "T_2 is empirically adequate," it also will favor "T_1 is true" over "T_2 is true." This follows from the fact that, for any observation O, $Pr(O|T_i$ is empirically adequate$) = Pr(O|T_i$ is true$)$ $(i = 1,2)$. Given this fact about likelihoods, what would it mean to say that the goal of science is to solve the first discrimination problem but not the second– that solving the second is merely a byproduct? Observations can be brought to bear on theories that make claims about unobservables; when such theories confer different probabilities on what we observe, it is perfectly possible to discover which theory is better supported. Various frequentist frameworks of inference – model selection theory, for instance – also allow that data can discriminate between theories that make reference to unobservables; this happens when the different theories make different predictions about matters we can observe.

Contrastive empiricism

Empiricism should not regard propositions that postulate unobservable entities with suspicion. Rather, empiricism should be formulated as a thesis about *testing problems*, not about *propositions* (Sober 1990, 1993, 1999). If two theories make different predictions about observations (and here we need to think of prediction probabilistically, not just deductively), science may be able to test the two hypotheses against one another; but if they are predictively equivalent, science has nothing to say about how the theories compare. To see the importance of formulating empiricism as a thesis about problems, not about single propositions, consider the parallel epistemological problems posed by the following two triplets:

(P_1) Quantum mechanics is true.
(P_2) Classical mechanics is true.
(P_3) Quantum mechanics is empirically adequate, but false.

(Q_1) Dinosaurs once roamed the earth.
(Q_2) There were no dinosaurs.
(Q_3) It is false that dinosaurs once roamed the earth, though all the evidence we will ever have suggests that they did.

Let us grant, for the sake of argument, that P_1 is about unobservable entities and that Q_1 is strictly about observables. For van Fraassen, this makes all the difference in the world, but according to the version of empiricism I am describing, it does not matter. Rather, the point of importance concerns the similarities that unite the Ps and the Qs, not their differences. Observations can discriminate between P_1 and P_2, just as observations can discriminate between Q_1 and Q_2. And observations cannot discriminate between P_1 and P_3, just as observations cannot discriminate between Q_1 and Q_3. The reason observations cannot discriminate between P_1 and P_3 has nothing to do with the fact that P_1 describes unobservable entities; the same impossibility attaches to testing Q_1 against Q_3. Science is in the business of addressing problems of the first kind, not problems of the second.

This version of empiricism, *contrastive empiricism*, maintains that the goal of science is to bring observations to bear on the comparison of theories (Sober 1990). This goal is *attainable*; in fact, it has frequently been attained. I do not deny that scientists often want to discover which theories are true and often think they have done so. However, the humbling fact of the matter is that scientists are able to consider only those theories that have been formulated thus far. And, for the most part, there is no reason to think that the theories we have at hand exhaust the range of possible theories (Stanford 2006). The same point shows that what van Fraassen regards as the goal of science is often not attainable. Scientists may seek theories that are empirically adequate; however since the theories they consider are rarely exhaustive, they are often in no position to say that the best of their theories is empirically adequate. It may be objected that finding true theories or theories that are empirically adequate must be among the goals of science, since scientists would be pleased if their pet theories had that status. My reply is that "the goals of science" in this context should be understood as the goals that scientific modes of inference are able to achieve; the hopes that scientists harbor for their theories are not at issue. The debate between realism and empiricism concerns the power of scientific inference, not the psychology of scientists.

Whither the super-empirical virtues?

Empiricists have sometimes been skeptical about the role of simplicity and unification in theory evaluation, thinking that their empiricism obliges them to hold that the simplicity of a hypothesis cannot be evidence that it is true or empirically adequate (see, e.g., van Fraassen 1980: 87). However, it is far from obvious that empiricist standards require this stance. Empiricists have the resources of mathematics and logic, as well as the observations, to bring to bear on competing theories. Perhaps, in an interesting range of circumstances, there is an empirically grounded reason why simplicity should be a defeasible guide to truth or empirical adequacy.

If the relative simplicity of theories H_1 and H_2 is epistemically relevant, the empiricist needs to explain why this is so without invoking the thesis that simplicity is an end in itself, a *sui generis* constraint on what it means to be a good scientific theory. Here is a simple example in which it is possible for the empiricist to make good on this commitment. Suppose some students are sitting in a seminar room that overlooks a lake. At time t, all of them come to believe that a red sailboat is crossing the lake. Why did the same belief suddenly take hold? Consider two hypotheses. H_1 says that there was a single red sailboat crossing the lake at time t; H_2 says that the students independently and simultaneously suffered hallucinations at time t. Why is H_1 a better theory than H_2? One thought is that H_1 is simpler; it postulates a single cause that explains the observations, whereas H_2 regards the simultaneous occurrence of the observations as an elaborate coincidence. But that is not the end of the story. It also is true that the students simultaneously having the same experience is rendered more probable by H_1 than by H_2. Here the simpler hypothesis is also the hypothesis of higher likelihood, in the sense of the *law of likelihood*. This is the sort of justification of simplicity that empiricists can embrace. There are less trivial examples that follow the same pattern. A longstanding question in evolutionary theory concerns the use of a parsimony criterion in phylogenetic inference. Biologists have so far identified two different models of the evolutionary process that each render parsimony and likelihood ordinally equivalent (Sober 2008). If we have empirical reasons to accept one or the other of these process models in a given problem, we thereby have a reason to think that parsimony is relevant to deciding which phylogenetic hypotheses are better supported by the data.

One complication that empiricists need to face is that *simplicity* may have different justifications in different inference problems. Even if a given model of the evolutionary process entails that parsimony and likelihood go hand-in-hand in phylogenetic inference, the situation seems very different in model selection problems in which more complex models fit the data better than simpler ones (Forster and Sober 1994). Unfortunately, empiricists must think about the so-called "super-empirical virtues" piecemeal. But so, too, should everyone else. The claim that simplicity and unification really are *super-empirical* guides to truth or empirical adequacy requires a positive argument. It is not enough that we presently do not understand the roles of simplicity and unification in theory evaluation. Empiricists and realists both have work to do here.

Concluding comments

Empiricism is best viewed as a thesis about the power of scientific reasoning; that power is not unlimited. Philosophers of science have long recognized that non-deductive reasoning is uncertain, but there are more limits than this on what science can achieve. At any moment, scientists are limited by the observations they have at hand. That limitation does not force them to restrict their attention to theories that are strictly about observables; still less does it force them to limit themselves to hypotheses that do not go beyond restating the evidence at hand. Rather, the limitation is that science is forced to restrict its attention to problems that observations can solve.

Acknowledgements

I am grateful to Juan Comesaña, Martin Curd, Fred Dretske, Malcolm Forster, Stathis Psillos, Susanna Rinard, Larry Shapiro, and Carolina Sartorio for discussion.

See also Bayesianism; Explanation; Inference to the best explanation; Logical empiricism; Metaphysics; Observation; Probability; Realism/anti-realism; Underdetermination; The virtues of a good theory

References

Churchland, P. (1985) "The Ontological Status of Observables: In Praise of the Superempirical Virtues," in P. Churchland and C. Hooker (eds) *Images of Science: Essays on Realism and Empiricism*, Chicago: University of Chicago Press, pp. 35–47.

Dretske, F. (1969) *Seeing and Knowing*, Chicago: University of Chicago Press.

Forster, M. and Sober, E. (1994) "How to Tell When Simpler, More Unified, or Less Ad Hoc Theories Will Provide More Accurate Predictions," *British Journal for the Philosophy of Science* 45: 1–36.

Hacking, I. (1965) *The Logic of Statistical Inference*, Cambridge: Cambridge University Press.

Jeffrey, R. (2002) *Probability and the Art of Judgment*, Cambridge: Cambridge University Press.

Kyburg, H. (1970) "Conjunctivitis," in M. Swain (ed.) *Induction, Acceptance, and Rational Belief*, Dordrecht: Reidel, pp. 55–82.

Maxwell, G. (1962) "The Ontological Status of Theoretical Entities," in H. Feigl and G. Maxwell (eds) *Minnesota Studies in the Philosophy of Science*, 3, Minneapolis: University of Minnesota Press.

Sober, E. (1990) "Contrastive Empiricism," in W. Savage (ed.) *Minnesota Studies in the Philosophy of Science*, Volume 14: *Scientific Theories*, Minneapolis: University of Minnesota Press, pp. 392–412.

—— (1993) "Epistemology for Empiricists," in H. Wettstein (ed.) *Midwest Studies in Philosophy*, Volume 18: *Philosophy of Science*, Notre Dame, IN: University of Notre Dame Press, pp. 39–61.

—— (1999) "Testability," *Proceedings and Addresses of the American Philosophical Association* 73: 47–76.

—— (2008) *Evidence and Evolution: The Logic Behind the Science*, Cambridge: Cambridge University Press.

Sorensen, R. (1999) "Seeing Intersecting Eclipses," *Journal of Philosophy* 96: 25–49.

Stanford, K. (2006) *Exceeding Our Grasp: Science, History, and the Problem of Unconceived Alternatives*, New York: Oxford University Press.

Van Fraassen, B. (1980) *The Scientific Image*, Oxford: Oxford University Press.

—— (2002) *The Empirical Stance*, New Haven, CT: Yale University Press.

Further reading

Van Fraassen (1980) reacted against the scientific realism defended by J. J. C. Smart in *Between Science and Philosophy* (New York: Random House, 1968), G. Maxwell (1962), and H. Putnam's *Philosophy of Logic* (New York: Harper & Row, 1971). The anthologies edited by P. Churchland and C. Hooker, *Images of Science: Essays on Realism and Empiricism* (Chicago: University of Chicago Press, 1985), and by J. Leplin, *Scientific Realism* (Berkeley: University of California Press, 1984), contain papers replying to van Fraassen. A. Kukla's *Studies in Scientific Realism* (Oxford: Oxford University Press, 1998) reviews this debate.

13

ESSENTIALISM AND NATURAL KINDS

Brian Ellis

Natural kinds and real essences

Essentialists believe that there are objective, mind-independent, kinds of things in nature. These are the so-called "natural kinds." To explain the existence of these natural kinds, essentialists postulate that the sources of the relevant similarities and differences are intrinsic, i.e. independent of circumstances, and independent of human knowledge or understanding. Things of the same natural kind are supposed to have certain intrinsic properties or structures that together explain their manifest similarities, whereas things of different natural kinds are supposed to be intrinsically different in ways that adequately account for their manifest differences. The properties or structures that distinguish the kinds are called their "real essences."

The real essences of natural kinds are to be distinguished from their nominal essences. The real essence of a kind is the set of properties or powers that a thing must have for it to be a thing of that kind. The nominal essence of a kind (whether natural or not) is the set of properties or powers that a thing must have, or perhaps just the set of predicates that must be satisfied, for it to be *called* a thing of that kind. In either case, the statement attributing the essence to the kind is necessarily true; for there is no possible world in which it would be false. But the two kinds of necessity are nevertheless different. The kind of necessity that is associated with real essences is *metaphysical*, or *de re*, necessity, while that associated with nominal essences is *analytic*, or *de dicto*. The difference lies not in the strength of the necessity that is attributed to the relationship, but in its grounding. *De re* necessities are grounded in the real world, and have to be discovered by scientific investigation. Specifically, we have to discover what sets of intrinsic properties or structures are required to constitute things of these kinds. *De dicto* necessities are grounded in our linguistic conventions, and can be discovered by competent speakers of the language just by reflecting on how the terms designating the kinds are used. *De re* necessities are thus *a posteriori* and need to be established empirically, whereas *de dicto* necessities are knowable *a priori*.

Natural kinds may be supposed to exist in many different fields of inquiry. Accordingly, we may distinguish between essentialists by their commitments to natural kinds. To be an essentialist in biology, for example, is to believe that there are natural biological kinds, each of which has its own distinctive real essence. To be an essentialist in chemistry is to believe that there are natural chemical kinds having real essences. To be an essentialist in ontology is to believe that at least some of the most fundamental existents in nature are members of natural kinds, and that things of these kinds are distinguished by their own real essences. Aristotle was a biological essentialist. He believed that animal species were natural kinds that were distinguished from one another by their essential natures. Hilary Putnam is a chemical essentialist, as his Twin Earth example illustrates. But most of us who would claim to be essentialists without qualification are ontological essentialists. That is, we believe that natural-kinds structures go all the way down to the most basic levels of existence. This does not mean that we believe that these same sorts of structures exist at all higher levels. In fact, very few essentialists these days would claim to be economic or even biological essentialists. Most would accept chemical essentialism, the case for which appears to be overwhelming, and some form of physical essentialism, but would be skeptical of essentialist claims about the existence of natural kinds at higher levels of complexity.

Every distinct type of chemical substance would appear to be an example of a natural kind, since the known kinds of chemical substances all exist independently of human knowledge and understanding, and the distinctions between them are all real and absolute. Of course, we could not have discovered the differences between the kinds of chemical substances without a lot of scientific investigation. But these differences were not invented by us, or chosen pragmatically to impose order on an otherwise amorphous mass of data. There is no continuous spectrum of chemical variety that we had somehow to categorize. The chemical world is just not like that. On the contrary, it gives every appearance of being a world made up of substances of chemically discrete kinds, each with its own distinctive chemical properties. To suppose otherwise is to make nonsense of the whole history of chemistry since Lavoisier.

What is true of the chemical kinds is not true of biological species. The existing species of animals and plants are clusters of morphologically similar organisms whose similarities are due to their genetically similar constitutions. Our species concepts are therefore generic cluster concepts. They are not, however, generic kinds that are categorically distinct from one another, as the generic chemical kinds are. The species "elephant" has a number of sub-species, which are sub-clusters within the elephant cluster. These sub-species are distinct enough to be reliably distinguished morphologically, and sufficiently different genetically to be said to be different kinds of animals. However, if we broadened our vision to include all of the ancestors of the current elephants in the world, we should find, I think, that the morphological clusters, and the genetic clusters that explain them, would shift about as we go back in time, and would eventually overlap. Therefore, neither the generic species nor any sub-species of elephant is a natural kind in the same sense as the generic and specific chemical kinds are. Chlorine, for example, is a generic chemical kind, the species of which include the various isotopes of chlorine. But there is no species of chlorine existing now or at any other time that could possibly be a species of any element other than chlorine.

Chlorine, the generic kind, has a fixed nature, and each species of chlorine has its own fixed nature.

There are not only natural kinds of substances, which are fixed in nature as the chemical kinds are, but there are also natural kinds of processes, which are fixed in nature in the same sort of way. For every chemical equation represents some kind of process of chemical combination or dissolution. Moreover, each such kind of process is categorically distinct from every other kind of process. There are no halfway-houses, i.e. no processes between which we have arbitrarily to draw a line and say: "This is a chemical process of this kind, represented by this chemical equation, whereas that is a chemical process of this other kind, represented by this other chemical equation." Chemistry presents us with no such choices, as it surely would if the kinds of chemical processes were not categorically distinct. Therefore, if there are substantive natural kinds, as indeed every distinct kind of chemical substance undoubtedly is, then there are also dynamic natural kinds, i.e., naturally distinct kinds or events or processes.

To develop the theory of natural kinds, it is important to make a distinction between an *infimic species* of a kind and an *instance* of it. An infimic species of a natural kind is any species of the kind that has no natural sub-species. The class of electrons, for example, is an infimic species of the fundamental particles, because there are no natural sub-species of electrons. But the class of electrons is itself a natural kind. So it is a species, not an instance. The instances of the fundamental particles are all of the particular fundamental particles that there are in the world. A particular instance of particle might well be an electron. But if it is, then it is an instance of the species of electrons. The class of fundamental particles is a natural kind, but it is not infimic, since it has sub-species. It is, therefore, a generic natural kind.

In my view, there is also a third kind of natural kind, viz. natural *properties* (or natural *relations*). For, plausibly, natural properties are just natural kinds of property instances (i.e., tropes). Consider, for example, the property of unit charge, i.e., the charge on an electron. This specific charge is an infimic species of the generic property, charge. The specific property, unit charge, is instanced in every electron and in every other particle in the universe with single negative charge. But, of course, these instances of unit charge are not the electrons themselves or any of the other particles with single negative charge, since these particles are not tropes of anything other than (perhaps) the corresponding substantive natural kinds. They could not in any case be tropes of unit charge because they are not all identical. An electron and an anti-proton, for example, both have unit charge, but no electron is identical to any anti-proton.

Whether this conception of natural properties and relations is accepted or not, every essentialist is committed to what David Armstrong (1997) calls a "sparse theory of properties." Sparse theories distinguish sharply between *properties* and *predicates*. Predicates are linguistic entities that would not exist if languages did not exist. Properties and relations are universals, or, at least, natural similarity classes. Consequently, the linguistic operations of negation, conjunction, and disjunction do not apply automatically to properties, as they do to predicates. Armstrong allows conjunctive universals, but not disjunctive or negative. I do not allow any of these constructed universals automatically, although I concede that there might be universals that are related to other universals as if they were their conjuncts, disjuncts or negations.

The generic natural kinds in every category are ontologically more fundamental than any of their species. For, the generic natural kinds and properties could exist, even though none of their existing species existed. But, conversely, no species of a generic kind or property could exist if that generic kind or property did not exist. Therefore, by the usual argument for ontological dependence, the genera must take precedence over their species in the order of being. In his *A World of States of Affairs*, Armstrong argues that the reverse is the case, and that the generic kinds must be constituted by their infimic species. His conclusion certainly appeals to our intuitive belief in the ontological primacy of the ultimately specific properties of particulars. Nevertheless, there is a strong argument against this conclusion, quite apart from the one concerning the direction of ontological dependence. It is the argument that the generic kinds cannot be constituted by their species. One might, for example, try to constitute a generic kind as the disjunct of its infimic species. Disjunctive kinds like this are highly suspect in any case, as Armstrong himself has argued. But there is a further, more telling, objection. Probably, there is no object anywhere in the universe with mass $m/2$, where m is the mass of an electron. But the generic kind, mass, surely includes this species of mass as a logical possibility.

The conclusion that generic kinds are ontologically prior to their species has one very significant and pleasing consequence: it explains the overriding importance of generic kinds in the order of nature. For the laws of nature would all appear to be concerned with generic kinds of things. (See "Laws of nature" below.) Quantities are clear cases of generic properties, i.e., properties that have specific measures as their infimic species. Therefore, to the extent that the laws of nature are quantitative, they must be concerned with generic kinds.

Essentialist metaphysics

According to the theory developed in *Scientific Essentialism* (Ellis 2001; hereafter *SE*), the world consists ultimately of things belonging to natural kinds. Three kinds of natural kinds are described: substantive; dynamic; and tropic. The *substantive* natural kinds include all of the natural kinds of substances; the *dynamic* natural kinds include all of the natural kinds of events and processes; and the *tropic* natural kinds include all of the natural properties and relations. These three categories of natural kinds are hierarchically structured by the species relation. At the summit of each category, there is assumed to be a global kind, which includes all of the other natural kinds in its category. For example, the global substantive kind would be the class of all physical systems. At the base of each hierarchy are the infimic species of the global kind, i.e., the species that have no sub-species. Electrons are presumably infimic species in the category of substances. In the middle are all of the generic kinds of greater or lesser generality that exist in the world. The world is thus assumed to be a highly structured physical world. This is my *basic structural hypothesis*.

It is further assumed that every natural kind of thing, at every level of generality, has its own distinctive real essence, i.e., its unique set of intrinsic properties or structures in virtue of which things are of the kinds they are. This is the hypothesis of essentialism. For substantive kinds, it is argued that these intrinsic properties or structures must include at least some causal powers. Complex objects may have distinctive structures. Isomers, for example, may be thus distinguished. But as we descend to more elementary things, structure, involving relationships between parts necessarily drops out, and, at the most elementary level, there is no structure at all. Therefore, the most elementary things existing in the world must be essentially distinguished from each other, not by their structures, but by their causal powers alone. Electrons, for example, must be distinguished from other kinds of fundamental particles just by their causal powers.

The essence of a causal power, though, depends on what it does. Hence the causal power itself must be an intrinsically dispositional property, the full description of which must tell us what things having this property must thereby be disposed to do in the various possible circumstances in which they might exist. If the causal power is a propensity, then its full description must describe all its possible effects and the conditional probabilities of their occurring in whatever the given circumstances might be. Therefore, according to essentialist metaphysics, the most fundamental natural properties must be (a) the dispositional properties of the basic natural kinds and (b) the properties of the various possible circumstances in which they might exist. To describe the circumstances of a thing's existence, it is necessary to specify what other things exist with which it might interact, what their intrinsic properties and structures are, and how these other things are related spatio-temporally to the thing itself. Essentialist metaphysics therefore seems to require that there be at least two kinds of properties in nature: dispositional properties (causal powers, capacities and propensities) and categorical ones (spatio-temporal and numerical relations). An essentialist should therefore be a categorical realist as well as a dispositional one.

Laws of nature

Essentialists believe that the laws of nature describe the essences of the natural kinds. This is the thesis of *dispositionalism*. The global laws describe the essences of the global kinds, and hence refer to all things in their respective categories; the more specific laws refer only to the more specific kinds and their various sub-species. The applications of the laws to specific cases describe the behavior predicted of the infimic species involved in these cases. If this is true, then there are two important consequences of essentialism for the theory of laws of nature:

- There are hierarchies of laws of nature that are uniquely correlated with the hierarchies of natural kinds.

In fact, this appears to be the case.

(a) There are global laws that apply to all things in the global category of substances. Lagrange's principle of least action, for example, is a law that applies to all physical systems. The law of conservation of energy states that every event or process of the global kind, i.e., every physical event or process, is intrinsically conservative of energy. I do not know what the global laws are in the category of properties and relations, but some of the most general must surely be the fundamental laws in the theory of quantitative relationships, for example, those of spatio-temporal and of numerical relationships.

(b) There are laws concerning various kinds of substances and fields. The laws of electromagnetism, for example, are very general, but they are not really global, i.e., they do not range non-vacuously over all things in any particular category. The laws of chemistry, of particle interactions and of radioactive decay processes, are also in the intermediate range. The objects and processes described in these laws are, of course, subject to the global laws, because the global essences are ubiquitous. But the global laws do not entail the more specific ones, which depend on the more specific essences of the kinds to which they refer. What we call the applications of the laws to specific cases are more specific still, since they depend on the essences of the infimic species of the kinds of things involved.

- The laws of nature are metaphysically necessary: electrons are necessarily negatively charged; physical systems are necessarily Lagrangean; physical processes are necessarily intrinsically conservative of energy; water is necessarily H_2O; and so on.

If essentialists are right in thinking that the laws of nature describe the essences of the natural kinds, then the laws of nature are in a class of their own. For they are necessary, but are neither analytic nor formally logically necessary. Like accidental generalizations, they are *a posteriori* and can be established only by empirical inquiry; but unlike such generalizations, they are not contingent.

Objections

The metaphysics of SE have been challenged in a number of ways. John Heil (2005) does not like the theory of universals that is used, and would prefer an ontology of tropes (modes in his terminology), grouped by similarity relationships. Stephen Mumford (2005) has questioned the essentialist hypothesis (that every ontologically basic natural kind has its own distinctive real essence). John Heil and Alexander Bird (2005) have supported Sydney Shoemaker (1980, 1998) in arguing that the fundamental properties in nature must all be causal powers. Their arguments were presented at the "Ratio Conference" in Reading in 2004, and were subsequently published, along with my replies, in *Metaphysics in Science*, edited by Alice Drewery (2006). Here I take up some other issues that seem to me to need further discussion.

Counterfactuals

Scientific essentialists are thought to have great difficulty in giving an adequate account of counterfactual conditionals. John Bigelow first raised such concerns in his paper,

"Scientific Ellisianism" (1999). Bigelow's point was this: real or metaphysical possibilities are sometimes very hard to determine: "It is true that if there were a beer in front of me, I should drink it," says John. But how does anyone know that it is really possible that there could be a beer in front of him. I do not know enough about the ultimate constitution of the world to know whether this is really possible, and nor does anyone else. Certainly, it is epistemically possible, i.e., possible for all anyone knows. But how could I possibly know whether there are real possibilities of past events, which would have resulted in a beer being in front of him and which would not, at the same time, have affected his thirst or his taste for beer? Realistic evaluation of such a conditional is therefore impossible.

Bigelow is right about this. With counterfactual conditionals, we generally have to content ourselves with epistemic rather than real possibilities. That is, we must consider epistemic possibilities of counterfactual realization, and evaluate conditionals in the kind of way that Lewis does, but with reference to epistemically, rather than logically or metaphysically, possible worlds. For example, to consider the counterfactual that if there were a beer in front of John then he would drink it we have to consider what we should expect to be the case in the epistemically possible worlds most like ours in which the antecedent supposition is realized. If this is a possible world in which John would drink the beer, then the counterfactual conditional is epistemically true. If not, it is epistemically false. This concession does not worry me much, because I have long held that counterfactual conditionals are capable only of epistemic evaluation, and that a system of logic based on an epistemic concept of truth is needed to evaluate arguments involving them, as explained in my book *Rational Belief Systems*. Nevertheless, the proposed method of determining whether a given counterfactual conditional is epistemically true is open to the charge of ad hocness. For, as Marc Lange (2004) has pointed out, I have to consider epistemically possible worlds that have the same laws of nature as ours to be more like our world than any that differs from it only in matters of particular fact. Otherwise, my judgments of epistemic truth will be absurd. But this is clearly parallel to the objection that Lewis has had to face. As a Humean, Lewis was unable to provide any principled reason for judging logically possible worlds that have the same laws as ours to be more similar to our own world than any that differed from it only in matters of particular fact.

As far as I know, the charge of ad hocness has arisen in the literature only in connection with counterfactual conditionals of the form: If X were an A, then X would be a B, *where it is believed to be a law of nature that all As are Bs*, and the counterfactual supposition is being made against the background belief that X *is neither an A nor a B*. In these circumstances, there are two ways in which the antecedent supposition that X is an A could, in principle, be accommodated. One is to preserve the background information that X is not a B, and reject the law. The other is to retain the law, and reject the background information that X is not a B, thus allowing for the (undoubtedly correct) conclusion that if X were an A, then it would be a B. The allegedly ad hoc assumption (involved in the second response) is that laws take precedence over matters of contingent fact in evaluating conditionals. The charge against Lewis and others is that this move to protect the law of nature rather than the matter of particular fact in moving to accommodate the antecedent supposition is unprincipled. A Humean, who thinks that all events are loose and separate, has no obvious reply to this objection. Lange thinks that the essentialist theory of counterfactual conditionals developed in SE fares no better than Lewis's theory in its response to this charge of ad hocness.

I reject the charge of ad hocness. The theory of conditionals developed in SE was based on an essentialist ontology whose rationale had nothing to do with the theory of conditionals, and was only indirectly connected with the laws of nature. This essentialist ontology derived from my earlier physicalist one, in which all objects, events, processes, properties, and relations were supposed to be ultimately physical. The main difference is that I would now insist that the physical world is a highly structured one. Consequently, in writing SE, I began by developing an ontology that had structure built into it. My older physicalist ontology was unstructured, and so still fundamentally Humean in that respect. But the world evidently consists of vast numbers of things belonging to intrinsically exact similarity classes, the members of which have exactly similar intrinsic properties, and participate in exactly similar events and processes. I took the view that these similarity classes must reflect a natural-kinds structure of the world. On closer examination, it became clear that the natural-kind classes of this structure exist in hierarchies in each of the principal categories of existence. That is, there are hierarchies of natural kinds of objects, of events and processes, and of natural properties (i.e. natural kinds of tropes). My ontology thus became that of a physical world structured by natural-kind hierarchies. This was all contained in my basic structural hypothesis (SE: Ch. 2).

Lange argues that an essentialist is in no better position than a Humean, when it comes to making judgments concerning similarities between (epistemically) possible worlds. Therefore, my essentialist theory of conditionals is no better than a Humean one in this respect. Not so. Given the structured physicalist ontology outlined, similarities between worlds would have to be judged by similarities of both content and structure. A world with non-physical content would have to be very different from this world, as would one with a different natural kinds structure. But if the theory of laws of nature proposed in SE is accepted, sameness of natural kinds structure implies sameness of laws. For the hypothesis of essentialism is that the laws of nature describe, or derive from, the essential properties of the natural kinds.

There is nothing arbitrary or ad hoc about any of this, and it is certainly not unprincipled. The basic structural hypothesis not only explains what the laws of nature are, it also provides an explanation of the hierarchical structure of the whole system of laws, the dependence relationships among the laws, and the natural necessity of laws. So, there are good independent reasons to take the basic structural hypothesis seriously, and hence the criteria for similarity of worlds implied by it. Two epistemically possible worlds will be basically similar, according to this theory, if and only if they have the same sort of physical constitution and structure. To gauge the degree of similarity between epistemically possible physical worlds, one might give greater weight to the more general kinds of objects, properties or processes than to the more specific ones (since they are ontologically more fundamental), and hence to the most general laws of nature. But the theory of conditionals developed in SE does not depend on any such extended theory. To resolve the issue at hand, where the supposition of the truth of the antecedent of a conditional would force us to choose between a law and a particular matter of fact, it is clear that we must choose to preserve the law. For the law derives ultimately from the natural-kinds structure that defines the nature of the world in which we live.

Meinongianism

David Armstrong (1999a, 1999b) thinks that if dispositions are genuine properties that support counterfactual conditionals, then those properties must somehow *point to* the consequents of those conditionals. And this, he thinks, poses a special problem for dispositions that are never manifested. For in those cases the displays never occur and the consequents are never realized. Therefore, anything that is the bearer of an unmanifested disposition must somehow *point to* a non-existent, but presumably possible, object. Such a relationship of *pointing to*, he says, is Meinongian. Therefore, he argues, anyone who embraces dispositional realism must also be willing to accept this form of Meinongianism.

In my view, genuine dispositional properties are not essentially different from categorical ones. For the tropes of both are just relationships of *possession* between objects and universals. The difference is just in the nature of the universals involved. A trope of triangularity is a relationship between a triangular object and a tropic universal (triangularity). The same sort of thing is true of the tropes of causal powers. A trope of the causal power to dissolve sugar is an instance of the relationship between an object (e.g., the tea in the teacup) and the dynamic natural kind that is the process of dissolving sugar. Therefore, if one believes in dynamic universals, as I do, then one should have no difficulty in believing that there are tropes of causal powers, such as that of having the power to dissolve sugar, even if some of those tropes are never displayed.

Dynamic universals are universals. Therefore, a dynamic universal exists if any instance of it exists. Therefore, a natural kind of process exists if any instance of the process exists. That is all. It does not require that every possible instance of it should exist. Nor does it depend on whether any instance of it that involves the object in question exists. Therefore, the existence of a trope of a causal power in an object has nothing to do with whether it is ever exercised. It depends only on whether the dynamic universal that is the natural kind of process in question exists – which is a very different matter. The natural kind of process that is involved in the dissolving of sugar certainly does exist, and the tea in the teacup certainly exists. Why then should there be any problem with the existence of the *having* relationship between those two entities, implying that the tea in the teacup has the power to display the process of dissolving sugar? The Meinongian objection would appear to be just a storm in a teacup.

See also Biology; Chemistry; Laws of nature; Metaphysics; Philosophy of language.

References

Armstrong, D. M. (1997) *A World of States of Affairs*, Cambridge: Cambridge University Press.

—— (1999a) "Comment on Ellis," in H. Sankey (ed.) *Causation and Laws of Nature*, Dordrecht: Kluwer.

—— (1999b) "The Causal Theory of Properties: Properties According to Shoemaker, Ellis and Others," *Philosophical Topics* 26: 25–37.

Bigelow, J. C. (1999) "Scientific Ellisianism," in H. Sankey (ed.) *Causation and Laws of Nature*, Dordrecht: Kluwer.

Bird, A. (2005) "Laws and Essences," *Ratio* 18: 437–61.

Drewery, A. (ed.) (2006) *Metaphysics in Science*, Oxford: Blackwell.

Ellis, B. D. (2001) *Scientific Essentialism*, Cambridge: Cambridge University Press.

—— (2002) *The Philosophy of Nature: A Guide to the New Essentialism*, Montreal: McGill–Queen's University Press.

Heil, J. (2005) "Kinds and Essences," *Ratio* 18: 405–19.

Lange, M. (2004) "A Note on Scientific Essentialism, Laws of Nature and Counterfactual Conditionals," *Australasian Journal of Philosophy* 82: 227–41.

Mumford, S. D. (2005) "Kinds, Essences, Powers," *Ratio* 18: 420–36.

Shoemaker, S. (1980) "Causality and Properties," in P. van Inwagen (ed.) *Time and Cause*, Dordrecht: Reidel.

—— (1998) "Causal and Metaphysical Necessity," *Pacific Philosophical Quarterly* 79: 59–77.

Further reading

The most important pioneering work in the development of modern essentialism was undoubtedly R. Harré and E. H. Madden's *Causal Powers: A Theory of Natural Necessity* (Oxford: Blackwell, 1975). Important recent works on modern essentialism include J. Heil's *From an Ontological Point of View* (Oxford: Clarendon Press, 2003), G. Molnar's *Powers: A Study in Metaphysics*, edited by S. Mumford (Oxford: Oxford University Press, 2004), and S. Mumford's *Laws in Nature* (London: Routledge, 2004). The papers by S. Shoemaker (1980, 1998) are seminal, as is C. B. Martin's "Power for Realists," in K. K. Campbell and L. Reinhardt (eds) *Ontology, Causality and Mind: Essays in Honour of D. M. Armstrong* (Cambridge: Cambridge University Press, 1993). My own principal works on essentialism are (2001) and (2002).

14
ETHICS OF SCIENCE
David B. Resnik

What is the ethics of science?

The ethical questions and issues that arise in scientific inquiry correspond to the traditional branches of ethics: meta-ethics; normative ethics; and applied ethics. Thus, the *meta-ethics* of science considers the meaning and justification of ethical norms in science; the *normative ethics* of science addresses the theories, concepts, and principles that guide conduct in the sciences; and *applied ethics* of science examines specific ethical problems and dilemmas that arise in science, such as the allocation of credit, sharing data, and so on. The ethics of science also encompasses social and political issues, such as the funding of research and the intellectual property system.

The meta-ethics of science

Meta-ethics deals with questions concerning the foundations of ethics. Two of the central meta-ethical problems are the justification of ethical norms and the universality of ethical norms. These questions arise also in the ethics of science.

Justifying ethical norms in science

Science's ethical norms are part of the social epistemology of science and can be justified insofar as they are necessary for achieving the goals of scientific communities. These goals include seeking truth, avoiding error, explaining phenomena, and controlling nature. For example, honesty and objectivity are essential for acquiring truth, avoiding error, and explaining phenomena. Some ethical norms, such as openness, fair credit allocation, respect for colleagues, and respect for intellectual property, help to promote trust among scientists, which is vital to achieving the community's goals. Most scientists conduct research in groups ranging in size from several to hundreds to even thousands of researchers. Scientists share information, methods, tools, and resources; publish data and results; review and criticize each other's work; and educate and train future researchers. All of these social activities require a high degree of cooperation and trust. Finally, ethical norms also promote the goals of science by helping to secure the public's support for science. The public provides economic and social resources for scientific research, and enacts laws and regulations that pertain to science. Unethical behavior in science can erode the public's confidence in science and lead to declining public support, and increased regulation and oversight.

Since scientific communities exist in larger societies, scientific norms must also answer to broader social and moral norms and rules. For example, ethical rules and guidelines pertaining to the use of human subjects in research are based on moral norms, such as beneficence, justice, and respect for persons. Dishonesty in science is unethical because it prevents scientists from achieving their goals and because it is a form of lying, which is morally wrong. Misappropriating intellectual property is unethical in science because such conduct destroys cooperation and trust among scientists and because it is a form of theft, which is immoral. In addition to possibly violating moral norms, unethical conduct in science may also be illegal, since there are many different laws and regulations governing scientific research, including rules concerning the use of human or animal subjects, intellectual property, laboratory safety, fraud, sexual harassment, and so on.

The universality of ethical norms in science

Questions concerning the universality of science's ethical norms rehash, in some ways, traditional debates in philosophy about moral relativism. The basic problem is: Are there ethical rules that apply to all scientific disciplines at all times in all societies? Questions about the universality of ethical norms in science have arisen in contro- versies about authorship, plagiarism, treatment of data, intellectual property, human research, and animal research. In countries such as the U. S., which value individual contributions to research, scientists are concerned about receiving appropriate credit for their accomplishments, such as authorship and citation. Failure to acknowledge individual contributions is a serious ethical transgression in these countries, and can lead to accusations of plagiarism in some instances. In countries that place less weight on individual contributions, such as China and India, scientists pay less attention to accurate authorship attribution and citation. When foreign scientists and students come to the U. S. for research, education, or training, they sometimes have difficulties with adjusting to the U. S.'s rules for authorship and citation practices.

Many different questions have arisen concerning the universality of various rules for conducting research on human subjects. According to some, ethical standards for research on human subjects should be the same everywhere in the world. Informed consent is an aspect of human research that shows considerable variation around the world. In Western industrialized nations, such as the U. S., informed consent of the research subject (or the subject's legal representative) is a cornerstone of research ethics. Informed consent is usually documented with consent forms. These Western standards of informed consent can be difficult to implement in some developing countries, because communities often make medical decisions for individuals, and the people have little understanding of modern medicine or even the purpose of signing a consent document. In some cases, there may be no written language.

Ethical dilemmas have also arisen in using placebo control groups in clinical trials in the developing world when there is an effective treatment available in the developed world. In the U. S. and other Western nations, it is regarded as unethical to give research subjects with a serious illness a placebo if an effective therapy is available, since this would deny subjects in the placebo control group necessary medical treatment. In the mid-1990s, HIV researchers used placebo groups in clinical trials in developing nations to test the efficacy of an affordable treatment to prevent perinatal (mother–child) transmission of HIV, even though a more expensive therapy was available in the developing world. Critics of those clinical trials argued that it was unethical to use a placebo group, because an effective therapy was available. Defenders of the trials responded that even though an effective therapy was available in Western nations, the therapy was not available in developing nations, due to its high cost. Subjects who received the placebo were no worse off than they would have been had they not participated in the research. Critics of the trials argued also that a single standard for research on human subjects should apply throughout the world, not one standard for developed nations and another standard for developing ones. Defenders of the trials replied that ethical standards should take into account local circumstances, and that it is ethical imperialism to insist that developing nations must adhere to the same research rules and regulations that prevail in developed nations.

Questions concerning the universality of ethical standards in science have arisen in the discussion of the behavior of important figures in the history of science, such as Robert Millikan. Millikan conducted experiments with oil drops to measure the smallest electrical charge (or the charge on an electron). In his experiments, he dripped oil through electrically charges plates and measured the effect of those charges on the oil drops. Millikan rated each observation that he made as "good," "fair," or "poor." In a paper that he published on the charge of an electron, he reported only 140 of the 189 observations that he had recorded in his laboratory notebooks. Some scholars and scientists have accused Millikan of unethically trimming his data, while others have claimed that Millikan should be judged by the ethical standards of his own time – an era in which scientists were not as careful with the treatment of data as they are today. Most twenty-first-century scientists would agree that it is not appropriate to exclude data points from analysis and interpretation, unless one has a good reason to believe that they are statistical outliers or have resulted from human or experimental error. One should also discuss the decision to exclude data points from analysis and interpretation when one presents one's results to the public.

Variations among the research traditions and practices of distinct scientific disciplines also give rise to questions about the universality of ethical norms in science. There is some evidence, for example, that the various disciplines have different traditions and practices concerning authorship. While almost all disciplines hold that those listed as authors should have made a significant contribution to the publication in question, they interpret "significant contribution" differently. In some disciplines, sharing data or methods is a significant contribution; in others, it is not. In some disciplines, securing resources and funding is a significant contribution; in others, it is not. While almost all disciplines hold that the order in which authors are listed in a publication is important, there is some variation: in some disciplines, the person who makes the most significant contribution to the publication is listed ahead of the others; in other disciplines, the author whose name appears last is the most important. There is also some evidence that different disciplines have different traditions and practices concerning the sharing of data prior to publication and after publication. Some disciplines have a strong commitment to sharing data before, during, and after publication; other disciplines, especially those where patents play a key role in the research, have a weaker commitment to sharing data.

While it seems reasonable to hold that there should be some cultural, disciplinary, and historical variation in the ethical norms in science, it does not seem reasonable to hold that that there are *no* ethical norms that transcend different cultures, disciplines, and historical periods. There must be some core norms (or values) common to all of the different practices that we regard as "scientific." For example, we would not consider a discipline with no ethical prohibitions against faking data or deliberately distorting results to be a scientific discipline. Thus, adherence to the norms of *honesty* and *objectivity* constitutes a part of our definition of what it means to think or act scientifically, even though there may be some variation in the interpretation and application of those norms. Other core (or definitional) norms might be *openness* and *freedom of inquiry*. Norms that do not play a role in defining scientific research, such as respect for animal or human subjects, might function as peripheral norms rather than core norms. For example, seventeenth- and eighteenth-century anatomists performed many vivisections on animals without anesthesia or analgesia, and apparently had little concern with minimizing animal suffering. We would still call their research "science" even though it violated modern norms concerning the treatment of animals in research. By calling a norm "peripheral" I do not mean to devalue or belittle the norm, since a norm might have considerable moral or political value or significance even if it is not part of the definition of scientific inquiry. Respect for human subjects is certainly one of the most important norms in science, even though it is conceivable that some researchers, such as the Nazi scientists at Nuremburg, have flouted it while conducting methodologically sound experiments on human beings.

The normative ethics of science

The normative ethics of science focuses on the general norms (standards, values, or principles) that should guide scientific conduct. There are several different approaches to the normative ethics of science, which correspond to different approaches to normative ethics. According to the top–down (or theory-based) approach, general ethical theories, such as utilitarianism, Kantianism, natural rights, or virtue ethics, should guide scientific conduct. According to the bottom–up (or casuist) approach, precedents set by different cases should guide scientific conduct. According to the mid-level (or principle-based) approach, ethical values, such as honesty, social responsibility, and the like, should guide scientific conduct.

While ethical theories can provide valuable insight into ethical dilemmas and problems in science, and while it is also important to examine previous cases when deciding how to act in a particular case, I think that the principle-based approach offers the best account of the normative ethics of science. I reject the theory-based approach because ethical theories can be very difficult for scientists to understand and apply. Scientific norms should provide researchers with guidance concerning particular decisions and actions. Theories are not well-suited to that task. I reject the casuist approach because it does not provide scientists with a reasonable method for justifying their decisions to supervisors, colleagues, clients, and the public. Scientific norms should provide researchers with a consistent, coherent framework that they can use in accounting for their conduct. Casuistry is not well-suited to this task, because it does not develop general rules or principles.

What follows is a list of ethical norms that should guide scientific reasoning and conduct. The first ten apply to all scientific disciplines, but the final two – humane treatment of animal subjects and respect for human subjects – apply only to those disciplines that use animal or human subjects.

Honesty

Scientists should practice honesty in research and publication, and in their interactions with peers, research sponsors, oversight agencies, and the public. As noted earlier, this norm helps to promote the goals of science and is supported by broader moral norms. Dishonesty in science may also violate laws or regulations. Legal prohibitions against data fabrication and falsification are based on the scientific commitment to honesty.

Objectivity

Scientists should strive for objectivity in research and publication, and in their interactions with peers, research sponsors, oversight agencies, and the public. If one assumes that truth and knowledge are objective, then this norm also helps to promote science's epistemic goals of truthfulness and error-avoidance. Strategies and methods designed to minimize bias and error in research, such as good record-keeping practices, the peer review system, replication of results, and conflict of interest rules, are based on a commitment to objectivity. Scientists also have an obligation to strive for objectivity when giving expert testimony in court, or when serving on government panels and committees.

Openness

Scientists should share data, results, ideas, methods, tools, techniques, and resources. As noted earlier, science is a social activity that involves cooperation and trust. It is important, therefore, for scientists to share with one another. To paraphrase Isaac Newton, all scientists stand on the shoulders of giants. Openness is vital to publication, peer review, replication, and other strategies and methods that promote objectivity. Even though openness is a very important norm in scientific research, it sometimes conflicts with legitimate demands for secrecy and confidentiality. For example, researchers are justified in not sharing unpublished data and results in order to protect their claims to priority or intellectual property and their work from premature dissemination. Secrecy is also justified in peer review, personnel decisions, research on human subjects, and in research sponsored by the military or private industry.

Freedom

Scientists should be free to conduct research without political or religious intimidation, coercion, or censorship. This norm applies to institutions and organizations that support and oversee science, as well as the political systems in the countries where science is conducted. Freedom is vital to innovation, discovery, and criticism in science, since scientists need to be free to develop or pursue new ideas and to question old ones. For hundreds of years, scientists have had to defend their intellectual freedom against opponents. In the seventeenth century, the Inquisition put Galileo Galilei under house arrest for disobeying the Roman Catholic Church's demand that he recant his contention that the earth is not the center of the universe. In the twentieth century, the Soviet Union punished, intimidated, suppressed, and exiled biologists who did not agree with Lysenkoism, a biological theory endorsed by the communist regime. Although freedom of inquiry is crucial to science, there are some limits to the extent of such freedom. First, a right to free inquiry is not a right to receive funding. Research sponsors, such as private corporations and governments, can decide how best to invest their research and development (R&D) budgets. In making R&D funding decisions, corporations have an obligation to earn profits for the company and its shareholders; and in deciding how to allocate R&D funds, government agencies have an obligation to promote the public good. Second, a right to free inquiry is not a right to violate laws, rules, or regulations designed to protect human or animal research subjects, intellectual property, the public health, national security, or other important social goods.

Fair credit allocation

Scientists should give credit, but only where credit is due. This principle is important in promoting scientific collaboration and cooperation, since people who work together on a project or publication deserve to receive credit for their contributions. People who publish their research also want to be cited properly when others use their findings. Prohibitions against plagiarism, and rules pertaining to scientific authorship reflect science's commitment to fair credit allocation. Although disputes about credit allocation do not seem to have as much moral significance as debates about respecting human or animal subjects, they mean a great deal to scientists. Publication, priority, and citation are the coinage of science. Indeed, there is evidence that a large percentage of the ethical disputes in science involve controversies about credit allocation.

Respect for colleagues

Scientists should treat their peers, subordinates, students, and supervisors with respect. This norm is important for building and maintaining cooperation and trust among scientists, and is supported by the moral requirement to respect persons. It implies ethical duties to refrain from engaging in practices that show disrespect for colleagues, such as sexual and non-sexual harassment, discrimination, abuse, and exploitation.

Respect for property

Scientists should respect physical and intellectual property belonging to individuals, institutions, and organizations. This norm is also important in building and maintaining cooperation and trust in scientific research, and promotes collaboration among researchers and among institutions and organizations that support research. People are less likely to share their property when they believe that it may be damaged, destroyed, or stolen. Physical properties in research include such items as cell and tissue samples, reagents, organisms, scientific instruments, and computer technology. Intellectual properties include data, patented inventions, and copyrighted original works.

Respect for laws

Scientists should comply with the laws, regulations, policies, and guidelines that pertain to their work. There are many different laws that govern scientific research, including government rules and regulations, institutional and organizational policies, and professional guidelines and codes. Compliance with those rules is important in securing public support for science and in promoting trust among scientists and research institutions and organizations. Additionally, scientists have a moral obligation to obey laws because laws protect people from harm and promote social stability. Laws and other rules govern many areas of research, such as experimentation on human or animal subjects, laboratory practices, radiation safety, conflict of interest, harassment, discrimination, controlled substances, restricted biological agents, technology transfer, record-keeping, management of funds, fraud, and intellectual property. Even though scientists have an obligation to adhere to laws and other rules that govern their work, they have a right to protest or deliberately violate laws they believe to be immoral, unjust, or antithetical to scientific progress. Conscientious objection sometimes has a place in scientific research. For example, during the sixteenth century, it was illegal in many European countries to dissect the human body, but Andreas Vesalius disobeyed such laws in order to advance the study of human anatomy. One might argue that Vesalius was justified in violating the law because it placed unethical restrictions on human freedom and stifled progress in research on human anatomy. As noted earlier, Galileo disobeyed the Church in the name of scientific progress.

Stewardship of research resources

Scientists should take appropriate care of physical, human, technological, and financial resources used in research. Scientists make use of many resources in conducting research, including equipment and tools; money and investments; laboratories, rooms, and buildings; samples and specimens; geographical sites and regions; and human communities. Stewardship of resources is important to help advance the goals of science and to promote public support for scientific endeavor. For example, in studying the remains of an ancient city, it is important for archeologists to avoid damaging the site, so that other researchers may also study it. If scientists mismanage or waste public funds, then the public will be less inclined to trust them with public money in the future.

Social responsibility

Scientists engage in activities that enhance or promote social goods, such as human health, public safety, education, agriculture, transportation, and scientists therefore should strive to avoid harm to individuals and society. There are many different ways that scientists can fulfill their social responsibilities, such as: testifying in legal proceedings or government hearings; educating the public about science; promoting science education in elementary, high school, and college education; warning government agencies and the public about dangerous substances, activities, or conditions; and conducting research which benefits the public. Some of the most significant events in the history of modern science have involved researchers exercising what they regarded as their responsibilities to society. For instance, during the Second World War, Albert Einstein wrote to President Franklin Roosevelt urging him to develop the atomic bomb before Nazi Germany would be able to develop the weapon. After the war, many scientists who were involved in the effort to develop atomic weapons turned their attention to preventing the spread of nuclear weapons and promoting peaceful uses of nuclear power. Scientists have social responsibilities for several reasons. First, like other people in society, scientists have a moral duty to benefit others and avoid doing harm. Second, since scientists receive a great deal of public support through their careers, they have an obligation to repay society for its investment in their education and research. Third, socially responsible science helps to promote public support: people will be less inclined to fund science if they regard researchers as socially irresponsible, "mad scientists."

Humane treatment of animal subjects

Scientists should protect and promote the welfare of animals used in research. Scientists use animal subjects in many different areas of biomedical research, ranging from toxicity testing on mice to neurological studies of pigeon brains, to studies of primate behavior. There is not sufficient space in this essay to cover arguments for and against using animals in research. Although many people have voiced moral objections to using animals in research, there is little doubt that animals make important contributions to our understanding of biology and human health. There are three principles pertaining to the humane treatment of animals in research: *reduction* (whenever feasible, one should reduce the total number of animals used in research); *replacement* (whenever feasible, one should replace animal subjects with, for example, animal tissues or cells); and *refinement* (one should refine experimental techniques to minimize pain and distress in animals). There are several reasons why researchers should treat animals humanely. First, inhumane treatment of animals can bias research results, because animals experiencing tremendous pain or distress do not react like animals under minimal pain or distress. Second, scientists, like all other members of society, have an obligation to minimize pain and suffering in animals. Third, humane treatment of animals helps to promote public support for science, because most people are morally opposed to unnecessary animal pain and suffering.

Respect for human subjects

Scientists should respect the rights of human subjects and protect them from harm and exploitation. Human subjects participate in many types of research, ranging from psychological studies of human cognition, emotion, and behavior, to social and anthropological studies of human societies, to biomedical studies of treatments for human diseases. The reasons for treating human subjects with respect are familiar and obvious. First, scientists, like in the rest of society, have obligations to refrain from violating the rights of other people or harming or exploiting them. Second, respect for human subjects helps to promote public support for science, since most people will disapprove of research that violates human rights or harms or exploits people. A range of ethical principles relate to respect for human subjects in research. While there is not sufficient space in this essay to discuss them in depth, I mention five:

- *informed consent* (human subjects should not be used in research without their informed consent or the consent of their legal representatives);
- *beneficence* (researchers should promote the welfare of human subjects and implement procedures designed to minimize harm to human subjects);
- *privacy* (researchers should protect the privacy and confidentiality of human subjects);
- *justice* (researchers distribute the benefits and burdens of research fairly and should select subjects equitably);
- *scientific validity* (researchers should not enroll human subjects in experiments that are poorly designed and are unlikely to yield scientifically useful results).

Comments about science's ethical norms

It will be useful now to make a few comments about the norms.

First, the norms should be understood as entailing *prima facie* obligations. The norms (or principles) are rules of thumb, rather than exceptionless rules. The norms may sometimes conflict with each other or with various regulations, laws, or policies. When conflicts arise, scientists must decide which norm, regulation, law, or policy to follow. For example, *openness* may conflict with *social responsibility* if sharing information can cause significant harms to society. Thus, if a researcher develops a method for modifying a common virus to make it increase its virulence, he or she might decide against publishing the research out of concern that the information could be used by terrorists to make a bioweapon. If a scientist has signed a contract with a company that requires her to not divulge the company's confidential information, and she discovers that the company is keeping important information from the scientific community concerning the hazards of a drug manufactured by the company, then she must decide whether to adhere to the requirements of the contract or to fulfill her social responsibilities by disclosing that confidential information. To decide on the best course of action to take when conflicts arise, scientists must carefully weigh and balance different norms, rules, and policies in light of the relevant facts.

Second, the norms of scientific research should be understood as prescribing conduct not as describing it. The norms instruct scientists how they ought to act; they do not state facts about what scientists usually do. Sociologists of science, most notably Robert Merton, have attempted to describe norms adopted by scientists. The prescriptive norms discussed in this essay are not based on empirical research into the practice of science. Rather, they are derived from a philosophical and conceptual analysis of the role of ethics in scientific inquiry. This need not imply, however, that scientists seldom or never adhere to the prescriptive norms discussed here; far from it. It is likely that most scientists (and scientific organizations) follow most of those norms most of the time. Indeed, it is difficult to conceive how science could have progressed if scientists (and scientific organizations) have not adhered to most of these norms most of the time. The ethics of scientific research thus helps to explain the successes of science.

Third, as is often the case with ethical principles and standards, some of these norms overlap with or duplicate laws, regulations, institutional policies, and professional codes. Scientists do not face an ethical dilemma when the norms of science agree with laws, regulations, codes, or institutional policies, but, as noted above, they do face a dilemma when such a conflict arises.

Acknowledgements

This research is supported by the Intramural Program of the NIEHS/NIH. The ideas and opinions in this essay do not represent the views of the NIEHS, the NIH, or the U. S. Government.

See also Biology; Values in science.

Further reading

For books that cover the philosophical foundations of the ethics of science, see D. Resnik, *The Ethics of Science* (New York: Routledge, 1998); and K. Shrader-Frechette, *Ethics of Scientific Research* (Lanham, MD: Rowman & Littlefield, 1994). For books that explore ethical and policy dilemmas in scientific research, see A. Shamoo and D. Resnik, *Responsible Conduct of Research* (New York: Oxford University Press, 2003); F. Macrina, *Scientific Integrity*, 3rd edn (Washington, DC: American Society of Microbiology Press, 2005); and N. Steneck, *ORI Introduction to Responsible Conduct of Research* (Washington, DC: Office Research Integrity, 2004). For an overview of social epistemology, see A. Goldman, *Knowledge in a Social World* (New York: Oxford University Press, 1999). For an exegesis of the social epistemology of science, see P. Kitcher, *The Advancement of Science* (New York: Oxford University Press, 1994).

15

EXPERIMENT

Theodore Arabatzis

It might, of course, be the case, that in experimental physics the method for establishing general laws were the same as in astronomy… But it is not so. And that is small wonder. The physicist has full liberty to interfere with his object and to set the conditions of experiment at will. This empowers him to invent methods widely different from, and largely superior to, the placid observation of the astronomer. (Schrödinger 1955: 13)

Although experimentation has been a staple feature of modern science since the seventeenth century, it was only recently, during the 1980s, that experimental practice attracted the attention of philosophers of science. This chapter addresses some of the salient philosophical issues concerning experiment and its relation to theory that emerged in that period. I will argue that the philosophical analysis of experimentation compels us to reconsider a central tenet of post-positivist philosophy of science, namely the theory-ladenness of observation and its implications for theory choice. To place contemporary philosophical debates on experiment in historical perspective, I start with a brief sketch of the birth of systematic experimentation in the seventeenth century. (For a more detailed history and a bibliography see Arabatzis 2005.)

The early history and philosophy of experiment

In Aristotelian natural philosophy, which had been dominant until the seventeenth century, unaided observation and everyday experience played a prominent role in the investigation of nature. In the seventeenth century that role was gradually taken over by experiment – the active *interrogation* of nature, an intervention in natural processes, and a manipulation of nature's forces. The rise of experimentation, of which Francis Bacon was an early and influential advocate, was accompanied by the invention of new scientific instruments that performed three different functions. First, they expanded the senses (e.g., the telescope, the microscope). Second, they made possible the production of controlled and, sometimes, artificial conditions (e.g., the air-pump); under those conditions new phenomena were created. Third, they were used to register the quantitative changes of a physical magnitude (e.g., the barometer).

The new "experimental philosophy" was greeted with skepticism on two different grounds. Its critics pointed out two difficulties with regard to experimentation. First, in contrast to the phenomena that could be observed with the unaided senses, the phenomena created by experiment were neither familiar nor accessible to everyone. Second, it was unclear why the manipulation of nature by means of instruments would reveal, rather than distort, its workings. Those difficulties were two aspects of the same issue, namely the authentication of experimental results; an issue which had to be resolved before experimentation could become a proper foundation for natural philosophy. Experimental philosophers addressed this issue in two ways. First, they stressed that experimentally produced phenomena could be replicated at will and, therefore, could not be idiosyncratic artifacts of particular experimental setups. Second, they performed many of their experiments in public and presented their results in meticulously detailed experimental reports. In this manner the readers of those reports could *witness* the experiments in question and convince themselves of the validity of the results obtained. Thus, in the eighteenth century the validation of experimental knowledge, which had been hotly debated in the preceding century, was no longer regarded as a significant philosophical issue.

In the nineteenth and the early twentieth century the few philosophers who wrote on experiment focused their reflections on different issues. John Stuart Mill, for instance, was mainly interested in the potential of experiment for establishing causal links between phenomena. Echoing Bacon, he stressed the "inherent imperfection of direct induction when not founded on experimentation" (Mill 1886: 252). The imperfection he had in mind concerned the detection of causal relations: "Observation … without experiment … can ascertain sequences and co-existences, but cannot prove causation" (*ibid.*: 253). His analysis of experimental methodology aimed at formulating a number of, more or less effective, methods for inferring the presence of causal connections (see *ibid.*: 253–66).

Another prominent example of a late nineteenth-century philosopher–scientist who discussed experiment is Pierre Duhem. His reflections on experiment concerned its outcome, experimental results, and their relationship to scientific theory. Duhem put forward three theses which set the stage for many subsequent debates in the philosophy of science. The first thesis is that experimental results are theory-laden:

> An experiment in physics is the precise observation of phenomena accompanied by an *interpretation* of these phenomena; this interpretation substitutes for the concrete data really gathered by observation abstract and symbolic representations which correspond to them by virtue of the theories admitted by the observer.
>
> […]
>
> The result of the operations in which an experimental physicist is engaged is by no means the perception of a group of concrete facts; it is the formulation of a judgment interrelating certain abstract and symbolic ideas which theories alone correlate with the facts really observed. (Duhem 1954: 147)

Thus, according to Duhem, theoretical knowledge is essential for the expression and interpretation of an experiment's outcome.

The theory-ladenness of experimental results led Duhem to a second thesis, namely that there is a gap between the observed facts and the corresponding experimental results. Scientists who believe in different theories will interpret the same observations using different theoretical terms (cf. *ibid.*: 160–1). This gap is also due to another factor, namely the limited precision of our measuring instruments. Because of the approximate character of our measurements, it is possible to formulate, using the same theoretical concepts, infinitely many rival hypotheses that are compatible with the same data:

> The same practical fact may correspond to an infinity of logically incompatible theoretical facts; the same group of concrete facts may be made to correspond in general not with a single symbolic judgment but with an infinity of judgments different from one another and logically in contradiction with one another. (*Ibid.*: 152; see also pp. 162, 199)

For example, one could come up with infinitely many experimentally indistinguishable hypotheses that differ merely in the values they assign to a constant.

Finally, Duhem's third thesis concerns the theory–experiment relationship and it has become one of the most widely discussed issues in twentieth-century philosophy of science. Duhem stressed the holistic character of theory-testing. Experimental results falsify or confirm "a whole group of hypotheses" (*ibid.*: 187). Predictions cannot be derived from isolated hypotheses; rather "a whole group of hypotheses" is necessary to obtain a prediction. When the prediction is contradicted by experiment, "at least one of the hypotheses constituting this group is unacceptable and ought to be modified; but the experiment does not designate which one should be changed" (*ibid.*). When, on the other hand, a prediction is experimentally confirmed, the confirmation applies to the whole set of hypotheses under test:

> the agreement of the calculated predictions with the results of the measurements no longer, then, confirms this or that isolated proposition of ... [a] theory, but the whole set of ... hypotheses that must be invoked in order to interpret each of ... [the] experiments. (Ibid.: 199)

Duhem's analysis of experiment focused on its end-products, rather than on the process and practice of experimentation. In this respect it differs from more recent philosophical work on experiment, which has returned to some of the epistemological issues that occupied natural philosophers in the seventeenth century.

The place of experiment in twentieth-century philosophy of science

The debates over the legitimacy of experiment were largely over by the end of the seventeenth century. Ever since, experiment has become a crucial driving force in the development of the natural sciences. It is worth pointing out that before the late nineteenth century very few scientists, even in physics, confined themselves solely to theory. Even such famous theoreticians as James Clerk Maxwell and Hermann von Helmholtz were adept experimentalists, and physicists, then as now, took a keen interest in experimental results. But despite the indisputable importance of experimentation for science, it was ignored by philosophers of science for most of the twentieth century. It was considered either uninteresting or insignificant from an epistemological point of view.

Logical empiricists did not focus their philosophical talents on experimental practice. The only aspect of experimentation that interested those philosophers was its final product, namely observations and experimental results. These were deemed to play a crucial role in the formulation and testing of empirical laws, which were in turn systematized and explained by higher-level scientific theories.

Karl Popper and his followers, who also formed an influential school in twentieth-century philosophy of science, had more to say about experimental practice, but they portrayed it as an activity guided entirely by theoretical questions and interests. An experiment, according to Popper, is always performed to answer a question or to test a conjecture which has been posed by a theoretician. In that sense, experiment has no independence from theory (Popper 1968: 107). I will have more to say about this below.

With the historicist turn in the philosophy of science in the 1960s and 1970s, the autonomy of experimentation was downplayed still further. Post-positivist philosophers of science (Norwood Russell Hanson, Thomas Kuhn, and Paul Feyerabend, among others) attributed a primary role to theory and claimed that even the most elementary observations are "theory-laden." Those philosophers, like Duhem long before them, pointed out that observational reports are couched in theoretically loaded language; but they moved beyond Duhem in highlighting the crucial influence of theoretical beliefs and expectations on perception. Drawing on psychological experiments, they argued that two observers with different theoretical beliefs will see different things when they look at the *same* object. In the heated debates that followed in the wake of the historicist turn it was widely assumed that the theory-ladenness of observations and experimental results undermined completely its privileged status as a neutral arbiter between competing theories.

While philosophy of science as a discipline was oriented for a long time towards the theoretical aspects of the scientific enterprise, that one-dimensional orientation has now been exposed and criticized. Ian Hacking's work has been decisive in redressing the neglect of experiment and in bringing out its philosophical significance (Hacking 1983). Following Hacking's, by now, classic *Representing and Intervening*, experimental activity became a subject of philosophical scrutiny and post-positivist theses, such as the theory-ladenness of observation, were reconsidered and challenged. Besides Hacking, several "experimentalist" historians, philosophers, and sociologists of science have contributed to the exploration of experimental practice (see, e.g., Collins 1992; Franklin 1986; Galison 1987, 1997; Gooding et al. 1989). The focus of these more recent discussions has been on the authentication of experimental results and the epistemological import of instrumentation.

I touch on three of the issues highlighted by the new experiment-oriented philosophy of science. The first concerns the significance of observation for obtaining scientific knowledge. In Hacking's words, "Observation, as a primary source of data, has always been a part of natural science, but it is not all that important" (1983: 167). What is important is experimental practice: the design, construction, and running of experimental setups which reveal or produce phenomena in a reliable manner. An essential aspect of this practice

> is getting to know when the experiment is working. That is one reason why observation in the philosophy-of-science usage of the term, plays a relatively small role in experimental science. Noting and reporting of dials ... is nothing. Another kind of observation is what counts: the uncanny ability to pick out what is odd, wrong, instructive or distorted in the antics of one's equipment. (*Ibid.*: 230)

As this passage indicates, the focus of philosophical analysis has shifted from the final product of experimentation, experimental reports and observational results, to experimental practice itself. The point now is to understand the process of discovering, or creating, new experimental facts and thereby to develop an epistemology of experiment, a theory of experimentally obtained knowledge.

Second, several commentators on experiment have stressed that the function of experimentation is not limited to the testing of scientific theories. Its scope is much wider, extending from the measurement of physical constants to aiding the construction of scientific theories and the systematic exploration of phenomena. Experiments are often made for the purposes of exploring a new domain, without having any systematic high-level theory to guide their design and implementation (Steinle 2002).

The third issue concerns the thesis that observation is theory-laden. The philosophical analysis of experimental practice has been used to downplay the significance of that thesis. In particular, the view that the theory-ladenness of the experimental process hinders the objective evaluation and testing of scientific theories has come under attack. I examine these issues below in more detail.

Towards an epistemology of experiment

The study of experimental practice has raised several issues whose significance had been overlooked. One such question is: "How does an experiment end?" This question is crucial for understanding the process of experimentation because in every experiment there are many (potentially infinite) factors which may influence the phenomenon under investigation and distort the experimental results. The decision to terminate an experiment is taken when the experimentalist has good reasons to believe that all the likely sources of "noise" have been identified and eliminated (Galison 1987).

What is involved in this decision can be shown by means of an example (adapted from *ibid.*: 2–3). At the end of the eighteenth century Henry Cavendish designed an apparatus for measuring the gravitational force between two objects. On either end of a wooden arm he hung a lead ball and suspended the arm horizontally by a thin wire. Near each of those balls he placed a larger lead ball. The attraction between the larger and the smaller balls would cause the arm to rotate, but the force in question was minute (0.000002 percent of the weight of the small ball). To detect it accurately the temperature throughout the room where the experiment was performed had to be constant. If not, then the temperature differences would give rise to currents that would rotate the arm. To eliminate such currents, Cavendish placed his apparatus in a sealed room and employed a remote-control mechanism. Furthermore, he observed the motion of the arm with a telescope. In these ways, he tried to eliminate possible distortion of the measurements he obtained. The design of his apparatus was based on his prior theoretical and experimental knowledge of the various factors that could influence its operation.

As the above example illustrates, one way to eliminate "noise" is by experimental design. Often, however, this is not possible. In those cases experimentalists attempt to either measure or calculate the likely distorting factors and, thereby, to figure out whether they influence their results. Cavendish, for instance, placed his apparatus in a wooden case to protect it from the wind. He wondered whether the gravitational attraction exerted by the case on the suspended balls would be strong enough to distort his measurements. He calculated the force in question and showed that the effect was insignificant.

The question concerning the end of an experiment may now be reformulated as follows: When does the experimenter decide that he or she has eliminated all the significant sources of "noise" and, therefore, that the obtained results are valid? Sometimes the experimenter's decision is based on the stability of experimental results. The achievement of stability is a good indication that the sources of "noise," which usually vary randomly, have been screened off (Galison 1987; Steinle 2002). In general, experimenters use various methods to ensure the validity of their results. Whenever similar experiments lead to discordant results, these methods are essential for figuring out which of those results are faulty. The analysis and explication of these methods is a central task of the epistemology of experimentation.

Of course, the application of these methods is not algorithmic. They require judgment and thus leave room for disagreement. Realist philosophers of experiment recognize the essential role of judgment in experimentation, but they insist that disagreements about the validity of experimental results are rationally resolved, on the basis of good reasons and persuasive arguments (see, e.g., Franklin 2002). Relativist sociologists of science, on the other hand, have capitalized on the non-algorithmic character of experimental practice to throw doubt on the veracity of experimentally established facts (see, e.g., Collins 1992). The fact that the experimenters' decisions involve various judgments has been used to argue that scientific facts are social constructions. According to the early and most radical version of social constructivism, the constraints of nature on the products of scientific activity are minimal. Data are selected or even constructed in a process which reflects the social interactions within the relevant scientific community. Therefore, one should not appeal to the material world to explain the generation and acceptance of scientific knowledge.

When pressed, social constructionists concede that arguments and reasons play a role in scientific debates over experimental results, but they deny that those reasons and arguments determine the choices made by scientists. Those choices may be reasonable, but they are not rationally compelling. The closure of scientific controversies is never solely the result of rational argumentation. Other contingent social factors (e.g., professional interests) affect scientific decision making and play a role in bringing protracted debates to a conclusion.

The social constructionists' case is based on detailed empirical studies of scientific controversies and, therefore, its rebuttal would be more effective if it were based on a scrutiny of those studies. I think, though, that one may also offer a more general response to the constructionist challenge. One should grant that scientists' decisions are the outcome of judgments which cannot be reduced to an algorithm. This point goes back to Duhem, who stressed: "Pure logic is not the only rule for our judgments," which rely essentially on "good sense" (Duhem 1954: 217). He also pointed out, however, that good sense is the key for understanding scientific controversies. These do "not last forever. The day arrives when good sense comes out so clearly in favor of one of the two sides that the other side gives up the struggle *even though pure logic would not forbid its continuation*" (*ibid*.: 218). It may be true that what counts as good sense is sometimes subject to *negotiations* within the scientific community, but one should recognize that this social process leads to "experimental conclusions [which] have a stubbornness not easily canceled by theory change" (Galison 1987: 259). The robustness and stability of experimental knowledge would be hard to understand if it were solely a product of contingent, non-epistemic, factors. To avoid this difficulty, one could view *good sense* as an evolving product of a long learning process. Its explication is an important task facing the philosophy of experiment.

The exploratory role of experiment and its relationship to theory

It used to be the prevailing view of experiment that its main aim is to test theoretical predictions:

> The theoretician puts certain definite questions to the experimenter, and the latter, by his experiments, tries to elicit a decisive answer to these questions, and to no others ... the theoretician must long before have done his work, or at least what is the most important part of his work: he must have formulated his question as sharply as possible. (Popper 1968: 107)

By tying experiment to theoretical expectations, this view compromises the autonomy and exploratory character of experimental practice. The new philosophy of experiment, on the other hand, denies that there must "be a conjecture under test in order for an experiment to make sense" (Hacking 1983: 154). Many experiments are performed without the guidance of an articulated theoretical framework and aim to discover and explore new phenomena. If by "theory" we mean a developed and articulated body of knowledge, then the history of science abounds in examples of pre-theoretical observations and experiments. For instance, many electrical phenomena were discovered in the eighteenth century by experiments which had not been guided by any developed theory of electricity. The systematic attempts to detect and stabilize those phenomena were part and parcel of their conceptualization and theoretical understanding (Steinle 2002).

To investigate the relationship between experiment and theory one should take into account that "theory" has a wide scope, extending from vague qualitative hypotheses to precise mathematical constructs. These different kinds of theory influence experimental practice in different ways. A *desideratum* in the philosophy of experiment is to understand the role of various levels of theoretical commitment in the design and implementation of experiments. It is clear, for instance, that theoretical beliefs often help experimentalists to isolate the phenomena they investigate from the ever-present "noise" and "provide essential ... constraints on acceptable data" (Galison 1987: 73).

Furthermore, the role of experiment in the testing of scientific theories has to be re-examined. In particular, we have to rethink the post-positivist view that the theory-ladenness of observation (or, rather, experimentation) undermines the objectivity of theory choice. For that purpose we have to understand the kinds of theoretical knowledge employed in the design, implementation, and description of experiments. In philosophical analyses of theory-testing, the theory that informs the design and understanding of the instruments employed in an experiment is often confused with the theory under test. Duhem, for example, thought that "when the theory to be subjected to test by the facts is ... a theory of physics ... it is impossible to leave outside the laboratory door the theory that we wish to test, for without theory it is impossible to regulate a single instrument or to interpret a single reading" (Duhem 1954: 182). If that were the case, the confirmation of a physical theory by an experiment would be suspect, the expected outcome of a circular procedure. If an experiment presupposed the very theory under test, then it would occasion no surprise if the obtained results ended up confirming the theory. Moreover, the comparative testing of two different theories on the basis of experimental evidence would be jeopardized, since experimental results would not provide a neutral ground for comparing the two theories. Suppose, for instance, that the results of an experiment support one theory (T_1) and oppose another (T_2). If the experiment presupposed T_1, then the proponents of T_2 might reasonably dispute the validity of the experiment's results.

In practice, there is usually no overlap between the background knowledge that makes an experiment possible and the theory that the experiment is supposed to test. In Hacking's aptly chosen words, "Seldom is the modeling of a piece of apparatus or an instrument the same as the theory in question" (1992: 45). The theory-ladenness of experimentation does not have to compromise the comparative evaluation of theories, because the crucial experiments that are designed and carried out for that purpose do not usually involve any of the competing theories. A historical example will illustrate this point. In 1896 the Dutch physicist Pieter Zeeman discovered that the spectral lines of a radiating substance split under the influence of a magnetic field. In the design and running of his experiments Zeeman relied on substantial theoretical and experimental knowledge to eliminate several factors which could have distorted his results. Furthermore, those results were obtained by means of a sophisticated instrument, the so-called "Rowland grating," whose operation was informed by the wave theory of light. That theory and the rest of the knowledge that Zeeman drew upon were independent of the theoretical explanations of his results which were subsequently put forward. Somewhat simplifying the historical situation, we could say that there were two alternative theoretical accounts of the Zeeman effect: one based on classical electromagnetic theory; the other on the quantum theory of the atom. For a long time neither theory was able to explain fully the complex experimental data associated with the Zeeman effect. Finally, in 1925 the quantum theory, supplemented by the novel concept of spin, made possible a satisfactory explanation of the phenomenon in question, which superseded the corresponding classical account. The important point is that the design of Zeeman's experiments and the reasons that convinced the physics community of the validity of his results did not involve either of the two theories that were subsequently put forward to account for them. Thus, the results in question provided a neutral ground, with respect to the two theories, which made possible their objective comparative evaluation (for details see Arabatzis 1992).

It is worth pointing out here that even when the theory employed in the design of an experiment is the same as the theory under test, its confirmation is not *a priori* guaranteed. As Dudley Shapere has remarked, the fact that the theory under test coincides with the theory which informs the experimental process

> by no means makes it impossible that ... [this] theory might be questioned, modified, or even rejected as a consequence of the experiment. It is not a logical or necessary truth that it could be so questioned; but *as a matter of fact*, we find that, despite the employment of the same theory ... disagreement between prediction and observation results. And that disagreement could eventuate in the alteration or even rejection of [the] theory despite its pervasive role in determining the entire observation-situation. (Shapere 1982: 516)

Suppose, for example, that we want to test the hypothesis that metals expand when they are heated. For that purpose, we need to obtain measurements of the temperature of various metals. If we use a mercury thermometer to perform those measurements, then there is no guarantee that the hypothesis of the thermal expansion of metals will be confirmed, even though our beliefs about how the thermometer works are based on that very hypothesis.

Furthermore, in cases such as the above the refuting import of disconfirming results would be more clear-cut than in situations where the hypothesis under test and the auxiliary hypotheses informing the experiment are different. In the latter, but not in the former, one could retain the hypothesis under test by modifying some of the auxiliary hypotheses.

Concluding remarks: the autonomy of experimental practice

I have argued that experimental practice is largely independent of high-level explanatory theories. The recognition of this autonomy prompts us to rethink the history of the sciences and, in particular, how we divide that history into periods. The well-known revolutions in the history of the physical sciences (e.g., the transition from classical physics to relativistic and quantum physics) were theoretical upheavals that were not accompanied by corresponding changes in the practices of experimental scientists. Conversely, important breaks in experimental practice did not have an immediate effect on the theoretical understanding of nature. For example, in the advancement of twentieth-century experimental microphysics there were, at least, two significant breaks. First, there was a transition from experiments with instruments that provided information for the average behavior of particles to experiments with instruments that could detect individual particles. The second break was the transition from relatively low-scale and low-cost tabletop experiments to extremely expensive and collectively performed experiments on an enormous industrial scale. These transitions were not immediately followed by corresponding breaks in physical theory. Thus, the development of experimentation and instrumentation requires its own history, which will turn out to be largely independent of the development of high-level theory (Galison 1997).

The philosophy of experimentation reflects a promising shift from an exclusive philosophical preoccupation with the end products of scientific activity to a systematic investigation of that activity itself. This shift has led to a novel view of science. Science, on this view, is not simply a changing body of knowledge, codified in textbooks and research papers, but an evolving array of practices. Those practices have many aspects. Besides those familiar to philosophers of science, such as the formulation and testing of theories, there are other, more *pedestrian*, aspects, such as the design and construction of instruments, the statistical analysis of experimental results, and the management of collaborative large-scale experimentation. Although it has become widely accepted that philosophers of science should also attend to those neglected dimensions of scientific practice, the implications of this more inclusive point of view are not yet fully worked out.

An example will illustrate how this broadened perspective may affect our understanding of a central issue in the philosophy of science, the *Duhem thesis*. As I already mentioned, Duhem pointed out that if the results of an experiment do not agree with the predictions of a theory, then one may either reject the theory in question or, alternatively, modify one of the auxiliary hypotheses concerning the operation of the instruments employed. Hacking (1992), drawing on Andy Pickering's work, gave an interesting twist to Duhem's thesis. He claimed that scientists have more leeway than that allowed by Duhem. To obtain an agreement between theory and experiment they have the option to change the experimental apparatus itself. Experimental results, according to Hacking, are plastic resources and not fixed constraints on theorizing. This claim may or may not survive philosophical scrutiny. In either case, it would have been inconceivable without the recent turn to practice.

The many faces of scientific practice have also been the focus of recent history of science. In fact, the historiography of experimental practice has been one of the few areas where philosophical questions and issues have motivated and guided historical work. The philosophy of experiment may, thus, provide novel opportunities for a much-needed renewal of the dialogue between history and philosophy of science.

Acknowledgements

I would like to thank Martin Curd, Kostas Gavroglu, and Stathis Psillos for many helpful comments.

See also Critical rationalism; Evidence; The historical turn in the philosophy of science; Logical empiricism; Measurement; Observation; Realism/anti-realism; Structure of theories; Underdetermination.

References

Arabatzis, T. (1992) "The Discovery of the Zeeman Effect: A Case Study of the Interplay between Theory and Experiment," *Studies in History and Philosophy of Science* 23: 365–88.
—— (2005) "Experiment", in M. Horowitz (ed.) *New Dictionary of the History of Ideas*, Detroit: Charles Scribner's Sons, Volume 2, pp. 765–69.
Collins, H. M. (1992) *Changing Order: Replication and Induction in Scientific Practice*, Chicago: University of Chicago Press.
Duhem, P. (1954) *The Aim and Structure of Physical Theory*; trans. from the 1914 edn by P. P. Wiener, Princeton, NJ: Princeton University Press.
Franklin, A. (1986) *The Neglect of Experiment*, Cambridge: Cambridge University Press.
—— (2002) *Selectivity and Discord: Two Problems of Experiment*, Pittsburgh, PA: University of Pittsburgh Press.
Galison, P. (1987) *How Experiments End*, Chicago: University of Chicago Press.
—— (1997) *Image and Logic: A Material Culture of Microphysics*, Chicago: University of Chicago Press.
Gooding, D., Pinch, T., and Schaffer, S. (eds) (1989) *The Uses of Experiment: Studies in the Natural Sciences*, Cambridge: Cambridge University Press.
Hacking, I. (1983) *Representing and Intervening*, Cambridge: Cambridge University Press.
—— (1992) "The Self-Vindication of the Laboratory Sciences," in A. Pickering (ed.) *Science as Practice and Culture*, Chicago: University of Chicago Press, pp. 29–64.
Mill, J. S. (1886) *A System of Logic Ratiocinative and Inductive*, London: Longmans, Green, & Co.
Popper, K. R. (1968) *The Logic of Scientific Discovery*, New York: Harper & Row.
Schrödinger, E. (1955) "The Philosophy of Experiment," *Il Nuovo Cimento* 1: 5–15.
Shapere, D. (1982) "The Concept of Observation in Science and Philosophy," *Philosophy of Science* 49: 485–525.
Steinle, F. (2002) "Experiments in History and Philosophy of Science," *Perspectives on Science* 10: 408–32.

Further reading

The role of instrumentation in experimentation is explored in R. J. Ackermann's *Data, Instruments and Theory: A Dialectical Approach to Understanding Science* (Princeton, NJ: Princeton University Press, 1985); and D. Baird's *Thing Knowledge: A Philosophy of Scientific Instruments* (Berkeley: University of California Press, 2004). The constructionist literature on experiment and instruments is surveyed in Jan

Golinski's *Making Natural Knowledge: Constructivism and the History of Science* (Chicago: University of Chicago Press, 2005). A moderate constructionist study that attributes to the material world a significant role in the production of scientific knowledge is A. Pickering's *The Mangle of Practice: Time, Agency, and Science* (Chicago: University of Chicago Press, 1995). The interweaving of experimentation and concept formation is discussed in D. Gooding's *Experiment and the Making of Meaning* (Dordrecht: Kluwer Academic Publishers, 1992). The significance of error statistics for the epistemology of experiment is meticulously argued in D. G. Mayo's *Error and the Growth of Experimental Knowledge* (Chicago: University of Chicago, 1996). Finally, an up-to-date introduction to the philosophy of experiment is H. Radder (ed.) *The Philosophy of Scientific Experimentation* (Pittsburgh, PA: University of Pittsburgh Press, 2003); among the topics discussed in this volume are the metaphysics of experimentation and the distinction between the natural and the artificial.

16

EXPLANATION

James Woodward

Introduction

Although issues having to do with the nature of explanation, both in science and in ordinary life, have figured importantly in philosophy from the pre-Socratics onwards, discussion of this topic in contemporary philosophy of science really begins with the formulation of the *deductive–nomological* (D–N) model in the middle part of the twentieth century. As is almost always true in philosophy, there are many earlier (and roughly contemporaneous) statements of the basic idea, but what has come to be regarded as the canonical version is due to Carl Hempel (1965a). Hempel's work initiated extensive discussion and the development of a number of competing models of scientific explanation, developments that continue to this day.

The D–N model

The basic idea of the D–N model is straightforward: an explanation (at least insofar as this involves deterministic, rather than statistical, laws) has the structure of a sound deductive argument, in which the fact to be explained (called the *explanandum*) is deduced from a set of premises (called the *explanans*) which do the explaining. (This is the *deductive* part of the D–N model.) The premises in the *explanans* must (i) have empirical content and be true and (ii) must include at least one "law of nature." This law must figure "essentially" or non-redundantly in the deduction, in the sense that the derivation of the *explanandum* from the *explanans* will no longer be deductively valid if this law-premise is removed. (This is the *nomological* component of the D–N model, "nomological" being just a philosopher's term of art for "lawful".) Typically, the *explanans* will also include other premises which are not laws – statements of "initial" or "antecedent" conditions. The *explanandum* may be either a particular matter of fact or itself a generalization.

To draw an illustration from Hempel (1965b), a D–N explanation of the expansion and contraction of soap bubbles on some particular occasion will have the following structure:

$$C_1, C_2, \ldots, C_k$$

$$L_1, L_2, \ldots, L_r$$

Explanans

—————————————————

E

Explanandum sentence

C_1, C_2, etc., represent *particular facts*, such as the temperature of the air inside the bubbles in comparison to the surrounding air. L_1, L_2, etc., represent laws describing *uniformities*, such as the ideal gas laws. E, which describes the fact that bubbles first expand and then contract, is deducible from the conjunction of the C_i and L_i.

Of the two components of the D–N model, the notion of a deductively valid argument is (at least in this context) unproblematic. The notion of a law of nature, however, has been the subject of continuing controversy, both regarding the criteria that distinguish laws from non-laws and regarding the role that laws play in science in general (see, e.g., Giere 1999). For reasons of space, I do not enter into this controversy here, except to observe that the development of adequate criteria for lawfulness remains an important project for defenders of the D–N model (and for other theories that assign the notion of *law* a central role in explanation and causation).

The I–S model

Hempel was aware that in many areas of science, generalizations are statistical rather than deterministic in form. When such generalizations take the form of statistical *laws*, Hempel suggests that we should think of them as explaining individual outcomes, in accordance with a distinctive form of explanation which he calls "inductive–statistical" (I–S) explanation (Hempel 1965b: 376–412). The technical details of the I–S model are complex but the basic idea is that statistical laws explain individual outcomes to the extent that they show those outcomes are highly probable. For example, suppose that it is a statistical law that

(S) Any human exposed to the measles virus has probability 0.8 of developing measles.

Suppose that Jones is exposed to the measles virus (*E*) and does develop measles (M). Then we may explain M by appealing to S and E because together S and E confer a high probability on M. I–S explanation is thus a sort of inductive analogue of D–N explanation, in the sense that I–S explanation involves showing that the *explanandum* phenomenon was at least likely, even if not certain, given the relevant laws and initial conditions.

Motivation for the D–N/I–S model

Why think that successful explanation must have a D–N or an I–S structure? Hempel appeals to two interrelated ideas. The first has to do with the point, or goal, of explanation: According to Hempel, a D–N/I–S explanation shows that the phenomenon to be explained "was to be expected" on the basis of a law and "it is in this sense that the explanation enables us to understand why the phenomenon occurred" (Hempel 1965b: 337). The second idea that motivates the D–N/I–S model has to do with an assumed connection between causation and the instantiation of laws or regularities – what we might call the assumption of the nomological character of causation. According to Hempel, causal claims always "implicitly claim" or "presuppose" the existence of some associated law or laws according to which the candidate for cause is part of some larger complex of "antecedent conditions" which are linked via a regularity to the *explanandum* phenomenon. These laws and antecedent conditions will provide a D–N (or at least an I–S) explanation for the *explanandum* phenomenon. Thus, according to Hempel, any causal explanation is always (at least implicitly) a D–N or an I–S explanation.

Counterexamples to the D–N/I–S model

A number of well-known *counterexamples* have been advanced against both the sufficiency – (1) and (2) – and the necessity – (3) – of the D–N/I–S requirements on explanation.

(1) Many explanations exhibit *directional* or asymmetric features that do not seem to be captured by the D–N/I–S model. From information about the height (h) of a flagpole, the angle (a) of the sun above the horizon and the laws (L) governing the rectilinear propagation of light, one may deduce the length of the shadow (s) that the pole casts. This derivation satisfies the D–N requirements and seems, intuitively, to be explanatory. However, by running the derivation in the *opposite* direction, one may deduce h from a, s, and L. This derivation again satisfies the D–N requirements but does not seem to explain the height of the pole (see Bromberger 1966).

(2) The presence of certain kinds of irrelevant information seems to undermine the goodness of explanations, even if these satisfy the D–N requirements. From the generalization (H) "All hexed salt dissolves in water" and the additional premise that s is a sample of hexed salt, one can deduce that s dissolves in water. Arguably H counts as a law according to the criteria usually employed by philosophers. But the resulting derivation seems defective as an explanation because, intuitively, whether or not salt is hexed is irrelevant to whether it will dissolve (see Salmon 1984).

(3) Suppose (see Scriven 1959) that only those who have latent syphilis (s) develop paresis (p), but that the probability of p, given s, is low, – say, 0.3. If Jones develops p, we can, according to Scriven, explain this by pointing to the fact he has s. But, in doing so, we have not cited laws and conditions that make p certain or even highly probable.

The reaction of many philosophers has been that such counterexamples show that something essential is missing from the D–N/I–S model and that this has to do with the failure of this model to do justice to the role of *causal* information in explanation. For example, (1) seems to illustrate the point that causation has directional features that are omitted from the D–N/I–S model and (2) seems to trade on the point that (barring complications having to do with overdetermination, etc.) causes must make a difference to their effects. Hexing salt does not cause it to dissolve (whether or not a salt is hexed does not make a difference to whether it dissolves) and in consequence hexing does not explain dissolving. More generally (2) shows that a factor can be (or can be part of) a nomologically sufficient condition for an outcome and yet not cause it. In part because of such considerations, subsequent discussion of explanation has tended to focus largely (but by no means entirely) on the role of causation in explanation and on the development of a more adequate theory of causation.

The CM model

Salmon's early work on explanation involved the development of his *statistical relevance* (or SR) model of explanation which attempted to characterize explanation (and causation) purely in terms of statistical regularities. In later work (1984), Salmon concluded that this approach was not fully adequate and instead devised a new account of explanation – the *causal/mechanical* (CM) model – that attempts to capture the *something more* that he concluded was involved in causation besides mere statistical relevance relationships. The CM model rests on several key ideas. A *causal process* is a physical process, such as the movement of a baseball through space. Such processes have the ability to "transmit a mark", so that if the causal process is altered in some appropriate way (e.g., the ball is scuffed) this alteration will persist in the absence of an additional external interference. More generally, causal processes have the ability to propagate their own structure from place to place and over time, in a spatio-temporally continuous way, without the need for further outside interactions. Causal processes contrast with *pseudo-processes* (such as the successive positions of a spot of light on the surface of a dome which are cast by a rotating searchlight) which lack those characteristics. A *causal interaction* occurs when two causal processes (spatio-temporally) intersect and modify one another, as when a collision between two billiard balls results in a change in momentum of both. According to the CM model, an explanation of some phenomenon (E) involves tracing the causal processes and interactions (or some portion of these) that lead up to E.

The CM model represents an attempt to characterize causation in, as it were, physical or material (or, as Salmon says, "ontic") terms, rather than in terms of the more formal or mathematical relations emphasized in the D–N/I–S and SR models. The paradigmatic application of the model is simple mechanical systems in which causal influence is transmitted by spatio-temporal contact, and involves the transfer of quantities like momentum and energy that are locally conserved. The model nicely captures the sense that many people have that there is something especially intelligible about such interactions (and the theories that describe them) and something fundamentally unsatisfying, from the point of view of explanation, about theories that postulate action at a spatio-temporal distance, non-local causal influences, and so on.

Despite these attractions, the CM model, like its predecessors, suffers from some serious limitations. For reasons of space, I describe just one of these (see Hitchcock 1995). If we imagine a "witch" touching her wand to a sample of salt and "hexing" it, there will be a spatio-temporally continuous process running from the motion of the wand to the sample and spatio-temporally continuous processes involved in the dissolution of the salt in water, all satisfying laws having to do with the conservation of energy and momentum. The process running from the hexing to the dissolution seems to be a causal process, rather than a pseudo-process, but the hexing is irrelevant to the dissolution. Intuitively, the problem is that the CM model does not seem to have the resources to explicate the difference between those features of a causal process that are relevant to the outcomes it produces and those that are irrelevant. Capturing this second contrast seems to require reference to laws or generalizations showing how the features of the *explanandum* phenomenon depend on (or would change under changes in) some features of the associated causal process and not others or in the identification of the features of the causal process which *make a difference* to the *explanandum* phenomenon. For example, the irrelevance of hexing to salt dissolution seems to have a lot to do with the fact that changing whether salt is hexed makes no difference to whether it dissolves, a fact that can be easily ascertained experimentally.

Unificationist models

The final class of models of explanation to be considered in this essay are *unificationist* models. These draw their inspiration from the very intuitive idea that explanatory theories unify a range of different phenomena, in the sense of showing them to be the result of the operation of the same fundamental principles. The most detailed and influential development of this idea is due to Philip Kitcher (see especially Kitcher 1989).

For reasons of space, I will not describe Kitcher's technical apparatus in detail, but the basic idea is that successful unification is a matter of repeatedly using the same argument patterns to derive a range of different conclusions – the fewer the number of patterns required, the more restrictions they impose on the particular arguments that instantiate them, and the larger the number of conclusions derivable via them, the more unified the associated explanation. Thus, like the D–N model, Kitcher's model takes explanation to consist of derivations from principles of great generality. However, according to Kitcher, his theory avoids the standard counterexamples to the D–N model in the following way: derivations that seem intuitively unexplanatory turn out to be associated with argument patterns that are less unified than derivations associated with competing alternative argument patterns, where the latter vindicate our usual explanatory judgments. For example, a derivation running from the height of a flagpole of the length of its shadow belongs to a set of argument patterns that are more unified than the set to which a derivation running from the length to the height belongs, and there is also an alternative argument pattern associated with a derivation of the height from other premises (having to do with the origin of the pole), and this is more unified than the pattern associated with the length-to-height derivation. Thus the asymmetries of causation and explanation, illustrated by the flagpole example, are in some sense generated by or fall out from facts about the comparative degrees of unification achieved by competing deductive systemizations. According to Kitcher, this illustrates a more general point: the "because of 'causation' is always derivative from the 'because' of explanation" (1989: 477). In other words, it is the notions of explanation and unification that are primary, and the relationships we describe as causal are just those relationships that are associated with derivations connected to our most unified theories.

Unificationist accounts have a number of attractive features. Plainly, there is *some* connection between explanation (in some sense of that protean word) and unification, again on some understanding of that notion. In some areas of science (particularly fundamental physics, but not limited to this) a drive toward unification is a very conspicuous goal of theory construction, and theories that are thought of as unifying what were previously seen as very disparate phenomena are seen as important explanatory achievements. This is true, for example, of Newton's unification of terrestrial and celestial mechanics, and of the unification of the electromagnetic and weak forces achieved by Salam and Weinberg. More generally, successful explanation surely has something to do with generality, and with exhibiting inter-connections or showing how things hang together, and again all these seem connected to unification.

Despite these attractions, it has proved difficult to articulate the intuitive relationship between explanation and unification in a precise and satisfying way or so as to reproduce intuitive explanatory judgments in the way that Kitcher hoped. Part of the problem is that there are many different possible kinds of unification and only some of them seem to be connected to explanation – that is, there are non-explanatory as well as explanatory unifications (Morrison 2000). For example, one sort of unification consists in the use of the same mathematical structures and techniques to represent very different physical phenomena, as when both mechanical systems and electrical circuits are represented by means of Hamilton's or Lagrange's equations. This unified representation allows for the derivation of the behavior of both kinds of systems, but would not be regarded by physicists as giving a common unified explanation of both kinds of systems or as constituting an explanatory unification of mechanics and electromagnetism. A closely related observation, developed by several authors, is that it simply does not seem to be true that considerations of comparative unification always yield familiar judgments about causal asymmetries and causal irrelevancies – these seem to have (at least in part) an independent source. So we seem left with the assessment that although there is very likely something deeply right about the general idea that underlies unificationist approaches, current formulations probably require some rethinking.

Open issues and future work

In a perceptive review essay, Noretta Koertge (1992) noted that although the literature on explanation is immense, comparatively little attention has been paid, in the construction of the various competing models of explanation, to the question of what they are to be used *for* or what their larger point, or purpose, is (other than capturing our notion of explanation). Relatedly, relatively little attention has been paid to how explanation itself is connected to or interacts with other goals of inquiry. As a result, it is sometimes unclear how to assess the significance of our intuitive judgments about the goodness of various explanations or to determine what turns on our giving one judgment rather than another. For example, as we have noted, the intuitive judgment of most people is that one cannot explain the height of a pole by appealing to the length of its shadow. However, a determined defender of the D–N model (e.g., Hempel 1965b: 353–4) might well ask why we should be so impressed by this. Perhaps our pre-analytic assessment is confused or mistaken in some way, or perhaps it reflects merely pragmatic considerations that should have no place in the theory of explanation. To respond to this skepticism we need a non-trivial account of what of importance would be lost or left out if we failed to distinguish between explanations of shadow lengths in terms of pole heights and explanations running in the opposite direction. One possible answer would appeal to the epistemic goal of having information relevant to manipulation and control; one may manipulate the length of the shadow by, among other things, manipulating the height of the pole, but not conversely. This difference is real regardless of one's intuitions about explanation in the two cases (see Woodward 2003: 197ff).

My interest here is not in defending this particular answer but rather in suggesting the more general point that one way forward in assessing competing models of explanation is to focus less (or not just) on whether they capture our intuitive judgments and more on the issue of whether and why the kinds of information they require are valuable (and attainable), and how that information relates to other goals we value in inquiry.

As another illustration of this point, consider the CM model. Underlying the model is presumably some judgment to the effect that tracing causal processes is a worthy goal of inquiry. Now, of course, one might try to defend this judgment simply by claiming that the identification of causes is an important goal and that causal process theories yield the correct account of cause. But a more illuminating and less question-begging way of proceeding would be to ask how that goal relates to other epistemic values. For example, what is the connection between the goals of identifying causal processes and of constructing unified theories? Or between identifying causal processes and the discovery of information that is relevant to manipulation and control? Are these the same goals? Independent but complementary goals? Competing goals in the sense that satisfaction of one may make it harder to satisfy the other? Obviously one may ask similar questions about the goal of unification.

An important part of the original appeal of the D–N/I–S model was that it served a critical function: it was used by Hempel and others to criticize claims of explanation, particularly in history and the social sciences. For example, Hempel (1965c) criticized certain kinds of functional explanation on the grounds that they did not provide (and could not readily be replaced by explanations that provided) nomologically sufficient (or high probability conferring) conditions for their *explananda*. He also claimed (1965d), again by appealing to the D–N/I–S model, that explanations in history should invoke explicit generalizations, and he attacked claims that historical explanations were fundamentally different in structure from explanations in the natural sciences. By way of contrast, in more recent work on explanation, this critical function often has receded into the background, and the focus has instead been on capturing the structure of widely accepted examples of successful explanation – as the reader can see from the above descriptions of the models that have followed the D–N model. Clearly, though, if models of explanation are to play a useful role in inquiry, they should yield plausible judgments about when explanations are bad as well as good, and they should make achievable recommendations for the improvement of explanations.

It is uncontroversial that explanatory practice – what is accepted as an explanation, how explanatory goals interact with others, what sort of explanatory information is thought to be achievable, discoverable, testable, etc. – varies in significant ways across different disciplines. Nonetheless, all of the models of explanation surveyed above are universalist in aspiration – they claim that a single, *one-size* model of explanation fits all areas of inquiry in so far as they have a legitimate claim to explain. Although the extreme position that explanation in biology or history has nothing interesting in common with explanation in physics has (in my view) little to recommend it, in my opinion it would be worthwhile to develop models of explanation that are more sensitive to disciplinary differences. Such models should reveal commonalities across disciplines; but they should also enable us to see why explanatory practice varies as it does across different disciplines and the significance of such variation. For example, biologists, in contrast to physicists, often describe their explanatory goals as the discovery of mechanisms rather than the discovery of laws. Although it is conceivable that this difference is purely terminological, it is also worth exploring the possibility that there is a distinctive story to be told about what a mechanism is for the purposes of biology, and how information about mechanisms contributes to explanation.

A closely related point is that at least some of the models described above impose requirements on explanation that may be satisfiable in some domains of inquiry, but are either unachievable (in any practically interesting sense) in other domains; or, to the extent that they may be achievable, bear no discernible relationship to generally accepted goals of inquiry in those domains. For example, many scientists and philosophers hold that there are few, if any, laws to be discovered in biology and the social and behavioral sciences. If so, models of explanation that assign a central role to laws may not be very illuminating regarding how explanation works in these disciplines. Appealing to this sort of link to *achievable*, worthwhile goals may strike some philosophers as an unwelcome intrusion of merely practical or epistemic considerations into the theory of explanation; but, looked at in a more positive light, such considerations are a source of additional constraints that can be used to choose among such theories.

As already noted, many of the difficulties faced by the models described above seem to derive from their (often tacit) reliance on inadequate accounts of causation and causal relevance. So another part of the way forward in the study of scientific explanation will be the development of more adequate accounts of causation and their integration into models of explanation. As this survey shows, focusing just on a general notion of explanation and hoping that the causal component would fall out as a sort of afterthought has not been a very successful strategy; it seems clear that attention needs to be focused in a more direct and unapologetic way on causation itself.

Does this mean that a focus on causation should entirely replace the traditional project of developing models of explanation? I think this would be to lose connections with some important issues. For one thing, causal claims themselves seem to vary greatly in the extent to which they are explanatorily deep or illuminating. Causal claims found in Newtonian mechanics seem deeper or more satisfying from the point of view of explanation than causal claims of "The rock broke the window" variety. It is usually supposed that such differences are connected to other features – for example to how general, stable, and coherent with background knowledge a causal claim is. However, as I have noted, not all kinds of generality and stability seem explanatorily relevant. So even if one focuses only on causal explanation, there remains the important project of trying to understand better what sorts of distinctions among causal claims matter for goodness in explanation.

There is also the important question of whether all legitimate forms of *why*-explanation are causal. For example, some writers (e.g. Nerlich 1979) contend that there is a variety of physical explanation which is *geometrical* rather than causal, in the sense that it consists in explaining phenomena by appealing to the structure of spacetime rather than to facts about forces or energy/momentum transfer. A really satisfying theory of explanation should provide some principled answer to the question of whether all *why*-explanation must be causal (and according to what notion of causal this is so), rather than just assuming an affirmative answer to this question.

Explanation, the D–N model, and other areas of philosophy

As noted above, there are a number of apparently compelling (and decades-old) counterexamples to the D–N/I–S model. Moreover, in its pure, unvarnished form the model has few defenders among researchers working specifically on the topics of explanation–causation. It is thus a very curious fact that the basic commitments of the model remain enormously influential in other areas of philosophy. As an illustration, consider contemporary treatments of the problem of mental causation in philosophy of mind. A central focus of this discussion is whether mental content (e.g. the content of Jones's decision to hail a cab) can be *causally relevant to* (or *make a difference for*) the production of behavior by Jones – e.g., a certain hand signal. A common suggestion is that this notion of causal relevance can be captured by the notion of nomological sufficiency. For example, Fodor (1989) claims that a property makes a difference if "[i]t's a property in virtue of the instantiation of which the occurrence of one event is nomologically sufficient for the occurrence of another" (see Robb and Heil 2005). Although the D–N model is not explicitly mentioned in this remark, it reveals the clear influence of a D–N-inspired picture of explanation (or at least causal–explanatory relevance), with these notions being understood in terms of *nomological sufficiency*.

Fodor and others who offer this explication of what it is for one property to make a difference to another are either unaware of counterexamples like (1) and (2) – the flagpole and the hexed salt discussed on p. 173 – or do not see their relevance to the topic of mental causation. However, these examples (as well as many others) show about as unequivocally as it is possible to show anything in philosophy that it simply is not true that nomological sufficiency is a sufficient condition for causal or explanatory relevance, or for making a difference. Instead, the lesson of examples like that of the hexed salt is that causal relevance and nomological sufficiency are very different notions, with the former, but not the latter, having to do with the contrast between what happens under the presence of the putative cause and its absence – a contrast which might be naturally captured by some sort of counterfactual account, although these tend to be dismissed as obviously inadequate in the philosophy of mind literature (Robb and Heil 2005). Although I lack the space for detailed discussion, I believe that a similar pattern of failure to recognize the apparent lessons that have emerged from the literature on explanation can be found in many other areas of philosophy as well.

What accounts for this disconnect between work carried out by "specialists" who focus directly on the notion of explanation and the use of this work elsewhere in philosophy? Several factors seem to be at work. First, none of the alternatives to the D–N model has won general acceptance among those working on explanation – there is no clear winner even among those who think that the D–N model is mistaken. Another factor is that often it is hard to see exactly how to apply these alternative models to many of the problems about explanation–causation that interest philosophers. For example, the psychological information that is relevant to judgments of mental causation (or to the causal relevance of the mental) is arguably information about the subject's beliefs, desires, and intentions, and perhaps generalizations of some kind connecting these to behavior. It is hard to see how to apply the CM model to such explanations since they do not seem to work by conveying information about spatio-temporally continuous processes. Perhaps there is a unificationist account of the causal relevance of the mental, but again it is far from obvious how this would go, and no one seems to have undertaken to provide such an account. The upshot is that the D–N model, or something in its neighborhood, has seemed to be the natural default to many philosophers working in this area, and similarly elsewhere in philosophy. I thus close with a dual appeal: philosophers constructing models of explanation should be more willing to explicitly discuss the implications of their models for issues elsewhere in philosophy; and philosophers and others who are not direct contributors to the explanation literature should be more willing to take on board what has been discovered in this literature over the past several decades.

See also Causation; Inference to the best explanation; Laws of nature; Mechanisms; Scientific method; Unification.

References

Barnes, E. (1992) "Explanatory Unification and the Problem of Asymmetry," *Philosophy of Science* 59: 558–71.

Bromberger, S. (1966) "Why Questions," in R. Colodny (ed.) *Mind and Cosmos: Essays in Contemporary Science and Philosophy*, Pittsburgh, PA: University of Pittsburgh Press.

Giere, R. (1999) *Science Without Laws*, Chicago: University of Chicago Press.

Hempel, C. (1965a) *Aspects of Scientific Explanation and Other Essays in the Philosophy of Science*, New York: Free Press.

—— (1965b) "Aspects of Scientific Explanation," in Hempel (1965a), pp. 331–496.

—— (1965c) "The Logic of Functional Analysis," in Hempel (1965a), pp. 297–330.

—— (1965d) "The Function of General Laws in History," in Hempel (1965a), pp. 231–43.

Hempel, C. and Oppenheim, P. (1948) "Studies in the Logic of Explanation," *Philosophy of Science* 15: 135–75; reprinted in Hempel (1965a), pp. 245–90.

Hitchcock, C. (1995) "Discussion: Salmon on Explanatory Relevance," *Philosophy of Science* 62, 304–20.

Kitcher, P. (1989) "Explanatory Unification and the Causal Structure of the World," in Kitcher and W. Salmon (eds) *Minnesota Studies in the Philosophy of Science*, Volume 13: *Scientific Explanation*, Minneapolis: University of Minnesota Press, pp. 410–505.

Koertge, N. (1992) "Explanation and its Problems," *British Journal for the Philosophy of Science* 43: 85–98.

Morrison, M. (2000) *Unifying Scientific Theories*, Cambridge: Cambridge University Press.

Nerlich, G. (1979) "What Can Geometry Explain?" *British Journal for the Philosophy of Science* 30: 69–83.

Robb, D. and Heil, J. (2005) "Mental Causation," in Edward N. Zalta (ed.) *The Stanford Encyclopedia of Philosophy* (spring 2005 edition), available: http://plato.stanford.edu/archives/spr2005/entries/mental-causation.

Salmon, W. (1984) *Scientific Explanation and the Causal Structure of the World*, Princeton, NJ: Princeton University Press.

—— (1989) *Four Decades of Scientific Explanation*, Minneapolis: University of Minnesota Press.

Scriven, M. (1959) "Explanation and Prediction in Evolutionary Theory," *Science* 30: 477–82.

Woodward, J. (2003) *Making Things Happen: A Theory of Causal Explanation*, New York: Oxford University Press.

Further reading

Hempel's classic statement of the D–N model can be found in Hempel (1965b). Salmon's CM model is described in Salmon (1984), and Kitcher's unificationist model is described in Kitcher (1989). Salmon (1989) and S. Psillos, *Causation and Explanation* (Montreal: McGill–Queen's University Press, 2002) provide detailed surveys of the entire subject. Woodward (2003) develops my own position.

17

THE FEMINIST APPROACH TO THE PHILOSOPHY OF SCIENCE

Cassandra L. Pinnick

The notion that there are "feminist approaches" to science appears in *Feminism, Science, and the Philosophy of Science*, edited by Lynn Hankinson Nelson and Jack Nelson. According to Nelson and Nelson (1996), a feminist approach promised important contributions to traditional philosophy of science. As they expressed it:

> We take philosophers of science and scientists, feminists and non-feminists alike, to share an interest in the nature of objectivity, truth, evidence, cognitive agency, scientific method, and the relationship between science and values. (1996: ix)

But, the Nelsons pointed as well to a difference between traditional philosophy of science and a feminist approach.

> We also take there to be substantive issues that divide feminists and their mainstream colleagues [in traditional philosophy of science], not including interest in the notions just listed [objectivity, truth, etc.] ... questions concerning the explanatory principles that should figure in the philosophy of science are among the more pervasive and contested issues. (*Ibid.*)

This chapter on the feminist approach to philosophy of science proceeds in four sections. The first explains why a traditional approach to philosophy of science dismisses a feminist approach. The second gives reasons why a feminist approach is, or can be, a philosophy of science. The third has two sub-parts that assess the extent to which a feminist approach is a better philosophy of science than is traditional philosophy of science. The final section is a plea to abandon the aims of the feminist approach and return to feminist philosophy understood as a thesis about worthy and correct political goals.

Dismissal

It may surprise readers to find that the "Major debates" part of this anthology includes a chapter on the feminist approach to philosophy of science. The surprise would be due to the not well-hidden fact that the so-called "feminist approach" is dismissed, widely among philosophers of science, as having nothing to contribute to debates concerning core questions in the philosophy of science. When in a charitable mood, philosophers may allow that a feminist approach conceivably has something to say about the human or social sciences, but they judge it to be of no moment when it comes to the *hard-core* physical sciences, the sub-disciplines of science that are the very height of conceptual abstraction, removed from the possible distortion of context.

As viewed from within traditional philosophy of science – of the sort discussed in other chapters of this book – "feminist" philosophy of science is akin to "Republican" or "Korean" or "Blond" or "Aquarian" philosophy of science. These kinds of modifiers may signal information about bias, perhaps keenly relevant from other perspectives such as a sociological view, but reach not at all to epistemic merit. Feminist modifiers are irrelevant from the philosophical point of view, particularly so because, on the traditional view, the gender of the inquirer does not weigh in on the analysis of science, especially not on the justification side of science. Therefore, insofar as the feminist approach is no more than a bold conjecture about the relevance of gender, traditional philosophy of science has no role for it. Hence the dismissal.

Philosopher of science Noretta Koertge describes the dismissal in this way:

> Feminist epistemology is motivated by feminist views about the role of [non-cognitive] values in science and what makes science valuable. Scientists and philosophers of science have traditionally considered the principal aims of science to be explanation and application. On this view only cognitive values should influence what is taken to be explanatory. (2003: 222)

We should note that the dismissal is predicated on the methodological presupposition, first, that there is an agreed set of core questions and, second, that whatever else might be said about the feminist approach, the battery of feminist argumentation about science is irrelevant to the set of core questions. In all likelihood there is a set of core questions about science that philosophy ought to be able to answer, although probably the set is more like Wittgenstein's "rope" than it is like a delineated and immutable list, girdled from the historical vicissitudes of scientific inquiry with Lakatos's protective belt. The likely members of the set of core questions range from the high arcana of philosophy of science: questions about truth and the aims of science, to the more pedestrian questions that engage scientific practice: questions about experimental design and interpretation. It is no secret that our scientific and philosophical epoch wishes science to be both metaphysical guide to the deep structure(s) of reality and epistemological (and methodological) feedback mechanism, so that we continue to learn how to learn about the world.

Perhaps feminist philosophers of science have an interesting and philosophically important response to the customary dismissal. If Koertge gives a correct descriptive account of the standoff as between the feminist approach and traditional philosophy of science, then there is at least one means by which feminists can land a swift rebuff to the dismissal: namely, show that feminist values (as Koertge calls them) or feminist categories play a *necessary* role in any adequate theory or philosophy of science. In other words, if feminist philosophy of science demonstrates a necessary epistemic and methodological role for feminist values or categories that gender entails, then traditional philosophy of science must redefine itself to incorporate the feminist approach. In brief then, we are asking this question: *Is the feminist approach a serious challenge such that, if correct, it forces a redefinition of philosophy of science?*

The next section explores that question. Of course, even if the feminist approach is a serious challenge to traditional philosophy of science, we must ask another question: Does the challenge succeed? That question is also addressed below, in the sections following the next.

The feminist approach as a philosophy of science

The best philosophy of science, just like any theoretic or definition, will be of the widest scope possible. However, in this essay I construe philosophy of science narrowly, considering the feminist approach insofar only as it targets the physical sciences. The rationale for this narrow focus is that, for the feminist approach to be taken seriously, it must be a compelling theory of not only the *soft* (social) sciences but also a philosophy of the *hard* (physical) sciences. After all, it is hardly a surprise, nor the basis of a challenge, to be told that bias is, or has been, rampant in social science; but it is quite another thing to adopt the view that the hard sciences are fundamentally biased and that a better philosophy of science would use feminist values to explain (the epistemology) and guide (the methodology) science. To their credit, proponents of the feminist approach are the first to acknowledge that fact. Sandra Harding and Merrill Hintikka themselves narrow the focus as follows:

> A more fundamental project now confronts us. We must root out sexist distortions and perversions in epistemology, metaphysics, methodology and the philosophy of science – in the "hard core" of abstract reasoning thought most immune to infiltration by social values. (Harding and Hintikka 1983: ix)

So, I take my cue from Harding and Hintikka and note that I am not concerned with the feminist approach *qua* social or political theory. Most importantly, I am not concerned with feminist arguments that call for fair play and a level playing-field, whether in science or any other area of expertise. I am concerned solely with the feminist approach insofar as it represents a challenge to the traditional philosophical analysis of science. Thus, as I consider it, the feminist approach *qua* philosophy of science is not a socio-political thesis based in a concern for gender diversity or any related social goal. Nor do the formulations that constitute a serious challenge contest traditional methodology, such as the discovery–justification divide. Feminist approaches to science *qua* a feminist philosophy of science must be understood, as the proponents themselves state, as a thesis about the best epistemic and methodological criteria to ground philosophy of science.

From the above, it follows that the feminist approach ought to be taken seriously. If the feminist approach has merit, then, as currently conceived, philosophy of science is demonstrably too narrow – by its own lights. (Readers should note that, even if it is shown that traditional epistemology of science is too narrow in its explanatory categories, an additional argument would be necessary to show how best to widen the range of categories. See Slezak 1991; Pinnick 1994; Intemann forthcoming 2008.)

Now, as philosophers of science – or, more narrowly, as epistemologists of science – we are bound to assess the strength of the feminist arguments. To do so, we will take into consideration arguments that are well formulated. This criterion may appear odd, but it is important for the reason that our focus rules out a certain swathe of the full feminist critique of science: namely, feminist critiques the authors of which self-consciously eschew argumentative form. Our focus rules out, for example, Donna Haraway's contributions. And, titles such as "Beyond Epistemology" (mentioned in a recent APA *Newsletter* on feminism and philosophy) and discussions that the feminist "epistemological project" would overcome "traditional 'malestream' epistemology" (Code, Mullett, and Overall 1988) probably drop off the radar, as well.

Assessing the feminist challenge to traditional philosophy of science

Within the feminist critique, two philosophers, Sandra Harding and Helen Longino, stand out from the rest – indeed, insofar as we consider the feminist approach as applied to science, all the rest is derivative on the works of these two philosophers. In saying so, let me note that there is a difference, even if highly nuanced, as between feminist epistemology and feminist epistemology (or philosophy) of science. There are many authors in the former category and a few other than Harding and Longino in the latter category. But Harding and Longino are without competitors, if not quite *sui generis*, in their role as premiere feminist philosophers of science advocating for the feminist approach. The arguments made variously by Harding and Longino are innovative and provocative, and present the kind of serious challenge to traditional philosophy of science that warrants a response for the reason that, if correct, philosophy of science ought to be radically revamped to include, especially, the consideration of gender as a necessary element in the epistemology of science.

Both Harding and Longino have a wide corpus of philosophical contributions. Longino especially has made important contributions to other areas, in particular her contributions to the history of science; readers may wish to consult the historical essays in Kohlstedt and Longino (1997). But it is as philosophers of science only that I consider Harding and Longino here.

Sandra Harding on women and science: the epistemic challenge

Harding presents her arguments as friendly to science in the sense that her theoretic would improve science. What is at issue is whether or not it is possible for science to achieve the very epistemic aims it enunciates for itself. In Harding's view, science will achieve its self-stated aims only if gender plays an essential role in the epistemology of science. We may simplify: Harding's arguments promise the necessary conditions on scientific rationality – and, given success in stating the necessary conditions, Harding may then proceed to detail the sufficient conditions, as well.

Let us look now to the details of Harding's feminist approach. To grasp the logical structure of Harding's argumentation and to put her ideas in context, we need to consider the following passages from her book, *Is Science Multicultural?*:

> Women and men in the same culture have different "geographical" locations in heterogeneous nature, and different interests, discursive resources, and ways of organizing the production of knowledge from their brothers ... it is more accurate and useful to understand women and men in any culture as having a different relationship to the world around them ... starting off research from women's lives can provide for increasing human knowledge of nature's regularities and the underlying causal tendencies anywhere and everywhere that gender relations occur. (1998: 90)

> In many ways they [men and women] are exposed to different regularities of nature that offer them different possible resources and probable dangers and that can make some theories appear more or less plausible than they do to those who interact only with other environments. (96)

> When science is defined in terms of these linked meanings of objectivity and masculinity ... science itself is distorted. (139)

> Standpoint approaches can show us how to detect values and interests that constitute scientific projects ... Standpoint approaches provide a map, a method, for maximizing a "Strong Objectivity" in the natural and social sciences. (163)

Let me summarize these passages. Women, due to living in different "environments" than men, have different insight into "regularities of nature." If we "start off research from women's lives" we can increase knowledge in "the natural and social sciences". The means by which we may do better science – which is to say: remark on and, presumably, rid science of distortion and bias – is to revamp traditional philosophy of science to adopt the new feminist epistemic category that Harding terms "Strong Objectivity."

Harding's argumentation relies on two empirical claims. The first is that gender biases scientific reasoning. (Recall that we are considering the philosophical, or epistemological, import of Harding's argumentation only, not any warranted complaint about a lack of equal access or the like.)

Presumably Harding intends to rely on the notion that gendered bias is *negative* in the case of a male orientation, whereas gendered bias is *positive* (or at least potentially so) in the case of a female orientation. It is not plain how Harding would demonstrate her position on bias and science, without assuming the truth of the very claim that must be proved – that there is an epistemic link between gender and bias – thereby begging the question rather than showing the truth of the empirical claim. Harding can – and she does – recite evidence for her bias claim, based in the history of science. Readers will find that Harding's typical historical example is drawn from biological science.

This kind of argument, based on a historical induction, is not only legitimate – and thus provides yet another reason to take the feminist challenge seriously – but is to be preferred to quixotic *a priori* efforts to show philosophical conclusions about science. Harding's argument, based in the historical study of science, is a good foil for historically informed philosophy of science such as the naturalized approach advocated by Larry Laudan.

Although we may admire Harding's use of the very kind of argumentation prized among philosophers of science – namely, the historical induction – one must note that the most glancing view of the history of science does little to support Harding's idea that from the standpoint of female (positive) bias, on nature and its regularities and underlying causal tendencies, we gain a strong(er) evidentiary base to argue for the feminist approach. Rather, the history of science, patently dominated by male achievers, amounts to a thumping good induction to the conclusion that male bias – whatever it is and to the exclusion of identifiably different kinds of bias – ought to be maximized in science.

The second empirical premise is that including more women in science can boost the aims of science. In other words, Harding aims to conclude not only that women's lives will make a difference, but also that women's lives "can provide for increasing human knowledge of nature's regularities and the underlying causal tendencies anywhere and everywhere that gender relations occur." Harding is explicit about this. In the words just quoted, she states plainly that the feminist approach is a means by which to change the epistemology of science, doing so by an infusion of women's standpoints on nature.

In some later works (e.g., 2004), Harding distances herself from "standpoint" theory. Thus, Harding prefers in her later publications to rely on different categorical labels, such as "multiculturalism," as the preferred epistemological standard. However, this tactic is transparent relabeling, not re-theorizing. Politically, Harding's pluralism is commendable; philosophically, it is self-defeating (see Pinnick 1994). And the notion of a standpoint as having epistemic importance is believed still by many feminists (cf. Harding's own 2004 *The Feminist Standpoint Theory Reader*).

To assess the feminist approach as Harding enunciates it, we must assess the empirical strength of the claim that women's standpoints – or some preferred epistemic category that is peculiar to women – will promote a better philosophy of science. The redefined philosophy of science is better, minimally, because it does the best possible job of achieving the very cognitive aims that traditional epistemology of science itself values. Understood in this way, Harding's arguments are impressive for the promise they make that the very goals and values associated with traditional epistemology of science are better served by a feminist approach – in her case, by an epistemology built on women's standpoint.

Yet in the end we have *promise* only, for the reason that there is a complete lack of data that would tell, one way or the other, about the propriety of Harding's provocative epistemological claims. Harding's arguments do present a serious challenge to the traditional approach. But in what is perhaps the most impressive aspect of Harding's kind of argument – its empirically based claims about women and science – lies the ultimate downfall of this attempt to enshrine the feminist approach. Where there should be empirical support, one way or another, there is none. As Robert Klee says,

> Harding and her sister feminist science critics present no empirical evidence for their centrally important claim that when marginalized and oppressed persons do science their substantive results are more "objective" than when the male power elite does science. (Klee 1997: 187–8)

The support that is available rises to the level of anecdotal reportage (such as one finds in Evelyn Fox Keller's narratives about cellular activity) or untested counterfactual assertions about case histories (as in the case of the oft-mentioned primatology studies, which readers may begin to explore in Longino's writings).

Helen Longino on women and science: the methodological challenge

In considering the feminist approach found in works by Helen Longino, it should be remembered that I am considering Longino's contributions to philosophy of science and the epistemology of science only. Longino has made significant contributions to the history and sociological critique of science, but I am not concerned here with these. In some ways, Longino's arguments are not strictly feminist or part of a feminist approach, because her arguments are expressed primarily in the form of a concern for the social or the community-based nature of science. (In similar fashion, Sandra Harding prefers now to talk about multicultural perspectives rather than about her former methodological rubric, "women's standpoints".) It is quite plain that, for Longino, there are other epistemic communities than those of just women or feminists; but insofar as women form a community within science, it is legitimate to consider Longino as part of the feminist approach. In a 1996 essay, Longino described the feminist approach as a philosophy of science in this way:

> I wish in this essay to explore some of the tensions between descriptivism and normativism (or prescriptivism) in the theory of knowledge, arguing that although many of the most familiar feminist accounts of science have helped us to redescribe the process of knowledge (or belief) acquisition, they stop short of an adequate normative theory. (Fox Keller and Longino 1996: 264–5)

Even if Longino does not speak in terms exclusively of the feminist approach, her argumentation is an apt case study. This is because her focus is on evidence and objectivity. She relativizes evidence to background beliefs and, on that basis, says that she shows both the opportunity and the need for a feminist critique of evidence. In other words, Longino argues that background beliefs are tainted with bias, but that if we use better background beliefs – such as those contributed by the feminist community of inquirers – then we will likely have better science. Robert Klee has remarked that this kind of philosophy of science amounts to the thesis that "doing accurate science is a question of putting politically progressive people in charge of making up the facts and the methods that will produce them" (1997: 188).

In her more recent work, Longino (2001) promises to develop a new account of scientific knowledge that integrates the social – which includes social groups of women in science – and the "cognitive." She argues that social interaction secures scientific knowledge. Reminiscent of Bacon's *New Atlantis*, Longino describes a scientific community and the optimal methods by which the community will adjudicate what the community deems scientific knowledge. There is no question but that Longino's goal is to argue for new methodological categories that challenge traditional philosophy of science and, if warranted, would transform philosophy of science.

In the case of Longino's arguments, the transformation would require that philosophy of science widen its explanatory scope to include an array of inquiring communities. It is not entirely clear how to draw communities, and this is an abiding problem in sociology and its cognate social sciences. But let us presume some method by which to individuate a community. We surely want to know how the new, social epistemology does a better job than traditional philosophy of science of justifying scientific belief and – especially given our focus on Longino as methodologist – in guiding the practice of science.

Regardless of how a communitarian-style philosophy of science is dressed up, in the end the community is the final arbiter, not evidence. In the long run, there are no objective grounds on which belief is justified, only grounds for a particular community. Just as Longino writes, justification is "dependent on rules and procedures immanent in the context of inquiry" (Longino 2001: 92). This evades a pernicious epistemological relativism (if it does) only by appeal to normative sociology, not by appeal to (normative) epistemology.

In any case, does Longino show that social interaction secures knowledge? To say, merely, that social interaction contributes to the success of science is neither new nor the special provenance of the feminist approach (cf. Laudan 1984; Hull 1988). If we want a methodological boost, then it needs to be shown that science is improved by means of the feminist *qua* communitarian approach.

Whatever one's views on a communitarian approach, Longino's theoretic nowhere demonstrates that feminist background beliefs (whatever these may turn out to be) are associated with, much less that they cause, better science. Indeed, it is nowhere shown even that when scientists are self-professed feminists or are allied in some programmatic way with the feminist approach that the science produced is better – or even that it is different. Nowhere is it shown in Longino's argumentation that peculiarly feminist means (or, by extension, that of any other special *community* of inquirers) have a special claim to rooting out the negative impact of sexist bias in science or in the philosophy of science. There is no reason to believe that a community of inquirers will get us closer to unadulterated evidence than do, say, individual male inquirers.

As with Sandra Harding, Helen Longino offers a bold theory about gender and science, but it is a theory in need of testing. Just as is the case with Harding's argumentation, Longino's communitarian-based philosophy of science falls short of the targeted conclusion, namely, that our scientific understanding – or our philosophical understanding of science – is improved when voices from a specific political or social – or gendered, or marginalized – swathe of the community of science participate.

The feminist approach and liberal ideals for inquiry

At one point in time, feminist philosophy was a political thesis. It was a political thesis that was based, primarily, on a call for fair play and a level playing-field for women. The feminist approach to philosophy of science is a different thesis. This thesis is, in every case, some version of the key idea that women will make distinctive and unique contributions to science and our philosophical understanding of it.

We have seen that, although the arguments in support of the feminist approach are worthy of serious consideration, those arguments fail. Therefore, at least as matters stand for women as based on a feminist approach, there is no reason either to believe the key idea associated with the feminist approach or to put the thesis into practice and push women into science. In important practical ways the failure of the feminist approach is a setback for what could be for women in science. For example, were the feminist approach a justified thesis about women and science, then it would follow that public policy ought to favor pouring money into educational support for women in science and that women ought to be promoted to the top scientific positions in universities, industry, and research institutes.

The high profile that the feminist approach enjoys, and has enjoyed for a significant time, and the failure of the arguments associated with the feminist approach to be anything other than unsubstantiated promises, risk the conclusion that efforts to promote women in science – in education and in careers – amount to misallocated scant resources. It is easy to read the shortcomings that are evident in the feminist approach on to feminist philosophy *per se*.

This would be a profound error. The political thesis that motivates feminist philosophy remains timely. This is because there is abundant evidence to show that women remain on the *outside* when it comes to the hard-core sciences. In the private sector, women head far fewer labs than do their male counterparts. Although academics may pledge themselves to liberal political ideals, there is no reason to be sanguine; for there is a trend that shows women to have better access to top career echelons in the private sector than in academe (Smith-Doerr 2004). This is contrary to the prevailing view, expressed by colleagues with whom I would otherwise agree, "that sexist discrimination, while certainly not vanished into history, is largely vestigial in the universities" (Gross and Leavitt 1994: 110). This belief is in error (see

National Research Council of the National Academies 2006). The facts show that despite the rise in the number of women who seek and complete degrees in hard-core science, women have not moved into the top academic ranks of science faculties. There is a persistent absence of women full professors in science, and their absence is most apparent at flagship universities. Thus, those who are concerned to support equal access for women in science would do well to reconsider feminism as a political thesis.

It remains important for all who are interested in philosophy of science, and in science itself, to understand and assess the feminist approach. That approach is not just irrelevant for the reason that its best arguments fail for lack of empirical testing or confirmation, but for the reason that it becomes dangerous when it diverts or obscures attention away from the abiding educational and career needs of women in science.

See also Relativism about science; Social studies of science; Values in science.

References

Code, L., Mullett, S., and Overall, C. (eds) (1988) *Feminist Perspectives: Philosophical Essays on Method and Morals*, Toronto: University of Toronto Press.

Gross, P. R. and Levitt, N. (eds) (1994) *Higher Superstition: The Academic Left and its Quarrels with Science*, Baltimore, MD: Johns Hopkins University Press.

Harding, S. G. (1998) *Is Science Multicultural?* Bloomington: Indiana University Press.

—— (ed.) (2004) *The Feminist Standpoint Theory Reader: Intellectual and Political Controversies*, New York: Routledge.

Harding, S. G. and Hintikka, M. (eds) (1983) *Discovering Reality*, Dordrecht: Reidel.

Hull, D. L. (1988) *Science as a Process: An Evolutionary Account of the Social and Conceptual Development of Science*, Chicago: University of Chicago Press.

Intemann, K. (forthcoming 2008) "Increasing the Number of Feminist Scientists: Why Feminist Aims Are Not Served by the Underdetermination Thesis," *Science & Education*.

Fox Keller, E. and Longino, H. E. (eds) (1996) *Feminism and Science*, Oxford: Oxford University Press.

Koertge, N. (2003) "Feminist Values and the Value of Science," in C. L. Pinnick, N. Koertge, and R. F. Almeder (eds) (2003) *Scrutinizing Feminist Epistemology*, Piscataway, NJ: Rutgers University Press.

Klee, R. (1997) *Introduction to the Philosophy of Science*, New York: Oxford University Press.

Kohlstedt, S. G. and Longino, H. E. (eds) (1997) *Women, Gender, and Science*, Osiris 12 (second series), Chicago: University of Chicago Press, Journals Division.

Laudan, L. (1984) *Science and Values*, Berkeley: University of California Press.

Longino, H. E. (2001) *The Fate of Knowledge*, Princeton, NJ: Princeton University Press.

National Research Council of the National Academies (2006) *To Recruit and Advance: Women Students and Faculty in Science and Engineering*, Washington, DC: National Academies Press.

Nelson, L. H. and Nelson, J. (eds) (1996) *Feminism, Science, and the Philosophy of Science*, Norwell, MA: Kluwer.

Pinnick, C. L. (1994) "Feminist Epistemology: Implications for Philosophy of Science," *Philosophy of Science* 61: 646–57.

Slezak, P. (1991) "Bloor's Bluff: Behaviourism and the Strong Programme," *International Studies in the Philosophy of Science* 5: 241–56.

Smith-Doerr, L. (2004) *Women's Work: Gender Equality vs. Hierarchy in the Life Sciences*, Boulder, CO: Lynne Rienner.

Further reading

Three resources provide the best basis to assess the empirical claims made within the feminist approach. These are National Research Council of the National Academies (2006), and two works by Gerhard Sonnert and Gerald Holton: *Who Succeeds in Science? The Gender Dimension*; and *Gender Differences in Science Careers: The Project Access Study*, both published by Rutgers University Press, Piscataway, NJ, in 1995. Another recent empirical work is Laurel Smith-Doerr (2004), which more narrowly considers women in the life sciences. In 1992 and 1993, *Science* (March 13, 1992, vol. 255 and April 16, 1993, vol. 260) published annual special sections of "Women in Science." See especially the 1992 section, which is not so dated. Feminist approaches to philosophy of science and epistemology more generally can be found in H. E. Longino, *Science as Social Knowledge* (Princeton, NJ: Princeton University Press, 1990); J. Duran, *Philosophies of Science/Feminist Theories* (Boulder, CO: Westview Press, 1998); and M. Griffiths and M. Whitford (eds) *Feminist Perspectives in Philosophy* (Bloomington: Indiana University Press, 1998). For critical responses, see D. Patai and N. Koertge (eds) *Professing Feminism* (New York: Basic Books, 1994); N. Koertge (ed.) *A House Built on Sand* (New York: Oxford University Press, 1998); C. L. Pinnick, "Feminist Philosophy of Science," *Metascience* 9, no. 2 (2000): 257–66; C. L. Pinnick, N. Koertge, and R. F. Almeder (eds) *Scrutinizing Feminist Epistemology* (Piscataway, NJ: Rutgers University Press, 2003).

18
INFERENCE TO THE BEST EXPLANATION

Peter Lipton

Introduction

Science depends on judgments of the bearing of evidence on theory. Scientists must judge whether an observation or the result of an experiment supports, disconfirms, or is simply irrelevant to a given hypothesis. Similarly, scientists may judge that, given all the available evidence, a hypothesis ought to be accepted as correct or nearly so, rejected as false, or neither. Occasionally, these evidential judgments can be made on deductive grounds. If an experimental result strictly contradicts a hypothesis, then the truth of the data deductively entails the falsity of the hypothesis. In the great majority of cases, however, the connection between evidence and hypothesis is non-demonstrative, or inductive. In particular, this is so whenever a general hypothesis is inferred to be correct on the basis of the available data, since the truth of the data will not deductively entail the truth of the hypothesis. It always remains possible that the hypothesis is false even though the data are correct.

One of the central aims of the philosophy of science is to give a principled account of these judgments and inferences connecting evidence to theory. In the deductive case, this project is well-advanced, thanks to a productive stream of research into the structure of deductive argument that stretches back to antiquity. The same cannot be said for inductive inferences. Although some of the central problems were presented incisively by David Hume in the eighteenth century, our current understanding of inductive reasoning remains remarkably poor, in spite of the intense efforts of numerous epistemologists and philosophers of science.

The model of *inference to the best explanation* (IBE) is designed to give a partial account of many inductive inferences, both in science and in ordinary life. One version of the model was developed under the name "abduction" by Charles Sanders Peirce early in the twentieth century, and the model has been considerably developed and discussed over the last four decades (e.g., Harman 1965; Thagard 1978; Day and Kincaid 1994; Barnes 1995; Psillos 2002; Lipton 2004). Its governing idea is that explanatory considerations are a guide to inference, that scientists infer from the available evidence to the hypothesis which would, if correct, best explain that evidence. Many inferences are naturally described in this way. Darwin inferred the hypothesis of natural selection because, although it was not entailed by his biological evidence, natural selection would provide the best explanation of that evidence. When an astronomer infers that a galaxy is receding from the earth with a specified velocity, she does this because the recession would be the best explanation of the observed red-shift of the galaxy's spectrum. When a detective infers that it was Moriarty who committed the crime, he does so because that hypothesis would best explain the fingerprints, bloodstains, and other forensic evidence. Sherlock Holmes to the contrary, this is not a matter of deduction. The evidence will not entail that Moriarty is to blame, since it always remains possible that someone else was the perpetrator. Nevertheless, Holmes is right to make his inference, since Moriarty's guilt would provide a better explanation of the evidence than would anyone else's.

IBE can be seen as an extension of the idea of self-evidencing explanations, where the phenomenon that is explained in turn provides an essential part of the reason for believing that the explanation is correct. The galaxy's speed of recession explains why its spectrum is red-shifted by a specified amount, but the observed red-shift may be an essential part of the reason the astronomer has for believing that the galaxy is receding at that speed. Self-evidencing explanations exhibit a curious circularity, but this circularity is benign. The recession is used to explain the red-shift and the red-shift is used to confirm the recession; this reciprocal relationship may leave the recession hypothesis both explanatory and well-supported. According to IBE, this is a common situation in science: hypotheses are supported by the very observations they are supposed to explain. Moreover, on this model, the observations support the hypothesis precisely because it would explain them. IBE thus partially inverts an otherwise natural view of the relationship between inference and explanation. According to that natural view, inference is prior to explanation. First the scientist must decide which hypotheses to accept; then, when called on to explain some observation, she will draw from her pool of accepted hypotheses. According to IBE, by contrast, it is only by asking how well various hypotheses would explain the available evidence that she can determine which hypotheses merit acceptance. In this sense, IBE has it that explanation is prior to inference. Here it is important to distinguish between *actual* and *potential* explanation, where a potential explanation is something that satisfies all the conditions on actual explanation, with the possible exception of truth. Thus all actual explanations are potential explanations, but not conversely. Stories of alien abduction might explain certain observations – to that extent they are potential explanations – but they are not actual explanations because they are not true. According to IBE, we infer that what would best explain our evidence is likely to be true, that is, that the best potential explanation is likely to be an actual explanation.

There are two different sorts of problem that an account of inference in science might purport to solve. The problem of *description* is to give an account of the principles that govern the way scientists weigh evidence and make inferences. The problem of *justification* is to show that those principles are sound or rational, for example, by showing that they tend to lead scientists to accept hypotheses that are true and to reject those that are false. One popular application of IBE has been the attempt to mount a philosophical inference to the best explanation to justify scientific realism, arguing that the truth of certain scientific theories, and so the reliability of scientific methods, would be the best explanation of their predictive successes. I return briefly to this justificatory gambit at the end of this essay, but my main focus is on the descriptive problem: not whether letting inferences be governed in part by explanatory considerations would be a good way to think, but whether, for better or worse, scientists *do* think that way.

The difficulties of the descriptive problem are sometimes underrated, because it is supposed that inductive reasoning follows a simple pattern of extrapolation, with *more of the same* as its fundamental principle. Thus we predict that the sun will rise tomorrow because it has risen every day in the past, or that all ravens are black because all observed ravens are black. This picture of enumerative induction has, however, been shown to be strikingly inadequate as an account of inference in science. On the one hand, a series of formal arguments, most notably the raven paradox and the new riddle of induction, have shown that the enumerative model is wildly permissive, treating virtually any observation as if it were evidence for any hypothesis or prediction (Hempel 1965: Ch. 1; Goodman 1983: Ch. 3). On the other hand, the enumerative model is also much too restrictive to account for most scientific inferences. Scientific hypotheses typically appeal to entities and processes not mentioned in the evidence that supports them and often unobservable and not merely unobserved, so the principle of *more of the same* does not apply. For example, while the enumerative model might account for the inference that a scientist makes from the observation that the light from one galaxy is red-shifted to the conclusion that the light from another galaxy will be red-shifted as well, it will not account for the inference from observed red-shift to unobserved recession.

The best-known attempt to account for these *vertical* inferences that scientists make from observations to hypotheses about often unobservable entities and processes is the *hypothetico-deductive model* (Hempel 1966: Chs 2–3). According to this model, scientists deduce predictions from a hypothesis (along with various other auxiliary premises) and then determine whether those predictions are correct. If some of them are not, the hypothesis is disconfirmed; if all of them are correct, the hypothesis is confirmed and may eventually be inferred. Unfortunately, while this model does make room for vertical inferences, it remains (like the enumerative model) far too permissive, counting data as confirming a hypothesis which are in fact totally irrelevant to it. For example, since a hypothesis (H) entails the disjunction of itself and any prediction whatever (H or P), and the truth of the prediction establishes the truth of the disjunction (since P also entails (H or P)), any successful prediction will count as confirming any hypothesis, even if P is the prediction that the sun will rise tomorrow and H the hypothesis that all ravens are black.

What is wanted is thus an account that permits vertical inference without permitting absolutely everything, and IBE promises to fill that bill. IBE sanctions vertical inferences, because an explanation of some observed phenomenon may appeal to entities and processes not themselves observed; but it does not sanction just any vertical inference, since a particular scientific hypothesis would not, if true, explain just any observation. A hypothesis about raven coloration will not, for example, explain why the sun rises tomorrow. Moreover, IBE discriminates between different hypotheses all of which would explain the evidence, since the model sanctions an inference only to the hypothesis which would best explain it.

Articulating the slogan

IBE thus has the advantages of giving a natural account of many inferences and of avoiding some of the limitations and excesses of other familiar accounts of non-demonstrative inference. If, however, it is to provide a serious model, IBE needs to be developed and articulated, and this has not proven an easy thing to do. More needs to be said, for example, about the conditions under which a hypothesis explains an observation. Explanation is itself a major research topic in the philosophy of science, but the standard models of explanation yield disappointing results when they are plugged into IBE. For example, the best-known account of scientific explanation is the *deductive–nomological model,* according to which an event is explained when its description can be deduced from a set of premises that essentially includes at least one law (Hempel 1965: Ch. 12). This model has many familiar weaknessses. Moreover, it is virtually isomorphic to the hypothetico-deductive model of confirmation, so it would disappointingly reduce IBE to a version of hypothetico-deductivism.

The challenge of articulating IBE is compounded when we turn to the question of what makes one explanation better than another. To begin with, the model suggests that inference is a matter of choosing the best from among those explanatory hypotheses that have been proposed at a given time, but this seems to entail that at any time scientists will infer one and only one explanation for any set of data. This is not promising, since scientists will sometimes infer more than one explanation and will sometimes refuse to infer at all. But this is not a fatal objection to explanationism, since the account should be understood to permit multiple compatible inferences (e.g., more than one cause of a phenomenon) and no inference at all, if the *best* is not sufficiently good. Thus "inference to the best explanation" must be glossed by the more accurate, but less memorable, phrase "inference to the best of the available competing explanations, when the best one is sufficiently good." But under what conditions is this complex condition satisfied? How good is "sufficiently good"? Even more fundamentally, what are the factors that make one explanation better than another? Standard models of explanation are virtually silent on this point. This does not suggest that IBE is incorrect but, unless we can say more about explanation, the model will remain relatively uninformative.

Some progress has, however, been made in analysing the relevant notion of the best explanation. Consider a basic question about the sense of "best" that the model requires. Does it mean the most probable explanation, or rather the explanation that would, if correct, provide the greatest degree of understanding? In short, should IBE be construed as inference to the *likeliest* explanation, or as inference to the *loveliest* explanation? A particular explanation may be both likely and lovely, but the notions are distinct. For example, if one says that smoking opium tends to put people to sleep because opium has a "dormitive power," one is giving an explanation that is very likely to be correct but not at all lovely: it provides very little understanding. At first glance, it may appear that *likeliness* is the notion IBE ought to employ, since scientists presumably infer only the likeliest of the competing hypotheses they consider. This is, however, probably the wrong choice, since it would severely reduce the interest of the model by pushing it towards triviality. Scientists do infer what they judge to be the likeliest hypothesis, but the main point of a model of inference is precisely to say how these judgments are reached, to give what scientists take to be the *symptoms* of likeliness. If IBE is along the right lines, explanations that are lovely will also be likely, but it should be in terms of loveliness that the inference is made. For to say that scientists infer the likeliest explanations is perilously similar to saying that great chefs prepare the tastiest meals, which may be true, but is not very informative if one wants to know the secrets of their success. Like the "dormitive power" explanation of the effects of opium, "inference to the likeliest explanation" would itself be an explanation of scientific practice which provides only little understanding.

The model should thus be construed as "inference to the loveliest explanation." Its central claim is that scientists take loveliness as a guide to likeliness, that the explanation that would, if correct, provide the most understanding is the explanation that is judged likeliest to be correct. This at least is not a trivial claim, but it raises three general challenges. The first is to identify the explanatory virtues, the features of explanations that contribute to the degree of understanding they provide. The second is to show that those aspects of loveliness match judgments of likeliness, that what are judged the loveliest explanations tend also to be those that are judged likeliest to be correct. And the third challenge is to show that, granting the match between judgments of loveliness and likeliness, the former are in fact the scientist's guide to the latter.

Identification, matching, and guiding

To begin with the challenge of *identification*, there are a number of plausible candidates for the explanatory virtues, including scope, precision, mechanism, unification, and simplicity. Better explanations explain more types of phenomena, explain them with greater precision, provide more information about underlying mechanisms, unify apparently disparate phenomena, or simplify our overall picture of the world. Some of those features, however, have proven surprisingly difficult to analyze. There is, for example, no uncontroversial analysis of unification or simplicity, and some have even questioned whether they are genuine features of the hypotheses deployed in scientific explanations, rather than artifacts of the way those hypotheses happen to be formulated, so that the same hypothesis will count as simple if formulated in one way but complex if formulated in another.

A different but complementary approach to the problem of identifying some of the explanatory virtues focuses on the contrastive structure of many why-questions. A request for the explanation of some phenomenon often takes a contrastive form: one asks not simply "Why P?" but "Why P rather than Q?" What counts as a good explanation depends not just on fact P but also on the foil Q. Thus the increase in temperature might be a good explanation of why the mercury in a thermometer rose rather than fell, but not a good explanation of why it rose rather than breaking the glass. Accordingly, it is possible to develop a partial account of what makes one explanation of a given phenomenon better than another by specifying how the choice of foil determines the adequacy of contrastive explanations. Although many explanations both in science and in ordinary life specify some of the putative causes of the phenomenon in question, the structure of contrastive explanation shows why not just any causes will do. Roughly speaking, a good explanation requires a cause that *made the difference* between the fact and the foil. Thus the fact that Smith had untreated syphilis might explain why he rather than Jones contracted paresis (a form of partial paralysis), if Jones did not have syphilis; but it will not explain why Smith rather that Doe contracted paresis, if Doe also had untreated syphilis. Not all causes provide lovely explanations, and an account of contrastive explanation helps to identify which do and which do not (cf. van Fraassen 1980: Ch. 5; Lipton 2004: Ch. 3).

Assuming that a reasonable account of the explanatory virtues is forthcoming, the second challenge to IBE concerns the extent of the *match* between loveliness and judgments of likeliness. If IBE is along the right lines, then the lovelier explanations ought also in general to be judged likelier. Here the situation looks promising, since the features we have tentatively identified as explanatory virtues seem also to be inferential virtues, that is, features that lend support to a hypothesis. Hypotheses that explain many observed phenomena to a high degree of accuracy tend to be better supported than hypotheses that do not. The same seems to hold for hypotheses that specify a mechanism, that unify, and that are simple. The overlap between explanatory and inferential virtues is certainly not perfect, but at least some cases of hypotheses that are likely but not lovely, or conversely, do not pose a particular threat to IBE. As we have already seen, the explanation of opium's soporific effect by appeal to its dormitive power is very likely but not at all lovely; but this is not a threat to the model, properly construed. There surely are deeper explanations for the effect of smoking opium, in terms of molecular structure and neurophysiology, but those explanations will not compete with the banal account, so the scientist may infer both without violating the precepts of IBE.

The structure of contrastive explanation also helps to meet this matching challenge, because contrasts in why-questions often correspond to contrasts in the available evidence. A good illustration of this is provided by Ignaz Semmelweis's nineteenth-century investigation into the causes of childbed fever, an often fatal disease contracted by women who gave birth in the hospital where Semmelweis did his research. Semmelweis considered many possible explanations. Perhaps the fever was caused by "epidemic influences" affecting the districts around the hospital, or perhaps it was caused by some condition in the hospital itself, such as overcrowding, poor diet, or rough treatment. What Semmelweis noticed, however, was that almost all of the women who contracted the fever were in one of the hospital's two maternity wards, and this led him to ask the obvious contrastive question and then to rule out those hypotheses which, though logically compatible with his evidence, did not mark a difference between the wards. It also led him to infer an explanation that would explain the contrast between the wards: namely, that women were inadvertently being infected by medical students who went directly from performing autopsies to obstetrical examinations, but examined only women in the first ward. The hypothesis was confirmed by a further contrastive procedure, when Semmelweis had the medics disinfect their hands before entering the ward: the infection hypothesis was now seen also to explain not just why women in the first rather than in the second ward contracted childbed fever, but also why women in the first ward contracted the fever before but not after the regime of disinfection was introduced. This general pattern of argument, which seeks explanations that not only would account for a given effect, but also for particular contrasts between cases where the effect occurs and cases where it is absent, is very common in science, for example wherever use is made of controlled experiments (Hempel 1966: Ch. 2; Lipton 2004: Ch. 5).

This leaves the challenge of *guiding*. Even if it is possible to give an account of explanatory loveliness (the challenge of identification) and to show that the explanatory and inferential virtues coincide (the challenge of matching), it remains to be argued that scientists judge that an hypothesis is likely to be correct *because* it is lovely, as IBE claims. Thus a critic of the model might concede that likely explanations tend also to be lovely, but argue that inference is based on other considerations, having nothing to do with explanation. For example, one might argue that inferences from contrastive data are really applications of Mill's method of difference, which makes no explicit appeal to explanation, or that precision is a virtue because more precise predictions have a lower prior probability and so provide stronger support as an elementary consequence of the probability calculus (Howson and Urbach 1989).

The defender of IBE is here in a delicate position. In the course of showing that explanatory and inferential virtues match up, he will also inevitably show that explanatory virtues match some of those other features that competing accounts of inference cite as the real guides to inference. The defender thus exposes himself to the charge that it is those other features rather than the explanatory virtues that do the *real* inferential work. Meeting the matching challenge will thus exacerbate the guiding challenge. The situation is not hopeless, however, since there are at least two ways to argue that loveliness is a guide to judgments of likeliness. Other accounts of inference may fail to get the extension right: they are inapplicable to many scientific inferences and incorrect about others. If it is shown that IBE does better in this respect, then this is a powerful reason for supposing that loveliness is indeed a guide to likeliness. Second, if there is a good match between loveliness and likeliness, as the guiding challenge grants, this is presumably not a coincidence and so itself calls for an explanation. Why should it be that the hypotheses that scientists judge likeliest to be correct are also those that would provide the most understanding if they were correct? IBE gives a very natural answer to the question, similar in structure to the Darwinian explanation for the tendency of organisms to be well-suited to their environments. If scientists select hypotheses on the basis of their explanatory virtues, the match between loveliness and judgments of likeliness follows as a matter of course. Unless the opponents of the model can give a better account of the match, the challenge has been met.

Explanationism and Bayesianism

Bayesians hold belief to be a matter of degree that can be represented in terms of probabilities. Thus $P(E)$ is the probability the scientist gives to the statement E, which may range from 0, if she is certain E is false, to 1, if she is certain E is true. By representing beliefs as probabilities, it is possible to use the mathematical theory of probability to give an account of the dynamics of belief and, in particular, an account of inductive confirmation. The natural thought is that evidence E supports hypothesis H just in case the discovery of E causes (or ought to cause) me to raise my degree of belief in H. To put the point in terms of probabilities, E supports H just in case the probability of H, after E is known, is higher than the probability of H beforehand. The standard axioms of probability theory yield an equation that appears to tell us just when this condition of confirmation is satisfied, and so to give us a precise theory of induction. That equation is Bayes's theorem, which in its near simplest form looks like this:

$$P(H\,|\,E) = P(E\,|\,H)P(H)/P(E).$$

On the left-hand side, we have the conditional probability of H given E. Bayesians treat this as the posterior probability of H, so the figure on the left-hand side represents the degree of belief the scientist should have after evidence E is in. The right-hand side contains three probabilities, which together determine the posterior. The first of these – $P(E\,|\,H)$ – is the probability of E given H, known as the "likelihood" of H, because it represents how likely H would make E. The other two probabilities on the right-hand side – $P(H)$ and $P(E)$ – are the priors of H and E respectively. They represent degree of belief in hypothesis H before the evidence described by E is in and degree of belief in E itself before the relevant observation is made. This process of moving from prior probabilities and likelihood to posterior probability by moving from right to left in Bayes's theorem is known as "conditionalizing" and is claimed by the Bayesian to characterize the dynamic of degrees of belief and so the structure of inference (Howson and Urbach 1989).

Bayesianism has been taken by some to pose a threat to IBE (van Fraassen 1989: Ch. 7; Salmon 2001); but it may rather be an opportunity for collaboration. For in real life it is often not easy to work out the probabilities that are required in order to move from prior to posterior probability simply on the basis of a (presumably tacit) grasp of the abstract principles of the probability calculus. Explanatory considerations of the sort to which IBE appeals are often more accessible than those principles to the enquirer on the street or in the laboratory, and may provide an effective surrogate for certain components of the Bayesian calculation. On this proposal, the resulting transition of probabilities in the face of new evidence might well be just as the Bayesian says, but the mechanism that actually brings about the change is explanationist (Okasha 2000; Lipton 2004: Ch. 7).

One way explanatory considerations might fit into the Bayesian scheme is by helping enquirers to assess likelihoods, an assessment essential to Bayesian conditionalizing. For although likelihood is not to be equated with loveliness, it might yet be that one way we judge how likely E is, given H, is by considering how well H would explain E. This would hardly be necessary in cases where H entails E (since here the likelihood is simply unity), but in real-life inference this is rarely the case and, where H does not entail E, it is not so clear how in fact we do work out how likely H makes E (and how likely not-H makes E). Here explanatory considerations might help, if in fact loveliness is reasonably well correlated with likelihood. What would be required is that lovelier explanations tend to make what they explain likelier (even if high likelihood is no guarantee of good explanation), and that we sometimes exploit this connection by using judgments of loveliness as a barometer of likelihood. Perhaps explanatory loveliness is used as a symptom of likelihood, and likelihoods help to determine likeliness or posterior probability. This is one way in which IBE and Bayesianism may be brought together.

Another way in which explanatory considerations may play an important role in a Bayesian calculation is in the determination of prior probabilities. Choices between competing potential explanations of some phenomenon are often driven by judgments of which of the explanations has the higher prior. The defender of IBE need not deny this, but may claim that those priors were themselves generated in part with the help of explanatory considerations. Insofar as explanatory considerations play a role in conditionalizing, explanatory considerations also have a role to play in the determination of priors, since priors are partially determined by earlier conditionalization. Explanatory considerations may also enter into the determination of priors in other ways, since various aspects of explanatory loveliness, such as simplicity and unification, may directly influence judgments of prior probability.

The justificatory project

In addition to offering a description of aspects of inductive inferences, IBE has been used to justify them, to show that those hypotheses judged likely to be correct really are so. For example, it has been argued that there is good reason to believe that the best scientific theories are true, since the truth of those theories is the best explanation of their wide-ranging predictive success. Indeed it has been claimed that the successes of our best scientific theories would be inexplicable unless they were at least approximately true.

This argument has considerable plausibility; nevertheless, it faces serious objections. If scientific theories are themselves accepted on the basis of inferences to the best explanation, then an argument of the same form to show that those inferences lead to the truth may beg the question. Moreover, it is not clear that the truth of a theory really is the best explanation of its predictive success. For one thing, it seems no better an explanation than would be the truth of a competing theory that happens to share those particular predictions. For another, to explain why our current theories have thus far been successful may not require an appeal to truth, if scientists have a policy of weeding out unsuccessful theories (van Fraassen 1980: 39–40).

The explanation that the truth of a theory would provide for the truth of the predictions that the theory entails appears to be logical rather than causal. This may provide some answer to the circularity objection, since the first-order scientific inferences that this overarching logical inference is supposed to warrant are at least predominantly causal. But it may also give rise to the suspicion that the real source of the plausibility of the argument is the plausibility of inferring from the premise that most false hypotheses would have yielded false predictions to the conclusion that most hypotheses that yield true predictions are themselves true. Perhaps the premise of this argument is correct, but the argument is fallacious. Most losing lottery tickets get the first three digits of the winning number wrong, but most tickets that get the first three digits right are losers too. It remains to be shown why the predictive success of a general causal hypothesis is any better reason to believe that hypothesis to be true than getting the first few digits of a lottery ticket right is a reason to think that ticket is a winner.

See also Bayesianism; Explanation; Mechanisms; Realism/anti-realism; Scientific method; Unification; The virtues of a good theory.

References

Barnes, E. (1995) "Inference to the Loveliest Explanation," *Synthese* 103: 251–77.
Day, T. and Kincaid, H. (1994) "Putting Inference to the Best Explanation in its Place," *Synthese* 98: 271–95.
Goodman, N. (1983) *Fact, Fiction and Forecast*, 4th edn, Indianapolis: Bobbs–Merrill.
Harman, G. (1965) "The Inference to the Best Explanation," *Philosophical Review* 74: 88–95.
Hempel, C. (1965) *Aspects of Scientific Explanation*, New York: Free Press.
—— (1966) *The Philosophy of Natural Science*, Englewood Cliffs, NJ: Prentice-Hall.
Howson, C and Urbach, P. (1989) *Scientific Reasoning: The Bayesian Approach*, La Salle, IL: Open Court.
Lewis, D. (1986) "Causal Explanation," in *Philosophical Papers*, New York: Oxford University Press, Volume 2, pp. 214–40.
Lipton, P. (2004) *Inference to the Best Explanation*, 2nd edn, London: Routledge.
Okasha, S. (2000) "Van Fraassen's Critique of Inference to the Best Explanation," *Studies in the History and Philosophy of Science* 31: 691–710.
Psillos, S. (2002) "Simply the Best: A Case for Abduction," in A. C. Kakas and F. Sadri (eds) *Computational Logic: Logic Programming and Beyond*, Berlin: Springer-Verlag, pp. 605–26.
Salmon, W. C. (2001) "Explanation and Confirmation: A Bayesian Critique of Inference to the Best Explanation," in G. Hon and S. S. Rakover (eds) *Explanation: Theoretical Approaches and Applications*, Dordrecht: Kluwer, pp. 61–91.
Thagard, P. (1978) "The Best Explanation: Criteria for Theory Choice," *Journal of Philosophy* 75: 76–92.
Van Fraassen, B. (1980) *The Scientific Image*, Oxford: Oxford University Press.
—— (1989) *Laws and Symmetry*, Oxford: Oxford University Press.

Further reading

David Hume's *Enquiry Concerning Human Understanding*, ed. T. L. Beauchamp (Oxford: Clarendon Press, 2000 [1748]) is the seminal discussion of problems of inductive inference. Hempel (1965) is the source of much of the subsequent discussion about the nature of scientific explanation. Linking those two topics, Harman (1965) is a powerful early advertisement for IBE. For more recent discussion of IBE, see Thagard (1978); Day and Kincaid (1994); Barnes (1995); Psillos (2002); and Lipton (2004).

19
LAWS OF NATURE
Marc Lange

Introduction

On the standard view, there are three kinds of facts. First, there are the *logical* or *metaphysical* necessities: facts that absolutely could not have been otherwise. These include the fact that triangles have three sides and that either you are now sitting down or it is not the case that you are now sitting down. The rest of the facts are *contingent*. They divide into two classes: the *nomic necessities*, which follow from the laws of nature alone, and the *accidents*, which do not. Among the accidents are that all of the coins in my pocket today are silver-colored and that all solid-gold cubes are smaller than a cubic mile. (For the sake of argument, let's suppose that these are truths.) The laws, according to our best current science, include that all gold is electrically conductive and that electric charge is conserved. Both laws and accidents are contingent: just as magnetic monopoles could possibly have existed and material bodies could possibly have been accelerated from rest beyond 3×10^8 ms^{-1} (contrary to natural law), so a solid-gold cube larger than a cubic mile could have existed (contrary to accidental fact).

Notice that the accidental regularity concerning gold cubes is just as general, universal, and exceptionless as the law that all solid cubes of uranium-235 are smaller than a cubic mile. (Large clumps of U-235 undergo nuclear chain-reactions, as in an atomic bomb.) Notice also that a law may currently be undiscovered (though I can't give you an example of one of those!) and that, after it has been discovered, it need not be officially called a "law" (as with the axioms of quantum mechanics, Bernoulli's principle, and Maxwell's equations). Some things that are still called "laws" (such as Newton's law of gravity and Bode's law) may not currently be regarded as genuine laws (or even as facts at all).

Philosophers have drawn many distinctions among the laws of nature. Some laws are causal (such as laws governing what happens whenever two chemical substances are combined under certain conditions), whereas others are not (such as conservation laws). Some laws are fundamental; others are derived (such as Galileo's law that any body falling from rest freely to earth covers a distance proportional to the square of the time it has spent falling). Some laws are deterministic; others are probabilistic – that is, statistical (such as that any atom of beryllium-11 at any moment has a 50 percent chance of decaying over the subsequent 13.81 seconds). Some laws are more theoretical or model-driven, whereas others are more phenomenological. Many laws are instantiated, but some are vacuous (as when a law specifies what would happen if two substances were combined under certain conditions, but in fact, they never are). Some philosophers believe that there are laws of *special*, or "inexact," sciences, such as population genetics, ecology, mineralogy, psychology, and economics; that these laws frequently include *ceteris-paribus* clauses; and that their irreducibility to the laws of physics is responsible for the explanatory autonomy of those scientific fields. Other philosophers believe that such "laws" are either fictions (such as that all human beings have ten fingers), accidents (such as the "frozen accident" of the genetic code), or logical necessities (such as the principle that a creature with greater evolutionary fitness is more likely to reproduce than is a less fit creature), and that the genuine laws require no elastic escape clauses. Laws of nature tie into a host of topics of perennial metaphysical and epistemological interest, including causation, chance, confirmation, counterfactuals, determinism, dispositions, emergence, explanation, models, natural kinds, necessity, properties, reduction, unification, and universals.

Some philosophers have even denied the "standard view" ("There are three kinds of facts …") with which I began. Scientific *essentialists* (such as Ellis 2002) regard laws as metaphysically necessary: it is part of electric charge's essence that it involves the causal power to exert and to feel forces in accordance with certain particular laws. Cartwright (1983) has argued that some processes are not governed by any laws and that statements of the laws of nature are not even truths – at least, when they are interpreted as describing exceptionless regularities, though perhaps they are true as describing causal powers. Giere (1999) and van Fraassen (1989) contend that the philosophical tradition has been led astray in employing the concept of natural law to rationally reconstruct science.

In this chapter, I confine myself to two questions (and even then, I can do little more than ask them). First, what difference does it make, in scientific reasoning, whether some truth is believed to be a law or an accident? Second, what is it about the world that makes some fact a law rather than an accident? Ideally, the answer to the second question should account for the answer to the first question. If these questions cannot be answered satisfactorily within the "standard view," then perhaps something more radical will be necessary.

What laws do

How do laws differ from accidents in the role they play in scientific reasoning? To begin with, an accidental truth just happens to obtain. A gold cube larger than a cubic mile could have formed, but the requisite conditions happened never to arise. In contrast, it is no accident that a large cube of uranium-235 never formed, since the laws governing nuclear chain-reactions prohibit it. In short, things *must* conform to the laws – the laws have a kind of *necessity* (weaker than logical, conceptual, mathematical, or metaphysical necessity, according to the standard view) – whereas accidents are just giant coincidences.

That is to say, had Bill Gates wanted to build a large gold cube, then (I dare say) there would have been a gold cube greater than a cubic mile. (As Lewis 1973 puts it: in the closest possible world where Gates wants to build a large gold cube, there is a gold cube exceeding a cubic mile.) But even if Gates had wanted to build a large cube of uranium-235, all U-235 cubes would still have been less than a cubic mile. The laws govern not only what actually happens, but also what would have happened under various circumstances that did not actually happen. The laws underwrite various facts expressed by subjunctive (counterfactual) conditionals, i.e., statements of the form "Had p been the case, then q would have been the case" (where p is false). That is why scientists use the laws in figuring out what earth would have been like, had it been farther from the sun. In contrast, for any accident a, there exists some p that is "nomically possible" (i.e., consistent with all of the laws' logical consequences) such that a would not still have held had p been the case. That there is some such p follows simply from the fact that an exception to an accident is nomically possible. For example, had there been a gold cube exceeding a cubic mile (a nomic possibility), then it would not have been the case that all gold cubes are smaller than a cubic mile.

Counterfactuals are notoriously context-sensitive. In Quine's famous example, the counterfactual "Had Caesar been in command in the Korean War, he would have used the atomic bomb" is correct in some contexts, whereas in others, "... he would have used catapults" is correct. What is preserved under a counterfactual supposition, and what is allowed to vary, depends on our interests in entertaining the supposition. But according to many philosophers (notably Goodman 1983), in any context, the laws tell us what would have happened, under any nomic possibility p. (Lewis (1973, 1986) is a notable dissenter, as we shall see.).

Because of their necessity, laws have an explanatory power that accidents lack. For example, a certain powder burns with a yellow flame, not another color, because the powder is a sodium salt and it is a law that all sodium salts, when ignited, burn with a yellow flame (as explained by more fundamental laws). The powder *had* to burn with a yellow flame, considering that it was a sodium salt – and that *had-to-ness* reflects the laws' necessity. In contrast, we cannot explain why my wife and I have 2 children by citing the fact that all of the families on our block have 2 children – since that fact is an accident. Were a childless family to try to move onto our block, it would not encounter an irresistible opposing force. (A counterfactual!) This is the origin of Hempel's *covering-law* conception of scientific explanation.

The distinction between laws and accidents makes itself felt not only metaphysically, but also epistemologically. We believe that it would be mere coincidence if all of the coins in my pocket today turn out to be silver-colored. So we consider it accidental that every coin from my pocket today *that we have checked so far* has been silver-colored. Therefore, we regard this evidence as failing to confirm that the *next* coin to be examined from my pocket today will also be silver-colored. To know that all of the coins in my pocket today are silver-colored, we would have to examine every single coin in my pocket today. (If we know that there are two coins in my pocket, select one at random, and find it to be silver-colored, then typically we confirm the hypothesis that all of the coins in my pocket are silver-colored, but we do not confirm that the coin we did not select is silver-colored.) In contrast, a candidate law is confirmed differently: that one sample of a given chemical substance melts at 383°K (under standard conditions) confirms, for every unexamined sample of that substance, that its melting point is 383°K (in standard conditions). Accordingly, many philosophers (e.g., Dretske 1977; Goodman 1983) have held that a hypothesis believed to be a law, if true, is confirmed differently by its *positive instances* from a hypothesis believed to be accidental, if true. Only a *law-like* hypothesis is *confirmed inductively*. (For dissent, see Sober 1988 and van Fraassen 1989; for an attempted reconciliation, see Lange 2000.)

That the very same claims play all of these special roles in scientific reasoning – in connection with necessity, counterfactuals, explanations, and inductive confirmations – would suggest that scientific reasoning draws an important distinction here, which philosophers characterize as the difference between laws and accidents. However, it is notoriously difficult to capture the laws' *special roles* precisely. Take counterfactuals. The mathematical function relating my car's maximum speed on a dry, flat road to its gas pedal's distance from the floor is not a law (since it reflects accidental features of the car's engine). Yet this function supports counterfactuals regarding the car's maximum speed had we depressed the pedal to a half-inch from the floor. This function has invariance with respect to certain hypothetical changes, though not with respect to certain changes to the engine. Indeed, for nearly any accident, there are *some* hypothetical changes with respect to which it is invariant. All gold cubes would have been smaller than a cubic mile even if I had been wearing a differently colored shirt today. Likewise, past instances exhibiting my car's pedal-speed function confirm the function's holding of certain unexamined cases. (But they do not confirm the function's continuing to hold, were the car's engine altered.) Moreover, my car's pedal-speed function (together with the road's condition and the pedal's current position) explains the car's current maximum speed.

So even if a fact's lawhood makes a difference to science, it is difficult to identify exactly the difference it makes. Furthermore, even if it is true that in any context, the laws tell us what would have happened under any nomic possibility, this does not allow us to pick out the laws, since it uses the laws to pick out the relevant range of counterfactual suppositions. It is circular to specify the laws as exactly the truths that would still have held under any counterfactual supposition that is logically consistent with the laws.

What if we allow a set of truths containing some accidents to pick out the relevant counterfactual suppositions: those that are logically consistent with every member of that set? Take, for instance, a logically closed set of truths that includes the accident that all gold cubes are smaller than a cubic mile but omits the accident that all of the coins in my pocket are silver-colored. Here's a counterfactual supposition that is consistent with every member of this set: had there been either a gold cube that is *larger* than a cubic mile or a coin in my pocket that is *not* silver-colored. What would the world then have been like? In many conversational contexts, we would deny that of the two accidents I have mentioned, the one in the set ('All gold cubes are smaller than a cubic mile') would still have held. (Perhaps it is the case, of neither the gold-cubes accident nor the silver-coins accident, that it would still have held.) The same sort of argument could presumably be made regarding any logically closed set of truths that includes *some* accidents but not *all* of them. Given the opportunity to pick out the range of counterfactual suppositions convenient to itself, the set nevertheless is not invariant under all of those suppositions. (Trivially, every member of the set of *all* truths would still have held under any counterfactual supposition logically consistent with all of them, since *no* counterfactual supposition is so consistent.)

Here, then, is my rough suggestion for the laws' distinctive relation to counterfactuals. Take a set of truths that is *logically closed* (i.e., that includes every logical consequence of its members) and is neither the empty set nor the set of all truths. Call such a set "stable" exactly when every member, *g*, of the set would still have been true had *p* been the case, for each of the counterfactual suppositions, *p*, that is logically consistent with every member of the set. My rough suggestion: *g* is a nomic necessity exactly when *g* belongs to a stable set. (For a more careful discussion, see Lange 2000.)

What makes the nomic necessities special is their stability: *taken as a set*, they are invariant under as broad a range of counterfactual suppositions as they *could* logically possibly be. *All* of the laws would still have held under *every* counterfactual supposition under which they *could all* still have held. No set containing an accident can make that boast (except for the set of all truths, for which the boast is trivial). Because the set of laws (and their logical consequences) is non-trivially as invariant under counterfactual perturbations as it could be, there is a sense of *necessity* corresponding to it; necessity involves possessing a *maximal* degree of invariance under counterfactual perturbations. No sense of necessity corresponds to an accident, even to one (such as my car's gas pedal–maximum speed function) that would still have held under many counterfactual suppositions. The notion of *stability* allows us to draw a sharp distinction between laws and accidents, accounts for the laws' necessity, and gives us a way out of the notorious circle that results from specifying the nomic necessities as the truths that would still have held under those counterfactual suppositions consistent with the nomic necessities.

Even if this proposal (once suitably refined) distinguishes the nomic necessities from the accidents, it fails to distinguish the laws from the nomic necessities that are not laws. Scientific practice appears to recognize that not all contingent logical consequences of nomic necessities are laws (though of course, all possess nomic necessity). For instance, it is physically necessary that anything that is an emerald or a ruby is green or red, but this fact fails to help explain why a given stone is green or red; that it is an emerald (let's say) together with the law that all emeralds are green explains why the stone is green and why it is green or red. Likewise, in the nineteenth century it was believed to be coincidental (albeit physically necessary) that all alkane hydro-carbons differ in their atomic weights by multiples of the atomic weight of nitrogen. Laws correspond to natural kinds (such as emerald and ruby), but (as Fodor 1974 emphasizes) this could not be so if every logical consequence of laws is a law.

What laws are

Lewis (1973, 1986) gives the most sophisticated *Humean* or *regularity* account of natural law. According to Lewis, facts about laws "supervene" on the spacetime geometry and the spatio-temporal mosaic of instantiations of the properties belonging to a certain elite class. (That is, two possible worlds cannot differ in their laws without differing in their spacetime geometry or their mosaics.) These elite properties are the properties meeting the following conditions:

- They are perfectly natural – unlike, for instance, the property of being an emerald or greater than 3 inches long; that is, they are among the *sparse* properties – non-gerrymandered ones, not mere shadows of predicates.
- They are categorical – that is, *Humean*: they involve no modalities, propensities, chances, laws, counterfactuals, dispositions … (Scientific essentialists deny that there are any such properties; see Ellis 2002.)
- They are qualitative in the sense that they do not involve the property, which (according to some philosophers) a given thing intrinsically possesses, of being the particular individual thing that it is. (Such a property is called a "haecceity.") For example, the property of being identical to Jones is not elite.
- They are possessed intrinsically by spacetime points or occupants thereof.

Also supervening on the Humean mosaic are facts about single-case objective chances, such as this atom's having a 50 percent chance of undergoing radioactive decay in the next 13.81 seconds. Consider the deductive systems of truths regarding instantiations of elite properties and claims regarding the objective chances at various times that certain elite properties will be instantiated at later times (where the system says A only if it also says that A never had any chance of not obtaining). These systems, Lewis says, compete along three dimensions:

(a) *informativeness* (in excluding or in assigning chances to possible arrangements of elite-property instantiations);
(b) *simplicity* (e.g., in the number of axioms and the order of polynomials therein, as expressed in terms of natural properties, spacetime relations, and chances); and
(c) *fit* (which is greater insofar as the actual course of elite-property instantiations receives higher probability).

These three criteria stand in some tension. Greater informativeness can be achieved by adding facts to the system, which often (though not always) brings a loss of simplicity. Likewise, if property P is instantiated at time t_2, then, by adding to a system the claim that c is the chance at t_1 of P being instantiated at t_2, we may add informativeness (though not as much as we would had we added that P is instantiated at t_2) and we may add fit (though not as much as we would had c been greater).

Perhaps some single system is by far the best on balance in meeting these three criteria. Perhaps which system *wins* the competition is relatively insensitive to any arbitrary features of our sense of simplicity or our rate of exchange among the three criteria. In that case, the laws of nature are the contingent generalizations belonging to the best system, and the facts about chances at a given moment are whatever the best system (and the history of elite-property instantiations until that moment) entails them to be.

Lewis's account has the virtue of using only Humean resources to distinguish between laws and accidents. It also nicely accommodates vacuous laws. Take *Coulomb's law*, which specifies the electrostatic force between any two point charges long at rest. Suppose we replace Coulomb's law in the best system by a generalization that agrees with Coulomb's law except in the case of a point body of exactly 1.234 statcoulombs at exactly 5 centimeters from a point body of exactly 6.789 statcoulombs. If there never exists such a pair of bodies, then the replacement generalization is true, just like Coulomb's law. However, it is not as simple as Coulomb's law, since it treats this hypothetical pair of bodies as a special case. So the best system contains Coulomb's law, replete with uninstantiated cases.

On the other hand, it might be wondered whether the laws really do supervene on the Humean mosaic. Could not two possible worlds involve the same Humean mosaic, but whereas in one world it is a law that all Fs are G, this regularity is accidental in the other world? Perhaps there it is a law that all Fs have 99.99 percent chance of being G. Or suppose there had been nothing in the entire history of the universe except a single electron moving uniformly forever. (Presumably, this impoverished world is nomically possible.) Lewis's account apparently dictates that the laws would then have included "At all times, there exists only one body." But intuitively, perhaps, the laws of nature would have been no different had there been only a single lonely electron (i.e., in the closest possible world where there is nothing but a single electron). Only the universe's initial conditions would have been different. In some possible lone-electron worlds (such as the closest one), the laws say that like electric charges repel, whereas in other possible lone-electron worlds, the laws say that like charges attract. The laws thus fail to supervene. (For more sophisticated arguments for nomic non-supervenience, see Tooley 1977: 669–72 and Carroll 1994: 60–8.)

On Lewis's behalf, it might be replied that were there nothing but a lone electron, then a great many actual laws would be vacuous (such as Coulomb's law, not to mention "All emeralds are green"). They would then be true, trivially, but what would there be to make them laws? Furthermore, if laws fail to supervene on the Humean base, then how could we ever know – even if all observable facts were available to us – what the laws are?

Clearly, we have here a major philosophical dispute. Lewis regards the laws as arising *from below*, out of the Humean mosaic; they are constituted by that mosaic. Non-Humean accounts, in contrast, take the laws as governing the universe, and so as being imposed on the Humean mosaic *from above*; the laws are facts over and above the facts they govern. Dretske (1977), Tooley (1977), and Armstrong (1983) have proposed broadly similar non-Humean accounts, according to which the laws are irreducible, contingent relations among universals. That emeraldhood (a universal) stands in a relation of *nomic necessitation* to greenness (another universal) metaphysically demands that all emeralds are green (a regularity).

Any account of natural law must account for the laws' special roles in science – notably in connection with induction, counterfactuals, and explanation. Armstrong, Dretske, and Tooley argue that if a law is merely a regularity (even one belonging to the best system), then for the law that all Fs are G, together with Fa, to explain why it is the case that Ga would amount either to Fa & Ga explaining itself, or to spatio-temporally remote instances of the regularity explaining this one (and vice versa), or to the entire Humean mosaic (including irrelevant events) effectively figuring in the explanation. So a regularity view cannot account for the laws' explanatory power. Lewis replies that to explain a fact just is to place it within the simplest, most comprehensive system of the world, i.e., to locate it in relation to the "best system." In contrast, without some further, independent characterization of the relation of *nomic necessitation*, Lewis says, it is unclear why Ga should be explained by Fa and such a relation's holding between F-ness and G-ness. That relation is merely stipulated to be explanatorily potent.

Although a relation of nomic necessitation is contingent, its advocates say that it would still have held had things been different in some nomically possible way (e.g., had I missed my bus to work this morning); relations among universals are not vulnerable to being overturned by such counterfactual perturbations among the particulars they govern. Hence, the laws would still have been laws, had I missed my bus to work this morning. Lewis replies that, once again, non-Humeans are merely stipulating their lawmaker to have whatever properties they believe it must have in order to account for scientific reasoning. Furthermore, Lewis believes that in a deterministic world, the counterfactual supposition that I missed my bus to work this morning requires a "small miracle" (a single localized violation of the actual laws) in order for this departure from actuality to be accommodated in the least disruptive fashion: without modifying the past by including this supposition's nomically necessary causal antecedents. Hence, the laws would have been different had I missed my bus to work this morning; some actual laws would have been violated (by the "miracle"), so not all actual laws would still have been true and, since the laws must at least be facts, not all actual laws would still have been laws. On Lewis's view, that the laws are not "held sacred" under counterfactual suppositions is best explained by a Humean view, according to which there is no great metaphysical gulf separating laws from accidents.

Armstrong contends that Lewis's account cannot explain why the law that all emeralds are green underwrites the fact that, had there been another emerald, then all emeralds would still have been green. That the best system includes the fact that all emeralds are green gives us no basis, in supposing that there were another emerald, for believing that it would be green. We are arbitrarily extending the regularity to cover a new case. Lewis replies that part of the logic of counterfactual reasoning is that the best system is especially influential in determining which possible world where there is another emerald is closest to the actual world. A scientific essentialist, on the other hand, turns Armstrong's objection to Lewis against Armstrong himself. Whereas Armstrong believes that a certain relation's holding among universals forces a regularity on to the world, making that regularity (nomically) necessary, a scientific essentialist argues that a relation's holding contingently among universals has no necessity to impart to a regularity; a regularity isn't made necessary in virtue of following from a relationship among universals unless that relationship is itself necessary. (Lewis 1983: 366 (cf. van Fraassen 1989: 106) agrees with this critique of Armstrong: that Armstrong's posited relation is called "nomic necessitation" does not give it the power to confer necessity on a regularity.) A brute, contingent relation of nomic necessitation is insufficient to sustain counterfactuals; there is no reason why a contingent relation among universals should still obtain, had there been another emerald. A metaphysically necessary relation is required.

Yet some counterfactual conditionals seem sustained by mere accidents, such as counterfactuals regarding the car's maximum speed had we depressed the pedal to a half-inch from the floor. Furthermore, the laws' metaphysical necessity makes the laws true in every possible world. How, then, do we account for the truth of counterfactuals with nomically impossible antecedents? For example, if it is an accident that all of the wires on the table are made of copper, then (in some conversational contexts, at least) it is true that had copper been electrically insulating, then all of the wires on the table would have been useless. Likewise, physicists tell us that the existence of living things is the result of exquisite coordination among the laws of nature: had the electromagnetic force been a little stronger relative to the strong nuclear force, then nuclei larger than carbon would not have been stable. How should these counterlegals be understood, if laws are metaphysical necessities?

In future years, philosophers will undoubtedly continue to develop various accounts of what laws are that aim to explain what laws do.

See also Causation; Confirmation; Determinism; Essentialism and natural kinds; Explanation.

References

Armstrong, D. M. (1983) *What Is a Law of Nature?* Cambridge: Cambridge University Press.
Carroll, J. (1994) *Laws of Nature*, Cambridge: Cambridge University Press.
Cartwright, N. (1983) *How the Laws of Nature Lie*, Oxford: Clarendon.
Dretske, F. (1977) "Laws of Nature," *Philosophy of Science* 44: 248–68.
Ellis, B. (2002) *The Philosophy of Nature: A Guide to the New Essentialism*, Montreal and Kingston: McGill–Queen's University Press.
Fodor, J. (1974) "Special Sciences," *Synthese* 28: 97–115.
Foster, J. (2004) *The Divine Lawmaker*, Oxford: Clarendon.
Giere, R. (1999) *Science Without Laws*, Chicago: University of Chicago Press.
Goodman, N. (1983) *Fact, Fiction, and Forecast*, 4th edn, Cambridge, MA: Harvard University Press.
Lange, M. (2000) *Natural Laws in Scientific Practice*, New York: Oxford University Press.
Lewis, D. (1973) *Counterfactuals*, Cambridge, MA: Harvard University Press.
—— (1983) "New Work for a Theory of Universals," *Australasian Journal of Philosophy* 61: 343–77.
—— (1986) *Philosophical Papers*, Volume 2, New York: Oxford University Press.
Sober, E. (1988) "Confirmation and Law-Likeness," *Philosophical Review* 97: 93–8.
Tooley, M. (1977) "The Nature of Law," *Canadian Journal of Philosophy* 7: 667–98.
Van Fraassen, B. C. (1989) *Laws and Symmetry*, Oxford: Clarendon.

Further reading

Many important papers (including many of the works cited above) appear in Carroll, *Readings on Laws of Nature* (Pittsburgh, PA: University of Pittsburgh Press, 2004). In "Humean Supervenience Debugged," *Mind* 103 (1994): 473–90, Lewis gives his final statement of his account of laws. Armstrong's *A World of States of Affairs* (Cambridge: Cambridge University Press, 1997) includes a useful overview of his approach. Shoemaker's "Causality and Properties," in P. van Inwagen (ed.) *Time and Cause* (Dordrecht: Reidel, 1995 [1974]) has strongly influenced scientific essentialism. Fodor (1974) is the classic defense of the autonomy of special sciences; for a different defense, see Lange, "Who's Afraid of Ceteris Paribus Laws?" *Erkenntnis* 57 (2002): 407–23; every paper in this issue concerns *ceteris paribus* laws. Beatty's "The Evolutionary Contingency Thesis," in G. Wolters and J. Lennox (eds) *Concepts, Theories, and Rationality in the Biological Sciences* (Pittsburgh, PA: University of Pittsburgh Press, 1995, pp. 45–81) gives a powerful argument that any biological generalization is an evolutionary accident, not a law. Cartwright's *The Dappled World* (Cambridge: Cambridge University Press, 1999) elaborates her views on the limits of lawfulness in nature.

20

NATURALISM

Ronald N. Giere

Introduction

Naturalism is a general program for all of philosophy, including ethics, the philosophy of language and mind, epistemology, and the philosophy of science. There are some general features of naturalism shared by all these different philosophical projects. Yet, in each of those areas, the impulse to naturalization has had various motivations and a distinctive history. I begin this essay by attempting to characterize the general naturalistic program before moving on to considering the specific project of naturalizing the philosophy of science.

Naturalism as a methodological stance

Characterizing a general naturalistic program turns out to be far from easy. If one agrees that little outside the realm of abstract constructions, such as a geometrical circle, has anything like an essence to be captured in an explicit definition, there can be no strict definition of naturalism. In this case one can hardly do better than begin with a passage from the later writings of the foremost American champion of naturalism, John Dewey. "Naturalism," he wrote, "is opposed to idealistic spiritualism, but it is also opposed to super-naturalism and to that mitigated version of the latter that appeals to transcendent *a priori* principles placed in a realm above Nature and beyond experience." This passage is typical of commentaries on naturalism in emphasizing what naturalism opposes over what it proposes. In this passage Dewey is opposing "idealistic spiritualism" (Hegel?), "super-naturalism" (religion?), and "transcendent *a priori* principles" (Kant?).

Here is a suggestion for at least the form of a positive characterization: *Naturalists insist that all aspects of the world can be accounted for naturalistically*. Scientific accounts are the obvious exemplars for naturalistic accounts, but one should not rule out historical accounts in the form of narratives expressed in everyday concepts or, indeed, everyday accounts, so long as they make no overt appeals to a transcendent realm.

What, one might reasonably ask, constitutes a scientific account of anything? The best general answer a naturalist can give is: *A scientific account is one sanctioned by a currently recognized science*. To say more is to risk going beyond the bounds of naturalism. At the most general level naturalists, not being willing to appeal to essences, cannot attempt to solve the demarcation problem by providing a definition that separates scientific accounts from non-scientific ones. At a less abstract level, naturalists know that what counts as a scientific account changes over time. For most of the seventeenth century, for example, mechanical accounts appealing to action at a distance would have been rejected. In the eighteenth century, after the success of Newton's *Principia*, such accounts became commonplace. Ultimately, naturalists can do no more than follow such historical developments. This does not mean that naturalists cannot criticize some current scientific practices, but such criticism can be based only on common sense or on a critical understanding of other scientific practices, there being no extra-scientific basis for any other sort of appeal.

A major problem with this positive characterization of naturalism is that it invites the charge of begging the question against all those who would appeal to the super-natural or to *a priori* principles. How could anyone know that all aspects of reality have a scientific explanation? A danger here is that a would-be naturalist might fall into the trap of trying to provide an *a priori* argument for naturalism. That would be self-defeating. So the problem is to find a way of defending naturalism from *within* a naturalistic perspective.

Although it is tempting to think that naturalism may be defended empirically, there is no empirical way to test the general claim that everything can be accounted for naturalistically. There is, of course, good evidence for more specific naturalistic claims. During the nineteenth century there were still many who claimed that life could not be explained in terms of natural causes. By the beginning of the twenty-first century, particularly after the development of molecular biology, few doubt that life is a wholly natural phenomenon. Now a primary candidate for non-naturalistic explanations is human consciousness or, maybe, self-consciousness. In advance of an accepted scien-tific explanation of consciousness, the best one can do is offer the inductive argument that, since we have successfully explained life and many other things naturalistically, probably a naturalistic explanation of consciousness will eventually be forthcoming.

My recommendation for naturalists is to take a *methodological* turn. Characterize naturalism not as a thesis, but as a method. A general formulation of the method would be something like this: *For any aspect of the world, seek a naturalistic rather than a super-naturalistic (or a priori) explanation.* It is a virtue of a methodological stance that its adoption does not even seem to require an *a priori* justification. Commitment to the method can be sufficiently justified by appealing to past successes at finding naturalistic explanations, such as that for organic life. One might argue even that the success rate has been going up for the past 300 years. More than that one cannot do without going outside a naturalistic stance. I think naturalists should settle for the methodological stance. Of course, naturalists can also help themselves to currently accepted scientific conclusions, remembering that such conclusions are always subject to revision or even outright rejection.

A corollary to the general methodological stance of always seeking naturalistic accounts is that, once a sufficient naturalistic explanation is at hand, there is no need to look for any further non-naturalistic explanations. This is in line with a standard interpretation of the relationship between evolution and special creation. By showing how species could evolve through natural processes, Darwin undercut projects for a natural theology based on an argument from design. The apparent design in nature is only apparent, so there is no basis for positing an intelligent designer. The justification for this corollary is also methodological. The general aim of understanding the world, which presumably we all share, is not advanced by adopting hypotheses with no empirical support. The discovery of a naturalistic explanation of a previously disputed phenomenon undermines any non-naturalistic explanation.

Naturalism in the philosophy of science

Projects for naturalizing the philosophy of science were advanced independently within the Vienna Circle by Otto Neurath and in the United States by John Dewey from roughly 1925 to 1945. A decade later, Ernest Nagel, a philosopher of science familiar with both Neurath and Dewey, defended a general philosophical naturalism in his presidential address to the American Philosophical Association. In 1969, W. V. Quine published his influential article "Epistemology Naturalized." Nevertheless, recent interest in naturalization in the philosophy of science dates only from the1980s. Three influences stand out. First, a growing dissatisfaction with logical empiricism and, more generally, with any philosophy of science conceived of as the logical or conceptual analysis of scientific and methodological concepts. Second, this dissatisfaction was in part sparked by a growing interest in the history of science, particularly as employed in Thomas Kuhn's 1962 book *The Structure of Scientific Revolutions*. Finally, beginning in the 1970s, there was a challenge from a newly militant and explicitly naturalistic sociology of science claiming to provide the whole story of how science works.

In thinking about science, it is usual to distinguish between the *process* of doing science, scientific practice, and the *product* of that process, usually understood as scientific knowledge. The project of naturalization applies to both processes and products. The naturalist project for examining knowledge in various special fields rejects claims to special forms of logical and philosophical analysis, preferring to employ fundamentally the same tools employed by the relevant scientists themselves. But philosophers may ask different questions from those that typically concern working scientists. For example, a philosopher of science may ask how the concept of causality in quantum mechanics differs from that in classical mechanics, or how the theories and methods of classical genetics differ from those of molecular genetics. The answers will be framed in terms that can be understood by both scientists and educated lay-persons. No peculiarly philosophical concepts are required. This essay focuses on the naturalizing project for understanding the process of science, including methods for certifying particular knowledge-claims.

Any naturalizing project must face the question: "Naturalize to what?" Scientific subject matter, of course, but what? For the philosophy of science there have been three prominent resources for naturalization: evolutionary theory, cognitive science, and the sociology of science. It is all too often assumed that one of these resources is the only resource needed. My view is that all three are needed, and probably more besides.

Naturalism and evolutionary theory

In addition to providing a paradigm case of the successful application of naturalistic methodology, evolutionary theory provides a resource for a naturalistic study of science itself. For a naturalist, one of the most important facts about humans is that they evolved by natural selection. Thus, even before the development of language and culture humans were sufficiently attuned to their environments successfully to survive and reproduce. For early humans, there never was a general "problem of the external world." Their problems were the very specific ones of doing the right things enough of the time. Thus, human physical and cognitive abilities evolved together to promote appropriate actions, not to promote the discovery of anything like general truths about the world. In fact, these two goals are often in conflict. For example, given that one has to act quickly and thus on the basis of only partial information, it is usually better for long-run survival to overestimate the presence of predators and take evasive action even when it is not really necessary. Failure to take evasive action when it is necessary has a much higher cost. I thus reject the arguments of some evolutionary theorists and philosophers of science that early humans evolved an understanding of some inductive principles along the lines of, say, the consilience of inductions. Similar problems arise for any strictly evolutionary epistemology.

Apart from putting to rest Cartesian doubts about the possibility of human knowledge of the world, the fact that humans are evolved creatures does more to frame the problem of a naturalistic theory of science than to provide resources for solving it. The problem is this: How did creatures with the evolved physical and cognitive capacities of contemporary humans come to create the vast body of scientific knowledge that now exists, including evolutionary theory itself?

There is another, altogether different, role that evolutionary theory has played in naturalist theories of science: namely, as a model for changes in scientific knowledge over time. The strongest such position is that the evolution of scientific knowledge is structurally isomorphic to the evolution of populations of organisms. This requires, for example, finding counterparts to genotypes and phenotypes in the process of science itself, a project many view with suspicion. Most people impressed with evolutionary ways of thinking about the course of science take a much looser approach. They note the great amount of chance in

(a) the ideas that get proposed or the experiments that get done (*variation*);
(b) which ideas and results become accepted and used (*selection*); and
(c) which ideas and results get passed on for future researchers (*transmission*).

This approach has the advantage that it need not deny the obvious fact that individual scientists are highly purpose-driven: they propose hypotheses to solve known problems and experimentally test these hypotheses to help decide which are worth pursuing. As a general framework for thinking about the historical development of science, such evolutionary thinking provides a useful counterbalance to the Kuhnian stage theory and other developmental accounts of scientific change.

Naturalism and cognitive science

Even if one adopts a broadly evolutionary account of scientific change, there is still a need for some more specific account of the mechanisms that produce the variation, selection, and transmission of scientific concepts – the counterpart of genetics in the evolutionary synthesis. Some of these mechanisms are surely cognitive in the sense of cognition studied in the cognitive sciences and, more specifically, in the small subfield of the cognitive study of science.

The operation of cognitive processes is most salient in the generation of new theoretical concepts as well as new strategies for experimentation, and also the design of new instruments. Examples of such cognitive processes include mental modeling, creating analogies, and devising thought experiments. Such processes presuppose the use of language and other symbolic artifacts, the operation of which a naturalist expects eventually to be explained within the cognitive sciences. The extent to which the experimental testing and acceptance or rejection of specific claims can be subsumed under the cognitive categories of judgment or decision-making is considered below. One would expect that the mechanisms for the transmission of knowledge are primarily social, though presupposing underlying cognitive processes.

One of the most promising recent developments in the cognitive sciences for the cognitive study of science is the study of distributed cognitive systems. The dominant idea in the cognitive sciences that cognition is computation has presupposed that cognition is located in a limited space, such as in a computer or a brain. This limitation is abandoned in the consideration of distributed cognitive systems which include combinations of humans, computers, and other artifacts. Large experimental systems such as the Hubble Space Telescope or a gene-sequencing laboratory are prime examples of such systems. Here one regards the process of cognition as distributed throughout the whole system. It is the whole system, and not any one component, that produces the cognitive output, typically some kind of knowledge. Whether the whole system is still usefully thought of as computational is an open question.

Also open is the issue of whether one should ascribe other cognitive attributes to the system as a whole. Does the system as a whole "remember" anything? Does it "know" anything? Does it "believe" anything? Does it have "intentions" or "desires"? Is it "responsible" for the results produced? Is it "conscious"? My view is that we should keep "cognition" as a technical term of cognitive science so we can talk about distributed cognitive systems, but limit the other traditional cognitive attributes to the human components. This avoids creating unnecessary puzzles and keeps a naturalistic philosophy of science compatible with the history of science, where only human actors are recognized.

A major benefit of introducing the notion of a distributed cognitive system is that it eliminates much of the perceived conflict between cognitive and social explanations of scientific processes. The social organization and interactions among all components, human and non-human alike, are part of the system as a cognitive system in that they all contribute to the quality of the cognitive output. Typically, it is the social organization among the humans that determines just how the cognitive processes are to be distributed throughout the whole system.

Naturalism and the sociology of science

Continuing with a generally evolutionary picture of scientific change, it is undeniable that many of the mechanisms of change are social. This is particularly clear in the case of mechanisms for the transmission of scientific knowledge. It takes a fairly elaborate social superstructure, including a system of education, to ensure that scientific knowledge is transmitted to a new scientific cohort.

But social organization also plays a crucial role in the certification of scientific knowledge. One can give a cognitive account of how individuals come to know various scientific claims. Yet, individual knowledge is not yet scientific knowledge. Scientific knowledge is *public* knowledge. To become public it has to pass through various public processes. Earlier, to become scientific knowledge a claim had to be published in the transactions of a scientific body such as the Royal Society. Today, certification as scientific knowledge typically requires peer review and publication in a recognized journal (which might be only electronic). This is a social, not merely individual, process. If one thinks of scientific knowledge as produced by a distributed cognitive system, then that system is very distributed indeed, including the process of review, publication, and distribution.

Naturalism and normativity

The most common objection to the general naturalist project is that it cannot account for normative aspects of life. This objection is perhaps most serious in the case of naturalistic ethics, but it is raised against all naturalist projects, including naturalistic semantics where it is argued that, because some uses of any particular language are correct and others incorrect, normativity is unavoidable. These objections seem to me to be based on an unduly narrow understanding of naturalism, equating it with a crude materialism. So one asks how anything merely material can embody norms. Here an evolutionary perspective helps. Humans are material objects, to be sure, but highly complex objects. A human society, even a small group of hunter–gatherers, will develop some division of labor, even if based mainly on sex differences. So some activities will be regarded as proper for some members and not for others. Thus, as Nietzsche argued, we have at most a genealogy of morals, not a justification for any particular moral practices. There is no naturalistic distinction between a social practice being regarded as normative and its somehow really being normative. Similarly for the evolution of language. For humans, one could say, normativity is natural. One only must resist the non-naturalistic urge to seek beyond nature or history for something further on which to ground our moral and other normative judgments.

Returning to the philosophy of science, it is argued that, because the whole project of naturalized philosophy of science is based only on scientific findings, it can at most describe actual scientific practice; it cannot provide a normative basis for distinguishing good science from pseudo-science. Naturalism, it is concluded, leads straight to relativism. Naturalists point out that this objection assumes that there exists an extra-scientific criterion for demarcating good science from pseudo-science.

It assumes science has a discoverable essence, something naturalists deny. This is borne out, naturalists argue, by the repeated failure to find an agreed demarcation criterion. Still, it is a fact that scientists and others claim to distinguish good science from mere pretenders to that status. Naturalists need an account of the bases for such judgments.

The usual naturalist account is that the norms operative in science are all conditional norms of the general form: if the goal is G, use method M. The justification for such norms is itself empirical, consisting of evidence that employing M is a relatively reliable means of obtaining G. This reply itself gives rise to several problems. One is the specification of the goal, or goals, of scientific inquiry. Is this not itself a normative issue? A second problem is the threatened regress of methods, since taking the determination of whether M is a reliable means to G as a goal of inquiry seems to require another method of inquiry whose reliability also needs to be investigated. Pragmatism, it will be seen, provides a response to this latter objection.

The most commonly proposed goal for science is truth. Is it not a non-naturalist norm that scientists should seek truth? How could a naturalist justify such a norm? Furthermore, if truth is the goal, and claims to truth are to be based on empirical evidence, then must there not be some rules of rational inference licensing claims to truth based on empirical findings? Surely, it is claimed, these rules are normative and cannot be justified naturalistically.

This non-naturalist appeal to the concept of truth is too quick. First, as has often been pointed out, the simple injunction to seek the truth is useless. Which truths? There is a multitude of truths that one might seek, most of them quite trivial. Presumably scientists are to seek truths that are in some sense important or otherwise significant, but judgments of importance or significance can come only either from within a scientific community or from a surrounding society. Those judgments arise in the natural course of events. No non-natural normative injunction to seek significant truths is needed. Second, the idea that scientists are in the business of producing truths is on oversimplification. Looking at actual scientific practice, one finds scientists producing more or less elaborate models which well represent some aspects of the world, but never perfectly or completely. One might argue that producing such models is a goal of much scientific activity. But, if so, this is just a historical fact about science, though a very significant one, and not a response to a normative injunction grounded outside the practice of science itself.

Naturalism and model choice

There remains the question of whether the process of testing models empirically requires principles of inference that cannot themselves be naturalistically grounded. Here I suggest one way of testing models without invoking non-naturalistic principles, which is enough to show that it is possible. The crucial step is not to think of empirical testing as involving principles of inference at all, but, rather, as a process of decision-making. This moves the issue to the naturalistic ground of seeking reliable means to given ends.

Here I focus on the special case of a crucial experiment with two rival models. The experiment is assumed to have an observable output which, for purposes of illustration, we can represent schematically as a one-dimensional range, R, of numerical values. The models and the experimental setup should be related as follows:

- If the model M_1 provides a good fit to the real world, then it is very probable that the experiment will yield an outcome in the range R_1 and very improbable that it will yield an outcome in the range R_2.
- If the model M_2 provides a good fit to the real world, then it is very probable that the experiment will yield an outcome in the range R_2 and very improbable that it will yield an outcome in the range R_1.

The *decision rule* is: if the setup yields a reading in the range R_1, choose model M_1 as the best fitting model; if the setup yields a reading in the range R_2, choose model M_2 as the best fitting model. The *conditional norm* is: if one wishes to decide empirically which of two rival models better fits the world, design an experiment satisfying the conditions stated above. The justification for the utility of this norm is that an experiment satisfying those conditions provides a basis for a reliable decision between the two models. To see why this is so, one need only review the situation as presented above. Given the stated design features, if M_1 does provide a good fit to the world, it is very likely that one will observe a reading in the range R_1 and, correctly, choose M_1; similarly, if M_2 in fact best fits the world. In either case one has a good chance of making the correct choice. Of course there is always the possibility that neither model fits the world very well and the experiment yields a result in some intermediate range. In that case, the whole experiment is simply inconclusive.

There are a number of possible objections to this account of empirical testing. One is that it is comparative. A second is that it is subject to a regress. That is, applying the principles of design requires substantive knowledge of the physical probabilities of the experimental setup. If that knowledge were based on previous experiments, they would require similar assumptions, and so on. Pursuing this line of argument leads to a quest for a foundational inductive method that can be applied with no prior general knowledge whatsoever and whose use can be justified *a priori*. Naturalists doubt that any such quest could be successful. In any case, both of these objections can be met by adopting a pragmatist stance.

Naturalism and pragmatism

It is no accident that prominent naturalists of earlier generations embraced pragmatism. Naturalism needs a philosophical orientation that makes sense of its rejection of *a priori* metaphysical and epistemological principles. Pragmatism provides that orientation for contemporary naturalistic philosophers of science. The relevant pragmatist doctrine is that one always begins from the current state of what is taken to be known. From that point, anything can be questioned and subjected to experimental test, provided that there is some basis for doubt. But not everything can be questioned at once. Universal

Cartesian doubt is ruled out. Thus, in place of a foundationalist picture of knowledge of either rationalist or empiricist persuasion, one has claims to knowledge regulated by a method of motivated doubt and empirical investigation.

Given that pragmatist stance, it is not a problem that empirical tests of the fit of models to the world always require some general empirical claims in order to determine the probability of possible outcomes of an experiment if one or another model in fact fits its subject matter fairly well. Such claims can themselves be tested if they are seriously questioned, but, if among currently accepted claims, they need not be questioned for a test to be regarded as reliable. Similarly, the fact that good tests of the fit of a model are comparative fits with the pragmatist idea that empirical testing should be motivated by a specific need to know how well a particular model fits the world. Such a need is generated by consideration of a potentially viable alternative.

Naturalism and realism

Realism and empiricism may be understood as two opposed views of the goals of science. Given the long-standing associations between naturalism and pragmatism, and between pragmatism and empiricism, it might seem problematic that a naturalist could be a realist.

In fact, naturalists should be skeptical that there is any such thing as *the* (singular) goal of science. Apart from their personal goals, which might include fame and fortune, scientists *qua* scientists have historically pursued different goals along the spectrum between empiricism and realism. Before Galileo and Newton, most astronomers were satisfied if they could "save the phenomena," that is, come up with a geometrical arrangement that would predict the observed apparent motions of the sun, the moon, the planets, and other stars – as observed with the naked eye from the earth. After Galileo's introduction of telescopes for observing the heavens, other phenomena, such as the phases of Venus, needed also to be explained. And after Newton, it was required also to give an account of the forces, especially gravity, producing the observed motions. In the nineteenth century, thermodynamics was pursued without speculations about a possible atomic structure of gasses. Finding relations among thermodynamic variables was enough. Discovering an underlying microscopic structure was not a goal. Later it became a goal and was pursued quite successfully. With the emergence of quantum theory, predicting observable results became the professed aim as physicists became convinced that finding an intelligible, realistic account was impossible. In light of this historical diversity, it is difficult to argue that there is some single goal that scientists ought, normatively, always to pursue. This leaves naturalists free to be either empiricists or realists in different contexts, depending on the particular circumstances.

Here it should be noted that the schema outlined above for empirically testing the relative fit of alternative models required only a distinction between models and data, not a distinction between what is observable and what is not. Thus, for example, the flux of solar neutrinos detected on earth might be used as data with which to distinguish rival models of nuclear reactions deep inside the sun. A neutrino flux would traditionally be regarded as a non-observable phenomenon. But it is reliably detectable, and that is all that matters for a naturalist. Thus, in many circumstances, naturalists can be realists.

Naturalism and secularism

By definition, naturalism implies the rejection of super-naturalism, and thus the rejection of the metaphysical claims of religions that posit the existence of a super-natural being. Given naturalism's reliance on the methods and findings of the sciences, naturalism elicits science in the cause of secularism. The details of how this relationship might function in practice deserve some consideration.

Naturalists need not be guilty of a simple scientism that recognizes only scientific knowledge as legitimate. We all know many things about our everyday lives that were not learned through any process of scientific investigation. Most people in techno-logically advanced societies, for example, know their birthday. This was not the case in pre-industrial societies. In Europe, name-days were better known, being the dates associated with the Christian saints after whom most people were named. Yet all our current scientific knowledge supports the view that one's birthday is the kind of thing that people now can know even though they might not have done in the past.

The naturalist principle here is that claims to knowledge should at least be compatible with currently accepted scientific knowledge. Put the other way around, current scientific knowledge acts as a constraint on claims to knowledge of the natural world. Thus, any claim to knowledge of specific events in the universe outside the light cone of the claimant would be rejected on naturalistic grounds as incompatible with special relativity. More significantly, the all-too-common belief that evolution has been guided by an intelligent designer to insure the existence of humans is also ruled out by evolutionary theory. On evolutionary principles, the existence of a mutation is probabilistically independent of how favorable or unfavorable that mutation might be in the given environment. Interference in that process, however it might be accom-plished, would destroy that independence. And, of course, the creation of the earth, let alone the universe, in six days is incompatible with established knowledge in many fields.

But naturalism puts stronger constraints on claims to knowledge. To take a somewhat fanciful example, someone might claim that there is an advanced civilization now operating under the surface of Mars. That possibility might well be compatible with all existing scientific knowledge. Yet it is naturalistically unacceptable because it has not been tested by any known reliable method. Imagination or intuition is not a reliable method for generating knowledge of the world. Most of the metaphysical claims made by religions fall into this category. This is particularly true of claims based on ancient texts such as the Bible or the Koran. Ancient texts are notoriously unreliable.

The above naturalistic restrictions on religious beliefs apply only to empirical or metaphysical claims, not to claims about what is ethically correct. A separation between facts and values is preserved, but restricted. The metaphysical claims of religions are taken by their adherents as grounds for the ethical prescriptions. Naturalism undercuts such claims to authority. It forces ethical claims to be argued for in secular terms. So, although naturalism generates no specific ethical claims, it does constrain debates over ethical issues to be conducted in secular terms.

See also Explanation; The historical turn in the philosophy of science; Logical empiricism; Pragmatism; Scientific method; Social studies of science.

Further reading

Donald Campbell's "Evolutionary Epistemology," in P. A. Schilpp (ed.) *The Philosophy of Karl Popper* (La Salle, IL: Open Court, 1974), pp. 413–63, is the founding paper for what became evolutionary epistemology. My book *Explaining Science: A Cognitive Approach* (Chicago: University of Chicago Press, 1988) develops a naturalistic theory of science drawing on resources from the cognitive sciences. My *Science Without Laws* (Chicago: University of Chicago Press, 1999) includes the papers "Philosophy of Science Naturalized" and "Naturalism and Realism"; my latest book, *Scientific Perspectivism* (Chicago: University of Chicago Press, 2006), contains a chapter on distributed cognition in science. For a feminist approach to naturalized philosophy of science by a leading feminist philosopher of science, see Lynn Hankinson-Nelson's "A Feminist Naturalized Philosophy of Science," *Synthese* 104 (1995): 399–421. Clifford Hooker's "Evolutionary Naturalist Realism: Circa 1985," in *A Realistic Theory of Science* (Albany, NY: State University of New York Press, 1987) is an assessment of evolutionary naturalist approaches to a realistic theory of science by one of the major proponents of evolutionary naturalism. David Hull's *Science as a Process: An Evolutionary Account of the Social and Conceptual Development of Science* (Chicago: University of Chicago Press, 1988) is a monumental attempt to show that the social and conceptual developments of science are structurally identical with that of organic evolution. Philip Kitcher's "The Naturalists Return," *Philosophical Review* 101 (1992): 53–114, reviews naturalistic developments in philosophy during the second half of the twentieth century. Larry Laudan's *Beyond Positivism and Relativism* (Bolder, CO: Westview Press, 1996) includes papers expounding and defending his signature normative naturalism. Nancy Nersessian's "Interpreting Scientific and Engineering Practices: Integrating the Cognitive, Social, and Cultural Dimensions," in M. E. Gorman, R. Tweney, D. Gooding, and A. Kincannon (eds) *Scientific and Technological Thinking* (Mahwah, NJ: Erlbaum, 2005), pp. 7–56, is an authoritative review of recent connections between cognitive and social studies of science. Joseph Rouse's *How Scientific Practices Matter: Reclaiming Philosophical Naturalism* (Chicago: University of Chicago Press, 2002) is a sophisticated development of philosophical naturalism applied to science. Finally, John Ryder's *American Philosophical Naturalism in the Twentieth Century* (Amherst, NY: Prometheus Books, 1994) includes a good selection of papers, mostly from the first half of the century.

21
REALISM/ANTI-REALISM
Michael Devitt

The main realism/anti-realism issue in the philosophy of science is the issue of *scientific realism*, concerned with the unobservable entities of science. However, there is also a more general issue, often known as "realism about the external world," concerned primarily with the observable entities of common sense, but which spreads to scientific entities, both observable and unobservable. The issue of scientific realism is best approached from a perspective on the more general issue.

What are the realism issues?

The literature provides a bewildering variety of answers to this question, far too many to discuss here. I provide answers along what seem to me the right lines and then allude briefly to others.

I think that we should take these issues to be concerned with realism doctrines having two dimensions. The *existence dimension* of the general doctrine is a commitment to the existence of, primarily, the observable physical entities posited by common sense: stones, trees, cats, and the like. The existence dimension of scientific realism is a commitment to the existence of most of the unobservables posited by science: atoms, viruses, photons, and the like. Idealists, the traditional opponent of realists, have typically not denied this dimension; or, at least, have not straightforwardly denied it. What they have typically denied is *the independence dimension*. According to some idealists, the entities identified by the first dimension are made up of mental items, *ideas* or *sense data*, and so are not external to the mind. In recent times, under the influence of Kant, another sort of idealism has been much more common. According to these idealists, the entities are not, in a certain respect, *objective*: they depend for their existence and nature on the cognitive activities and capacities of our minds; we partly *construct* them by imposing our concepts. Furthermore, since we often differ in our worldview and hence differ in our concepts, we construct different worlds. This *constructivism* is the view of the very influential philosopher of science Thomas Kuhn (1970). Realists reject all such mind dependences.

Though the focus of the debate has mostly been on the independence dimension, the existence dimension is important. First, it identifies the entities that are the subject of the dispute over independence. In particular, it distinguishes a realism worth fighting for from a commitment to there merely being *something* independent of us. Second, in the discussion of unobservables – the debate about *scientific* realism – the main controversy has been over existence.

We can capture the general doctrine's commitment to observables well enough as follows:

> *Common-sense realism*: Most of the observable physical entities of common sense and science exist mind-independently.

Scientific realism is our main concern and we need to be a bit more careful before defining it. So here are some clarifications. First, talk of the "commitments of science" is vague. In the context of the realism debate it means the commitments of *current* scientific theories. The realist's attitude to past theories will be the concern of the section "Arguments against scientific realism." Second, the realist's commitment is to *most* of the unobservables posited by science. It would be foolhardy to hold that current science is not making any mistakes, and no realist would hold this. Third, this cautiousness does not seem to go far enough: it comes too close to a blanket endorsement of the claims of science. Yet scientists themselves have many epistemic attitudes to their theories. These attitudes range from outright disbelief in a few theories that are useful for predictions but known to be false, through agnosticism about exciting speculations at the frontiers, to a strong commitment to thoroughly tested and well-established theories. The realist is not less skeptical than the scientist: she is committed only to the claims of the tested and established theories. Furthermore, realism has a critical aspect. Theories may posit unobservables that, given their purposes, they need not posit. Realism is committed only to *essential* unobservables. In brief, realism is a cautious and critical generalization of the commitments of well-established current theories.

Utilizing the language of these clarifications we can define a doctrine of scientific realism well enough as follows:

> *Scientific realism*: Most of the essential unobservables of well-established current scientific theories exist mind-independently.

This is a commitment only to the existence of unobservables. Realists often want a stronger doctrine than this *entity*-realism: they want a *fact*-realism committed to scientific theories mostly being right about the properties of those entities. But to keep it simple my focus is on the weaker doctrine.

According to definitions like these, the realism issues that concern us are *metaphysical* ones about the nature of the world. The literature contains a bewildering variety of other definitions, many of which seem very different. I have discussed these matters at length elsewhere (1997: Chs 2–4, 2005) and must be very brief here. Some of this variety are *epistemic* definitions about what we know about the world. Others are *apparently semantic* definitions about the truth and reference of our theories. These definitions do not differ in any *significant* way from straightforwardly metaphysical ones. However, there are others that do differ significantly. Most important are those that really have a semantic component. "Scientific realism" is often now taken to refer to some combination of a metaphysical doctrine like scientific realism with a correspondence theory of truth (Putnam 1978; Fine 1986a; Kitcher 1993). The combination is strange. Skepticism about unobservables, which is indubitably at the center of the realism debate, is simply not about the nature of truth. The issue of that nature is surely fascinating but is orthogonal to the realism issue. No doctrine of truth is constitutive of metaphysical doctrines of scientific realism.

I turn now to the metaphysical issues. I start with common-sense realism because, manifestly, anyone who rejects that will reject scientific realism: if one has doubts about the independent existence of observables one will surely have doubts also about the independent existence of unobservables. So, scientific realism arises as a *distinct* issue only once common-sense realism has been accepted.

Common-sense realism

Realism about the ordinary observable physical world is a compelling doctrine. It is almost universally held outside intellectual circles. It is aptly named "common-sense realism" because it is the core of common sense. What, then, has persuaded so many philosophers out of it? The tradition provides a clear answer: the problem of extreme skepticism. In the *First Meditation* Descartes famously doubted the evidence of his senses. Is he right to believe that he is sitting by the fire? Perhaps he is suffering from an illusion, perhaps he is dreaming, perhaps he is being stimulated by an evil demon. In the face of such doubts, how can it be rational to believe realism?

Idealists think that it is not rational. They see an unbridgeable *gap* between the knowing mind and the independent world the realist believes in. They propose to close the gap between us and the world by abandoning the independence dimension: the world is made up of ideas or is partly constructed by the knowing mind. Only thus, it is thought, could the world be knowable.

A semantic variant of this argument can be abstracted from contemporary anti-realist discussions (Kuhn 1970; Putnam 1978, 1981). Just as traditional philosophers argued for epistemological doctrines that show that we could not *know* the realist world, we can see contemporary philosophers as arguing for semantic doctrines that show that we could not *refer to* the realist world. So the world we refer to cannot be that world but must be a world we make.

Abandoning realism and adopting idealism is, however, very costly. Idealism strikes many as bizarre. Thus, consider constructivism, according to which we partly make the familiar world by imposing our concepts. But how could we literally make dinosaurs and stars? It seems fantastic to suppose that we do.

I have argued elsewhere (2002) for two other responses we might make to the arguments against common-sense realism. First, there is a Moorean response that the arguments proceed in the wrong direction. The arguments are based on speculations about what we could know and refer to. Yet surely realism is much more plausible than these epistemological and semantic speculations that are thought to undermine it. So we should *put metaphysics first* and argue from realism against these speculations. The second response stems from naturalism. From a naturalistic perspective, these speculations cannot be supported *a priori* and they do not come close to having the empirical support enjoyed by realism. The arguments against realism use the wrong method and proceed in the wrong direction.

One final point about the issue of common-sense realism is very important to the issue of scientific realism. Extreme skepticism demonstrates that the evidence we have for any of our beliefs about the external world is *logically compatible* with other views of the world, for example, with the view that we are manipulated by an evil demon. So the following *weak underdetermination* thesis is true:

WU: Any theory has rivals that entail the same actual given observational evidence.

Not even a theory about observables can be simply *deduced* from any given body of evidence; indeed, not even the very existence of an observable can be deduced *from experience*. If we are to put extreme skepticism behind us we must rely on some *non*-deductive, or *ampliative*, method of inference that will support common-sense realism over the likes of the evil-demon hypothesis. This reliance might appeal to *a priori* insight or to empirical considerations, but without it there is no escape from extreme skepticism. Now, given that scientific realism arises as a distinct issue only once common-sense realism has been accepted, it follows that the issue arises only once we have adopted *some* ampliative method of inference that is sufficient to escape from extreme skepticism. The issue then arises because, armed with that method, and confident enough about the observable world, there is thought to be a *further* problem believing what science says about unobservables. So the defense of scientific realism does not require that we refight the battle with extreme skepticism, just that we respond to this special skepticism about unobservables.

We turn now to the most influential arguments for and against scientific realism. The arguments *for* are the "success argument" and related explanationist arguments (see next section). The arguments *against* are the "underdetermination argument," which starts from the claim that theories always have empirically equivalent rivals; and the "pessimistic meta-induction," which starts from a bleak view of the accuracy of past scientific theories ("Arguments against scientific realism").

Arguments for scientific realism

The most famous argument for scientific realism is the argument from the success of science (Putnam 1978: 18–19). Scientific theories tend to be successful in that their observational predictions tend to come out true: if a theory says that S, then the world tends to be observationally as if S. Why are theories thus successful? The best explanation, the realist claims, is that the theories' theoretical terms typically refer – scientific realism – and the theories are approximately true: the world is observationally as if S because, approximately, S. For example, why are all the observations we make just the sort we would make if there were atoms? Answer: because there *are* atoms. Sometimes the realist goes further: it would be "a miracle" that theories were so successful if they were not approximately true. Realism does not just have the best explanation of success, it has *the only good* explanation.

Larry Laudan (1981) mounted a sustained attack on this argument. In the first prong of this attack, Laudan offers a list of past theories – phlogiston theory is a favorite example – that were successful but are now known not to be approximately true. The realist has a number of responses. First, the success of a theory can be challenged: although it was thought to be successful, it was not really so. But unless the criterion of success is put so high that not even contemporary theories will qualify, some theories on Laudan's list will surely survive. Second, it can be argued that a theory was not, in the appropriate sense, well-established and hence not the sort that the realist is committed to; or that entities it posited were not essential to its success. But surely some theories on the list will survive this test too. Third, the realist can insist that there are many other past theories, ones *not* on Laudan's list, for which the realist's explanation of success works fine.

Still, the realist faces a problem with the theories that survive on Laudan's list. In my view (2005), the realist should modify the explanation for such a surviving theory, explaining its success by appealing to the unobservables of replacement theories.

But perhaps anti-realists *can* explain success? There have been attempts:

- Bas van Fraassen offered a Darwinian explanation: "any scientific theory is born into a life of fierce competition, a jungle red in tooth and claw. Only the successful theories survive" (1980: 39). But this explanation is not relevant because it is not explaining the same thing as the realist's success argument. It is explaining why we humans hold successful theories. It is not explaining why those particular theories are successful.
- Arthur Fine (1986b) claimed that anti-realism can explain success as well as realism can by appealing to a theory's instrumental reliability (Fine is not committed to this anti-realist explanation). Jarrett Leplin develops this proposal and labels it "surrealism." The basic idea is that although the world has a *deep structure* this structure is *not experientially accessible*. "The explanation of the success of any theory ... is that the actual structure of the world operates at the experiential level as if the theory represented it correctly" (Leplin 1997: 26). Leplin goes on to argue that the surrealist explanation is not a successful alternative to the realist one.

In the second prong of his attack on realism, Laudan has criticized the realist's success argument for its dependence on inference to the best explanation, or *abduction*. Fine (1986a: 113–22) has made a similar criticism. Abduction is a method of inference that an anti-realist might reject. Van Fraassen (1980), for one, does reject it. Is the realist entitled to rely on abduction? Richard Boyd (1984: 65–75) has argued that the anti-realists are not in a position to deny entitlement because scientists regularly use abduction to draw conclusions about *observables*.

Boyd's argument illustrates an important, and quite general, realist strategy to defend unobservables against discrimination, to defend "unobservable rights." The realist starts by reminding the anti-realist that the debate about *scientific* realism is not over extreme skepticism: the anti-realist claims to have knowledge of observables (see "Common-sense realism"). The realist then examines the anti-realist's justification for this knowledge. Using this justification she attempts to show, positively, that the epistemology it involves also justifies knowledge of unobservables. And, she attempts to show, negatively, that the case for skepticism about unobservables produced by the anti-realist is no better than the case for skepticism about observables, a skepticism that all parties to the scientific realism dispute have rejected.

So the anti-realist's criticism of the success argument leaves him with the task of showing that he can save his beliefs about observables without using abduction. If he cannot manage this, the criticism fails. If he can, then the realist seems to face the task of justifying abduction.

How concerned should the realist be about this? Perhaps not much. After all, the *anti*-realist must rely on some methods of ampliative inference, even if not on abduction, to overcome extreme skepticism. How are those methods justified? The anti-realist may well have little to say about this, relying on the fact that these methods are widely and successfully used in science and ordinary life and on there being no apparent reason to abandon them. But, of course, that seems to be true of abduction as well. If further justification for a method is required, where could we find it? Any such justification would have to be either *a priori* or empirical. Either way, it is not obvious that the justification of abduction will be more problematic than the justification of the methods of inference relied on by the anti-realists.

The literature contains two other explanationist arguments for scientific realism:

1   Why is our scientific methodology *instrumentally reliable* in that it leads to successful theories, theories that make true observational predictions? Boyd (1984) offers the realist explanation that the methodology is based in a dialectical way on our theories and those theories are approximately true. He argues that anti-realists cannot explain this methodological success.
2   I have offered elsewhere (1997: 113–17) a very basic argument: by supposing that the unobservables of science exist, we can give good explanations of the behavior and characteristics of observed entities, behavior and characteristics which would otherwise remain inexplicable.

In sum, there are some good arguments for scientific realism provided the realist is allowed abduction. It is not obvious that anti-realists are in a position to disallow this.

Arguments against scientific realism

The underdetermination argument

This empiricist argument starts from a doctrine of *empirical equivalence*. Let *T* be any theory committed to unobservables. Then,

EE: *T* has empirically equivalent rivals.

This is taken to imply the *strong underdetermination* thesis:

SU: *T* has rivals that are equally supported by all possible observational evidence for it.

So, doctrines like scientific realism are unjustified.

What is it for two theories to be *empirically equivalent*? The basic idea is that they have the same observational consequences. We shall soon see the importance of looking very closely at this basic idea.

SU should not be confused with other underdetermination theses, particularly the obviously true WU (from the earlier section on common-sense realsim) that leads to the challenge of extreme skepticism. SU is stronger than WU in two respects. First, SU concerns an *ampliative* relation between theories and evidence and not merely a deductive one. Second, SU is concerned with *T*'s relation to *all possible* evidence not merely to the given evidence. If we are to avoid skepticism in the face of WU, we noted, some ampliative method of inference must be accepted. But if SU is true, we face a *further* challenge: ampliative methods do not support *T* over its rivals either on the given evidence or even on all possible evidence. So what *T* says about the unobservable world can make no evidential difference. Surely, then, commitment to what the theory says is a piece of misguided metaphysics. Even with extreme skepticism behind us, realism is threatened.

A good reason for believing EE is that there is an empiricist algorithm for constructing an equivalent rival to *T*. Consider T_0, the theory that the observational consequences of *T* are true. T_0 is obviously empirically equivalent to *T*. Now form *T** by combining T_0 with the negation of *T*. *T** is an empirically equivalent rival to *T*. So EE is established.

It is tempting to respond that *T** is produced by trickery and is not a *genuine* rival to *T*. But this response seems question-begging. We need a principled basis for dismissing rivals as *not genuine*. Following the earlier-described realist strategy, I have argued for such a basis (1997: 150–3, 2002, 2005): in counting the likes of *T** as rivals, EE as it stands is too weak to sustain SU. For, with extreme skepticism behind us, we *are* justified in choosing *T* over empirically equivalent rivals like *T**. If the underdetermination argument is to work, it needs to start from a stronger equivalence thesis, one that does not count any theory as a genuine rival to *T* that can be dismissed by whatever ampliative inferences enable us to avoid extreme skepticism. Precisely how far we can go in thus dismissing rivals remains to be seen, of course, pending an account of how to avoid extreme skepticism. And, given the realist strategy, the account that matters is the one given by the anti-realist.

With EE now restricted to such *genuine* rivals, the next step in assessing the underdetermination argument is a careful consideration of how to interpret EE's talk of empirical equivalence. Given the basic idea of empirical equivalence, a natural interpretation is:

EE1: *T* has genuine rivals that entail the same possible observational evidence.

Whether or not EE*1* is true, it is easy to see that it is inadequate to support SU. This inadequacy arises from the fact that *T* is likely to entail few observations on its own and yet the conjunction of *T* with auxiliary hypotheses, theories of instruments, background assumptions, and so on – briefly, its conjunction with *auxiliaries* – is likely to entail many observations. *T* does not face the tribunal of experience alone (Duhem–Quine). As Laudan and Leplin (1991) point out in their influential critique of the underdetermination argument, by failing to take account of these joint consequences, EE*1* leaves many ways in which evidence could favor *T* over its rivals, contrary to SU. To sustain SU and challenge realism, we need another interpretation of EE.

Consider this interpretation:

EE2: *T* has genuine rivals which are such that when *T* and any of the rivals are conjoined with A$_t$, the auxiliaries that are accepted at a time *t*, they entail the same possible observational evidence.

Whether or not EE2 is any threat at all to realism, it is clearly too weak to sustain the threat posed by SU. Let *T'* be an empirically equivalent rival to *T* according to this interpretation. So *T*&A$_t$ and *T'*&A$_t$ entail the same observations. This sort of equivalence is *relative to* A$_t$. It amounts to the claim that *T* and *T'* cannot be discriminated observationally if conjoined only with those auxiliaries. But this does not show that *T* and *T'* could not be distinguished when conjoined with *any* acceptable auxiliaries at *any* time. And that is what is needed, at least, to sustain the claim that *T* and *T'* cannot be discriminated by *any possible* evidence, as SU requires. SU demands a much stronger answer to the interpretative question:

EE3: *T* has genuine rivals which are such that when *T* and any of the rivals are conjoined with any possible acceptable auxiliaries they entail the same possible observational evidence.

If *T* and *T'* were thus related they would be empirically equivalent not just relative to certain auxiliaries but *tout court*, *absolutely* equivalent. Only then would they be observationally indiscriminable. So if EE is to support SU, it must be interpreted as EE3.

The main point of Laudan and Leplin's critique can be put simply: we have no reason to believe EE3. If *T* and *T'* cannot be discriminated observationally relative to, say, currently accepted auxiliaries, they may well be so relative to some future accepted auxiliaries. Some currently accepted auxiliaries may cease to be accepted and some new auxiliaries are likely to become accepted. This point becomes particularly persuasive, in my view (1997: 119), when we note our capacity to invent new instruments and experiments to test theories. With a new instrument and experiment come new auxiliaries, including a theory of the instrument and assumptions about the experimental situation. Given that we can thus *create* evidence, the set of observational consequences of any theory seems totally open. Of course, there is *no guarantee* of successful discrimination by these means: a theory may really face a genuine empirically equivalent rival. Still, we are unlikely to have sufficient reason for believing this of any particular theory. More importantly, we have *no reason at all* for believing it of *all* theories, as EE3 requires. We will seldom, if ever, have a basis for concluding that two genuine rivals are empirically equivalent in the absolute sense required by EE3. *There is no known limit to our capacity to generate acceptable auxiliaries.*

What about EE2? We have already seen that EE2 will not sustain SU but maybe it could otherwise threaten realism. But is it true? There are surely some theories that face a genuine rival that is empirically equivalent relative to the accepted auxiliaries at a certain time. But do *all* theories face such rivals at that time, let alone at *all* times? EE2 *guarantees* that all theories do at all times. But the ampliative methods, whatever they may be, that support our knowledge of the observable world and avoid extreme skepticism will count many rivals as not genuine, so many as to make this guarantee seem baseless. There is no basis *a priori* for supposing that T must always face such a genuine rival.

In sum, we have no reason to believe EE2 or EE3, and so the underdetermination argument fails.

The pessimistic meta-induction

A powerful argument against scientific realism, called a "meta-induction" by Putnam (1978), runs as follows: the unobservables posited by past theories do not exist; so, probably the unobservables posited by current theories do not exist. The argument rests on a claim about past theories from the perspective of our current theories. And the pessimistic suggestion is that, from a future perspective, we will have a similarly critical view of our current theories. Laudan (1981) has supported these claims about the past with a list of theoretical failures.

Scientific realism already concedes something to the meta-induction in exhibiting *some* skepticism about the claims of science. It holds that science is more or less right, but not totally so. It is committed only to well-established theories not exciting speculations. It leaves room for a theoretical posit to be dismissed as inessential to the theory. According to the meta-induction, reflection on the track record of science shows that this skepticism has not gone nearly far enough.

The realist can respond to the meta-induction by attacking the premise or the inference. Concerning the premise, the realist can, on the one hand, resist the bleak assessment of the theories on Laudan's list, claiming that while some of the unobservables posited by these theories do not exist, others do; or claiming that while there is a deal of falsehood in these theories, there is a deal of truth too. On the other hand, the realist can claim that the list is unrepresentative, that other past theories do seem to be approximately true and to posit entities that do exist.

Clearly, settling the status of the premise requires close attention to the historical details. What would such an attempt be likely to reveal? I think that it would reveal a good deal of indeterminacy about what does or does not exist, but also much determinacy. Among the determinate cases there will surely be some of non-existence: phlogiston is a good candidate. But there will surely also be some of existence: the atoms posited in the nineteenth century are good candidates. So, we should conclude that the premise of the meta-induction is overstated, at least. But how much is it overstated? That depends on the *success ratio* of past theories, the ratio of the determinately existents to the determinately non-existents + indeterminates. Where is this ratio likely to leave scientific realism? To answer this we need to consider the meta-induction's inference.

The first point to note is that even if history were to show that *most* of the unobservables posited by past theories do not exist that would *not* be sufficient to show that, probably, most of the unobservables posited by current theories do not exist. The problem is what Marc Lange (2002) calls "the turnover fallacy." Because false theories turn over much more often than true ones, the premise might be true even though, at any time, most of the unobservables posited at that time exist. So, if the inference is to be good, and so threaten scientific realism, it must start from the premise that most of the unobservables posited by theories *at all – or most – past times* do not exist.

I think (1997: 162–5) that we have good reason for doubting the inference even from this stronger premise. If the premise were right it would show that our past theories have failed rather badly to get the unobservable world right. Why would that show that our present theories are failing similarly? It clearly would show this if we supposed that we are *no better* at finding out about unobservables now than we were in the past. But why suppose that? Just the opposite seems more plausible: we are now *much better* at finding out about unobservables. Science has for two or three centuries been getting better and better at this. Indeed, scientific progress is, to a large degree, a matter of improving scientific methodologies often based on new technologies that provide new instruments for investigating the world. If this is so – and it seems fairly indubitable – then we should expect an examination of the historical details to show improvement over time in our success ratio for unobservables. If the details do show this, it will not matter to realism that the ratio for, say, two centuries ago was poor. What will matter is that we have been improving enough to now have the sort of confidence reflected by scientific realism. And if we have been improving, but not fast enough for scientific realism, the realist can fall back to a more moderate commitment to, say, a high proportion of the unobservables of currently well-established theories.

Improvements in scientific methodologies make it much harder to mount a case against realism than seems to have been appreciated. For, the appeal to historical details has to show not only that we were nearly always wrong in our unobservable posits but that, despite methodological improvements, we have not been getting increasingly right. It seems to me most unlikely that this case can be made.

Conclusions

The realism doctrines that concern philosophy of science are best seen as straightforwardly metaphysical. Extreme skepticism poses the background issue: it threatens realism about observables. Sustaining this *common-sense realism* requires adopting some ampliative method of inference. Only then does a realism about unobservables, *scientific realism*, arise as a distinct issue. Various explanationist arguments for scientific realism succeed provided that the realist is entitled to abduction. The underdetermination argument against realism fails because we have no good reason to believe an empirical equivalence thesis that would serve as its premise. The pessimistic meta-induction, with its attention to past theoretical failures, does pose a problem for realism. But the problem may be manageable. For, the anti-realist must argue that the historical record shows not only that past failures are extensive but also that we have *not improved* our capacity to describe the unobservable world sufficiently to justify confidence that the accounts given by our current well-established theories are to a large extent right. That is difficult to argue.

See also Empiricism; Inference to the best explanation; Models; Naturalism; Theory-change in science; Underdetermination; The virtues of a good theory.

References

Boyd, Richard N. (1984) "The Current Status of Scientific Realism," in Jarrett Leplin (ed.) *Scientific Realism*, Berkeley: University of California Press, pp. 41–82.

Devitt, Michael (1997 [1984]) *Realism and Truth*, 2nd edn, Princeton, NJ: Princeton University Press.

—— (2002) "Underdetermination and Realism," in Ernest Sosa and Enrique Villanueva (eds) *Realism and Relativism: Philosophical Issues 12*, Cambridge, MA: Blackwell, pp. 26–50.

—— (2005) "Scientific Realism," in Frank Jackson and Michael Smith (eds) *The Oxford Handbook of Contemporary Analytic Philosophy*, Oxford: Oxford University Press, pp. 767–91.

Fine, Arthur (1986a) *The Shaky Game: Einstein, Realism, and the Quantum Theory*, Chicago: University of Chicago Press.

—— (1986b) "Unnatural Attitudes: Realist and Instrumentalist Attachments to Science," *Mind* 95: 149–77.

Kitcher, Philip (1993) *The Advancement of Science: Science without Legend, Objectivity without Illusions*, New York: Oxford University Press.

Kuhn, Thomas S. (1970 [1962]) *The Structure of Scientific Revolutions*, 2nd edn, Chicago: University of Chicago Press.

Lange, Marc (2002) "Baseball, Pessimistic Inductions, and the Turnover Fallacy," *Analysis* 62: 281–5.

Laudan, Larry (1981) "A Confutation of Convergent Realism," *Philosophy of Science* 48: 19–49; reprinted in Leplin (1984).

Laudan, Larry, and Leplin, Jarrett (1991) "Empirical Equivalence and Underdetermination," *Journal of Philosophy* 88: 449–72.

Leplin, Jarrett (ed.) (1984) *Scientific Realism*, Berkeley: University of California Press.

—— (1997) *A Novel Defense of Scientific Realism*, New York: Oxford University Press.

Putnam, Hilary (1978) *Meaning and the Moral Sciences*, London: Routledge & Kegan Paul.

—— (1981) *Reason, Truth and History*, Cambridge: Cambridge University Press.

Van Fraassen, Bas C. (1980) *The Scientific Image*, Oxford: Clarendon Press.

Further reading

Leplin (1984) is an excellent collection containing many of the arguments discussed. Paul M. Churchland and Clifford A. Hooker (eds) *Images of Science: Essays on Realism and Empiricism, with a Reply from Bas C. van Fraassen* (Chicago: University of Chicago Press, 1985) is another helpful collection. Paul Feyerabend's *Against Method* (London: New Left Books, 1975) is an influential source of constructivism (along with

Kuhn 1970). J. J. C. Smart's *Philosophy and Scientific Realism* (London: Routledge & Kegan Paul, 1963) is a classic defense of realism. Ian Hacking's *Representing and Intervening* (Cambridge: Cambridge University Press, 1983) is a lively and persuasive defense of entity-realism. Laudan's *Beyond Positivism and Relativism: Theory, Method, and Evidence* (Boulder, CO: Westview Press) reprints Laudan and Leplin (1991) and contains much else of interest. Stathis Psillos's *Scientific Realism: How Science Tracks Truth* (New York: Routledge, 1999) is a thorough discussion, and sustained defense, of scientific realism. André Kukla's *Studies in Scientific Realism* (New York: Oxford University Press, 1998) is a careful critical analysis of the arguments both for and against scientific realism. J. Worrall's "Structural Realism: The Best of Both Worlds," *Dialectica* 43 (1989): 99–124, is an interesting defense of a weaker form of realism.

22

RELATIVISM ABOUT SCIENCE

Maria Baghramian

Epistemic relativism is the view that claims to knowledge are invariably bound by particular historical, cultural and conceptual frameworks and are true or legitimate only relative to their conditions of production. Relativism about science, a species of epistemic relativism, claims that scientific knowledge is the product of specific social, economic and cultural conditions, and contrary to its stated ambitions, cannot attain the universality or objectivity it aspires to. Scientific theories, the claim goes, are true or justified only relative to their cultural or conceptual backdrop.

Relativistic views of science are frequently formulated negatively, through the rejection of what may be called the "objectivist conception of science" (or OC), in particular relativists reject:

(OC1) *Scientific realism* The view that scientific theories are attempts to describe the one real world – a world that exists independently of human thinking – and that there is a single correct description of that world.

(OC2) *The universality of science* Genuine scientific laws apply to all times and places and are invariant and value neutral.

(OC3) *A univocal scientific method* There is such a thing as a uniquely correct scientific method.

(OC4) *Context-independence* There is a sharp distinction between the context of justification of a scientific theory and the context of its discovery. The social, economic and psychological circumstances that give rise to a scientific theory should not be confused with the methodological procedures used for justifying it.

(OC5) *Meaning invariance* Scientific concepts and theoretical terms have stable and fixed meanings. They retain their meaning as theories change.

(OC6) *Convergence* Diverse and seemingly incompatible scientific views will ultimately converge into one coherent theory.

(OC7) *Scientific knowledge is cumulative* There is a steady growth in the range and depth of our knowledge in any given area of science and progress in science is made possible by such accumulation. (Baghramian 2004: 182–3)

The rejection of OC1–7 is guided by a variety of philosophical worries and impulses. Most importantly, relativists about science argue that scientific knowledge, like all *knowledge*, is inevitably informed by our all too local human perspectives and since we cannot step out of our cultural or conceptual frameworks and study the world *as it is*, the claims to universality or objectivity of science could not be justified. Furthermore, they point out that different historical epochs and cultures produce different standards and paradigms of rationality and *correct* reasoning, and hence no ahistorical criterion of adjudication between these differing perspectives is available. Relativism about science is also frequently motivated by a mistrust of the political and economic effects of science. Science is seen as a repressive institution which serves the interests of the dominant economic and cultural groupings and marginalizes dissenting views, particularly those of women and non-Western people.

In recent decades relativistic views of science have been advanced and defended by sociologists of science, some feminist epistemologists and postmodernists.

Sociology of science

The Strong Programme, associated with a number of sociologists of science at Edinburgh, particularly Barry Barnes and David Bloor, and so-called "science studies" influenced by Bruno Latour and other social constructionists are at the forefront of relativistic approaches to science. According to the social constructionist sociologists of science, scientific facts, and even reality – or what we call "the world" with its objects, entities, properties and categories – are not out there to be discovered by scientists, rather they are constructed via interactive norm-governed processes and practices such as negotiations, interpretations and manipulation of data (as well as accidental and opportunistic developments). Scientific discoveries and theoretical knowledge are the products of socially sanctioned norms and practices and are guided by projects that are of cultural, economic, or political importance. As Latour and Woolgar in their influential work *Laboratory Life: The Construction of Scientific Facts* put it: "Our point is that 'out-there-ness' is the consequence of scientific work rather than the cause" (1979: 180). Although the existence of a world or a reality independent of us is not in dispute, they insist that so-called "scientific facts," or the objects scientists study, for instance subatomic particles, emerge out of social and conceptual practices, in the context of laboratory work, and are constituted by these practices (hence the subtitle of their book).

The constructionist approach echoes the views of Nelson Goodman who maintains that in science, as well as in arts, we are engaged in an act of *world-making*. We make constellations by picking out and putting together certain stars rather than others, and we make stars and planets by drawing certain boundaries rather than others. Nothing in nature, Goodman claims, dictates whether the sky shall be marked off into constellations or other objects. Latour, in a similar vein, argues that bacteria were "invented," and not discovered as it is commonly assumed, through the laboratory practices of the nineteenth-century scientists. The constructionist approach relativizes scientific knowledge insofar as it implies that different social and conceptual conditions can lead to the construction of different systems of knowledge; for the products of science are "contextually specific constructions which bear the mark of the situated contingency and interest structure of the process by which they are generated" (Knorr-Cetina 1981: 226).

The sociological perspective on science has been a useful corrective measure to the decontextualized understanding of science advocated by the logical positivist and other analytic philosophers in early twentieth century. It is undoubtedly true that science is a social activity and that scientists follow norms and procedures that are sanctioned by and through their practices; in that sense the activities of the scientific community have the imprint of their group thinking. It is also useful to be aware of the consensual nature of scientific practice and to take account of the connections between science and other aspects of our lives, politics and economics in particular. But none of these concessions to the sociologists of science should compel us to move from non-contentious observations about the processes involved in any scientific enquiry to the startling conclusion that *what* scientists discover or investigate are mere social constructs.

Feminist epistemology and relativist interpretations of science

Feminist epistemologists are also skeptical about the value of any account of knowledge that ignores the social and personal conditions of its production. According to feminist epistemologists, the history of philosophy and science shows that the supposedly generic, universal epistemic subject is, in fact, the white affluent male and that what passes as scientific knowledge is inherently masculine and androcentric. The more radical wing of feminist epistemology rejects the ideal of objectivity altogether, characterizing it variously as incoherent, unapproachable, or undesirable. It argues that male bias is not simply a question of intellectual error or bad faith; rather, the whole idea of objectivity is an invention of male scientists and philosophers and hence it bears the imprint of its inventors. The so-called "scientific method" and its practice do not take the views and experiences of women seriously, often dismissing them as "subjective," "intuitive," "irrational," "illogical," "emotional," etc. Thus science falls well short of its claim to universality and neutrality (OC2).

Feminist epistemologists, like the social constructionists, often deny the legitimacy of the distinction between context of discovery and context of justification (OC4) and claim that the so-called "neutral" epistemic virtues of objectivity and rationality, seen as essential components of the scientific method, are often the means of furthering patriarchal interests at the expense of women and other disadvantaged groups (Anthony 1993: 206). Some feminist epistemologists go even further and argue that there are fundamental differences between the male and female cognitive, emotional and social experiences of the world, and hence the ideal of a universal and neutral conception of rationality is simply a chimera. Evelyn Fox-Keller puts it this way: "Recent developments in the history and philosophy of science have led to a re-evaluation that acknowledges that the goals, methods, theories, and even the actual data of science are not written in nature; all are subject to the play of social forces" (1990: 15). Different social forces present us with different methods and theories, therefore both in the practice of science and in our construction of a theory of knowledge we should take into account the individual, social and historical particularities of the subjects of knowledge in their diverse forms and accord subjectivity the respect it deserves. As with the social constructionists, the key claim is "that knowledge is a *construct* produced by cognitive agents within social practices" and these practices may vary across social groups (Code 1993: 15). If all knowledge, including scientific knowledge, is perspectival and informed by the specific context of its production, then its evaluation would also be contextual. Feminine knowledge, the claim goes, has its own justificatory sphere as does masculine knowledge; scientific knowledge is thus relativized to gender, which in turn is a socially constructed, rather than a natural category.

Relativism, for many feminist epistemologists, is seen as the most effective defense against the imposition of universal sameness; it is a battle cry against the repressive imperialism of the Western scientific worldview and the claim by the privileged that they, and only they, have access to the *one true story*. Such a strategy, however, risks the ghettoization of women. To argue for a feminine sphere of knowledge and furthermore to characterize it as subjective, non-logical, and not governed by norms of rationality would simply confirm the long held stereotypes about women and reinforce the very barriers and prejudices that feminists had initially set out to dismantle.

Postmodernist relativism and science

Postmodernist relativist attitudes towards science are inspired by the writings of French poststructuralist philosophers such as Jacques Derrida, Jean Lyotard and, in particular, Michel Foucault. Postmodernist philosophers, and their followers in science studies, claim that the so-called "tools of science" – reason, logic and rationality – are instruments of political and cultural domination; they not only embody and replicate the power relationships already in place in society, but are also intellectual vehicles for their perpetuation. According to Foucault, a historical analysis of reason and knowledge shows that "all knowledge rests upon injustice (that there is no right, not even in the act of knowing, to truth or a foundation for truth) and that the instinct for knowledge is malicious" (1970: 160).

Foucault believes that each historical period, with its distinct political and economic order, proposes a claim to power, and thereby to knowledge and truth. For instance, the Renaissance, the Classical Age (seventeenth and eighteenth centuries) and the Modern Age (nineteenth and twentieth centuries) as key historical periods with diverse conceptions of knowledge, or *epistemes*, have generated their own diverse truths and moral imperatives. Conceptions of truth vary according to these historically constituted *epistemes*, which provide their practitioners with implicit but distinct views concerning 'the order' or the relationship between things. For example, the Renaissance emphasized the relationship of resemblance while the Classical Age prioritized the relationship of identity (see Foucault 1970). The Enlightenment project of favoring reason and rationality and the subsequent emphasis on the scientific method as the most secure way of attaining objective knowledge gave rise to modern science, but the authority of its claims is no more universal than the views preceding it. Science, particularly in the form of social sciences, is an instrument of social control to such an extent that its very constitution is inseparable from the exercise of social and political power. For Foucault, as with feminist epistemologists, the rejection of dominant norms of objectivity, truth, and reason, is an exercise in political activism rather than a neutral intellectual stance. Relativism is thus a political ideology of emancipation as well as a particular conception of how science works.

Postmodernism has fanned some of the more extreme relativistic claims about science. The heated debates on these issues took a new twist with the publication of the infamous "Sokal hoax" and the ensuing "science wars" (see Sokal and Bricmont 1998). Although the debates are still continuing, they seem to be losing their intensity.

Despite some important differences in approach and points of emphasis, the postmodernists, feminist epistemologists, and sociologists of science are united in their rejection of the view that scientific theories and methodologies could be divorced from their socio-political context. With the denial of this key tenet of the objectivist conception of science, OC4 above, the rejection of OC1–3 immediately follows. If the methods of science are guided, or even governed, by prevailing social and political conditions, then given the variability of these conditions OC3 or the belief in the existence of a uniquely correct methodology in science becomes untenable. Furthermore, if scientific theories are not free of the limitations of their time and place, then they cannot be universal (OC2). OC1, or scientific realism, is also undermined, for a socially constructed world cannot readily be identified with the scientific realists' mind-independent world.

Underdetermination and its consequences

Much of the philosophical inspiration behind relativism about science comes, not from French postmodernism, but from the Duhem–Quine thesis of *underdetermination of theory by data* and the Kuhn–Feyerabend thesis of *incommensurability*.

The thesis of the underdetermination of scientific theories is a claim about the relationship between theories and the data or evidence adduced in their favor. Evidence, the claim goes, underdetermines theory in so far as it does not uniquely provide warrant for its acceptance or proof of its truth. Since a single body of empirical data can support more than one theory, rival hypotheses may be equally justified by the same set of observation or be equally compatible with the same body of evidence. In Quine's words, "Physical theories can be at odds with each other and yet compatible with all possible data even in the broadest possible sense. In a word they can be logically incompatible and empirically equivalent" (1970: 179).

The so-called "Duhem–Quine thesis of underdetermination of theory by data" makes the even stronger claim that since it is only with the help of auxiliary hypotheses that we can decide if a specific set of observational consequences follow from given theory, it is always possible for any theory, together with suitable auxiliary hypotheses, to accommodate all recalcitrant data and experimental results. So Quine, in his more radical moments in the "Two Dogmas of Empiricism," maintains that as a consequence of underdetermination scientists can hold on to any theory come what may, or more precisely, "any statement can be held true come what may, if we make drastic enough adjustments elsewhere in the system" (1953: 43).

Irrationalist and relativist interpretations of Quine's thesis are legion. Larry Laudan (1990), for instance, interprets Quine as denying that there can be any rational grounds for preferring one theory to another when all the competing theories are consistent with observation. Paul Feyerabend, on the other hand, uses the under-determination thesis to defend his "democratic relativism" – the view that different societies may look at the world in different ways and regard different things as acceptable (1987: 59). According to his democratic relativism "for every statement, theory, point of view believed (to be true) with good reason there exist arguments showing a conflicting alternative to be at least as good, or even better" (ibid.: 76). This position is much weaker than the epistemic relativist claim that truth, knowledge, reality, etc., are relative to prevailing cultural norms or their historical contexts. Nonetheless, Feyerabend believes that privileging one conception of truth, ration-ality or knowledge in the name of scientific objectivity runs the risk of imposing a repressive worldview on members of other cultural groupings who may not share our assumptions or intellectual framework. His democratic relativism is a plea for intel-lectual and political tolerance and a denunciation of dogmatism both in science and in politics: "It says that what is right for one culture need not be right for another" (ibid.: 85). But it coincides with stronger relativistic claims insofar as it denies OC6, or the claim that diverse and seemingly incompatible scientific theories will ultimately converge into one coherent theory. Feyerabend's views, in turn, have been echoed by feminist epistemologists. Lorraine Code, for instance, acknowledges Feyerabend's influence in providing her with the necessary conceptual tools to resist what she sees as the intellectual tyranny of the traditional conceptions of science.

Quine's arguments for underdetermination have also been used extensively in support of various relativistic positions in science studies by the strong theorists and social constructionists. Andrew Pickering, for instance, in *Constructing Quarks* argues that since "choice of a theory is underdetermined by any finite set of data ... it is always possible to invent an unlimited set of theories ... capable of explaining a given set of facts" (1999: 5–6). This is where the scientists' judgments, as individuals and groups, come to play their role in theory choice. Scientific method, by itself, is not sufficient to determine theory choice, scientists are obliged to rely on their judgments and such judgments are inevitably colored by social, historical and personal conditions as well as by the prevailing cultural norms and values. The thesis of underdetermination points out a logical gap between theory and evidence; the social constructionists, feminist epistemologists and other relativists claim that this gap is often filled by economic and political motives and interests. The traditional assumption that scien-tists follow a determinate set of methodological guidelines (OC3) is no longer tenable as no single methodology is available to overcome the inevitable underdetermination of all theories.

Incommensurability and relativism

The most profound influence on relativistic conceptions of science, particularly in sociology of science, has come from Thomas Kuhn and Paul Feyerabend's historicist approach. From a traditional inductivist perspective, progress in science occurs through the accumulation of data, the gathering of facts, and a process of theory-building, by way of induction from available data. According to Karl Popper's falsificationist approach, on the other hand, progress occurs when scientists come up with bold speculations or hypotheses that explain larger numbers of observations and survive the tests that have falsified earlier theories. But even in this case, there is continuity between earlier and later theories in that successive theories reflect past successes and improve upon them. Kuhn, on the other hand, questioned the very ideas of linear progress in science. According to him history of science consists of a series of radical shifts and fundamental changes in scientific worldviews or paradigms. During what he calls a "period of normal science," theorizing, research, and discovery take place within specific paradigms. Paradigms are the core cluster of concepts, theoretical assumptions, rules and standards for scientific practice associated with particular traditions of scientific research, which shape the approach scientists take to their subject. "In learning a paradigm the scientists acquire theory, methods, and standards together, usually in an inextricable mixture. Therefore, when paradigms change, there are usually significant shifts in the criteria determining the legitimacy both of problems and of proposed solutions" (Kuhn 1970: 109).

During a scientific revolution the entire theoretical structure and the methodological and metaphysical framework of a given area of research – the prevailing paradigm – is replaced with new and radically different ones that on many points may be incompatible with their predecessors. Paradigm shifts are discontinuous and scientific knowledge is non-cumulative, largely because questions posed in older paradigms and the answers provided for them may become irrelevant in a new paradigm. When a scientific revolution takes place, there is a shift of professional commitment from one paradigm to another. In a revolution, scientists reject one respected and well-established paradigm in favor of another; and with this comes a shift of perspective in the choice of problems to be studied to such an extent that different paradigms bring about different and *incommensurable* ways of looking at and seeing the world and of practicing science in it. "Though the world does not change with a change of paradigm, the scientist afterward works in a different world" (*ibid.*: 121).

Such pronouncements have, understandably, given rise to social constructionist interpretations of Kuhn and have frequently been used to justify relativist thinking about science. For it seems that if all assessments of the success, and even the truth, of a particular scientific theory can be made only within a given paradigm, there remains no room for extra-paradigmatic, non-relative evaluation in science. Furthermore, Kuhn seems to maintain that agreement between scientists and professional allegiances are the ultimate authority for theory choice, that "in paradigm choice – there is no standard higher than the assent of the relevant community" (*ibid.*: 94). He thus emphasizes the consensual character of scientific research, a sentiment shared by the constructionists. Kuhn in later life explicitly disassociated himself from science studies, constructionism, and relativism by aligning himself with traditional approaches to science; but his disavowals had little effect on what by then had become a canonical interpretation of his work.

The term "incommensurability" – meaning the impossibility of comparison by a common measure – has its origins in mathematics and geometry but its current philosophical usage, and its role in supporting relativism about science, dates back to 1962 and the writings of Kuhn and Feyerabend. The term appears in Kuhn's *Structure of Scientific Revolutions* and in Feyerabend's "Explanation, Reduction, and Empiricism." The objectivist claim (OC7 above) that there is cumulative progress in science is based on the assumption of the *meaning invariance* of both theoretical and observational terms employed by scientists. Progress presupposes continuity in the use, interpretation and definition of theoretical terms (OC5). Paul Feyerabend, like Kuhn, claims that the hypothesis of meaning invariance is not supported by the history of science, for the meaning of scientific terms change with each scientific revolution. Successive paradigms, according to Kuhn, give us different and sometimes conflicting accounts of the world, its constituents and its composition. The research methodology, the theoretical language and the overall worldviews governing different paradigms are irreconcilable and hence incommensurable with one another. This is in part because there is "no theory-independent way to reconstruct phrases like 'really there'; the notion of a match between the ontology of a theory and its 'real' counterpart in nature now seems to me illusive in principle" (Kuhn 1970: 206). More generally, observation language, Kuhn argues, presupposes a paradigm and a theory, and hence a change in paradigm brings about a change of observation language as "the data itself changes." New paradigms do inherit and incorporate elements from the theoretical vocabulary and apparatus of the older paradigm, Kuhn admits, but these inherited elements are used in new ways. For instance, the term "mass" as used in Newtonian mechanics, denotes a property, while in relativity theory it refers to a relation; thus it would be a mistake to assume that "mass" has an invariant meaning across theories. Similarly, space and time are separate and independent entities in Newton's theory, while in Einstein's theory both are replaced by the single concept of spacetime; hence the concepts of space and time in the two theories, strictly speaking, are not commensurable. This is why scientists debating the merits of their respective paradigms, the Newtonians and the Einsteinians in this case, often talk slightly at cross-purposes. The view of both Kuhn and Feyerabend is that "the meanings of scientific terms and concepts – 'force' and 'mass,' for example, or 'element' and 'compound' – often changed with the theory in which they were deployed. And ... when such changes occurred, it was impossible to define all the terms of one theory in the vocabulary of the other" (Kuhn 1982: 669). Scientific revolutions also bring about a change in the most fundamental assumptions and principles in the theory and practice of science. This "change of universal principles brings about a change of the entire world. Speaking in this manner we no longer assume an objective world that remains unaffected by our epistemic activities, except when moving within the confines of a particular point of view" (Feyerabend 1978: 70).

It is useful to distinguish between the semantic and the epistemic varieties of *incommensurability*. Two conceptual systems or theories are semantically incommensurable if they are not inter-translatable, i.e., if the meaning and the reference of terms used in one cannot be equated with or mapped into the terms used in another. Kuhn argues that theories from different paradigms are incommensurable because there is no neutral "observation language" into which both can be fully translated (Kuhn 1970: 126–7). Feyerabend also links the incommensurability of scientific theories with questions of meaning and translation more directly. According to him, "Two theories will be called incommensurable when the meanings of their main descriptive terms depend on mutually inconsistent principles" (1965: 227, n.19) and believe that incommensurability "occurs when the conditions of meaningfulness for the descriptive terms of one language (theory, point of view) do not permit the use of descriptive terms of another language (theory, point of view)" (1987: 272). Semantic incommensurability seems to lead to relativism, for if theories, worldviews and languages are not inter-translatable then they are not comparable either and hence we cannot adjudicate between their possibly conflicting truth-claims. In such an event we could either take a skeptical attitude towards the truth-claims of all paradigms or resort to relativistic permissiveness whereby diverse theoretical claims could be true according to their internal criteria. Semantic incommensurability also supports relativism, defined negatively, in so far as it leads to the denial of OC5–7. For instance, if scientific theories belonging to different paradigms or disciplinary matrices prove to be semantically incommensurable then convergence between incompatible scientific views may prove impossible. Similarly, the very idea of progress in science presupposes continuity in meaning as well as the continuous growth of knowledge and the incommensurability thesis denies both.

Many have found the possibility of semantic incommensurability unintelligible. This charge of unintelligibility is the cornerstone of Donald Davidson's famous argument against the coherence of relativism (Davidson 1974: 190). For Davidson something counts as a language, and hence a conceptual scheme or a theory, only if it is translatable. He, thus, makes it *a priori* impossible for languages or paradigms to be incommensurable or untranslatable. According to Davidson, the idea of a language forever beyond our grasp is incoherent in virtue of what we mean by a system of concepts; a worldview allegedly governed by a paradigm radically different from ours will necessarily turn out to be very much like our own. Davidson equates semantic incommensurability, and through it relativism, with a total breakdown of translatability. Kuhn and Feyerabend, however, thought of semantic incommensurability as *partial* failures of translation only: for instance, Kuhn says that proponents of competing paradigms "are bound *partly* to talk through each other" (Kuhn 1970: 148 emphasis added) and that communication across paradigms or revolutionary divides "is inevitably partial" (*ibid.*: 149), but he does not believe that there is ever a complete and insurmountable breakdown of communication between incommensurable theories. Languages that are not translatable, in the strict word-for-word sense, may still be interpretable and hence allow for the possibility of comparisons. Davidson, on the other hand, denies that there are any significant differences between the translation and interpretation of a language; for him an act of translation is simultaneously one of interpretation. (See Baghramian 2004: 250–66.)

Feyerabend also denies the claim to total breakdown of communication. According to him, "incommensurable languages (theories, points of view) are not completely disconnected – there exists a subtle and interesting relation between their conditions of meaningfulness" (1987: 272). But Davidson's doctrine of meaning holism – or the view that the meaning of any part of a language is dependent on the meaning of every other part – does not allow the possibility of partial translatability; according to him languages succeed or fail to be translatable as a whole. Thus he identifies semantic incommensurability, and relativism, with complete breakdown of communication, a very strong claim that was never advocated by either Kuhn or Feyerabend.

Unlike semantic incommensurability, epistemic incommensurability emphasizes the divergences between styles of reasoning and methods of justification. Different paradigms, societies or cultures, it is suggested, have different modes of reasoning, standards and criteria of rationality, and we are not in a position to evaluate or choose between them. Kuhn for instance claims, "the proponents of competing paradigms ... must fail to make complete contact with each other's viewpoints" (Kuhn 1970: 148); "the proponents of different, competing paradigms practice their trades in different worlds... Practicing in different worlds, the two groups of scientists see different things when they look from the same point at the same direction" (*ibid.*: 150).

Feyerabend's democratic relativism, as we saw above, both acknowledges and advocates epistemic incommensurability. Norms of rationality, even the laws of logic, Feyerabend maintains, may vary with local cultural norms or historical contexts and such variations should be accepted and respected. Epistemic incommensurability leads to relativism insofar as it precludes the possibility of having a cross-paradigmatic criterion for adjudicating between different styles of reasoning. It also denies (OC3) or the belief that there is, or could be, such a thing as a single, universal, scientific method. Kuhn and Feyerabend's account of the history of science, and the role they assign to incommensurability, make science amenable to relativistic interpretations, hence their prominent positions in the writings of the constructionists and their allies.

Conclusion

Relativism about science is a heady and subversive idea that has attracted many partisan champions. Its force mainly lies in its ability to make us reconsider some of the basic tenets of the more traditional conceptions of science. However, a great majority of philosophers of science in the analytic tradition, as well as practicing scientists, have remained unconvinced by the image of science it conveys. The success of science in enabling us to explain, manipulate and control the world we live in, and the fact that this success is repeated irrespective of the cultural background, political affiliation or the gender of its practitioners undermine the more extreme claims of relativists about science.

See also Confirmation; Critical rationalism; The feminist approach to the philosophy of science; The historical turn in the philosophy of science; Philosophy of language; Probability; Social studies of science; Scientific method; Underdetermination.

References

Anthony, L. (1993) *A Mind of One's Own: Feminist Essays on Reason and Objectivity*, Boulder, CO: Westview Press.

Baghramian, M. (2004) *Relativism*, London: Routledge.

Barnes, B. (1977) *Interests and the Growth of Knowledge*, London: Routledge.

Bloor, D. (1976) *Knowledge and Social Imagery*, London: Routledge & Kegan Paul.

Code, L. (1993) "Taking Subjectivity into Account," in L. Alcoff and E. Potter (eds) *Feminist Epistemologies*, London: Routledge.

Davidson, D. (1974) "On the Very Idea of a Conceptual Scheme," in D. Davidson (1984) *Inquiries into Truth and Interpretation*, Oxford: Oxford University Press.

Feyerabend, P. (1962) "Explanation, Reduction and Empiricism," in H. Feigl and G. Maxwell (eds) *Minnesota Studies in the Philosophy of Science*, Volume 3: *Scientific Explanation: Space and Time*, Minneapolis: University of Minnesota Press.

—— (1965) "Problems of Empiricism," in R. Colodny (ed.) *Beyond the Edge of Certainty*, Englewood Cliffs, NJ: Prentice-Hall, pp. 145–260.

—— (1975) *Against Method*, London: New Left Books.

—— (1978) *Science in a Free Society*, London: New Left Books.

—— (1987) *Farewell to Reason*, London: Verso.

Foucault, M. (1970) *The Order of Things*, trans. A. Sheridan, London: Tavistock.

Fox-Keller, Evelyn (1990) "Long Live the Difference between Men and Women Scientists," *The Scientist* 4(20): 15.

Goodman, N. (1978) *Ways of Worldmaking*, Indianapolis, IN: Hackett.

Knorr-Cetina, K. (1981) *The Manufacture of Knowledge*, Oxford: Pergamon Press.

Kuhn, T. S. (1970 [1962]) *The Structure of Scientific Revolutions*, 2nd edn, Chicago: University of Chicago Press.

—— (1982) "Commensurability, Comparability, Communicability," in P. Asquith and T. Nickles (eds) *PSA: Proceedings of the Biennial Meeting of the Philosophy of Science Association*, East Lansing, MI: Philosophy of Science Association, Volume 2, pp. 669–88.

Latour, B. and Woolgar, S. (1979) *Laboratory Life: The Social Construction of Scientific Facts*, London: Sage.

Laudan, L. (1990) "Demystifying Underdetermination," in C. Wade Savage (ed.), *Minnesota Studies in the Philosophy of Science*, Volume 14: *Scientific Theories*, Minneapolis: University of Minnesota Press.

Pickering, A. (1999) *Constructing Quarks: A Sociological History of Particle Physics*, Chicago: University of Chicago Press.

Quine W. V. (1953) *From a Logical Point of View*, Cambridge MA: Harvard University Press.

—— (1970) "On the Reasons for Indeterminacy of Translation," *Journal of Philosophy* 67: 178–83.

Sokal, A. and Bricmont, J. (1998) *Intellectual Impostures*, London: Profile Books.

Further reading

There are several collections on epistemic relativism with very useful articles. See M. Krausz and J. W. Meiland (eds) *Relativism: Cognitive and Moral* (Notre Dame, IN.: University of Notre Dame Press, 1982), in which G. Doppelt's "Kuhn's Epistemological Relativism: An Interpretation and Defense" is particularly noteworthy. Another good collection is Martin Hollis and Steven Lukes (eds) *Rationality and Relativism* (London: Routledge, 1982). "Rationalism and the Sociology of Knowledge" by Barnes and Bloor and W. Newton-Smith's "Relativism and the Possibility of Interpretation" are two strong statements of opposing views on this topic. Paul Boghossian's *Fear of Knowledge* (Oxford: Oxford University Press 2005) offers strong arguments against postmodernist and social-constructionist brands of relativism. K. M. Ashman and P. S. Baringer (eds) *After the Science Wars* (London: Routledge, 2001) also deals with the "Sokal hoax" but adopts a more conciliatory tone. S. Fuller's "The Reenchantment of Science: A Fit End to the Science Wars" is one of the many interesting articles in that collection. L. Laudan, *Beyond Positivism and Relativism: Theory, Method and Evidence* (Oxford: Westview Press, 1996) presents a strong anti-relativistic view and is particularly good at analysing the connections between relativism and logical positivism. Much has been written on feminist epistemology: K. Lennon and M. Whitford (eds) *Knowing the Difference: Feminist Perspectives in Epistemology* (London: Routledge, 1994) is one good example.

23
SCIENTIFIC METHOD
Howard Sankey

Philosophers have long held there to be something special about science that distinguishes it from non-science. Rather than a shared subject-matter, the distinction is usually taken to reside at the methodological level. What sets the sciences apart from non-scientific pursuits is the possession of a characteristic method employed by their practitioners. It is customary to refer to this characteristic method of science as the "scientific method." Those disciplines which employ the scientific method qualify as sciences; those which do not employ the method are considered not to be scientific.

While most philosophers agree that science is to be characterized in methodological terms, they disagree about the nature of this method. Many take the fundamental method of science to be an inductive method. Others belittle induction or deny its use altogether. It was once taken to be virtually axiomatic that the method of science is a fixed and universal method employed throughout the sciences. Yet, at the present time, it is not uncommon to hold that method depends on historical time-period or cultural context, or that it varies from one field of science to another. While it was once widely believed that there is a single scientific method characteristic of all science, it is now more common to hold that the method of science consists of a multifaceted array of rules, techniques and procedures which broadly govern the practice of science. Indeed, some have concluded that there is, strictly speaking, no such thing as *the* scientific method.

It is possible to distinguish a number of different levels at which methods may be employed in science. At the ground level of data collection and experimental practice, there are methods which govern the proper conduct of an experiment or the correct employment of a piece of equipment. At a slight remove from experimental practice, there are methods of experimental design or test procedure, such as the use of random trials or double-blind tests in clinical trials. At a more remote level are methods for the appraisal, or evaluation, of theories, and possibly theory construction. The methods described in what follows tend, for the most part, to comprise methods of theory appraisal which are designed to provide the warrant for theory choice or theory acceptance. For it is at this level that the bulk of the philosophical debate about scientific method has been conducted.

Philosophers sometimes distinguish between two contexts in which a method might be employed in science. The first context, in which a new idea emerges in the mind of a scientist, has been called the "context of discovery." The second context, in which the idea receives scientific validation, is known as the "context of justification." The bulk of methodological discussion relates to the second context. This reflects the once-dominant view that the process of having a new idea is an inscrutable matter of individual psychology, rather than a matter of logic or method. Contemporary philosophers of science place less weight on this traditional distinction than was previously the case. Indeed, many would be prepared to grant a role to method in the context of discovery.

Naive inductivism

The first view of method I consider is one that is usually presented as part of the common-sense view of science rather than credited to any particular philosopher of science. This is the *naive inductivist* view that the method of science consists simply of inductive inference on the basis of observation. On this naive view, induction is understood in a rudimentary sense as enumerative induction. An inference is inductive in this sense if it proceeds from a limited number of positive instances which have been observed to a generalization that covers all instances whether or not they have been observed.

The naive inductive method may be presented in simplified terms as a two-step procedure for arriving at theories on the basis of observation. Suppose, to begin with, that a specific domain of phenomena is under investigation. The first step in a scientific investigation consists of the collection of empirical data from the domain. Scientists gather empirical data by employing unbiased sense perception to detect observational facts. Only after the collection of empirical data may scientists proceed to the second step, which is the formulation of scientific laws and theories by a process of inductive generalization. Scientists employ inductive reasoning to infer from empirical data to generalizations about the behavior of the items found in the domain under investigation. The generalizations which result constitute empirical laws, which may be conjoined with other such laws to serve as the basis of scientific theories. Induction plays a fundamental role in this method because it is required in order to draw an inference from the limited data provided by observation to the generalizations which apply to items beyond those which have been observed.

This account of method provides both a method of discovery and a method of justification. It provides an account of how scientists arrive at laws and theories, as well as an account of the validation of laws and theories. Armed with the empirical data they have collected, scientists employ inductive generalization to discover laws, which form the basis of theories. At the same time, scientists' use of the inductive method provides the warrant for their acceptance of the laws and theories that result. For the method consists of the use of perception and inductive inference, which are themselves epistemically well-grounded means of belief formation.

Despite its simplicity, the naive inductive method faces a number of serious problems. In the first place, it is not clear that the process of data collection may precede or be independent of theory in the way that the naive inductivist suggests.

For in order to collect data it must already be known which domain of phenomena is the relevant focus of study. Indeed, even to identify data as relevant some prior judgment of the significance of various kinds of data must already have been made. Such judgments depend on previous knowledge, which may include prior theory about the domain under investigation. But this means that science cannot begin with pure observation and only afterwards proceed to the theoretical level. A background of knowledge, which may include theoretical knowledge, must *already* be in place before the work of data collection may even begin.

In the second place, naive inductivism fails to provide an adequate account of scientific theory formation. Scientific theories typically postulate the existence of unobservable theoretical entities (e.g., genes, atoms, electrons) whose behavior underlies the observable phenomena which scientists seek to explain. But while the simple inductive model may have some plausibility as an account of the discovery of low-level empirical laws, it has little plausibility as an account of the formation of theories about the unobservable entities that underlie the observed phenomena. The reason is that theoretical discourse about unobservable entities is typically couched in terms of theoretical vocabulary. Given this, it is not possible for scientists to infer by enumerative induction from premises which are stated in an observational vocabulary to conclusions, stated in a theoretical vocabulary, about unobservable entities. In short, naive inductivism does not have the resources to sustain an inference from observation to theory.

Third, naive inductivism is beset by a range of foundational problems, of which the most significant for present purposes is Hume's *skeptical problem of induction* (though the *paradoxes of confirmation* deserve mention). Since Hume's problem plays such a central role in the philosophy of scientific method, it is important to introduce the problem at this stage in the discussion. The problem is that of providing a rational justification for the use of inductive inference. Because induction is not a form of deductive inference, it is difficult to see how it may be justified on the basis of deductive logic. Nor does it seem possible to justify induction by appeal to the past success of induction, since that would be to use induction to support induction in a circular manner. Neither may induction be grounded in a principle of the uniformity of nature, since such a principle is unable to be justified in an *a priori* manner, and appeal to past uniformity would be circular. As will be seen when I turn to Karl Popper's *falsificationist account of method*, this problem has motivated the search for non-inductivist theories of method.

Before turning to the next theory of method, it is important to emphasize that the naive inductive method presented here is just that. It is a *naive* version of the inductivist method. More refined inductive methods are available. On the one hand, many inductivists favor forms of eliminative induction (e.g., Mill's methods) which take into account negative rather than only positive instances. On the other hand, inductivists have sought to develop an inductive logic and confirmation theory on the basis of the probability calculus. Such technical aspects of the inductive method are dealt with in other contributions to this collection. Rather than explore technical developments, I consider instead a somewhat more sophisticated inductivist theory of method which deals with the first two problems described above.

The hypothetico-deductive method

The second theory of method with which I deal is a more sophisticated inductive method which treats induction solely as a matter of justification. This is the *hypothetico-deductive method*, or, as it is also called, the *method of hypothesis*. The hypothetico-deductive method has enjoyed broad support, from nineteenth-century methodologists such as Jevons and Whewell to logical empiricists such as Hempel and Reichenbach in the twentieth century. According to the hypothetico-deductive view of method, theories are to be evaluated by testing the observational predictions which follow from them as deductive consequences. True predictions confirm a theory; false predictions disconfirm it.

Proponents of the hypothetico-deductive method take induction to serve as a method of *justification* rather than a method of *discovery*. The confirmation which a verified prediction provides for a theory constitutes non-conclusive inductive support for the theory, since the theory will typically have content which extends well beyond the specific prediction which supports it. But while the support provided by such evidence is inductive, there is no requirement that the theory be arrived at by means of an inductive inference. Arriving at a theory is a creative process which may involve intuition, inspired guesswork and imagination, as well as various kinds of deductive and inductive reasoning. What matters, as far as the justification of a theory is concerned, is how the theory fares when its observational consequences are subjected to scrutiny. And the relation of confirmation between verified prediction and theory, which is the only relation of relevance to the justification of a theory according to hypothetico-deductivists, is a relation that is inductive in nature.

The hypothetico-deductive method represents an advance over the naive inductive method with which I began. While it remains subject to foundational problems such as inductive skepticism, it avoids the first two problems with naive inductivism described above. The hypothetico-deductive method does not require that a scientific investigation begin with observation prior to theory. It is entirely possible for scientists who seek to explain a phenomenon to first propose a hypothesis and then to undertake observations in an attempt to verify the predictions entailed by the hypothesis. Nor is there any need for scientists to arrive at theories solely by means of an enumerative induction on the basis of observation. Scientists are free to postulate the existence of unobservable theoretical entities in the context of the development of scientific theories. Theoretical claims about such entities may receive indirect confirmation when the predictive consequences of the theories are subjected to empirical test.

But while the hypothetico-deductive method marks an advance over the naive inductive method, it faces several problems, of which two of the most telling are as follows. The first problem relates to the fact that theories are typically formulated in terms of universal generalizations. But it is impossible to derive a testable prediction from a universal generalization without specification of the initial conditions obtaining in the domain to which the generalization applies. In addition, it is usually the case that a range of further auxiliary hypotheses must also be employed about the objects in the domain, as well as the techniques and apparatus employed to investigate the domain. The result is that theoretical generalizations from which predictions are derived are not capable of being tested in isolation from all other empirical assumptions. The outcome of a prediction may therefore fail either to confirm or disconfirm the theory from which it is derived, since the initial conditions or auxiliary hypotheses might be responsible for the success or failure of the prediction. The ambiguous character of such tests means that the verification of a prediction does not necessarily provide a theory with genuine support. This problem provides an illustration, in the case of the hypothetico-deductive method, of the general problem of the underdetermination of theory by empirical data. In the specific form described here, the problem is known as the Duhem–Quine problem, after Pierre Duhem (1954: 180–200) and W. V. Quine (1953: 41), who brought the problem to the attention of philosophers of science.

While the first problem is an instance of a more general one, the second problem arises specifically with respect to the assumption that theories receive confirmation solely by way of their *predictive content*, as suggested by the hypothetico-deductive method. The problem may be illustrated by considering a scenario in which two or more alternative theories entail exactly the same empirically verified prediction. If the only source of empirical confirmation is by way of the verification of such predictions, then it is difficult to avoid the conclusion that all theories which entail the same predictive consequence receive exactly the same degree of confirmation from that prediction. But, without denying the importance of verified predictions, it should be clear that exclusive reliance on prediction in the confirmation of theories is problematic; for it assumes that there are no other factors of an evidential or methodological nature that might be of relevance to the empirical support of a theory. Yet it seems mistaken to assume, for example, that a coherent and an incoherent theory should be equally supported by the same prediction, or that both a theory and the theory conjoined with an irrelevant proposition should receive equivalent support from the same prediction. At the very least, it should be allowed that success in prediction may convey differential support to various theories in light of relevant differences in the theories and their circumstances. Just which factors should be taken into account is a matter of dispute among philosophers. But factors such as prior probability, fit with background knowledge, and explanatory power are worthy of note.

In recent years, an attempt to modify the hypothetico-deductive method that emphasizes the *explanatory role of hypotheses* has attracted considerable support. If a hypothesis can be shown to be the best available explanation of a set of phenomena, then this fact provides a reason to prefer that hypothesis to alternative hypotheses which provide inferior explanations.

Popper's falsificationist theory of method

The next account of method which we will consider is the *falsificationist theory of method* proposed by Karl Popper. Popper agrees with Hume that induction cannot be justified, and proposes instead a method which makes no use of induction. According to Popper, the method of science is a method of "trial and error – of conjectures and refutations" (Popper 1963: 46). Scientists propose bold, speculative theories in an attempt to explain phenomena which appear problematic in light of background knowledge and expectation. But rather than support such theories by means of experience, scientists seek to disprove theories by means of rigorous tests of the predictions that the theories entail. Those theories which fail such tests are rejected. Those theories which survive all attempts to refute them are then tentatively accepted as the best currently available.

Popper's theory of method may be thought of as an anti-inductivist version of the hypothetico-deductive method. Popper rejects the idea that scientific theories are arrived at by means of induction. Along with advocates of the hypothetico-deductive view of method, he regards the process of theory construction as an imaginative process of discovery incapable of rational reconstruction in terms of the logic or method of science. But, unlike the hypothetico-deductivists, he does not regard the positive outcomes of empirical tests as providing theories with inductive support. For not only does Popper reject induction as a method of theory formation, he rejects it also as a method of confirmation. Indeed, Popper's falsificationist philosophy of science is sometimes called "deductivism" because he rejects induction as a myth, and insists that deduction is all the logic that is needed for the methodology of science.

But while Popper rejects induction, this does not mean that there is no basis on which scientists may accept a theory. According to Popper, a theory receives support of a non-inductive nature as a result of passing empirical tests, and that provides a reason to accept the theory. Popper says that a theory which passes a test is "corroborated" by the test, a term he uses to avoid the inductivist overtones of "confirmation." Corroboration is not just a matter of the number of tests a theory passes. Theories receive greater corroboration the more testable they are. Indeed, Popper argues that the more improbable a theory is, the greater will be the corroboration it receives from a test that it does pass.

Popper's theory of method has itself been the subject of much critical discussion (e.g., Putnam 1974; Grünbaum 1976). Most controversial has been his outright dismissal of induction, which has met with sustained resistance on the part of inductivist philosophers of science. An important example of such resistance may be seen in an objection that is developed in detail by Wesley Salmon in his paper "Rational Prediction" (1981). Salmon focuses attention on the practical case in which one must decide on a course of action on the basis of a theory. Salmon asks how one is to choose between alternative theories which make conflicting predictions as a basis on which to act. According to Popper, the action should be based on the most highly corroborated of the competing theories. But this suggests that corroboration has inductive force. For while corroboration relates to a theory's past success in surviving tests, if it is to serve as a basis for future action then past survival of tests must be of relevance to what will take place in the future. But if corroboration is to be taken into account in determining a future course of action, this amounts to an inductive inference from past success in surviving tests to the likely continuation of such success into the future. It therefore appears that Popper's falsificationist philosophy of science rests at base on an assumption that is inductive in nature.

Another influential line of criticism of Popper derives from consideration of the history of science. Popper's theory of method suggests that theories are to be rejected the moment they entail a false prediction. But such ruthless elimination of theories does not appear to be the norm in actual science. Scientists often retain theories in the face of conflicting evidence. A failed prediction may simply be regarded as a problem for further investigation, rather than grounds for outright rejection of a theory. An established theory may be so thoroughly entrenched in a field of scientific activity that scientists are prepared to tolerate a range of discrepancies between theory and data. Indeed, they may adhere to a theory until a replacement theory has compiled an equally compelling track record and has shown outstanding additional promise. In the face of such behavior, the falsificationist might reply by distinguishing between the actual practice of science and the normative dictates of a theory of scientific method, and noting that actual practice need not always conform to the dictates of method. Alternatively, they might seek to show that resistance to apparent refutation of theories is associated with the introduction of testable modifications of theories, rather than conventionalist stratagems. But those philosophers of science who hold that the actual practice of science is of relevance to the normative methodology of science will be little inclined to adhere to the Popperian picture in the face of historical evidence of anti-falsificationist practice in science.

From paradigms to pluralism

Perhaps the most significant development in twentieth-century philosophy of science was the emergence in the 1960s of a historical approach to the philosophy of science. The influential work of T. S. Kuhn, as well as that of authors such as P. K. Feyerabend and N. R. Hanson, posed a challenge to orthodoxy in the philosophy of science, as represented by the logical empiricists and by Popper. Whereas philosophers had previously sought to characterize science by identifying its special method, the historical philosophers of science tended to see science as an evolving process which takes place in a variety of shifting circumstances. On the more historically attuned conception of science which has subsequently become prevalent, the notion of *a scientific method* plays a less pivotal role than it once did. Indeed, methodological factors are deemed to be of little more than rhetorical significance by practitioners of the sociology of science, which has arisen as one prominent response to the historical movement.

The historical movement in the philosophy of science was characterized by a number of themes in addition to increased sensitivity to the historical character of science. Historical philosophers of science tended to reject a sharp distinction between empirical fact and scientific theory. They argued that neither perceptual experience nor the observation statements prompted by such experience are independent of the scientific theories proposed to explain observed facts. They also emphasized the way in which scientific concepts and vocabulary are developed as part of the process of theory formation, and are subject to variation as theories themselves undergo variation.

Most importantly in the present context, historical philosophers of science challenged the idea of a theory-neutral scientific method that is invariant with regard to historical time-period and scientific discipline. This may be illustrated by means of Kuhn's views about method. In his masterwork *The Structure of Scientific Revolutions*, Kuhn characterized science in terms of periods of routine "normal science" based on an accepted scientific "paradigm," which is broken at intervals by periods of revolution in which the reigning paradigm is replaced by another. He suggested that the rules of scientific method depend on, and therefore vary with, the paradigm that is in place in a scientific community at a given time. However, in later work, Kuhn took the view that there is a set of methodological criteria of theory appraisal which are, by and large, invariant throughout the history of the sciences. The criteria – which include accuracy, consistency, simplicity, breadth, and fertility – are employed by scientists in the comparative choice between alternative theories. Kuhn claimed that the criteria "function not as rules, which determine choice, but as values, which influence it" (1977: 331). But while the criteria may provide scientists with a rational basis for choice of theory, they may enter into conflict in application to particular theories and may also be subject to alternative interpretations. As a result, appeal to the methodological criteria may fail to yield an unequivocal outcome. Scientists may choose to adopt opposing theories even though they adhere to a common set of methodological standards. (For related discussion, see Duhem 1954: 216–18.)

The flexibility of Kuhn's methodological values is complemented by a well-known theme from Feyerabend's "epistemological anarchist" philosophy of science in his book *Against Method*. According to Feyerabend, all methodological rules have limitations, and are therefore defeasible. Although Feyerabend typically expressed this view in more extravagant terms, the main thrust of his claim is simply that there may be particular circumstances in which any given methodological rule ought not to be applied.

In an attempt to restore objectivity to the methodology of science, Imre Lakatos (1970) proposed a synthesis of Popper's falsificationism with Kuhn's model of science. Instead of paradigms, Lakatos spoke of research programs, which are characterized by a "hard core" of laws embedded in a "protective belt" of auxiliary hypotheses. He argued that there is an objective basis for choice between competing research programs, since a progressive program that successfully predicts novel facts is to be preferred to a degenerating one that fails to predict such facts.

Despite their initial opposition to the historical approach, many philosophers of science have taken its central message on board. Whether the rules of method vary with paradigm or remain stable throughout theory change, the view that there is a plurality of methodological rules operative in the sciences is now widespread. Indeed, it seems to represent current orthodoxy. Philosophers who embrace such a pluralist conception of method typically hold that the scientific method does not consist of some single method, such as the hypothetico-deductive or falsificationist method. Rather, the method consists of a plurality of rules which may be employed in the evaluation of scientific theories or in the certification of empirical results. But, while some see such pluralism as being opposed to traditional theories of method, there are others who see in the variety of methodological rules the true nature of the inductive method.

The justification of method

No survey of the philosophy of method would be complete without consideration of the *problem of the justification of method*. The question of how a method, or a rule of method, is to be justified is a meta-level question about the method or the rule of method. It is a question, not of methodology, but of *meta-methodology*. It is at this level that the philosophy of method intersects with the central justificatory concerns of normative epistemology. For it is at this level that questions about the nature of the epistemic warrant of rules and methods must be confronted.

The problem of justification may be illustrated by considering the two major sources of justificatory problems which relate to method. The first source is one that we have already encountered. It is the problem of inductive skepticism, which is the problem of replying to the Humean skeptic by showing that induction may be given a non-circular justification. The second source is the problem of epistemological relativism, which arises from the methodological variation and pluralism highlighted by Kuhn and other historical philosophers of science. For if no single shared method exists, but rather a variety of potentially shifting methodological norms, then it is not clear that there may be any objective, rational basis for scientific theory choice or theory acceptance. Provided only that a theory satisfies standards which happen to be adopted by some scientist or group of scientists, virtually any theory is capable of being accepted on a rational basis. Without a shared method, there would seem to be no genuine difference between right and wrong in matters of theory choice.

Strictly speaking, the problems of skepticism and relativism are different problems. The skeptic denies the existence of objective knowledge or rationally justified belief. By contrast, the relativist allows that knowledge and rational belief exist, but asserts that they are relative to context. But while the problems of skepticism and relativism are distinct problems, both problems raise the question of how a given method is to be provided with a sound rational basis.

This way of looking at the problem of justification suggests that the solution may require a unified approach that addresses both the skeptic and the relativist. The literature on the problem of methodological justification is too vast to summarize here (but for extended coverage, see Nola and Sankey 2000). In the current philosophical climate, however, one particular unified approach is especially worthy of mention.

In recent years, a great many philosophers have embraced a naturalistic approach to philosophical matters. In the context of the problem of the justification of method, an *epistemological naturalist approach* has a great deal to offer. Such a naturalist sees philosophy as continuous with the sciences, so that epistemological matters are to be dealt with in a broadly empirical fashion. On such a naturalistic approach, the challenge of the epistemic skeptic is dissolved by noting that the skeptic sets unrealistically high standards of justification. No higher standards of justification exist over and above those employed in successful scientific practice or in common-sense interaction with the world. Indeed, it may even be possible to respond to the inductive skeptic using an inductive argument from the success of past induction in a manner that avoids vicious circularity (see Papineau 1992).

As for the threat of relativism, the naturalist may simply deny that no distinction may be drawn between right and wrong in relation to methodological matters. For it is possible to subject alternative methods to empirical test in an attempt to determine which methods work and which do not in actual scientific practice. Those methods which pass such tests may be accepted as the normatively correct methods to follow; those which fail such tests are to be rejected as incorrect, and should not be employed. This way of determining the warrant of a method is known as "normative naturalism" (Laudan 1996). It is a form of reliabilist epistemology, since it takes reliable performance as a crucial component in the warrant of a method.

It would be wrong to suggest that the naturalistic meta-methodology just outlined currently enjoys universal assent among philosophers of science (for dissenting views, see Worrall 1999 and Field 2000). Nevertheless, an analysis of the arguments which might be provided for or against such a position will take one straight to the heart of current discussion in the philosophy of method. For the question of whether the problem of justification may be resolved by epistemic naturalism is one of the key questions of concern to contemporary philosophers of scientific method.

See also Bayesianism; Confirmation; Critical rationalism; Evidence; The historical turn in the philosophy of science; Logical empiricism; Naturalism; Social studies of science.

References

Duhem, P. (1954) *The Aim and Structure of Physical Theory*, Princeton, NJ: Princeton University Press.

Feyerabend, P. K. (1993) *Against Method*, 3rd edn, London: Verso.

Field, H. (2000) "Apriority as an Evaluative Notion," in P. Boghossian and C. Peacocke (eds) *New Essays on the A Priori*, Oxford: Clarendon Press, pp. 117–49.

Grünbaum, A. (1976) "Is Falsifiability the Touchstone of Scientific Rationality? Karl Popper versus Inductivism," in R. S. Cohen, P. K. Feyerabend and M. W. Wartofsky (eds) *Essays in Memory of Imre Lakatos*, Dordrecht: Reidel, pp. 213–52.

Kuhn, T. S. (1977) "Objectivity, Value Judgment, and Theory Choice," in T. S. Kuhn, *The Essential Tension*, Chicago: University of Chicago Press, pp. 320–39.

—— (1996) *The Structure of Scientific Revolutions*, 3rd edn, Chicago: University of Chicago Press.

Lakatos, I. (1970) "Falsification and the Methodology of Scientific Research Programmes," in I. Lakatos and A. E. Musgrave (eds) *Criticism and the Growth of Knowledge*, Cambridge: Cambridge University Press, pp. 91–196.

Laudan, L. (1996) *Beyond Positivism and Relativism*, Boulder, CO: Westview Press.

Nola, R. and Sankey, H. (2000) "A Selective Survey of Theories of Scientific Method," in R. Nola and H. Sankey (eds) *After Popper, Kuhn and Feyerabend: Recent Issues in Theories of Scientific Method*, Dordrecht: Kluwer, pp. 1–65.

Papineau, D. (1992) "Reliabilism, Induction and Scepticism," *Philosophical Quarterly* 42: 1–20.

Popper, K. R. (1963) *Conjectures and Refutations*, New York: Routledge & Kegan Paul.

Putnam, H. (1974) "The 'Corroboration' of Theories," in P. A. Schilpp (ed.) *The Philosophy of Karl Popper*, La Salle, IL: Open Court, pp. 221–40.

Quine, W. V. (1953) "Two Dogmas of Empiricism," in W. V. Quine, *From a Logical Point of View*, New York: Harper & Row, pp. 20–46.

Salmon, W. (1981) "Rational Prediction," *British Journal for the Philosophy of Science* 32: 115–25.

Worrall, J. (1999) "Two Cheers for Naturalised Philosophy of Science," *Science and Education* 8: 339–61.

Further reading

Alan Chalmers's *What Is This Thing Called Science?* 3rd rev. edn (St. Lucia: University of Queensland Press, 1999) remains one of the best introductions to leading themes in the methodology of science. C. G. Hempel's *The Philosophy of Natural Science* (Englewood Cliffs, NJ: Prentice-Hall, 1966) is a classic which contains lucid discussion of key topics. Comprehensive coverage of the various theories of scientific method may be found in *Theories of Scientific Method: An Introduction* (Chesham: Acumen, 2007) by Robert Nola and Howard Sankey. The historical origins of the hypothetico-deductive method are explored by Larry Laudan in *Science and Hypothesis* (Dordrecht: Reidel, 1981). Popper's major treatise on method is *The Logic of Scientific Discovery* (London: Routledge, 1959). Criticism of Popper's method may be found in W. C. Salmon and A. Grünbaum (eds) *The Limitations of Deductivism* (Berkeley: University of California Press, 1988). Peter Lipton provides clear discussion of problems with enumerative induction and hypothetico-deductivism as a preliminary to his account of inference to best explanation in *Inference to the Best Explanation*, 2nd rev. edn (London: Routledge, 2004). An important discussion of methodological issues arising from the historical turn is Larry Laudan's *Science and Values* (Berkeley: University of California Press, 1984). Two excellent works on Kuhn are Alexander Bird's *Thomas Kuhn* (Chesham: Acumen, 2000) and Paul Hoyningen-Huene's *Reconstructing Scientific Revolutions: Thomas S. Kuhn's Philosophy of Science* (Chicago: University of Chicago Press, 1993).

24

SOCIAL STUDIES OF SCIENCE

Robert Nola

Francis Bacon on knowledge, power, and method

That science has a *social* dimension has been long recognized, though the extent to which science is social is a hotly debated topic. The slogan "knowledge is power" is commonly attributed to Francis Bacon (1561–1626), but he hardly endorsed such an implausible identity claim when talking about scientific knowledge. Lurking behind the slogan are two Baconian truisms: science and its applications have social consequences; also both are brought about, in part, by social factors. The first truism says in effect that unless we have correct scientific knowledge we cannot apply it to enhance our powers over nature and ourselves, thereby leading to greater human benefits. Situated at the beginning of modern science, Bacon is optimistic about the use of science to improve our lives; and he hardly envisages any negative effects of its applications, intended or not, of which we are now too well aware (from climate change to the possibility of nuclear warfare).

The second truism is expressed in his utopian fantasy *New Atlantis*. Through his account of Salomon's House, Bacon envisages a vast research institute in which there is a necessary division of labor within science and its consequent need for social organization in order to produce applied scientific knowledge. Putting these truisms together produces a third: science and its applied technologies exist within a causal nexus involving important social, political, and cultural elements, both as causal preconditions and as outcomes. This is a suggestive heuristic for the development of empirically testable hypotheses about specific connections between science and society; as such it remains an important part of current social studies of science. In our times Bacon's idea of a "Salomon's House" can be extended, in ways that Bacon could not have envisaged, to include universities and research institutes, whether government, private or military, as important drivers of the kinds of research to be carried out. How science is shaped by these is an important object of research for sociologists and others. For example Greenberg (2001) gives us an account of how a modern "Salomon's House" of government and private funding agencies have become intermeshed with scientific research in ways which bear out the subtitle of his book: *Political Triumph and Ethical Erosion*.

Are all aspects of science situated within a social causal nexus? For Bacon some lie outside it, such as matters concerning the truth or falsity of scientific hypotheses or methods for testing those hypotheses (whether they are Bacon's methods or those of others). Unlike those who advocate a strong involvement of the social in science, Bacon would not have held that the truth-values of scientific claims are a social construct; and, being an important contributor to methodology, he would not have held that scientific method lacks autonomy and is itself yet another social item within the nexus of knowledge–power. Underlying this is some version of an *internal–external* distinction in which there are aspects of science to be explained by appeal to matters internal to science, such as its methods, while other aspects are external in that they can be given an explanation in terms of the social, cultural, historical, and political context of science. Autonomous internalist features such as principles of Baconian method (or any other method) can be used to determine, say, the evidential support for scientific hypotheses about heat or magnetism, or even particular sociological hypotheses about the science–society nexus. This suggests what might be called a "rational model" of explanation of the scientific beliefs held by persons; what does the explaining must include in its explanatory premises rules of method which scientists employ in forming their scientific beliefs. Where these principles do not, or can not, have a role in explaining some aspect of science, then alternative socio-political explanations can come to prevail. Here quite different, non-rational, social, causal models of explanation are commonly employed. Though individual writers draw the internal–external distinction differently, or they give each different explanatory priority and weighting, there is a measure of agreement that some such distinction *can* be drawn and that it has some use. But more radical sociological positions mentioned later claim that there is no such distinction and all allegedly internalist explanations of aspects of science are ineradicably social.

Marx on science and production

Karl Marx also adopted a version of the external–internal distinction, but placed externalist accounts of science and its technological applications at the center of his "materialist conception of history." On the often-invoked, simple, two-tiered model, in which there is an economic basis which *determines* a superstructure, science and its applications appear in the economic basis in two different ways. The first concerns science as embodied in the skills (knowing *how to*) and the knowledge (knowing *that*) of laborers engaged in productive processes. The second concerns the instruments and other technologies that laborers use in any productive process. For Marx, labor power and the instruments of production are not a given but are relative to levels of scientific and technological development that prevail at each historical period; moreover they evolve together. Examples of these are early humans and their skills in using simple adzes and axes, or humans using a spinning jenny, or humans using a computer (e.g., as a wordprocessor or in developing new software). Marx even extends these ideas to the case of the labor power of teachers who transform pupils into active members of an advanced "knowledge economy."

Marx's two-tiered view is the first of several theories of *technological determinism* in which science and/or technology are the major, if not the only, drivers of historical and social changes. Some of Marx's remarks suggest that he adopts technological determinism; but as Cohen (1978) argues, a better understanding of his model of explanation is not causally *deterministic*, but *functionalist*. The task then is to discover what functional role science plays in the complex of items that make up the two-tier model of base and superstructure. It is important to note that science as a system of ideas or theories does not appear directly in the economic base, either as one of the means of production or as part of the relations of production (viz., patterns of ownership). Nor is it, as some claim, part of the superstructure of "ideological forms of consciousness" which the economic base is said to determine. Science and its applications are often treated as a third, relatively independent, item within the forces of production alongside labor power and the means of production (see *Capital*, Vol. 1, Ch. XIV, section 5). That science is an independent force of production would undercut some of the over-simple accounts, proposed since the 1920s by Hessen, Bernal and others, of the role of science in the two-tier model. Marx also endorsed Bacon's view that scientific method is separate from the nexus of items in the two-tiered model.

On the functionalist model the role of science and its applications within capitalist (and other) social systems is to facilitate and promote the growth of surplus value (and thus profit) at increasing rates through innovation in the technological basis of production, and through the transformation of the abilities and knowledge of laborers who use that technology (another aspect of the "knowledge economy"). At best this is schematic, and alleged instances need to be empirically explored, such as Marx's own claims in *Capital* on the role of chemistry (see *Capital*, Vol. 1, Ch. XV, section 1). There Marx presents a case for the claim that, with the development of new ways of weaving cloth through the mechanization of spinning, capital accumulation could proceed apace on this technological basis only if new ways of making dyes other than the prevailing traditional ones could come into existence. Here a technological change in methods of spinning, along with capital accumulation, created a need for research in pure and applied chemistry to discover new ways of making dyes, a function that the newly emerging chemical industry did perform.

Merton's ethos of science

Although Robert Merton is a severe critic of the simple two-tier model that gives rise to technological determinism, he shares with Marx a functionalist orientation, as do many other sociologists of science. This is nowhere more evident than in his influential, but controversial, account of the ethos of science. In Merton's view the "institutional goal for science is the extension of certified knowledge" (1973: 270). He accepts a version of the internal–external distinction in which there is a scientific method autonomous from its socio-historical context by which this certification takes place (though Merton has an over-simple view of what this might be). What is important for him are not just the methodological norms which do the certifying but also the institutional norms whose functional role is to realize the goal of extending certified knowledge. Merton wrote at a time of growing fascism in Europe where various kinds of racially based science were advocated. Racial science is not only morally reprehensible; it is also dysfunctional with respect to the overriding goal in that the exclusion of certain peoples from science (e.g., the attacks on Einstein as a Jew) lowers the probability of achieving that goal. To combat this, Merton proposed a norm of *universalism* according to which the nationality, race, religion, class, etc., of individual scientists ought to be irrelevant to their participation; the participation of *all* qualified scientists best promotes the goal.

A second norm of *communism* (later often referred to as "communalism") claims that certified scientific knowledge ought to be available in the public domain, and so communally owned. Any attempts to keep scientific discoveries private, as in the case of commercial firms conducting research to further their own commercial interests, can only detract from that goal.

A third norm is that of *disinterestedness*, a demand of integrity according to which scientists ought not to allow personal interests to influence their scientific judgments. Violations of that norm, as in cases of scientific fraud, are part of the dark side of science that has been scrutinized by sociologists and historians of science.

A fourth norm of *organized skepticism* requires that whatever support a theory may have from religious, political, and other groups, it ought not to be accepted unless it has been examined according to the norms of scientific method and has passed the critical scrutiny of one's peers (a social aspect of theory acceptance through consensus). Violations of the norm can be detected in some aspects of the promotion of *intelligent-design* theory at the expense of Darwinian evolution. There is in some countries a growing tendency to overrule scientific findings on political grounds (such as the debate over climate change). Though this is not quite the same as the subversion of scientific testing on political or religious grounds, the fourth norm can still be of relevance in cases of the application of science in politically charged contexts.

Merton's theory of an ethos of science lies behind much of his other work in the sociology of science, such as his studies of the reward systems of science, the nature of priority disputes, and social aspects of the processes of scientific evaluation. Other sociologists have extended Merton's approach by developing a theory of the ethical norms of science to accompany his institutional norms and epistemic norms of method.

Critics of Merton's ethos of science ask whether his theory of institutional norms (including the above norms and others) is complete or needs supplementation. They also investigate the extent to which norms have been violated, and, in cases where violation has been extensive, they consider whether this counts against the claim that there is such an institutional norm at all. They ask whether the norms are invariant across all sciences at all times and places, or whether they vary; and they ask whether an institution as broad as science has the one and only goal that Merton attributes to it, or whether science has a set of goals, or merely quite diverse goals in different circumstances. In abandoning Merton's ethos for science (which is quite abstract and can be hard to apply), sociologists have moved towards a more contextualist and local account of what norms and goals there may be and the different uses to which scientists might put them. Despite this, Merton has captured an important feature of science, one that is coming under renewed investigation in a more highly politically and ethically charged twenty-first century science than that which prevailed in the second half of the twentieth century after Merton had written his seminal papers.

The social construction of scientific knowledge

Social studies of science have not been content with merely investigating the external socio-historical context of science but have also looked at the very claims that are made within science itself. This takes us into the arena of the sociology of *knowledge* or, more accurately, of *belief*. The difference here is a distinction philosophers make and sociologists often ignore, viz., between belief, which is a naturalistic notion, and knowledge or rational belief, which are normative notions in that they involve rationality conditions such as reasons and justifications for belief, or coherence of belief. Another important difference sociologists often overlook is that knowledge, unlike belief, must involve truth (truth being a notion about which most sociologists remain quizzical or skeptical). Importantly, any explanation of why a person *knows* something must refer to the norms of knowledge and thus fits best the *rational model* of explanation; in contrast, explanations of why a person *believes* something need not be within the context of the model. The involvement of knowledge with normativity, unlike belief, places it outside the realm of empirical sociological investigation. As will be seen, more radical sociologists do not think that there is an autonomous realm of the normative and so knowledge, as well as belief, becomes a field of empirical investigation. Within the sociology of knowledge there are moderate positions which accept some version of the internal–external distinction, and a concomitant knowledge–belief distinction. But more radical sociologists abandon both distinctions since, in their view, all science, including its claims to knowledge and its methods, is inextricably bound up with the social. On the more moderate side is one of the founders of the sociology of knowledge, Karl Mannheim.

Mannheim speaks of the "existential determination of thought" but is never particularly clear about the way in which one's social existence determines thought. He rejects the idea that there is a "mechanical cause–effect" relation, but otherwise leaves wide open to empirical research just how strict the "correlation" might be. However, he does say that "the existential determination of thought may be regarded as a demonstrated fact in those realms of thought in which we can show that the process of knowing does not actually develop historically in accordance with immanent laws … or from pure logical possibilities" and that it is not driven by an "inner dialectic" (1960: 239–40). That remark supposes a version of the internal–external distinction in which some thought and/or knowledge has no existential basis and is driven by its own "inner laws"; moreover this has priority in demarcating the boundaries between the internal and the external. It is not too hard to see in this an autonomous realm for scientific belief which arises from the application of scientific methods.

Mannheim is chastised by advocates of the "strong programme" (SP) of the sociology of scientific knowledge (SSK) for putting forward such a weak claim. In contrast they advocate a strong thesis based on four tenets in which all scientific beliefs (or knowledge – any distinction here is downplayed) are drawn into the realm of social–causal explanation and none are left to explanation by "inner laws." As a consequence the *rational model* of explanation of belief, and also functionalist explanations, are rejected in favor of a purely social–causal model which makes no reference to norms of method.

The naturalistic orientation of SP is spelt out in four tenets. The *causality* tenet says that all scientific beliefs of all persons are to be causally explained in terms of the purely naturalistic factors that lead to belief formation, from non-social matters such as our brain and cognitive structures, perceptual apparatus, and sensory input, to social matters, such as a person's socio-political and cultural context, or a person's interests in these. If SP is to be a distinctive thesis then the role of the social must be given considerable weight and cannot be absent from any causal explanation of occurrences of belief; if it were absent then both the social character and the strength of SP would be impugned. The *impartiality* tenet tells us that, for the purposes of explanation, it does not matter what epistemic properties our scientific beliefs have, viz., whether they are true or false, rational or irrational, or lead to success or failure; all are to be explained. Explained in what way? The third tenet, *symmetry*, tells us that "the same types of cause would explain, say, true and false beliefs." The strength of SP is underlined again in the talk of "same type" of explanation: it admits only the causal model mentioned in the causality tenet and excludes all others, especially the rational model. The final tenet, *reflexivity*, tells us that the above tenets also apply to beliefs within sociology – and to the tenets of SP itself (Bloor 1991: 7). In this way, one half of the internal–external distinction is deemed empty since internalist *rational* models of explanation are not to be countenanced.

The fourth tenet follows readily from the first. Sociological beliefs are simply more of the beliefs that are to be found in science and are to be explained socio-causally. Some have argued that this raises difficulties for the status of SP itself. On what grounds do its advocates believe SP? They point to the large number of case studies which show that, for particular scientific beliefs held by particular persons at particular times, the causes of their belief have a social component. This has been a fertile ground of research, but also of controversy in that for many case studies in which social factors are allegedly involved, there are counter studies of the same episode in which it is alleged that there is no social involvement. Setting these important controversies aside, SP is said to get its support by induction from these case studies. But isn't induction a principle of methodology? "No," they say, arguing that it is not a normative principle of method but a naturalistic propensity we possess as reasoners – a point to be addressed shortly.

The impartiality tenet also follows directly from the causality tenet; but it makes explicit that all scientific beliefs are candidates for explanation regardless of their epistemic status. However this ignores the fact that most methodologies – such as Popper's critical rationalism, Lakatos's methodology of scientific research programs, or Bayesianism – can apply equally as well to the false as the true, a point that these methodologists emphasize. So, rational models of explanation which appeal to methodological principles cannot be ruled out on the ground that they deal with only the true. The symmetry tenet introduces something new over and above the first tenet. Some version of the symmetry tenet is widely adopted within SSK – but such symmetry claims can vary widely in their formulation. The stated version needs to be supplemented with an account of the types of cause that are to be admitted, and the grounds, not always clear, as to why the social–causal model of the first tenet is the only explanatory model to adopt.

Bloor gives a quite different ground for accepting the symmetry tenet when he says in reply to critics: "The symmetry requirement is meant to stop the intrusion of a non-naturalistic notion of reason into the causal story. It is not designed to exclude an appropriately naturalistic construal of reason, whether this be psychological or sociological" (1991: 177). Although the appeal to believers as natural reasoners fits well with the overall naturalism of SP, it is undermined by the evidence from cognitive psychology showing how poor we are at reasoning, especially in probabilistic contexts. If this aspect of naturalism is at the core of SP, then we can have no account of why the beliefs formed within science are epistemically worthy at all.

Another aspect of naturalism emerges in unpacking the claim that the norms of reason are an intrusion on the natural causal realm; it is as if the norms of reason are *ex machina* supernatural entities from another world, zapping into the realm of the natural world quite indeterministically. Underlying this aspect of naturalism is an important issue about the status of norms, especially within naturalism. SP adopts an implausible stance towards norms by supposing that they are an intrusion of something non-natural into the natural realm. More plausibly it is we humans – already understood to be items in the natural world – who use norms in coming to form scientific beliefs. No account of ourselves as users or followers of norms should be committed to the view that the way norms play a role in determining our scientific and other beliefs involves non-natural causation. What this shows is that the symmetry tenet is not as straightforward as it appears and is open to quite divergent interpretations, some implausible.

Let us grant the central claims of SP, viz., that the causes of scientific belief are mainly the socio-political context of the scientists or the interests each has in his or her context. Then what kind of explanation would this offer of the evident success we have had in the theories we have selected, where that success can be cashed out as the empirical success of a theory, or its success in making a number of quite novel true predictions, or in leading to successful technological applications? For those who adhere to some version of the *rational* model of explanation, there is an explanation at hand. It is the methodological principles we have applied to the historical sequence of rival theories that have led us to select those theories which exhibit this success. There is something right or correct about our principles of method that makes it highly probable that when they are applied to theories they will select those which are successful in the sense specified.

Advocates of SP cannot appeal to such principles; they can appeal only to matters such as the socio-political context of believers, or their interests in those contexts. Now we can ask: how probable is it that the socio-political contexts of believers or their interests in their socio-political context will lead them to select theories which are successful in the sense mentioned? This would appear to be either low or a matter of indifference. It is hard to see what bearing the socio-political context of scientists or their interests could have on the success of the theories they select. That they come up with any successful theories would seem to be more a matter of luck than anything else. In contrast, this would not be the case for the application of our principles of method by which, on the whole, we do arrive at successful theories. Thus in comparing the two explanations of how it is that we have arrived at the historical sequence of successful theories in science that we have, SP cannot account for this or has to treat it is a matter of luck. In that respect it is deficient when contrasted with a rival explanation, viz., that we apply principles of method which have good epistemic credentials, and it is those credentials that provide a much more plausible explanation of success.

The philosophy of the later Wittgenstein has had a strong influence on SSK. His view that philosophy ought to be a purely descriptive enterprise and not imitate science by adopting causal explanatory models has influenced ethnomethodologists when they come to apply their methods to science (see Lynch 1993). Under Wittgenstein's influence they regard the social studies of science as a descriptive rather than an explanatory enterprise. This has led to a spate of studies, now subsiding, in which the activities of scientists, along with their notebooks, recorded conversations, gossip, and the like, are viewed with the eye of an anthropologist visiting a strange tribe. But this has not precluded ethnomethodologists from adopting a range of different philosophies, from phenomenology to constructivism, in their meta-comments on what they observe (see for example the constructivism that permeates Latour and Woolgar 1986).

Advocates of SP draw quite different lessons from Wittgenstein, as is evident from Kripke's interpretation of his views on rule-following developed by Bloor (1997) within a naturalistic context. On this account what makes norms objective is the consensus of the community of rule-followers. This is the doctrine of meaning finitism. Briefly expressed, for any individual following a rule there is no correct next case to be found objectively in the nature of things or in some alleged transcendent meaning of words; it is as if any item can come next in the sequence of things that is to be called, say, "swan." What objectivity there is arises from the constraints imposed on individuals by what the community at large will sanction by endorsement or reprimand. Overall consensus gives what sense there is to the idea of an individual having got it right in saying "swan." In that sense, all rule-following inescapably involves a social element. Meaning finitism is extended not only to all the terms of science from "swan" to "electron," but also the methodological norms of science themselves; there is nothing more to their status other than what the community of scientists is willing to endorse. If this differs from science to science, from community to community, and over time, then that is something with which the communitarian theory of rule-following can cope.

Some salvos in the science wars

Such a position on the meaning of scientific terms can also be found in Kuhn (1977: Ch. 12). His protean book *The Structure of Scientific Revolutions* (1962) has had a strong influence on the development of SSK, especially in the ways Kuhn admitted a role for sociological considerations concerning theory choice and in determining what counts as a paradigm for a community. However, sociologists of science have not followed the modification he made to his earlier stance. The later Kuhn advocated the non-historical nature of some values in science (Kuhn 2000: Chs 9 and 11). And he rejected a role for negotiation and power in theory acceptance: "I am amongst those who have found the claims of the strong program absurd; an example of decon-struction gone mad" (2000: 110). Notions of power have been widely employed in science studies, especially under the influence of Michel Foucault's popular, but often obscure, doctrine of power–knowledge. However, the sensible core of that doctrine was already well expressed by one of its first advocates, Francis Bacon.

There are many other currents shaping recent social studies of science. One of these is feminism, with its distinctive approach to science studies (e.g., Harding 1986). There has also been a resurgence of interest in social epistemology on the part of philosophers, especially in areas such as the nature of testimony and the social character of knowledge, which has added to philosophical aspects of social studies of science (Goldman 1999 and Kusch 2002). But it is postmodernism that has excited the greatest amount of public controversy and has fanned the so-called "science wars." A large salvo was fired by the "Sokal Hoax" in which Alan Sokal managed to get the editors of the journal *Social Text* to publish what was later revealed to be a spoof of postmodernist writing on science (see Editors of Lingua Franca (2000) for the original spoof and a collection of responses). A further critique was developed in Sokal and Bricmont (1998). Already matters had been bubbling away with the earlier publi-cation of Gross and Levitt (1994), followed by the papers in Koertge (1998).

What is the reception by scientists themselves of the studies that have been made of them, their laboratory activities, and their theories? The Nobel Prize-winning Jonas Salk tells us that he was willing to have Bruno Latour in his laboratory to produce the study that led to Latour and Woolgar (1986). He thought that, on the positive side, their work was important enough so that "in the future many institutes and laboratories may well include a kind of in-house philosopher or sociologist"; but on the negative side he adds that we can find their work "uncomfortable and even painful in places" (1986: 14). Other scientists have not been so generous in confining their negative remarks to just responses to the findings of sociologists; rather the very character of the social studies of science themselves is uncomfortable and painful. For one thing scientists hardly recognize themselves in these studies, a point that other sociologists of science have raised. They also complain of the distortions of scientific theories in the writings of postmodernists. But ultimately they reject the theories, epistemological and social, in which much current social studies of science has been couched. This attitude on the part of scientists is well expressed in Wolpert (1993) and Weinberg (2002). The battlefront of the science wars is now moving in the direction of a truce, but with as yet no way forward about how to conduct the peace. What is needed is a peacetime redeployment of social studies of science which, drawing on the long history of its engagement with science, can give us a renewed perspective on the considerable influence science has on our lives, for better or worse.

See also The epistemology of science after Quine; Naturalism; Scientific method; Social sciences.

References

Bloor, D. (1991) *Knowledge and Social Imagery*, Chicago: University of Chicago Press; first edition 1976.
—— (1997) *Wittgenstein, Rules and Institutions*, London, Routledge.
Cohen, G. A. (1978) *Karl Marx's Theory of History: A Defence*, Oxford: Clarendon Press.
Editors of Lingua Franca (2000) *The Sokal Hoax*, Lincoln: University of Nebraska Press.
Goldman, A. (1999) *Knowledge in a Social World*, Oxford: Clarendon Press.
Greenberg, D. S. (2001) *Science, Money and Politics: Political Triumph and Ethical Erosion*, Chicago: University of Chicago Press.
Gross, P. and Levitt, N. (1994) *Higher Superstition*, Baltimore, MD: Johns Hopkins University Press.
Harding, S. (1986) *The Science Question in Feminism*, Ithaca, NY: Cornell University Press.
Koertge, N. (1998) *A House Built on Sand: Exposing Postmodernist Myths About Science*, Oxford: Oxford University Press.
Kuhn, T. S. (1977) *The Essential Tension*, Chicago: University of Chicago Press.
—— (2000) *The Road Since Structure*, Chicago: University of Chicago Press.
Kusch, M. (2002) *Knowledge by Agreement: The Programme of Communitarian Epistemology*, Oxford: Clarendon Press.
Latour, B. and Woolgar, S. (1986) *Laboratory Life: The Social Construction of Scientific Facts*, 2nd edn, Princeton, NJ: Princeton University Press.
Lynch, M. (1993) *Scientific Practice and Ordinary Action*, Cambridge: Cambridge University Press.
Mannheim, K. (1960 [1936]) *Ideology and Utopia*, London: Routledge & Kegan Paul.
Merton, R. K. (1973) *The Sociology of Science: Theoretical and Empirical Investigations*, Chicago: University of Chicago Press.
Sokal, A. and Bricmont, J. (1998) *Intellectual Impostures*, London: Profile Books.
Weinberg, S. (2002) *Facing Up*, Cambridge, MA: Harvard University Press.
Wolpert, L. (1993) *The Unnatural Nature of Science*, Cambridge, MA: Harvard University Press.

Further reading

As well as the books listed above, two useful forays by philosophers into the sociology of scientific knowledge are J. R. Brown, *Who Rules in Science? An Opinionated Guide to the Wars* (Cambridge, MA: Harvard University Press, 2001) and S. Haack, *Defending Science – Within Reason* (Amherst, NY: Prometheus Books, 2001). A useful survey by sociologists of science is B. Barnes, D. Bloor, and L. Henry, *Scientific Knowledge: A Sociological Analysis* (Chicago: University of Chicago Press, 1996). An account of the broad field of STS not discussed here can be found in S. Sismondo, *An Introduction to Science and Technology Studies* (Oxford: Blackwell, 2004).

25

THE STRUCTURE OF THEORIES

Steven French

Introduction

From one perspective, theories are the sorts of things that we have beliefs about, that we may believe to be true, for example, or that we accept as empirically adequate. From another, they are related to each other, to models, and of course, to the *phenomena*. It is from this latter perspective that we consider how the interrelationships between theories contribute to our understanding of scientific progress, for example, or how the relationship between a theory and the phenomena allows us to get a grip on the notion of scientific explanation. In such cases we might get a better understanding of what's going on if we were to open theories up, as it were, and examine their internal structure, on the grounds that knowing how the various components of a theory fit together might shed some light on these interrelationships.

In the following I present two important analyses of the structure of theories, the so-called "syntactic" and "semantic" views. I'll consider some of the problems with each before critically discussing a kind of "hybrid" position. I conclude by considering the question of whether these analyses can be said to tell us what theories *are* or are merely different modes of description.

The "syntactic" view

The so-called "syntactic" view of theories gets its name from the way it represents the structure of theories syntactically in terms of logico-linguistic expressions related by a deductive calculus. According to this approach, then, the structure of scientific theories consists of:

(i)   an abstract formalism F;
(ii) a set of theoretical postulates (axioms) T;
(iii) a set of "correspondence rules" C.

F consists of a language L in terms of which the theory is formulated and a deductive calculus defined. L will contain logical and non-logical terms; the latter can be divided into the set of observation terms and the set of theoretical terms; the "correspondence rules" function as a kind of dictionary by relating the former to the latter.

A *partial interpretation* of the theoretical terms and the sentences of L containing them is then provided by the theoretical postulates – which contain only theoretical terms – and the correspondence rules, which correlate the non-logical, theoretical terms with observable phenomena by allowing for the derivation of certain sentences containing observation terms from certain sentences containing theoretical ones. The interpretation is partial because the theoretical terms are not explicitly defined and there is room, as it were, for the addition of further correspondence rules as science advances, thus extending the interpretation of these terms.

If T is the conjunction of theoretical postulates and C the conjunction of the correspondence rules, then a scientific theory is taken to consist of the conjunction TC. Furthermore, by expressing the structure of theories within the framework of a logical calculus, the resources of the latter can be drawn upon to capture other aspects of scientific practice. This view meshes nicely with the *deductive–nomological* account of explanation, for example, according to which some phenomenon is deemed to be explained by a theory if a sentence describing it can be logically deduced from the set of sentences expressing the relevant laws – which are typically, but may not necessarily be, theoretical – plus appropriate initial or boundary conditions.

What about other aspects of scientific practice? It is often emphasized that scientists use different kinds of models in their work, rather than theories *per se*. Putting things rather crudely, one can say that in a model, certain terms which one believes refer or might refer to actual entities in the world, are replaced by terms which one knows do not refer, at least not in the relevant domain anyway, because they involve significant idealizations, or the introduction of objects from an entirely different domain for example. Thus, in the classic billiard ball model of a gas, certain theoretical terms – "gas atoms" say – are replaced by other, more familiar terms – "billiard balls" – while keeping the laws the same – Newton's laws of mechanics, for example. The model is deemed to be false, since we know that gas atoms are not billiard balls – they're the wrong size, are not made of ivory, do not have colors painted on to them and so forth – yet it is argued that the substitution of familiar objects for unfamiliar ones helps to increase our understanding and further, by exploring the similarities and differences between these objects, can aid progress.

However, problems arise on this account. First of all, the structure of a model must be the same as that of the theory from which it is obtained, which seems implausible in practice. Furthermore, it has been argued that a lot of model construction is actually independent from theory in methods and aims (Cartwright, Shomar, and Suárez 1995) and that some models are, in a certain sense, *autonomous* from theories, in a way that allows them to *mediate* between theories and the phenomena (Morrison 1999). Now one way of responding to these concerns would be to acknowledge that scientific practice involves at least two features – theories and models – that are separate foci of scientific activity and separate sources of scientific knowledge. Thus we would have to consider not only the structure of theories but also that of models, as well as the further issues of the role such models play in explanation, confirmation and so on. Alternatively, the advocate of the syntactic approach could insist that models can be embraced as well, by treating them as "little theories" with a deductive structure and appropriate theoretical statements, correspondence rules, and all the rest. Of course, the issue of how all these "little theories" are interrelated would still have to be addressed.

Nevertheless, there are other problems that the syntactic approach must face. In particular, if the correspondence rules change, then we have a different theory, since these are a constitutive part of the theory's structure. But these rules embody experimental procedures, etc., so if someone comes up with a new way of testing a given theory, and thus a new experimental technique, that requires a new correspondence rule to be added and hence, strictly speaking, we have a new theory. Now the evolution of one theory into another may be regarded as a fluid business, but whatever one's view of scientific progress, it certainly seems implausible to maintain that one has a new theory every time one introduces a new experimental technique.

Furthermore, the logico-linguistic nature of the structure presented on this view leads to the worry that a change in *language* also leads to a change in theory. Again, there are cases where this seems totally implausible: whether Newtonian mechanics is presented in English or Portuguese, it is still Newtonian mechanics. Of course, a defender of the syntactic view can easily respond by insisting that the postulates and statements of a theory, although couched in a particular language, express certain *propositions*. That then ties this view to some account of the latter – whatever they are, that is what a theory will be. At the other extreme, there are cases for which we might indeed want to say that couching the theory in a different formal framework has given us an entirely new theory. In between these extremes, however, are non-trivial cases where a change in the language used to express the theory does not lead to a new theory and it is not clear whether the syntactic view can accommodate such changes.

It is also worth noting that this view represented the structure of theories in terms of the best framework to hand, namely that of predicate logic. This gives theories a nice, deductive structure in terms of which one can accommodate scientific explanation and prediction, as well as the relationship between theoretical statements and their observational counterparts. However, strictly speaking, an infinite number of propositions can be deduced from any given set of theoretical axioms, effectively bloating a theory to implausible proportions. Fortunately, the early twentieth century saw the development of other formal devices that could be used to represent the structure of theories. In particular Tarski, in formalizing the intuitive idea of *truth in a structure*, introduced the set-theoretical notion of a model, where a model provides a semantic interpretation for our language. This gave philosophers of science a further set of resources that they could use. Crucially, it was recognized that the relationship between theory and phenomena was much more complex than could be captured by correspondence rules; there were models of experiment, models of data, models of phenomena, all interrelated and related to theoretical models. And finally, it was suggested that philosophers of science should draw on the same sorts of resources to represent theories as scientists use to represent phenomena, namely mathematical, rather than meta-mathematical (i.e., logical) tools.

The "semantic" approach

According to the so-called "semantic," or model-theoretic approach, the structure of theories is described in terms of classes of mathematical models. The central idea is that theories can be characterized by what their linguistic formulations refer to when the latter are interpreted semantically, in terms of those models. In this sense theories can be seen as extra-linguistic and it is often claimed that according to the semantic approach theories *are* families of such mathematical models. In particular, what the syntactic view designated as the "axioms" of the theory is then understood as serving to pick out the relevant models (by virtue of the fact that the axioms are true in those models). In order to present a theory on this view, we define the relevant class of models directly.

This approach has been put into service on behalf of both realism and anti-realism. Van Fraassen's constructive empiricism (1980) has, at its heart, the notion of empirical adequacy, taken to be the aim of science and characterized in model-theoretic terms. A theory is said to be empirically adequate if it *saves* the phenomena by representing that phenomena in terms of *appearances* which are effectively embedded in the theory. The notion of *embedding* used here is a mathematical one in the sense that there is an isomorphism (a mapping that is one-to-one and onto) between the appearances and sub-structures of the theory, known as the "empirical substructures." Giere (1988), on the other hand, suggests that models should be regarded as similar in certain respects and degrees to physical systems and that such talk of "similarity" can function as a surrogate to the usual talk of "truth" in this context. From this perspective, the laws of a theory, represented logico-linguistically within the syntactic approach, and treated as being of crucial importance by many philosophers of science, merely serve to delineate the class of models, since they come out true in the latter by virtue of the nature of those semantic models.

This approach, it is claimed, better represents the complex relationships between theories, data, and phenomena (Suppes 1962) and also, crucially, the role of models in scientific practice. This last feature in particular has come under criticism, since the semantic approach appears to tie the construction and role of scientific models too closely to theories (Cartwright, Shomar, and Suárez 1995; Morrison 1999). However, no matter how they are constructed, there appears to be nothing to prevent scientific models from being represented in terms of set-theoretical structures; nor is there anything to prevent their relationship, if any, to theories (also represented in terms of set-theoretic structures), from being represented using the resources of that approach (da Costa and French 2003: 54–7).

Of course, there is more to the structure of theories than this. The *structuralist* program of Stegmuller, Sneed and others has developed from an early form of the semantic approach and offers a complex and layered set-theoretic analysis of theories.

It begins with certain general conditions (so-called "frame conditions") that define the relevant scientific concepts which feature in the theory. These conditions are satisfied by what are called the "potential" models of the theory. Some of the concepts expressed by a theory are internal to that theory, whereas others are determined from *outside*, as it were. The models satisfying the axioms for these *outsider* concepts are called "partial potential models." The "actual models" are then those models that in addition satisfy the laws of the theory.

Models of the same theory and models of different theories will be interrelated, of course, via "constraints" and "links," respectively, and taken together, these various components constitute the "core" of the theory. However, in order to identify a theory, we also need to specify the "domain of intended applications." This is delimited by the above *outsider* concepts, and hence the intended applications constitute a subclass of the partial potential models of the theory. The relationship between the theory and its domain of intended applications can be expressed by the claim that the latter can be subsumed under the theoretical content of the core of the theory.

The core, taken together with the intended applications constitute a "theory element." These can then be aggregated in a "theory net" yielding a synchronic structure, with a single fundamental law at the top, under which hold various "specializations" of that law, each determining a new theory-element (see Balzar and Moulines 1996: 11). From a diachronic perspective, if certain conditions are satisfied, then a sequence of theory-nets constitutes a "theory-evolution" (*ibid.*: 11–12). Theory-nets which differ in their classes of potential models may also be interrelated and form what is called a "theory-holon."

A standard criticism of this view is that when it comes to the application of theories it effectively betrays its model-theoretic origins by opening the door to elements of the syntactic view: the empirical claims of the theory are expressed through a logico-linguistic statement that states that certain theoretical and non-theoretical properties of the entities within the theory's domain are related in terms of the prescribed structure. Thus, in application, at least, it seems as if we cannot get away from linguistic formulations.

A broader concern is that despite its application to numerous case studies, the formalism deployed in this approach sets it as too far removed from actual scientific practice. In particular, the "domain of intended applications" would appear to be, in practice, *open* in a way that cannot be straightforwardly captured using the standard tools of set theory. And certain defenders of the structuralist line do themselves no favors by accommodating *social* or *pragmatic* considerations through the set-theoretic representation of whole scientific communities or generations within diachronic theory elements!

The *openness* inherent in various features of scientific practice is something that has been emphasized in a variant of the model-theoretic approach which attempts to accommodate it through the introduction of *partial structures* (da Costa and French 2003).

Partial structures

As already mentioned, a fundamental issue within the model-theoretic approach concerns the relationship between theories and the kinds of models that scientists regularly deploy in their practice. Critics of this approach insist that the latter are just too diverse to be accommodated by a set-theoretic construction and recent studies have even drawn on apparently inconsistent models to push this claim (Frisch 2005). However, it has been argued that by appropriately amending the set-theoretic notion of model such criticisms can be met (da Costa and French 2003). The central idea here is to introduce *partial relations*, defined over the elements of the model. So, in a partial structure we have

$$\mathfrak{A} = <D, R_i>_{i \in I},$$

where D is a non-empty set and each R_i is (crucially) a partial relation, which is not necessarily defined for all n-tuples of elements of D. (Such relations can be taken to represent the "partialness" of our information about the actual relations linking the elements of D.) More formally, each partial relation R can be viewed as an ordered triple, $<R_1, R_2, R_3>$, where R_1, R_2, and R_3 are mutually disjoint sets, with $R_1 \cup R_2 \cup R_3 = D^n$, and such that: R_1 is the set of n-tuples that belong to R, R_2 is the set of n-tuples that do not belong to R, and R_3 is the set of n-tuples for which it is not defined whether they belong or not to R. (Note that when R_3 is empty, R is a normal n-place relation that can be identified with R_1.) A partial structure can then be extended into a total structure such that each partial relation is extended in the sense that each extended relation is defined for every n-tuple of objects of its domain (Mikenberg, da Costa, and Chuaqui 1986).

Introducing such structures widens the framework of the model-theoretic approach and allows various features of models and theories – such as analogies, iconic models, and so on – to be represented (da Costa and French 2003). Indeed, it is argued that even inconsistencies in science – such as Bohr's model of the atom – can be accommodated within this framework. One can then define partial isomorphisms holding between the partial structures, which captures the idea that they may share parts of their structure and, it is claimed, allow one to capture various relationships between models and theories. In particular, the existence of a hierarchy of models stretching from the data up to the level of theory can also be captured and by introducing partial homomorphisms one can go even further, to incorporate the relationship between theories and mathematical structures (Bueno, French, and Ladyman 2002).

However, the fundamental criticism has been leveled that the crucial issue here is not that of formally establishing isomorphisms between models and other models or between models and systems but rather that of ruling out those which are uninteresting (Collier 1992: 294–5). Weakening the relationship to admit partial isomorphisms just makes matters worse by increasing the number of possible relationships to select from. One response is to appeal to heuristic factors in order to account for why one model rather than another was adopted. Such factors might include adherence to well-established symmetry principles, for example (da Costa and French 2003). This line can be extended to other criticisms as well. It has been claimed that the semantic approach cannot accommodate the way in which scientists may prefer certain idealizations over others, even though such idealizations are equivalent in model-theoretic terms. Again, additional factors can be introduced which describe the relationship of those idealizations to the relevant background theories. Of course, what we are doing here is bringing in non-formal factors but to do so is to acknowledge what we can expect from a formal representation. By allowing for such factors, and adopting what might be seen as a *lighter* touch with regard to the formal representation of inter- and intra-theoretical relationships, this version of the Semantic Approach occupies the *middle ground* between the structuralists, above, and those who eschew such formal representations altogether.

Nevertheless, the question remains: can we eschew linguistic elements entirely in favor of models? Van Fraassen, for example, writes that "the semantic view of theories makes language largely irrelevant to the subject" (1989: 222), but by "subject," here, he is referring to the description of the structure of theories and in terms of such a description the semantic approach does appear to offer significant advantages. Nevertheless, Giere characterizes the statements that assert how models are related to systems – that is, that assert claims of similarity – as "theoretical hypotheses" and insists that it is with regard to those hypotheses, rather than the models *per se*, that we form our epistemic judgments. Now when we turn from a discussion of the structure of theories to a consideration of our epistemic attitudes towards them, it seems that we have no choice but to resort to some sort of linguistic formulation. When I say "I believe *p* is true/false/adequate in some sense or other," *p* is standardly taken to be a statement, expressing a proposition. Indeed, unless *p* is taken in this way, we cannot employ Tarski-like formulations of truth, which understand the truth of a statement in terms of its satisfaction within a model.

There are then two ways we can go. We can take Giere's theoretical hypotheses as constitutive elements of theories and thus, since they are clearly linguistic, as fatally undermining the stance that language is largely irrelevant. Alternatively, we can take seriously the above expression of turning from a discussion of structure to a consideration of epistemic attitudes and articulate this in terms of adopting different perspectives on theories. This may then allow us to accommodate the claim that the semantic approach offers at least a useful and perhaps even the best set of resources for representing the structure of theories, whilst also acknowledging that in presenting them and characterizing our epistemic attitudes towards them we cannot avoid linguistic expressions.

The first kind of move can be seen in attempts to conceive of theories as *hybrid* entities, consisting of both model-theoretic and linguistic elements. The second takes us back to a view originally espoused by Suppes himself.

The hybrid view

In an attempt to accommodate the above concerns, Hendry and Psillos take as their starting point Hertz's famous answer to the question "What is Maxwell's theory?" – "Maxwell's Theory is Maxwell's system of equations" (Hendry and Psillos 2007). Taken as it stands, such a claim might seem too spare a view of what theories are, but as they point out, it is on the right track since equations such as Maxwell's are clearly a central component of many scientific theories. However, such equations are equally clearly *linguistic*.

But this is not the whole story. These equations describe the interrelationships between the magnitudes referred to by the relevant terms. This description is typically idealized and hence is not of the real-life system itself but of a (theoretical) *model* of it. These models are similar to real physical systems, with similarity coming in appropriate respects and degrees. Thus on this account, theories are regarded as complex entities, in which both language and models are used to represent the world.

Now, when it comes to representation, there appears to be general agreement that a *pure* form of structuralism in the context of the semantic approach is a non-starter (French and Saatsi forthcoming). Even a hard line adherent of this approach might agree that when it comes to the *mechanism* of representation, linguistic and non-linguistic elements will be involved. However, when it comes to the nature of theories themselves, taking them to be "consortia of representational elements" (*ibid.*) seems less plausible. Consider: on the syntactic view, a theory is a closed set of statements or propositions, where closure is imposed through (classical) logical consequence. On the semantic view, theories are – typically – taken to be families of set-theoretical models, interrelated via partial isomorphisms, say. In both cases the interrelationships between the various components of a theory are comparatively straightforward to represent, since these components are all of the same kind and the kind that they are determines the nature of the interrelationship.

But it is not easy to see how one could tell a similar story on the hybrid approach. There we have two kinds of thing – mathematical equations and models – and they are interrelated by virtue of interpretation: providing an interpretation of the equations yields a model, such that the relationship between equation and model is definitional, as the adherents of the semantic view insist. But then it is not clear how theories can be characterized as hybrid entities, since the two components are not on a par; one is defined by the other. The worry now is that if pushed, the hybrid view collapses into either the syntactic or semantic view, depending on where the emphasis is placed.

Let's now turn to the second route indicated above, which suggests that when we consider our epistemic attitudes to theories, we need to shift our perspective and here linguistic considerations cannot be avoided.

Truth and meta-representation

Theories are also – on most accounts – truth-apt; that is, they can be true or false. This also raises problems for the semantic approach, since, as Chakravartty has emphasized, if theories are identified with families of models then realism – as it is standardly conceived – cannot even be entertained because there is no way of expressing the requisite sense of *correspondence* with the world (Chakravartty 2001). If we are going to be realists about a particular model, in the sense of asserting that some aspect(s) has a counterpart in reality, then we are going to have to make some sort of statement asserting a correspondence between a description of that aspect and the world. But this in turn requires the deployment of a linguistic formulation to be interpreted in such a way that we can understand what exactly the model is telling us about the world. Again, it seems, we must associate models with linguistic expressions, such as mathematical equations, and interpret such expressions in terms of correspondence with the world. The conclusion is: "Theories can't tell us anything substantive about the world unless they employ a language" (*ibid.*: 330–1).

Now, again, one can argue that even if it is granted that models must be *associated* in some way with linguistic expressions, this does not mean that such expressions must be understood as constituent parts of the theory concerned. However, the following dilemma also arises: suppose theories are *identified* with families of set-theoretic models and it is also held that these theories can be true, in the usual correspondence sense as formalized by Tarski. But the models themselves *cannot* be taken to be true in this sense since it is precisely their role to satisfy the sentences of the theory in its linguistic formulation.

How can we resolve this dilemma? One response goes as follows: first, move away from the *identification* of theories with set-theoretic models and take the latter to simply *represent* the former; second, adopt a useful distinction first introduced by Suppes, between what he calls the "extrinsic" and "intrinsic" characterizations of a theory (1967: 60–2). The former concerns the structure of the theory, and the relationships between theories themselves and between theories and *the world*, understood in terms of that structure. From the "extrinsic" perspective we regard theories from "outside" a particular logico-linguistic formulation and it is in this respect that models play a *representational* role. From the intrinsic perspective, however, theories can be taken to be the objects of epistemic attitudes, and be regarded as true, empirically adequate, approximately true, or whatever.

What this means is that we must be careful in shifting from one perspective to another (da Costa and French 2003: 33–5). When we consider the claim "So-and-so believes theory *T* to be true," we must acknowledge that we are working – as philosophers of science – from within the "intrinsic" perspective, since our epistemic attitudes are expressed by belief reports that are sentential in nature. Here the models play the role of *possible realizations* that satisfy the sentences of the belief reports and thus allow truth to be defined. Of course, just because belief *reports* are expressed in terms of sentences, that does not imply that the *objects* of the beliefs themselves are sentential in character. Adopting the "intrinsic" stance allows us to focus on the relevant set of propositions for the purposes of applying the formal machinery of truth but we must not make the mistake of thinking that the theory can be identified with such a set, lest we run into precisely the sorts of problems the semantic approach is supposed to resolve. And likewise, when we talk of theories or models being interrelated via partial isomorphisms or whatever, we need to recognize that we have now moved to the extrinsic characterization which affords us access to such notions as isomorphisms and the like. Indeed, it is only from "outside" a particular logico-linguistic characterization that we can formulate the question whether "a certain theory" can be logically axiomatized in the first place: "To ask if we can axiomatize the theory is then just to ask if we can state a set of axioms such that the models of these axioms are precisely the models in the defined class" (Suppes 1967: 60). Of course, maintaining this dual perspective means refusing to identify theories with either sets of propositions or classes of models. What we are doing in each case is choosing the appropriate representational tools for the purposes at hand.

This approach can be understood as a move away from taking the role of models to be *constitutive*, in the sense that the class of models actually constitutes the theory, and adopting them as *representational*, in the sense that we draw on set theory to represent the structure of the theory. This leaves open the question "What, then, is a theory?" and we might be accused of not offering a clear account of the ontological status of theories. But then, identifying theories with either sets of propositions or classes of models merely pushes the answer to this question back a step, since the questions then arise: "What is a proposition?" and "What is a model?" or "What is a set?" The former leads us into the philosophy of language, the latter into the philosophy of mathematics, both of which offer multiple sources of contention and dispute. Accepting the accusation, we might actively refuse to offer such an account and adopt a *quietist* attitude which maintains that what is important from the point of view of the philosophy of science is to appropriately represent the various features of scientific practice we are interested in. Representation is thus the focus at multiple levels: within science, with theories and models representing phenomena; and within the philosophy of science with set-theoretical structures representing theories and models, and their interrelationships.

Quietism in philosophy is typically associated with anti-realist, anti-metaphysical and anti-representationalist stances and it is important to insist that what is *not* being suggested here is that we adopt such an attitude towards the objects of science, such as quarks, genes, or whatever, but towards the putative objects of the philosophy of science, namely theories, models, or whatever. Quietism in philosophy is also associated with a broadly pragmatic attitude that separates *genuine* doubts from the *make-believe* kind. Of course, how we draw that line is crucial, but typically, again, the separation is based on issues of relevance for understanding practice, of some sort or other. Similarly, we can ask whether the ontological status of theories and models is relevant for our understanding of scientific practice. If we agree that it is not, then doubts about such status can be dismissed as not 'genuine' and the related issues taken to be irrelevant.

A quietest attitude towards the objects of science will find itself coming up against something like the *no miracles argument*, but it is hard to see how a form of the latter could be constructed in defense of the objects of the philosophy of science. Positing the reality of quarks or genes may contribute to the explanation of certain features of the physical world; adopting a similar approach towards theories and models does little if anything to explain the features of scientific practice. It is better, then, to simply turn away from this issue and ask, instead, how can we best represent these features in order that we can understand this practice? In this context, the unitary framework of the semantic approach – suitably modified – offers the best way forward.

See also Idealization; Logical empiricism; Models; Realism/anti-realism; Representation in science; Theory change in science.

References

Balzer, Wolfgang and Moulines, C. Ulises (eds) *The Structuralist Theory of Science: Focal Issues, New Results* (Berlin and New York: Walter de Gruyter, 1996)

Bueno, O., French, S., and Ladyman, J. (2002) "On Representing the Relationship between the Mathematical and the Empirical," *Philosophy of Science* 69: 452–73.

Cartwright, N., Shomar, T., and Suárez, M. (1996) "The Tool Box of Science (Tools for Building of Models with a Superconductivity Example," in W. E. Herfel et. al. (eds) *Theories and Models in Scientific Processes*, Amsterdam: Rodopi, pp. 137–49.

Chakravartty, A. (2001) "The Semantic or Model-Theoretic View of Theories and Scientific Realism," *Synthese* 127: 325–45.

Collier, J. D. (1992) "Critical Notice: Paul Thompson, *The Structure of Biological Theories*," *Canadian Journal of Philosophy* 22: 287–98.

da Costa, N. C. A. and French, S. (2003) *Science and Partial Truth: A Unitary Understanding of Models and Scientific Reasoning*, Oxford: Oxford University Press.

French, S. and Saatsi, J. (forthcoming) "Realism about Structure: The Semantic View and Non-Linguistic Representations," *Philosophy of Science* (*Proceedings of the 2004 PSA Meeting*).

Frisch, M. (2005) *Inconsistency, Asymmetry, and Non-Locality: A Philosophical Investigation of Classical Electrodynamics*, Oxford: Oxford University Press.

Giere, R. (1988) *Explaining Science: A Cognitive Approach*, Chicago: University of Chicago Press.

Hendry, R. and Psillos, S. (2007) "How to do Things with Theories: An Interactive View of Language and Models in Science," in J. Brzeziński et al. (eds) *The Courage of Doing Philosophy: Essays Dedicated to Leszek Nowak*, Amsterdam and New York, NY: Rodopi, pp. 59–115.

Mikenberg, I. F., da Costa, N. C. A., and Chuaqui, R. (1986) "Pragmatic Truth and Approximation to Truth," *Journal of Symbolic Logic* 51(1): 201–21.

Morrison, M. (1999) "Models as Autonomous Agents," in Morgan, M. and Morrison, M. (eds) *Models as Mediators*, Cambridge: Cambridge University Press, pp. 38–65.

Moulines, C. U. (1976) "Approximate Application of Empirical Theories," *Erkenntnis* 10: 201–27.

Suppes, P. (1962) "Models of Data," in Nagel, E., Suppes, P., and Tarski, A. (eds) *Logic, Methodology and the Philosophy of Science: Proceedings of the 1960 International Congress*, Stanford, CA: Stanford University Press, pp. 252–67.

—— (1967) "What is a Scientific Theory?," in S. Morgenbesser (ed.) *Philosophy of Science Today*, New York: Basic Books, pp. 55–67.

Van Fraassen, B. (1980) *The Scientific Image*, Oxford: Oxford University Press.

—— (1989) *Laws and Symmetry*, Oxford: Oxford University Press.

Further reading

Fred Suppe's *The Semantic View of Theories and Scientific Realism* (Urbana and Chicago: University of Illinois Press, 1989) presents an *insider's* comparison of the syntactic and semantic approaches and for an illustrative application of the latter to biological theory, see Elizabeth Lloyd's *The Structure and Confirmation of Evolutionary Theory* (Princeton, NJ: Princeton University Press, 1994). Perhaps the most famous "structuralist" text is Wolfgang Stegmüller's *The Structure and Dynamics of Theories* (New York:

Springer-Verlag, 1976) and recent articulations are presented in Balzer and Moulines (1996). An excellent survey is provided in Roman Frigg and Stephan Hartmann's "Models in Science," in Edward N. Zalta (ed.) *The Stanford Encyclopedia of Philosophy* (spring 2006 edition), available: http://plato.stanford.edu/archives/spr2006/entries/models-science. Peter Achinstein's *Concepts of Science: A Philosophical Analysis* (Baltimore, MD: Johns Hopkins University Press, 1968) is a rich source of examples illuminating the diversity of models and theories. The late Daniela Bailer-Jones offers a useful account in "Tracing the Development of Models in the Philosophy of Science," in Lorenzo Magnani, Nancy Nersessian and Paul Thagard (eds) *Model-Based Reasoning In Scientific Discovery*, Dordrecht: Kluwer, 1999), pp. 23–40, and explores the supposed differences between theories and models in her unpublished monograph "Models in Philosophy of Science."

26

THEORY-CHANGE IN SCIENCE

John Worrall

Introduction

According to an historical sketch enjoying wide circulation, once upon a time, in the "bad old days" of logical empiricist hegemony, philosophers of science believed that the progress of science is cumulative. When a new scientific theory replaces a previously accepted one, it simply generalizes the older one (or perhaps two or more older theories). The (alleged) paradigm case was Newton's "synthesis" of the laws of Kepler and of Galileo: Kepler's laws govern planetary motions; Galileo's govern terrestrial free fall and projectile motion; Newton's theory provides an account of *all* motion anywhere in the universe that, when applied to the planets and to terrestrial objects respectively, yields Kepler's and Galileo's laws as special cases.

Despite tenacious defense, this cosy picture – so the widespread story continues – could not indefinitely resist the impact of the two great revolutions of the twentieth century. For two centuries Newton had been supposed to have discovered the truth about the universe, but then his theory was rejected in favor of a relativistic rival that fundamentally contradicts it in several important ways: for example, replacing the Newtonian assertion that time is absolute, with the claim that two events may be simultaneous in one frame of reference but not in another. The "quantum revolution" involved breaks with entrenched ideas that seem, if anything, even more radical – for example, classical physics is deterministic, quantum theory seemingly inherently probabilistic.

And, so this story concludes, once these changes had been seen as "revolutionary," commentators (most notably Thomas Kuhn in his celebrated *Structure of Scientific Revolutions*) could emphasize that there had in fact been revolutionary change across the board in science. For example, the accepted view of the nature of light has changed from material particle, to wave in an elastic medium, to wave in a *sui generis* electromagnetic field, to photons – "particles" without rest mass obeying probabilistic laws.

Unsurprisingly, this sketch is at best a *highly* reconstructed rational reconstruction of history; but what *is* true is that many of the most important problems in philosophy of science since the 1960s have involved attempts to come to terms with (apparently *radical*) theory-change in science. Kuhnian theory-change seems to challenge the two most basic theses that single science out as epistemically privileged: the thesis of *scientific realism* and the still more basic thesis of *scientific rationality*.

Theory-change and scientific rationality

Kuhn claims that not only do successive theories separated by a "revolution" contradict one another, they are embedded within "paradigms" that involve different methodo-logical standards. This certainly appears to entail a particularly striking version of relativism – if there are no "trans-paradigmatic" standards standing outside the scien-tific fray, then it seems impossible to deliver the verdict that the newer "revolutionary" theory is objectively superior to the older one: all one can do is record the empirical fact that (most of) those in the relevant scientific community came to believe that it was superior by dint of embracing the new paradigm.

Laudan (1984) agrees that if everything – theories *and* methods of appraisal (and also for him the aims of science) – were taken to change all at once in science then we would indeed be landed with "big-picture relativism." But Laudan holds that, while Kuhn may have been wrong that methods of appraisal of theories *always* change when fundamental theory does, he is certainly right that methods of appraisal are not fixed but are subject to at least occasional change. We learn *how* to do science better as we do better science! Delivering this (seemingly attractive) verdict requires some way of underwriting the claim that later scientific theories are in general better than earlier ones, while at the same time allowing that the methodological standards through which we make such judgments are themselves rationally modifiable. Laudan argues that this feat can in fact coherently be achieved via his *reticulated model* of theory-change.

The basic idea of this model is that a theory T_1 may be accepted as superior to some erstwhile entrenched rival T while some methodology M is in force, but then T_1 itself, once accepted, turns out to justify a change in methodology from M to M_1. Laudan sees this idea as a version of *normative naturalism* that somehow delivers norms which are both genuinely normative and empirically-governed.

There are however difficulties with Laudan's interesting attempt. He claims, for example, that the wave theory of light was accepted while Newton's inductivist methodology, which eschews genuine theories and theoretical notions, was applied in science; but this acceptance then forced the abandonment of the inductivist methodology in favor of a more liberal hypothetico-deductive approach. It is easy to see how, *once accepted*, Fresnel's theory, with its commitment to the undeniably theoretical "luminiferous aether," would fail to cohere with inductivism as Laudan construes it. But how could Fresnel's theory have been accepted in the first place if Newton's methodology really did rule against any genuinely theoretical entities and if that methodology really was accepted by scientists?

Laudan's claims tend to conflate *professed* and *real* methodology, and also, like many of Kuhn's, seem to result from an over-inflated understanding of the admittedly vague term "methodology." If *any* claim about what types of theory for a given area are likely to prove successful is counted as "methodological," then it is no news that there has been clear methodological change over time in science. Many such "rules" are unsurprisingly paradigm- or research programme-dependent. Once, for example, Fresnel had produced a successful account of diffraction, scientists applied the "rule" that other optical phenomena should be explained in terms of waves in an elastic medium. But there is surely a *reason* why classical wave theories were once thought likely to work, but then the idea was abandoned. A reason based on judgments (about empirical support and the avoidance of ad hoc assumptions) that remained fixed. While classical wave theories were initially far and away the best empirically supported accounts of light, eventually a theory came along – Maxwell's theory – that was still better empirically supported, on those same principles, and yet rejected the luminiferous ether. There is no indication either from the history of science or from anything that Laudan or Kuhn says that there has been any change in these core principles of "little methodology."

Even if this is true, two questions immediately arise: *first* what *are* those core principles? and *secondly* what is their status – how can they themselves be defended?

Suppose, concerning the second question, we have agreed on some basic, abstract principles of empirical support. How could those principles themselves be justified? This issue – essentially of how, if at all, the principles of rationality can themselves be rationally defended – is one that has often arisen in the history of philosophy. It would seem that deductive logic dictates that the basic principles of rationality *cannot* in fact themselves be rationally defended – there is nowhere deeper to go (and even if there was, the issue would arise again with respect to those "deeper" principles). And hence it seems that the adoption of rationality must itself be arational. The best we can do is to defend those basic principles as very general, abstract *givens* or "dogmas."

This is, however, an uncomfortable admission for a rationalist to make and in philosophy of science, as in more general epistemology, a good deal of effort has gone into attempting to avoid making it. These efforts have often involved claims that certain logical circles, far from being vicious, are somehow acceptable (see Van Cleve 1984, though the idea goes back at least to Braithwaite and Goodman); they have also often involved defenses of *externalist* epistemological views (e.g., Papineau 1993); and finally, and cutting across these various efforts, it has been claimed, as we saw in discussing Laudan, that methodological rules can be regarded as themselves subject to empirical assessment and hence as *naturalized* (without sacrificing the normative force of those rules).

All these approaches have their adherents and the issues remain open – though my own view is that they each face insuperable objections.

Aside from the issue of their own status, what could the basic core principles of scientific rationality be? Despite many difficulties, it still seems clear that they somehow have to do centrally with *empirical support*. Moreover they will have to be principles of empirical support that deal adequately with the *Duhem problem*.

Kuhn's most direct challenge to scientific rationality was his claim that scientists normally treat difficulties for their theories as *anomalies* rather than as Popper-style refutations: as problems for further research and not as reasons to give up the paradigm. As anomalies mount up, both those who declare a "crisis" and look for a new paradigm and those who continue to believe that the older paradigm will eventually resolve its anomalies, are *equally rational*. This clearly threatens the idea that theory-change is invariably justified in terms of the newer theory/paradigm proving better empirically supported than the older one.

Kuhn's notion of an *anomaly* is easily, and better, explained via a Duhemian analysis. Duhem (1906) pointed out that although we often speak of testing single scientific theories against empirical data – Newton's theory against planetary positions and so on – when the deductive structure of such tests is properly analysed, the situation is seen to be more complex. Auxiliary assumptions are always needed – any attempt to test Newton's theory of mechanics plus gravitation against the observed positions of some planet will, for example, implicitly rely on an assumption (clearly a theoretical assumption) about the amount of refraction that light reflected from the planet undergoes in passing into the earth's atmosphere. Moreover, at least for many theories, the central theory itself breaks down into a 'core' component and a set of more specific assumptions. For example, there is really no such thing as *the* wave theory of light. Instead, and in line with Lakatos's idea (1970) of competing research programs, there is a core idea: that light consists of some sort of waves in some sort of medium, together with an evolving set of more specific claims about the type of medium, about the waves therein and so on. Thus the full structure of an empirical test is more like the following:

Central theory
Specific assumptions
Auxiliary theories
Initial conditions

_____

Therefore, empirical result *E*

Assume that, when the observation is made, *E* turns out to be false. All that logic guarantees is that at least one of the premises is false – it does not dictate which one and in particular it does not dictate that it is the central theory. Those scientists whom Kuhn describes as treating recalcitrant data as "anomalies" are just taking it that, at least as a first move, the "blame" for getting the data wrong lies either with an auxiliary theory or with one of the specific assumptions rather than with any theory basic to the paradigm.

There are many cases in the history of science showing that this type of move, far from being under suspicion of possible "irrationality", has produced some of the greatest scientific breakthroughs. Perhaps the most famous was the discovery of Neptune: by holding on to Newton's theory despite its apparent clash with the facts about Uranus's orbit, Adams and Leverrier were led successfully to predict the existence of a hitherto unknown planet.

Treating a negative result as an anomaly is, therefore, *sometimes* good science. But in other cases it seems to be the very essence of pseudoscience. Consider, for example, creation "scientists" defending their basic theory that god created the universe in 4004 BC against the evidence of the fossil record by assuming, as Gosse famously did, that god created the rocks with the fossils already in them.

And even within science, such defenses of an entrenched theory often seem to be clearly bad science. When, for example, the wave theory of light made impressive predictions about the results of various diffraction experiments, some corpuscularists, just as Kuhn would suggest, "held out" for their preferred theory and claimed that these results were merely "anomalies" for their theory: eventually, by making the right (and clearly quite complex) assumptions about the "diffracting forces" that affect the particles as they pass the edges of opaque objects, these results could be given a corpuscularist account. Duhem's analysis shows that such a move is always logically possible. However, although corpuscularists might produce tailor-made assumptions about diffracting forces to accommodate, say, the outcome of the two-slit experiment, the strong intuition remains that this is a telling result in favor of the wave theory.

If we are to show that theory-change in science has been rational in the precise sense that later theories are invariably better empirically supported than their predecessors, then we shall need an account of empirical support that underwrites this intuition.

An obvious distinguishing feature in these cases is that the newer theory standardly *predicts* the empirical results, while the defenders of the older theory *accommodate* those results after the fact. So Fresnel's theory *predicted* the white spot at the centre of the geometrical shadow of a small opaque disc; corpuscularists suggested *after the event* that this result might be accounted for within their approach by making suitable assumptions about "diffracting forces". Darwinian theory predicts (in a way) the fossil record; creationists only accommodate the facts after the event by supposing that god chose to draw pretty pictures in some rocks when creating them. If then there were a general defensible rule of empirical support that *predictions count more* then we would have the rationale we are seeking.

The issue of *prediction vs. accommodation* is a long-running one that continues to be hotly debated. There seem, however, to be two obvious problems with the suggestion that predictions carry more supportive weight than explanations of (otherwise equivalent but) already established facts. The *first* is that while the suggestion yields the intuitively correct judgments in *some* cases, it does not do so in all. The facts about the precession of Mercury's perihelion were, for example, well known before the general theory of relativity was articulated, and yet all serious commentators regard that theory's explanation of Mercury's orbit as constituting important empirical support for it – at least as strong support as it received from the prediction of any temporally novel fact. The *second* problem is more general: the suggestion seems to stand without any epistemic justification – why on earth *should* the time-order of theory and evidence have any epistemological import?

It seems then that for all its sharpness, the *predictions-count-more* view cannot be the correct solution to the Duhem problem. And in fact the main defect of the creationist account of the fossil record, for example, is surely not that the facts were already known when the specific theory that captures them was first formulated, but rather that they *had to be* known since they were used in the construction of that specific theory. The basic idea of creationism gives no indication whatsoever that there should be particular "pictures" found in particular rocks – the specific theory that has them as part of creation is based entirely on the observations themselves. Similarly, in the optics case, the basic idea that light consists of material particles subject to forces gives no indication whatsoever that the particular "diffracting forces" emanating from a small disc should be such as to draw the particles passing the edge so that they hit the center of the geometrical shadow: that fact had to be given and to form the starting point of the construction of some force function that would do the job. On the other hand, those cases in which some already-known result seems to supply strong empirical support to a theory are characterized by the fact that the result follows from the central theory concerned, using only *natural* auxiliaries – not special assumptions that are tailored to the fact concerned. For example, planetary stations and retrogressions fall out naturally from the Copernican theory as straightforward consequences of the fact that we are making observations of the other planets from a moving observatory: a given planet's stations occur when we overtake or are overtaken by it. The issue is not about prediction versus accommodation, unknown vs. known facts, but rather all about non-ad hoc vs. ad hoc accounts of phenomena whether already known or not (though of course a scientist cannot tailor an assumption to an empirical result she does not yet know about!).

This is not to assert that ad hoc maneuvers are automatically scientifically illicit. Adams and Leverrier created a theory specifically so that it would entail the already known (and initially anomalous) details of Uranus's orbit. Often, indeed, scientists obtain specific theories by *deduction from the phenomena* – where this really means deduction from the phenomena plus a general theory (or set of such theories) that they already accept. As I argued in "New Evidence for Old" (2002), we need in fact to differentiate two types of empirical support. *Deductions from the phenomena* supply support for the deduced theory, but *only* against the already-given background of the general theory: they supply no further support for that general theory. Thus, the creationist theory with the fossils gets (conditional) support from the fossils – they provide a very good reason to hold that particular version of the creation story if you are going to hold any version of that story at all; but the fossils give no (unconditional) support whatsoever to the general story. Similarly, in the Adams and Leverrier case the data from Uranus give very good support to their version of the Newtonian account involving a change in the number of planets presupposed, but the data alone give no unconditional support, I would say, to the general Newtonian theory. The difference in the two cases is, of course, that there is independent evidence in the Newtonian case: the revised theory is *read off* the Uranian data but then *predicts* the existence of a new planet, a prediction that can, of course, be checked observationally and which turned out to be true. In the creation case there is patently no such independent testability – writing the fossils into creation simply avoids the initial problem presented by those data but yields no further prediction that can be checked.

One important issue is whether the currently most widely held formal account of empirical support – that of the personalist Bayesians – can adequately capture the intuitive judgments of confirmation. However the merits and demerits of Bayesianism are discussed elsewhere in this collection.

Theory-change and scientific realism

The issue of *scientific realism* is clearly related to the question of scientific rationality, but is logically independent of it. It is logically possible to hold that there are fixed, objective rules of theory appraisal in the light of evidence that have governed all instances of theory-change in mature science, while at the same time being entirely agnostic as to whether following those rules is likely to take science ever closer to some aim – whether that aim be total empirical adequacy or the whole truth (as in scientific realism). Logically possible, but distinctly odd! Games specify their own aims – your team wins at football if it scores more goals, and there is nothing more to be said. But science is surely more than a game. Suppose we have agreed on the rules that dictate what it means for one theory to have greater empirical support than any of its rivals. It seems counterintuitive to claim that *all* we can say about the currently winning (*best-supported*) theory in some field is that it is indeed winning according to those rules. We would expect to be able to say something about what that judgment implies in terms of the likely relationship between that theory and the universe.

What (epistemological) scientific realists want to say, of course, is that the very best theories in the light of the rules of evidence are approximately true – not only at the empirical level but also at the level of "deep structure." The main motivation behind realism is the sometimes stunning empirical success of some theories in science: quantum electrodynamics, for example, turns out to predict the value of the magnetic moment of the electron correctly to better than one part in a billion! Intuitively speaking, realists have argued that it would be a miracle if some theory made such an amazing prediction and yet were not at least approximately true in what it said was going on *behind* the phenomena.

The chief obstacles to this view are precisely those posed by the facts about theory-change in science. If we accept that earlier theories in the history of science were quite radically false and yet enjoyed striking predictive success, then it can scarcely be claimed that it would be a miracle if present theories enjoyed the success they do and yet were not even approximately true. The history of science would be a history of *miracles*!

How (if at all) can realism about current theories be reconciled with the facts about theory-change? One line is the heroic one: accept that theories in the past were radically false but yet insist that our current theories are true. One might even *try* to make the line look less heroic by pointing out that, assuming a positive solution of the rationality problem, our theories now are epistemically superior to their historical predecessors; so why should not current theories be approximately true even though their predecessors were not? But this line is surely unsustainable. Suppose we really must admit that Newton's theory now looks radically false in the light of Einstein's theory. Although, of course, the evidence that we have now for Einstein's theory is more extensive than that for Newton's theory in the nineteenth century, the difference is only one of degree. On what grounds, then, could the realist deny the possibility that Einstein's theory might itself eventually be replaced by a theory bearing the same relation to it as it does to Newton's (of course, this would be on the basis of still more extensive evidence) and therefore come itself to look radically false?

Realists well-grounded in the facts about theory-change have not taken the heroic line, but instead have argued against the thesis that those theory-changes have invariably been *radical*. One possibility is to accept that there have indeed been radical changes in *fundamental* theory, but to point out that such changes do not seem to affect theories *lower down* the theoretical hierarchy. Correspondingly, any claim of approximate truth in the case of *fundamental* theories (e.g., concerning the basic structure of space and time) would be abandoned, and realism restricted to theories lower down the hierarchy (maybe those concerning atoms). Such an approach might be called "partial scientific realism."

A different approach – at least *allegedly* – is the widely discussed view called "entity-realism" (see, e.g., Hacking 1983). This claims to be different since it claims to eschew realism about theories altogether in favor of realism about entities. But how do we know that some (alleged) thing is an entity rather than a nonentity, that is, how do we (take ourselves to) know that there is something in reality corresponding to some term involved in our theoretical framework? The answer given is that we know this if we can *manipulate* the "entity" in question. But *why do we believe* that we are *manipulating* an electron in certain circumstances? We certainly do not ever see the electrons, let alone the *manipulation* of them. The answer is, of course, that we believe this because we accept certain *theories* that tell us that this is what we are doing and in the light of which we interpret certain observable signs (tracks in a cloud-chamber or whatever) as produced by electrons. Theories are inevitably involved. Entity-realists seem simply to be telling us that we should be realists about certain types of theory (ones that are sufficiently low-level and well entrenched) and not about others (ones that are more fundamental).

Like other versions of partial realism, entity-realism is at best agnostic about realism concerning our fundamental theories. Yet it is fundamental theories like Newton's theory with its prediction of the hitherto-unsuspected existence of Neptune that provide the most striking predictive successes and, hence, the seemingly best reason for being a realist. No one, independently of any issue about theory-change, should be a fully gung-ho realist about our fundamental theories. Quantum mechanics and general relativity are, for example, to say the least, uneasy bed-fellows, so all informed commentators expect one or both to be *corrected* in some not-yet-fully articulated "synthesis." Hence no one should claim that our current fundamental theories are outright true, but surely one should not give up so easily on the view that they are *approximately* true?

There are two versions of scientific realism on the market that – unlike partial realism – do not give up. One is defended by Philip Kitcher (1993: Ch. 5) and Stathis Psillos (1999: Ch. 5). They suggest that we should be realist about fundamental theories all right, but only about *parts* of those fundamental theories. Kitcher proposed a distinction between the *working* and *presuppositional posits* of a theory. It is *only* the latter that are rejected in *scientific revolutions*, while the working posits are invariably preserved. It therefore seems reasonable to make the optimistic meta-induction that those working posits will continue to be preserved through all future theory-changes – the reason for that preservation being that, unlike the presuppositional posits, they are *true*. Kitcher claims, for example, that Fresnel's assumptions about light waves are working assumptions, his claims about the elastic ether that carries the waves being merely presuppositional. The working posit – in the form of the idea that light is a (transverse) wave – was thus carried over in the theory-change to Maxwell's electromagnetic theory; and only the presuppositional (or idle) assumptions were abandoned.

This sounds like an attractive position. But it may be overly optimistic about what claims are really preserved through change – if we think not of the differences between Fresnel's theory and the next theory of optics, namely Maxwell's, but between it and our current theory of light, then since this involves probabilistic waves associated – by an entirely new quantum mechanics – with particles without rest mass, it is just as difficult to see Fresnel's waves preserved within that theory as it is his elastic solid ether. (Waves, that is, in some full-blooded contentual sense; there are, of course, wave *functions* in quantum mechanics – but this points toward *structural realism*. Indeed it can be argued that Kitcher and Psillos's position, when fully articulated, merges with the latter.)

Structural realism (SR), pioneered by Poincaré, attempts to deliver the "best of both worlds" (see Worrall 1989). It respects the pro-realist intuitions by agreeing that their striking predictive success is a clear indication that theories in the mature sciences have latched on to reality (no doubt in some approximate way); and at the same time it insists that, after all, the development of theoretical science, including fundamental theory, *is* cumulative (or quasi-cumulative) – but at the level of *structure*. Essentially, metaphysical ideas about how the mathematical structures involved in our best theories are instantiated in reality may seem to change radically as science progresses, but those mathematical structures themselves are invariably retained (usually *modulo* the *correspondence principle*). Maxwell's theory may do away with the elastic solid ether on which Fresnel's theory was based, and so Fresnel was indeed as wrong as he could be about *what* waves to constitute the transmission of light, but his theory continues to look structurally correct from the vantage point of the later Maxwell theory, which agrees with it that optical effects fundamentally depend on *something or other* that waves at right angles to the direction of the transmission of light. Hence Fresnel's equations – though not his preferred interpretation of the terms within them – are retained in the later theory. According to this view, Fresnel was, from the vantage point of the successor theory, as wrong as he could be about the *nature* of light (there is no such thing as the elastic solid ether and *a fortiori* no such thing as waves transmitted through it), but he was correct about its *structure* (light really does depend on *something or other* that vibrates at right-angles to its direction of transmission).

The question of whether SR is defensible currently attracts lively debate. The general feeling underlying many criticisms appears to be that SR is not strong enough to count as *really* a version of realism. Whether this is correct is an open question. Certainly SR is not a version of realism on Putnam's much-discussed 1978 characterization. This requires a realist to assert that the theoretical terms in successful theories have real world reference; it can then be admitted that the theory's assertions about those "entities" are only approximately, rather than strictly, true, but the realist must assert that the theoretical terms refer. This approach was incorporated into any number of attempts to slay the demon of *incommensurability*: if the various theories of Johnstone Stoney, Thomson, and later scientists were not all talking about the same thing (namely an "electron"), then how can we possibly compare the likely truth-values of those claims?

SR, to the contrary, is just as fallibilist (or approximativist) about *reference* as it is about *truth*. Indeed, it emphasizes that standard referential semantics points us in the wrong direction by pretending that we have some theory-unmediated access to the real world, against which to compare our theories. Once articulated, this surely is immediately seen to be an untenable position: *all* our access to the "deep structure" of the universe is through our theories; the so-called "causal theory of reference" is a clear non-starter, at least for the sorts of (alleged) entities involved in physics. (How would one "ostend" *the* electromagnetic field, say, in order to "baptize" it, without presupposing theory?) SR takes it that the mathematical structure of a theory may globally reflect reality without each of its components referring to a separate item of that reality; and that the indication that the theory does reflect reality is exactly the sort of predictive success that motivates the *no miracles argument*. This may seem like a hand-waving sort of realism to some, but it is arguably the strongest form of realism compatible with the history of theory-change in science.

See also Bayesianism; The historical turn in the philosophy of science; Naturalism; Observation; Philosophy of language; Prediction; Realism/anti-realism; Scientific method; Truthlikeness.

References

Duhem, P. (1906) *The Aim and Structure of Physical Theory*, Princeton, NJ: Princeton University Press.
Hacking, I. (1983) *Representing and Intervening*, Cambridge: Cambridge University Press.
Kitcher, P. (1993) *The Advancement of Science*, Oxford: Oxford University Press.
Kuhn, T. S. (1970 [1962]) *The Structure of Scientific Revolutions*, 2nd edn, Chicago and London: University of Chicago Press.
Lakatos, I. (1970) "Falsification and the Methodology of Scientific Research Programmes," in I. Lakatos and A. Musgrave (eds) *Criticism and the Growth of Knowledge*, Cambridge: Cambridge University Press.
Laudan, L. (1984) *Science and Values*, Berkeley: University of California Press.
Papineau, D. (1993) *Philosophical Naturalism*, Oxford: Blackwell.
Psillos, S. (1999) *Scientific Realism: How Science Tracks Truth*, London: Routledge.
Putnam, H. (1978) *Meaning and the Moral Sciences*, Boston, MA: Routledge & Kegan Paul.
Van Cleve, J. (1984) "Reliability, Justification, and the Problem of Induction," *Midwest Studies in Philosophy* 9: 555–67.
Worrall, J. (1989) "Structural Realism: The Best of Both Worlds," repr. in D. Papineau (ed.) *The Philosophy of Science*, Oxford: Oxford University Press (1996).
—— (2002) "New Evidence for Old," in P. Gärdenfors et al. (eds) *In the Scope of Logic, Methodology and Philosophy of Science*, Amsterdam: Kluwer.

Further reading

The main sources of the recent concern with the rationality of theory-change are Kuhn (1970 [1962]) and Lakatos (1970). References to some of the social-constructivist ideas inspired by Kuhn can be found in Kitcher (1993) which attempts to chart a middle course between earlier overly optimistic views of the epistemic status of science ("legend") and the more recent and negative, Kuhn-inspired, constructivist views (of the "legend bashers"). Probably the currently most widely advocated account of scientific rationality is the personalist Bayesian one: the most detailed accounts are contained in John Earman's *Bayes or Bust? A Critical Examination of Bayesian Confirmation Theory* (Cambridge, MA: MIT Press, 1992) and in Colin Howson and Peter Urbach, *Scientific Reasoning: The Bayesian Approach*, 3rd edn (La Salle, IL: Open Court, 2006). Bas van Fraassen's *The Scientific Image* (Oxford: Clarendon Press, 1980) develops his *constructive empiricist* view, probably the strongest rival to scientific realism currently available. The best overview of the scientific realism debate is provided by Psillos (1999). The influential "Newman objection" to the structural realist view defended in Worrall (1989) was reintroduced into philosophy of science through William Demopoulos and Michael Friedman's "Critical Notice: Bertrand Russell's *The Analysis of Matter* – its Historical Context and Contemporary Interest," *Philosophy of Science* 52 (1985): 621–39. The attempt to re-secure reference, despite theory-change, for theoretical terms such as "electron" relies on the causal theory of reference developed in Putnam (1978) and in Saul Kripke's *Naming and Necessity* (Oxford: Blackwell, 1980).

27
UNDERDETERMINATION
Igor Douven

Underdetermination is a central issue not only in the philosophy of science, but in other areas of analytic philosophy as well. Underdetermination claims are at least often adduced to argue that our epistemic position *vis-à-vis* a given part of reality is less impressive than we would have hoped or thought it was, and in any event there is almost invariably a lot at stake in arguments concerning some underdetermination claim(s). Some well-known philosophical debates can be regarded as turning, at bottom, on whether or not a given underdetermination claim must be accepted, and, concomitantly, on whether or not we must resign ourselves to some (typically very) modest epistemic position concerning whatever part of reality is at issue.

What does it mean to say that one thing is underdetermined by another?

In the philosophy of science one frequently encounters claims to the effect that a particular theory is (or is not) "underdetermined by the evidence," or even that all scientific theories, or at least all those belonging to a certain interesting class of theories, are underdetermined by the evidence, even all evidence we might ideally possess. What is typically, and roughly, meant by such claims is that having all the available evidence will not allow us to determine the truth-value of the theory, respectively, of any theory or any theory belonging to some designated class. To make this both more precise and more general, we can let underdetermination be a relationship between distinct classes of propositions, and hold for different combinations of *know* and *justifiedly believe*. (To make this *entirely* general, one might even consider any combination of epistemic attitudes, though I doubt that others than the just-mentioned ones will yield philosophically interesting underdetermination claims.) We might, for instance, say that one class of propositions C_1 <know, know>-underdetermines another class of propositions C_2 if and only if knowing every member of C_1 is not enough to know any member of C_2. Similarly, C_1 <know, justifiedly believe>-underdetermines C_2 if and only if knowing every member of C_1 is not enough even to be justified in believing any member of C_2.

While not usually stated in this way, most underdetermination claims encountered in the philosophy of science seem to be about <know, justifiedly believe>-underdetermination of a class of propositions expressing (relevant) evidence and some given class of rival scientific theories – and not just those in the philosophy of science. What is one of the most central underdetermination claims in epistemology can be rendered as: the class of propositions expressing all your sense data throughout your entire life, as well as those you might have had at some moment, <know, justifiedly believe>-underdetermines the class of propositions {You are a brain-in-a-vat, You are an embodied brain}. And a well-known underdetermination claim from the philosophy of mind is that the class of truths about a person's behavior <know, justifiedly believe>-underdetermines, among many others, the class of hypotheses {The person has an "inner life", The person does not have an "inner life"}. In any event, below, by "underdetermination" will be meant <know, justifiedly believe>-underdetermination throughout.

Why is underdetermination philosophically interesting?

Nothing philosophically really interesting follows from an underdetermination claim in itself. Suppose C_1 underdetermines C_2, so that knowing every member of C_1 will not justify us in believing any member of C_2. That does not mean that we cannot justifiedly believe any member of C_2. Perhaps we simply do not need to know any member of C_1 in order to come to have justified beliefs in, or even knowledge of, the members of C_2, for instance because we have direct epistemic access to the latter, or epistemic access via some other class of propositions C_3.

In interesting underdetermination claims, there is always some alleged important epistemic distinction between the two classes of propositions referred to in the claim. To one class we are supposed to have a fairly direct cognitive access, or at least a direct access given certain idealizing assumptions which in the context of the discussion are mostly deemed innocuous (or, at any rate, permissible). To the other class we at least *prima facie* seem to have cognitive access, if at all, only via the former, that is, it seems that the propositions in the latter class can be known, or at least justifiedly believed, if at all, only because we can know the propositions in the former.

Arguments involving underdetermination claims come in two main varieties. One is meant to establish either the existence of a class of data to which we have some kind of cognitive access – though typically it is not obvious that we have that access – or the existence of one or more rules of inference that we justifiably rely on, though typically it is not obvious that we rely on those rules, or at least that we are justified in doing so. The other variety is meant to establish some form of skepticism.

In arguments of the first type, it is standardly presented as a given that we know/ justifiedly believe all or at least some members of a class of propositions C, and that there is at least some initial plausibility to the thought that our knowledge of/justified belief in these propositions entirely depends on our knowledge of (some of) the members of another class of propositions C'. But – it is then claimed – C' underdetermines C. The point then typically argued for is *either* that our knowledge of/justified belief in the elements of C (insofar as we have it) must, appearances to the contrary notwithstanding, depend on more than just our knowledge of (some of) the members of C' (if it depends on that at all) *or* that there must be other rules than those most obviously available to us (like the rules of first-order logic) by dint of which we can come to have knowledge of/justified beliefs in (some of) the elements of C on the basis of our knowledge of the members of C′. This is almost invariably accompanied by some proposal as to what the something more, or the other rule(s), could be.

Underdetermination claims in the philosophy of language often are of this type. For instance, in pragmatics it is often claimed that sentence-meaning underdetermines speaker-meaning; that we usually are justified in believing we know, and even know, what a speaker means by what she says; and thus that we must have more to go on in figuring out what a speaker means than only sentence-meaning, the something more – according to most authors – consisting of contextual clues.

In a similar vein, David Lewis (1986: 107), discussing the requirements for a functional theory of mental content, argues that in order to be able to assign content to functional states, we must rely on principles of fit, roughly to the effect that the assignment of contents to a person should tend to make her behavior come out as serving her desires according to her beliefs. But, says Lewis (*ibid.*),

> principles of fit can be expected to underdetermine the assignment of content very badly. Given a fitting assignment, we can scramble it into an equally fitting but perverse alternative assignment. Therefore a theory of content needs a second part: as well as principles of fit, we need "principles of humanity," which create a presumption in favour of some sorts of content and against others.

This is a kind of attempted transcendental deduction of the existence of principles we use in interpreting each other, where – note – it is taken as a given that interpretations (or assignments of contents) are not generally underdetermined.

The other type of argument involving underdetermination claims is the one more common in the philosophy of science and also epistemology. The common structure of arguments of this type is the following: we can know/justifiedly believe the members of a class of propositions C, if at all, only because we can know the propositions in another class C′; but C′ underdetermines C; hence we cannot know any member of C. Well-known examples of this type are the Cartesian argument for external-world skepticism and various arguments for more restrictive forms of skepticism, such as skepticism about other minds. To this type also belongs one of the main arguments – if not *the* main argument – for scientific anti-realism, the position in the philosophy of science which counsels agnosticism as the proper epistemic attitude *vis-à-vis* scientific theories, because, it is claimed, scientific theories are underdetermined by the evidence.

What reason(s) do we have to believe underdetermination claims?

From here on the focus is entirely on underdetermination in the philosophy of science. The standard anti-realist argument for the thesis that scientific theories are underdetermined by the evidence involves two premises. The first is this:

(EE) For each scientific theory there are empirically equivalent rivals, where an empirically equivalent rival to a theory is a contrary (a theory inconsistent with it) that at least in the light of the evidence alone – any possible evidence – will necessarily be accorded the same confirmation-theoretic status. Naturally one could consider weaker versions of EE ("for most theories ...," "for many theories ...," "for some theories ...," "for all theories with such-and-such features ...," and so on), which, in combination with the premise KE (see below), would all seem to yield somewhat different versions of scientific anti-realism, but for simplicity we stick to EE here.

The important thing to note is that if EE is correct, then no matter how many empirical tests a theory has already passed, such success cannot be taken as an indication that the theory is true, for each of its empirically equivalent rivals will or would pass the same tests just as successfully. Thus, unless the data refute a theory, no amount of them suffices to determine its truth-value.

While on its own EE does not yield any anti-realist conclusions, it does do so together with a premise sometimes called "knowledge empiricism":

> (KE) If the data alone do not suffice to determine a theory's truth-value, then nothing does.

Indeed, from EE and KE it follows straightforwardly that the truth-value of any scientific theory must forever remain beyond our ken. Notice that KE says, in effect, that what are sometimes called the "theoretical virtues" – factors such as simplicity, scope, coherence with other accepted theories, and, more generally, explanatory force – which many philosophers and scientists regard as (not necessarily unfailing) marks of truth, and thus as being of epistemic significance, are at most of pragmatic value.

Arguments for EE either extrapolate from supposed historical cases of empirical equivalence or try to prove formally the existence of empirically equivalent rivals to any scientific theory. As to the former, we are often pointed to the empirical equivalence of the theory of special relativity and the ether theory in the Lorentz–Fitzgerald–Poincaré version and, respectively, that of standard quantum mechanics and Bohmian mechanics. As to the latter, John Earman (1993) has proposed various plausible formalizations of the notion of empirical equivalence and used them to prove some propositions all of which can be regarded as establishing interesting versions of EE. Similar results have been obtained by other authors.

Arguments for KE typically try to raise doubts about the truth-conduciveness of any *prima facie* reasonable candidate criterion for theory choice beyond conformity with the data. For instance, anti-realists have argued that there is no *a priori* reason to believe that reality is simple rather than complex. A further point they have raised is that, even if it is granted that the world is "simple" in *some* sense of that word, it still need not be "simple" in the mundane sense that its nature or structure is easy to grasp for creatures with *our* cognitive capacities.

What can one say in response to underdetermination claims?

Not many philosophers are happy to accept scientific anti-realism. It is not surprising, then, that a number of responses to the above anti-realist argument for underdetermination are to be found in the literature. It merits remark that most of those responses, now to be discussed, have close parallels in debates about other (skeptical) underdetermination arguments.

One type of response against the anti-realist argument denies EE, or at least maintains that currently we have no reason to believe that there exist (interesting) empirically equivalent rivals to any scientific theory. We might regard as an early token of this the logical positivists' argument that apparently empirically indistinguishable rivals are really just notational variants of one another. But their response was based on a verificationist view of meaning that nowadays is almost universally regarded a failure.

It seems a better strategy to tackle directly, or at least try to raise doubts about, the arguments that have been given in support of EE. For instance, it may be pointed out that the historical evidence for the thesis is rather meager. Advocates of the thesis time and again point to the two historical cases mentioned in the previous section. Patently, however, having two actual cases of empirical equivalence seems hardly enough to support the claim that all scientific theories have empirically equivalent rivals – or even that an interesting number of theories have such rivals. Yet that is about all the historical evidence we have ever been given! It might be countered to this objection that the sparseness of actual examples of empirically equivalent rivals is explained by the fact that in scientific practice it is typically quite hard to come up with even one theory that fits the data and is also consistent with accepted background theories, let alone that we could find a number of such theories. But one can also, and perhaps with more right, draw an altogether different moral from this fact, as, for instance, Gerard 't Hooft (1994: 27) does about the fundamental laws of physics when he says:

> The requirement that [the fundamental laws of physics] must agree with the very restrictive postulates of both quantum mechanics and general relativity has up to now proved so difficult to realize in any physical model that one is tempted to suspect that not more than one model will exist which agrees with all this.

In their influential "Empirical Evidence and Underdetermination" (1991), Larry Laudan and Jarrett Leplin have argued that in fact no amount of actual examples of allegedly empirically equivalent theories can support EE, for such theories may really be only temporarily indistinguishable by the data. They do not mean to suggest that cases of theories that happen to be indistinguishable in the light of the data we currently have are unable to support EE. Rather their point is that, first, our conception of data may be due to change over time and, in particular, the line between the observable and the unobservable may shift due to technological advances; and second, as is widely acknowledged, theories have observational consequences only when conjoined with so-called auxiliaries, and over time we may come to hold different views about the hypotheses we deem eligible to figure as "auxiliaries" in the derivation of observational consequences from theories, so that over time theories may come to have different observational consequences.

It is worth emphasizing, though, that it would seem to be within the rights of the anti-realist to insist on a conception of data, or at least the observable, that is *not* susceptible to change over time. Specifically, Bas van Fraassen (1980) has argued that there is an epistemically significant distinction between claims whose truth-value can be ascertained by observation with the naked eye and ones whose truth-value cannot thus be ascertained. And, almost by definition, no technological advances are going to affect that distinction. As for the variability of auxiliaries, Richard Boyd (1984: 201) may be right that advocates of EE can successfully respond to this point by reformulating the thesis in terms of "total sciences," which include both theories and auxiliaries.

In their 1991 paper Laudan and Leplin further complain that, while many philosophers of science seem to believe that there exists some algorithm for generating empirically equivalent rivals to any given theory, such an algorithm is nowhere to be found in the literature. This seems right. At the same time one wonders why such an algorithm should be called for. It seems that a proof of EE – whether or not that shows how *effectively* to construct empirically equivalent rivals – would offer the advocates of EE all they could wish for. And, as we saw above, such proofs do exist. (It should be noted that those proofs appeared after the publication of Laudan and Leplin's paper; they were, at least partly, meant as a response to that paper.)

It must be admitted, though, that at least the extant proofs of EE appear to rely on assumptions that are open to dispute. For instance, the proofs given in Earman (1993) crucially depend on the assumption that theories can be formulated in a first-order language, an assumption which may well be false. It may in effect be very hard to prove EE in a way which could suit the anti-realist's needs. The main stumbling-block here is that there seems to be no purely logical characterization of the notion of empirical equivalence. Of course, it is not uncommon to find empirically equivalent rivals defined as contraries that have the same logical consequences in the observational part of some designated vocabulary – which *is* a logical characterization. But while this characterization of empirical equivalence may be perfectly all right if hypothetico-deductivism is assumed, that confirmation theory is certainly not part of the current orthodoxy, to put it mildly. Indeed, it would be a mistake to think that the notion of empirical equivalence can be defined without (at least implicit) reference to a confirmation theory.

To buttress this point, it will help briefly to consider the underdetermination problem from a Bayesian perspective. It is easy to appreciate that, given Bayesian confirmation theory, EE would be unable to establish any (interesting) underdetermination claim were empirical equivalence to be defined in the way just suggested. For, that two or more theories have the same observational consequences does not imply that they bestow the same likelihood on all evidence statements they do not entail (but are consistent with). And the latter are, from a Bayesian point of view, just as relevant to determining a theory's confirmation-theoretic status as are its observational consequences. In fact, given a purely subjective version of Bayesian confirmation theory, which imposes no constraints on rational degrees of belief beyond the axioms of probability theory, no underdetermination claim would seem to follow from EE, even if empirically equivalent theories were defined to be ones that bestow the same likelihood on all evidence statements. That confirmation theory would, for instance, allow one to assign a prior probability of 0 to all empirically equivalent rivals to a given theory, so that, unless the data refute it, the theory may eventually come to have a probability of 1 (which is typically thought to suffice for justified credibility). On the other hand, for versions of Bayesian confirmation theory that are only slightly stronger, interesting underdetermination claims *can* be derived if the existence of empirically equivalent rivals in the just-defined sense is assumed. Suppose, for instance, we add to the subjective theory the apparently still quite weak principle that, given any set of empirically equivalent theories, there is no *unique* element of that set which receives highest prior probability. Then it is a direct consequence of Bayes's theorem that at no point in time will any of the theories have a unique highest posterior probability, no matter what evidence one may come to possess.

Thus, since it depends at least partly on the confirmation theory that is being assumed whether two theories will have the same confirmation-theoretic status given any amount of evidence, proofs of EE may be of limited interest at best: even if it can be shown that all theories have empirically equivalent rivals given our current best confirmation theory, there may be no guarantee that they will have these rivals given some still-to-be-developed confirmation theory which we may come to prefer one day.

However, it may be questioned whether EE is really all that important for anti-realist purposes. For instance, one may wonder why an argument for underdetermination must be based on the claim that there *actually* exist empirically equivalent rivals to any scientific theory. Is it not enough to observe that any scientific theory *might* have such rivals? But, first, whether the mere possibility that these rivals exist really undercuts any confirmation we might otherwise have for a given scientific theory will (again) depend on one's confirmation theory. Furthermore, it is reasonable to say that most philosophers of science would regard a position based on an assumption of the mere possibility of empirically equivalent rivals as being of academic interest at best, and not as a live option (which may explain why no scientific anti-realist has tried to argue for underdetermination along the lines suggested here).

There may be a more viable way to argue that an interesting argument for underdetermination can go through even if EE cannot be maintained. For consider that it may be rather simple to devise – on paper, that is – an experiment that would enable us to distinguish between two theories while practically it is impossible to carry out the experiment. This possibility is anything but academic. For instance, David Atkinson (2003: 216) argues that, while string theory is testable in principle, in order to really test it "one would have to produce energies that are ten to the power sixteen ... times higher than those that [the biggest particle accelerator] will produce in 2005." Indeed, he concludes that it "seems safe to say that we will never be able to produce energies anywhere near this value, and that string theory can never be confronted with the crucial test of experiment" (*ibid.*). One does not necessarily have to agree with Atkinson's pessimism regarding the testability of string theory in order to appreciate how similar practical considerations might apply quite generally in science. And if every scientific theory should have rivals that are indistinguishable from it by any evidence we might be able to obtain given the practical constraints under which we are bound to labor – even if the theories *are* distinguishable by the evidence we could obtain in principle – that would seem to serve an underdetermination argument for scientific anti-realism no less than does EE. Patently, since every empirically equivalent rival to a theory is a rival that is indistinguishable from it given the evidence that could practically be obtained, but not vice versa, the claim that every theory has rivals indistinguishable from it by that sort of evidence is weaker than EE.

The other main type of response to the argument from underdetermination, one that may well be more promising than the attack on EE, is of course to deny KE. Such denials nowadays mostly take the form of an attempt to defend the rule of *inference to the best explanation* (IBE), which accords confirmation-theoretic import to explanatory force in the sense that, very roughly, if of two theories that both conform to the data one better explains those data (on the supposition that it is true), then that gives *prima facie* reason to believe it is true (or is closer to the truth than the other). While there may be some intuitive plausibility to this rule, it has proved no easy matter to defend it. Few believe that the connection between *explanatory force* and *truth* (or approximate or probable truth, or probable approximate truth, or some such) is, if it exists, *a priori*.

It thus seems that a defense of IBE, if it can be had at all, must be empirically based. But while it is tempting to argue – and indeed it has been argued – that the hypothesis that IBE is a reliable rule of inference is credible because it best explains the empirical successes scientists have had by using the rule, that argument is obviously question-begging, as it relies on IBE itself. However, it may be, as some philosophers think, that this is only a defect of the argument if we conceive of it as a means to convert the anti-realist, or more generally the disbeliever in IBE, and that the argument still is of value as a means of giving reassurance of the reliability of the rule from a *realist* perspective.

Moreover, there have been attempts to argue for IBE via a straightforward enumerative induction. The common idea of these attempts is that every newly recorded successful application of IBE adds further support to the hypothesis that IBE is a reliable rule of inference in the way in which every newly observed black raven adds some support to the hypothesis that all ravens are black; no appeal is made to the potential explanatory force of the hypothesis. A seeming problem for these attempts is that claims of the successful application of IBE to the realm of the unobservable – for instance, the claim that the tobacco mosaic virus was once postulated on explanatory grounds and later discovered by experimental means – would appear to beg the question against the anti-realist, who denies, after all, that we have the kind of access to the unobservable which would permit us to speak of, for example, the *discovery* of the tobacco mosaic virus. And it seems clear that if IBE is to be of any use in arguing against anti-realism, it is not enough to establish its reliability in the observable realm.

A third, less common, type of response is the pragmatists' one. According to this, KE is false because the theoretical virtues are truth-conducive by definition: possessing those virtues is simply constitutive of being true, together of course with being in accordance with the data. (So note that for pragmatists the connection between truth and explanation *is a priori*: being a good explanation is, in part, what *makes* a theory true.) But what if two empirically equivalent theories that are in accordance with the data do equally well in light of the theoretical virtues, too? Surely there is no guarantee that this will never happen. Here the pragmatist answer is that, even though such theories may appear to be rivals, they are not really. Rather they are different, equally legitimate, conceptualizations of reality, and may both be true ("true in their conceptual schemes," as it is then often put). In this vein, W. V. Quine (1992: 100) suggests that one may "oscillate" between the different conceptualizations "for the sake of added perspective from which to triangulate on problems." Very similar passages are to be found in the writings of Hilary Putnam after his conversion to pragmatic realism (see, for example, Putnam 1981). Needless to say, those responses share all the problems that beset pragmatist accounts of truth and language generally (such as, most notably perhaps, the problem that they seem to issue in what many think is a self-refuting relativism).

See also Bayesianism; Confirmation; Inference to the best explanation; Logical empiricism; Realism/anti-realism; The virtues of a good theory.

References

Atkinson, D. (2003) "Experiments and Thought Experiments in Natural Science," in M. C. Galavotti (ed.) *Observation and Experimentation in the Natural and Social Sciences*, Dordrecht: Kluwer, pp. 209–25.

Boyd, R. (1984) "On the Current Status of Scientific Realism," *Erkenntnis* 19: 45–90; reprinted in R. Boyd, P. Gasper, and J. D. Trout (eds) *The Philosophy of Science*, Cambridge MA: MIT Press, 1991, pp. 195–222 (the page reference is to the reprint).

Earman, J. (1993) "Underdetermination, Realism, and Reason," in P. French, T. Uehling, Jr., and H. Wettstein (eds) *Midwest Studies in Philosophy*, Volume 18: *Philosophy of Science*, Notre Dame, IN: University of Notre Dame Press, pp. 19–38.

Laudan, L. and Leplin, J. (1991) "Empirical Equivalence and Underdetermination," *Journal of Philosophy* 88: 449–72.

Lewis, D. (1986) *On the Plurality of Worlds*, Oxford: Blackwell.

Putnam, H. (1981) *Reason, Truth and History*, Cambridge: Cambridge University Press.

Quine, W. V. (1992) *Pursuit of Truth*, Cambridge, MA: Harvard University Press.

't Hooft, G. (1994) "Questioning the Answers or Stumbling upon Good and Bad Theories of Everything," in J. Hilgevoord (ed.) *Physics and Our View of the World*, Cambridge: Cambridge University Press, pp. 16–37.

Van Fraassen, B. C. (1980) *The Scientific Image*, Oxford: Clarendon Press.

Further reading

Most modern textbooks in the philosophy of science contain a chapter on underdetermination; the relevant chapters in Peter Kosso, *Reading the Book of Nature* (Cambridge: Cambridge University Press, 1992) and James Ladyman, *Understanding Philosophy of Science* (London: Routledge, 2001) are especially helpful. The chapters on underdetermination in André Kukla, *Scientific Realism* (Oxford: Oxford University Press, 1998) and Stathis Psillos, *Scientific Realism: How Science Tracks Truth* (London: Routledge, 1999) contain more advanced material. Readers undeterred by technicalities should certainly have a look at Kevin Kelly's very sophisticated – though also somewhat idiosyncratic – study of underdetermination in his *The Logic of Reliable Inquiry* (Oxford: Oxford University Press, 1996), which makes ample use of results from recursion theory and formal learning theory. Igor Douven and Leon Horsten's "Earman on Underdetermination and Empirical Indistinguishability," *Erkenntnis* 49 (1998): 303–20, uses the framework developed in Earman (1993) to derive some further formal results concerning underdetermination. See Anthony Brueckner, "The Structure of the Skeptical Argument," *Philosophy and Phenomenological Research* 54 (1994): 827–35, for a clear discussion of the place of underdetermination claims in epistemology, in particular in the standard type of argument for external-world skepticism. For a defense of external-world realism that invokes IBE, see Jonathan Vogel, "Cartesian Skepticism and Inference to the Best Explanation," *Journal of Philosophy* 87 (1990): 658–66.

28
VALUES IN SCIENCE
Gerald Doppelt

Value-free science?

It is hard to find a more distinctive mark of modern society than the trust placed in scientific knowledge. Science is regarded as perhaps the best exemplar of objectivity, rationality, and progress in human affairs. On the other hand, some of the worst horrors of the twentieth century – Nazi eugenics and Stalin's purges – were undertaken in the name of science. Mindful of these distortions, logical positivists saw their attempt to draw a demarcation between science and pseudo-science as a matter of human survival. Genuine scientific claims necessarily depend on clearly definable connections to the court of sense experience. Lacking those connections, pseudo-scientific claims might express values, masked in the language of fact. Such claims are emotive expressions removed from rational justification and any status as genuine scientific claims. Anglo-American philosophy of science is thus motivated by a powerful commitment to the idea that genuine science is *value-free*.

Today, philosophers mostly reject the emotive account of value-judgments. Yet many remain tied to the idea that political values corrupt scientific inquiry when they have an undue influence over its direction, results or uses. On the other hand, studies of science reveal that social values shape scientific inquiry in various contexts. Now, some philosophers of science argue that social values "can be good for science."

This essay aims to clarify the role of values in scientific knowledge. It defends a distinctive conception of the *value-ladennesss of scientific knowledge* which preserves its rationality.

Social and epistemic values

It is useful to distinguish the many ways that social values influence the practice of science. "Social values" refers to features of society which are taken to be good-making ones (e.g., justice, universal health care, the conquest of disease, national self defense, etc.). It is evident that social values shape all of the following: the direction of scientific funding; scientists' motives for doing science; the particular questions and problems they tackle; what they seek knowledge of and for; the uses to which the results of their inquiry are put, etc. In each case, we can evaluate the results and argue that other more reasonable values ought to have been in play. Better values yield better scientific practice. This is important, but straightforward. Nevertheless, once we recognize these various lines of influence of social values, none of them imply that scientific knowledge is itself value-relative. The above value dimensions of science aside, the question of whether scientists succeed in producing knowledge may simply be a matter of whether their theories are empirically adequate, accommodating the relevant evidence in the right ways. Such empirical adequacy is not a social value in the above sense and is not obviously determined by social values. Indeed it seems entirely independent of social values.

Is scientific knowledge itself value-free? This essay argues that scientific knowledge is value-laden, but that the values necessary for knowledge are *epistemic*, in the final instance. This account allows a role for social values only if they are embodied in appropriate *epistemic values*. Appropriate epistemic values are features of scientific theories which are, and are taken to be, good-making features of theories that motivate and justify their acceptance. Epistemic values include properties of theories such as simplicity, unification, accuracy, novel in prediction, explanatory breadth, empirical adequacy, etc. While these epistemic values or goals demarcate science from other activities, the standards governing their application change – leading to new versions of, for instance, simplicity or empirical adequacy, determining in a new way what counts as a good theory and thus as scientific knowledge.

Does this leave any legitimate room for the influence of social values? The present account defends the view that social values can legitimately enter scientific knowledge only if they provide good reasons for adopting certain epistemic values; or more precisely, certain standards for their realization. Social values corrupt scientific knowledge when they determine knowledge-claims, independently of (1) their effective embodiment in appropriate epistemic values and (2) the empirical success of scientists in realizing those values. This account steers a middle course between the classical view that social values necessarily corrupt scientific knowledge and the optimistic view that social values of the right sort can only enhance scientific knowledge, for human benefit. The resulting two-tier model of scientific knowledge allows that social values can provide good reasons for adopting certain epistemic values, while epistemic values can provide good reasons for believing the theories which actualize them.

The value-ladenness of scientific knowledge would be self-evident if the epistemic value in question is taken to be truth and the standard, a principle of confirmation, unitary and universal throughout science. Then, scientific knowledge could be accounted for as the acceptance of whatever theoretical beliefs best succeed in fulfilling the unitary epistemic value/standard. The value-ladenness of scientific knowledge becomes an epistemologically important thesis when conjoined with a Kuhnian insight; namely, that the history of science involves normative shifts concerning the epistemic values and standards chosen to define scientific knowledge in a field. An adequate philosophy of science will need new conceptions of *rationality*, *objectivity*, and *progress* to show how such normative shifts in values can exhibit these classical ideals.

There are four types of value-commitment which shift in the development of scientific knowledge.

1 *Value-laden phenomena* Scientists in a given area of inquiry must be committed to the value of certain kinds of phenomena and problems as the core of the domain. This core is what a theory is expected to predict or explain in order to constitute scientific knowledge in that area. Many of the observational phenomena (the sensible qualities of things, such as their metallic features) valued as essential for a chemical theory to explain, on the standards of the pre-modern chemistry of neo-Aristotelians and alchemists, are excluded from the domain and replaced by other sorts of phenomena (e.g. weight-gain in combustion), on the standards of Lavoisier and, later, Daltonian chemistry (Doppelt 1978; Shapere 1984).

2 *Value-laden inferences* Scientists in a given area of inquiry need a shared commitment to the value of certain kinds of inference as what is required in order to establish a theory on the basis of observational phenomena. For example, Newtonians held that a hypothesis is knowable only if it is a strict inductive generalization from observed phenomena. Ether theorists endorsed the method of hypothesis on which hypotheses concerning unobservables (various "ethers" to account for heat, light, gravitation) could be known indirectly on the basis of evidence that they imply or explain (abduction), but do not inductively generalize (Laudan 1981).

3 *Value-laden theoretical virtues* Scientists require a shared commitment to the value of certain kinds of theories, and not others, concerning the virtues which theories in an area of inquiry should possess to constitute scientific knowledge. Is "action-at-a-distance" an acceptable feature of a theory of bodies, or do the phenomena of gravitation require a mechanistic theory with contact-action? Is the capacity of a theory to make novel predictions a virtue required for it to gain the status of scientific knowledge? Phenomena deducible from a theory which are previously unknown or are different in kind from those the theory is designed to accommodate have unique value on the standards of scientific knowledge embraced by Herschel and Whewell, which they completely lack for Mill and others (Laudan 1981). Einstein rejected quantum physics because it was fatally incomplete, arguing that it failed to capture determinate aspects of reality required by the principle of locality.

4 *Value-laden standards of empirical accuracy* Scientists need to agree on acceptable degrees of approximation or margins of error in comparing the predictions of a theory with the measured values of observed phenomena. Otherwise, there is no shared way of determining when data support a theory.

The thesis that scientific knowledge is value-laden can be reformulated by analogy with the more familiar idea that human knowledge is always relative to available evidence. The value-ladenness thesis extends this traditional view to encompass "the relativity of knowledge to appropriate epistemic values and standards" of the above kinds. The scientific ideal of objective evidence is a changing normative notion in the history of science. This is not to discount the powerful continuities in what counts as relevant evidence in any given scientific tradition, such as the enduring importance of the motions and orbits of the planets in astrophysics. Nonetheless, scientific traditions undergo significant transformations in (1) how the domain of phenomena taken to constitute relevant evidence is defined; (2) what sort of inferential connection is required for phenomena to constitute evidence for a theory; (3) what sorts of theories with which virtues are capable of gaining support from evidence; and (4) what standard of accuracy is required for observed phenomena to count as evidence for a theory.

Justifying the value-ladenness thesis

What justifies the thesis of the value-ladenness of scientific knowledge? It is useful to contrast the argument presented here with that of Helen Longino (1990). Her approach begins with the classical argument concerning the underdetermination of theory by observation. She uses the fact of underdetermination to show that the link between theory and evidence cannot be that of induction, abduction, or logic alone. Rather, the link is provided by scientists' background assumptions, which involve wider social values, as well as more internal epistemic values. On this view, values fill the gap between theory and evidence, which the pure logic of inference opens up. Longino's starting point is an apt one, given the centrality of logical models of confirmation, within twentieth-century Anglo-American empiricism.

The thesis of value-ladenness is justified here as providing the best explanation of the historical development of science and the kinds of rationality it arguably possesses. Arguments concerning underdetermination are not a suitable starting point, because, in the post-Kuhnian environment little follows from them. In particular, such arguments show that standards of confirmation cannot be captured in purely logical terms. Many a realist, reliabilist, naturalist, and instrumentalist now accepts this point without being pushed to value-ladenness. Why? The argument from underdetermination allows many options for defending a non-logical but universally applicable standard, or cognitive mechanism, of theoretical knowledge in science – free of any value-ladenness. The scientific realist's appeal to *inference to the best explanation* and the normative naturalists' appeal to *truth-conducive, reliable mechanisms of belief-formation*, provide two examples. The defense of value-ladenness does not get much support from underdetermination. Its best defense consists in establishing that it provides a better explanation of the historical development of science, successful science, and scientific debates than its rivals.

Thus the present argument starts not from the logic of underdetermination but rather from the history of science. This argument begins with a distinctive interpretation of Kuhn's *The Structure of Scientific Revolution* (Doppelt 1978). Previous interpreters of Kuhn developed a standard, deflationary reading on which the key to scientific revolution, or *paradigm* change for Kuhn, is a wholesale change in language, meaning, ontology, and worldview, generating a radical incommensurability between scientific paradigms or theories (Shapere 1964, 1966; Scheffler 1967). On the counter-reading, the more plausible and epistemologically significant key to scientific revolution or, paradigm change, in Kuhn's work is a normative shift in the epistemic problems, data, standards, and values taken to be required of theories for genuine scientific knowledge. This line of argument in Kuhn does not imply radical incommensurability or wholesale change. But such historical shifts in the standards and goals of theoretical inquiry pose challenges to several influential accounts of scientific rationality, knowledge, and progress (Doppelt 2000). In addition, this essay argues that the thesis of value-ladenness can be deployed to develop a critical theory of scientific argument which promises to make social controversies over what is known more rational.

How can we determine when background assumptions are just empirical beliefs, and when they function as values? There are three kinds of evidence in the behavior of scientific groups to establish that a shared belief constitutes a fundamental epistemic value:

(1)   their choices concerning what sorts of theories to accept or reject;
(2)   their grounds or reasons for these choices; and
(3)   the principles they appeal to in scientific controversies.

The value-ladenness thesis is confirmed if and only if the attribution of a shared epistemic standard(s) of theory assessment to the group is part of *the best explanation* of (1), (2), and (3).

Consider how to explain the transition from alchemy to the chemistry of Lavoisier and, later, Dalton. Many of the chemical effects explained by the new chemistry were unrecognized by the alchemists (Kuhn 1970: 99–100, 107, 133). Similarly, the alchemists sought to account for many observed phenomena (concerning the sensible qualities of things) that are abandoned, by the new chemistry. On standard accounts, these transitions are represented as changes in scientific concepts and beliefs, often accompanied by the assumption that the more modern beliefs were better confirmed by *the* observational evidence. The thesis of value-ladenness provides a richer explanation. Using the three sorts of evidence mentioned above, we may learn that the change in the practice of chemistry involves more than the standard change in belief plus greater empirical success with *the* observational evidence. We may learn that rival epistemic values were at stake concerning how to define the chemical phenomena that different groups took to be essential to a genuine knowledge of nature. This account can explain losses, as well as gains, in the observational *explicanda* of science: for example, how a new chemistry could succeed, even though it fails to explain obvious phenomena (why all metals have metallic qualities in common) at the center of previous chemistry (alchemy), and in principle, still awaiting some theoretical explanation (which is achieved in twentieth-century science). While this does involve new beliefs and empirical success, bringing in the shift to new epistemic values provides a better explanation of why chemists at some points cease to accord any scientific legitimacy to the phenomena at the center of alchemy.

Clearly, such a new normative consensus, while necessary for the attainment of scientific knowledge, is *not* sufficient. Knowledge requires success in the achievement of epistemic values. Scientific knowledge is contingent on

(1) the way the world is – as realists argue;
(2) how effectively scientific groups are able to renegotiate their common values, when they conflict – as social constructivists argue; and
(3) the ability of scientific groups to develop theories, techniques, etc. that provide empirical success and meet their standards – as empiricists stress.

The best way to provide a defense of this view is to consider objections.

Postmodernism: it's politics all the way down

Postmodern scholars of the politics of knowledge may object that the notion of epistemic values depends on a false separation between the epistemic and the social. Epistemic values are social standards governing the way members of a scientific community identify the good-making features of theories. This distinguishes them from *social values* as characterized above (good-making features of societal practices). Scientists often have reasons for their commitments to epistemic values rooted in social values. Yet, it is only when social values get expressed in the appropriate epistemic values that scientific knowledge becomes possible. Furthermore, the causal influence of social values over knowledge-claims is rational only when these values provide good reasons for the adoption of appropriate epistemic values.

For example, it is undeniable that the development of modern meteorology by Vilhelm Bjerknes and his collaborators in the first quarter of the twentieth century is motivated by powerful social interests in more reliable weather forecasts for aviators, fishermen, and farmers, in the context of commercial, military, and political goals (Friedman 1989). The emergence of such practical interests – especially with the age of flight (airships, aviation, etc.) – justifies a redefinition of the domain of weather phenomena by Bjerknes to include atmospheric motions and conditions. This redefinition of the weather provides a key epistemic standard of *empirical success* for the new meteorology of the Bergen School and its quest for a physics of the atmosphere. The social value of forecasting certain phenomena of "weather" provides both a motivation and good practical reason for embracing the new epistemic standards for meteorological knowledge concerning what a science of "the weather" needed to include. Only at the point where reasonable social values are effectively embodied in appropriate epistemic standards of cognitive success does the possibility of scientific knowledge exist. Indeed this provides a good example of the way a reasonable social value justifies the practical commitment to a new epistemic value for circumscribing the domain of relevant phenomena.

But, epistemic values may be justified independently of social values. Consider the range of practical aspirations that have motivated astronomers to understand the positions and movements of heavenly bodies. Long after astronomers give up any hope of reading the heavens to discern the will of God(s), the outcome of human endeavors, etc., the epistemic value of certain astronomical phenomena remains central to various branches of scientific knowledge. So while the practices of science are often shaped by social values, the value-ladenness of knowledge cannot be reduced to these social values.

There are three more important objections to the value-ladenness of scientific knowledge:

(a) Against the value-relativity thesis, there are neutral, external, and universal standards of knowledge.
(b) Normative naturalism and externalist reliabilism, characterize scientific knowledge without value-relativity.
(c) The value-relativity thesis carries with it the threat of relativism.

Universal values

It is plausible to hold that there are universal epistemic values in all scientific inquiry – empirical success, predictive accuracy, breadth of explanatory scope, unification, simplicity, problem-solving effectiveness, etc. – though scientific groups strike different trade-offs between them. Such values distinguish scientific inquiry from pseudo-science and other non-scientific types of inquiry. Nonetheless, such values can function as criteria of scientific knowledge only when they are given flesh, and articulated in terms of more local standards. Predictive accuracy cannot function as a mark of scientific knowledge in the absence of standards of acceptable empirical approximation. Breadth of explanatory scope and unification do not function as virtues of theory in the absence of standards that indicate which domains of phenomena ought to be unified; and whether or not unification is taken to require common explanatory and causal mechanisms across domains, or only common mathematical and formal principles lacking explanatory force (Morrison 2000).

Empirical success in *saving the phenomena* cannot function as a criterion of knowledge until questions like the following are answered: What sorts of phenomena are most important to *save*, and which can be neglected? What kind of theory is valuable or useless to *save* the phenomena? What type of reasoning or proof is valuable if the phenomena are to be saved by a theory or empirical law? If a theory saves *the* phenomena, does this provide good reason for taking the theory to be true? In the history of science, groups answer such questions in quite different ways – linking the very possibility of scientific knowledge to the epistemic values to which such communities are actually committed.

Normative naturalism and externalist reliabilism

Normative naturalists recognize the value-ladenness of scientific practices while resisting the conclusion that knowledge is value-relative. They propose that we evaluate the value-laden practices in science empirically, as more or less effective means to the ultimate aim(s) of science (Laudan 1987).

Normative naturalism comes in different versions. On one view, scientific groups embrace different aims – for example, prediction, rather than explanation. This version of normative naturalism concedes the value-ladenness thesis. If it evaluates the efficacy of local values relative to aims, and allows aims to vary from one scientific group to another, then, scientific knowledge will be relative to the larger epistemic values/aims to which some but not all scientific groups are committed.

On a second version of naturalism, there is but one unitary aim of all science – for example, to discover the truth about nature. It is not clear how the naturalist will adjudicate the disagreements concerning *the* goal of science among realists, instrumentalists, pragmatists, unificationists, empiricists, etc. Suppose we are realists and fix the aim of science as the attainment of true theories. Then the naturalist can characterize knowledge as whatever local epistemic values, methods, theories, etc., prove in fact to be the most effective means to this aim. The normative naturalist's language of unitary aim, efficiency, and empirical evidence, is deceptive. The attainment of theoretical truth is no more a value-neutral unitary aim than is empirical success. Suppose we set out to determine which of the value-laden practices of scientific groups is in fact most effective in producing true theories. What epistemic standards must be satisfied by true theories? Should true theories be explanatory or predictive, or simple and unifying, or deterministic, in each case – as some but not all scientific groups have insisted? Do we count as true any theory which succeeds in implying already well-known kinds of phenomena? Or, do we restrict the theories that we count as true to theories which succeed in predicting previously unknown, surprising phenomena, different in kind from those they were designed to explain? The normative naturalist cannot circumvent these value-laden choices.

Reliabilist epistemologists embrace an externalist standpoint which promises to make knowledge independent of the epistemic values internal to the knower. Knowledge is simply a matter of whether the knower is using a reliable, or truth-conducive, mechanism of forming beliefs. Can the naturalist gain a scientific knowledge of reliability without a commitment to specific epistemic values? How is the naturalist supposed to adjudicate the normative dispute between scientific realists and instrumentalists or empiricists? They disagree over whether inference to the best explanation is ever a reliable method or mechanism for arriving at theoretical truths. Reliabilism is as value-laden as the bodies of scientific knowledge it hopes to evaluate *externally* and *naturalistically*. The externalist enjoys no epistemological privilege in determining whose standards of truth and reliability define scientific knowledge.

On the other hand, once a scientific community has implicitly committed itself to the value of predicting and explaining certain sorts of phenomena, the value of certain standards of reasoning, and the value of certain virtues of theory (or models), then judgments of reliability may be achieved.

Objectivity, rationality, relativism, and critique

Should the value-ladenness thesis be rejected because it is incompatible with scientific rationality, objectivity and progress? On the present account, scientific knowledge requires the exercise of practical rationality in the choice of epistemic values, as well as the rationality of belief in theories which satisfy them. What conception of practical rationality is appropriate?

When scientific groups choose appropriate epistemic values and standards, typically they have good reasons for those decisions. In some cases, social values provide good reasons for these epistemic commitments, as in the example of the Bergen School's interest in the weather discussed above. On the other hand, epistemic considerations themselves often inform the reasons that justify commitments to new epistemic standards. A good example is the debate concerning epistemic standards in the eighteenth and nineteenth centuries, concerning value-laden inference models (Laudan 1981:111–14; Doppelt 1990: 10–18). The triumph of Newtonian mechanics convinced many natural philosophers that all genuine empirical knowledge depends on strict inductive generalization from observed phenomena and excludes speculative hypothesis involving unobservable entities.

The subsequent development of empirical inquiry generated good reasons for rejecting the inductivist methodology as *the* standard of genuine scientific knowledge. By the second half of the eighteenth century, the most successful theories of electricity, magnetism, heat, light, and other phenomena violated the inductivist standard by positing various unobservable, ethereal media to explain these phenomena. This situation generated an inconsistency between the ether theorists' fruitful theories and the dominant inductivist standard of proof. George Le Sage developed the *method of hypothesis* in order to justify the claim that ether theories could be a form of genuine knowledge. On this standard, if a hypothesis entails a large variety of true observational consequences, then it is empirically well-founded and counts as genuine knowledge, even if it reaches beyond sense experience in order to posit unobservable entities (the ethereal media). Le Sage cleverly argued that this hypothetico-deductive standard provided a better account of the great Newtonian achievements than the strict inductivist methodology. Further, he argued that the method of hypothesis could be rigorously formulated so that it could exclude spurious hypotheses like those of Cartesian mechanics. While conceding that the method of hypothesis was fallible, Le Sage showed that the requirement of infallibility was unrealizable.

Because epistemic standards and values, theories, techniques of observation, bodies of observed phenomena, and projects of problem-solving evolve together, the exposure of inconsistencies and the maintenance of coherence provide scientific groups with powerful epistemic reasons to revise their value commitments. Practical rationality is involved because specific groups always need to *decide* how to maintain coherence – what to abandon and what to preserve in the corpus of beliefs and values. Yet the ether theorists' decision to embrace the method of hypothesis was rational because it allowed them to develop effective explanations for whole domains of phenomena closed to the inductivists. At the same time, their decision was also a powerful contribution to scientific progress because it helped produce better standards of scientific inference. By defending the value of appropriate *inferences to unobservables*, the ether theorists set the stage for enlarging the sorts of theories scientists could develop and the enormous range of phenomena that science would eventually explain with such theories.

The thesis of value-relativity does not imply the Kuhnian picture of scientific revolution in which one set of epistemic values is replaced wholesale by another. Provided there are good reasons for changes in epistemic values, and empirical success in realizing them, the value-ladenness of science does not justify relativism, or any view which undermines the possibility of scientific progress. The fact that scientific inquiry inevitably responds to the normatively salient aspects of nature, theory-construction, and reasoning, does not undermine the existence of scientific knowledge, reality, and cognitive progress.

The value-ladenness thesis opens the way onto a critical theory of scientific argumentation. Some arguments over scientific knowledge may be normative conflicts concerning epistemic values. Conflict over the facts may embody rival epistemic value commitments. Extreme relativism threatens only if we assume that value commitments are beyond the scope of reason. What forms of reasoning can be exploited by a critical theory of scientific argument grounded in the value-ladenness of knowledge?

(a) Such a theory may be used to expose the *rival* epistemic value-commitments at stake in scientific controversies.

(b) A critical theory may seek to *clarify* the social values possibly at stake in groups' rival epistemic value-commitments. Such reasoning can show whether these provide good reasons for embracing particular epistemic values.

(c) A critical theory of scientific argument asks which social values are embodied in a scientific practice, and seeks to determine whether they are reasonable or unreasonable social values.

How might such a critical theory enhance the rationality of scientific debate?

When air traffic controllers (ATCs) went on strike during the Reagan administration, the President fired them and hired non-union replacements to restore the flow of air traffic in the USA (Tesh 1988). The strike demands rested on the claim that the ATCs were victimized by conditions of work that generated oppressive patterns of stress. Congress held hearings to investigate the claim. The ATCs had complaints about their work – forced overtime, conflicting demands, disrespect, speed-up, lack of control, demands for absolute accuracy, etc. Their advocates (the union, occupational safety and health officials) decided that the best strategy in the hearings was to represent the complaints in the scientific discourse of "stress." Medical researchers linked stress to a heightened likelihood of illnesses such as coronary heart disease, stroke, peptic ulcers, diabetes, etc. By invoking the notion of stress, the ATCs' advocates hoped to give their complaints scientific legitimacy and medical urgency.

Unfortunately, the strategy backfired. Congressional investigators solicited the testimony of scientific experts on stress who discredited the ATCs' complaints. The experts were behavioral scientists who embraced a paradigm of stress which identifies it with physiological, biochemical, and psychological measurements. On these standards, the experts reached the conclusion that it was empirically unsound to describe the work of ATCs as stressful. The scientific facts spoke against the claims of the ATCs, and they were discredited by the very medicalized concept of "stress" which they had invoked.

Nevertheless, there was a very different account of stress which *might* have better served the interests of the ATCs, the value of occupational health and safety, and public safety. For the ATCs, stress was something different from the body's bio-chemical reactions to the debilitating experiences of work. For them, stress referred to an excessive pace of work and demands for accuracy that left them no time for thought, double-checking, error, and self-correction – with thousands of lives at stake in hazardous landings. Stress referred to the experience of staring at a radar screen for long periods of time without breaks, making life and death decisions, under intense demands, and unrelenting time pressure.

As such, stress was a commonly experienced dimension of the ATCs' lives in the work environment; many noticed that it was followed by common experiences of sleeplessness, irritability, inability to maintain relations of family and friendship outside of work, lower capacity for pleasure and enjoyment, etc. The common experiences of the ATCs point to different standards for defining stress, and explaining its causes and consequences.

Of course, these experiences by themselves do not amount to any scientific knowledge of stress. The laborers' experiences might have produced scientific knowledge that would vindicate their claims. We cannot foreclose the possibility of such a counter-knowledge of stress – based on objective investigation seeking causal links between certain conditions of work, patterns of experience, and negative outcomes in and beyond the world of work. Informed by a set of epistemic standards at odds with those of the behavioral scientists (e.g., over the definition of "stress"), such a scientific inquiry might become successful and provide a well-grounded challenge to the facts-of-the-matter concerning stress in such a case.

The thesis of the value-ladenness of scientific knowledge may provide the basis for a critical theory of scientific argument for use in cases like this one. This theory awakens actors to the possibility of the play of rival social values and epistemic values in such conflicts. The controllers paid a terrible price because the epistemological politics at issue were invisible, and their experiences of stress were not embodied in any authoritative scientific voices or knowledge claims. Had the debate been refocused, in this light, it might have been more rational and truth-conducive. When rival epistemic values are at stake, the rationality of science is best served if these normative differences are made visible; and it is understood that we are involved in indissolubly linked commitments concerning what to value, how to know, and what to believe. When there are good reasons for these commitments, and they inspire an empirically successful practice of science, then practical rationality, the advance of scientific knowledge, and new aspects of nature are linked together in a human narrative of cognitive progress.

See also Confirmation; Inference to the best explanation; Logical empiricism; Naturalism; Prediction; Relativism; Social studies of science; Underdetermination; Unification; The virtues of a good theory.

References

Doppelt, G. (1978) "Kuhn's Epistemological Relativism: An Interpretation and Defense," *Inquiry* 21: 33–86; reprinted in J. W. Meiland and M. Krausz (eds) (1982) *Relativism: Cognitive and Moral*, Notre Dame, IN: University of Notre Dame Press, pp. 113–46.

—— (1990) "The Naturalist Conception of Methodological Standards," *Philosophy of Science* 57: 1–19.

—— (2000) "Incommensurability and the Normative Foundations of Scientific Knowledge," in P. Hoyningen-Huene and H. Sankey (eds) *Incommensurability and Related Matters*, The Netherlands: Kluwer Academic Publishers, pp. 159–79.

Friedman, R. M. (1989) *Appropriating the Weather: Vilhelm Bjerknes and the Construction of a Modern Meteorology*, Ithaca, NY: Cornell University Press.

Kuhn, T. (1970) *The Structure of Scientific Revolution*, 2nd edn, Chicago: University of Chicago Press.

Laudan, L. (1981) *Science and Hypothesis*, Dordrecht: Reidel.

—— (1987) "Progress or Rationality? The Prospects for Normative Naturalism," *American Philosophical Quarterly* 24: 19–31.

Longino, H. E. (1990) *Science as Social Knowledge*, Princeton, NJ: Princeton University Press.

Morrison, M. (2000) *Unifying Scientific Theories: Physical Concepts and Mathematical Structures*, Cambridge: Cambridge University Press.

Scheffler, I. (1967) *Science and Subjectivity*, Indianapolis, IN: Bobbs-Merrill.

Shapere, D. (1964) "The Structure of Scientific Revolutions," *Philosophical Review* 73: 383–94.

—— (1966) "Meaning and Scientific Change," in R. Colodny (ed.) *Mind and Cosmos: Essays in Contemporary Science and Philosophy*, Pittsburgh, PA: University of Pittsburgh Press, pp. 41–85.

—— (1984) *Boston Studies in the Philosophy of Science*, Volume 78: *Reason and the Search for Knowledge*, Dordrecht: Reidel.

Tesh, S. (1988) *Hidden Arguments: Political Ideology and Disease Prevention Strategy*, Piscataway, NJ: Rutgers University Press.

Further reading

In the last four decades, many central works and debates in philosophy of science bear on the role of epistemic values and standards in science, and its implications for the unity of scientific method, scientific rationality, theory evaluation, cognitive progress in science, and scientific realism. The work of Lakatos contains important discussions of rival standards of scientific rationality in the history of science. In particular, see "Falsification and the Methodology of Scientific Research Programmes," in I. Lakatos and A. Musgrave (eds) *Criticism and the Growth of Knowledge* (Cambridge: Cambridge University Press, 1970). Many of Kuhn's works provide historical examples of scientific developments in which shifts in epistemic values and standards are central, and imply relativism, on his view. In addition to *The Structure of Scientific Revolution* listed above, see Kuhn, *The Copernican Revolution: Planetary Astronomy in the Development of Western Thought* (Cambridge, MA: Harvard University Press, 1957) and *The Essential Tension: Selected Studies in Scientific Tradition and Change* (Chicago: University of Chicago Press, 1970). Laudan's work takes up the challenge of Kuhnian relativism and advances his own successive accounts of how to incorporate changing epistemic values into a non-relativist conception of scientific rationality and progress. See Laudan: *Progress and its Problems* (Berkeley and Los Angeles: University of California Press, 1970); *Science and Values* (Berkeley and Los Angeles: University of California Press, 1984); and *Beyond Positivism and Relativism* (Boulder, CO, and Oxford: Westview Press, 1996). For value-based Kuhnian challenges to the work of Laudan and Shapere, see Doppelt, "Laudan's Pragmatic Alternative to Positivism and Historicism," *Inquiry* 24 (1981): 253–71; "Relativism and the Reticulation Model of Scientific Rationality," *Synthese* 69 (1986): 225–52; and "The Philosophical Requirements for an Adequate Conception of Scientific Rationality," *Philosophy of Science* 55 (1988): 104–33. For works which explicate or challenge Kuhn's account of the value-relativity of scientific knowledge, see Alexander Bird, *Thomas Kuhn* (Princeton, NJ: Princeton University Press, 2000) and Paul Hoyningen-Huene, *Reconstructing Scientific Revolution: Thomas S. Kuhn's Philosophy of Science* (Chicago: University of Chicago Press, 1993). For additional approaches to the place of values in science, and an extensive bibliography on this subject, see J. Dupré, H. Kincaid, and A. Wylie (eds) *Value-Free Science: Ideal or Illusion?* (Oxford: Oxford University Press, 2007).

Part III
CONCEPTS

29
CAUSATION
Christopher Hitchcock

Introduction

In a paper read before the Aristotelian Society, Bertrand Russell (1913: 1) claimed:

> All philosophers, of every school, imagine that causation is one of the fundamental axioms or postulates of science, yet, oddly enough, in advanced sciences such as gravitational astronomy, the word "cause" never appears... To me, it seems that ... the reason why physics has ceased to look for causes is that, in fact, there are no such things. The law of causality, I believe, like much that passes muster among philosophers, is a relic of a bygone age, surviving, like the monarchy, only because it is erroneously supposed to do no harm.

Russell was hardly alone in that opinion. Other writers of the period, such as Ernst Mach, Karl Pearson, and Pierre Duhem, also rejected as unscientific the notion of causation. Their view was shared also by most of the logical positivists. Indeed, the concept of causation was regarded with suspicion by philosophers, as well as by many statisticians and social scientists, throughout much of the twentieth century.

Contrary to Russell's claim, however, the most casual perusal of the leading scientific journals reveals that causal locutions are commonplace in science. The 2006 volume of *Physical Review Letters* contains articles with titles like "Inverse Anderson Transition Caused by Flatbands" (by Masaki Goda, Shinya Nishino, and Hiroki Matsuda) and "Softening Caused by Profuse Shear Banding in a Bulk Metallic Glass" (by H. Bei, S. Xie, and E. P. George). Indeed, physicists refer to a variety of phenomena as "effects": the "Hall effect," the "Kondo effect," the "Lamb-shift effect," the "Zeeman effect," and so on. Presumably where there are effects, there are causes as well. Causal claims are even more common in the medical sciences: for example, a 2005 editorial by E. K. Mulholland and R. A. Adegbola in the *New England Journal of Medicine* bore the title "Bacterial Infections – a Major Cause of Death among Children in Africa." Given the ubiquity of causal claims in the sciences, *causation* deserves to be a concept of great interest to philosophers of science.

Analyses of causation

Diverse attempts have been made to analyze causation, and many of the debates that surround the concept of causation stem from fundamental disagreements about the best way to go about the project. Proposed analyses of causation can be divided into two broad categories: *reductive* and *non-reductive*. Reductive analyses of causation aim to provide truth-conditions for causal claims in non-causal terms. Non-reductive analyses of causation aim to establish systematic relationships between causation and other concepts of interest to philosophers; those relationships can then be used to derive interesting non-causal consequences from causal claims, even when the causal claims cannot themselves be paraphrased without causal remainder.

Pressure to provide a reductive analysis of causation comes from at least two sources: epistemology and metaphysics. Epistemological pressure stems from the unobservability of causal relations: we may observe the hot sun and the soft wax, but we do not observe the sun's *causing* the wax to soften. Thus, it seems that in order to assess the truth-value of a causal claim, it must be possible to translate that claim into one that does admit of direct epistemic access. Metaphysical pressure stems from Ockham's razor: in metaphysical system-building, it is preferable to analyze causal relations away rather than posit them as additional ingredients of the world.

Both of these pressures are capable of being resisted. Epistemologically, causal claims may be treated as akin to claims about theoretical entities such as electrons. We do not expect to be able to translate a claim such as that "every hydrogen atom contains one electron" into purely observational terms. All that a reasonable epistemology can demand of us is that such claims be susceptible to empirical confirmation or disconfirmation, for example, by entailing various observational consequences or by rendering some observations more probable than others. Causal claims are regularly subjected to empirical test in the sciences. In the medical sciences, for example, causal claims are often tested using controlled clinical trials. Such tests are capable of providing strong evidence in support of causal claims without the need to reduce those claims to non-causal claims. Metaphysically, systems that include causation as a basic feature of our world need not be unnecessarily complex: causal relations may well be the sorts of basic constituents of our world into which other relations are analyzed.

Challenges

There are a number of challenges that an adequate account of causation must meet. First, an account of causation must be able to distinguish between genuinely causal relationships and merely accidental relationships. Suppose, for example, that only a small handful of human beings eat a particular kind of fruit before the species of plant that bears it becomes extinct. By sheer coincidence, all of these people die shortly after eating the fruit. A theory of causation should not then rule that consumption of this particular fruit causes the death: the relationship between eating the fruit and death is merely accidental. In other words, an adequate theory of causation should entail that *post hoc ergo propter hoc* is, at least sometimes, a fallacy.

A second challenge is to distinguish causes from effects. Typically, perhaps even universally, when one event C causes another event E, it is not also the case that E causes C. In such typical cases, an adequate theory of causation must correctly rule that C causes E, but not vice versa. Some philosophers have attempted to address this problem by stipulating that, *by definition*, causes occur earlier in time than their effects. Thus if we have two events C and E that are related as cause and effect, we can identify the cause as the one that occurs earlier, and the effect as the one that occurs later. This solution to the problem has the disadvantage that it renders claims of backward-in-time causation false by definition. For example, there are solutions to the general field equations of general relativity that permit closed causal curves: time-like trajectories along which an object could travel from spatio-temporal region A to the distant spatio-temporal region B, and then back to A. Along such a trajectory, it may happen that the state of the object at A causes the state of the object at B, and the state of the object at B causes the state of the object at A. While such models may not describe the actual universe, that would seem to be an empirical matter, and not one to be settled *a priori* by our definitions of "cause" and "effect." Thus it would be desirable for a theory of causation to provide an independent account of the directionality of causation.

A third challenge is to distinguish causes and effects from effects of a common cause. It may be, for example, that smoking causes both stained teeth and lung cancer, with the former occurring before the latter. If so, then it may be common for individuals with stained teeth to develop lung cancer later in life. But stained teeth do not cause lung cancer; rather, stained teeth and lung cancer are effects of a common cause. An adequate theory of causation had better be able to mark the distinction.

Finally, an account of causation ought to be able to distinguish between genuine causes and pre-empted backups. Suppose, for example, that a building receives its electricity from the city's main power grid. In addition, the building has a backup generator that will kick in if there is a power failure. When the city's power grid is functioning properly, it is that power source, and not the backup generator, that causes the lights in the building to be on. A successful theory of causation must be able to mark the difference.

Regularity theories of causation

Perhaps the best-known attempt to analyze causal relations is that of David Hume: "we may define a cause to be *an object, followed by another, and where all the objects similar to the first, are followed by objects similar to the second*" (Hume 1977 [1748]: 76; italics in original). Hume, then, analyzes causation in terms of constant conjunction: a cause is always conjoined with its effect. According to Hume, our experience of such a constant conjunction produces in us a customary transition in the mind. Thus "[w]e may … form another definition of cause; and call it, *an object followed by another, and whose appearance always conveys the thought to that other*" (ibid.: 77; italics in original). It is our impression of that mental operation from which our idea of causation is derived.

In the nineteenth century, John Stuart Mill pointed out that simple causes will not invariably be followed by their effects. Thus, for example, smoking will not always be accompanied by lung cancer: some smokers may not be susceptible, or may die of other causes before cancer develops. In order to account for this sort of case, John Mackie (1974) developed his theory of INUS conditions. An INUS condition is an insufficient but non-redundant part of an unnecessary but sufficient condition. Thus C will be an INUS condition for E if there is a conjunction of factors ABCD ... such that whenever these factors occur together, they are followed by E, but where the factors ABD... without C are not invariably followed by E. This account allows that C may sometimes occur without E and vice versa.

One problem with this account is that it may be an accident that all conjunctions of ABCD ... are followed by E. One strategy for dealing with this problem is to require that the regularity be a consequence of *laws of nature*; that is, it must be possible to derive E from ABCD ... together with statements describing laws of nature. This strategy is essentially that adopted by Carl Hempel in his Deductive–Nomological model of scientific explanation. There is a sense, however, in which this approach simply relocates the problem, for now we must have an account of laws that distinguishes genuine laws of nature from mere accidental generalizations.

As Hume defined them, causes precede their effects in time. It is hard to see how a regularity theory of causation can capture the asymmetry between causes and effects without this stipulation. For example, critics of Hempel's *deductive–nomological model of explanation* have pointed out that the same laws that can be used to deduce the length of a shadow from the height of a flagpole and the angle of the sun can also be used to derive the height of the flagpole from the length of its shadow; but only the former derivation captures the right causal direction. Similarly, regularity theories of causation have difficulties with effects of a common cause. If there are conditions that when conjoined with smoking are invariably followed by lung cancer, then there may well be further conditions that, when conjoined with stained teeth, are always followed by lung cancer (these further conditions would include, for example, the absence of factors other than smoking that might account for stained teeth).

Finally, regularity theories have trouble distinguishing genuine causes from pre-empted backups. For example, it may well be that whenever a backup generator is in good working order, the lights in a certain building will be on – either because the generator itself is powering them or because the city's power grid is working effectively. But only in the former case would we consider the backup generator to be a cause of the lights being on. These difficulties with regularity theories of causation have led some philosophers to search for alternative accounts of causation.

Probabilistic theories of causation

The success of quantum mechanics in the twentieth century raises the possibility that our world may be indeterministic at the most fundamental level. If so, then causes need not be constantly conjoined with their effects, even if we specify all of the other relevant conditions. It may be that a complete specification of relevant factors ABCD ... suffices only to fix a certain probability for E to occur. Probabilistic theories of causation embrace this possibility. The central idea is that causes need not be sufficient for their effects, but need only raise the probabilities of their effects. The most natural way to make this precise is through conditional probability: C raises the probability of E just in case $Pr(E|C) > Pr(E)$, where $Pr(E|C)$ is defined to be $Pr(E\&C)/Pr(C)$.

One worry with this approach is that E may chance to happen more often in the presence of C than in its absence, even though there is no causal relationship between C and E. This is the analog of the problem of accidental generalizations that plagues regularity theories of causation. In order to guard against this possibility, the function Pr must refer to the true underlying probabilities, and not merely to statistical frequencies. This gives rise to the question of how to interpret the relevant probability claims. In particular, since causal relations are objective features of the world, the probabilities should correspond to objective features of the world, and not just to our state of uncertainty about the world.

The basic idea that causes raise the probabilities of their effects does not, by itself, do anything to solve the problems associated with the direction of causation. Indeed, it is easy to show that if $Pr(E|C) > Pr(E)$, then $Pr(C|E) > Pr(C)$. Moreover, if A and B are effects of a common cause, then typically we will have $Pr(A|B) > Pr(A)$ and $Pr(B|A) > Pr(B)$. For example, if A represents lung cancer, and B stained teeth, we would expect to find a greater prevalence of lung cancer among people with stained teeth than in the population at large, for the former group will have a higher proportion of smokers. If we look only at the probability relations among pairs of events, those problems are insoluble; matters change, however, once we consider the probability relationships between three or more events. If C is a common cause of A and B, then it will typically be the case that C *screens-off* A from B, that is, $Pr(A|BC)$ = $Pr(A|C)$. (Screening-off will fail, however, if A and B share a further common cause in addition to C.) Thus while B might raise the probability of A overall, it does not raise the probability of A conditional on the common cause C. Thus, in judging whether C is a cause of E, we need to consider not the simple probabilities $Pr(E|C)$ and $Pr(E)$ but more complicated conditional probabilities of the form $Pr(E|C\&K)$ and $Pr(E|K)$, where K represents various other causal factors that need to be held fixed. Screening-off relations can also help us to distinguish causes from effects. If C is a common cause of A and B, then, as we have noted, C will typically screen-off A from B. On the other hand, if E is an effect of both A and B, then typically E will not screen-off A from B. We can thus appeal to these distinctive probabilistic signatures to determine whether the causal arrows are pointing into or out of A and B.

Most recent probabilistic approaches to causation are non-reductive. The reason for this is that in order to assess whether C is a cause of E, we must look at the conditional probabilities $Pr(E|C\&K)$ and $Pr(E|K)$, where K includes common causes of C and E. If we cannot specify which factors must be included in K in non-causal terms, then we will not be able to analyze the claim that C causes E into probabilities without causal remainder.

Probabilistic approaches to causation have problems discriminating genuine causes from pre-empted backups. Suppose, for example, that the connection between the city's power grid and a particular building is faulty, so that the building might fail to receive electricity even when the power grid is otherwise running properly. Then the presence of the backup generator might raise the probability that the lights will be on in the building, even when we hold fixed the functioning of the power grid. Yet on a given occasion it might still be the power grid, rather than the backup generator, that is powering the lights. In such a case, probabilistic approaches to causation would incorrectly rule that the backup generator is also causing the lights to be on.

Counterfactual theories of causation

Counterfactual approaches to causation take from jurisprudence the central idea that causes are conditions *sine qua non* for their effects. In other words, when C causes E, then the counterfactual conditional "If C had not occurred, E would not have occurred" is true. This counterfactual then becomes the test for causation. According to the standard possible-world semantics for counterfactuals, this counterfactual will be true just in case there is at least one possible world in which C does not occur and E does not occur that is closer to the actual world than any possible world in which C does not occur but E does occur. In other words, the counterfactual will be true just in case E does not occur in the closest possible worlds in which C does not occur. Thus, to specify the truth-values of counterfactual claims, it is necessary to specify the metric that determines the relative closeness of possible worlds.

Suppose that as a matter of accident, conjunctions of events of type ABCD ... are always followed by events of type E, while conjunctions of events ABD ... without C are not. Now consider one particular incident in which a conjunction of events of type ABCD ... occurs, and is followed by an event of type E. In this case, C is not a genuine cause of E. Consider the counterfactual "If C had not occurred, then E would not have occurred." In order for this counterfactual to be true, the closest not-C worlds where E does not occur would have to be closer to actuality than any not-C worlds where E does occur. The (not-C, not-E) worlds might seem to be further from actuality than the (not-C, E) worlds, because the (not-C, not-E) worlds differ from the actual world with respect to the occurrence of E, while the (not-C, E) worlds do not. But there is another sense in which the (not-C, not-E) worlds might seem to be closer to actuality: in these worlds, the conjunction ABD ... is not followed by E. In order to avoid the conclusion that C is a cause of E, the relevant metric of similarity must put more weight on similarity with respect to the occurrence of E than on similarity with respect to accidental generalizations. On the other hand, if the connection between C and E is lawful, then the closest worlds in which C fails to occur and E occurs anyway would involve a violation of the laws of the actual world, and this sort of difference would be accorded a much greater significance. Indeed, the ability to support counter-factuals is often taken to be a feature that distinguishes genuine laws from accidental generalizations.

In order to capture the directionality of causation, the relevant counterfactuals must themselves be directional in the appropriate way. Suppose, for example, that Julian smokes, and as a result his teeth become stained, and he develops lung cancer. Then it seems plausible to say that if he had not smoked, he would not have stained teeth and he would not have lung cancer. These counterfactuals correctly entail that Julian's smoking caused his stained teeth and his lung cancer. But we must not say that if Julian did not have stained teeth, it would have to be because he did not smoke, and hence he would not have had lung cancer either. If counterfactuals are allowed to *back-track* in this way, then our counterfactual criterion will rule that C is a cause of E when in fact C is an effect of E or C and E are effects of a common cause. One challenge, then, is to provide an account of the metric of similarity over possible worlds that preserves this directionality. If this cannot be done in non-causal terms, then it will not be possible to provide a reductive analysis of causation in terms of counterfactuals.

Counterfactual theories of causation face problems with pre-emption. Unlike regularity and probabilistic theories, the problem is not that counterfactual theories judge pre-empted backups to be causes, but rather that they fail to recognize pre-empting causes. Suppose, for example, that the city's power grid is functioning properly, causing the lights in the building to be on. Now it is false that if the power grid were not functioning properly, the lights would not be on; for if the power grid were not functioning, the backup generator would come on. There are a number of attempts to rescue the counterfactual approach to causation from the problem of pre-emption: this is currently a lively area of research.

Manipulability theories of causation

Manipulability approaches to causation take as their point of departure the idea that causes are means for producing their effects. This means that agents can exploit the link between C and E as a handle for bringing about E. Agents are not merely passive observers, but intervene in the normal course of nature to bring about events that would not otherwise have occurred. The relationship between C and E can be used as a means for producing E only if it remains stable under this sort of intervention. Suppose, for example, that E is in fact a cause of C, rather than vice versa. It may well be that events of type C are typically accompanied by events of type E. Nonetheless, if an agent were to intervene in order to produce an event of type C, we would no longer expect it to be accompanied by its usual cause E. This is because the intervention is by itself sufficient to produce C; it breaks the customary link between C and E. Similarly, if A and B are both effects of a common cause C, we would not expect that an intervention to produce A would result in the occurrence of B. Once again, the intervention breaks the link between A and its usual cause C. Similarly, if the relationship between C and E is accidental, there would be no reason to expect that a novel event of type C produced by an intervention would be accompanied by an event of type E.

One worry is that this account makes reference to the interventions of an agent. This might seem to make the account of causation too anthropocentric: what of causal relationships where intervention is not practicable or even possible; for instance, causal relationships in astrophysics or in the early universe? While reference to the actions of an agent is a useful heuristic, it is possible to characterize the relevant notion of intervention without making reference to human beings or other agents. The important feature of an intervention is not its origin in the intentions of an agent, but rather its status as an independent cause that overrides the customary causal mechanisms for the production of C. The notion of an intervention is itself a causal notion, hence an account of causation in terms of interventions will be non-reductive.

Manipulability approaches to causation face problems with pre-emption in much the same way that counterfactual theories do. It may be that the city's main power grid is causing the lights to be on in a certain building, even though, due to the presence of the backup generator, the lights cannot be controlled by intervening on the city's power grid. Many of the strategies that have been proposed for counterfactual theories to deal with this problem may be adapted for manipulability theories as well.

Difference-making

All four approaches to causation discussed above share a common idea: causes are difference-makers for their effects, in the sense that the cause makes a difference to whether or not the effect occurs. The various approaches differ over precisely how the notion of *making a difference* is to be understood. According to regularity theories, the presence or absence of the cause C makes a difference for whether the effect E regularly follows from the conjunction of additional factors ABD... According to probabilistic theories of causation, the presence or absence of the cause C makes a difference to the probability of the effect E. In the counterfactual framework, the presence or absence of the cause C in nearby possible worlds makes a difference to whether the effect E occurs in those worlds. And in manipulability theories, interventions that make C occur or fail to occur make a difference to whether or not E occurs.

Process theories of causation

Process theories of causation are quite different from the difference-making approaches to causation already described. Instead of focusing on causal relationships between discrete events, process theories focus on continuous causal process. Causal processes include ordinary physical objects like baseballs and automobiles, more esoteric objects like photons and neutrinos, as well as various kinds of waves, such as sound waves and water waves. These processes need to be distinguished from pseudo-processes, such as shadows and spots of light. One important difference between them is that causal processes are restricted by the *first-signal principle* of the special theory of relativity, whereas pseudo-processes are not. For example, if one were to shine a very bright light on the wall of a large circular stadium, it would be possible in principle to rotate the light source so that the spot of light traveled along the wall with a velocity greater than the speed of light. By contrast, no causal process can be accelerated across the speed of light.

A central challenge for process theories of causation is to distinguish between causal processes and pseudo-processes. According to one leading approach, causal processes differ from pseudo-processes in their ability to transmit conserved quantities, such as energy, linear momentum, and charge. Baseballs, automobiles, photons, neutrinos, and sound waves are all capable of carrying energy from one place to another. Shadows and spots of light are not capable of transmitting conserved quantities. Here the process theorist must take care to distinguish between the *transmission* of a conserved quantity and the mere *presence* of a conserved quantity at various locations. For example, as a spot of light moves along a wall, energy will be present at each point along the wall as it is illuminated. Nonetheless, energy is not *transmitted* from one point on the wall to another; rather the energy is supplied to the various points along the wall from the central source. The spots of light on the wall are related not as cause and effect, but as effects of a common cause. The challenge for the *conserved-quantity theory* is to characterize the relevant notion of transmission in order to make this distinction.

Process theories of causation can easily solve the problem of pre-emption. We know that it is the city's power grid rather than the backup generator that is causing the lights in a building to be on because there are causal processes – electrons, which transmit the conserved quantity charge – that connect the city's power grid to the light sources in the building. There are no analogous processes connecting the backup generator to the lights. On the other hand, process theories offer little that is new to the problem of the direction of causation. If there is a causal process connecting C to E, then there will be a causal process connecting E to C. The process theorist can, of course, define the cause to be the earlier of the two events, a strategy that is available to all of the approaches to causation that we have canvassed.

One approach to causation, which is closely related to the process theories, analyzes causal relationships in terms of the *mechanisms* that connect causes with their effects.

Conclusion

It is fair to say that there is no one account of causation that has won the allegiance of the majority of philosophers who have thought about these issues. Nonetheless, sufficient progress has been made that few philosophers today continue to regard the concept of causation with the same suspicion voiced by Russell and his contemporaries.

See also Determinism; Explanation; Laws of nature; Mechanisms; Physics; Probability.

References

Dowe, P. (2000) *Physical Causation*, Cambridge: Cambridge University Press.
—— (2004) "Causation: Causal Processes," in Edward N. Zalta (ed.) *The Stanford Encyclopedia of Philosophy* (winter 2004 edition); available: http://plato.stanford.edu/archives/win2004/entries/causation-process.
Eells, E. (1991) *Probabilistic Causality*, Cambridge: Cambridge University Press.
Gasking, D. (1955) "Causation and Recipes," *Mind* 64: 474–87.
Hitchcock, C. (2001) "The Intransitivity of Causation Revealed in Equations and Graphs," *Journal of Philosophy* 98: 273–99.
—— (2002) "Causation: Probabilistic," in Edward N. Zalta (ed.) *The Stanford Encyclopedia of Philosophy* (fall 2002 edition); available: http://plato.stanford.edu/archives/fall2002/entries/causation-probabilistic.

Hume, D. (1977 [1748]) *Enquiries Concerning Human Understanding and Concerning the Principles of Morals*, ed. L. A. Selby-Bigge, 3rd edn, rev. P. H. Nidditch, Oxford: Clarendon Press.

—— (1978 [1739–40]) *A Treatise of Human Nature*, ed. L. A. Selby-Bigge, 2nd edn, rev. P. H. Nidditch, Oxford: Clarendon Press.

Lewis, D. K. (1973) "Causation," *Journal of Philosophy* 70: 556–67; reprinted with postscripts in Lewis, *Philosophical Papers*, Oxford: Oxford University Press, 1986, Volume 2, pp. 159–213.

Mackie, J. (1974) *The Cement of the Universe*, Oxford: Oxford University Press.

Menzies, P. (1989) "Probabilistic Causation and Causal Processes: A Critique of Lewis," *Philosophy of Science* 56: 642–63.

—— (2001) "Causation: Counterfactual Theories," in Edward N. Zalta (ed.) *The Stanford Encyclopedia of Philosophy* (spring 2001 edition); available: http://plato.stanford.edu/archives/spr2001/entries/causation-counterfactual.

Mill, J. S. (1843) *A System of Logic: Ratiocinative and Inductive*, London: J. W. Parker.

Reichenbach, H. (1956) *The Direction of Time*, Berkeley and Los Angeles: University of California Press.

Russell, B. (1913) "On the Notion of Cause," *Proceedings of the Aristotelian Society* 13: 1–26.

Spirtes, P., Glymour, C. and Scheines, R. (2000) *Causation, Prediction, and Search*, 2nd edn, Cambridge, MA: MIT University Press.

Woodward, J. (2001) "Causation and Manipulability," in Edward N. Zalta (ed.) *The Stanford Encyclopedia of Philosophy* (fall 2001 edition); available: http://plato.stanford.edu/archives/fall2001/entries/causation-mani.

—— (2003) *Making Things Happen: A Theory of Causal Explanation*, Oxford: Oxford University Press.

Further reading

Russell's critique of the concept of causation is presented in Russell (1913). Hume presents his account of causation in Book I, Part III of *A Treatise of Human Nature* (1739–40) and in section VII of *An Enquiry Concerning Human Understanding* (1748). Mill presents his regularity theory of causation in Volume I, Chapter V of his *System of Logic* (1843). Mackie (1974: Ch. 3) contains a detailed discussion of Mill's theory, and presents the theory of INUS conditions. Reichenbach (1956, Part IV) is an influential early presentation of a probabilistic theory of causation, including the central idea of screening-off relations. Eells (1991) is a book-length treatment. Spirtes, Glymour, and Scheines (2000) is a very technical but important work on the connection between causation and probability. The problem of pre-emption for probabilistic theories of causation is presented in Menzies (1989). Hitchcock (2002) is a survey article covering probabilistic approaches to causation. Lewis (1973) is the classic presentation of the counterfactual approach to causation. Hitchcock (2001) is one recent attempt to address the problem of pre-emption. Menzies (2001) surveys the counterfactual framework. Gasking (1955) is an early defense of the manipulability theory of causation; Woodward (2003) is a recent book-length treatment while Woodward (2001) is an article-length survey. Dowe (2000) presents the conserved quantity theory of causal processes, and Dowe (2004) is a survey of process theories of causation.

30
DETERMINISM
Barry Loewer

Determinism is a contingent metaphysical claim about the fundamental natural laws that hold in the universe. It says:

> The natural laws and the way things are at time t determine the way things will be at later times.

The mathematician Pierre-Simon Laplace (1820) expressed his belief that determinism is true this way:

> We ought to regard the present state of the universe as the effect of its antecedent state and as the cause of the state that is to follow. An intelligence knowing all the forces acting in nature at a given instant, as well as the momentary positions of all things in the universe, would be able to comprehend in one single formula the motions of the largest bodies as well as the lightest atoms in the world, provided that its intellect were sufficiently powerful to subject all data to analysis; to it nothing would be uncertain, the future as well as the past would be present to its eyes. The perfection that the human mind has been able to give to astronomy affords but a feeble outline of such intelligence.

The physics of Laplace's day (the first decades of the nineteenth century) was Newtonian (classical) mechanics. Isaac Newton formulated principles that he thought express the laws describing how forces determine the motions of bodies ($F = ma$) and how the positions of bodies and other factors determine gravitational and other kinds of forces. Using these principles, Newton and physicists following him were able to predict and explain the motions of celestial and terrestrial bodies. For example, these laws account for the orbits of the planets, the trajectories of cannon balls, and the periods of pendulums. Like Newton, Laplace did not know all the forces there are but he envisioned that, once those forces (and the corresponding force laws) were known, Newtonian physics would be a *complete* physical theory. That is, its laws would account for the motions of *all* material particles. And since he thought that everything that exists in space is composed of various kinds of very small material particles (or atoms) he thought that Newtonian mechanics (once all the forces were known) would be what today we would call *the theory of everything*. It seemed clear to him that the completed Newtonian theory would be deterministic and that it would thus be in principle possible accurately to predict the future (and retrodict the past) from complete knowledge of the present. It should be noted, however, that there are subtleties concerning whether Newtonian mechanics is deterministic in the way Laplace imagined it to be. It has been shown that there are initial conditions compatible with the laws for which the laws do not determine all future positions. However, those conditions are unusual and it is plausible that they can be ruled out as obtaining in our world.

Many people find the idea of determinism abhorrent and incredible. It is felt to be abhorrent by those who think that determinism is incompatible with free will and human dignity. It may seem that if determinism obtains then people are like marionettes whose movements are under the control of impersonal laws of nature. It also strikes many as incredible because it seems that so much of what happens – not just deliberate human action, but also the weather, the stockmarket, falling in love, and so on – is irremediably unpredictable and so, they think, constitutes proof that determinism is false.

On the other hand, some people find determinism to be an attractive and even inspiring metaphysical view. It seems to imply that every event (except perhaps the first event, if there is one) has a *scientific explanation*. And while it is granted that we cannot predict much of the future it might be argued that the reason is not that determinism is false, but, as Laplace suggests, that our intellect is too feeble to acquire the relevant information and make the required calculations.

Whatever visceral reaction one has to determinism, it is widely believed that debates concerning it belong to a previous era since it is now known that Newtonian mechanics is false and the theories that replace it – in particular quantum mechanics – are not deterministic. But, as we will see, the situation is more complicated and interesting.

Clarifying determinism

In the formulation of determinism, "determine" means "logically necessitates." The Newtonian laws are (modulo the remark about unusual initial conditions above) two-way deterministic because they and the state at t logically necessitates both the future and the past of t. Some philosophers have something stronger in mind by "determines." Their idea is that the present (and the laws) do not just logically imply the future but that they *bring about* future states. On this understanding, a temporal direction is built into the characterization of determinism since we think of the past as bringing about the future but not the other way around. I will say more about "bringing about" when discussing *laws*.

The *state at t* is explained in terms of the space–time and the fundamental ontology and magnitudes. The existence of the state at t presupposes a view about space–time and fundamental ontology on which there is a complete temporal ordering of all events and the fundamental magnitudes are exemplified instantaneously. The values of all these quantities specify the state at t. In Newtonian mechanics the state at t is specified in terms of the positions, momentum and intrinsic quantities, like mass and charge, of each particle at time t. In field theories the state at t is specified in terms of the field values (which can be vectors) at all spatial points at time t. There are fundamental theories that posit space–times and ontologies that do not share those presuppositions. For example, in the space–times of Einstein's theory of special and general relativity there are events that are not temporally comparable. Nevertheless, versions of determinism can be formulated for many of those space–times by finding something that plays the role of the state at a time such that it and the laws determine the events throughout all of the space–time (Earman 1986).

The most controversial and philosophically significant concept in the characterization of determinism is that of *law of nature*. The idea that there are *laws of nature* and that it is the job of the sciences to discover them developed during the seventeenth and eighteenth centuries with the rise of classical mechanics. An overly simple suggestion that may have a grain of truth is that laws as the basis of explanation came to be seen as an intermediary between God's will and his creation or even as a replacement for theological explanation. It became a central tenet of physics (and many of the other sciences) that knowledge of the laws of nature is the key to scientific explanation and reliable prediction. Not every true generalization (equation or function that maps each state on to its future) is or is associated with a law. If it were, then determinism would be trivial. So the question is, What makes a generalization or equation lawful? Part of the answer is provided by the connections between laws and other central notions in the sciences, in particular explanation, counterfactuals, causation, and confirmation. Explanations often involve specifying how a law and initial conditions entail the event to be explained. Laws support counterfactual statements: for example, if the distance between the earth and the sun were r meters then the gravitational force between them would be $F = Gm_e m_s/r^2$. Further, propositions that are apt for expressing lawful generalizations are confirmed by their instances.

While the features just mentioned help to identify laws, there is still a question of what laws are. There are two main philosophical positions concerning the metaphysics of laws, which I will call "Humean" and "metaphysical" accounts. The most sophisticated version of the Humean view is due to David Lewis (1994) and the most sophisticated version of the metaphysical view is due to Tim Maudlin (see Maudlin 2007).

On Lewis's account the laws are contingent generalizations implied by the *best systematization* of the distribution of fundamental entities, magnitudes, etc. Here is the idea. Let L be a language whose atomic predicates express only fundamental magnitudes and relations and mathematical notions and let W be the set of all truths of L. The laws (call them "L-laws") are defined as follows:

> Take all deductive systems whose theorems are true. Some are simpler, better systematized than others. Some are stronger, more informative, than others. These virtues compete: an uninformative system can be very simple,

an unsystematized compendium of miscellaneous information can be very informative. The best system is the one that strikes as good a balance as truth will allow between simplicity and strength. How good a balance that is will depend on how kind nature is. A regularity is a law iff it is a [contingent] theorem of the best system. (Lewis 1994: 478)

According to Maudlin's metaphysical account, laws (call them "M-laws") are not themselves generalizations or regularities but rather fundamental elements of the world's ontology that *produce* the lawful regularities. Maudlin says little more about what laws are and exactly how a law *produces* regularity. His idea seems to be that laws are described by dynamical equations (e.g., $F = ma$). Given the state of the universe at t the laws evolve that state into subsequent states, producing a regularity satisfying the equation.

The question is whether the fundamental laws of our world are L-laws or M-laws (or some other account). On Lewis's account the best system of a world is determined by the entire history of states of the universe. It follows that the L-laws *supervene* on the totality of states. In contrast, M-laws (if there are any) do not supervene on the totality of states since different laws can *produce* the same total histories. For some advocates of M-laws this contrast is enough to establish that L-laws are too weak to do the work that laws are supposed to do. They say that L-laws are incapable of explaining state-evolution since they are determined by the states. But the issue is more subtle since L-laws and the state do *entail* subsequent states. Advocates of L-laws go on to say that we have no idea of how M-laws *produce* states. We cannot settle the issue here but will note some other differences between the two accounts.

The two accounts of laws may render different verdicts concerning determinism since the generalizations entailed by the world's best theory (if there is one) may be different from the generalizations brought about by the world's M-laws (if there are any). The two accounts also differ with respect to the connections they make between laws and time. The metaphysical account presupposes a temporal direction since the laws evolve the world toward the future. The L-view does not presuppose any intrinsic temporal direction but attempts to account for temporal direction in terms of the distribution of the structure of the totality of states.

It has been suggested that views about laws have consequences for the threat that determinism poses to the existence of free will. It has been argued as follows: we have no control over the past and/or the laws, and if determinism is true it seems to follow that we have no control over the future either. Some philosophers have responded to this argument by observing that while the argument may be sound if laws are M-laws, it fails if laws are L-laws. The reason is that the L-laws are determined by the totality of facts including facts about what we chose; so, rather than constraining our choices, they are partly determined by them (Mele and Beebee 2002; Hoefer 2005). I do not assess the strength of this response here, except to note that if it proves a good response, it would cast doubt on the claim that L-laws can explain and support counterfactuals.

The belief that determinism entails predictability is a reason why some people find determinism abhorrent. They might fear that if determinism is true, then others (or a superior intelligence) would be able to calculate what they will do and thus thwart their plans. But determinism and predictability are quite different claims, and neither entails the other. Determinism is a *metaphysical* claim about the fundamental laws of the universe; predictability is an *epistemic* claim about what we can *know* about the future.

There are a number of considerations that show why determinism does not entail predictability. First it may be impossible (because of our natures and the laws themselves) for us to know what the laws are. Even if we knew the laws we might not be able to use them to gain knowledge of certain future events because accurate predictions require knowing an enormous amount – possibly an infinite amount – about the present. In the case of Newtonian mechanics, perfectly reliable predictions of the *exact* future motions of particles require knowledge of the exact present positions and motions of all the particles in the universe, and the exact position of a particle will typically be represented by an infinitely long decimal. It may turn out that the laws themselves entail that the knowledge required to make certain predictions is impossible to obtain. Further, small differences at one time can make for very big differences a short time later with respect to matters that concern us. Another obstacle to prediction is that the mathematical equations expressing the laws may not be solvable except approximately. This, in fact, is the case for the simple Newtonian world when three or more particles are involved. Laplace was idealizing enormously when he suggested that an "intelligence" could predict future states from the present state and the laws.

On the other hand, the failure of determinism does not preclude the possibility of reliable predictions about the future. Of course, the extent to which we can reliably predict the future depends on exactly what the laws are. If the laws are probabilistic, it may turn out that, given the state or even a partial description of the state at t, the laws specify probabilities very close to 1 for some future events. Thus, even if coin-tosses are fundamentally random, we can pretty accurately predict that 1,000 tosses of an ordinary coin will result in between 450 and 550 heads. The moral of all this is that we should keep in mind that determinism is a metaphysical claim about the laws while predictability is an epistemic claim about what we can reliably predict, and neither entails the other.

Determinism and quantum theory

Laplace considered determinism to be true because he accepted that Newtonian mechanics is the true theory of everything and that it entails determinism. But Newtonian mechanics has been superseded by quantum mechanics (QM), and so the question arises of its consequences for determinism.

In non-relativistic QM the state of an isolated system is specified, not by the positions and momenta of particles as in Newtonian mechanics, but by a vector-valued *wave function* $\psi(t)$ that specifies the probabilities of the values of measurements made at t of the *observable* quantities of the system. The observable quantities, corresponding to position, momentum, total energy, spin, and so on, are the properties of quantum systems. They need not literally be observable. No state ψ assigns a probability of 1 for every observable. In particular, no ψ assigns a probability of 1 to values of both the momentum and the position observables associated with, for example, an electron. This is an instance of Heisenberg's *uncertainty principle*. On the orthodox, or "Copenhagen," interpretation of QM, an observable O (e.g., a particle's momentum) is said to have a *determinate* value if and *only if* ψ assigns a probability 1 to a particular value of that observable. (The "Copenhagen" interpretation refers to a collection of ways of thinking about QM associated with Niels Bohr and Werner von Heisenberg that came to be accepted as the orthodox way of understanding QM. A good discussion can be found in Cushing 1994.) It follows that no electron (or any other QM system) has both a determinate position and a determinate velocity. In fact, for typical states of elementary particles, neither position nor momentum, nor any other familiar quantities, possess determinate values. QM also includes a dynamical law – Schrödinger's *equation* – describing ψ's evolution. Schrödinger's law is deterministic and linear. So the question naturally arises of how probabilities come into the picture. On the orthodox account, the answer is that ψ obeys Schrödinger's deterministic law *except* when a system is being measured (or observed). When a measurement of O is made, the system randomly jumps into a state in which O has the determinate value with the probabilities specified by ψ.

There are a number of novel and peculiar features of QM. The most striking is the claim that quantities like position may not be determinate. This lack of determinateness is different from a failure of determinism since it says that at a given time a certain quantity, for instance position, has no specific value. Underlying this is the QM principle of superposition. If ψ_1 is a state corresponding to a particle being located in region 1 and ψ_2 corresponds to the particle being located in a distinct region 2, then there are *superpositions* of these states, $a\psi_1 + b\psi_2$, that correspond to the particle being located somewhere in the union of the two regions *but at no specific* place within the union of the two regions. The coefficients a and b determine the probabilities of the outcomes of position measurements in the respective regions. On the orthodox interpretation, it is not just that we do not *know* the exact location of the particle but that its location is *indeterminate*. Another peculiar feature is the role of *measurement* (or *observation*) in the formulation of the laws. This seems to make QM peculiarly subjective and certainly makes it inexact, without a precise characterization of measurements. A third peculiarity is *non-locality*. It turns out that there are states of, for example, a spatially separated pair of electrons for which, when a measurement of one of the electrons is made, the state of it *and the other electron* jumps into a new state (Bell 1987; Albert 1992).

The peculiarity of these features encouraged many physicists to take an instrumentalist attitude towards the theory. Instrumentalists think of QM as *merely* providing rules for predicting the outcomes of measurements. So understood, QM is silent about the ontology and the laws, whatever they might be, that lie behind its predictions. Some physicists believed it to be impossible to supplement or modify QM while preserving its predictions and impossible to remove the notion of observation from the theory. If this were the last word about QM then QM would be silent on whether determinism is true.

However, there are realist ways and also deterministic ways of understanding QM that are now beginning to be taken seriously by some physicists and philosophers. The most important deterministic account is the so-called "hidden variables theory" devised by David Bohm in 1952 (see Bell 1987; Albert 1992; Cushing 1994). The ontology of Bohmian mechanics consists of particles (that always possess definite positions) and a quantum field that corresponds to the wave function. The state of a system at t is determined by the positions of the particles at t and the values of the quantum field at t. The dynamical laws are Schrödinger's law and a law (the "guidance equation") that specifies the velocities of the particles. These laws are thoroughly deterministic. Probabilities come into the picture through a probability distribution that is posited to hold over initial positions of particles of a system compatible with its wave function. Measurements are simply interactions between two systems that result in the value of a quantity of the measured system being correlated with a macro-state of the measurement instrument. The predictions of the results of measurements on Bohm's theory are exactly the same as those of orthodox QM. In particular, Bohmian mechanics entails the uncertainty principles and all the other probabilistic predictions of QM. The uncertainty is irremediable since it follows from the laws and the initial probability distribution that it is impossible to know the complete state of a system.

There are also realist versions of QM whose dynamical laws are indeterministic. The most fully worked out of these is the GRW theory, so called after its formulators: Ghirardi, Rimini, and Weber (see Albert 1992; Ghirardi 2005). The GRW theory replaces the deterministic Schrödinger law with an indeterministic law that specifies the probabilities of the state at t "jumping" into various possible states at subsequent times. The law has the consequence that for a system whose quantum state involves few degrees of freedom (with respect to particle position) the evolution will be as specified by Schrödinger's equation, except for very rare "jumps" that localize particle position. (The basic idea of the GRW theory is that the quantum state of a system evolves in accord with Schrödinger's law, except that there is a probability per unit time of the wave function of the state being multiplied by a very narrow Gaussian: see Ghirardi 2005.) But in macroscopic systems (e.g., a measuring device that consists of many particles) it is very likely that at least one of those particles will undergo a jump in a fraction of a second. Since the positions of the particles are correlated, when one jumps into a localized position state, the rest must follow. The consequence is that measurements and other macroscopic interactions result in quantum states in which macroscopic objects have determinate positions. There is no need to introduce the notions of "measurement" or "observer" into the formulation of the theory.

The most important point for our discussion is that orthodox quantum theory, GRW, and Bohmian mechanics are, for all practical purposes, empirically equivalent even though the first two are incompatible with determinism and the latter entails it. (There are, in principle, empirical differences between theories with collapses, like the orthodox theory and GRW, and no-collapse theories like Bohm's. However, it is plausible that they are empirically equivalent for all practical purposes, since it is unlikely that it will ever be possible to conduct an experiment whose outcomes discriminate among these theories.) This is a dramatic case of the *underdetermination of theory by all possible evidence.* Although neither of these theories is true (since they fail to take into account relativity), it is very plausible that if there is a theory of everything, there will be also be empirically equivalent theories that are deterministic and indeterministic. So it is very likely that the question of whether or not determinism is true is plausibly something that we will never be in a position to answer.

Determinism and statistical mechanics

Even if the dynamical laws are deterministic, as in Newtonian mechanics and Bohm's theory, probabilities are required for explanation and prediction. Suppose that, as Laplace thought, the world consists of point particles and the laws are given by classical mechanics. The macroscopic state of a system (even the universe) at a time is specified by the values of macroscopic quantities like temperature, average frequency of radiation, average mass, and charge density, in small, but not too small, volumes of space. The macroscopic state is typically insufficient to pin down, for example, whether or not there is an ice-cube floating in a pail of warm water in some particular room (or whether a room is full of people and other macroscopic features). For a given macroscopic state of a system at *t* there are infinitely many possible micro-states (states characterized by precise positions and momenta of all the particles that compose the system) only one of which *actually* composes the system at *t*. In Newtonian mechanics with a particle ontology (similar remarks apply to quantum theories) *the macroscopic state of the universe (or an isolated system) at *t* and the deterministic dynamical laws determine very little about *the macroscopic* states at other times. For example, the macro-state of an ice-cube in warm water is compatible with "maverick" micro-states whose futures (as entailed by the deterministic laws) involve the ice-cube growing bigger or even forming the shape of Jimmy Durante's nose and jumping out of the water. So, if we just know the macro-state of the system (that it is an ice-cube floating in warm water), the deterministic laws are not sufficient to predict that the ice-cube will melt. The same point applies to the prediction of the motions of the planets and every other application of Newton's laws, if we think of planets, as Laplace did, as composed of atoms that obey Newton's laws.

Ludwig Boltzmann faced this problem when he tried to explain how the laws of thermodynamics are related to the fundamental dynamical laws. Thermodynamics includes laws that are temporally asymmetric and that reliably and deterministically predict how a system evolves. For example, the *second law of thermodynamics* says that *the entropy* of an isolated system never decreases. The entropy of a system is, roughly, the size of the collection of micro-states that are compatible with the system's macro-state. The increase in entropy of the ice-cube in warm water corresponds to the ice-cube's melting. So, the problem Boltzmann faced was how to square the temporally directed second law with the temporally symmetric fundamental laws. Boltzmann's solution is based on the observation that micro-states which the laws evolve to states realizing macro-states with greater entropy – maverick micro-states – are, in a certain sense, "rare." The sense in which maverick states are rare is not that there are fewer of them – there are infinitely many – but that a very natural measure on the set of micro-states assigns the set of maverick states a measure close to 0. (See Sklar 1993 and Albert 2000 for philosophical discussions of statistical mechanics.)

Boltzmann construed this measure as a probability distribution over the micro-states that are compatible with a given macro-state, and this has the consequence that maverick micro-states (e.g., those that spontaneously form into the shape of a nose) are exceedingly unlikely. It turns out (again not surprisingly since the dynamical laws are temporally symmetric) that the uniform distribution over the micro-states compatible with the ice-cube in warm water entails that it is highly likely that in the past (just as in the future) the pail contained water at a uniform temperature. A way of avoiding this consequence while preserving the good consequences is to posit the uniform distribution over micro-states compatible with the macro-state of the universe immediately after the Big Bang and to posit that the entropy of this is very, very low. This has the consequence that it is very likely that the entropy of the entire universe (and its relatively isolated subsystems) increases over time.

Given the dynamical laws and the initial micro-state, the statistical–mechanical probability distribution implies that the evolution at a macroscopic level appears to be indeterministic. Very small differences in the micro-states that realize a macro-state entail very different future evolutions. Even if a demon knows a very detailed macro-description of the roulette wheel and the motions of the croupier's hand, and so on, and knows the dynamical laws and could perform the relevant calculations, he could not predict the outcome of a turn of the wheel. Our world is apparently full of macroscopic phenomena (so-called "chaotic systems") whose future evolution is very sensitive to the initial micro-states that realize their macro-states.

There is controversy concerning exactly what "probability" means in statistical mechanics since the dynamical laws are deterministic. The same issue arises in Bohmian mechanics, as its dynamical laws are also deterministic. Since the outcome of a turn of the roulette wheel is strictly determined by the laws and the complete micro-state of the world prior to the turn of the wheel, it is often said that the probabilities involved in deterministic theories must reflect *merely* subjective ignorance. But this doesn't seem quite right, since these probabilities are based on objective facts about our world and are supposed to explain the second law. For that reason it is plausible to consider them objective and lawful. (There are proposals for how to understand probabilities objectively if determinism obtains, including a generalization of Lewis's best-system account of laws discussed earlier: see Loewer 2001 and 2004.)

Conclusion

At the turn of the twenty-first century, physicists have not realized Laplace's dream of a theory of everything and if there is such theory, it is not known whether it is deterministic. Nonetheless, the success of QM and statistical mechanics (which must be accounted for by any complete theory) provides very strong reason to believe that scientific account of the universe will involve probabilities either in indeterministic dynamical laws (as in orthodox QM and GRW) or as initial-condition probabilities (as in statistical mechanics and Bohmian mechanics). Further, it is very likely that if there is an empirically adequate proposal for a complete theory whose dynamical laws are probabilistic, there will also be an empirically equivalent account in which the fundamental laws are deterministic. The upshot is that it is likely that we will never know whether or not determinism is true; but it is certain that if it is true then there can be no predicting the future with certainty. This conclusion will doubtlessly be frustrating to those who think that whether or not determinism obtains has vast consequences for free will and other philosophical issues.

See also Laws of nature; Physics; Probability; Underdetermination.

References

Armstrong, David (1983) *What Is a Law of Nature?*, Cambridge: Cambridge University Press.
Albert, David (1992) *Quantum Mechanics and Experience*, Cambridge, MA: Harvard University Press.
—— (2000) *Time and Chance*, Cambridge, MA: Harvard University Press.
Bell, J. S. (1987) *Speakable and Unspeakable in Quantum Mechanics*, Cambridge: Cambridge University Press.
Carroll, John (ed.) (2004) *Readings on Laws of Nature*, Pittsburgh, PA: University of Pittsburgh Press.
Cushing, J. T. (1994) *Quantum Mechanics: Historical Contingency and the Copenhagen Hegemony*, Chicago: University of Chicago Press.
Earman, John (1986) *A Primer on Determinism*, Dordrecht: Reidel
Ghirardi, Giancarlo (2005) "Collapse Theories," in Edward N. Zalta (ed.) *The Stanford Encyclopedia of Philosophy* (spring 2002 edition); available: http://plato.stanford.edu/archives/spr2002/entries/qm-collapse.
Hoefer, Carl (2005) "Causal Determinism," in Edward N. Zalta (ed.) *The Stanford Encyclopedia of Philosophy* (summer 2005 edition); available: http://plato.stanford.edu/archives/sum2005/entries/determinism-causal.
Kane, Robert (1996) *The Significance of Free Will*, Oxford: Oxford University Press.
Laplace, P. (1820) *Essai philosophique sur les probabilités*, forming the Introduction to his *Théorie analytique des probabilités*, Paris: V Courcier; trans. F. W. Truscott and F. L. Emory as *A Philosophical Essay on Probabilities*, New York: Dover, 1951.
Lewis, D. (1994) "Chance and Credence: Humean Supervenience Debugged," *Mind* 103: 473–90.
Loewer, Barry (2001) "Determinism and Chance," *Studies in the History and Philosophy of Modern Physics* 32: 609–20.
—— (2004) "David Lewis's Humean Theory of Objective Chance," *Philosophy of Science* 71: 1115–25.
Maudlin, Tim (2007) *The Metaphysics Within Physics* Oxford: Oxford University Press.
Mele, Alfred and Beebee, Helen (2002) "Humean Compatibilism," *Mind* 111: 201–23.
Sklar, Larry (1995) *Physics and Chance*, Cambridge: Cambridge University Press.
Tooley, Michael (1987) *Causation*, Oxford: Clarendon Press.

Further reading

The best book-length discussion of determinism is Earman (1986). For various views about the nature of laws, see Carroll (2004) and Lange's contribution to this collection. For Maudlin's view of laws, see Maudlin (2007). For elementary but philosophically sophisticated discussions of quantum mechanics and statistical mechanics, see Albert (1992) and (2000). For advanced discussions of the philosophy of quantum mechanics see Bell (1987). For advanced discussions of the philosophy of statistical mechanics, see Sklar (1995).

31

EVIDENCE

Peter Achinstein

Four concepts of evidence

In 1883 Heinrich Hertz performed experiments on cathode rays in order to determine whether these rays carry an electric charge (Hertz 1896). In one experiment he separated cathode rays from ordinary electricity produced in a cathode tube and caused the cathode rays to enter an electrometer that would determine the presence of electric charge. In his experiment no electrical effect was produced. In a second experiment he introduced oppositely electrified plates into the tube to see if the cathode rays were deflected electrically. No deflection was produced. Hertz concluded, mistakenly as it turns out, that cathode rays carry no electric charge and hence are not composed of charged particles. His mistake, as J. J. Thomson (1897) showed experimentally fourteen years later, was to assume that the air in the cathode tube was sufficiently evacuated to allow electrical effects to occur. Thomson demonstrated those effects, concluded that the rays are indeed composed of electrically charged particles (later called "electrons"), and experimentally measured their ratio of mass to charge. (For his experiments with cathode rays Thomson received the Nobel Prize in 1906; he is credited with the discovery of the electron.)

Concentrating just on Hertz's negative experimental results in 1883, are (or were) these results evidence that cathode rays are electrically neutral? Several different answers are possible.

1 The results of Hertz's experiments are evidence that cathode rays are not charged. Given what was known by Hertz and others in 1883, and what was technically feasible then, Hertz and others were completely justified in believing that cathode rays are neutral. Anyone in Hertz's epistemic situation would be justified in drawing this conclusion.
2 From 1883 to 1897 Hertz's results were evidence that cathode rays are not charged. After that this was not the case. During this period the physics community regarded these results as the best information available on this topic. After Thomson's new results in 1897 physicists no longer regarded Hertz's experiments as evidence of the neutrality of cathode rays.
3 The results of Hertz's experiments are not, and never were, evidence that cathode rays are electrically neutral. They do not and never did provide a good reason to

believe this hypothesis, since the results were based on an experimental flaw (the cathode tubes were not sufficiently evacuated to demonstrate electrical effects), and since the conclusion itself is false.

Which answer is correct? A plausible case can be made for each, suggesting that in using the term "evidence" we are operating with different concepts.

The first is based on the idea of providing a justification for belief that is relativized to an epistemic situation. Hertz's negative results were evidence for Hertz and others in his epistemic situation. Such persons were justified in believing what they did. Hertz's results were not evidence for anyone in Thomson's epistemic situation. This type of evidence can be called epistemic-situation or ES-evidence. Although this concept is relativized to an epistemic situation, there need be no actual person in that situation, and if there is, such a person need not know or believe that he is. In this sense the concept, although relativized, is objective.

The second use is thoroughly subjective and historical. The negative results were evidence for Hertz and others simply because they took them to be so. They were not evidence for Thomson, because he regarded Hertz's experiments as based on a flaw and did not take these results to be evidence. This subjective use of "evidence" does not carry with it the implication that the person for whom it is evidence is justified in believing the hypothesis in question on that evidence.

The third answer, appealing to a good reason to believe a hypothesis, contains two ideas that can be separated. One is that Hertz's results were not a good reason to believe his hypothesis since they were based on the mistaken assumption that his cathode tubes were sufficiently evacuated to show electrical deflection. The other is that Hertz's results were not a good reason to believe his conclusion since that conclusion is in fact false. Two concepts of *good reason for belief* are possible, each related to one of these ideas: a *strong* concept requiring, in Hertz's case, not only the absence of a flaw in the design of the experiment but the truth of the hypothesis as well; and a *weaker* one that requires the absence of a flaw, but not the truth of the hypothesis.

There is a concept of evidence based on each of the latter concepts of good reason to believe: *veridical* evidence, which provides a good reason to believe a hypothesis in a sense that requires the truth of that hypothesis, and *potential* evidence, which provides a good reason to believe a hypothesis in a sense that does not require this. Both concepts are completely objective. Whether a fact e is evidence that some hypothesis h is true, in either the veridical or the potential sense, does not depend on what anyone knows or believes. Nor, like ES-evidence, is it relativized to an epistemic situation. It is not evidence for anyone in some epistemic situation.

With these four concepts we can describe Hertz's situation as follows. There are two senses in which his experimental results were evidence that cathode rays are electrically neutral, and two senses in which they were not evidence for this. They were Hertz's subjective evidence, since they were what Hertz took to be evidence. They were also ES-evidence for Hertz, since anyone in his epistemic situation would be justified in believing in the electric neutrality of cathode rays, given these results.

However, they were not potential evidence, since the fact that there was a flaw in the design means that the results did not provide a good reason to believe the hypothesis. They were not veridical evidence since the hypothesis is false. By contrast, Thomson's later experimental results were evidence for Thomson's charged particle hypothesis in all four senses of "evidence."

The question now is whether and, if so, how these four concepts can be defined in a more basic and illuminating way. Let us begin with accounts that have become standard in the literature.

Five standard theories of evidence

Subjective Bayesian definition

On this view, evidence for a hypothesis is defined simply as anything that increases the probability of the hypothesis. In formal terms,

$$e \text{ is evidence that } h, \text{ given } b, \text{ if and only if } P(h/e\&b) > P(h/b), \tag{1}$$

that is, if and only if the probability of h on e and b is greater than its probability on b alone, where b is background information being assumed. The concept of probability used is subjective. It is relativized to a particular person X at a time t, and it measures the degree of X's belief in hypothesis h at time t. The only requirement is that X's degrees of belief in various propositions are probabilistically "coherent," i.e., they satisfy the axioms of mathematical probability.

Returning to the Hertz example, since the null results of his experiments increased Hertz's degree of belief in the hypothesis that cathode rays are electrically neutral, those results were his evidence for this hypothesis in 1883 (assuming that his degrees of belief were probabilistically "coherent"). Hertz's results did not constitute evidence for Thomson for the neutrality hypothesis in 1897, since the results did not increase Thomson's degree of belief then.

This Bayesian view obviously yields a type of subjective evidence. Subjective Bayesians insist that this is the only legitimate concept of evidence. They argue that rationality in one's set of degrees of belief requires only that the set be probabilistically "coherent." Evidence for a proposition, then, is whatever increases one's rational degree of belief in it. (See Howson and Urbach 2006 for a defense of this idea.)

Objective Bayesian definitions

According to the objective Bayesian, probability is to be construed objectively, not subjectively. It does not depend on what any particular person or group believes. One of the most influential views of this kind is due to Rudolf Carnap (1962), who distinguished two probability concepts of evidence. One is the increase-in-probability (or "positive relevance") account given in (1) above. The other is a high-probability definition according to which

$$e \text{ is evidence that } h, \text{ given } b, \text{ if and only if } P(h/e\&b) > k, \qquad (2)$$

where k represents some threshold of high probability. Carnap defines the probability of h given e in purely syntactical terms, invoking only logical–linguistic properties of the sentences h and e and properties of the linguistic system in which those sentences are expressed. Whether a given probability statement of the form

$$P(h/e) = r \text{ (where } r \text{ is a real number between 0 and 1)} \qquad (3)$$

is true is for Carnap a matter of *a priori* calculation.

Among the semantic interpretations Carnap offers for his syntactically defined concept of probability, one of the most important is this. If a sentence of the form (3) is true, then for any person X, if X's total observational information is e, then X is rationally justified in believing h to the degree r. This is different from subjective interpretations of probability, since, on Carnap's view, a sentence of form (3) if true is so whether or not there exists anyone whose total observational information is e or who believes h to the degree r.

With this semantic interpretation of probability, the objective Bayesian interpretations of (1) and (2) furnish a type of ES-evidence. Such evidence provides a justification for certain degrees of belief for anyone in certain epistemic situations, whether or not any such person exists.

The error-statistical view

A very different probabilistic definition of evidence is developed by Deborah Mayo (1996). It rejects the standard Bayesian views that invoke *posterior* and *prior* probabilities of a hypothesis, i.e., $P(h/e)$ and $P(h)$, while appealing to the probability that a test for a hypothesis h will yield the result e. Her basic idea is that e is evidence that h if and only if h has passed a good test with the result being e. Passing a test T with result e counts as a good test for a hypothesis h if and only if e "fits" h, and T is a "severe test" of h.

Let us write the probability that the test T will yield the putative evidence e, given that the hypothesis h is true, as $P(e(T)/h)$, and the probability that the test T will yield e, given that h is false, as $P(e(T)/\sim h)$. Mayo's requirement of "fit" is that the former probability is not low, or at least that it is greater than the latter. Her requirement of "passing a severe test" is that the probability is very high that test T would produce a result that fits h less well than e does if h were false. Accordingly, we can write:

(*Error-statistical*) e is evidence that h, relative to test T, if and only if $P(e(T)/h)$ > $P(e(T)/\sim h)$, and $P(T$ produces a result that fits h less well than $e/\sim h)$ is very high. (4)

Since the concept of probability that Mayo employs, viz. relative frequency, is an objective one that is not relativized to a person or an epistemic situation (4) seems best construed as a definition of potential evidence.

Hypothetico-deductivism (h-d)

This conception of evidence derives from the h-d view of scientific method. The scientist begins by proposing a hypothesis h, from which, together with other assumptions b he is making, he deduces some testable conclusion e that is not deducible from b alone. If e is tested and turns out to be false, either h, or some assumption in b, must be revised or discarded. If e turns out to be true, then this fact provides evidence for h, on the assumption of b. So, on a simple version of this view:

> (*Simple h-d view*) e is evidence that h, given b, if and only if h together with b entails e, but b by itself does not entail e.   (5)

More elaborate versions of the h-d view have been proposed, which impose further conditions on h, b, or e. One is due to the nineteenth-century scientist, historian and philosopher of science William Whewell (1840), who imposes three further conditions. The first is that the evidence should include not just facts that have already been established, but ones newly predicted. The second is what Whewell calls "consilience," the idea that the evidence should include not just facts of a type that prompted the hypothesis in the first place, but ones of a different type that did not. The third, which Whewell calls "coherence," is based on the idea that scientific theories change over time as a result of new investigations. If a theory becomes more coherent (unified, simple), we are more convinced of its truth. So we might say that e is (strong) evidence that h, given b, only if h, b, and e satisfy the idea of coherence. Accordingly, we have:

> (*Whewellian h-d*) e is evidence that h, given b, if and only if (5) above is satisfied, and h, e, and b also satisfy Whewellian prediction, consilience, and coherence (the more these are satisfied the stronger the evidence).   (6)

The simple h-d view (5) provides a concept of *potential* evidence. (It could be transformed into a concept of *veridical* evidence by adding the further requirement that h is true.) It is not relativized to any epistemic situation or to any person or group. The Whewellian concept (6) is quite different. It is best understood as a subjective concept of evidence that is relativized to a person or group. Whether e constitutes (Whewellian) evidence that h, given b, for a particular person or group depends on whether e contains facts that are predictions for that person or group, and facts in addition to those that prompted that person or group to propose the hypothesis in the first place. It also depends on whether h was modified over time by its proponents and on the character of these modifications. So it could be that e provides evidence that h for some actual persons or groups but not for others.

Satisfaction definitions

On these definitions data constitute evidence that a hypothesis is true only if the data provide instances that "satisfy" the hypothesis in a sense that can be defined in formal–logical terms. A simple version was introduced by Hempel in his "Studies in the Logic of Confirmation" (1945). To formulate it Hempel introduces the concept of the *development* of a hypothesis of the form "All As are Bs" for a class of individuals x_1, x_2, …, x_n as what that hypothesis would assert if only those individuals existed. In this case the development is a conjunction consisting of sentences of the form

If x_i is an A, then x_i is a B (for each x_i in the class of individuals).   (7)

The individuals mentioned in the conjunction "satisfy" the hypothesis "All As are Bs." Hempel then defines two evidential concepts, *direct confirmation* and *confirmation*, as follows:

(a) *e* directly confirms *h* if *e* deductively entails the development of *h* for the class of individuals mentioned in *e*.
(b) *e* confirms *h* if *h* is deductively entailed by a class of sentences each of which is directly confirmed by *e*.   (8)

A more elaborate version, the so-called "bootstrap" definition of Clark Glymour (1980), is based on the idea that one can use a theory *T* containing an hypothesis *h* to confirm that very hypothesis *h*:

(*Bootstrap evidence*): *e* is evidence that *h* with respect to theory *T* if, using *T*, it is possible to derive from *e* an instance of *h*, and the derivation is not such as to guarantee an instance of *h* no matter what *e* is chosen.   (9)

Glymour's specific conditions are complex. For a more detailed exposition that also contains examples as well as counterexamples the reader is invited to consult Achinstein (1983: 355–62).

Both of these "satisfaction" definitions provide concepts of potential evidence, rather than subjective or ES-evidence. Whether *e* is evidence that *h*, on those definitions, is not relativized to any person or time, nor to an epistemic situation.

Two assumptions about evidence

Most of the previous definitions make, or at least satisfy, one or both of the following · very basic assumptions about evidence, which will be called the "weakness" and "*a priori*" assumptions.

The weakness assumption

Evidence is a weak idea. You do not need very much to have evidence that a hypothesis is true.

For example, on Bayesian definition (1), construed either subjectively or objectively, all you need for evidence that *h* is information that increases the probability of *h*. So the fact that I buy one ticket in a fair lottery containing 1 million tickets, one of which will be drawn at random, is evidence that I will win, since it increases the (subjective or objective) probability. To be sure, it is not a lot of evidence, but on this definition, it is some.

Examples such as this are precluded by the second of the two Bayesian definitions (2), which requires high probability for evidence. But (2) allows a different kind of weakness in evidence. It allows putative evidence to have little, if anything, to do with the hypothesis in question. For example, let e be that the former basketball star Michael Jordan eats the breakfast cereal Wheaties (he used to advertise the product on TV). Let b include the fact that men have not become pregnant. And let the hypothesis h be that Michael Jordan will not become pregnant. Then, since $P(h/e\&b)$ is very high, definition (2) would require us to conclude that, given b, the fact that Michael Jordan eats Wheaties is evidence that he will not become pregnant. A concept of evidence that allows this conclusion is very weak indeed.

The weakness assumption is also satisfied by the simple h-d definition (5). The fact that the sun exists is entailed by Kepler's first law that the planets revolve around the sun in elliptical orbits. By (5), then, the fact that the sun exists counts as evidence that Kepler's first law is true. Again, we have a very weak concept of evidence.

The weakness assumption is also implicit in the "satisfaction" definitions (8) and (9). Let e be that I have drawn one red ball from an urn containing 1 million balls. Let h be that all of the balls in this urn containing 1 million balls are red. Then e "directly confirms" h, since e deductively entails the development of h for the class of individuals mentioned in e. So the fact that one ball is red is evidence that all of them are. Glymour's bootstrap definition (9) can also be shown to make very weak demands on evidence. (See Achinstein 1983: 358–61.)

Of the definitions given earlier the ones providing the strongest concept are the error-statistical definition (4) and the Whewellian definition (6). The former requires that a hypothesis pass a severe test, while the latter requires "prediction," "consilience," and "coherence" in addition to the basic h-d idea. Even so, those definitions yield concepts that some regard as insufficiently strong.

First, with reference to Whewell, as John Stuart Mill (1872) noted in his important mid-nineteenth-century debate with Whewell, there may well be several incompatible theories which entail the data, all of which satisfy "prediction," "consilience," and "coherence" to an equal extent. If so, then e becomes Whewellian h-d evidence that each of these theories is true. Mill argued that this concept allows too much, and that the requirement needs to be strengthened by the addition of an inductive condition that, where the hypothesis is a general law, the evidence include reports of a sufficient number of observed instances of that law.

Second, the error-statistical definition permits e to be evidence that h, indeed very strong evidence, even when the epistemic probability of h, given e, is vanishingly small. Some believe that this makes the error-statistical account too weak. (See Howson 1997 and Achinstein 2001: 134–40 for examples and arguments, and Mayo 2005 for a defense of her position against these.)

The second assumption often made about evidence is this:

The *a priori* assumption

The evidential relationship is *a priori*, not empirical. Whether *e*, if true, is
evidence that *h* is a matter to be determined completely by *a priori* calculation, not empirical investigation.

This assumption is satisfied by a number of the previous definitions. For Carnap,
whether probability statements of the form $P(h/e) = r$ are true is a matter of *a priori*
calculation. Therefore so is whether *e* increases *h*'s probability and whether *h*'s
probability on *e* is high. Therefore, whether *e*, if true, is evidence that *h*, on Carnap's
definitions (1) and (2) is *a priori* decidable. Similarly, since whether *h* and *b* together,
but not *b* alone, entail *e* is *a priori* decidable, the simple h-d definition (5) yields a
concept of evidence satisfying the *a priori* assumption. So do the "satisfaction" definitions (8) and (9) given by Hempel and Glymour, respectively.

The exceptions are the subjective Bayesian interpretation of definition (1), the
error-statistical definition (4), and Whewell's h-d version (6). For the subjective
Bayesian, as well as for Whewell, whether *e* is evidence that *h*, given *b*, is relativized to
a particular person or group and time. For the subjective Bayesian it depends on that
person's degree of belief in *h* on *e* at the time in question, which is an empirical issue,
not an *a priori* one. For Whewell it depends on an empirical fact about when *h* was
formulated and why. But notice that these are empirical issues not about the alleged
facts reported in *h* and *e*, but about someone's *beliefs* about those facts (in the case
of the subjective Bayesian) or (in the case of Whewell) about when and why those
alleged facts were cited. For the error-statistical definition (4), whether $P(e(T)/h)$ is
higher than $P(e(T)/-h)$ can be an empirical matter about the nature of the test *T*
and about the probabilities in question – matters not resolvable simply by *a priori*
calculation.

Rejection of these assumptions

Previous examples used to show that certain standard definitions of evidence satisfy
the weakness assumption may also be employed as a basis for rejecting this very
assumption along with the definitions that satisfy it. The fact that I bought 1 ticket
out of 1 million in a fair lottery is not evidence that I will win, despite the fact that
the latter's probability is increased. The fact that Michael Jordan eats Wheaties is not
evidence that he will not become pregnant, despite the fact that the probability of the
latter, given the former, is high. The fact that the sun exists is not evidence that all
the planets revolve around the sun in elliptical orbits, despite the fact that the latter
entails the former.

What is missing here? Why do scientists want evidence? What does it give them? A
plausible answer is that scientists want evidence because it gives them a good reason to
believe a hypothesis. And in none of the examples previously cited does the putative
evidence provide a good reason for believing the hypothesis. Accordingly, we might
drop the weakness assumption and replace it with a much stronger one:

Good-reason-to-believe assumption: e is evidence that h, given b, only if, given b, e provides a good reason to believe h.

This assumption is satisfied by potential and veridical evidence as characterized in the opening section. For the subjective concept of X's evidence that h, it would be required that person X believe that e provides a good reason to believe h. For ES-evidence it would be required that e be a good reason to believe h for anyone in the epistemic situation in question. The important issue, then, is whether and how a definition of evidence can be formulated so as to satisfy this new assumption.

Before attempting this, let us turn to the second of the previous assumptions, the *a priori* assumption that whether e if true is evidence that h is completely *a priori*. It might be claimed that when scientists attempt to establish or refute a claim of the form "e is evidence that h, given b" they always do so solely by *a priori* calculation. But this is clearly false. When Thomson attempted to refute Hertz's evidential claim that the null-results of Hertz's cathode-ray experiments are evidence that cathode rays are electrically neutral, Thomson gave an empirical argument, not an *a priori* one. He appealed to the screening-off effect produced by not sufficiently evacuating the tube, and to the results of his own experiments. And when Thomson defended the claim that his results were evidence that cathode rays are electrically charged he appealed to the fact that the air in his cathode tube was sufficiently evacuated to prevent the screening-off effect.

Accordingly, let us replace the *a priori* assumption with the following:

Empirical assumption: For at least some e, b, and h, whether e, if true, is evidence that h, given b, is an empirical issue. It can be determined, at least in part, by empirical investigation of facts pertaining to e, h, and b.

Final definitions

We seek a definition of evidence that satisfies the *good-reason-to-believe* and the *empirical* assumptions just formulated. Let's start with the former.

Two claims will be made. First, if e is a good reason to believe h, then the probability of h, given e, must be sufficiently high. The second claim is that if e is a good reason to believe h then e cannot be a good reason to believe the negation of h. The fact that I am tossing a fair coin cannot be a good reason to believe it will land heads and also a good reason to believe it won't. In such a case there is no reason to believe either, but rather to suspend belief.

From these two claims it can be shown to follow that

e is a good reason to believe h only if the probability of h, given e, is greater than ½. (10)

Accordingly, Carnap's earlier definition (2) provides a necessary condition for evidence, as long as k, the threshold for high probability, is ½. However, recalling the

Michael Jordan Wheaties example, high probability is not a sufficient condition. The probability of h on e may be greater than ½ even though e has nothing to do with h; it does not provide a good reason to believe h.

How can the good-reason assumption be satisfied? It can if we adopt the following principle, which introduces the idea of the probability of an explanatory connection between e and h:

> If, given e and b, the probability is greater than ½ that there is an explanatory connection between h and e, then, given b, e is a good reason to believe h.   (11)

There is an explanatory connection between h and e if and only if h correctly explains why e is true, or if e correctly explains why h is true, or if some hypothesis correctly explains both why e is true and why h is true. In the Michael Jordan example, given e – that Michael Jordan eats Wheaties – and given the standard background information b, the probability is very low that there is an explanatory connection between the fact that e is true and the hypothesis h that he will not become pregnant.

Suppose we make the explanatory connection requirement in (11) a requirement for evidence, so that

> e is evidence that h, given b, only if $P(E(h,e)/e\&b) > $ ½,   (12)

where $E(h,e)$ means that there is an explanatory connection between h and e. From (11) and (12) together it will follow that

> If e is evidence that h, given b, then, given b, e is a good reason to believe h (thus satisfying the good-reason-to-believe requirement for evidence).   (13)

Moreover, since it can be shown mathematically that

> $P(E(h,e)/e\&b) = P(h/e\&b) \times P(E(h,e)/h\&e\&b),$

it follows that if the quantity on the left is greater than ½, then each of the quantities on the right is also greater than ½. Therefore, from (10) we get

> e is evidence that h, given b, only if $P(h/e\&b) > $ ½.   (14)

So if e is evidence that h, given b, then (10) above is satisfied.

Two other conditions for evidence will be imposed: that e and b be true (false information can't provide evidence), and that e not entail h (entailment would be *proof* not evidence). Putting this together we get the definition

> e is evidence that h, given b, if and only if (a) $P(E(h,e)/e\&b) > $ ½; (b) e and b are true; (c) e does not entail h.   (15)

This can be used to define each of the four concepts of evidence distinguished in the opening section. If we employ an "objective epistemic" notion of probability that measures degrees of reasonableness of belief but is not relativized to any particular epistemic situation (see Achinstein 2001), then (15) yields a definition of *potential evidence*. Adding the further condition that *h* is true and that there is an explanatory connection between *h* and *e*, we generate a definition of *veridical evidence*. To obtain *subjective evidence*, we can say that *e* is X's subjective evidence that *h* if X believes that *e* is veridical evidence that *h*, and X's reason for believing that *h* is true is that *e* is true. And we obtain a concept of ES-*evidence* by saying that *e* is ES-evidence that *h* (with respect to an epistemic situation) if and only if *e* is true and anyone in that epistemic situation is justified in believing that *e* is veridical evidence that *h*.

Definition (15) satisfies not only the assumption that (potential) evidence provides a good reason for belief, but also the assumption that the evidential relationship can be an empirical one. The definition requires that *e* and *b* be true, which is an empirical matter. More important is the fact that objective epistemic probability of the kind in condition (a) can be empirical. The claim that the probability is high that there is an explanatory connection between Hertz's null results and the hypothesis that cathode rays are neutral was rejected by Thomson on empirical grounds, not *a priori* ones.

Thomson's experimental results *e* (electrical deflection in his experiments) constitute (potential) evidence that *h* (cathode rays carry electrical charge). The three conditions in definition (15) are all satisfied. Moreover, since *h* is true, and since there is an explanatory connection between *h* and *e* (cathode rays are deflected by an electric field because they carry an electric charge), Thomson provided veridical evidence for his hypothesis.

In seeking evidence for a hypothesis *h*, if a scientist is attempting to provide a good reason to believe *h*, where this is a strong sense of "good reason" (requiring the truth of *h*) and where the goodness of the reason does not vary from one epistemic situation to another, then what the scientist seeks is veridical evidence. Usually when a scientist claims that some experimental result is evidence that a hypothesis is true, he can be understood as making a claim using this concept. In evaluating such a claim, if *we* know or believe there is some flaw in the experiment, or if we have information not available to the scientist that casts doubt upon his hypothesis or refutes it, we can describe his experimental result using one or more of the other three concepts of evidence, depending on the situation. We might say that it is potential but not veridical evidence, or that it is evidence for anyone in his epistemic situation, or just that, in the subjective sense, it is his evidence.

See also Bayesianism; Confirmation; Explanation; Probability; Scientific method.

References

Achinstein, Peter (1983) *The Nature of Explanation*, New York: Oxford University Press.
—— (2001) *The Book of Evidence*, New York: Oxford University Press.
—— (ed.) (2005) *Scientific Evidence*, Baltimore, MD: Johns Hopkins University Press.

Carnap, Rudolf (1962) *Logical Foundations of Probability*, Chicago: University of Chicago Press.

Glymour, Clark (1980) *Theory and Evidence*, Princeton, NJ: Princeton University Press.

Hempel, Carl G. (1945) "Studies in the Logic of Confirmation," *Mind* 54: 1–26, 97–121; reprinted in Hempel, *Aspects of Scientific Explanation*, New York: Free Press, 1965, pp. 3–46.

Hertz, Heinrich (1896) *Miscellaneous Papers*, London: Macmillan.

Howson, Colin (1997) "A Logic of Induction," *Philosophy of Science* 64: 268–90.

Howson, Colin and Peter Urbach (2006) *Scientific Reasoning*, 3rd edn, La Salle, IL: Open Court.

Mayo, Deborah (1996) *Error and the Growth of Experimental Knowledge*, Chicago: University of Chicago Press.

—— (2005) "Evidence as Passing Severe Tests: Highly Probable versus Highly Probed Hypotheses," in Achinstein (2005), pp. 95–127.

Mill, John Stuart (1872) *A System of Logic: Inductive and Ratiocinative*, 8th edn, London: Longmans.

Thomson, J. J. (1897) "Cathode Rays," *Philosophical Magazine* 44: 293–316.

Whewell, William (1840) *The Philosophy of the Inductive Sciences*, London: John Parker; reprinted London: Routledge–Thoemmes Press, 1996.

Further reading

For a more extensive discussion of the four concepts of evidence in the opening section and the definitions of evidence in the final section, see Achinstein (2001); critical discussions and scientific applications of this material by various authors can be found in Achinstein (2005). Cathode ray experiments of Hertz and of Thomson are described in: Hertz (1896) and Thomson (1897), as well as in Achinstein (2001) and in Theodore Arabatzis, *Representing Electrons: A Biographical Approach to Theoretical Entities* (Chicago: University of Chicago Press, 2006). The five standard theories of evidence discussed in this chapter are best defended by their proponents listed in the References. The reader might also consult Sherrilyn Roush, *Tracking Truth: Knowledge, Evidence and Science* (Oxford: Oxford University Press, 2005), which defends an objective Bayesian view against objections given in Achinstein (2001); and Laura J. Snyder, *Reforming Philosophy* (Chicago: University of Chicago Press, 2006), in which the views of Whewell and Mill are extensively discussed.

32
FUNCTION
D. M. Walsh

It is common practice among biologists to attribute functions to biological traits. Examples abound: the function the vertebrate kidney is to purify the blood; the function of an image-forming eye is vision. Yet the concept of *biological* function is far from unproblematic. The explanatory role and the ontological commitments of functions have been the source of intense debate over the last thirty years or more. The issue is that, as intuitively appealing, as evidently instructive, as function ascriptions are they appear to deploy a mode of thinking that, by all accounts, has been thoroughly discredited since the Scientific Revolution. Function ascriptions, taken at face value, are *teleological*. A function ascription answers the question "What is it *for?*" where the answer to the question cites some effect that the trait ought to have for the good of the organism of which it is a part. Moreover, in a functional explanation, the appeal to "what a trait is for" is called on to explain the presence of the entity functionally characterized. The most vivid analogy for the role of functions in biology comes from the functions of artifacts. Artifact function is unreservedly teleological. The function of an artifact is determined by the intentions of the designer (or user).

Much of the recent philosophical literature on function addresses this tension between the presumed explanatory role of function ascriptions, on the one hand, and their naturalistic credentials, on the other. Two general strategies for naturalizing function emerge from the recent debates. The first, by far the more common – I call it *reductive non-teleological* – attempts to recast the concept of function in a way that eliminates the apparent commitment to unreduced natural teleology. The second strategy – I call it *non-reductive teleological* – accepts at face value the teleological implications of function ascriptions and functional explanations. It attempts to demonstrate, nevertheless, that genuine teleological functions are naturalistically acceptable.

Reductive non-teleological function

There are two broad categories of reductive non-teleological approaches to the analysis of biological functions. One attempts to preserve as much as possible of the pre-theoretic conception of function explanations. It offers an *ersatz*, naturalized teleology that emulates genuine teleological explanations, while avoiding the latter's ontological commitments. On this view, to cite a biological trait's function really is to explain its presence. Furthermore, the function of a trait token entails a commitment concerning what that trait token *ought* to do. The other strand in the reductive tradition argues that to suppose that functional explanation in biology genuinely resembles teleological explanation is simply a misapprehension.

Ersatz teleological function

Among those reductive approaches that seek to emulate genuine teleological explanation, the most influential originates with Wright (1973). A central insight of Wright's analysis, and those that follow it, is that to ascribe a function to a trait, artifact, entity, is to cite some effect it has, which effect explains its presence. Wright claims that the statement "*x* is for *y*" is interchangeable with "*x* is there because it does *y*." More specifically, according to Wright (1973), the function of *x* is *z* means:

1 *x* is there because it does *z*; and
2 *z* is a consequence (or result) of *x*'s being there.

Wright's account is strictly neutral between non-reductive teleological and reductive non-teleological approaches. In the case of artifact functions, for example, *z* may meet conditions 1 and 2 as a consequence of a designer's intentions. By the same token, Wright's schema is satisfied by a biological trait that has undergone natural selection. If a trait *x* has been selected for its capacity to do *z*, then not only, typically, does it do *z*, but it is in the population because it does *z*. Thus Wright offers a unified account of function ascription and functional explanation that applies indifferently to artifacts and to organisms.

Despite its avowed ecumenism, Wright's etiological analysis of function has provided a significant impetus to a family of explicitly reductionist approaches to biological function (Neander 1991), according to which the function of a trait is the effect it has been selected for in the past. Natural selection is a strictly causal, mechanical process. So this *selected effects* variant on the Wright account of function concedes no irreducible role to biological teleology.

Adherents of the selected effects account of biological function claim that it captures a set of crucial distinctions implied by function ascriptions. There is a distinction between those effects of a trait that constitute its function and those that are mere accidents. Famously, the heart both pumps blood and produces electrical pulses. Only the former of these effects is its function; the other is a mere accident. Similarly, a trait may have a function even when it is incapable of producing the effect which constitutes its function. A heart that cannot pump blood still has the function of doing so. When a trait cannot perform its function in propitious conditions, it is malfunctioning. Tradition has it that the *function–malfunction* and *function–accident* distinctions are normative. They depend on there being some effect that a trait *ought* to have. The selected effects approach evidently underwrites those distinctions without invoking any sort of non-natural norms. If the function of a trait is what it has been selected to do, then that is the effect which explains its presence. Other effects are mere accidents. A trait that fails to have the selected effect, in propitious conditions, is malfunctioning.

The selected effects account of function has had an enormous influence on the philosophy of biology and the philosophy of mind (Millikan 1984). While the fecundity of the selected effects approach is beyond doubt, its correctness has been repeatedly challenged. There are two lines of objection. The first is that the selected effects account fails accurately to capture the purposes to which function ascriptions are applied in biology. The second, related, complaint is that it fails accurately to capture the extension of the *function* concept in evolutionary biology.

Amundson and Lauder (1994) argue that the selected effects account distorts the practices of working biologists. They claim that not only is it extremely difficult to determine just what a trait has been selected for in the past, but that doing so is seldom the motivation for providing a function ascription. Biologists working in the disciplines of functional anatomy, physiology, immunology, and ethology, for instance, investigate the *current* causal roles of an organism's traits without presuming that those roles have been forged by natural selection in the past. All this may be so, but it does not follow from the fact that biologists are not specifically concerned to reconstruct the history of selection that the interesting effects they designate as "functions" are not the result of natural selection in the past. Biologists typically ascribe functions to traits that they take to be of particular significance to the survival and reproduction of organisms. These may well be *effects* that have been promoted by natural selection in the past.

A more telling line of criticism is that the selected effects account fails accurately to capture the extension of the function concept as it is deployed by biologists. One reason to believe this is that biologists are often willing to apply the concept of function to an effect that is novel, yet evolutionarily significant: at least some function ascriptions are overtly not historical (Bock and von Wahlert 1965; Bigelow and Pargetter 1987; Walsh 1996). Moreover, detractors claim, the selected effects approach misidentifies the explanatory role of function in biology. Those functions that are evolutionarily significant identify some typical effect that accounts for a trait's propensity to persist within a population, whether that propensity be an occurrent or historical one (Walsh 1996). Current functions and historical functions play the same explanatory role. The selected effects account accords that role only to historical functions.

A further weakness of the selected effects approach becomes apparent when we note that a trait type can have such an explanatorily significant disposition even when that disposition has not been selected for (Buller 1998). Suppose an established trait begins to make a novel yet significant contribution to organisms' well-being, due perhaps to a change in the environment. The trait will persist into the future by dint of its capacity to produce the new effect; it will have a new function. All the same, there will be no selection for the new function, as *ex hypothesi*, the population does not vary with respect to the trait. Furthermore, a trait may have an evolutionary function even if it is being selected *against*. Suppose that in a population two alternate alleles, or traits, x and y, exist, each of which contributes to an organism's well-being by doing z, yet because of the marginally greater efficiency of y, x is being slowly displaced in the population. Trait *x* will usually be thought by biologists to have the same function as *y*, namely to perform *z*, even though it has been selected *against*. The selected effects approach, then, places two quite stringent restrictions on the ascription of biological functions: it restricts function to historical function; and it ties functions to the effects of selection *for*. The practices of working biologists suggest that neither of these strictures is appropriate.

Contribution to fitness

The uses of the function concept in biology motivate a range of alternatives to the etiological/selected effects approach. Nagel (1961) proposes that the function of a trait is to be identified with the way it contributes to the well-being of the organism of which it is a part. This suggestion has been criticized on the grounds that it introduces an unreduced, teleological, or evaluative concept – *well-being* – into the definition of function. Instead, Bigelow and Pargetter (1993) propose that a function is a particular kind of occurrent disposition. Amundson and Lauder (1994) suggest that the function of a biological trait is some particular kind of causal role. These accounts have been criticized for their lack of specificity: *which* dispositions? *which* causal roles? Walsh (1996) argues that the sorts of evolutionary explanations to which biologists apply the concept of function suggest that the function of a trait, in a particular context, is the typical contribution that the trait type makes to organismal *fitness*. Fitness is the propensity of an organism to survive and reproduce. There is also a sense in which fitness is a measure of an organism's *well-being*, but it does not involve biological function ascriptions in any irreducible teleological commitment. The fitness of an organism is simply a particularly salient disposition.

If function is contribution to fitness, there is little reason to suppose that function ascriptions should carry normative import. To be sure, there are significant function–accident and function–malfunction distinctions to be made, and these can be captured by the contribution to fitness approach, but there is little reason to believe that function ascriptions are genuinely normative. The evolutionarily significant effects of a trait type are its functions. Other effects a trait might have that do not contribute significantly to fitness are mere accidents. If a token, *t*, of type *T* cannot contribute to fitness in the way that other tokens of *T* do, *t*'s bearer suffers a fitness decrement on that account: *t* is malfunctioning (Walsh 1996). The function–malfunction and function–accident distinctions are wholly captured by the contribution to fitness account, but their usage in evolutionary biology suggests that these distinctions are not normative.

The question remains of how much the contribution to fitness account preserves of the pre-theoretic intuitions about functional explanation that motivate the reductive *ersatz* teleological approach. The answer, it seems, is "Not much." The ascription of a function, on this account, does not explain the presence of a trait token in an organism. Evolutionary function ascriptions explain merely the persistence of a trait type in a population. There seems to be nothing resembling teleology in these sorts of explanations. Nor is there any normative commitment: evolutionary function ascriptions entail nothing about what a trait *ought* to do in propitious conditions.

Causal role function

Robert Cummins (1975) has argued strenuously that the central motivation behind ersatz teleological approaches to function, that of preserving as much as possible of the pre-theoretic notion of function, has seriously misled most philosophical analyses of function. Function ascriptions, according to Cummins, do not explain the presence of a trait, much less identify what a trait token ought to do. A function ascription merely identifies the causal contribution of part of a system (e.g., a trait token) to the characteristic activities of the system of which it is a part. Cummins's influential account of functional analysis goes as follows: "the function of x in s is to φ . . . relative to an analytic account A of s's capacity to ψ just in case x is capable of φ-ing in s and A appropriately and adequately accounts for s's capacity to ψ by, in part, appealing to the capacity of x to φ in s" (*ibid.*: 64). More simply, the function of some part of a system, with respect to some analysis, is the causal role it plays in producing some activity (of interest) of the system as a whole. This is often dubbed the "causal role" account of function.

One of the presumed advantages of the causal role approach is that it unifies the practice of ascribing functions across a wide range of scientific and engineering contexts. We speak of the function of nitrogen-fixing bacteria in the energy flow of an ecosystem, the function of ancestor worship in traditional societies, the function of interest-rate manipulation in the control of economic growth, the function of a carburetor in an internal combustion engine, the function of the impedance-matching ear in vertebrates. In all these contexts, function is simply some interesting causal contribution to the activity of the system as a whole.

The causal role approach has been roundly criticized for its evident incapacity to capture the salient features of the pre-theoretic notion of function and the purpose of function ascription. (See, e.g., Millikan 1989; Neander 1991.) There are two, related, lines of attack, one based on the putative specificity of function, the other based on the presumed normativity of function.

Causal role functions, it is said, are insufficiently specific. Given enough imagination, we could think of a system with respect to which *any* effect of anything constitutes a causal role function. For any entity, there are any number of systems of which it is a part, and any number of analyses of interest such that, with respect to that system, and that analysis, the entity has an effect that constitutes a function. In short, any effect that an entity might have constitutes a function. But the whole motivation behind applying the concept of function in biology (and elsewhere) is to differentiate those effects of a part of a system that have genuine explanatory importance from those that have only trivial or minor importance.

Similar considerations support the arguments from the so-called "normative" distinctions. Causal role function cannot, it is said, discriminate function from accident or function from malfunction. The human heart circulates blood. This is certainly an effect of most hearts. But hearts have other effects too. They produce electrical spikes due to muscle contractions. Intuitively, the former effect is a function and the latter is a mere accident. The causal role account, however, is committed to ascribing to hearts the function of producing electrical impulses. In the system comprising a heart and an ECG machine, this is precisely the causal contribution that the heart makes to the overall working of the system. Causal role function privileges no particular effect. So, the Cummins approach cannot distinguish genuine functions from accidents.

A comparable complaint is lodged on behalf of the function–malfunction distinction. A malfunction, as we have seen, occurs when, under propitious conditions, a part of a system fails to do what it is its function to do. If anything a part of a system (trait) does is a function, and nothing it does not do isn't, then a part of a system cannot malfunction.

There are obvious, and compelling, responses to be made on behalf of the causal role approach. The claim that causal role function ascriptions are radically indiscriminate misrepresents a crucial feature of that approach. The ascription of function is set against the context of an analysis of some activity of the system *of interest*, *with respect to* some analysis or other. Function ascriptions are thus relativized to a particular system and analysis of interest. It will seldom be the case that *with respect to* a particular analysis, a part of a system will have multifarious functions. The specificity argument is misplaced.

Attention to the specifics of the causal role approach also helps deflect the normativity charge. The Cummins approach explicitly denies that function ascriptions have normative import, and on good grounds. So the claim that causal role function fails to capture the normative import of function ascriptions begs the question. Nevertheless, as we have seen, there is a real difference between an effect that is a function and one that is an accident. They have different explanatory roles. In defense of causal role function, it should be noted that explanation has a pragmatic dimension, and the pragmatic element in the Cummins definition of functional analysis is designed to exploit it. We engage in functional analysis in order to explain a particular activity of *interest*. With respect to an analysis of the heart's contribution to human well-being, the most explanatorily significant effect is its capacity to pump blood. This is its function with respect to that particular analysis. The heart's capacity to make a pulse or to emit electrical discharges is of little explanatory interest with respect to that particular analysis; those effects are accidents. The function–accident distinction, on this way of thinking, is a pragmatic one, but an important one nonetheless. Similarly, there is available a pragmatic analogue of the function–malfunction distinction. If most hearts pump blood, and if doing so constitutes a significant contribution to survival and reproduction, there is an explanatorily relevant distinction between typical hearts and those atypical hearts that do not have this effect. This is simply the function–malfunction distinction (in extension).

The causal role approach to function is strongly deflationary, perhaps too much so. It appears not to support one of the most significant features of function ascription in evolutionary biology: function explains the persistence of a trait type in a population. But this use of function ascriptions can be accommodated by the causal role approach. After all, evolutionary function, as construed by the contribution to fitness theory, is a special case of causal role function. An evolutionary function, according to the contribution to fitness approach, is a causal role function with respect to an analysis in which the system of interest is the entire organism and the activity of interest is survival and reproduction (Walsh and Ariew 1996). Given that, an evolutionary function is an evolutionarily significant contribution to fitness for a trait type. One discovers the evolutionary function of a trait by performing a Cummins-style functional analysis. Evolutionary function is a special instance of Cummins's function.

Non-reductive teleological function

The non-reductive teleological approach to evolutionary function is, nowadays, a minority position. In general, on this family of views, the function of a trait token is constituted by its contribution to some *goal* of the organism. The potential advantage of a genuinely teleological theory of function is that it offers the prospect of preserving the pre-theoretical intuitions about the explanatory role. Natural function could explain the presence of traits in the way that design function explains the presence of artifacts. Its unpopularity stems from its avowed commitment to natural teleology. Though it is an unpopular position, it does have adherents. Thomas Nagel (1961, 1977) has advocated it and it has recently been comprehensively defended by Boorse (2002). For those authors, function is contribution to survival and reproduction (as in the fitness accounts of function). Survival and reproduction, furthermore, are goals.

Mere contribution to a goal is not sufficient to constitute a genuinely teleological function. It must also be that contributing to the goal explains the nature and the presence of those parts that contribute to the attainment of the goal.

The central problem for the non-reductive teleological conception of function concerns its presumption that *goals explain*. One set of objections arises from the claim that the concept of a goal is essentially evaluative. For a state of affairs to be a goal it must be *good* and the goodness of the goal must figure in the explanation of why the trait in question is present (Bedau 1992). But goodness is not a natural property. Worse still, if it is the function of a trait to bring about its goals, and the presence of the trait in question precedes the attainment of the goal, and goals explain the presence of the trait, then teleological function explanations must appeal to *unactualized* goals.

There are plausible responses available to the non-reductive teleology approach, and these exploit insights from the cybernetics research of the 1940s–60s and have been supplemented recently by research into complex adaptive, self-organizing systems (Kauffman 1995). The basic concept in cybernetics and complex adaptive systems research is that of a goal-directed or adaptive system. Such systems are capable of attaining and maintaining robustly persistent states by the implementation of complex, adaptive, compensatory changes (Sommerhof 1950). When systems exhibit this goal-directed behavior, the causal roles of the component parts are regulated by the overall goal-seeking capacity of the system. Here the goal-directedness of a system explains the causal roles of the system's parts. When a goal-directed system, like an organism, builds itself, it may well be that the pursuit of the developmental goals explains the presence of the system's parts.

This conception of how goal-directedness explains the presence and the nature of the traits of an organism (or the components of a system) seems to be at once both wholly natural and genuinely teleological. It is natural inasmuch as it makes no appeal in its explanations to unactualized states of affairs. Nor does it require that the concept of a goal is an irreducibly normative or evaluative one. It is teleological in that it explains the presence of a token trait by appeal to the capacity of the organism (or system) to attain its goals. The appeal to an organism's (or system's) goals does not tell us what a trait (or part) ought to do, in any irreducibly normative sense of "ought". It simply tells us what a trait (or part of a system) ought to do if it is to contribute to the attainment of the goals. A function ascription explains the presence of a trait (or a part of a system) by demonstrating that it is, in Aristotle's terms, "hypothetically necessary" for the attainment of the goal. The prevalent presumption that genuine teleological function is normative needs to be reappraised.

The nature of goal-directed, adaptive complex systems is becoming increasingly important in understanding the evolutionary importance of organismal development. The development of organisms exhibits an enormous amount of goal-directed, adaptive plasticity (West-Eberhard 2003). Each part of a developing organismal system has the capacity to produce a wide array of phenotypes. The particular phenotype that each part produces on an occasion is largely the result of adaptive regulation by the organism as a whole. The organism is capable of regulating the activities of its component parts during development, in order to produce traits that subserve and maintain the viability of the organism. It appears, then, that to explain the development of a particular organismal phenotype requires us to specify its contribution to the goals of survival and reproduction and *further* to specify how the organism's pursuit of those goals underwrites the occurrence of the trait in question. This is a genuine, unreduced, teleological explanation. As evolutionary developmental biology gains currency, it may demonstrate that evolutionary explanation requires a commitment to a category of unreduced teleological functions after all.

See also Biology; Explanation; Reduction.

References

Amundson, Ron and Lauder, George (1994) "Function Without Purpose: The Uses of Causal Role Function in Evolutionary Biology," *Biology and Philosophy* 9: 443–69.

Bedau, M. (1992) "Where's the Good in Teleology?" *Philosophy and Phenomenological Research* 52: 781–805.

Bigelow, J and Pargetter, R. (1987) "Functions," *Journal of Philosophy* 86: 181–96.

Bock, W. and von Wahlert, G. (1965) "Adaptation and the Form–Function Complex," *Evolution* 19: 269–99.

Boorse, C. (2002) "A Rebuttal on Functions," in A. Ariew, R. Cummins, and M. Perlman (eds) *Functions: New Essays in the Philosophy of Psychology and Biology*, Oxford: Oxford University Press, pp. 63–112.

Buller, D. (1998) "Etiological Theories of Function: A Geographical Theory," *Biology and Philosophy* 13: 505–27.

Cummins, R. (1975) "Functional Analysis," *Journal of Philosophy* 72: 741–65.

Kauffman, S. (1995) *At Home in the Universe*, Oxford: Oxford University Press.

Millikan, R. G. (1984) *Language, Thought, and Other Biological Processes*, Cambridge, MA: MIT Press.

—— (1989) "In Defense of Proper Functions," *Philosophy of Science* 56: 288–302.

Nagel, E. (1961) *The Structure of Science: Problems in the Logic of Scientific Explanation*, New York: Harcourt, Brace, & World.

—— (1977) "Teleology Revisited," *Journal of Philosophy* 84: 261–301.

Neander, K. (1991) "Functions as Selected Effects," *Philosophy of Science* 56: 288–302.

Sommerhof, G. (1950) *Analytical Biology*, Oxford: Oxford University Press.

Walsh, D. M. (1996) "Fitness and Function," *British Journal for the Philosophy of Science* 47: 553–74.

Walsh, D. M. and Ariew, A. (1996) "A Taxonomy of Functions," *Canadian Journal of Philosophy* 126: 493–514.

West-Eberhard, M. J. (2003) *Developmental Plasticity and Phenotypic Evolution*, Cambridge: Cambridge University Press.

Wright, L. (1973) "Functions," *Philosophical Review* 82: 139–68.

Further reading

Most of the major recent papers on biological function can be found reprinted in one (or both) of two compendia: C. Allen, M. Bekoff, and G. Lauder (eds) *Nature's Purposes: Analyses of Function and Design in Biology* (Cambridge, MA: MIT Press, 1998) is a comprehensive collection of influential papers; D. Buller (ed.) *Function, Selection, and Design* (Albany: State University of New York Press, 1999) is a judicious selection of papers with a very useful Introduction by the editor. A series of original papers on function can be found in A. Ariew, R. Cummins, and M. Perlman (eds) *Functions: New Essays in the Philosophy of Psychology and Biology* (Oxford: Oxford University Press, 2002). Lowell Nissen's *Teleological Language in the Life Sciences* (New York: Rowman & Littlefield, 1997) is a valuable survey of theories of function. Peter McLaughlin's *What Functions Explain* (Cambridge: Cambridge University Press, 2001) and Tim Lewens's *Organisms and Artifacts* (Cambridge, MA: MIT Press, 2005) offer distinctive and authoritative discussions of the issues touched on in this essay.

33
IDEALIZATION

James Ladyman

Introduction

Idealization is ubiquitous in science, being a feature of both the formulation of laws and theories and of their application to the world. There are many examples of the former kind of idealization: Newton's first law (the principle of inertia) refers to what happens to a body that is subject to no external forces, but there are probably no such bodies; the famous ideal gas laws do indeed idealize the behavior of real gases (which violate them in various ways, sometimes significantly); and economics refers to perfectly rational agents. Theory application is largely about idealization. Philosophers of science often focus their attention on scientific theories as expressed by a relatively small set of fundamental axioms, laws, and principles: for example, the laws of Newtonian mechanics plus the principle of the conservation of energy in the case of classical mechanics, or some variant of von Neumann's axioms in the case of quantum mechanics. However, if real science were restricted to making use of such resources, then it would be much less empirically and technologically successful than it is. The reason is that often the systems being studied are not amenable to a complete analytical treatment in the terms of fundamental theories. This may be because of the sheer complexity and size of systems in which scientists are interested; for example, it is not possible to use Newtonian mechanics to describe the individual motions and collisions of particles in a gas because there are so many of them. Another factor is that some mathematical problems cannot be solved exactly, as is the case, for example, with the famous three-body problem of classical mechanics.

Scientific knowledge is at least as much about how to overcome these problems with idealization as it is about fundamental theory. This may mean abstracting the problem by leaving out certain features of the real situation, or approximating the real situation by using values for variables that are close enough for practical purposes, but strictly speaking wrong, and/or using approximating mathematical techniques. So, for example, in physics, large bodies such as planets are often treated as if they are spherically symmetrical; in chemistry, crystals are often treated as if they were free of impurities and deformities; and, in biology, populations of reproducing individuals are often treated as if their fitness is independent of how many of them there are in the population.

Indeed idealization is fundamental to the use of language of any kind. Diverse entities are described as if they are all the same in some respect despite the subtle differences between them, and a single sortal term, for example, "dog," or predicate, for example, "is red," is applied to them. This is successful if we manage to describe the natural world in terms that readily capture the regularities in the behavior of things, and relevant causal and counterfactual facts. There is a long tradition of arguing that the world is split into a natural kinds structure that our language must reflect. In science, the categorization of the world in terms of complex theoretical languages is carefully designed on the basis of existing theories, and so as to facilitate further successful theorizing. Scientists do not usually deal with phenomena, events in the world, *simpliciter*, but with phenomena interpreted by means of theory and organized in stable patterns. Idealization is necessary to render complex real systems tractable by theoretical descriptions, and, as some philosophers have emphasized, the "raw" data of experiments are passed through a "conceptual grinder" (Suppes 1967: 62) to give data models, each specific to a particular experimental technique and correspondingly theory-laden in a specific way. Models of the phenomena may be inferred from such data models (Bogen and Woodward 1988). For example, it is routine to use exact linear, polynomial, or exponential curves to represent scientific data, rather than plotting the actual data points, as long as the latter are within experimental error of the curve. No real system that is measured ever exactly fits the description of the phenomena that become the target of theoretical explanation.

For these reasons theoretical explanations often contradict the description of the phenomena they were designed to cover. Consider Kepler's laws of planetary motion; these described the kinematical properties of the paths of the planets in a heliocentric model of the solar system that fitted the extensive data gathered by Brahe. They were explained by Newton's inverse square law of gravitation; yet the exactly elliptical orbits of Kepler are impossible if the gravitational effects of the planets on the sun and on each other are taken into account in the application of that law.

Mathematical idealization

One of the most ubiquitous forms of idealization in science is the application of mathematics to the world by imposing a precise mathematical formalism on a physical system. For Pierre Duhem, because the theoretical claims of physics are expressed in terms of concepts that are applied only with the help of artificially precise mathematics, the former are quite different from the ordinary truth-valued propositions of everyday life. Hence, he argued that physical concepts are abstract and merely symbolic formulae that describe only imaginary constructions. One perennial example of mathematical idealization concerns the representation of physical quantities as real numbers. The real-number continuum in mathematics has bizarre properties such as having as many points in a unit interval as there are in any other finite interval, no matter how much bigger in extent. Many properties of functions depend on their being defined on such continuous spaces, but if these are used to represent features of the real world it is reasonable to wonder whether a certain amount of falsification follows.

This has become important in recent years as some theoretical physicists have come to think that, although the representation of space–time as a continuous manifold is convenient for applying mathematics to physical problems, it may ultimately mislead us since the fine structure of space–time is discrete.

The use of mathematics in science is nonetheless often appealed to as the main reason to be some kind of realist about the abstract realm of mathematical entities such as functions and sets, geometrical and topological spaces, and abstract algebras. All these and other mathematical structures are apparently indispensable in physics and increasingly so in all other sciences too. It also seems to many, including, famously, the physicist Eugene Wigner (1953), that the effectiveness of mathematics has been surprisingly successful given the weirdness of the mathematical flights of fancy that have come to find application. It is not to be forgotten that the mathematical precision of much of contemporary science is extraordinary compared to what was achievable a few hundred years ago. Galileo famously said that the book of nature is written in the language of mathematics, but others have pointed out that the attempts we have made to copy the book must be regarded as literally false. The above *indispensability argument* for mathematical realism will be undermined if scientific realism cannot be justified. Conversely, if scientific theoretical descriptions of the world ineliminably involve mathematical idealization, and yet mathematical entities and properties are not correctly thought of as real, then this might give grounds for rejecting scientific realism. (The final section briefly returns to these issues.)

One particularly productive form of reasoning in science depends on idealizing physical structures so that they are treated as obeying exact symmetries. For example, someone calculating how many tiles will be needed to cover a certain area assumes the tiles to be exactly symmetrical; but, of course, there are imperfections in any production process and each tile is distorted in numerous ways compared to a geometrical object such as a square. Similarly, Galileo provided a dynamics that made the hypothesis of a heliocentrism intelligible. It depends on treating physical systems that are moving more or less uniformly as if they are moving exactly uniformly, and then reasoning about their behavior on the assumption that they obey the symmetries now known as the "Galilean group." For example, the behavior of a system that is at rest with respect to the surface of the earth is idealized and treated as an inertial system, even though the earth is in fact rotating. This is acceptable only when the relative distances in the model are small compared to the diameter of the earth, so that the earth is effectively flat from the point of view of the system. The search for symmetries was fundamental to the development of the various quantum field theories united in the *standard model* of particle physics.

Idealization and representation: models and theories

Idealization seems to give approximate truth. Many thought-experiments are based on idealized symmetry reasoning, yet they are essentially falsifying in nature. It is not clear what distinguishes legitimate idealizations from outright falsehoods. For example, a perfectly reversible (or maximally efficient) Carnot engine is impossible to build in practice, and yet is considered a respectable part of the subject matter of thermodynamics. On the other hand, a perpetual-motion machine of the second kind, the sole effect of which is the complete conversion of heat into work, is regarded as fundamentally impossible. What is the difference between an impossibility that can be considered possible in ideal circumstances and an impossibility that remains so no matter how idealized the scenario we envisage? A possible answer to this question is that a perpetual-motion machine of the second kind is incompatible with the laws of nature (in particular the *second law of thermodynamics*), whereas a perfect Carnot engine is compatible with the laws of nature. This does not get us very far, however, since the laws themselves involve idealizations. Other examples further complicate matters. In thermodynamical modeling it is common to make use of devices such as frictionless pistons, yet that there are no such real pistons is surely a law-like rather than an accidental fact.

Mathematical logic, developed in the early twentieth century, has ever since been used by many eminent philosophers of science to represent scientific theories. At one stage, the emphasis was on syntax, and theories were treated as linguistic entities. Confirmation, explanation, and laws, among other important features of science, were all analyzed by formulating theories as sets of axioms using a combination of obser-vation and theoretical languages. This *syntactic* account of scientific representation is rivaled by the *semantic* approach due to Patrick Suppes and others. Suppes emphasizes models rather than sets of sentences. Many of those who developed the semantic approach were concerned to do justice to scientific practice and, in particular, to the application of fundamental theory to real systems by the construction of models. For example, Ronald Giere's *Explaining Science* includes detailed analyses of models of concrete systems such as the simple harmonic oscillator in classical mechanics, which he describes as a "constructed," "abstract" entity having certain features ascribed in the standard physics texts (1988: 6). The construction is situated within a model in which those features are related, these relations being expressed at the syntactic level by the force law $F = -kx$, for example. Such idealized systems in physics provide exemplars for the application of the theory. In the sciences the term "model" usually refers to a description of a specific system or kind of system. So, for example, there are models of the earth's atmosphere that describe it as a large number of cells and seek to predict large-scale phenomena by computing the interaction between those cells; there are models of populations of predators and prey that describe them as if the animals in each species were all identical to each other; and there are models of physical systems like the famous billiard-ball model of a gas. In each case, the laws and principles of theories are applied to a real system only by being applied to a model of it. Clearly, models are usually less general than theories; theories often apply to idealized systems; and models are used to make real systems theoretically tractable. R. I. G. Hughes (1989: 198) provides a formulation of the semantic approach that makes the concept of idealization central: "On the semantic view, theories present a class of mathematical models, within which the behavior of ideal systems can be represented."

A number of different kinds of idealization in science are described by Ernan McMullin (1985). Both Cartwright (1983) and McMullin emphasize the distinction between theories and models. McMullin (1985: 255) argues that Galileo originated the contemporary methods of idealization in science, and that "Galilean idealization can proceed in two very different ways, depending on whether the simplification is worked on the conceptual representation of the object, or on the problem situation itself." The former is *construct* idealization, whereas the latter is *causal* idealization. Examples of the former given by McMullin include the idealization that represented a small part of the earth's surface as flat, or the idealization that weights suspended from a beam hang at exact right-angles to it. Construct idealization is performed within a model and, according to McMullin, divides further into *formal* and *material* idealization. The former is a matter of simplifying factors for mathematical–conceptual tractability, even where those factors are known to be relevant to the situation, as, for example, when the sun is treated as being at rest in a calculation of the orbits of the planets, even though its motion will in fact affect their paths. The latter is a matter of completely leaving out irrelevant factors, for example, the fact that the sun is made of gaseous and not solid matter is not relevant to its gravitational effect on the planets and the model of the solar system simply leaves unspecified the composition of it and the planets. Causal idealization, on the other hand, is the simplifying of the *tangle of causal lines* present in real situations by separating them out, either in an experiment designed to minimize or eliminate the contribution of some causes to the effect (*experimental* idealization) or in the imagining of counterfactual circumstances (*subjunctive* idealization).

Nancy Cartwright (1983) makes much of the distinction between idealization of concrete objects or situations and idealization where the simplifying assumptions involve abstracting so that we are no longer dealing with concrete, but rather with abstract (and fictional), entities. The former she calls "idealization," and characterizes it as the theoretical or experimental manipulation of concrete circumstances to minimize or eliminate certain features. For example, a real surface is idealized to become a perfectly flat and frictionless plane, and a coefficient for friction with a convenient mathematical form can be reintroduced to make the idealized model more accurate. In such cases, the laws arrived at are approximately true, and in the laboratory it is possible to apply them directly, if approximately, to very smooth surfaces. Hence, she argues that the laws arrived at by idealization are still *empirical* or *phenomenological*, and concern *concreta*. The second kind of idealization she calls "abstraction." This often involves eliminating details of the material composition of real systems and, importantly, eliminating interfering causes. The laws that are produced by this kind of idealization are *fundamental* laws.

Newton's first law, as mentioned above, refers to the behavior of bodies which are not acted on by external forces, despite the fact that there are no such bodies. Thermodynamics refers to systems in equilibrium despite the fact that no real system is ever genuinely in equilibrium. In her well-known *How the Laws of Physics Lie* (1983), Cartwright turned traditional philosophy of science on its head by arguing that fundamental laws depend on abstracting from the real causes that operate in the world, and which therefore achieve their generality only by losing their empirical adequacy. They describe not the world but only abstract and general features of theoretical models. Hence, she argues that fundamental theories are so idealized as not even to be candidates for the truth, whereas models with all their messy details are capable of describing the world accurately, but at the expense of universality: "The phenomenological laws are indeed true of the objects in reality – or might be; but the fundamental laws are true only of the objects in the model" (1983: 4).

Cartwright also argues that the fundamental laws, because of their abstract nature, may be explanatory, but they do not describe what happens at all, unless they are interpreted as *ceteris paribus* laws. However, Cartwright maintains that the list of ways in which things might not be equal is potentially infinite and does not admit of explicit characterization. Hence, fundamental laws are linked to the appearances only by phenomenological laws, which are non-explanatory but descriptive, and at the theoretical level scientists construct models that are overtly of a sort that the real things do not fit. In order to relate those models to specific phenomena, they have to carry out a two-stage "theory entry" process (*ibid.*: 132–4), whereby the phenomena are connected to theoretical models through a description that is overtly incorrect. Hence, says Cartwright, the fundamental laws are not even approximately true since relevant causal features have been subtracted and the laws are therefore not about concrete situations. They can be interpreted as *ceteris paribus* laws, but since all other things are never equal, they are not true of any actual, concrete situation. Hence, she denies that any single set of fundamental laws describes the world.

Cartwright says that fundamental laws refer to entities that are abstract and to which we ought not to be ontologically committed, for example, Hilbert spaces, inertial systems, and incompressible fluids. She proposes that fundamental laws be understood as being about causal dispositions, powers, or capacities: the "converse processes of abstraction and concretisation have no content unless a rich ontology of competing capacities and disturbances is presupposed" (1989: 184). She goes on to state that "laws in microphysics are results of extreme abstraction, not merely approximating idealizations, and therefore are best seen as laws about capacities and tendencies" (*ibid.*: 188). Scientists construct theoretical models that real things cannot satisfy, and the metaphysics of capacities explains "why one can extrapolate beyond ideal cases" (186).

This has profound implications for the plausibility of a very influential account of explanation in science, namely the covering-law model of Hempel. According to this account, to explain something is to subsume it under the laws of nature together with a number of initial conditions. In the context of determinism, this means that the *explanandum* must be deduced from a set of premises that includes at least one law of nature. If Cartwright is correct that laws are abstractions from concrete causal structures, and if we assume that scientific explanation needs to specify the causes of things, then it seems as if the task of deducing real-world occurrences from fundamental laws is hopeless, for if the extra premises undo the abstraction of the law then the presence of the law in the explanation will become redundant. If this is so, then perhaps the right account of explanation will not mention fundamental laws at all, in favor of singular causes, and only phenomenological laws will feature in scientific explanations. This would be a radical discovery because most scientists and philosophers of science have thought that one of the great successes of science is the explanation of natural phenomena by the fundamental laws of nature.

Many philosophers agree with Cartwright that there is a fundamental distinction between theories and models, and that the former are so abstract as not to be candidates for the truth but rather are about fictional objects. Nowak (1995), for example, adopts the extreme stance that idealization terms should be taken as referring to entities which exist in other, possible, worlds. In recent philosophy of science it has become common to emphasize models as the locus of scientific knowledge, and to treat theories as tools for model-building rather than as true claims about the deep structure of reality (Morgan and Morrison 1995).

However, this view has several problems. Firstly, it is not true that only *derivations* from fundamental laws involve abstraction as well as approximation. As Cartwright herself claims, "idealization would be useless if abstraction were not already possible" (1989: 188). If idealization presupposes abstraction, and if, as Cartwright thinks, abstraction by its nature is inconsistent with the approximately true representation of concrete reality, then phenomenological laws and models cannot represent concrete reality either.

Secondly, the distinction between theories and models, and that between the abstract and the concrete, are plausibly matters of degree rather than of kind. Indeed Cartwright sometimes talks of the "more or less concrete." If they are indeed only matters of degree then they may not be able to bear the metaphysical weight attached to them. The same equivocation affects examples of the concrete objects that phenomenological laws describe, "concrete objects in concrete situations, such as the simple pendulum, a pair of interacting harmonic oscillators, or two masses separated by a distance" (Cartwright 1993: 262). However, these objects are not conceptually free of abstraction as opposed to idealization. For example, the so-called "concrete" functional law of the simple pendulum holds only when the angle of displacement of the bob is less than 10° (so that $\sin\theta \approx \theta$ approximately). So, concrete objects are not simple pendula if they are oscillating with a greater amplitude. Or the other way round: simple pendula are not concrete objects but abstract pictures of concrete objects under some circumstances. Furthermore, models too often involve idealizations, as when the effects of particular forces, such as those resulting from air resistance, are treated as negligible or when a system is described as internally homogeneous, even though no real systems are exactly so.

Thirdly, Cartwright talks as if phenomena, and thus the laws about them, are concrete, while capacities, and the theoretical laws that describe them, are abstract. Yet even the so-called "phenomenological laws" need *ceteris paribus* clauses. No phenomenological law will ever be exactly descriptive of concrete happenings.

Idealization and scientific realism

The discussion above suggests that idealization occurs at every level of representation, from the *phenomenological* to the *theoretical*, with the consequence that, if Nowak were right, all reference in science would be to entities existing in other, possible, worlds.

A metaphysically more conservative account is suggested by Grobler (1995: 42) who asserts that "idealization consists in specifying in advance the kinds of predicates expected to occur in claims being made in a given context about objects of a given kind, rather than in referring to some fictitious, idealized objects." Thus, for example, describing an electron as a mass-point does not amount to adopting some Platonic object as a substitute; rather the description merely indicates the relative irrelevance of the particle's dimensions in the theoretical context, since we are obviously excluding spatial dimension from the list of predicates characterizing it. Nevertheless, other properties (like mass, spin, charge, and so on) of the electron are retained (otherwise, we would not refer to what is being described as "an electron"); and that description features in, and is part of, the construction of an appropriate model. Anti-realists may seize on this and argue that on such a view scientific theories are, if taken literally, either false or, if they are not to be taken literally, not even candidates for truth about the world.

The debate about scientific realism is usually couched in terms of claims about our best scientific theories. In particular, realists claim that we ought to believe in the unobservable entities posited by the latter. (Although a proper appreciation of the role of idealization in the application of theories to phenomena may induce some skepticism about the degree of confirmation that theories really enjoy.) Those who follow Cartwright in regarding the empirically adequate parts of science as models rather than theories may also abandon realism about theories in favor of realism about models, and so defend entity realism against theoretical realism. On the other hand, some have argued, against Cartwright, that theories and models are not so different and, in particular, that even the latter involve abstraction and not just approximation. If this is right, then models are no less problematic and abstract in principle than are theories, and the latter are simply higher-order representations (rather than being non-representational). This is taken by some to motivate a unitary account of scientific representation with respect to both theories and models. According to the *partial structures* account of scientific representation developed by Newton da Costa and Steven French (2003), these models of the phenomena are then related by means of partial isomorphisms and homomorphisms through a hierarchy of further models to the high-level theoretical structures. It has been argued that these fit best with structural forms of realism emphasizing the relational structure that scientists attribute to the world (Worrall 1989; Ladyman 1998).

See also Essentialism and natural kinds; Explanation; Laws of nature; Mathematics; Models; Realism/anti-realism; Representation in science; Structure of scientific theories; Symmetry.

References

Bogen, J. and Woodward, J. (1988) "Saving the Phenomena," *Philosophical Review* 12: 303–52.
Cartwright, Nancy (1983) *How The Laws of Physics Lie*, Oxford: Clarendon Press.
—— (1989) *Nature's Capacities and Their Measurement*, Oxford: Clarendon Press.

—— (1993) "How We Relate Theory to Observation," in P. Horwich (ed.) *World Changes: Thomas Kuhn and the Nature of Science*, Cambridge, MA: MIT Press, pp. 259–73.

da Costa N. C. A. and French, S. (2003) *Science and Partial Truth: A Unitary Approach to Models and Scientific Reasoning*, Oxford: Oxford University Press.

Giere, R. N. (1988) *Explaining Science*, Chicago: Chicago University Press.

Grobler, Adam (1995) "The Representational and the Non-Representational in Models of Scientific Theories," in W. E. Herfel, W. Krajewski, I. Niiniluoto, and R. Wójcicki (eds) *Theories and Models in Science: Poznan Studies in the Philosophy of the Sciences and the Humanities*, 44, Amsterdam: Rodopi, pp. 37–48.

Hughes, R. I. G. (1989) "Bell's Theorem, Ideology and Structural Explanation," in J. T. Cushing and E. McMullin (eds) *Philosophical Consequences of Quantum Theory: Reflections on Bell's Theorem*, Chicago: University of Chicago Press, pp. 195–207.

Ladyman, James (1998) "What Is Structural Realism?" *Studies in History and Philosophy of Science* 29: 409–24.

McMullin, Ernan (1985) "Galilean Idealization," *Studies in History and Philosophy of Science* 16: 247–73.

Morgan, M. and Morrison, M. (eds) (1995) *Models as Mediators*, Cambridge: Cambridge University Press.

Nowak, L. (1995) "Anti-Realism (Supra-)Realism and Idealization," in W. E. Herfel, W. Krajewski, I. Niiniluoto, and R. Wójcicki (eds) *Theories and Models in Science: Poznan Studies in the Philosophy of the Sciences and the Humanities*, 44, Amsterdam: Rodopi, pp. 225–42.

Suppes, P. (1967) "What Is a Scientific Theory?" in S. Morgenbesser (ed.) *Philosophy of Science Today*, New York: Basic Books, pp. 55–67.

Wigner, E. (1967) "The Unreasonable Effectiveness of Mathematics in Physics" (1953), in E. Wigner, *Symmetries and Reflections*, Bloomington: Indiana University Press.

Worrall, John (1989) "Structural Realism: The Best of Both Worlds?" *Dialectica* 43: 99–124.

Further reading

Cartwright's *How the Laws of Physics Lie* (1983) is a classic critique of received views of scientific representation, laws, and explanation. Her *Nature's Capacities and Their Measurement* (1989) is a follow-up work in which she develops a metaphysics of capacities. Mary Hesse, *Models and Analogies in Science* (Oxford: Oxford University Press, 1966) is a classic account of theory application. Suppes's 1967 article is a classic early defense of the semantic approach to scientific representation. McMullin's "Galilean Idealization" (1985) is a beautiful analysis of idealization in physics. Giere (1988) is a thorough introduction to the semantic approach, with numerous examples of models and idealizations. Herfel et al. (1995), N. Shanks (ed.) *Idealization in Contemporary Physics: Poznan Studies in the Philosophy of the Sciences and the Humanities*, 63 (Amsterdam: Rodopi, 1995), and Morgan and Morrison (1995) are all collections of papers by philosophers who emphasize the importance of models and idealization in science. Da Costa and French (2003) is a recent, comprehensive defense of the semantic approach to scientific representation in terms of partiality and pragmatism. Worrall (1989) is a classic appraisal of the scientific realism debate and an introduction to structural realism. Ladyman (1998) is an attempt both to develop Worrall's structural realism that introduced the – now standard – distinction between epistemic and ontic versions and to defend the latter.

34
MEASUREMENT
Hasok Chang and Nancy Cartwright

Introduction

Measurement is one of the most distinctive and pervasive features of modern science, but it is not easy to say what measurement actually is. Philosophers commonly define measurement as the correct assignment of numbers to physical variables. There are many difficult philosophical and practical questions about whether a measurement is made correctly and how we can know that it is. Various philosophical views surrounding these questions are discussed next; in the final two sections, we highlight concrete questions concerning the practice of measurement in the physical and the social sciences.

Epistemic questions

To the practitioner, the all-important question is whether measurements are carried out correctly. To the philosopher of science, that question acquires special significance in the context of the realism debate: does a measurement operation really measure what it purports to measure? Take one of the more controversial examples: does the IQ test really measure intelligence? To answer the question we need to consider not only whether the test results are in line with what we intuitively understand as "intelligence," but also whether the presumed quantity really exists. Two broad positions can be identified about the nature of measurement: one treats measurement methods as definitive of the concept; the other takes measurements as methods of finding out about objective quantities that we can identify independently of measurement. These positions could be characterized, respectively, as *nominalism* and *realism* about measurement.

The core of nominalism is a rejection of the realist question about the correctness of measurement. Within nominalism, we can again distinguish two positions. The more extreme is *operationalism*, which maintains that the meaning of a concept is fully specified by its method of measurement, implying that each measurement operation defines its own concept; consequently, it becomes a tautology that any measurement operation is the correct one for the concept associated with it. Operationalism is commonly associated with the American physicist Percy W. Bridgman, who once declared: "In general, we mean by any concept nothing more than a set of operations; the concept is synonymous with the corresponding set of operations" (1927: 5). Bridgman later regretted having formulated such a narrow view, distancing himself from the term "operationalism" or "operationism." Instead, he emphasized another strand that was always present in his writings: the usefulness of analyzing scientific practices and epistemic situations in terms of operations. Among other benefits, such operational analysis can reveal divergences in practice that careless linguistic and mathematical habits conceal. For example, consider the diversity of operations underlying the notion of "length": in everyday circumstances, we have operations like lining up meter-sticks against solid objects; measuring atomic dimensions requires putting together some complicated equations of electromagnetic theory or quantum physics with some observable quantities; measuring astronomical distances necessitates a host of different operations depending on the scale, starting with the measurement of the time light takes in reaching an object and traveling back after being reflected. According to operationalism, there are as many concepts of length as there are different types of operations used for measuring it.

The less extreme nominalist view is *conventionalism*, according to which we are free to choose by agreement the correct measurement method for a concept. Here it is useful to make a distinction between *definition* and *meaning*. We do not have to be close followers of the late Wittgenstein to admit that the meaning of a concept derives from all the different ways in which it is used. When we fix on a definition of a concept, the intention is to regulate its uses; the definition allows us to judge whether the use in question is correct or not. Pure operationalism defines concepts in terms of measurement operations, and then reduces down their meaning to such operational definitions. Conventionalism does not conflate meaning and definition but allows a convention, for example an agreed measurement operation, to regulate the use of the concept. Because nature does not dictate the correct method of measurement, we are left with convention as the highest epistemic authority. A prime example of conventionalism is Henri Poincaré's discussion of time measurement (2001 [1913]: 215): "time should be so defined that the equations of mechanics may be as simple as possible. In other words, there is not one way of measuring time more true than another; that which is generally adopted is only more *convenient*."

Nominalist positions are motivated partly by the recognition that many of the entities, properties, and relations that interest scientists are unobservable. This is not only about physics and chemistry venturing into the microscopic realm. One of the influences that pushed Bridgman toward operationalism was Albert Einstein's exposé of the impossibility of determining absolute simultaneity at a distance (Bridgman 1927: 1–9). It was an immense shock to many physicists and philosophers to realize that they had taken for granted the meaningfulness of the Newtonian notion of *distant simultaneity*, whereas critical thought should have made it obvious that it cannot be determined without adopting one measurement procedure or another, each lacking absolute justification. Bridgman, with his operational analysis, sought to "render unnecessary the services of the unborn Einsteins" (*ibid.*: 24).

Realism denies that measurement methods are definitive of concepts. For the realist, measurement is an activity aimed at discovering the true value of a specified quantity that exists independently of how we measure it, and the question of the correctness of method is certainly not vacuous. "Does some operation O measure concept C correctly?" is a question that must be taken seriously – and answered in the affirmative – by any empiricist who wishes to test the truth of any theories that involve C.

Within the sciences and even in philosophy, there is widespread *naive realism* about measurement that consists in the assumption that our familiar measurement methods correspond correctly to the concepts specified by our theories. In many cases, the situation is far more complex. For example, does the standard mercury thermometer measure temperature correctly? In common conception (though not in modern expert practice), the mercury thermometer is a mercury-filled cylinder of uniform bore, calibrated at the freezing- and boiling-points of water to read 0°C and 100°C, with the scale between those fixed points divided up uniformly and extrapolated beyond them. Such an instrument would give correct temperatures only if the mercury expands uniformly with temperature. How can we test that assumption? We need to monitor how the volume of mercury varies with real temperature; if the volume is a linear function of temperature, then our mercury thermometer is correct. But how can we get the real temperature values without already having a thermometer that we know we can trust, which is just what we are trying to obtain?

This problem of justification is common to all measurement methods based on empirical laws. Hasok Chang (2004: 59) has dubbed it "the problem of nomic measurement." We seek to determine quantity x via another, more easily observed, quantity, y, with the help of an empirical law expressing the former as a function of the latter: $x = f(y)$. In order to test our expression for f empirically we would need to observe values of x and y, but without f already established we cannot determine the x-values empirically. There are two obvious ways of trying to avoid this problem. First, determine the x-values by another measurement method; this only postpones the problem, as we would need to ask how that other method is justified. Second, derive f from a more general theory; this is not straightforward, either, as we would need to know that the theory was empirically justified, which would inevitably involve measurements of x itself or other unobservable quantities.

The problem of nomic measurement is a sharp manifestation of the more general problem of the theory-ladenness of observation. There are extreme types of theory-ladenness in modern measurements of many quantities, for example, very low temperatures, properties of elementary particles, and distances to faraway astronomical objects. Pierre Duhem (1962 [1906]) long ago noted how the necessity of justifying the workings of measuring instruments leads to holism in epistemology. In order to defend realism about measurement, one needs to have a way of dealing with theory-ladenness and holism in general. A mild version of operationalism can be seen as an attempt to avoid holism by avoiding theory-ladenness. If empirical concepts can be defined by well-specified measurement operations, observational data can be fixed without reference to theories and be made secure, while theoretical concepts and laws fluctuate and develop. Whether there are theory-free operations that can support sufficiently useful empirical concepts depends on the circumstance. Herbert Feigl (1970) noted that our most basic measurement operations are grounded in middle-level regularities that seem to have a remarkable degree of stability, such as Archimedes's law of the lever and Snell's law of refraction.

Whether nominalist or realist, those who practice measurement tend to be concerned about precision. In common parlance "precision" is often confused with "accuracy." *Accuracy* is a realist notion about whether measurement results agree with the true values; *precision* is a concept that is meaningful to the realist and nominalist alike, as it indicates merely how specific a measurement result is. One might say that precision is a necessary but insufficient condition for high accuracy. True precision requires consistency of results when repeated measurements of the same quantity are made. Different authors use different terms to express the accuracy–precision distinction. For example, statisticians commonly distinguish *validity* from *reliability*; the distinction also maps on to that between *error* and *uncertainty*. In some circumstances, the same operational measures or statistical data-processing techniques serve the goals of both accuracy and precision.

Some problems of measurement in the physical sciences

Quantification

Steeped in modern scientific thinking, we tend to think of all physical properties as numerical quantities amenable to measurement. It can be a shock to learn the list of physical concepts that used to be considered qualities to which numbers could not be attached. For example, Alistair Crombie (in Woolf 1961: 21–4) explains how fourteenth-century Oxford scholars struggled to quantify velocity, which had been considered by most Aristotelians as an unquantifiable quality. Another Aristotelian quality was heat, which was quantified during the seventeenth and the eighteenth centuries into the distinct modern concepts of *temperature* and the *quantity of heat*. Quantification of many other concepts in physics and chemistry followed. Acidity (and alkalinity) presents an interesting case: the modern measure of it is expressed in *pH* values, based on the concentration of hydrogen ions. That quantification of acidity made the meaning of the concept more specific than it had been and also ruled out certain previous concepts of acidity. A more extreme case of such narrowing and changing of meaning through quantification is that of color via wavelength.

Attempts at quantification do not always succeed, even in the physical sciences. One example is chemical affinity. Between the late eighteenth century and the early nineteenth century there were various schemes for measuring the strength of affinity between different chemical substances. This was an entirely sensible enterprise, since much chemistry in that period was based on ordinal rankings expressed in affinity tables which explained why certain combinations happen in preference to others. It was, therefore, a natural hope that coherent numerical values could be assigned to affinities. In this case quantification turned out to be a mirage, as further investigations revealed that even the ordinal rankings were not robust, being subject to flipping depending on external circumstances such as heat and wetness. Color is another interesting example. Psychologists studying color perception by mapping the perceived degrees of closeness between various hues found that the perceived relationships could be adequately represented only in a two-dimensional color circle, which cannot be mapped onto the linear spectrum of wavelengths.

The improvement of precision

Practically speaking, the best advertisement for quantification is precision. On the whole, the physical sciences have been extremely successful in improving the precision of measurements. Observational astronomy was probably the first field of science that developed specialized instruments and practices designed to increase precision, showing impressive achievements already by the sixteenth century, thanks to the likes of Tycho Brahe. By the mid- to late eighteenth century other physical quantities began to be measured with great precision. Fine balances for weight measurement were constructed, allowing Henry Cavendish, Antoine Lavoisier and others to weigh gases, and Count Rumford to argue that heat was not a substance because it had no detectable weight. Mechanical and pendulum clocks were developed well enough to show that the length of the day (from noon to noon) was not constant, and John Harrison with his famous marine chronometers led the pack of horologists searching for a method of making accurate longitude determinations at sea. Surveying techniques were sufficiently developed for teams of French scientists to determine the length of 1° of arc on different parts of the earth with precision; this helped to settle the debate between Newtonians and Cartesians about the shape of the earth, and also served as a basis for the definition of the meter adopted during the French Revolution. Charles Augustin Coulomb developed a torsion balance for the precise measurement of force, which he used in his investigations in electrostatics; Cavendish used a similar arrangement to measure the gravitational force between terrestrial objects. For the measurement of small lengths, micrometers were developed, and the engineering of other precision instruments depended crucially on the exact control of the dimensions of parts. Over the nineteenth century, a culture of precision took hold of experimental physics as a whole, to which the contributions of Victor Regnault were significant; gradually many other laboratory-based sciences followed suit.

Despite this impressive list of achievements, there is a deep epistemological question about how it is possible to increase precision, which can be illustrated with the case of temperature. If we only have thermometers that measure down to 1° to begin with, how will we be able to judge whether a new thermometer that measures down to 0.1° is correct? Relying on theory creates the same difficulties discussed earlier. If the justification is empirical, then a lower-precision instrument is being asked to underwrite a higher-precision instrument. This is a general problem, to which there is no simple realist solution. In the iterative development of precision, there is at each step a choice to be made between competing higher-precision standards, each compatible with the previously accepted lower-precision standard. How that choice can and should be made are serious philosophical and practical issues (Chang 2004: Chs 3 and 5).

The choice of convention

Once we allow a degree of nominalism about measurement, interesting issues emerge about the choice of convention. The competition between solar time and clock time gives a good illustration (Landes 1983: 122ff.). Clock time, which declares the movement of the sun irregular, appeared absurd to those who regarded astronomical regularities as the most important and even definitive aspects of the meaning of time. As noted in the previous section, a definition is an attempt to regulate the divergence of meaning. Any concept familiar to general society, such as time, is bound to have a multifaceted meaning. The measurement of such a concept with any precision is likely to sacrifice or alter some aspects of the meaning. In the case of time, any quantification at all is a departure from some aspects of the inner experience of it, as Henri Bergson argued.

There have been many debates about the choice of measurement unit and scale – some of them quite heated – as between Fahrenheit and Celsius, or metric and imperial. Philosophers may smile at these tussles over what seems an arbitrary issue, but the force of custom is considerable, as shown by the failure of the decimal clock and the ten-day week proposed, along with the metric system, during the French Revolution. Moreover, a unit is often not just about the size of the quantity we take as the base of counting. The choice of unit and scale is often tied up with the choice of measurement method, which is in turn based on substantive assumptions. For example, measuring distance in light-years is based on the assumption that the speed of light is constant. Similarly, it is too simple to say that *degrees Kelvin* is just *degrees Celsius* minus 273.15°. Lord Kelvin's absolute temperature concept sprang from his desire to avoid reference to any particular material substance in the definition of temperature, and it was based on the abstract theory of thermodynamics for that reason. The traditional Celsius scale was based on the system of two fixed points and relied on the assumption of the linear expansion of mercury. (In fact, the original temperature scale of Anders Celsius was *upside-down*, with 0° denoting the boiling-point of water and 100° the freezing-point; it is interesting to speculate about what exactly Celsius was trying to measure on that scale.)

Some problems of measurement in the social sciences

As Max Weber taught, the social sciences face a number of special problems with measurement that are more severe than those in the physical sciences. We discuss some of the more pressing issues here.

(1) Physical sciences look for exact laws involving unambiguously defined and measurable concepts, and they can adjust their choice of concept to serve this aim. If one candidate proves inconvenient, it can be replaced by another. Consider the acceleration of falling bodies, which go faster the longer and farther they fall. Medieval scholars tended to define acceleration as the increase of velocity as a function of distance traveled by the body. Modern physicists prefer to use dv/dt, the rate of increase of velocity with time; this formulation has many advantages, including its

role in Newton's second law of motion. The social sciences have no such latitude. They are supposed to help us understand the behavior of the factors we are interested in, which may not figure in strict laws nor be exactly measurable.

Measurement in the social sciences involves two kinds of activities: providing a theoretical definition for the quantity of concern, and devising and defending empirical procedures for determining when the concept applies in the world. The *theory of measurement* (see Suppes 1998 for an accessible introduction) concerns the first and, although its strictures apply equally in the natural and social sciences, social scientists are more attentive to its demands. The first task within measurement theory is to provide a mathematical representation of the targeted concept so that it can be integrated into a theory with an existing set of concepts. In the falling-body example above, both concepts of acceleration can be equally integrated with existing concepts.

The second task is to provide a *representation theorem* to show that this representation is adequate. A representation theorem first provides a set of characteristics taken to be true of the targeted concept, and then proves that the concept as defined has those characteristics. Consider economic freedom. We talk loosely of economic versus political freedom, of negative versus positive freedom, and the like. Can economic freedom be defined more exactly in the framework of, say, social choice theory? The simplest idea is a pure cardinality measure that identifies the degree of economic freedom agents have with the number of options available to them. Is this a good definition? Suppose we agree that economic freedom has some basic features: for example, if one set contains every option that a second contains and more, the first offers more economic freedom that the second. In a good exemplar of measurement theory at work, Pattanaik and Xu (1990) provide axioms describing three such features, then prove that an ordering among sets of options satisfies those axioms just in case it orders the sets according to their size. Later writers provide more nuanced definitions. In each case measurement theory requires that the definition be defended by a representation theorem.

Measurement theory regulates only half the job: once a concept has been defined within a theory, empirical procedures are required to tie it to the world. How, for instance, do we measure the size of someone's economic choice set? In psychometrics these two stages are often collapsed into one. Suppose a set of measurement procedures for a concept is on offer, say a questionnaire, to determine how depressed one is. Psychometrics offers a number of tests designed to provide evidence about whether the questionnaire is indeed a measure of depression. The analysis, defense, and improvement of such procedures are among the central tasks of methodology of the social sciences.

(2) Even if we assume that our social concepts pick out real quantities, there are other difficulties in the attempt to provide measurement procedures for them:

- Measurements of psychological states will always be indirect. Even honest and attentive self-reports cannot be taken as reliable without more corroboration.
- For the purpose of comparisons, measures and measurement procedures are required that can be applied across locations, populations, economies, and cultures. This

often results in measures that lose information – measures that are far from the best procedures that could be devised in the separate groups – and the more local measures often give dramatically different results from the more universal ones. Also, for theory-testing we need separate procedures that measure the same univocal concept, but for practical use we generally need a variety of purpose-specific concepts, each with measurement procedures appropriate to it. The two demands pull in opposite directions:

- Because people are self-conscious and reflective and because social institutions are often designed to be plastic and responsive to their environment, it is often difficult to design measurement procedures that do not significantly disturb the measured systems.
- Moral, political and cultural norms severely restrict the kinds of measurement operations that can be performed on people and their social institutions.
- We often want to measure aggregate and ambiguous concepts, like the total value of goods and services produced in a country. How do we do so since we cannot count them all; and how do we decide what is to be counted? For instance, is household labor to be included?

(3) Measures in social science are often not value-free despite our best efforts. Very frequently, they make sense as measures only in relation to certain values or purposes. This may be obvious in a case like the human development index, which includes life expectancy, level of education, and GDP. Should it include a measure of political freedom as well? That presumably depends on whether political freedom is accepted as a constituent of human flourishing.

The intrusion of values or purposes may be less expected elsewhere, but it seems exceedingly difficult to avoid. Consider the recent Boskin Commission proposals in the U. S. for revising the consumer price index (CPI). One proposal argued that the prices for many goods are overestimated because they are based on samples from retail stores, whereas the goods tend to be much cheaper in outlet stores, which are not properly represented when prices are sampled. But, as Julian Reiss (forthcoming) argues, adjusting the CPI in this way will disadvantage the elderly, those without cars, and other groups who have poor access to outlet stores, which are generally far from town centers.

A stock response to these problems urges that decisions involving value-laden choices in the construction of a measure be given to users of the measure – policy-makers of all sorts who will use the measure in their deliberations. This has major drawbacks. First, it leads to a proliferation of measures which become difficult to understand and keep track of; we also get the same problems of theory-testing and comparison discussed already with respect to universal versus purpose-built measures. Second, it is an extremely difficult strategy to execute. Consider poverty measures. Perhaps a legislative body or the populace is willing and able to think about whether the measure should be absolute or relative, and, if relative, relative to what. Should we set the poverty line at two-thirds of the median income? Should we count households or individuals? How should we weight individuals in a household? Those decisions both affect different groups in different ways and also can dramatically change the assessment of how much poverty there is and the poverty-rankings among different regions. To understand the impact of those decisions requires much thought and more economic and social knowledge than even experts have, let alone those who want to use the information. Here again is a problem that makes designing measures in the social sciences far more difficult than in the natural sciences.

See also Evidence; Scientific method; Social sciences; Values in science.

References

Bridgman, Percy Williams (1927) *The Logic of Modern Physics*, New York: Macmillan.

Chang, Hasok (2004) *Inventing Temperature: Measurement and Scientific Progress*, New York: Oxford University Press.

Duhem, Pierre (1962 [1906]) *The Aim and Structure of Physical Theory*, New York: Atheneum.

Feigl, Herbert (1970) "The 'Orthodox' View of Theories: Remarks in Defense as well as Critique," in Michael Radner and Stephen Winokur (eds) *Analyses of Theories and Methods of Physics and Psychology*, Minneapolis: University of Minnesota Press, pp. 3–16.

Landes, David (1983) *Revolution in Time: Clocks and the Making of the Modern World*, Cambridge, MA: Harvard University Press.

Pattanaik, Prasanta and Xu, Yongsheng (1990) "On Ranking Opportunity Sets in Terms of Freedom of Choice," *Louvain Economic Review* 56: 383–90.

Poincaré, Henri (2001 [1913]) "The Measure of Time," in *The Value of Science: Essential Writings of Henri Poincaré*, New York: Modern Library, pp. 210–22.

Reiss, Julian (forthcoming) *Error in Economics*, London: Routledge.

Suppes, Patrick (1998) "Measurement, Theory of," in E. Craig (ed.) *The Routledge Encyclopedia of Philosophy*, vol. 6, London: Routledge, pp. 243–49.

Woolf, Harry (ed.) (1961) *Quantification: A History of the Meaning of Measurement in the Natural and Social Sciences*, Indianapolis, IN: Bobbs-Merrill.

Further reading

Useful philosophical discussions about measurement in various sciences can be found in John Forge (ed.) *Measurement, Realism and Objectivity: Essays on Measurement in the Social and Physical Sciences* (Dordrecht: Reidel, 1987). Woolf (1961) gives very interesting historical views on quantification in the natural and the social sciences. Broader historical and cultural perspectives on precision measurement are provided in M. Norton Wise (ed.) *The Values of Precision* (Princeton, NJ: Princeton University Press, 1995). For those interested in following up on issues concerning economic measurements, an excellent place to start is Judy L. Klein and Mary S. Morgan (eds) *The Age of Economic Measurement* (Durham, NC, and London: Duke University Press, 2001). Broad surveys of measurements in a wide variety of fields can be found in David J. Hand, *Measurement Theory and Practice: The World Through Quantification* (London: Arnold, 2004), and Herbert Arthur Klein, *The Science of Measurement: A Historical Survey* (New York: Dover, 1974). Those interested in studying formal theories of measurement, introduced in Suppes (1998), can refer to David H. Krantz et al., *Foundations of Measurement*, 3 vols (New York: Academic Press, 1971–90).

35
MECHANISMS
Stuart Glennan

Introduction

While the term "mechanism" has a long and continuous use in scientific literature dating from the seventeenth century, the concept of mechanism has only recently become a major subject of discussion among philosophers of science. Mechanist philosophers of science argue that a vast variety of phenomena in the natural world are the product of the operation of mechanisms, and accordingly that any adequate theory of science should give an account of what mechanisms are, how they are discovered and represented, and the role that mechanisms play in scientific explanation. To a significant degree, a mechanistic philosophy of science can be seen as an alternative to an earlier logical empiricist tradition in philosophy of science that gave pride of place to laws of nature. Within that tradition, science was broadly conceived as a search for laws that described regularities in natural phenomena. Theories were understood to be deductive closures of sets of laws, explanations were understood as arguments from covering laws, and reduction was understood as a deductive relationship between laws of different theories. Mechanists argue that this approach is fundamentally at odds with the practice of science, especially in the life and social sciences, but even in many areas of physics and chemistry.

"Mechanism" is used to describe two distinct but related sorts of structures. First, mechanisms are systems consisting of a collection of parts that interact with each other in order to produce some behavior. So, for instance, a car's engine is a mechanism containing many parts whose interaction produces the motion of the drive shaft. Second, mechanisms are temporally extended processes in which sequences of activities produce some outcome of the mechanism's operation. For instance, photosynthesis is a mechanism in which by a series of activities involving water, carbon dioxide, and energy from light produces oxygen and sugar. There is a natural relationship between processes and systems, for the operation of systems gives rise to processes. Photosynthesis can, for instance, be conceived of as the activity of a system – the chloroplast – whose operation is a mechanical process.

The term "mechanism" is most widely associated with the seventeenth-century mechanical philosophy championed by philosophers such as Descartes and Boyle. Mechanism in the seventeenth century can be seen as embodying both a metaphysical doctrine and a scientific methodology (Des Chene 2001). Methodologically, mechanists sought to explain natural phenomena by identifying mechanisms – systems of interacting parts – that produce those phenomena. Metaphysically, the doctrine was closely related to atomism – the view that ultimately mechanistic operations would reduce to the kinetic interactions between atoms or corpuscles. Contemporary mechanists reject the metaphysical view while retaining much of the methodology. A seventeenth-century mechanist would be committed to the view that interactions governed by chemical, electrical, or gravitational forces would have to be explicable in terms of the operation of some atomistic, kinetic mechanism. Contemporary mechanists recognize that this part of the mechanical philosophy has simply not been borne out by scientific research. Accordingly they retain the strategy of explaining phenomena by identifying mechanisms, but they reject any fixed and limited list of the modes by which parts of mechanisms can act and interact.

Contemporary analyses of mechanism

In the recent mechanisms literature, considerable attention has been given to finding a suitable working definition of a mechanism. Two of the most widely cited are as follows:

> Mechanisms are entities and activities organized such that they are productive of regular changes from start or set-up to finish or termination conditions. (Machamer, Darden, and Craver 2000: 3)

> A mechanism for a behavior is a complex system that produces that behavior by the interaction of a number of parts, where the interactions between parts can be characterized by direct, invariant, change-relating generalizations. (Glennan 2002: S344)

These definitions share a number of common features:

Mechanisms are productive of phenomena or behaviors

Mechanisms always do something, and we identify a mechanism by first identifying the behavior it produces. For Machamer, Darden, and Craver, what the mechanism does is specified by its start-up and termination conditions. The constituents of mechanisms can be involved in the production of a variety of behaviors, and, depending on which behavior one focuses on, one will identify the parts, activities, interactions, and system boundaries differently. For instance, the mechanism that delivers blood to the brain will include the heart (and its parts) as well as a system of arteries, capillaries, and veins, while the mechanism that produces thumping in our chest will require a different description of the heart and will not include parts of the circulatory system outside the heart.

While many of the behaviors that mechanisms produce can be seen as teleological functions, the behaviors of mechanisms need not be the product of design or selection.

The regular behavior of synapses is the product of a long selective history, while the regular behavior of Old Faithful is not; yet both behaviors are produced by mechanisms.

Mechanisms consist of structured collections of parts

Mechanisms are made up of parts, and those parts are entities or objects. By calling parts "entities" or "objects," mechanists suggest that parts have properties that are relatively stable over time, and that at least theoretically these parts are subject to manipulation and isolation from the rest of the mechanism. Mechanisms are individuated not simply by what parts they have, but by how those parts are organized. A heap of parts does not make a mechanism. Rather the characteristic spatial, temporal, and functional organization of the parts explains the behavior of the mechanism.

Mechanisms behave in regular but not exceptionless ways

Because mechanisms have stable parts that have stable organization, those parts will characteristically interact in regular ways to produce regular behaviors – toilets flush, synapses fire, cars start. But the behaviors are subject to exceptions and breakdowns caused by perturbations of the mechanism or its environment. For instance, mechanisms of digestion will regularly digest foods and produce sugars, but the operation of those mechanisms depends on a variety of ambient conditions (e.g., an appropriate level of hydration, absence of disruptive bacteria, etc.).

One of the advantages of the move from nomological to mechanistic modes of explanation is that the latter allows for explanations involving exception-ridden generalizations. As I have argued elsewhere (Glennan 1996), many generalizations that have earned the honorific "law" (e.g., Mendel's laws, Kepler's laws, Hooke's law) are in fact generalizations describing the regular but not exceptionless behavior of mechanisms.

Mechanisms are hierarchical

Mechanisms are hierarchical because the parts of mechanisms can themselves be mechanisms, and the interaction between parts of a mechanism may involve the operation of further mechanisms. For instance, in the mechanism of human metabolism, one might begin with a description of a behavior that describes the digestion of food as it moves from mouth to stomach to small intestine and bowel. But these anatomical structures contain structured collections of parts that realize the mechanism responsible for each part's function within the larger mechanism. This embedding can proceed downward for many levels – in this case to the sub-cellular and molecular levels, and it can also proceed upward or outward, for instance to consider how animal digestive systems are parts of broader ecological mechanisms.

The analysis of mechanisms described above should be contrasted with Wesley Salmon's approach to mechanisms. In his classic 1984 book, Salmon develops an account of causation and explanation that he refers to as a "new mechanical philosophy." This account was meant to provide a foundation for a theory of explanation that avoided difficulties with traditional covering-law models. According to Salmon, causal explanations of events describe features of the causal processes that produce those events. Salmon does not actually define the term "mechanism," but instead gives an account of causal processes and interactions. Causal processes are entities that maintain their structure through space–time, and interactions between causal processes are intersections of such processes where changes in the properties of the processes occur. For instance a moving baseball and a swinging bat are both causal processes, and the striking of the ball with the bat constitutes an interaction between those processes. The striking of the bat has the effect of altering the properties of the process (e.g., the velocity of the ball and bat and the local deformation of the surface of the ball and bat).

Mechanisms in Salmon's sense have several things in common with mechanisms as characterized in this chapter. In both cases, mechanisms involve interacting entities that causally explain phenomena via productively continuous processes. But there are important differences as well. While Salmon's mechanisms are processes involving interactions, the interactions are not necessarily regular, and they do not involve the operation of systems. The mechanism of photosynthesis is a repeatable process that involves the continual operation of many cells with similar structure and function. When we consider a mechanistic explanation of photosynthesis, we are interested in a *general* account of the operation of that mechanism. But in the case of the baseball hitting the bat, we are interested in providing an explanation of a particular event, and we do so at one place and time.

Salmon's work on causal–mechanical explanation forms an important chapter in the recent history of philosophical discussions of causation and explanation, but it is related only tangentially to the more recent work on mechanisms. I turn now to a discussion of some recent debates in this latter body of work.

Discovering, representing, and explaining mechanisms

Mechanists claim that the chief virtue of their approach is that it is more faithful to the practices of science than approaches which suppose scientists to be seeking to understand nature by discovering laws. Accordingly, one of the projects of the mechanist program is to develop alternative theoretical accounts of the major areas of scientific practice – including theory structure, discovery, confirmation, and explanation.

Machamer, Darden, and Craver (2000) have argued that scientists represent a mechanism using a *mechanism schema*, which they define as "a truncated abstract description of a mechanism that can be filled with descriptions of known component parts and activities" (*ibid.*: 15). Others (including Bechtel and Abrahamsen, and myself) refer to representations of mechanisms as "models," but our views on the nature of the representations complement those of Machamer, Darden, and Craver. All of us emphasize that models should identify both the parts and their spatial, temporal, and functional organization. We also emphasize the practical importance of diagrams in addition to or in place of linguistic representations of mechanisms.

A number of mechanists have used case studies in an effort to develop an account of the general process by which scientists develop and test models of mechanisms.

Machamer, Darden, and Craver (2000) argue that scientists begin by identifying the overall behavior of a mechanism, and develop a "mechanism sketch," which identifies the purported gross structure of the mechanism. They cite an example of this, Watson and Crick's central dogma, which sketches a mechanism of protein synthesis, beginning with DNA, with an intermediate RNA stage and a final protein product. The sketch provides no details of the entities and activities that are at work in this mechanism. Guided by the sketch, scientists seek to fill in the black boxes, creating schemata of greater detail. If this process fails, scientists may need to revise the sketch.

Mechanists have explored a variety of techniques for identifying the entities and activities involved in the production of a mechanism's behavior. One generally begins by attempting to localize functions or activities in certain components, but in some cases localization fails and other strategies must be applied (Bechtel and Richardson 1993). One may use both top–down strategies, where one begins with a general view of the function of the mechanism and reasons to the structure and function of parts, and bottom–up strategies, where one identifies parts, and then looks at their activities to try to understand how they might be productive within the mechanism. Sometimes the entities and activities in a mechanism are directly observable, but at other times one must resort to indirect approaches (Glennan 2005) whereby one disrupts normal operating conditions of the mechanism, and uses the breakdown conditions to infer things about the mechanism's internal structure.

Mechanists generally believe that the relationship between mechanisms and their models is one of similarity rather than correspondence or isomorphism. Models thus cannot be verified or falsified, but can be shown only to be similar or dissimilar to modeled systems in certain degrees and respects of similarity. In response to observational and experimental data, models may be elaborated, tweaked, or abandoned. The fact that there are differing degrees and respects entails that there may be no definite ordering on the quality of models. Different models might be better for distinct purposes, and pragmatic considerations inevitably come into play.

An important theme in the literature on representation of mechanisms concerns the level of generality and abstraction of models of mechanisms. Mechanists believe that the mechanical systems and processes that are productive of natural phenomena are concrete particulars, and that few if any tokens of some type of mechanism will be identical with each other. Thus, for instance, in mechanisms of cellular metabolism, one should not expect that any two cells will have identical structures or will behave in exactly the same way. All models abstract away from details of a particular instance, but the level of abstraction and generality may differ. Thus, for instance, a highly abstract model of cellular metabolism will apply to all cells, while more detailed models will apply only to eukaryotes or prokaryotes, or cells of particular phyla or species, or cells belonging to particular organs within an organism.

In investigating mechanisms, scientists often begin by studying model systems or exemplars. For instance, scientists studying the mechanisms of synaptic transmission did much of their early work studying neurons in the giant squid (Bechtel and Abrahamsen 2005: 438). Testing models thus involves two distinct questions.

First, how good is the model of the exemplar? That is, in what degrees and respects does the model accurately represent the structure and operation of the exemplary mechanism? Second, if the model is a good model of the exemplar, how well does it generalize to related systems? These two questions are independent. Even if one has a well-confirmed model, for instance, of the behavior of action potentials in the giant squid, it does not follow that the model will apply to action potentials in mammals.

Mechanisms and causation

The concepts of mechanism and cause are intimately connected. Mechanisms cause, bring about, or produce events or states. These events or states are what in the various proposed definitions of "mechanism" are the phenomenon, or behavior, for which the mechanism is responsible. Moreover, mechanisms are characterized causally in terms of parts or entities that *act* and *interact*. While it is clear that there is some relationship between mechanisms and causation, it is not clear exactly what that relationship is. Mechanisms are causal, but can one give a theory of causation that is mechanistic?

I have argued (Glennan 1996) that causation can be analyzed in terms of mechanisms because (with the important exception of fundamental causal interactions, discussed below) causally related events will be connected by intervening mechanisms. A key may be said to cause a car to start because there is an intervening mechanism (involving a system of interacting parts) between the event of the key's turning and the event of the car's starting. This account may seem circular or at least unillumi-nating, since the intervening mechanism is defined as a system of interacting parts and the concept of interaction is transparently causal. But the problem can be mitigated by appealing to the hierarchical character of mechanisms. While the description of the intervening mechanism appeals to interacting parts, the parts themselves are mechanisms and the interactions between these parts can be explained mechanistically.

Although there can be a large number of levels of nested mechanisms, some interactions between parts cannot be explained by the operation of mechanisms. For instance, two electrons might interact with each other, but there is no mechanism connecting them. If mechanically explicable interactions are truly causal, the funda-mental interactions on which they ultimately depend must be causal as well, so a complete causal theory requires a theory of fundamental causal interactions. I have suggested (Glennan 2002) that fundamental causal connections can be explicated in terms of counterfactual dependence, but skeptics (e.g., Psillos 2004) may then wonder whether the mechanical theory then reduces to a counterfactual theory.

Salmon (1984, 1994) proposes a rather different sort of mechanistic theory of causation. Unlike my approach, the theory is reductionistic in the sense that it gives definitions of causal processes and interactions that do not ultimately appeal to other causal notions. Salmon has two versions of the theory, one which defines causal interactions in terms of a counterfactual criterion of mark transmission and one which defines them in terms of exchange of conserved quantities. Because Salmon-style mechanisms are not the focus of this discussion, I do not discuss the merits and difficulties of this "process" theory of causation here. For more information on the view, see chapter 29 of this collection.

Another important question about the relationship between mechanisms and causation concerns what Machamer, Darden, and Craver have called "activities." In their 2000 paper, they suggest that the chief innovation in their analysis of mechanisms is that mechanisms involve both entities and activities. They claim that activities represent a novel ontological category, and that without appeal to activities one cannot understand the productive (i.e., causal) character of mechanisms. The status of activities remains a matter of some dispute. Machamer (2004) has pressed the case for the importance of activities in any scientific ontology, while I have argued that the criticism of the interactionist formulation is based upon an unnecessarily impoverished notion of an interaction. Bogen (2004) has suggested that activities might form the basis for an account of causal processes that does not involve counterfactual dependency.

The scope of the mechanical paradigm

Proponents of the new mechanical philosophy claim that the chief virtue of the movement is that it provides a more accurate rendering of the objects and activities of scientific research than do more traditional approaches in the philosophy of science. They point out that science journals contain frequent references to mechanisms while references to laws are rare. But while it is undoubtedly true that the term "mechanism" is widely used in many scientific disciplines, questions remain about the range of applicability of the mechanical paradigm. Many advocates of the mechanistic approach are philosophers of biology and neuroscience, and many of the standard examples (protein synthesis, cellular respiration, the action potential, long-term potentiation, etc.) are drawn from these fields. What accounts for this fact, and does it suggest limitations on the scope of the mechanistic approach?

There are diverse reasons why mechanistic thinking is especially suitable for biology and neuroscience. In the first place, the objects of study in those disciplines behave in regular ways, but anything approaching exceptionless laws is very hard to come by. Moreover, standard examples of generalizations in biology (Mendel's laws, the central dogma, etc.) are both subject to exceptions and are themselves explicable – not by deduction from other laws – but by describing the mechanisms that produce the phenomena described by them.

Still one may question whether all biological mechanisms meet the constraints demanded by myself and by Machamer, Darden, and Craver. The most straightforward examples of mechanistic explanations involve systems with a relatively small number of parts (or at least kinds of parts), where these parts interact with each other at clearly defined places and times with clearly defined effects. In a system of intermeshed gears, for instance, each gear has a definite location, and a rotation of one gear brings about a rotation of an adjacent gear, and the interactions between the gears will be more-or-less identical on every occasion. But even in a paradigmatic biological example, like the mechanism of synaptic transmission, there are many parts and there is no presumption that the behavior of the mechanism at the level of an individual part (say an individual sodium ion) will be regular. But in those cases we can identify properties of relatively homogeneous aggregates of parts (e.g., concentrations of sodium ions) and describe regular interactions between the aggregates and other aggregates in ways that are recognizably mechanistic. But other examples may prove more difficult. Skipper and Millstein (2005) have, for instance, argued that the mechanism of natural selection is not amenable to analysis using either my account or that of Machamer et al., principally because the interactions between the entities that would most obviously count as parts – organisms and various entities in their environments – are not in the least regular or predictable.

Other instances in which systemic properties arise in ways which cannot be modeled or predicted from the local behavior of individual parts of a mechanism may include neural networks (Bechtel and Richardson 1993) and biochemical reaction networks (Boogerd et al. 2005). What seems to be called for in these cases is an analysis of *emergent mechanisms* – one which supports the mechanistic view that the behavior of systems should depend on the properties of and relations between their parts, while at the same time acknowledging and explaining the failures of standard mechanistic explanatory strategies (e.g., functional localization) for many complex systems.

Another area in which mechanisms and mechanistic explanation are prominent is the social sciences (see Bunge 1997). Like philosophers of biology, philosophers of social science have concerns about theories of inference and explanation which focus on laws. Social mechanisms help both to sort out correlations from causes and to explain why generalizations in the social sciences are subject to exceptions. But, as in the biological sciences, there are great difficulties in getting from the properties of individual parts of social systems to their overall behavior, and questions about holism and emergence loom large.

Recent mechanists see the mechanisms movement as part of a larger trend in which philosophers of science have ceased to think of theoretical physics as the paradigm science. Accordingly, one might expect the usefulness of the mechanistic approach in physics to be limited. As was seen in the discussion of mechanistic approaches to causation, certain causal relations in physics seem like they must be mechanically inexplicable. But while this fact places some limits on mechanistic explanation, it does not follow from this that there are no mechanistic explanations in physics. Many physical theories investigate how the behavior of a system consisting of a number of parts behaves in the aggregate. Classical models of planetary motion or the kinetic model of gases are cases in point. Still, one might argue that models of this kind can be thought of just as naturally in terms of the operation of exceptionless laws of nature. But some philosophers have argued that in physics, as in the life and social sciences, truly exceptionless laws of nature are hard to come by. Cartwright (1999), in particular, has advocated modes of explanation in physics that have much in common with the mechanistic approach.

See also Biology; Causation; Confirmation; Explanation; Metaphysics; Models; Social sciences.

References

Bechtel, William, and Abrahamsen, Adele (2005) "Explanation: A Mechanist Alternative," *Studies in the History and Philosophy of Biology and the Biomedical Sciences* 36: 421–41.

Bechtel, William, and Richardson, Robert C. (1993) *Discovering Complexity: Decomposition and Localization as Strategies in Scientific Research*, Princeton, NJ: Princeton University Press.

Bogen, Jim (2004) "Analysing Causality: The Opposite of Counterfactual is Factual," *International Studies in the Philosophy of Science* 18: 3–26.

Boogerd, F. C., Bruggeman, F. J., Richardson, R. C., Stephan, A., and Westerhoff, H. V. (2005) "Emergence and its Place in Nature: A Case Study of Biochemical Networks," *Synthese* 145: 131–64.

Bunge, Mario (1997) "Mechanism and Explanation," *Philosophy of the Social Sciences* 27: 410.

Cartwright, Nancy (1999) *The Dappled World: A Study of the Boundaries of Science*, Cambridge and New York: Cambridge University Press.

Darden, Lindley and Craver, Carl (2002) "Strategies in the Interfield Discovery of the Mechanism of Protein Synthesis," *Studies in History and Philosophy of Biological and Biomedical Sciences* 33: 1–28.

Des Chene, Dennis (2001) *Spirits and Clocks: Machine and Organism in Descartes*, Ithaca, NY: Cornell University Press.

Glennan, Stuart S. (1996) "Mechanisms and the Nature of Causation," *Erkenntnis* 44: 49–71.

—— (2002) "Rethinking Mechanistic Explanation," *Philosophy of Science* 69 (Supplement): S342–53.

—— (2005) "Modeling Mechanisms," *Studies in the History of the Biological and Biomedical Sciences* 36: 443–64.

Machamer, Peter (2004) "Activities and Causation: The Metaphysics and Epistemology of Mechanisms," *International Studies in the Philosophy of Science* 18: 27–39.

Machamer, Peter, Darden, Lindley, and Craver, Carl F. (2000) "Thinking about Mechanisms," *Philosophy of Science* 67: 1–25.

Psillos, Stathis (2004) "A Glimpse of the Secret Connexion: Harmonizing Mechanisms with Counterfactuals," *Perspectives on Science* 12: 288–319.

Salmon, Wesley C. (1984) *Scientific Explanation and the Causal Structure of the World*, Princeton, NJ: Princeton University Press.

—— (1994) "Causality Without Counterfactuals," *Philosophy of Science* 61: 297–312.

Skipper, Jr., Robert A. and Millstein, Roberta L. (2005) "Thinking about Evolutionary Mechanisms: Natural Selection," *Studies in History and Philosophy of Biological and Biomedical Sciences* 36: 327–47.

Further reading

Machamer, Darden, and Craver (2000) is the probably the most widely cited paper on mechanisms, and this paper along with Glennan (1996) are good places to start for general discussions of the mechanist approach. Readers interested in mechanistic explanation should refer to Glennan (2002) and Bechtel and Abrahamsen (2005). Bechtel and Richardson (1993) and Darden and Craver (2002) provide illuminating discussions of discovery and model-building. For questions about causation, Psillos (2004) provides a very readable overview that summarizes the mechanist approach and explores its relationship to counterfactual theories. *Studies in History and Philosophy of Biological and Biomedical Sciences* 36:2 (2005) is a special issue on mechanisms that contains a number of the papers cited above, and is also helpful for its Introduction, by Darden and Craver, that places the mechanisms movement in historical context and provides an extensive bibliography.

36
MODELS
Demetris Portides

Introduction

The many meanings of the term "model" that we encounter in scientific discourse make the possibility of giving an all-inclusive and precise definition of the concept seem remote. Possibly the most fruitful approach to understanding the concept is to explore its links to other equally complex concepts like *representation* and *idealization*. Despite the disparity of meanings in the use of the term "model," we can discern that most, if not all, of its uses indicate that "model" is strongly tied to *representation*, i.e. a model is meant to represent something else, whether an actual or an ideal state of affairs, whether a physical or an ideal system. For instance, a model of a building is a *representation* of an actual (or actualizable) building. Moreover, we can discern that "model" is also strongly linked with *idealization* and *abstraction*, i.e. a model represents a physical system in an abstract and idealized way. Thus, a model of a building is not meant as an exact replica but as an *idealized* and *abstract* representation of an actual building because, for instance, it represents only certain features of the actual system, e.g., the spatial relations; and ignores others, e.g., the plumbing system.

Philosophers have identified several kinds of models used in science, such as iconic or scale models, analogical models, and mathematical (or abstract) models, all of which are different means of representing respective target systems in idealized and abstract ways. Iconic or scale models are models that represent their target systems by displaying an idealized and abstract physical image of some of the latter's features and relations, e.g. the double helix macro-model of the DNA molecule. Analogical models represent their target systems by means of an analogy that is based on a similarity relation between aspects of the model and aspects of its target, for instance, the billiard-ball model of a gas. Mathematical or abstract models represent their target systems by means of language, predominantly mathematical language, for example, the classical simple harmonic oscillator model of the mass-spring system. Representation is a common function of all different kinds of models, and idealization–abstraction is the steering conceptual process by which this function is carried out. By highlighting this point I mean to suggest no more than that a better understanding of "model," as used in science, could be achieved if we examine it as a member of the aforementioned triad of concepts.

Although all of the above kinds of models in science are philosophically interesting, one kind sticks out: *mathematical* models. Representation with iconic or scale models, for instance, has a *local* character. It is local either in the sense that it applies only to a particular situation at a particular time or in the sense that it requires the mediation of a mathematical (or abstract) model in order to relate to other modes of scientific discourse and scientific representation, like theories. Representation via mathematical models, on the other hand, is of utmost interest because it has a *global* character. It is global because it is closely related to scientific theories and because it applies to *types* of target systems, but also because it can be used to draw inferences about the time-evolution of systems. Moreover, since mathematical language is the principal scientific mode of describing aspects of the world, philosophical analyses have centered, by and large, on the notion of scientific model as a *mathematical entity*. For these reasons it is on this notion that I focus here.

It is not just philosophers who focus their attention primarily on mathematical models. Physicists, for example, consider material and other kinds of models as auxiliary devices that help visualize or understand the propositions of theoretical physics and not as a central part of the latter. The construction of mathematical models, on the other hand, is considered central to their work, and in their meta-theoretical moments they go as far as to make – epistemological and methodological – distinctions among them. They commonly divide mathematical models roughly into two categories: theory-driven models and phenomenological models. The distinction is based on the consideration that theory-driven models are constructed in a systematic, theory-regulated way by supplementing the theoretical calculus with locally operative hypotheses. Phenomenological models, on the other hand, are constructed by the deployment of semi-empirical results, by the use of ad hoc hypotheses, or by the use of a conceptual apparatus that is not directly related to the fundamental concepts of a theory. In other words, physicists distinguish these two kinds of models on the grounds that the latter are not in any straightforward sense deductive consequences of a theory, whereas the former seem to be. The distinction provides valuable insight into the processes of construction of mathematical models in science that a philosophical analysis of "model" cannot ignore.

The background to philosophical views about scientific models

For much of the twentieth century, philosophical debates on the concept of *model* as a mathematical entity were dominated by attempts to give a unifying account of theories and models, that is, an account based on a definite logical relation between the two. Two important philosophical conceptions of scientific theories, known as the "received view" (RV) and the semantic, or model-theoretic, view (SV), emerged. The former is the conception of theories as formal axiomatic calculi whose possible logical interpretations are furnished by meta-mathematical models. Models in this (Tarskian) sense are structures that satisfy subsets of sentences of the formal calculus, and not vehicles of representation of physical systems. In the RV, the vehicles of scientific representation are sentences; models could be thought of as a secondary form of theorizing that facilitates the understanding of the formal calculus. The RV was criticized on several grounds that are by-products of its focus on syntax (see Suppe 1977): namely, that it requires a theoretical–observational distinction and an analytic–synthetic distinction in the vocabulary and sentences of a theory, both of which seem to be untenable; and also that it relies on the obscure notion of *correspondence rules* for giving a partial physical interpretation of the formal calculus. But more importantly for our purposes, RV was criticized because it withholds from models their representational role.

The SV, despite also being an attempt to pursue the same goal as its predecessor – that of giving a unifying account of theories and models – places the representational capacity of models on a par with that of theories. Indeed, the semantic conception is the view in which theories are identified with classes of model-types (structure-types) which would have been interpretations of a formal calculus were the theory formalized. However, the classes of model-types could be directly defined without recourse to a formal language. This could be done either by means of the mathematical language in which the particular theory is formulated, in which case the theory structure could be understood as a class of state-space types (e.g. van Fraassen 1980; Suppe 1989); or within a set-theoretical framework by defining a set-theoretical predicate, in which case the theory structure is exactly the class of model-types that satisfy the set-theoretical predicate (e.g., Suppes 2002; da Costa and French 2003).

An interesting question is whether there is an important logical difference between defining the class of models directly as opposed to meta-mathematically. Both Friedman (1982) and Worrall (1984) have argued that if the class of models that constitutes the theory, according to the SV, is identified with an *elementary* class that contains precisely the models of a theory formalized in first-order language, then the SV is equivalent to the RV. Van Fraassen (1987) has responded to this argument by accentuating that mathematical concepts, like the real-number continuum, which are assumed as part of the formal background of scientific theories, cannot easily be included in a Hilbert-style formalization that assumes only the apparatus of first-order logic. Whether or not there is an important logical difference between RV and SV is an issue that concerns the structure of theories and not the nature of scientific models. For our purposes, it is worth noting that the SV is the first systematic attempt to explore the nature and function of mathematical models in science, and that it has shed significant light on the importance of mathematical models as a guide to understanding the scientific representation of phenomena.

According to the SV, a model that belongs to the class that constitutes the theory is proposed for the representation of a target physical system. Since it is questionable whether such models fully capture the nature and function of actual scientific models, that is, mathematical models used in actual science for representing physical systems, let us – in order to distinguish them from the latter – label them "theoretical models" (following Giere 1988). Experimental data from measurements on the relevant apparatus are then used to construct what, following Suppes (1962), has been dubbed a "data-model." The theoretical model is then contrasted to the data-model. Because the two models are mathematical structures, the comparison between the two consists in mapping the elements and relations of one structure onto the other. Since on one side of the comparison we have a constitutive part of the theory structure and on the other a structured representation of the relevant data, the mapping relation between the two, according to the SV, fully captures the relation between theory and experiment. These are general theses of the SV that possibly all of its adherents would concur with.

Some differences among the various versions of the SV concern the interpretation of the mapping relation between theoretical and data models. Van Fraassen (1980) suggests that it stands for isomorphism between a data-model and an empirical substructure that is embedded in a theoretical model. Da Costa and French (2003) suggest that it stands for isomorphism between partial structures, that is, structures in which only some of its ordered n-tuples satisfy the sentences expressing the n-ary relations between the individuals concerned. Suppe (1989) interprets the mapping relation counterfactually and suggests that it indicates only that the theoretical model is "an abstract and idealized replica of" the target system. Giere (1988) suggests that the mapping relation should be construed as a relation that indicates "similarity in respects and degrees" between the theoretical model and the target.

Current debate on the nature and function of scientific models

Without dismissing the importance of the above differences between the various versions, I shall focus on the general contention of the SV that theoretical models, which are direct derivatives of theory, are candidates for representing physical systems by virtue of the fact that they stand in mapping relations to corresponding data-models. Indeed, this is an interesting claim about the theory–experiment relation that manages on the one hand to establish an understanding of models as representational agents, a characteristic that they were denied by the RV, and on the other to maintain a direct logical connection between theories and models. If this were a necessary and sufficient condition for explaining the theory–experiment relation, then actual scientific models would either have to be identified with theoretical models or in some way reduced to the latter. If this were the case, then the construal of scientific models as mere mathematical structures subsumed under a theory structure would be an adequate explication not only of how they actually relate to theory, but also of how they are constructed, of the nature of the conceptual resources used in their construction, of how they are used as sources of knowledge, and of their representational function.

As an objection to understanding scientific models in the manner advocated by the SV, it could be claimed that we rarely see in actual scientific modeling a sharp distinction between theoretical and data models, and that we rarely see working scientists relying merely on a mapping relation to infer the empirical reliability and the representational capacity of a scientific model. But this argument will not do, because the SV does not have to be regarded as a literal description of how scientific theorizing is conducted and of all of its ingredients (after all, scientific theories or models are rarely, if at all, handled e.g. in a set-theoretical formulation), but it could be understood as a rational reconstruction (i.e. a presentation of a logical – in this case set-theoretical – formulation into which the actual formulations of scientific theories could essentially be reformulated) of actual scientific theorizing and modeling.

Arguments against the SV conception of the theory–experiment relation and of scientific models have centered, by and large, on the nature of theoretical models *vis-à-vis* actual scientific models used for the representation of physical systems. One such objection (see Morrison 1998, 1999) is based on the claim that theories, and hence theoretical models as direct conceptual descendants of theory, are highly abstract and idealized descriptions of phenomena, and hence they represent only the general features of phenomena and do not explain the specific mechanisms at work in physical systems. In contrast, scientific models are distinct from theories and should be understood as partially autonomous mediators between theories and phenomena that are constructed in ways so as to explain the specific mechanisms, and they function as sources of knowledge about corresponding target systems and their constitutive parts. This argument, in which representational capacity is correlated to the explanatory power of models, achieves two goals. Firstly, it offers a way by which to go beyond the narrow understanding of scientific representation as a mapping relation. Secondly, it offers a general way to understand the representational function of both kinds of models that physicists call "phenomenological" and "theory-driven."

Both phenomenological and theory-driven models possess explanatory power because both represent their targets, although the ways by which they are constructed may differ. The SV could accommodate an explanation of why theory-driven models possess representational capacity – at least, for some theories, for example, classical mechanics – by appealing to their close logical (structural) relation to theory. However, it is forced to undervalue the representational capacity of phenomenological models because they do not relate to theory in any direct way, and especially because they cannot be reduced to theoretical models. The explanatory-power criterion, on the other hand, renders models *representational*, independently of the strength of their relation to theory, on the basis of how well they achieve the purpose of providing explanations for what occurs in physical systems.

There is an important difference between the SV approach and Morrison's approach to understanding the representational function of scientific models. The SV defines the representational function of models in terms of what it claims to be a primitive and more fundamental characteristic of science: namely, the mapping relation of structures. Morrison does not attempt to define the representational function of models, because in her view this function can be achieved in a variety of unrelated ways, but instead points to the reason why a model can be representational: because it can fulfil the explanatory-power criterion. The latter is a feature common to every representational model, hence it is a necessary characteristic for models to be representational.

The explanatory-power criterion is admittedly too general, and its different senses and instances need to be explored. For example, in one sense, theories explain the general aspects of phenomena, whereas models explain specific features of physical systems. I briefly sketch two examples in an attempt to elucidate the idea of *explanatory power* by contrasting it to that of a *mapping relation*. The first example concerns theory-driven models and the second phenomenological models. In doing so, I aim to expose the fact that the *mapping-relation* criterion, despite being a plausible suggestion for understanding the nature of theory-driven models, does not do justice to phenomenological models. My intention, however, is not to present an exhaustive analysis in order to establish the adequacy or inadequacy of each of the two criteria in explicating the representational function of models.

As a first example, I choose a standard modeling procedure in the application of classical mechanics, which demonstrates the strengths of the semantic approach and which, in fact, may be its best-case scenario. Let the physical system we wish to model be a horizontally oriented, flexible, stretched string held at its end-points by fixed supports, very much like the situation we encounter in various stringed musical instruments, which is plucked at one of its points; let us also imagine that at one of its end-points we place a force-meter of negligible weight calibrated in such a way as to measure force-magnitude along the longitudinal direction. If we assume, *inter alia*, that the two supports are rigid, that the transverse displacement by the plucking is infinitesimally small, that the tension on the string changes insignificantly (i.e., it is constant), and ignore all external forces acting on the string, then we can model the system by means of the well-known *scalar wave equation* of motion for the string. If, however, we assume all things about the physical system exactly as mentioned above but consider the tension acting on the string as a variable quantity then, we model the system by means of what we could call the *Euler–Lagrange equation* of motion for the vibrating string.

Despite the idealizations involved in their construction, both of these models are explanatory but their explanatory power is not the same. The difference lies in the fact that the wave equation does not explain (or predict) the variations in the tension (i.e., compressions and rarefactions of the string along the longitudinal direction) of the actual physical system detected by the attached force-meter, whereas the Euler–Lagrange equation predicts their occurrence and explains how longitudinal variations of the tension interact with transverse vibrations of the string. In other words, it explains how two different processes operate together in the physical system. Hence the latter is a better representation of the actual physical system than the former.

The SV also gives a good explanation of the difference in representational capacity between the two models. It appeals to the degree of idealization in each of the models claiming that the model that satisfies the Euler–Lagrange equation is less idealized than that which satisfies the wave equation. Both structures – if we were to speak the language of partial structures suggested by da Costa and French (2003) – are partially isomorphic to data about the physical system. That is to say, both share parts of their structure with the corresponding data-model, but the Euler–Lagrange equation for the string model, being less idealized, shares more parts than its competitor, and hence is a better choice for representing the physical system. It could be claimed that this understanding of the degree of representational capacity of models is based on the hypothesis that the process of idealization can be construed as a partial ordering of structures. This is a debatable issue, one that I do not explore here.

Although it is possible to look into the two criteria in more detail and discern minor differences in their strengths and weaknesses in explaining the representational capacity of theory-driven models, for the purposes of my argument (i.e., that the important differences are to be found in the explication of the representational capacity of phenomenological models), we could assume that they are equally good.

The second example I sketch here does, however, illuminate important differences in the two approaches. When physicists attempted to explore the structure of the nucleus, the theoretical models of quantum mechanics could not be used in modeling the target system. One reason for this was that when applied to an arbitrary number of nucleons the Schrödinger equation gives rise to the nuclear many-body problem for which no analytic solution is available. Hence no significant insight into the physics of the nucleus can be gained. The physics community proceeded by constructing Hamiltonians in phenomenological ways. The result was the construction of various models, such as the liquid-drop model, the shell model, and the unified model of nuclear structure (for a discussion of these models, see Morrison 1998; Portides 2005, 2006), each of which represents aspects of the nuclear structure. The three models are based on different conceptions of nuclear behavior and different hypotheses about nuclear motion. The liquid-drop model assumes that the nucleus is a collection of closely coupled particles and accounts only for collective modes of nuclear motion; the shell model assumes that the nucleons move in rather independent ways in an average nuclear field and accounts for nuclear motion only as an aggregate of independent nucleon motion. Finally, the unified model assumes that the nucleons move nearly independently in a common, slowly changing, nuclear potential, thus accounting for a collective nuclear motion that interacts with nucleon motion.

As a result of these differences each model explains features of the nucleus that its competitor models do not. Based on the explanatory-power criterion, each of these models may be understood to represent aspects of the nuclear structure, because on the one hand each explains the behavior of the nucleus due to those aspects, and on the other hand it explains the particular semi-empirical results that guide its construction. Furthermore, the same criterion leads to the conclusion that the unified model can be considered a better representation of the nucleus in comparison to its competitors, because it explains most of the known results about the nucleus. Hence, on the basis of the explanatory-power criterion we are able to classify phenomenological models as representational and also rank their representational capacity on the basis of the comparative degree of explanation. Indeed, explanatory power is not just a matter of counting the number of features of the target for which the model gives an account. The unified model outmatches its predecessors because it provides a specific explanation of how different processes operate together in the nucleus: namely, it explains how collective motion and particle motion in nuclei interact, and it offers an explanation of the structure of the nucleus based on that interaction.

If we focus solely on structural criteria to evaluate these models as representational agents, then we are faced with a number of problems. Firstly, it is not possible to evaluate the representational capacity of each model because when we look at the ways in which they are constructed it is not possible to reconstruct the essential requirement of structural representation, namely, a sharp distinction between a theoretical and a data model. Secondly, even if we were able to overcome the first problem, we would not be able to clearly rank the representational capacity of different models, because they do not represent the same aspects of the target system, but also because they represent the target system in different ways (see Morrison 1998, 1999). Thirdly, we would overlook the importance of the evolutionary history of models in achieving improvements in our representation of physical systems (see Portides 2006). Hence we would be forced to dismiss the representational capacity of some models on the basis of the requirement that representational models must be structurally related to theory. But the latter is a hypothesis about models and scientific modeling that needs to be grounded on evidence from actual models, and it seems that phenomenological models, by and large, disconfirm it.

Since scientific models are expressed in terms of mathematical equations and it is a trivial matter that equations satisfy a structure, the structural characteristics of models cannot be ignored. But understanding scientific models solely as mathematical structures subsumed under a theory structure is a highly restrictive perspective that makes us overlook important elements used in the construction of our most successful models, and thus does not enable us to understand all kinds of modeling in science. Moreover, understanding representation by means of models solely as a mapping relation between structures leads us to undervalue the representational function of important models in the history of science that fail to meet this criterion. The unified model, above, is unquestionably an important result in the history of nuclear physics: it is the outcome of an evolutionary history of which both the liquid-drop model and the shell model are important ingredients. If we were to dismiss the representational capacity of the latter two models (e.g., on the grounds that they do not share parts of their structure with theory) we would fail to evaluate correctly the reasoning involved in constructing the unified model, and consequently we would fail to understand the reasons it came to be considered successful. To avoid such drawbacks we are compelled, therefore, to regard the two models as representations of their target system, despite their shortcomings, just as we regard the wave equation as a representation of the vibrating string, despite its shortcomings. The explanatory-power criterion seems to be a better justification than the mapping relation criterion for such a conclusion. More generally, it could be argued that by identifying a representational model with only one of its modes, i.e., that of being a mathematical structure, it obscures the character of a model as an entity in which theoretical principles, semi-empirical results, and experimental findings are blended together to give it its distinct representational capacity. Furthermore, it detaches the model from its evolutionary history; hence it also blurs its characteristic of being an entity in which scientific concepts are formed.

Another kind of argument that also targets the SV, and in particular how theory application is conceived within the SV, is based on the claim that theories are highly abstract and thus do not, and cannot, represent what happens in actual situations (Cartwright 1999). This same characteristic is explicitly recognized by some proponents of the SV. It is, for instance, why Suppe (1989) opts for the view that the most science can achieve is to represent nature by means of abstract and idealized replicas, i.e., theoretical models. It is also implicitly present in the view advocated by da Costa and French (2003), who interpret the theory–experiment relation in terms of partial isomorphism precisely because they recognize that isomorphism between the two structures never obtains in scientific practice. But Cartwright's objection is much more robust: to claim that theories represent what happens in actual situations is to overlook that the concepts used in them – such as *force functions* and *Hamiltonians* – are abstract. Such abstract concepts could apply to the phenomena only whenever more concrete descriptions (such as those present in models) can stand in for them, and for that to happen the bridge principles of theory must mediate (see Cartwright 1999). Hence the abstract terms of theory apply to actual situations via *bridge principles*, and in order to be able to make sense of the application of theory to phenomena we must regard its bridge principles as an integral part of theory. It is only when bridge principles sanction the use of theoretical models that we are led to the construction of a model that represents the target system and is closely related to theory. Now Cartwright observes that there are only a small number of theoretical models that can be used successfully to construct representations of physical systems and also that there are only a handful of theory bridge principles. In most other cases, where no bridge principles exist that enable the use of a theoretical model, concrete descriptions of phenomena are achieved by constructing phenomenological models. Phenomenological models are also constructed with the aid of theory, but there is no deductive (or structural) relation between them and theory. The relation between the two should be sought in the nature of the abstract–concrete distinction between scientific concepts, which should not be interpreted as one of inclusion, as if the concrete concept can be defined in terms of the abstract concept plus differentia. This is so because the concrete concept has a sense of its own, independent of the abstract concept it falls under. So, models in science, whether constructed phenomenologically or by the use of available bridge principles, encompass descriptions that are in some way independent from theory because they are made up of more concrete conceptual ingredients.

A weak reading of this argument is that the SV could be a plausible suggestion for understanding the structure of scientific theories as foundational work. But in the context of utilizing the theory to construct representations of actual situations, focusing on the structure of theory is disorienting because it is insufficient as an account of the abstract–concrete distinction that exists between theory and models. A stronger reading of the argument is that the structure of theories is completely irrelevant to how theories represent the world, because they just do not represent it at all. Only models represent pieces of the world, and they are detached from theory because they are constituted by concrete concepts that apply only to particular physical systems.

Conclusion

Mathematical models are essential to the scientific representation of phenomena. A number of interconnected questions need to be addressed in order to reach an adequate understanding of the sort of entities that they are and how they function as representational agents:

- How do they relate to theory?
- How do they relate to experimental data?
- How are they constructed?
- What conceptual ingredients are used in their construction?
- How are they used as sources of knowledge?
- How does their idealizational nature affect their representational function?
- What is the nature of their representational function?

Whether all these questions can be adequately addressed, so that an understanding of theory application to phenomena can be attained without violating a unifying view of theories and models, is a controversial issue. Theory, of course, constrains scientific modeling within its domain, but that alone is not sufficient reason to resort to the view that the interplay between theory and models is as simple as that suggested by unifying approaches.

See also Idealization; Measurement; Mechanisms; Representation in science; The structure of theories.

References

Cartwright, N. D. (1999) *The Dappled World: A Study of the Boundaries of Science*, Cambridge: Cambridge University Press.

Da Costa, N. C. A. and French, S. (2003) *Science and Partial Truth*, Oxford: Oxford University Press.

Friedman, M. (1982) "Review of Bas C. van Fraassen: *The Scientific Image*," *Journal of Philosophy* 79: 274–83.

Giere, R. (1988) *Explaining Science: A Cognitive Approach*, Chicago, University of Chicago Press.

Morrison, M. C. (1998) "Modeling Nature: Between Physics and the Physical World," *Philosophia Naturalis* 35: 65–85.

—— (1999) "Models as Autonomous Agents," in M. Morgan and M. Morrison (eds) *Models as Mediators: Perspectives on Natural and Social Science*, Cambridge: Cambridge University Press, pp. 38–65.

Portides, D. (2005) "Scientific Models and the Semantic View of Scientific Theories," *Philosophy of Science* 72: 1287–98.

—— (2006) "The Evolutionary History of Models as Representational Agents," in L. Magnani (ed.) *Model-Based Reasoning in Science and Engineering*, Texts in Logic, vol. 2, London: College Publications, pp. 87–106.

Suppe, F. (1977) "The Search for Philosophic Understanding of Scientific Theories" (1974), in F. Suppe (ed.) *The Structure of Scientific Theories*, Urbana: University of Illinois Press, pp. 3–241.

—— (1989) *The Semantic Conception of Theories and Scientific Realism*, Urbana: University of Illinois Press.

Suppes, P. (1962) "Models of Data," in E. Nagel, P. Suppes, and A. Tarski (eds) *Logic, Methodology and Philosophy of Science*, Stanford, CA: Stanford University Press, pp. 252–61.

—— (2002) *Representation and Invariance of Scientific Structures*, Stanford: CSLI Publications.

Van Frassen, Bas C. (1980) *The Scientific Image*, Oxford: Clarendon Press.

—— (1987) "The Semantic Approach to Scientific Theories," in N. J. Nersessian (ed.) *The Process of Science*, Dordrecht: Martinus Nijhoff, pp. 105–24.

Worrall, J. (1984) "Review Article: An Unreal Image," *British Journal of the Philosophy of Science* 35: 65–80.

Further reading

In addition to the literature on models listed above the volume by M. S. Morgan and M. Morrison (eds) *Models as Mediators* (Cambridge: Cambridge University Press, 1999) includes a number of essays dedicated to model construction in science. Analyses on how the semantic approach could deal with issues concerning representational models can be found in N. C. A. da Costa and S. French, "The Model-Theoretic Approach in the Philosophy of Science," *Philosophy of Science* 57 (1990): 248–65; and in R. I. G. Hughes's "Models and Representation," in L. Darden (ed.) *PSA 1996, Philosophy of Science* (Supplement) 64 (1996): 325–36. For an analysis of the processes of idealization and abstraction in scientific model construction the work by Suppe mentioned above is a good starting point, but different approaches can be found in S. French and J. Ladyman's "A Semantic Perspective on Idealisation in Quantum Mechanics," in Niall Shanks (ed.) *Idealization IX: Poznan Studies in the Philosophy of the Sciences and the Humanities*, 63 (Amsterdam: Rodopi, 1998), pp. 51–73; in E. McMullin's "Galilean Idealization," in *Studies in History and Philosophy of Science* 16 (1985): 247–73; in L. Nowak's *The Structure of Idealization* (Dordrecht: Reidel, 1980); in D. Portides's "A Theory of Scientific Model Construction: The Conceptual Process of Abstraction and Concretization," *Foundations of Science* 10 (2005): 67–88.

37

OBSERVATION

André Kukla

Observation plays a unique role in philosophical accounts of the scientific enterprise. Traditionally it is what distinguishes science from other epistemic enterprises like mathematics, philosophy, theology, and many of the pseudo-sciences. Conventional wisdom has it that the content of our observations is given to us by nature itself – it constitutes our *data*. Hence its pronouncements are mandatory. We may adopt opinions that go beyond what has been observed. But (according to conventional wisdom) these opinions are minimally required to square with the data.

Everyone agrees that science goes beyond the observational given to some extent (or else it would be mere journalism or natural history). But different groups of scientists and different historical eras have held vastly different opinions about how far beyond the data it is permissible or desirable to travel. The more closely a scientist or a philosopher hews to the data, the more of an *empiricist* she is. A major peak of empiricism came in the 1920s and 1930s with the logical positivists. According to the early (and more extremely empiricist) proponents of that philosophical school, a statement is meaningless unless it can be translated, or *reduced*, to *observation language* – a language consisting of terms that describe only observable properties of observable things (Ayer 1936). Statements about unobservable electrons were thought to be reducible to statements about observable tracks on photographic plates; statements about unobservable mental states were to be translated into statements about observable behavior; and so on.

These translation exercises failed, in psychology as well as in physics. Almost all of the interesting and fruitful concepts of science resisted reduction to anything remotely like an observation language. Their failure impelled the positivists to liberalize their criterion of meaningfulness. The old requirement was that scientific hypotheses must be *logically equivalent* to an observation statement. The new requirement was that hypotheses need only *entail* one or more observation statements. Scientific theories were now permitted to contain unreduced theoretical terms, so long as the theories had observational consequences. This became the standard view of science at mid-century.

The standard view also encompassed the following account of how one should choose between competing theories of the same domain. To choose between theories T_1 and T_2, you find an observation statement O such that O is an observational consequence of T_1, and not-O, the negation of O, is an observational consequence of T_2. Then you observe whether O or not-O. The theory with the right observational consequence wins.

Kuhn's view

The standard view encountered a number of difficulties, the most famous of which was the critique in Thomas Kuhn's 1962 seminal study of scientific revolutions. Kuhn claimed that the theoretical framework of the observer determines the nature of his perceptual experience. Suppose that a physicist and a non-physicist are looking at one and the same cloud chamber at the same time. It was Kuhn's contention that, because their minds are furnished with different conceptual schemes, the physicist and the novice will literally see different things:

> Seeing water droplets or a needle against a numerical scale is a primitive perceptual experience for the man unacquainted with cloud chambers and ammeters. It thus requires contemplation, analysis, and interpretation (or else the intervention of external authority) before conclusions can be reached about electrons or currents. But the position of the man who has learned about these instruments and had much exemplary experience with them is very different, and there are corresponding differences in the way he processes the stimuli that reach him from them. Regarding the vapor in his breath on a cold winter afternoon, his sensation may be the same as that of a layman, but viewing a cloud chamber he sees (here literally) not droplets but the tracks of electrons, alpha particles, and so on. (1962: 97)

The same point – that expertise alters the perceptual experience of the expert – has been made more recently by Paul Churchland (1988). According to Churchland, a trained musician "perceives, in any composition whether great or mundane, a structure, development and rationale that is lost on the untrained ear" (1988: 20). Both Kuhn's and Churchland's examples involve a comparison between a sophisticated and a naive conceptual apparatus. But Kuhn and Churchland believe that the same thing happens when we compare two sophisticated conceptions. A radically different theory of cloud chamber tracks – say, an account that attributed them to fairy-dust – would generate another perceptual experience different from either the physicist's or the layman's.

The Kuhnian view of perception has drastic consequences for the standard view of theory choice. If scientists with different theories see different things, then theory-neutral observation is an impossibility. And if there is no theory-neutral observation, there can be no theory-neutral observation *language*, for the simple reason that there's nothing for such a language to be about. Every attempt to describe the given goes beyond it. There are no pure data. But then the standard view of theory choice is unworkable! Standard-viewers would have us resolve the conflict between T_1 and T_2 by finding an observation statement O such that T_1 entails O and T_2 entails not-O. But this presupposes that the consequences of T_1 and the consequences of T_2 can be formulated in one and the same language. If our observations are theory-laden, the observational consequences of T_1 will be neither the same as the observational consequences T_2 nor the negations of the observational consequences of T_2. If Kuhn is right, T_1 and T_2 will be *incommensurable*.

Then how do we choose between competing theories? The question dominated the philosophy of science in the closing decades of the twentieth century. There are various replies on the philosophical table. The most radical is *social constructivism* (Latour and Woolgar 1979). Constructivists bite the bullet and say that theory choice is not a rational process. Theories vanquish their rivals through a process of social influence. Their truth is negotiated, not discovered. Less radical, but still far from the standard view, is Paul Feyerabend's position (1975) that there is no need to make a choice between T_1 and T_2. Since they are incommensurable, they can't contradict each other. Thus we do not commit any logical errors by accepting both. The most conservative response to the Kuhnian dilemma is to repudiate Kuhn's view of perception and to defend the standard view. I will discuss Jerry Fodor's defense (1984, 1988).

Fodor's view

In a reply to Churchland's disquisition on the perceptual effect of musical expertise, Fodor says that Churchland merely begs the question whether this effect is, in fact, perceptual: "What Churchland has to show is … that *perceptual* capacities are altered by learning musical theory (as opposed to the truism that learning musical theory alters what you know about music) …" (1988: 195). Presumably, Fodor would say the same about Kuhn's physicist. In both cases, Fodor grants to his antagonists that experts are wont to describe their experiences in terms different from those of novices. Kuhn and Churchland want to say that they do this because their perceptual experience has been altered by their expertise. Fodor's point is that the differences in perceptual reports can as well be explained by the alternative hypothesis that the physicist and the musician enjoyed the same theory-neutral perceptual experience, but that when it came to reporting what they saw or heard they chose to correct their account of the event in light of their background theories.

Kuhn cited experimental evidence for his view. In the 1950s, the psychologist Jerome Bruner (1957) and his colleagues conducted a series of experiments which purported to show that one's expectations – more generally, one's background theories – influence perception. However, the results of most of their experiments could as well be explained by Fodor's alternative hypothesis. Moreover, Fodor pin-points a fundamental difficulty with the Kuhnian case for the impossibility of theory-free observation. Grant that Bruner et al. have established that one's background theories influence perception. It does not yet follow that scientists with different theories will see different things. We can accept Kuhn's and Bruner's hypothesis that cognition influences perception, while still maintaining that there are *some* cognitive differences between scientists that make no perceptual differences. But then, even if Kuhn's hypothesis is true, it is possible for scientists who hold different theories to see the same thing when they look in the same direction – it just may be that the cognitive difference between them is one of those that does not make any perceptual difference. In fact, it is possible that *none* of the theoretical differences among scientists makes any difference to perception. To show the impossibility of theory-neutral observation, you would have to establish that *all* cognitive differences have an effect on perception – and that goes beyond what Bruner's research has established on even the most sanguine reading.

Fodor claims that many of our background beliefs do *not* influence perception. The most persuasive evidence comes from the persistence of perceptual illusions:

> The Müller–Lyer illusion is a *familiar* illusion; the news has pretty well gotten around by now. So, it's part of the 'background theory' of anybody who lives in this culture and is at all into pop psychology that displays [of the Müller–Lyer illusion] are in fact misleading and that it always turns out, on measurement, that the center lines of the arrows are the same length. Query: *Why isn't perception penetrated by THAT piece of background theory?...* This sort of consideration doesn't make it seem at all as though perception is, as it's often said to be, saturated with cognition through and through. On the contrary, it suggests just the reverse: that how the world looks can be peculiarly unaffected by how one knows it to be. (1984: 34)

The persistence of illusions suggests that perception is *informationally encapsulated*: only a restricted range of information is capable of influencing the output of perceptual processes (Fodor 1983: 64). That conclusion is a part of Fodor's broader theory that perceptual systems are *modular* (the other characteristics of modules do not concern us here).

But if perception is modular, then the story that Kuhn tells about the physicist and the novice may very well be false:

> [I]f perceptual processes are modular, then, by definition, bodies of theories that are inaccessible to the modules *do not affect the way the perceiver sees the world*. Specifically, perceivers who differ profoundly in their background theories – scientists with quite different axes to grind, for example, might nevertheless see the world in *exactly* the same way, so long as the bodies of theory that they disagree about are inaccessible to their perceptual mechanisms. (1984: 38)

Moreover, the possibility of theory-neutral observation brings in its train the possibility of a theory-neutral observation *language*:

> Suppose that perceptual mechanisms are modular and that the body of background theory accessible to processes of perceptual integration is therefore rigidly fixed. By hypothesis, only those properties of the distal stimulus count as observable which terms in the *accessible* background theory denote. The

point is, no doubt, empirical, but I am willing to bet lots that 'red' will prove to be observational by this criterion and that 'proton' will not. This is, of course, just a way of betting that ... physics doesn't belong to the accessible background. (1984: 38)

As Fodor says, the point is empirical. But there are also conceptual problems with Fodor's purported dissolution of the Kuhnian dilemma. The most important of these also afflict Bas van Fraassen's treatment of observation.

Van Fraassen's view

I noted above that the positivists had to abandon their early claim that the theoretical statements of science were translatable into purely observational statements. The standard view that came next required only that theoretical statements have observational consequences. But what was one to make of the parts of the theory that *do not* describe observational consequences – the *theoretical* parts? Here the standard view divides into two streams. *Scientific realists* say that the confirmation of an observational consequence – observing what the theory leads you to expect – is (defeasible) evidence for the existence of the unobservable entities postulated by the theory. *Anti-realists* deny this on empiricist grounds. Anti-realists come in two varieties. *Instrumentalists* say that electrons and other theoretical entities are merely convenient fictions useful for predicting observations. *Constructive empiricists* concede that theoretical terms literally refer to unobservable entities, but maintain that we can never know whether those entities actually exist – the most that we can know about a theory is that it is *empirically adequate*, which means that all of its claims about observables are true.

Both types of anti-realist wish to ascribe a philosophically superior status to the observational – for instrumentalists, the superiority is metaphysical; for constructive empiricists, it is epistemological. Evidently, the coherence of these positions depends on there being a coherent way to distinguish the observational from the non-observational. On the standard view, the distinction rests on a difference between two parts of the scientific vocabulary: observation language and theoretical language. Kuhn argued that this linguistic distinction could not be made. Anti-realism would seem to be a non-starter if Kuhn is right. Fodor argues that Kuhn is not right. Now Fodor is not himself an anti-realist; but if *he* is right, anti-realists might be able to use his analysis in defense of their doctrine. However, the most influential anti-realist of the past couple of decades, van Fraassen, begins his own analysis by fully accepting the Kuhnian critique:

All our language is thoroughly theory-infected. If we could cleanse our language of theory-laden terms, beginning with the recently introduced ones like 'VHF receiver', continuing through 'mass' and 'impulse' to 'element' and so on into the prehistory of language formation, we would end up with nothing useful. The way we talk, and scientists talk, is guided by the pictures provided by previously accepted theories. This is true also ... of experimental reports. (1980: 14)

Van Fraassen believes that he can make the observational–non-observational distinction in a way which is compatible with Kuhn. His idea is to make the distinction in terms of *entities* instead of languages. Our scientific theories tell us, in their unavoidably theory-laden manner, that certain entities or events impinge on our sensory transducers, and that others do not. For example, science tells us that some middle-sized physical objects such as sticks and stones are of the right size and configuration for reflecting light in the portion of the spectrum to which our retina is sensitive. The objects are visually observable entities. On the other hand, our physical theories tell us that individual elementary particles are not observable. The language is equally theoretical in both cases; but anti-realists can choose to privilege theory-laden statements about observable entities such as sticks and stones over theory-laden statements about unobservable entities such as electrons. Of course, they need to justify the move; but if van Fraassen's distinction works, they can at least state their thesis coherently, thereby avoiding checkmate in one move.

Critique of Fodor's and van Fraassen's views

Unfortunately for anti-realists, van Fraassen's distinction is afflicted with a number of philosophical problems. The articles by Maxwell (1962), Churchland (1985), and Kukla (1996) offer up a generous selection of the problems. (Maxwell's critique was actually directed at the logical positivists' linguistic distinction; but it turns out that most of what he has to say applies as well to van Fraassen's distinction.) Because of limitations on space, I discuss only one critical argument. This is, however, one of the most persuasive (and most colorful) criticisms. It is discussed by all three of the cited critics. I call it the *electron-microscope eye argument*.

Maxwell notes that whether or not a particular entity is observable (in either the positivists' or van Fraassen's sense) depends on the currently available instruments of science. Much of what was unobservable in the past has now become observable on account of the development of new scientific instruments, and there is every reason to believe that some of the things that we are unable to observe at present will become observable by means of the new and improved observational technology of the future. If you equate observability with *current* detectability, observability becomes a context-dependent notion that will not sustain the anti-realist thesis. Anti-realists do not just want to say that there is a class of entities that we can't believe in *now* – they want to say that there is a class of entities that can't *ever* be believed in, no matter what happens in the worlds of science and technology. For that purpose, they need a concept of observability that is free of contextual dependence. One alternative is to say that entities are unobservable if and only if they are undetectable by any physically possible means of instrumentation. The problem with this formula is that there is no reason to believe that any entity postulated by science, if it exists, would fail to qualify as observable. The anti-realist has no argument against the possibility that this concept of observability posits a distinction without a difference.

Van Fraassen tries to decontextualize the concept of *observability* in a different manner: he restricts the observable to what can be detected by the unaided senses. But does this move really effect a decontextualization? Maxwell himself had brought up the possibility that mutations might give rise to human beings with sensory capacities beyond our own. They might be able to observe ultraviolet radiation, or even X-rays, with their unaided senses (1962: 11). Churchland, mounting the same objection, asks us to consider the possibility of human mutants – or extraterrestrials – with electron-microscope eyes (1985). Clearly, the possibilities of genetic improvement in observational capacities are as unlimited as technological improvements. Thus the stipulation that observation be restricted to what can be accomplished by the unaided senses is no restriction at all.

The same criticism can be leveled at Fodor's distinction: if you define *observability* as that which can be the output of an endogenously specified perceptual module, then there is no telling what may be deemed observable in the future, on encounters with human mutants or extraterrestrials who have radically different perceptual modules. Churchland has used his electron-microscope eye argument against Fodor (Churchland 1988) as well as against van Fraassen (Churchland 1985). Here is Fodor's reply:

> Churchland apparently wants a naturalistic account of scientific objectivity to supply a guaranty that an arbitrary collection of intelligent organisms (for example, a collection consisting of some Homo sapiens and some Martians) would satisfy the empirical conditions for constituting a scientific community. *Of course* there can be no such guaranty. (1988: 190)

A book could be written explicating the notion of a *scientific community*. For present purposes, the following characterization will do: two beings are in the same scientific community if their opinions converge under ideal epistemic conditions. If, as seems likely, observability plays a special role in epistemology, then it may be necessary that two scientists have to agree about what is observable in order to belong to the same scientific community. Fodor alerts us to the possibility that we and the Martians may fail to meet this requirement.

All this may be true, as far as it goes. But it doesn't yet fully answer Maxwell's and Churchland's objection. It's possible that we and the Martians may be so differently endowed with senses that there can be no fruitful contact between our science and theirs. But it is also possible that we and the Martians are differently endowed with senses, but that the differences are not so profound that there can be no fruitful contact between our respective sciences. The requirement that we agree on what is *observable* does not entail that we have the same sensory capacities. If A is able to observe a phenomenon that B can't observe, A and B may yet be part of the same scientific community. All that is required is that B be willing to *credit* A's observational reports about the events that B is unable to witness. After all, there are *blind* scientists who consider their sighted colleagues to be part of their scientific community. If we denied that one could ever regard as *observable* an event that we ourselves are unable to observe, then we would have to accuse such scientists of irrationality. I am not prepared to spell out when it is or is not appropriate to credit another's observational claims. But it seems sufficient for accreditation that there be significant overlap between the two beings' sensory capacities, as there is between blind and sighted human scientists. In any case, whatever the crucial factor may be that allows blind and sighted scientists to belong to the same scientific community, the same factor can surely be shared by sighted human scientists and mutant or extraterrestrial scientists. For example, human mutants might develop whose sensory capacities are exactly the same as ours, except that they can see further into the ultraviolet spectrum than we can. It seems compelling that this case be treated the same as the blind-versus-sighted case: if it is rational for the blind to credit the visual reports of the sighted, then it is equally rational for us non-mutants to credit the mutants' reports of ultraviolet perception.

But that is the first step onto a slippery slope. We've granted that any event is observable for *some* possible being, and that if the perceptual differences between us and other beings are sufficiently small, then it is rational to expand our scientific community to include them. Now consider a being M whose perceptual capacities are as different from ours as we like. There is going to be a *series* of possible beings that has the following properties: (1) its first member is us; (2) its last member is M; and (3) the perceptual differences between any two adjacent members in the series are so small that the rational thing for any being to do is to enlarge its scientific community so as to include the being immediately next to it in the series. It follows from (1), (2), and (3) that we and M would belong to the same scientific community, if all beings acted rationally. This argument will work with any being M possessing arbitrarily different perceptual capacities. Thus for *any* supposedly *theoretical* entity X that exists, there are possible circumstances under which we have to admit that X is observable – the circumstances being the existence of a series of beings having properties (1), (2), and (3), where M is a being that can perceive X. And so both Fodor's and van Fraassen's concepts of observability posit a distinction without a difference.

What van Fraassen has to do in order to avoid the collapse of his anti-realism, and what Fodor has to do to shore up his defense against Kuhnian relativism, is *not allow any flexibility in the composition of the scientific community*. If you're in, you're in, and if you're out, you're going to stay out no matter what happens. That's the only way to assure there's going to be a class of claims that can *never* be believed, come what may. But this is a big philosophical pill to swallow. After all, it is not as though van Fraassen or Fodor or anybody else had offered us an epistemically relevant criterion for who should and who should not get included in the community in the first place. It's hard to imagine that there could be a plausible criterion that allows blind and sighted scientists to be members of the same community, but disallows the communality of the sighted scientists of the present and mutant scientists of the future who are just like them except that they can see further into the ultraviolet range. The fact that the boundaries include the blind and the sighted, but not the extra-sighted is not *rationalized* in any way; it is presented to us as a *fait accompli*. In other words, the inflexible boundaries around the scientific community are drawn *arbitrarily*.

In sum, both Fodor's and van Fraassen's ways of distinguishing the observational from the non-observational are problematic. That is where my story ends. But the analysis of the topic has been pursued further in all directions. There have been attempts to defend van Fraassen's distinction against the electron-microscope eye argument; there have been additional arguments against van Fraassen's conception; and conceptions of observability have been proposed that are different from either Fodor's or van Fraassen's, to which the foregoing criticism may not apply. Relevant references will be found among the reading recommendations below.

See also Empiricism; Logical empiricism; Psychology.

References

Ayer, A. J. (1936) *Language, Truth and Logic*, Oxford: Oxford University Press.

Bruner, J. (1957) "On Perceptual Readiness," *Psychological Review* 64: 123–52.

Churchland, P. M. (1985) "The Ontological Status of Observables: in Praise of Superempirical Virtues," in P. M. Churchland and C. A. Hooker (eds) *Images of Science*, Chicago: University of Chicago Press, pp. 35–47.

—— (1988) "Perceptual Plasticity and Theoretical Neutrality: A Reply to Jerry Fodor," *Philosophy of Science* 55: 167–87.

Feyerabend, P. K. (1975) *Against Method: Outline of an Anarchistic Theory of Knowledge*, New York: Humanities Press.

Fodor, J. (1983) *The Modularity of Mind*, Cambridge, MA: MIT Press.

—— (1984) "Observation Reconsidered," *Philosophy of Science* 51: 23–43.

—— (1988) "A Reply to Churchland's 'Perceptual Plasticity and Theoretical Neutrality'," *Philosophy of Science* 55: 188–98.

Kuhn, T. S. (1962) *The Structure of Scientific Revolutions*, Chicago: University of Chicago Press.

Kukla, A. (1996) "The Theory–Observation Distinction," *Philosophical Review* 105: 173–230.

Latour, B. and Woolgar, S. (1979) *Laboratory Life: The Social Construction of Scientific Facts*, London: Sage.

Maxwell, G. (1962) "The Ontological Status of Theoretical Entities," in H. Feigl and G. Maxwell (eds) *Scientific Explanation, Space, and Time*, Minneapolis: University of Minnesota Press.

Van Fraassen, B. C. (1980) *The Scientific Image*, Oxford: Clarendon Press.

Further reading

Some of the most important writings on observation are cited in the bibliography. Ayer's(1936) book – the logical positivists' manifesto – notoriously tries to reduce all meaningful statements to an observational base. P. W. Bridgman's *operationalism* is an early venture in reductionism in physics: *The Logic of Modern Physics* (New York: Macmillan, 1927). J. B. Watson's *behaviorism* promulgates the reductionist program for psychology: *Behaviorism* (New York: Norton, 1930). Kuhn's 1962 thesis of the theory-ladenness of data transformed the discussion of observation, which in turn had repercussions throughout the philosophy of science. D. Gilman assesses Kuhn's reliance on perceptual psychology to sustain his thesis in "What's a Theory to Do ... with Seeing? Or Some Empirical Considerations for Observation and Theory," *British Journal for the Philosophy of Science* 43 (1992): 287–309. The best things to read on Fodor's and van Fraassen's distinctions are the original presentations by Fodor (1984) and van Fraassen (1980). For a defense against the electron-microscope eye argument, see van Fraassen's "Empiricism in the Philosophy of Science," in Churchland and Hooker (eds) *Images of Science*, pp. 245–308. Less entertaining than the electron-microscope eye argument but even more devastating to van Fraassen's distinction is Michael Friedman's argument in his "Review of van Fraassen (1980)," *Journal of Philosophy* 79 (1982): 274–83. For an example of another way to conceive of observability, which may be immune to Churchland's and Friedman's objections, see the discussion of the "third distinction" in Kukla (1996).

38

PREDICTION

Malcolm Forster

Suppose I choose a card and place it face down on the table. You have to predict whether I chose a diamond. Even though the event you are predicting happened in the past, we are comfortable with using the word "predict," as opposed to "postdict." "Prediction" is the "diction" of an event, past, present, or future.

Deductive and probabilistic prediction

In the opening example, a person made the prediction. But in philosophy of science, we are interested primarily in predictions *made by theories*, and that is the notion to be explicated here. If a theory says that I selected the card from a group of ten diamonds, then the theory implies or entails that the selected card is a diamond. The prediction is *entailed by* the theory; this kind of prediction is timeless, for if an entailment holds at one time, it holds at all times.

Now modify the example in the following way: the theory is that only 9 of the 10 cards are diamonds and that the card placed on the table was *randomly* selected from those 10 cards (i.e., that each one had the same chance, 1 in 10 of being selected). The theory no longer entails that the selected card is a diamond, but the theory does imply that the *probability* that the card is a diamond is 9 in 10. To count as a prediction, it is normally understood that the prediction states the occurrence of an event, or state of affairs, that can be *observed* directly to be true or false. Probabilities are not directly observable, so the statement that the card is a diamond *with a probability* of 9 in 10 is not usually thought of as a prediction. In the case of probabilistic theories, we do not ask: "What does the theory predict?" Instead, we ask: "How well did the theory predict, or anticipate, the *actual* observed outcome?" Recent discussion of *prediction* and *predictive accuracy* (Forster and Sober 1994) use the term in this way because it fits with common parlance in statistics. The strength by which a theory is said to predict the observed outcomes is given by the probability it assigns to those outcomes, symbolized $P(e|h)$, where e is the observed outcome, and h denotes the theory in question. $P(e|h)$ is called the *likelihood* of h relative to e, not to be confused with the probability of h given e – written $P(h|e)$ – which is a different concept. Deductive prediction can be thought of as a special kind of probabilistic prediction, in which $P(e|h) = 1$.

If the likelihood is given by the theory itself, then prediction is an objective relation between theory and evidence, depending only on the logical relationship between a hypothesis h and the observed facts e. Either h entails e, in which case the prediction is deductive, or h predicts e with a degree of likelihood given by $P(e \mid h)$.

Rule-governed prediction

Even in the *exact* sciences, such as physics, deductions can be too complex to be tractable. A typical example is that of Clairaut's prediction of the return of Halley's comet in 1759. In that example, it was not the prediction that the comet would return that impressed the scientific community, for it doesn't take a rocket scientist to make the simple extrapolation that a comet previously observed at regular intervals will return again after the same interval of time. In fact, the simple extrapolation predicted that Halley's comet would reach its perihelion (the closest point to the sun) in the middle of 1759. The extraordinary fact was that Clairaut predicted that Halley's comet would return months earlier, near the beginning of 1759. His prediction was based on calculations of the gravitational effects of Jupiter and Saturn on the comet. Such calculations inevitably involve the truncation of higher terms in an equation, without there being any strict deductive justification that such a technique will accurately reflect what is deducible in principle. Nor were there any probability assignments of return dates deducible from the theory. So, strictly speaking, this is not a case of deductive or probabilistic prediction. But the calculation was based on well-established mathematical techniques, which count as *objective* in some sense. Let us refer to this third category as "rule-governed prediction", because it follows fixed rules, even though the rules are not purely deductive. Rule-governed predictions are still objective.

Prediction and confirmation

It is commonly thought that "in assessing the confirmation or evidential support of a hypothesis, we must take into account especially (and perhaps even exclusively) the success or failure of its *predictions*" (Musgrave 1974: 2). If confirmation and prediction are tied together in this way, then any controversy about the nature of confirmation automatically becomes a controversy about the nature of prediction. One such controversy is about whether confirmation is objective or subjective. On the objective view, confirmation is a relation between a hypothesis and its evidence or a comparison of two hypotheses and the evidence, or perhaps a relation between a hypothesis and its evidence given a background theory. On the subjective view, confirmation may also depend on the degree of belief, which may vary from one person to another. Such degrees of belief may depend, for example, on whether an hypothesis h is constructed or invented before or after the evidence e is known. It is uncontroversial, even on the objective view, that what someone *believes* about the confirmation depends on what someone *believes* about the relationship between theory and evidence. But to say that the confirmation relation *itself* depends on degrees of belief is the hallmark of a distinctly subjective view of confirmation.

How not to argue for a subjective theory of confirmation

Suppose we toss ten coins and observe a sequence of heads and tails, such as, HHTHTTTTHH, which we refer to as the evidence *e*. Now consider two possible scenarios. In scenario 1, someone formulates a theory and claims that it predicts *e*, but announces the prediction only after seeing the experimental outcome. In scenario 2, the person makes the same prediction, but announces the prediction in advance, *prior* to seeing the outcomes. Assuming that the predictions are correct in each case, then we are apt to *believe* that the evidence confirms the theory in scenario 2, but not in scenario 1. The only difference that we are told about concerns the timing of the predictions' announcement, which is irrelevant to any objective relationship between theory and evidence. Does it follow that confirmation is therefore subjective? No! For, an objectivist is committed only to the view that historical facts are irrelevant *once* the full logical facts are specified. In this example, the logical facts have not been stated. So, an objectivist can view the historical fact, about when the prediction was announced, as indicating something about the logical facts. In scenario 2, the prediction in advance rules out the possibility that the prediction was "fudged" by using the seen data to adjust parameters in the theory to ensure that the fitted theory produces the correct answer. When the data are unseen, this is impossible. If the difference between fudging and not fudging is objective, then we can explain why our *belief* that the *e* confirms *h* is stronger in scenario 2 than in scenario 1 without conceding that the confirmation relation itself depends on historical contingencies.

If the confirmation relation is objective, and we want to maintain a link between prediction and confirmation, then we need to view prediction as an objective commodity.

Beam balance example

It is essential that the objective view of prediction can be made precise in idealized cases. The beam balance is chosen because it is a real example that lends itself to a very simple mathematical treatment, and it is easily extended to illustrate more complex ideas (see below). Suppose a beam is supported at the center on a pivot (the fulcrum). Two objects will balance one another when hung on opposite sides of the fulcrum if and only if the distance from the fulcrum multiplied by the force acting on each object is equal for both objects. Let one object be a 1 kilogram mass, while the mass of the other object, denoted by θ, is unknown except for the assumption that is it greater than 0. Then the gravitational forces acting on each object are g and θg, respectively, where g is the gravitational field strength (the acceleration due to gravity). If x denotes the distance of the 1 kilogram mass from the fulcrum, and d is the distance that the other mass is hung on the other side, then $x = \theta d$. We can simplify this further by supposing that the object with the unknown mass θ is always hung at a fixed point, exactly 1 unit's distance from the fulcrum, while the kilogram mass is moved back and forth until the beam balances. Then the equation simplifies to $x = \theta$. From this equation, we see why a beam balance is a way of determining the unknown mass from the measured distance x. It is a mass-measuring device.

Prediction versus accommodation

Consider the beam balance equation $x = \theta$, together with the assumption that $\theta > 0$, to be an hypothesis H. Hypotheses with one or more adjustable parameters are often called "composite hypotheses," or *models*. We shall treat this example non-probabilistically, and allude very briefly to the probabilistic case in a separate paragraph. What predictions can be deduced from this hypothesis? It predicts that $x > 0$, but apart from that, no predictions can be deduced from the hypothesis alone. Now suppose we perform a single trial of the experiment; we hang our object on the balance, and adjust the kilogram mass until the beam balances. Denote the adjusted distance by x_1, and record the result of the experiment as $x_1 = 3$, which we might also denote as the statement e_1. H and e_1 now imply that $\theta = 3$. If we add the statement that $\theta = 3$ to the hypothesis, then we end up with a *fitted* hypothesis, which is predictively more powerful than H. The fitted hypothesis entails that $x_1 = 3$, and it therefore counts as a prediction. But the prediction in this case is plainly trivial because $H\&e_1$ entails e_1 no matter what H says.

Doesn't this show that we must deny a connection between prediction and confirmation? For surely the prediction does not confirm the hypothesis H in this case. Nor should it, because the hypothesis H does not predict that $x_1 = 3$. The example is an illustration of the problem of *irrelevant conjunctions*, or the *tacking problem*. From the fact that $H\&e$ entails e, we may conclude that e confirms $H\&e$, because e confirms e, but we must be careful *not* to conclude that e confirms H, unless H by *itself* entails e (which it does not in this case). So long as we are careful, we can maintain the connection between prediction and confirmation.

The fact remains that the fitted hypothesis entails $x_1 = 3$, and not $x_1 = 4$, and this is a limited kind of achievement. In such cases, we say that H *accommodates e* if and only if $H\&e$ is logically consistent or, equivalently, e does not refute H. (This definition applies to the deductive case only; in the probabilistic case we have to define the degree of accommodation as a degree of fit.) Accommodation is weaker than prediction, but it may fail in the beam balance example when the data are more complex. Suppose that in addition to the observation $x_1 = 3$, we perform the experiment a second time and observe that $x_2 = 4$. From the first observation, we conclude that $\theta = 3$ and from the second observation we infer that $\theta = 4$. But θ has only one value, by hypothesis, so the total set of observations is inconsistent with H. In other words, H does not accommodate e, where e is now the conjunction of two observation statements. Note that failure of accommodation is also a failure of prediction because the hypothesis H entails that $x_1 = x_2$, which is observed to be false. In other words, successful prediction entails that accommodation is successful. The converse is not true; we have already seen an example in which there is accommodation but no prediction.

To examine the relationship further, suppose we change the example so that the second trial of the experiment yields $x_2 = 3$, the same value of x as in the first trial. Now H does accommodate e, where e is the total evidence. Beyond accommodation, there is also a stronger relationship between H and e in this case; namely, that e *overdetermines* the value of the parameter in H, which leads to an agreement of independent measurements of θ. The observation $x_1 = 3$ implies that $\theta = 3$, using H, while the observation $x_2 = 3$, *independently* determines that $\theta = 3$, and the values agree (by "independent" we mean only that the measurements are derived from disjoint data sets). The agreement of independent measurements is something over and above an hypothesis merely being able to fit, or accommodate, the data.

There are other ways of viewing the stronger predictive relationship between theory and evidence. One way has already been noted: H predicts that $x_1 = x_2$, and this prediction has been observed to be true. But there is another way. Let e_1 denote the first observation $x_1 = 3$, while e_2 denotes the second observation $x_2 = 3$. Then $H\&e_1$ predicts e_2 and $H\&e_2$ predicts e_1. That is, H enables us to predict one datum *from* the other.

Let us call any hypothesis with one or more adjustable parameters a *model*. Accommodation concerns the capacity of a model to successfully *fit* a set of data. The *predictive* success of a model is something stronger.

In the case of probabilistic prediction, fit comes in degrees measured by the probability of the datum given by the fitted model. Let us denote the model H fitted to e by h, and we must assume that h confers a probability on any new or old data. Now assume that the data e consist of a sequence of N observations $e_1, e_2, \ldots, e_N$. Then the degree of accommodation of the model is just the degree of fit of h with e, which is commonly measured by the likelihood $P(e|h)$. Given assumptions about probabilistic independence that are commonly built into such models, this is equal to

$$P(e_1|h)P(e_2|h) \ldots P(e_N|h).$$

Let us now denote the model fitted to all the data with e_1 *left out* by h_{-1}, and so on. To measure the degree of predictive fit, or cross-validated fit (Forster, forthcoming) with the same e, we use a different formula:

$$P(e_1|h_{-1})P(e_2|h_{-2})\ldots P(e_N|h_{-N}).$$

The cross-validated measure of predictive fit avoids the double-use problem – each term measures the ability of the model to *predict* the data because the datum being predicted is not used to *construct* the fitted hypothesis that is doing the predicting. This is known in the statistics literature as *leave-one-out* cross-validation (CV), and it is asymptotically equivalent (for large N) to *Akaike's information criterion* (AIC) (Akaike 1973; Forster and Sober 1994).

When there are many observations, it makes little difference whether H is fitted to the full data or to the full data with one datum left out. For large and varied data sets, there is therefore little difference between measures of accommodation and measures of predictive fit, at least with respect to *the prediction of single data points*. This last qualification is very important because the overdetermination of parameters and the agreement of independent measurements is not exhaustively captured by leave-one-out CV fit even in the large data sets (the argument for this is sketched in a later section).

Single-point prediction is the Bayesian goal

Why do probabilistic measures of prediction play such a prominent role in philo-sophical theories of confirmation? According to Bayesianism, the goal is to evaluate an hypothesis by the probability that it is *true*, given the total evidence. By Bayes's theorem, $P(H|e) = P(H) \, P(e|H)/P(e)$, where $P(e|H)$ is called the "likelihood" of H relative to the evidence e. Given that H is actually an infinite disjunction of hypotheses of the form $h(\theta)$, where θ denotes a particular value of the parameter, the likelihood of H is a weighted average of the likelihoods of the disjuncts, denoted by $P(e|h(\theta))$, each of which measures the degree to which $h(\theta)$ succeeds in predicting e. It is Bayesians' use of average likelihoods that brings a subjective element into their notion of prediction. Since $P(e)$ drops out when we compare models against the same data, the most essential way that the data enter the analysis is via the likelihood terms $P(e|h(\theta))$. Bayesianism makes use of two kinds of subjective probabilities, called "prior probabilities." There is the prior degree of belief assigned to $P(H)$, and the there are the prior degrees of belief assigned to hypotheses in the model H, given H, which are used to calculate the (average) likelihood of H.

Bayesians sometimes claim that the subjective weights used to calculate $P(e|H)$ from the values of $P(e|h(\theta))$ are short-lived – in the large data limit the weights become unimportant because the likelihood function $P(e|h(\theta))$ becomes more and more sharply peaked around the maximum likelihood value $P(e|h)$, where h is the maximum likelihood hypothesis (that is, the hypothesis in H that has the greatest likelihood with respect to e). But now Bayesians face a dilemma. If their notion of prediction is objective, it is because $P(e|H)$ converges to $P(e|h)$ in the limit. But in the same limit, it is equal to the leave-one-out CV likelihood, which is clearly an indicator of how well the model is able to predict *single* data points. To the extent that the Bayesian notion of prediction is objective, it falls into the trap of evaluating models solely as instruments for the prediction of *single* data points. Are there other *attainable* goals that Bayesians have thereby overlooked? The example in the next section is intended to answer the question affirmatively.

Other kinds of prediction that emerge from the overdetermination of parameters

Consider a more complex experiment with three objects, labeled a, b, and c, hung on the same beam balance as before, by themselves and in pairs. There are six experiments. One with a, one with b, one with c, one with $a*b$, one with $b*c$, and one with $a*c$, where $a*b$ refers to the composite object consisting of a placed with b, and so on. In each experiment, we make a single measurement. Suppose the observations are, respectively, $x_1 = 3, x_2 = 4,$ $x_3 = 5, x_4 = 7, x_5 = 9,$ and $x_6 = 8$. Treat the masses of all six objects as unknown. Then the model, which we call the primitive model (PRIM) introduces 6 unknown quantities in 6 equations: $x_1 = m(a), x_2 = m(b), x_3 = m(c), x_4 = m(a*b), x_5 = m(b*c),$ and $x_6 = m(a*c)$. PRIM is not able to make any predictions of any part of the data from any other part of the data, and it therefore has no predictive success with respect to the seen data.

Now consider the usual Newtonian model (NEWT), which adds the *law of composition of masses* (LCM): it says that the mass of composite objects is equal to the sum of the masses of the component parts. For example, $m(a*b) = m(a) + m(b)$. NEWT has six equations in three unknowns, so each parameter has two independent measurements, which agree. The intuitively correct answer is that NEWT predicts the data better, and is therefore better confirmed by the data. But as average likelihoods converge to the maximum likelihood, the difference between NEWT and PRIM is washed away.

When we supplement the equations with an error term, PRIM and NEWT become probabilistic predictors. The model equation, in this case, becomes $x = \theta + u$, where u is an error term that the model may say is Gaussian (bell-shaped) with some specified variance (spread), such that small errors are more probable than larger errors. Bayesianism can reproduce the right relationship between the likelihoods $(P(e|NEWT) > P(e|PRIM))$ if the prior probabilities assigned to the parameters in the models are chosen one way; but it could also produce the wrong answer with a different choice. The power of Bayesianism to accommodate any answer is its shortcoming, for it seems clear in this example that the NEWT predicts better, and is therefore better confirmed by the evidence, *independently* of the prior probabilities assigned to the parameter values.

But there is another problem for Bayesianism. Clearly NEWT logically entails PRIM because $NEWT = PRIM \ \& \ LCM$. As Popper pointed out long ago, if A logically entails B, then, by the axioms of probability alone, $P(A|e) \leq P(B|e)$. So, there is no assignment of weights to the parameter values, and to $P(NEWT)$ and $P(PRIM)$, consistent with the axioms of probability that yields the result $P(NEWT|e) > P(PRIM|e)$. The usual Bayesian response is that PRIM should be understood as being PRIM minus LCM; that is, as PRIM with the specific assertion that at least one of the relations $m(a*b) = m(a) + m(b)$ is false. Then it is possible to adjust $P(NEWT)$ and $P(PRIM \ minus \ LCM)$ so that $P(NEWT|e) > P(PRIM \ minus \ LCM|e)$. The first point is that this changes the subject; it does not address the original example. Secondly, why should we think that $P(NEWT)$ is greater than $P(PRIM \ minus \ LCM)$ on *a priori* grounds when NEWT is so much more restrictive than PRIM minus LCM? Finally, the Bayesian reply flies in the face of the intuition that the correct answer is derived straightforwardly from the objective relationship between NEWT, PRIM, and the evidence.

Prediction and approximate truth

Consider a simple modification of the previous example in which each trial of the experiment is repeated n times, giving $6n$ data in total, with exactly the same numbers, except that the average value of x_6 is 8.001 instead of 8. Now PRIM minus LCM can have the best leave-one-out CV likelihood because it is, indeed, the best model at predicting a *single* data point from the remaining data. The higher likelihood of PRIM minus LCM will eventually cancel whatever advantage Bayesians give NEWT by the initial assignment of values given to $P(NEWT)$ and $P(PRIM \ minus \ LCM)$. And

Bayesians are correct to conclude that PRIM minus LCM is more probably true than NEWT, because there is a tiny but systematic error in the predictions of LCM, which provide strong evidence that NEWT is false. But this is not the only feature of the evidence worth looking at. For NEWT is partially successful in making predictions on which PRIM, and PRIM minus LCM, are silent. To ignore this is to ignore important *features* of the evidence, which tell us the ways in which the unified model, such as NEWT, is approximating the truth, even though it is probably not true. Such clues lead to better theories and models in a reliable way; to ignore them is to ignore an important heuristic element in science.

Conclusion

Prediction is a complicated concept; the standard subjective account of prediction (the Bayesian account) is monolithic in the way that it averages everything into a single number (the average likelihood). This melds together various kinds of predictive successes in a way that is appropriate only to evaluating our subjective degree of belief. Finer-grained relationships between theory and evidence tell us more about how a model is succeeding in some ways and failing in others, and how improvements may be made.

Acknowledgment

I am grateful to Ludovica Lorusso for helpful criticisms of a previous draft.

See also: Bayesianism; Confirmation; Evidence; Measurement; Models; Probability; Unification.

References

Akaike, H. (1973) "Information Theory and an Extension of the Maximum Likelihood Principle," in B. N. Petrov and F. Csaki (eds) *Second International Symposium on Information Theory*, Budapest: Akademiai Kiado, pp. 267–81.
Forster, M. R. (forthcoming) "A Philosopher's Guide to Empirical Success," *Philosophy of Science*.
Forster, M. R. and Sober, E. (1994) "How to Tell When Simpler, More Unified, or Less *Ad Hoc* Theories will Provide More Accurate Predictions," *British Journal for the Philosophy of Science* 45: 1–35.
Musgrave, A. (1974) "Logical Versus Historical Theories of Confirmation," *The British Journal for the Philosophy of Science* 25: 1–23.

Further reading

Alan Musgrave (1974) is a good introduction to the literature centered on the notion of novel prediction, which introduces a non-logical element into confirmation theory. It was Imre Lakatos, in "Falsificationism and the Methodology of Scientific Research Programmes," in I. Lakatos and A. Musgrave (eds) *Criticism and the Growth of Knowledge* (Cambridge: Cambridge University Press), pp. 91–196, who originally argued for the confirmational relevance of the novel prediction. The distinction between hypotheses, and families of hypotheses, or models, introduces new complications, and these are treated carefully in Forster and Sober (1994). Christopher Hitchcock and Elliott Sober, in "Prediction versus Accommodation and the Risk of Overfitting," *British Journal for the Philosophy of Science* 55 (2004): 1–34, discuss the issue of novel prediction in light of these complications. The Bayesian point of view is best summarized by Colin Howson and Peter Urbach in *Scientific Reasoning: The Bayesian Approach*, 3rd edn (La Salle, IL: Open Court, 2006).

39
PROBABILITY
Maria Carla Galavotti

Historical sketch

The origin of the notion of *probability*, taken in the quantitative sense that is nowadays attached to it, is usually traced back to the decade around 1660 and associated with the work of Blaise Pascal and Pierre Fermat, followed by that of Christiaan Huygens and many others.

Since its beginnings, the notion of probability has been characterized by a peculiar duality of meaning: its *statistical* meaning concerning the stochastic laws of chance processes; and its *epistemological* meaning relating to the degree of belief that we, as agents, entertain in propositions describing uncertain events. Such a duality lies at the root of the philosophical problem of the interpretation of probability, and has nurtured various schools animated by the conviction that a specific sense of "probability" should be privileged and made the essence of its definition. After a long period in which the "doctrine of chance" and the "art of conjecture" had peacefully coexisted, this absolutist tendency became predominant around the middle of the nineteenth century and gave rise to the different interpretations of probability that will be described in the following sections.

By the turn of the eighteenth century, probability had progressed enormously, having progressively widened its scope of application. Great impulse to its development came from the application of the notion of the *arithmetic mean* first to demographic data, then to fields like medical practice and legal decisions, and finally to the physical and biological sciences.

A pivotal role in the history of probability was played by the Bernoulli family, including Jakob, who started the analysis of *direct probability*, that is, the probability to be assigned to a sample taken from a population whose *law* is known, and proved the result usually called the "weak law of large numbers." The theorem holds for binary processes, namely processes that admit of two outcomes – such as "heads" or "tails" and the "presence" or "absence" of a certain property – and says that if p is the probability of obtaining a certain outcome in a repeatable experiment, and m the number of successes obtained in n repetitions of the same experiment, the probability that the value of m/n falls within any chosen interval $p \pm \varepsilon$ increases for larger and larger values of n, and tends to 1 as n tends to infinity. Bernoulli's result is based on the concept of *stochastic independence*, which receives an unambiguous definition for the first time. Bernoulli's work also sheds light on the relationship between probability and frequency, by keeping separate the probability and the frequency with which the events of the considered dichotomy can theoretically occur in any given number *n* of experiments, and sets the probability distribution over possible frequencies: 0, 1, 2, ..., *n*, usually called "binomial distribution." Bernoulli's work on direct probability was gradually generalized by other probabilists, including De Moivre, Laplace, and Poisson, to receive great impulse in the nineteenth and twentieth centuries, especially by Borel, Cantelli, and the Russian probabilists Chebyshev, Markov, Lyapunov, and Kolmogorov.

Other important members of the Bernoulli family were Nikolaus, who formulated the so-called "Saint Petersburg problem," and Daniel, who did seminal work on mathematical expectation and laid the foundations of the theory of errors, which reached its peak with the subsequent work of Gauss.

Special mention is due to Thomas Bayes, who proposed a method for assessing *inverse probability*, that is, the probability to be assigned to an hypothesis on the ground of available evidence. Whereas by direct probability one goes from the known probability of a population to the estimated frequency of its samples, by inverse probability one goes from known frequencies to estimated probabilities. Inverse probability is also called the "probability of causes," because it enables the estimation of the probabilities of the causes underlying an observed event. The method is based on the idea that the *final* or *posterior* probability $P(H \mid E)$ of a certain hypothesis (H), given a certain piece of evidence (E), is proportional to the product of the *initial* or *prior* probability $P(H)$ of the hypothesis calculated on the basis of background knowledge, and the so-called *likelihood* $P(E \mid H)$ of E given the considered hypothesis, namely on the assumption that the considered hypothesis holds. A general formulation of Bayes's rule, that takes into account a family of hypotheses $H_1 \ldots H_n$, is the following:

$$P(H_i \mid E) = [P(H_i) \times P(E \mid H_i)] / \Sigma_{i=1}^{n} [P(H_i) \times P(E \mid H_i)].$$

To illustrate this formula, let us take a factory that has 3 machines for the production of bolts, of which it produces 60,000 pieces daily. Of these, 10,000 are produced by machine A_1, 20,000 by machine A_2, and 30,000 by machine A_3. All three machines occasionally produce faulty pieces, F. On average, the rejection rates of the 3 machines are as follows: 4 percent in the case of A_1, 2 percent in the case of A_2, 4 percent in the case of A_3. Given a defective bolt taken from the rejects, we ask for the probability that it was produced by each of the three machines. In order to calculate such a probability by means of Bayes's rule, we start from prior probabilities, obtained in this case from the information concerning the production of the machines. They are as follows:

$P(A_1) = 10,000/60,000 = 1/6$
$P(A_2) = 20,000/60,000 = 1/3$
$P(A_3) = 30,000/60,000 = 1/2.$

The likelihoods are provided by information on the rejection rates:

$P(F \mid A_1) = 4/100$
$P(F \mid A_2) = 2/100$
$P(F \mid A_3) = 4/100.$

Posterior probabilities are calculated as follows:

$P(A_1 \mid F) = (1/6 \times 4/100) / [(1/6 \times 4/100) + (1/3 \times 2/100) + (1/2 \times 4/100)]$
$= 1/5 = 20\%$
$P(A_2 \mid F) = (1/3 \times 2/100) / [(1/6 \times 4/100) + (1/3 \times 2/100) + (1/2 \times 4/100)]$
$= 1/5 = 20\%$
$P(A_3 \mid F) = (1/2 \times 4/100) / [(1/6 \times 4/100) + (1/3 \times 2/100) + (1/2 \times 4/100)]$
$= 3/5 = 60\%.$

We therefore have a probability of 20 percent that a defective bolt taken at random was produced by machine A_1, a probability of 20 percent that it was produced by machine A_2 and a probability of 60 percent that it was produced by machine A_3. The obtained result shows that, although the machine A_2 works twice as well as A_1, it is equally probable that the defective piece originates from A_2 as from A_1, because the second machine produces twice as many pieces. Machine A_3, which supplies half of the total production, is nevertheless assigned probability 3/5 of having produced the defective piece because one of the two other machines works more reliably.

The crucial step in the application of Bayes's rule lies with fixing prior probabilities. This is a matter of debate. By allowing for the evaluation of hypotheses in a probabilistic fashion, Bayes's method spells out a canon of inductive reasoning. It was applied in the first place by Laplace, and later on came to be regarded as the cornerstone of statistical inference by the statisticians of the Bayesian School. The place of Bayes's inductive method within the whole of statistics is the subject of a major ongoing controversy.

The eighteenth century saw a tremendous growth in the application of probability to the moral and political sciences. Important work in this connection was done by Condorcet, the pioneer of the so-called "social mathematics," meant to produce a statistical description of society instrumental for a new political economy.

Between the nineteenth and twentieth centuries the study of statistical distributions progressed enormously thanks to the work of a number of authors, including Quetelet, Galton, Karl Pearson, Weldon, Gosset, Edgeworth, and others, who shaped modern statistics, by developing the analysis of correlation and regression, and the methodology for assessing statistical hypotheses against experimental data through the so-called "significance tests." Other branches of modern statistics were started by Fisher, who prompted the analysis of variance and covariance, and the *likelihood method* for comparing hypotheses on the basis of a given body of data. Also worth mentioning are Egon Pearson and Jerzy Neyman, who extended the methodology of tests to the comparison of two alternative hypotheses.

In the nineteenth century, probability gradually entered physical science, not only in connection with errors of measurement, but more penetratingly as a component of physical theory. Such developments started with the work of Robert Brown on the motion of particles suspended in fluid, which paved the way to the analysis of physical phenomena characterized by great complexity, leading to the kinetic theory of gases and thermodynamics, developed by Maxwell, Boltzmann, and Gibbs. Around 1905–6 von Smoluchowski and Einstein brought to completion the analysis of Brownian motion in probabilistic terms. More or less in the same years, the study of radiation led Einstein and other outstanding physicists, including Planck, Schrödinger, de Broglie, Dirac, Heisenberg, Born, Bohr, and others to formulate quantum mechanics, in which probability became an ingredient of the description of the basic components of matter.

In 1933 Kolmogorov spelled out his famous axiomatization, meant to shed light on the mathematical properties of probability, and to draw a distinction between probability's formal features and the meaning it receives in practical situations. Put simply, the formal properties of probability are the following: (1) for any event A, its probability is ≥ 0; (2) if A is certain, its probability equals 1; (3) probabilities are additive, that is, if two events A and B cannot both occur, $P(A \text{ or } B) = P(A) + P(B)$. Kolmogorov's axiomatization met with a wide consensus and obtained a twofold result: for one thing, it gained an equitable position for probability among other mathematical disciplines; and by tracing a clear-cut boundary between the mathematical properties of probability and its interpretations it made room for the philosophy of probability as an autonomous field of enquiry.

The classical interpretation

The "classical" interpretation is usually construed as the interpretation of probability developed at the turn of the nineteenth century by the mathematician–physicist–astronomer Pierre Simon de Laplace. Called "the Newton of France" for his work on mechanics, Laplace made a substantial contribution to probability, both technically and philosophically. His philosophy of probability is rooted in the doctrine of determinism, according to which the universe is ruled by a *principle of sufficient reason* stating that all things are brought into existence by a cause. The human mind is incapable of grasping every detail of the connections of the causal network underlying phenomena, but one can conceive of a superior intelligence able to do so. Making use of the methods of mathematical analysis and aided by probability, man can approach the all-comprehensive view of such a superior intelligence. Being made necessary by the incompleteness of human knowledge, probability is an epistemic notion, having to do with our knowledge, rather than being inherent in phenomena.

Laplace defines probability as "the ratio of the number of favorable cases to that of all possible cases," according to the statement known as the "classical" definition. This is grounded on the assumption that all cases in question are equally possible, lacking information that would lead us to believe otherwise. The stress placed on the dependence of the judgment of equal possibility on there being no reason to believe otherwise inspired the term "principle of insufficient reason" – also known in the literature as the "principle of indifference," after a terminology coined by Keynes – to refer to Laplace's assumption. In other words, for the sake of determining probability values, equally possible cases are taken as equally probable. This assumption is made for ease of analysis and is not endowed with metaphysical meaning. Laplace insists on the need to make sure that some outcomes are not more likely to happen than others, before applying his method. Moreover, Laplace's epistemic interpretation protects his definition of probability from the charge of being circular: once probability is taken as epistemic, it stands on a different ground from the possibility of the occurrence of events.

Dealing with inverse probability, Laplace enunciates a principle which amounts to Bayes's rule. Under the assumption of equally likely causes, he derives from it the method of inference called in the literature "Laplace's rule." In the case of two alternatives – like *occurrence* and *non-occurrence* – this rule allows us to infer the probability of an event from the information that it has been observed to happen in a given number of cases. If m is the number of observed positive cases, and n that of negative cases, the probability that the next case to be observed is positive equals $(m + 1) / (m + n + 2)$. If no negative cases have been observed, the formula reduces to $(m + 1) / (m + 2)$. Laplace's method is based on the assumptions of the equiprobability of priors and the independence of trials, conditional on a given parameter – like the composition of an urn, or the ratio of the number of favorable cases to that of all possible cases. The authors who later worked on probabilistic inference in the tradition of Bayes and Laplace – including Johnson, Carnap, and de Finetti – eventually turned to the weaker assumption of exchangeability.

Laplace's theory of probability was very influential. However, while it can handle a wide array of important applications, it gives rise to problems, such as the impossibility, in many situations, of determining the set of *equally likely* cases. In such situations – think for instance of the probability of a biased coin falling on either side or the probability that a given individual will die within a year – instead of looking for possible cases, we count the frequency with which events take place in order to calculate probability. Furthermore, when applied to problems involving an infinite number of possible cases, the classical interpretation generates the so-called "Bertrand's paradox," after the French mathematician Joseph Bertrand.

The frequency interpretation

According to the frequency interpretation, probability is defined as the limit of the relative frequency of a given attribute, observed in the initial part of an indefinitely long sequence of repeatable events. In other words, given that the attribute A has been observed with frequency m/n in the initial part of sequence B, its probability equals $\lim_{n \to \infty} F^n (A,B) = m/n$. The frequency interpretation is empirical and objective: probability is a characteristic of phenomena that can be empirically analyzed by observing frequencies. Probability values are in general unknown, but can be approached by means of frequencies. The frequency interpretation is fully compatible with indeterminism.

Started by Robert Leslie Ellis and John Venn, frequentism reached its climax with Richard von Mises, member of the Berlin Society for Empirical Philosophy and later professor at Istanbul and Harvard. Central to von Mises's theory is the notion of a *collective*, referring to the sequence of observations of a mass phenomenon or a repetitive event. Collectives are indefinitely long and exhibit frequencies that tend to a limit. Their distinctive feature is randomness, operationally defined as "insensitivity to place selection." It obtains when the limiting values of the relative frequencies in a given collective are not affected by any of all the possible selections that can be performed on it. In addition, the limiting values of the relative frequencies, in the sub-sequences obtained by place selection, equal those of the original sequence. This randomness condition is also called the "principle of the impossibility of a gambling system" because it reflects the impossibility of devising a system leading to a certain win in any hypothetical game. The theory of probability is restated by von Mises in terms of collectives, by means of the operations of *selection, mixing, partition*, and *combination*. This conceptual machinery is meant to give probability an empirical and objective foundation. Because probability, according to this perspective, can refer only to *collectives*, it makes no sense to talk of the probability of single occurrences.

A slightly different version of frequentism was developed by Hans Reichenbach, another member of the Berlin Society for Empirical Philosophy and co-editor of *Erkenntnis* together with Rudolf Carnap, later professor at the University of California at Los Angeles. Reichenbach made an attempt to extend the frequency notion of probability to the single case. Any probability attribution is a *posit* by which we infer that the relative frequencies detected in the past will persist when sequences of observations are prolonged. A posit regarding a single occurrence of an event receives a *weight* from the probabilities attached to the reference class to which the event has been assigned. Such a reference class must obey a criterion of homogeneity guaranteeing that all the properties relevant to the event under study have been taken into account. This obviously gives rise to a problem of applicability, because one can never be absolutely sure that the reference class is homogeneous. Reichenbach distinguishes between *primitive knowledge*, where no previous knowledge of frequencies is available so that *blind* posits are made on the basis of the sole observed frequencies, and *advanced knowledge* where *appraised* posits are obtained by combining known probabilities by means of the laws of probability, particularly Bayes's rule. There emerges a view of knowledge as a self-correcting procedure grounded on posits. Reichenbach's theory includes a pragmatic justification of induction, appealing to the success of probability evaluations based on frequencies.

The propensity interpretation

Anticipated by Charles Sanders Peirce, the *propensity theory* was proposed in the 1950s by Karl Raimund Popper to solve the problem of single-case probabilities arising in quantum mechanics. Probability as propensity is a property of the experimental arrangement, apt to be reproduced over and over again to form a sequence. This is the kernel of the so-called "long-run propensity interpretation." Popper regards propensities as physically real and metaphysical (they are non-observable properties), and this gives the propensity theory a strongly objective character. In the 1980s Popper resumed the propensity theory to make it the focus of a wider program meant to account for all sorts of causal tendencies operating in the world. He then saw propensities as *weighted possibilities*, or expressions of the tendency of a given experimental set-up to realize itself upon repetition, emphasizing single experimental arrangements rather than sequences of generating conditions. In so doing, he laid down the so-called "single-case propensity interpretation." Of crucial importance in this connection is the distinction between *probability statements* expressing propensities, which are statements about frequencies in virtual sequences of experiments, and *statistical statements* expressing relative frequencies observed in actual sequences of experiments, which are used to test probability statements. Popper's propensity theory goes hand in hand with indeterminism.

After Popper's work the propensity theory of probability enjoyed a considerable popularity among philosophers of science. Some authors, such as Donald Gillies, embrace a long-run perspective, while others, including Hugh Mellor, Ronald Giere, and David Miller, prefer a single-case propensity approach. Propensity theory has been accused of giving rise to a variety of problems. For one thing, the propensity theory faces a reference-class problem broadly similar to that affecting frequentism. Moreover, Paul Humphreys has claimed that it is unable to interpret inverse probabilities, because it would be odd to talk of the propensity of a defective bolt to have been produced by a certain machine. The notion of propensity exhibits an asymmetry that goes in the opposite direction to that characterizing inverse probability. For this reason various authors, including Wesley Salmon, appealed to the notion of propensity to represent (probabilistic) causal tendencies, rather than probabilities.

Other authors value the notion of propensity as an ingredient of the description of chance phenomena, without committing themselves to a propensity interpretation of probability. Among them is Patrick Suppes, who holds the view that propensities do not express probabilities, but can play a useful role in the description of certain phenomena, conferring an objective meaning on the probabilities involved.

The logical interpretation

According to the logical interpretation, the theory of probability belongs to logic, and probability is a logical relation between propositions, more precisely one proposition describing a given body of evidence and another proposition stating a hypothesis. The logical interpretation of probability is a natural development of the idea that probability is an epistemic notion, pertaining to our knowledge of facts, rather than to facts themselves. With respect to Laplace's classical interpretation, this approach stresses the logical aspect of probability, which is meant to give it an intrinsic objectivity.

Anticipated by Leibniz, the logical interpretation was embraced by the Czech mathematician and logician Bernard Bolzano and developed by a number of British authors, including Augustus De Morgan, George Boole, William Stanley Jevons, and John Maynard Keynes, the latter best-known for his contribution to economic theory.

For all of these authors the logical character of probability goes hand in hand with its rational character. In other words, they aimed to develop a theory of the reasonableness of degrees of belief on logical grounds. Keynes adopted a moderate form of logicism, permeated by a deeply felt need not to lose sight of ordinary speech and practice. Keynes assigned an important role to intuition and individual judgment, and was suspicious of a purely formal treatment of probability and the adoption of mechanical rules for its evaluation. He also attributed an important role to analogy, and held that similarities and dissimilarities among events must be carefully considered before quantitative methods can be applied.

Another supporter of logicism was the Cambridge logician William Ernest Johnson, who is remembered for having introduced the property of exchangeability under the name of "permutation postulate." According to that property, probability is invariant with respect to permutation of individuals, to the effect that exchangeable probability functions assign probability in a way that depends on the number of experienced cases, irrespective of the order in which they have been observed.

Logicism counts also among its followers the Viennese philosophers Ludwig Wittgenstein and Friedrich Waismann. Wittgenstein held that probability is a logical relation between propositions, which can be established pretty much as a deductive relation, on the basis of the truth-values of propositions. An active member of the Vienna Circle, Waismann saw the logical notion of probability as a generalization of the concept of deductive entailment to the case in which the scope of one proposition (premise) partially overlaps with that of another (conclusion), instead of including it. The measure of such a logical relation is defined on the basis of the scope of propositions. He also pointed out that in addition to its logical aspect, probability has an empirical side, having to do with frequency.

Waismann's conception of probability directly influenced the work of Rudolf Carnap, one of the prominent representatives of philosophy of science in the twentieth century. Starting from the admission that there are two concepts of probability – probability$_1$, or degree of confirmation, and probability$_2$, or probability as frequency, Carnap set himself the task of developing the former notion as the object of *inductive logic*. Inductive logic is developed as an axiomatic system, formalized within a first-order predicate calculus with identity, which applies to measures of confirmation defined on the semantic content of statements. Since it allows for making the best estimates based on the given evidence, inductive logic can be seen as a rational basis for decisions. Unlike probability$_2$, which has only one value that is usually unknown, logical probability may be unknown only in the sense that the logico-mathematical procedure leading to it is not figured out. Logical probability is analytic and objective: in the light of the same evidence, there is only one rational (correct) probability assignment. Carnap devised a *continuum of inductive methods*, characterized as a blend of a purely logical component and a purely empirical element, among which the so-called "symmetric" functions, having the property of exchangeability, occupy a privileged position. Carnap's methods belong to the broader family of Bayesian methods. When addressing the problem of the justification of induction, Carnap appealed to *inductive intuition*, in an attempt to keep inductive logic totally within an *a prioristic* domain, while dispensing with the pragmatic criterion of successfulness.

A further version of logicism was developed by the geophysicist Harold Jeffreys, who built on it a probabilistic epistemology having a strongly constructivist flavor, which shares some features of the subjective approach.

The subjective interpretation

According to the subjective interpretation probability is the *degree of belief* entertained by a person, in a state of uncertainty regarding the occurrence of an event, on the basis of the information available. The notion of degree of belief is taken as a primitive notion, which has to be given an operative definition, specifying a way of measuring it. A first option in achieving this goal is the method of bets, endowed with a long-standing tradition dating back to the seventeenth century. Accordingly, one's degree of belief in the occurrence of an event can be expressed by means of the odds at which one would be ready to bet. For instance, a degree of belief of 1/6 in the proposition that an unbiased die will turn up 3 can be expressed by the willingness to bet at odds 1:5 – namely, pay 1 if the die does not turn up 3, and gain 5 if it does. The general idea is to value the probability of an event as equal to the price to be paid by a player to obtain a unitary gain in case the event occurs. This method gives rise to some problems, like that of the diminishing marginal utility of money, in view of which various alternative methods have been devised.

Anticipated by the British astronomer William Donkin and the French mathematician Émile Borel, the subjective approach was given a sound basis by the multifarious genius of Frank Plumpton Ramsey. He adopted a definition of degree of belief based on preferences determined on the basis of the expectation of an individual of obtaining certain goods, not necessarily of a monetary kind, and specified a set of axioms fixing a criterion of *coherence*. In the terminology of the betting scheme, coherence ensures that, if used as the basis of betting ratios, degrees of belief should not lead to a sure loss. Ramsey stated that coherent degrees of belief satisfy the laws of probability. Thereby coherence became the cornerstone of the subjective interpretation of probability, the only condition of acceptability that needs to be imposed on degrees of belief. Once degrees of belief are coherent, there is no further demand of rationality to be met.

The decisive step towards a fully developed subjective notion of probability was made by Bruno de Finetti whose "representation theorem" shows that the adoption of Bayes's method, taken in conjunction with the property of exchangeability, leads to a convergence between degrees of belief and frequencies. This makes subjective probability applicable to statistical inference, which according to de Finetti can be entirely based on it – a conviction shared by the neo-Bayesian statisticians. For the subjectivist de Finetti *objective* probability, namely the idea that probability should be uniquely determined, is a useless notion. Instead, one should be aware that probability evaluations depend on both subjective and objective elements, and refine probability appraisals by means of calibration methods.

Concluding remarks

Of the various interpretations of probability outlined above, the classical interpretation is by and large outdated, especially in view of its commitment to determinism. Though the same cannot be said for the logical interpretation, its formalism, especially in connection with Carnap's work, has made it unpalatable to scientists. It should be added that philosophers of science of Bayesian orientation seem on the whole prone to embrace the more flexible approach based on subjective probability.

The frequency interpretation, due to its empirical and objective character, has long been considered the natural candidate for the notion of probability occurring within the natural sciences. But while it matches the uses of probability in areas like population genetics and statistical mechanics, it faces insurmountable problems within quantum mechanics, where probability assignments to the single case need to be made. The propensity interpretation was put forward precisely to solve that difficulty. In the debate that followed Popper's proposal, propensity theory gained increasing popularity, but also elicited several objections.

Subjective probability has an undisputable role to play in the realm of the social sciences, where personal opinions and expectations enter directly into the information used to support forecasts, forge hypotheses, and build models. Various attempts are being made to extend the use of subjective probability to the natural sciences, including quantum mechanics.

While the controversy on the interpretation of probability is far from settled, the pluralistic approach, which avoids the temptation to force all uses of probability into a single scheme, is gaining ground.

See also Bayesianism; Confirmation; Determinism.

References

Carnap, R. (1962 [1950]) *Logical Foundations of Probability*, 2nd edn, Chicago: Chicago University Press; reprinted 1967.
—— (1962) "The Aim of Inductive Logic," in E. Nagel, P. Suppes, and A. Tarski (eds) *Logic, Methodology, and Philosophy of Science*, Stanford, CA: Stanford University Press, pp. 303–18; repr. in S. Luckenbach (ed.) *Probabilities, Problems, and Paradoxes*, Encino-Belmont, CA: Dickenson, 1972, pp. 104–20.
de Finetti, B. (1937) "La prévision: ses lois logiques, ses sources subjectives," *Annales de l'Institut Henri Poincaré* VII: 1–68; translated as "Foresight: Its Logical Laws, its Subjective Sources," in H. Kyburg Jr. and H. Smokler (eds) *Studies in Subjective Probability*, New York: Wiley, 1964, pp. 95–158.
—— (1970) *Teoria delle probabilità*, Torino: Einaudi; translated as *Theory of Probability*, New York: Wiley, 1975.
Keynes, J. M. (1921) *A Treatise on Probability*, London: Macmillan; reprinted in *The Collected Writings of John Maynard Keynes*, Volume 8, Cambridge: Macmillan, 1972.
Laplace, P. S. (1814) *Essai philosophique sur les probabilités*, Paris: Courcier; translated from the 5th French edn of 1825 and edited by A. Dale as *A Philosophical Essay on Probabilities*, New York, Berlin, and London: Springer, 1995.
Popper, K. R. (1959) "The Propensity Interpretation of Probability," *British Journal for the Philosophy of Science* 10: 25–42.
—— (1990) *A World of Propensities*, Bristol: Thoemmes.
Ramsey, F. P. (1931) *The Foundations of Mathematics and Other Logical Essays*, ed. R. B. Braithwaite, London: Routledge & Kegan Paul.

Reichenbach, H. (1935) *Wahrscheinlichkeitslehre*, Leyden: Sijthoff; expanded and translated as *The Theory of Probability*, Berkeley and Los Angeles: University of California Press, 1949, 2nd edn 1971.
—— (1938) *Experience and Prediction*, Chicago and London: University of Chicago Press.
von Mises, R. (1928) *Wahrscheinlichkeit, Statistik und Wahrheit*, Vienna: Springer; translated as *Probability, Statistics and Truth*, London and New York: Allen & Unwin, 1939; repr. New York: Dover, 1957.

Further reading

On the history of probability and statistics, see I. Hacking, *The Emergence of Probability* (Cambridge: Cambridge University Press, 1975) and S. Stigler, *The History of Statistics. The Measurement of Uncertainty before 1900* (Cambridge, MA: Harvard University Press, 1986). A survey of the debate on the interpretation of probability can be found in M. C. Galavotti, *Philosophical Introduction to Probability* (Stanford: CSLI, 2005). Also of interest is D. Gillies, *Philosophical Theories of Probability* (London: Routledge, 2000). An excellent treatise on probability is W. Feller, *An Introduction to Probability Theory and its Applications*, 2 vols (New York: Wiley, 1950, 1966). For a rigorous but accessible introduction to probability see B. V. Gnedenko and A. Y. Khinchin, *An Elementary Introduction to the Theory of Probability* (New York: Dover, 1962). For more on the logical interpretation of probability see *Studies in Inductive Logic and Probability*, 2 vols (Berkeley and Los Angeles: University of California Press, 1971, 1980); vol. 1 was edited by R. Carnap and R. C. Jeffrey, and vol. 2 by R. C. Jeffrey. For more on the subjective interpretation see H. Kyburg, Jr. and H. Smokler (eds) *Studies in Subjective Probability* (New York: Wiley, 1964; 2nd edn Huntington, NY: Krieger, 1980).

40

REDUCTION

Sahotra Sarkar

Introduction

The metaphysical roots of modern science lie in the mechanical philosophy of the seventeenth century (see Sarkar 1989 for a history). Central to that philosophy were two claims: (i) explanations of events must only invoke past events; and (ii) the behavior of bodies must be explained by the contact interactions of their constituent parts. A body gets hot, for instance, because of the increased motion of its parts; getting cold corresponds to a decrease of motion. Moreover, any motion of or within a body must be a result of motions imparted to the body or its parts by some other body in the past. Causal influences always move from the past into the future. Teleology (including Aristotle's appeal to final causes) was illegitimate. Two types of locality were critical in causal interactions: *spatial* locality, because all interactions were contact interactions (there could be no action-at-a-distance); and *temporal* locality, which is implied by the fact that a contact interaction occurs only when cause and effect coincide in time. Longer chains of such primitive causal interactions allow one event to causally influence an event in a more distant future.

Contemporary science does not call into question the mechanical philosophy's first claim, the restriction of causes to those that emanate from the past, which amounts to an endorsement of Aristotle's efficient causes as the only legitimate type of cause. The second claim, which we will call "compositionality," is somewhat more controversial. It endorses what we now call "reductionism," though, as we shall see, there are many twists to the story. The mechanical philosophy was immensely successful, allowing modern science to liberate itself from its scholastic shackles, but there always remained a recalcitrant skeleton it its closet. Ever since the publication of Newton's *Principia* in 1687, the mechanical philosophers were faced with a superbly accurate theory – in fact the most quantitatively accurate theory yet seen in the history of science – that was based on action-at-a-distance, viz., Newton's theory of universal gravitation.

The eighteenth century saw many failed attempts to reconcile the mechanical philosophy with Newton's theory of gravitation. Finally, in a somewhat desperate move in the mid-nineteenth century, Helmholtz weakened the mechanical philosophy to allow interactions governed by a central force (besides contact interactions).

Action-at-a-distance was no longer problematic: it was simply a feature of the world. These weakened mechanical principles were subsequently used with spectacular success, most notably by Clausius, Maxwell, and Boltzmann, to provide explanations for the two laws of thermodynamics, perhaps the most important examples ever of successful reductions. Meanwhile, Maxwell's electromagnetic theory was used to reduce geometric optics to physical optics, and then to electromagnetism. Similarly the old, distinct theories of electricity and magnetism were reduced to the unified theory of electromagnetism.

Most importantly, the nineteenth century also began to see significant progress in the reduction of living phenomena to physical and chemical regularities, another project that went back to the seventeenth century and the efforts of early pioneers, including Harvey, to model living structures such as the heart as mechanical devices, for example pumps. Many twentieth-century debates over reductionism have been about biology (with the mind–body problem lingering unresolved in the background). Meanwhile the monumental changes in physics in the first decades of the twentieth century also influenced these debates. Special relativity eschews action-at-a-distance because it does not permit causal influences to propagate at speeds greater than that of light. This has led to the project of restricting causal interactions in physics to what are called "local interactions" mediated by local exchanges of energy and momentum. In contrast, there are many non-local effects in quantum mechanics, one of which (quantum entanglement) is discussed below. The tension between relativity theory and quantum mechanics in contemporary physics is partly because of the status of reductionism: relativity theory requires locality, which reductionism welcomes, while quantum mechanics is unable to avoid non-local effects.

Substantive issues

Modern philosophical discussions of reductionism go back to the logical empiricists, primarily Nagel (see 1961). Nagel distinguished between formal and non-formal conditions of reduction which he viewed as a form of inter-theoretic explanation. Explanation was characterized formally, and Nagel models reductionist explanations as deductive–nomological explanations, but with the *explananda* now consisting of the law to be reduced rather than an individual empirical fact. In other words, in a reduction, the laws of one theory were derived from those of another (*the condition of deducibility*) after the terms occurring in the two sets of laws were connected through bridge laws (*the condition of connectability*). The main contribution of Nagel's work was its emphasis on reduction as an epistemological rather than ontological issue. This is consonant with the position of most logical empiricists, especially Carnap, that ontological commitments depend on the epistemological success of theories: we should accept only those entities that occur in theories that explain the empirical facts in their domain (with explanation being construed as subsumption under general laws).

Nagel emphasized the importance of the non-formal conditions which determined whether a reduction was trivial or not. For instance, it critically mattered to Nagel whether a reduction led to fruitful development of theory. Even such non-formal or *substantive* issues – let alone the more scientifically oriented ones discussed below – were largely ignored in the 1960s and 1970s (with Nickles 1973 and Wimsatt 1976 providing important exceptions) because discussions of reduction focused primarily on formal issues, which were interpreted as linguistic issues. The question debated most often was whether reductions must connect type-terms in reduced theories to type-terms in reducing theories or whether it sufficed to connect type-terms in the former to token-terms in the latter. Most philosophers, especially those concerned with the mind–body problem, preferred the stricter view and used the inability to find type–type connections to reject the possibility of reducing mental phenomena to physical phenomena. The restriction of reduction to explanations in which type–type connections were necessary led to the strange consequence that there were apparently few, if any, reductions in the history of science, even though, within both physics and biology, it was generally accepted that many highly significant reductions had taken place. In fact, within biology, the acrimonious debates in the first half of the twentieth century about what was called "mechanism," which is identical to what we are calling "reductionism," was whether all explanations were mechanistic, that is, reductionist. The conclusion to be drawn from this situation is that philosophical discussions of reduction had veered off-track in the 1960s and 1970s.

To return on track we have to turn away from the formal issues that so fascinated the logical empiricists and their immediate followers. An additional reason for moving beyond formal issues is that the logical empiricist tradition regarded as best explanations those that brought empirical facts under the aegis of general laws. Consequently, discussions of explanation – including reductionist explanation – became embroiled in the disputes over the formal structure of laws and theories. Nonetheless, the formal structure of laws and theories is rarely important within the sciences, as Wimsatt emphasized in the 1970s (see, e.g., Wimsatt 1976). In any case, even if as philosophers we are interested in the structure of laws, theories, and explanations, those questions are largely independent of the question of reduction. What we must ask is what additional criteria must a successful explanation satisfy to constitute a reduction. In other words, and restricting attention to substantive issues, we must ask what substantive criteria distinguish reductionist explanations from other forms of explanation. *Reductionism* then becomes the empirical thesis that explanations in a particular discipline satisfy those criteria. In what follows, for expository simplicity I refer to "reduced" and "reducing theories and laws" but this should not be taken to imply that the entities connected by the reduction relation must be restricted to theories and laws: they may well be empirical generalizations in different disciplines or even individual facts.

The two most interesting substantive criteria in debates over reductionism have been (i) *hierarchy and compositionality* and (ii) *multiple realizability*.

Hierarchy and compositionality

The most important criterion for a successful reduction is that we have reason to expect that the reducing theory or law has *epistemological primacy* over (or is *more fundamental* than) its reduced counterpart: that is why explanation proceeds from the reducing theory or law to the reduced one. I assume that this criterion (sometimes also called "fundamentalism") is satisfied in all our discussions. However, when only this criterion is satisfied (that is, none of the others introduced below is satisfied) a reduction is *weak* because there is as yet no sense in which a whole is being explained by its parts. (Nickles 1973 and Wimsatt 1976 call these "intra-level" reductions.) Examples include the reduction of geometrical optics to physical optics, Newtonian mechanics to special relativity, and Newtonian gravitation to general relativity.

A stronger criterion of reduction is that an entity described by the reduced theory be modeled *hierarchically*, with the behavior of entities at higher levels of the hierarchy being explained using only *individual* properties of entities at lower levels. Here "individual" property means those properties of an entity that can be defined without reference to any other entity. The mass and charge of a body are examples of its individual properties; its membership in, say, a set of four bodies is not.

Note that there is as yet no commitment to this hierarchical organization being realized in physical space. Examples of reductions based on a non-spatial hierarchy include, most notably, the genetic explanation of the expression of phenotypic traits (structural features or behaviors) of organisms by its genotype. To show that genes explain the origin of a trait, the genotype is modeled hierarchically as multiple loci at which different alleles may occur. However, classical genetics is a formal enterprise: the hierarchy of genes (alleles and loci) described by genetic analysis need not map to a physical hierarchy and, in fact, does so only approximately (Sarkar 1998). The (statistical) laws of the transmission of genes, which refer to the hierarchical organization of the genotype, are then used to show that a particular set of genes (alleles) is statistically associated with a trait.

Within physics, problems emerge in the quantum domain (Shimony 1987). Interacting quantum systems (for instance, an electron and a proton which interact to form a hydrogen atom) may be in what are called "entangled" states in which we cannot attribute definite states to the parts though we can attribute a definite state to the composite system. (Moreover, systems that enter entangled states continue to remain in them. When one of these systems is a system being measured, and the other is the measuring apparatus, entanglement thus gives rise to the well-known *quantum measurement problem*.) For systems in entangled states, the properties of the composite system cannot be explained in terms of individual properties of their parts because the latter cannot be defined using such properties: any attempt to describe one of the sub-systems must refer to the others. There is thus no scope for hierarchical reduction, and this problem is so ubiquitous in quantum mechanics that Schrödinger (1936) viewed entanglement as the central interpretive problem of quantum mechanics. In fact, in the context of the natural sciences (that is, leaving aside questions of mind and culture), quantum mechanics produces the most serious challenge to reductionism to date – this is yet another way in which quantum mechanics continues to challenge our deepest philosophical commitments.

Finally, when we require that the hierarchy in question be one that is instantiated in physical space we return to where we started in the mechanical philosophy: spatial wholes are being explained in terms of their parts. This criterion of *composition-*

ality results in *strong* reductions: explanations that were traditionally sought by the mechanical philosophy, whether or not we restrict our interactions to contact (local) ones or admit central forces. Obviously, explanations that violate the hierarchy criterion *ipso facto* violate compositionality, as in the case of quantum entanglement. But genetic explanations of the sort discussed earlier do not satisfy compositionality since the hierarchy of loci and alleles from classical genetics can be spatially instantiated only approximately because of the existence of split genes, overlapping genes, etc. (Sarkar 2005). As a result, the abstract hierarchical structure of the classical genome, in which all loci are supposed to be discrete and non-overlapping, cannot be exactly realized by the genes as sections of DNA physically located on chromosomes.

Once compositionality is seen to be the critical criterion enabling strong reductions, contemporary molecular biology is seen as providing some of the most successful reductions in the history of science. Two examples emphasize this point, both of which were once believed to provide evidence for anti-reductionism (Monod 1971; Sarkar 1998). The first is *co-operativity*: some biological macromolecules, such as hemoglobin, consist of parts which enhance their functionality in the presence of other parts and molecules. In the case of hemoglobin, the ability to bind oxygen increases after the first oxygen molecule is bound to it. This phenomenon is known as "allostery." The second is *goal-directedness*: bacteria often produce enzymes necessary for the digestion of a substrate only in the presence of that substrate. In the early 1960s, Jacob and Monod, together with collaborators from a pioneering French group in molecular biology, succeeded in constructing reductionist models satisfying the compositionality criterion which successfully explained both of these phenomena. Allostery is explained by the fact that the physical conformation of the parts of molecules changes when in contact with other parts and the oxygen molecule, leading to an increased binding ability. The apparently goal-directed enzyme production of bacteria is explained by the *operon model*. The substrate physically interacts with and detaches from the DNA a repressor molecule that normally binds to the DNA and prevents expression of the enzyme that digests the substrate. However, any physically similar molecule which is not digestible by the enzyme will also remove the repressor molecule in the same way and lead to the production of the enzyme: there is no peculiar goal-directedness here. It is all a matter of the underlying molecular physics. The situation is somewhat surprising: traditionally biology, and not physics, was supposed to provide serious obstacles to the reductionist project. As it turns out, the opposite is the case.

Multiple realizability

One standard objection to reductionism in many contexts has been that a single term in a reduced theory may correspond to a multiplicity of entities in the reducing theory. In the context of discussions of the mind–body problem, this claim is sometimes formulated as that of a single mental kind (property, state, event) being realized by many distinct physical kinds (Bickle 2006). Such a situation is supposed to present a problem for construing the relevant explanations as reductionist, though it does not present a problem for (weak) supervenience (and *ipso facto* any version of [typically non-reductive] physicalism that relies only on – weak – supervenience): it may still be the case that there can be no change at the reduced (e.g., mental) level without some change at the reducing (e.g., physical) level. Similar objections were at one time raised to the reducibility of classical genetics to molecular biology (Rosenberg 1978).

The problem is obviously analogous to the problem of a type being reduced to tokens, but, in this version, the problem is interpreted substantively as one about entities rather than terms. Should a denial of multiple realizability be taken as a criterion for successful reduction? If so, one of the prototypical and most scientifically significant reductions will turn out to be deficient, viz., the reduction of thermo-dynamics to the kinetic theory of matter. Consider a cylinder of any typical gas. Each macroscopic state of the gas as, for instance, characterized by its pressure and temperature, corresponds to millions of different microscopic states with a frequency distribution at the microscopic level which provides a method to relate the two states. This is as extreme a case of multiple realizability as we can get, and the same situation typically arises in all instances of statistical explanation in both the natural and the social sciences. Arguably, this shows that multiple realizability cannot be used to rule out explanations as reductions. At the very least, it would be counterintuitive if we began with the goal of explicating a type of scientific change (viz., theory reduction), and then produced such an explication that the standard examples of that type of scientific change did not even approximately fit our account (in this case, because we proscribed multiple realizability). Reductionists should simply embrace multiple realiz-ability as a typical feature of many reductions rather than attempt to avoid it.

The status of reductionism

Throughout its history, reductionism has been a somewhat imperialist thesis purporting to bring under its purview all parts of science. This project's success was supposed to lead to the unification of science, with fundamental physics lying at the bottom of the hierarchy and enjoying epistemic primacy over all other disciplines. I discuss the status of this project before turning to the problems that frustrate its achievement. Finally, I briefly discuss the status of reductionism as a research strategy.

The unity and disunity of science

A very common belief among philosophers is that reduction leads to the unity of science. Strangely, this view has rarely been explicitly defended, with Oppenheim and Putnam (1958) and Causey (1977) being notable exceptions. Oppenheim and Putnam built a compositional hierarchy of the particles of matter, starting from the fundamental particles of physics all the way up to macroscopic objects, and suggested that explanations proceed seamlessly from lower levels to higher ones, resulting in a unified science of everything. In contrast, Causey gave a formal account of unification largely within the logical empiricist tradition.

That successful reduction should lead to unification gets support from several well-known episodes in the history of science: (i) Newton's reduction of Kepler's laws to his theory of gravitation led to the unification of celestial and terrestrial mechanics; (ii) Maxwell's reduction of the independent laws of electricity and magnetism to his laws of electromagnetism led to a unified theory embracing both domains; (iii) the same theory led to a unification of electromagnetism and optics through the reduction of the laws of the latter to those of the former; and (iv) Pauling's theory of valency reduced the rules of valency to quantum mechanics, thus unifying chemistry and physics to the extent that the disciplinary boundaries between them now largely reflect historical contingencies and convenience rather than deep conceptual differences.

There are, however, equally compelling counter-examples, most notably:

- the reduction of the laws of thermodynamics to the kinetic theory of matter has not led to the disappearance of an independent discipline of thermodynamics (which engineers must use every day) or even to its incorporation into a discipline unified with statistical mechanics; and
- classical genetics continues as an independent discipline in many contexts, particularly clinical contexts, in spite of its reduction to molecular biology.

What was just said about classical genetics can also be defended for many other areas of biology including cytology or neurobiology. In those cases, the molecular characterization of cell components neither prevents nor is always fully integrated with the continued traditional functional characterization of those components. In such examples, the older reduced theories and laws persist because they are adequate in their context. Introducing integrative or eliminative redescriptions from the reducing level would only result in irrelevant complexities of description.

Wimsatt (1976) argued that reductions show exactly when, and to what extent, the reduced theory or law is correct because the reducing theory or law is almost always more general than what gets reduced and includes the latter in its domain. This is one of the ways in which the reducing theory or law is more fundamental than its reduced counterpart. Nevertheless the reduced theory or law continues to be of value in its domain, the limits of which are better understood once a reduction has taken place. Thus, we know exactly when and how to use thermodynamics – and when not to – because we understand how it is related to the more fundamental kinetic theory. In this way reductions provide warrant for the use of a reduced theory or law. Far from producing the unity of science, successful reductions encourage the continued persistence of reliable special sciences to be used within their restricted domains. Such disunity is further encouraged by the details of the assumptions that must be made to carry out the derivation of a reduced theory or law from its reducing counterpart, as we shall see below.

Trouble in the details

Reductionist explanations can lead to genuine conceptual unification if the logical and mathematical inferences required can be justified on purely formal (that is, non-empirical) grounds, independently of the assumptions of the reducing theory or law. This point is best articulated using an example. Consider the relation between special relativity and classical mechanics. It is typically held that the latter is reduced to the former because classical mechanics leads to the same predictions as does special relativity when speeds are much lower than that of light. To derive the laws of classical mechanics from those of special relativity is mathematically trivial: we simply take the limit $c \to \infty$, where c is the speed of light. The trouble is that this limit is not only counterfactual but requires us to change counterfactually the value of a fundamental constant of nature. It is far from clear how to interpret what taking such a limit means.

Similar approximations and idealizations are commonplace in the explanation of much of macroscopic (for instance, condensed matter) physics from the microscopic level – Leggett has called them "physical" approximations and Sarkar has provided a detailed reconstruction of how these were deployed with uncanny skill in Einstein's reduction of Brownian motion to the kinetic theory of matter in 1905 (Leggett 1987; Sarkar 2000). Similarly, Boltzmann's derivation of the second law of thermodynamics involved a famous *Stosszahlansatz* of molecular randomness, the basis of which remains unclear even today. The orbitals used by Pauling to derive his rules for valency are equally difficult to justify from quantum mechanics (though, oddly, not from the older quantum theory). It is by now uncontroversial that the derivations involved in reductions are not simply straightforward deductions. Even in the 1960s, then working within the logical empiricist context, Schaffner (1967) noted that reducing theories often correct reduced theories.

The philosophically important aspect of physical approximations is that they go beyond mathematical (or logical) assumptions and may introduce empirical assumptions that cannot entirely be justified from the reducing theories as, for instance, in the case of the limit $c \to \infty$. Whether or not these assumptions vitiate the cogency of a reduction can only be determined by a careful examination of the context: if the assumptions introduce implausible assumptions about the reducing theory then the rational conclusion is that there has been no reduction; otherwise, we must recognize that a reduction is still tentative (until the assumptions are explicitly justified) or that its form more complex than what was ever envisioned in the models of reduction we inherited from the logical empiricists.

Thus, reductions are typically not simple logical deductions or even mathematical derivations. In the context of condensed matter physics, Batterman (2001) refers to these complexities as the "devil" in the details. But Wimsatt and I embrace those complexities, not as problems that confuse our picture of nature, but as suggestive prompts about how to construct richer models of phenomena. I argue that Einstein's physical approximations to solve the problem of Brownian motion led to a deeper understanding of the variety of stochastic phenomena, viz., the ways in which random noise may display different types of structure (Sarkar 2000).

The existence of such details has another even more important philosophical consequence. Reduction may not justify eliminating entities (on the grounds that all the functions of such entities can, following reduction, be taken over by their counterparts in the reducing theory). Such ontological eliminativism would be justified only if the reduction requires no assumptions other than those embedded in the reducing theory or law which, as we have seen, is often not the case. Moreover, the fact that reductions may involve new empirical assumptions supports the conclusion drawn earlier that they may not provide any ground for the claim that different theories are being unified through reduction.

Research strategy

Reduction has been viewed here as a form of explanation and reductionism as the thesis that explanations in a particular discipline will be reductionist. Endorsement of that thesis naturally leads to the pursuit of reductionist research strategies: methods of research that assume that the various substantive criteria for reduction will be satisfied. Reductionist research strategies have been among the most powerful heuristics ever deployed in the history of science, starting with the mechanical philosophy and continuing to research in molecular biology today. We will ignore weak reductions here because every research program which is not a purely descriptive (or classificatory) project is based on some assumption of epistemic primacy of some set of factors that will explain what is being studied. All potentially non-reductionist research strategies discussed satisfy the criterion of *epistemic primacy* required for weak reductions.

Even some apparently non-reductionist research strategies, reconstructed carefully, turn out not to be so. Consider, for example, explanations in classical genetics of the type mentioned above. As noted there, geneticists attempt to show whether or not some phenotypic trait of an organism is genetic by studying the statistical distribution of that trait among the organism's descendants. This is how, for instance, one shows that hemophilia is controlled by one gene residing on the X-chromosome of humans. There is apparently nothing reductionist in such an experimental design: we are merely measuring frequency distributions of the trait without probing into the inner structure of the genome. However, this is misleading. To design the experiment we presumed that genes explained traits and not vice versa. In that sense, the genetic level has epistemic primacy over the phenotypic level. Moreover, to apply the laws of transmission genetics we are already envisioning the genotype to have hierarchical structure. Thus, even though we only measure statistical associations, our research design implicitly incorporates reductionist assumptions.

However, there are exceptions both with respect to whether research strategies are reductionist and with respect to whether they are valuable rather than misleading. Wimsatt has pointed out that reductionist biases led to the design and misinterpretation of experiments in the units of selection controversy in evolutionary biology, biasing explanations in favor of lower levels of selection (Wimsatt 1980). Large scale data-mining techniques in contemporary biology which reconstruct phylogenies by matching DNA sequencing in massive databases often have no easy reductionist reinterpretation. The conclusion that should be drawn is that, while reductionist research strategies have been singularly successful in the history of science, we should remain pluralistic in our approach to research design, exploring any suggestion that leads to empirically adequate explanations of phenomena.

Acknowledgments

For discussions and comments on an earlier draft, thanks are due to the two editors, Martin Curd and Stathis Psillos, as well as James Justus, Alexander Moffett, and Bill Wimsatt.

See also Biology; Chemistry; Explanation; Mechanism; Physics; Unification.

References

Batterman, R. W. (2001) *The Devil in the Details: Asymptotic Reasoning in Explanation, Reduction and Emergence*, Oxford: Oxford University Press.

Bickle, J. (2006) "Multiple Realizability," in Edward N. Zalta (ed.) *The Stanford Encyclopedia of Philosophy* (fall 2006 edition); available: http://plato.stanford.edu/archives/fall2006/entries/multiple-realizability.

Causey, R. L. (1977) *The Unity of Science*, Dordrecht: Reidel.

Leggett, A. J. (1987) *The Problems of Physics*, Oxford: Oxford University Press.

Monod, J. (1971) *Chance and Necessity: An Essay on the Natural Philosophy of Modern Biology*, New York: Knopf.

Morgan, T. H. (1926) *The Theory of the Gene*, New Haven, CT: Yale University Press.

Nagel, E. (1961) *The Structure of Science*, New York: Harcourt, Brace and World.

Nickles, T. (1973) "Two Concepts of Inter-Theoretic Reduction," *Journal of Philosophy* 70: 181–201.

Oppenheim, P. and Putnam, H. (1958) "The Unity of Science as a Working Hypothesis," in H. Feigl, M. Scriven, and G. Maxwell (eds) *Concepts, Theories, and the Mind–Body Problem*, Minneapolis: University of Minnesota Press, pp. 3–36.

Rosenberg, A. (1978) "The Supervenience of Biological Concepts," *Philosophy of Science* 45: 368–86.

Sarkar, S. (1989) "Reductionism and Molecular Biology: A Reappraisal," Ph. D. Dissertation. Department of Philosophy, University of Chicago.

—— (1998) *Genetics and Reductionism*, New York: Cambridge University Press.

—— (2000) "Physical Approximations and Stochastic Processes in Einstein's 1905 Paper on Brownian Motion," in D. Howard, and J. Stachel (eds) *Einstein: The Formative Years, 1879–1909*, Boston, MA: Birkhäuser, pp. 203–29.

—— (2005) *Molecular Models of Life*, Cambridge, MA: MIT Press.

Schaffner, K. F. (1967) "Approaches to Reduction," *Philosophy of Science* 34: 137–47.

Schrödinger, E. (1936) "Probability Relations between Separated Systems," *Proceedings of the Cambridge Philosophical Society* 31: 446–52.

Shimony, A. (1987) "The Methodology of Synthesis: Parts and Wholes in Low-Energy Physics," in R. Kargon and P. Achinstein (eds) *Kelvin's Baltimore Lectures and Modern Theoretical Physics*, Cambridge, MA: MIT Press, pp. 399–423.

Wimsatt, W. C. (1976) "Reductive Explanation: A Functional Account," *Boston Studies in the Philosophy of Science* 32: 671–710.

—— (1980) "Reductionistic Research Strategies and Their Biases in the Units of Selection Controversy," in T. Nickles (ed.) *Scientific Discovery: Case Studies*, Dordrecht: Reidel, pp. 213–59.

Further reading

W. C. Wimsatt's "Reduction and Reductionism," in P. D. Asquith and H. E. Kyburg, Jr. (eds) *Current Research in the Philosophy of Science*, East Lansing, MI: Philosophy of Science Association, 1979), pp. 352–77, reviews much of the early work on reduction with an emphasis on biology. Many of the early papers are collected in the first edition of E. Sober (ed.) *Conceptual Issues in Evolutionary Biology* (Cambridge, MA: MIT Press, 1984), but not in later editions. Sarkar (1998) is the most extended discussion of reduction in biology, Batterman (2001), in physics. W. C. Wimsatt and S. Sarkar's "Reductionism," in S. Sarkar and J. Pfeifer (eds) *The Philosophy of Science: An Encyclopedia* (New York, NY: Routledge, 2006), pp. 696–703, provides a survey of recent work on reduction including the use of reductionist research strategies.

41
REPRESENTATION IN SCIENCE

Paul Teller

Representation in science: linguistic and otherwise

Many take scientific representation to be, in the main, linguistic, perhaps thinking of science as producing descriptions and natural laws, and thinking of the principal vehicles for results in science as the research article, textbook, monograph, and treatise. There is a general reason for suspicion about any such conclusion. To be applicable, language must be based on extra-linguistic skills: abilities to discriminate objects, properties, characteristics, generally that to which basic meaningful units of language apply such as colors, shapes, and re-identifiable objects; as well as much more complex skills such as those involved in using a microscope. Such skills involve perceptual and probably many other non-linguistic forms of representation. Now, apply T. H. Huxley's precept that science is scrupulously applied common sense. We should expect that science would make use of these extra-verbal representational tools and in fact build on, augment, develop, expand, and extend them.

When we look, this is just what we find: from the role of construction by compass and straight edge in Greek geometry, through the use and development of maps, illustrations, diagrams, and graphical methods, to the current explosion in the extra-linguistic tools enabled by information technology. Note that all of these provide a kind of epistemic access both to data and to theoretical (or modeling) conclusions that would otherwise be utterly out of reach. To emphasize with the extreme: imagine trying to understand the visual modeling output of sophisticated simulations in terms of a list of numbers or a print-out of the data and code used to produce the image!

How should we think about the use of mathematics in scientific representation? Did Galileo not say that the book of nature is written in the language of mathematics, and is mathematics not presented linguistically? But it is debatable whether mathematical representation should count as linguistic. For example, when we represent the motion of a pendulum with the function, $x = A \operatorname{Sin}(\omega t)$, the formula does not represent the motion directly. The formula represents a function, perhaps understood as a collection of ordered pairs of values, that, when interpreted as representing times and angles of deflection, in turn represent the motion of the pendulum. The representation succeeds to the extent that the function and the course of values are similar in respects that are of current concern.

The point generalizes. An abstract model – a piece of mathematics – can be used by representing agents to represent a target phenomenon by singling out form or structure shared by the model and its target. Often language facilitates picking out both the model and the relevant similarity used in the representation. Nonetheless it is the model, the abstract object, and the relevant similarity, not the language used to pick them out, which in the first instance function in the representational role. For that reason among others, an enormous amount of modern science is deeply extra-linguistic.

One must resist any temptation to wonder whether linguistic or extra-linguistic representation is the more important. Language cannot be applied without use of representation-driven tools of application – perceptual, abstract modeling, and probably much else. On the other hand, the recursive, combinatorial power of language to further structure, organize, and generally deploy representations – linguistic and others – immeasurably augments the power of our extra-linguistic representational tools. Linguistic and extra-linguistic representations are constitutively intertwined.

The ubiquitous inexactitude of human representation

I need to distinguish two ways in which a representation can be inexact. It will be crucial not to conflate "(im)precision" and "(in)accuracy". As I use these terms, to say that John's height is 6 feet *precisely* is to say something precise, but, if his height is not quite 6 feet, something not completely accurate. On the other hand, to say that John's height is 6 feet *close enough* is to say something imprecise, but, within the limits set by the imprecision, in no way inaccurate, even if John's height has an irrelevantly small deviation from 6 feet precisely. "Inexact" will be the umbrella term, meaning imprecise and/or inaccurate.

All will agree that "analog" representations, such as pictures, maps, and diagrams, are in some way inexact. It is too little appreciated that almost all human linguistic representation is also to some extent inexact in ways that science refines but does not eliminate. The only plausible exception is that part of mathematics not susceptible to unintended interpretations. To begin with the representation of perceptual qualities and objects, Galileo and his successors were already aware of the complications involved with the representation of so-called "secondary qualities." For example, our naive idea of the color red is of a monadic, intrinsic property of external objects. But color perception is a complex, multi-relational affair also involving facts about us and environmental factors. So our naive idea is a simplification, that is, it is inaccurate/idealized (in addition to being imprecise/vague). "Primary qualities" fare no better. Our naive ideas of time, space, duration, and distance are simplifications in view of the complexities revealed by quantum and relativistic theories. Even our conceptions of discrete, determinate, identity-bearing, everyday objects are idealizations in view of the problems of indefinite temporal and spatial boundaries and problems of constitution.

Where native human representational capacities fall short, many take science to provide exact theoretical refinements; but this is an illusion born of the belief that science identifies determinate natural kinds and quantities to which terms are directly attached that then function in exact, true, natural laws. We know that to date none of this has happened. To take only the restricted but particularly plausible case of fundamental physics: all fundamental theories in existing physics are idealizations, among other things idealizing the nature of the objects and quantities that they study. For example, mass was thought by Newtonians to be completely determinate. In special relativity, it splits into rest and relativistic mass. The theories of relativity blur the distinction between mass and energy, with gravitational mass–energy not being a localizable quantity. Quantum theories further cloud the status of mass where it functions as a renormalization parameter. It is a real stretch to think that at any point yet has "mass" been attached exactly to some univocal, completely determinate quantity. So likewise for "natural-kind terms" generally. Laws add an additional layer of idealization.

Human representation, scientific as well as pre-scientific, linguistic as well as extra-linguistic, is ubiquitously inexact. This is not a logical or conceptual matter: there is nothing in the nature of representation that requires it to fail of complete precision and accuracy. Rather, this is a matter of the limits of human representational powers relative to the – at least in practice – unlimited complexity of the world.

Evaluation of inexact representations

We evaluate representations with respect to how well they succeed in their function of representing things as they actually are. Such success can – apparently! – take different forms. When maps, diagrams, models, and the like succeed, we say that they are accurate – accurate enough in explicitly stated or tacitly understood respects, and in those respects to the required degree. In contrast, we say that statements are or are not true, period: for statements there appears to be no relativization to respects and degrees. This is an important way in which truth appears to differ from the much-maligned notion of *approximate truth* that is often rejected as incoherent. Incoherent it is if it is taken to be an absolute, context-independent notion. Like accuracy, approximate truth does make perfectly good sense, but only relativized to specific characteristics. A statement is approximately true when and to the extent that what it describes is similar to the way things actually are. But similarity is always in some specific respects and degrees. So, likewise, is approximate truth.

Truth is the only evaluative category for representational success that appears to be independent of relativity to respects and degrees. Such a conception of truth, understood as exact correspondence, does make perfectly good sense in as much as we can model it. But the ubiquitous inexactitude of the representations occurring in truth-evaluable vehicles (utterances, sentences, statements, propositions according to some) gives rise to the question of whether such independence ever, in practice, occurs. The application of any inexact representation will always, like the accuracy of maps, be evaluated relative to relevant respects and degrees. So, it would appear, must all truth-evaluable vehicles composed of inexact representations. The contextual respects and degrees are themselves never completely determinate, if only because they turn on incompletely determinate human interests. It follows, for this among other reasons, that statements have no exact truth conditions.

The foregoing argument, though cogent, tells us too little about what it is for an inexact statement to be true, and so about what is involved in evaluation for truth. For help one naturally looks to current accounts of vagueness – but in vain. Many accounts seek to provide exact truth conditions – thus denying the phenomenon of ubiquitous inexactitude of all our representational tools. Supervaluational accounts take a vague statement to be true just in case all its "appropriate precisifications" are true, but since "appropriate precisifications" is itself imprecise we are offered no help with the current question. Epistemicism insists that all terms are, after all, completely precise and that vagueness is exclusively a matter of our lack of access to that complete precision. The claims of epistemicists can here be set aside by application of the quali-fication *humanly accessible* to the claimed exactness of representations; and on the strength of a more direct worry that will appear below.

We need an alternative account, that, to be sure, will have its own idealizations, but that will offer a more exact understanding of truth and evaluation for truth in face of ubiquitous inexactitude. I suggest that evaluation for truth has much in common with evaluation of analog representations for representational success.

An approach to evaluating truth-evaluable representations

What is meant by saying that John's height is 6 feet? By this one could understand that John's height is 6 feet *precisely*. No one has a height of 6 feet precisely, but this false precise statement nonetheless functions as a truth if the discrepancy between 6 feet precisely and John's true height properties does not matter for current concerns. I will characterize this situation by saying that the *conditions of application* obtain for the statement that John's height is 6 feet precisely. This precise statement is inexact in virtue of its inaccuracy.

Or, one might intend that John's height is 6 feet *close enough*. This imprecise statement is in suitable circumstances literally true by virtue of being, within the limits of its imprecision, not in any way inaccurate. Which circumstances? None other than the foregoing conditions of application for the statement that John's height is 6 feet precisely. The new accurate statement is inexact in virtue of its imprecision.

An analysis based on this example will work for many similar cases, but often seems to fail. A clear case of John's height being 6 feet close enough will, it would appear, make it true that John's height is between 3 and 9 feet, without any possible reser-vation or qualification. But, of course, saying that John's height is between 3 and 9 feet no more succeeds in expressing a literally and exactly true statement than does saying that the present king of France is bald. There are no such things as (precise) heights that apply to people: heights go up and down half-an-inch a day. If we intend height at a moment of time (already an idealization) we still have to worry about posture, about how much of John's hair and dead surface skin to include. There is frame dependence from special relativity, indeterminateness of position from quantum mechanics, and so on.

Perhaps we should instead operationalize *height*. Any such effort will result in a conception that is now not inaccurate, but again is open-ended, and to that extent imprecise. Other candidates to remove the failure either of accuracy or of precision in *height* will face difficulties similar to one or another of the foregoing.

We conclude that the statement that John's height is between 3 and 9 feet faces the same kinds of reservations as faced by John's height being 6 feet. In one way the appeal to the interval, (3', 9'), is imprecise in as much as only an interval has been specified. But, in the way that is relevant to the applicability of unqualified truth, the appeal counts as perfectly precise since the interval has been precisely specified. However, the prior reservations still apply to *height*. We can understand this as a precise, but then inaccurate – because idealized – notion. Or we can go soft, perhaps by operationalizing *height*, and then have an accurate but no longer precise statement. Statements such as that there are some people in this room, that water is H_2O, that there are bears in the Rocky Mountains, etc., are likely to fare similarly.

We are now equipped to say something helpful about what is involved in an imprecise statement being true by appealing to the foregoing trade-off between impre-cision and inaccuracy. Imprecise and correlatively inaccurate statements in effect get the same representational work done, as kinds of *semantic alter egos*. To understand the representational force of an imprecise statement we refer it to a semantic alter ego, a correlatively precise (or relatively precise – see below on platforms) and, to that extent, idealized statement. The representational force of this semantic alter ego we under-stand, in turn, by analogy to maps, pictures, and other modes of representation that work on the strength of similarity of form or structure. The representational success of something like a map or a picture turns on whether it is similar enough to its target in respects that are of current interest. An idealized, and to that extent inaccurate, description picks out an "ideal" that is similarly evaluated for representational success. All these modes of representation involve at least an implicit relativization to respects and degrees of current concern.

To summarize, with an admittedly crude analogy. In practice, truth is, in certain respects, like being flat. In practice nothing is mathematically flat. But many things *are* flat, that is, flat enough for present concerns. Similarly, in practice, no perfectly precise statement is literally true. *Imprecise* statements *are* often true in a way analogous to something being flat in virtue of having a surface that, for current concerns, departs insignificantly from flat precisely. That is, imprecise statements are often true in virtue of some corresponding (precise, inaccurate) idealization being true enough, literal truth in the imprecise original then being accommodated by its imprecision, with the attendant relativization to current concerns. Truth achieved by smoothing over inaccuracy with imprecision can be thought of as a kind of generalization of the phenomenon illustrated by the case of flatness. Again, the only plausible exceptions to this generalization are some truths from mathematics.

Semantic contextualism

The ubiquitous inexactitude of representation is obscured by the fact that, when no difficulties result, it is something we do, and must, ignore. Consider the analogy with epistemic contextualism: knowledge is *epistemically contextual* insofar as change in context may require scrutiny of prior assumptions. In any discursive context we must start with some assumptions that are uncritically taken for granted with respect to justification. But we do this in a spirit of defeasibility: the challenge of a difficulty may require critical examination of the prior presumptions, of course on the basis of some new presumptions. By analogy, knowledge is *semantically contextual* insofar as changes in context may require tighter standards of precision and accuracy. Consider how, without any change in evidence, the status of "John's height is 6 feet" may change when there is a change in what we are willing to tolerate in the discrepancy from the ideal of 6 feet precisely. Knowledge is semantically contextual in the sense that the presumption of unproblematic starting points must, in practice, extend not just to justification but to what I call *platforms* of presumed exact truths. If we were forever refining, no examination or application could get started! But, again we proceed in a spirit of defeasibility. When problems arise, one option is to refine our representational tools.

The idea of platforms of semantic contextualism enables statement of what one suspects underlies the temptation of epistemicism: in effect, epistemicism conflates the belief that for every context there will be an adequate platform with the belief that there is one platform that suffices for any possible context – if only we knew what it was! Since any such platform is, at the very least, utterly out of human reach, we need a system for evaluating our representations for success that does not work in terms of any speculated ultimate precision.

Representation in science

Let us make a second use of Huxley's idea of science as scrupulously applied common sense, this time to suggest a highly idealized model, or rational reconstruction, of the historical development of scientific representations. We start with inexact, pre-scientific, representational tools. Using these we solve certain problems by correcting, extending, and refining our means of representation, which are then absorbed back into the overall conceptual toolkit. The process of improvement in accuracy and in precision continues. It is often recognized that further improvement stretches out indefinitely into accuracy's future. I emphasize that the same goes for precision. We can make some kind of sense of the process terminating in a Peircian long-run limit of inquiry where we could finally get a human grip on exact truth. But, as Keynes remarked in another context, in the long run, we are all dead.

See also Idealization; Models; The structure of theories; Truthlikeness.

Further reading

Ronald Giere's extensive work on the use of models in science fills in important parts of the foregoing sketch. See his most recent *Scientific Perspectivism* (Chicago: University of Chicago Press, 2006) and many of the references therein. Mark Wilson's leisurely *Wandering Significance: An Essay on Conceptual Behaviour* (Oxford: Oxford University Press, 2006) provides copious illustrations and bits of history relevant to my account. Bas van Fraassen's *Scientific Representation: Paradoxes of Perspective* (forthcoming) includes a broad introduction to the subject, with much historical background, relations to structuralism, and empiricists' questions about the relation of appearance and reality. A historical precursor to much of my thinking, and to much of the current modeling literature generally, can be found in Ludwig Boltzmann's "Theories as Representations," an excerpt from which is translated in Arthur Danto and Sidney Morgenbesser, *Philosophy of Science* (New York: Meridian Books, 1960), pp. 245–52. For more specialized topics, see Michael Lynch and Steve Woolgar (eds) *Representation in Scientific Practice* (Cambridge, MA: MIT Press, 1990), which provides a sampling of work by sociologists of science on issues about representation in science; and Edward Tufte's *The Visual Display of Quantitative Information*, 2nd edn (Cheshire, CT: Graphics Press, 2001), as well as other books by Tufte, for a marvelous account of the hows, whys and whats of that topic, with bits of history and striking illustrations. The five-volume series *Album of Science* (New York: Charles Scribner's Sons), with I. B. Cohen as general editor, gives a great deal of information on graphic representation throughout the history of science. Lorraine Daston and Peter Galison's "The Image of Objectivity," *Representations* 40 (1992): 81–128, gives a history of the ideal of objectivity of visual representation in science. For treatment of the impact of the information revolution, see Paul Humphreys, *Extending Ourselves: Computational Science, Empiricism, and Scientific Method* (New York: Oxford University Press, 2004). The history of mathematics is intertwined with that of science, especially physics. While I have not been able to find a general history of this interplay, see George Polya, *Mathematical Methods in Science* (Washington, DC: Mathematical Association of America, 1977) for an introduction, for those who don't know a great deal of mathematics, to some of the basic uses of mathematics in physics. Brian Baigre (ed.) *Picturing Knowledge: Historical and Philosophical Problems Concerning the Use of Art in Science* (Toronto: University of Toronto Press 1996) is a collection of essays investigating the use of illustrations, and other art forms, and their relation to text in the development and communication of science. Soraya de Chadarevian and Nick Hopwood (eds) *Models: The Third Dimension* (Stanford, CA: Stanford University Press, 2004) provides essays on the use of physical models in science. Not completely to neglect logical positivist views, a trimmed down and, many would argue, radically distorted version of these views can be seen as a refinement of long-standing empiricist approaches to language. These have been enormously influential, especially in the social sciences, but are now widely regarded as completely inadequate. For a summary of the ideas and difficulties, see Edward Hung, *The Nature of Science: Problems and Perspectives* (Belmont, CA: Wadsworth, 1997), which is especially thorough. The real history of logical positivism on representation has roots in the Kantian tradition, on which see, for example, Michael Friedman, *Reconsidering Logical Positivism* (New York: Cambridge University Press, 1999). For a treatment of current theories of vagueness, see Rosanna Keefe, *Theories of Vagueness* (Cambridge: Cambridge University Press, 2000). Timothy Williamson provides the definitive exposition and defense of epistemicism in *Vagueness* (New York: Routledge, 1996). For more on laws as idealizations, see Paul Teller, "The Law Idealization," *Philosophy of Science* 71 (2004): 730–41. Finally, I have an ever growing list of writings, filling in various parts of the thumbnail sketch provided here, that can be picked out from my vita and manuscripts on my website: http://philosophy.ucdavis.edu/paul.

42

SCIENTIFIC DISCOVERY

Thomas Nickles

Historical overview

The topic of scientific discovery presents us with a paradox. There are powerful skeptical arguments from logic, philosophy of science, historiography, and sociology of science against the very possibility of logics of discovery, and indeed of a general scientific method. Yet Bacon, Descartes, Newton, Leibniz, and other proponents of discovery methods would be delighted could they tour today's scientific facilities.

Bacon and the other founders of modern science – concerned that discovery had hitherto been sporadic and accidental, a product of luck rather than logic – attempted to provide general methods that would "level wits" and enable natural philosophers to engage in a systematic enterprise guaranteed to generate new knowledge. In their view the received logics and rhetorics of their day were sterile techniques for arranging what was already known.

In *Why Was the Logic of Discovery Abandoned?* Larry Laudan (1981: Ch. 11) noted that discovery was important to these investigators not only as a way to produce *new* knowledge but as a way to produce new *knowledge*. The discovery path was epistemologically relevant primarily because a reliable path to a conclusion is the strongest form of justification, in empirical science as in logical proof. This is a *generativist* view of justification. But by the turn of the nineteenth century, the method of hypothesis was increasingly touted as a legitimate and more flexible way to investigate nature and to communicate final results. In theoretically deep domains at the frontier of research, it is difficult or impossible to accumulate enough observational information to draw interesting inductive conclusions or to create new theoretical vocabularies. By contrast, an hypothesis can often be tested against a scattering of observational information, and the hypothesis guides research in telling us precisely what to look for.

For those and other reasons, generative methods gradually gave way to *consequentialist* methods in the maturing sciences, and methodologists detached *final justification* from *discovery*. Consequentialism's premise is that it does not matter how we hit upon our hypotheses, only how they are tested, the test predictions being logical consequences of the hypotheses. Tested, not proved (because of the fallacy of affirming the consequent), but natural philosophers were already coming to realize that certainty is impossible to attain, that science is better regarded as an ongoing, multi-pass, self-correcting enterprise in which scientists cycle back to refine previous results, investing them with greater theoretical and experimental richness.

During this period, then, we find a logical inversion in methodology, from generativism to consequentialism. The method of hypothesis, once an heuristic crutch to be thrown away when full *inductions* were achieved, now became the official method of science; and inductive methods were demoted to the Baconian, *historical* sciences. Since then, discovery methods have been associated with the data-driven, correlational sciences rather than with deep theoretical work.

During the twentieth century the logical empiricists and the Popperians, who made philosophy of science a professional, academic subject, institutionalized the consequentialist turn. Hans Reichenbach's 1938 distinction of *context of justification* from *context of discovery* eventually became a powerful criterion to demarcate the universal, normative, internalist, epistemological concern of philosophers with the "final *products*" of research from the supposedly particularist, externalist concern of historians and psychologists merely to describe the *process* of investigation. The most familiar statement of the two-context distinction is found in Karl Popper's *Logic of Scientific Discovery*, which portrays theories in an Einsteinean manner as "free creations of the human imagination." Thus discovery issues came to be ruled out-of-bounds as an epistemological topic until a revival of interest began around 1960. A major objection, anticipated by Charles Peirce in his work on economy of research, but soon forgotten, is that discovery path must be coupled to justification in the minimal sense that, unless some of the theory candidates to be tested have a chance of being truthful or fruitful, hypotheticalism has no chance at all of realizing its stated goal.

Interestingly, in his own work, Reichenbach bucked the strong consequentialism that inspired the two-context distinction, for he retained a generativist methodology of induction as epitomized by his *straight rule*: if m results in n trials produce outcome O, to infer that m/n of all cases are O. The rule is to be applied repeatedly, in a self-correcting manner, with a hoped-for long-run convergence on the correct result. And in his study of probabilistic causal relations, in which one cause can screen off others (a topic fruitfully developed by his student Wesley Salmon), Reichenbach anticipated the causal network approach described under "Some reasons for optimism," below.

Some reasons for pessimism

(1)   Bacon, Descartes, Newton, and other founding methodologists disagreed fundamentally about the correct method.

(2)   Their own methods were themselves discovered by luck and could not, at that time, have been regarded as reliable by any reasonable standard.

(3)   Early claims for one completely general, portable and, therefore, content-neutral method that would lead to truth were incredibly strong.
      (3a) It is unclear how the candidate methods can somehow implicitly contain all future discoveries and even provide the directions for finding them.

(3b) There is little evidence that appeal to such methods explains the success of modern science. By the late twentieth century it had become clear that the more powerful methods are not content-neutral and that neutral constraints such as simplicity are not truth-conducive. The "no free lunch" theorems of Wolpert and Macready (1997) attempt to make mathematically precise the intuition of Hume and Wittgenstein that which methods work better than others depends on the way the world is, that no method is *a priori* superior to any other.

(4) Romantics, reacting to the Enlightenment, pointed out that deeply creative theories owe as much to imagination as to method.

(5) The view that methods of discovery are supposed to deliver true laws and theories was challenged by arguments against strong scientific realism, among them skeptical attacks on induction by Humeans such as Bertrand Russell and Popper, and W. V. Quine's adaptation of Pierre Duhem's work to argue for a radical underdetermination of scientific theories.

(6) The new historiography of science seemed to point in the same direction as logic. Some philosophers of science took a historiographical turn during the 1960s, since Kuhn's *Structure of Scientific Revolutions* (1962) made the newly maturing historiography of science seem relevant for testing methodologies of science. The good news for the friends of discovery was Kuhn's showing that discoveries are not simply punctiform "aha" experiences, that they have an extended temporal and cognitive structure and thus are amenable to analysis. The bad news is that Kuhn noted how difficult it is to say precisely who discovered even such basic items as oxygen and the planet Uranus. Sociologists of science and social historians such as Simon Schaffer (1994) subsequently provided more detail about the extent to which individual investigators are socially conditioned, how much contingency and artifactual work (prepared samples, imaging representations, etc.) are typically involved, and the amount of social negotiation necessary to get something recognized as a discovery. They argue that "discovery" is better considered a complex social process than a psychological one. Augustine Brannigan (1981) contended that discoveries are social attributions rather than uncoverings of nature. Accordingly, many social historians avoid philosophers' talk of discovery altogether. However, much of the work described in this article can be framed in terms of "innovation" rather than "discovery" in a strongly realist sense.

(7) Artificial intelligence (AI) has also failed to live up to the early, grandiose claims for it, despite the fact that much of AI can be regarded as an explicit attempt to develop discovery logics in the sense of automated procedures for solving problems, computational procedures that avoid the vagueness characteristic of philosophical accounts. Sociologists note that AI programs typically incorporate individual–psychological rather than social–cognitive models of learning – the computer (program) as the lone scientist. Historical work is also often at odds with AI work on crisp, idealized problems, but there have been interesting attempts to straddle this boundary, for example, Thagard (1992) and Darden (2006).

Herbert Simon, one of the founders of AI, reduced discovery to problem-solving and problem solving to search through spaces of possible solutions (Simon 1977). This move jump-started the AI treatment of discovery since work on search was already underway. Simon and associates initially envisioned a General Problem Solver, incorporating basic, content-neutral heuristics such as hill climbing and backward chaining in addition to logic – the kinds of operations we typically use in searching for logic proofs. Unfortunately, the problem-solving power of this general approach turned out to be weak. Next Simon's group developed a series of more specific inductive programs that they claimed were capable of rediscovering famous laws of Kepler, Ohm, and so on (Langley et al. 1987). But since the problems were basically programmed in from the beginning and the data sets were relatively noiseless, these whiggish programs did not come close to capturing the messy research situation faced by the historical investigators. Rather, they are closer to the "discoverers' induction" of Herschel and Whewell, according to which, at the end of inquiry, we possess sufficient materials to construct a plausible discovery path (Snyder 2006). This is what I have called "discoverability" rather than original discovery. It represents a late stage of one type of multi-pass approach and is an important form of justification.

Meanwhile, AI produced a new generation of programs – knowledge-based expert systems – in which wide scope of application was sacrificed to problem-solving power within a specific problem domain such as a particular sort of medical diagnosis. There are many such programs in use today. While these programs can greatly improve the speed and reliability of many research tasks, they are not highly innovative discovery engines, for they answer routine questions by means of knowledge transferred from human experts who already possess it.

Some reasons for optimism

While the founders' claims were greatly overblown, the happy side of the opening paradox is that science today employs an impressive variety of knowledge amplifiers. We are not close to having methodical procedures that reliably generate imaginative deep theories or that think and act in the way that embodied, encultured, human beings do, but we need not set the bar so high. Isn't it just obvious that today we have many high-powered aids to discovery? Automatic gene sequencers and sophisticated computer programs come to mind. The latter, for instance, enable us to play with models of complex systems, models that give us access to processes previously hidden, processes sometimes suggestive of deep theoretical ideas such as that of a *strange attractor* in chaos studies.

There is a long tradition of data analysis broached by Bacon and continued by John Herschel and J. S. Mill ("Mill's methods") but more impressively developed in the probability, statistics, and experimental design traditions founded by Pascal and Fermat, and greatly developed by the French of Laplace's generation with their efforts to distill knowledge out of ignorance. The turn of the twentieth century saw another explosion of development, followed by an ongoing series of major advances. Today, students routinely run statistical "packages" of data analysis such as *ANOVA* on the computer. Leveling of wits indeed! Moreover, we have developed increasingly sophisticated means of mining the huge databases generated by today's instrumentation.

The last fifty years of work in the history and the sociology of science have taught us a great deal about paths of discovery. We now reject the view that discovery is an atomic event in which nature directly discloses itself to the ingenious or perceptive investigator. Laboratory life studies have helped us understand what community life is like at the frontier of research. Social studies of science helps philosophers adopt a more thoroughly naturalistic account of research, one that precludes simple appeals to reason or perception as clairvoyant faculties for grasping the truth. Still, it seems premature to abandon discovery-talk altogether. Granted that it is extremely difficult to say who discovered oxygen or Uranus, when, and under what description: do we really wish to deny that they have been discovered? The term "discovery" can mislead, but so can other terms, such as "social construction."

Historiography also discloses that history can be highly non-linear. Small causes can have big effects. A modest result including an instrumental innovation can eventually have revolutionary impact. Explaining major scientific change does not require positing huge, nearly instantaneous theoretical breakthroughs. Philosophers of science were too long seduced by the Romantic Einstein–Popper model.

There has also been progress on the logical front. In older senses of "method" and "logic," Enlightenment epistemology could be identified with method of science and the latter in turn with logic of science. Some logical empiricists retained the identification of method with logic after Gottlob Frege's severe reconceptualization of logic in terms of rules of valid deductive reasoning alone, a move that implies an epistemologically invidious discovery–justification distinction. For logic in the post-Fregean sense provides no direction to inquiry, no strategy for problem-solving such as is needed also in computer programs. Jaakko Hintikka (2004) has led the attempt to retain a broader, strategic conception of logic, including the logic of questions and answers. Investigators such as Ilkka Niiniluoto and Matti Sintonen in Helsinki and Atocha Aliseda in Mexico City, as well as many computer scientists, have applied this wider conception to the ampliative reasoning that Peirce termed "abduction." Other departures from standard logic include work on inconsistency-tolerant and adaptive logics by Diderik Batens and Joke Meheus at Ghent. Yet it is worth noting that even an ordinary deductive argument need not be sterile: it may be epistemically ampliative even though it is not logically ampliative, for we are not logically omniscient beings who see all the logical consequences of a set of propositions. Thus a mathematical proof may surprise us. By the same token, finding a deductive proof is itself a trial-and-error process, a fact often overlooked. In science the search for testable consequences of a theory or model is usually a difficult task. In this sense *discovery* is crucial to context of justification. As computer scientist Douglas Lenat once remarked, discovery is ubiquitous.

Kevin Kelly (1996) notes that whether a given sort of algorithmic procedure exists is not a historical existence question but an abstract mathematical existence question.

446

Nor need we require that a reliable method of inquiry tell us whether and when we have reached the truth. Given a sufficiently long data string as input, a learning machine may reliably converge on the correct structure and remain there ever after, whether or not the human users know this.

AI itself is far from dead. Case-based and model-based reasoning are promising for novel problem-solving and model-finding. In effect, case-based problem-solving implements Kuhn's insight that scientific problem-solving rarely starts from scratch. Rather, the new problem and solution are modeled on one or more successful solutions in the case library. Here, of course, it is crucial to have an appropriate similarity metric (corresponding to Kuhn's *acquired similarity relation*). Note that this approach explicitly recognizes the importance of such rhetorical tropes as similarity, analogy, and metaphor in creative problem-solving, whereas, historically, logic of science excluded rhetoric. Model-based reasoning is a broad, dynamical approach in which, for instance, mental or computer simulations replace static problems and solutions. Model-based approaches attempt to model human imagination, intuition, visualization, and tacit knowledge or expertise, and to explore forms of representation that improve human cognition.

The remainder of this section briefly describes evolutionary computation and Bayesian causal-network theory, the two most exciting recent developments in *logic of discovery*, both deriving from the computer revolution and latter-day AI.

The idea of evolutionary computation sounds crazy at first: we evolve problem solutions rather than solving the problems analytically! We start with a population of symbol strings or computer programs encoding knowledge already available. The genetic algorithm then tests those individuals against a fitness criterion and, on that basis, probabilistically selects and breeds or else mutates some of them. (If the individuals are computer programs, breeding consists in an exchange of sub-routines, producing two new individuals.) When run on a sufficiently powerful computer, the iterative process can often find satisfactory solutions to interesting problems in 50–100 generations. John Holland initiated this approach in the 1960s, but his work was largely ignored by the AI community until about 1990. Since then evolutionary computation has grown explosively as investigators have recognized its flexibility. Now thousands of scientific and engineering papers using these methods, sometimes in combination with others such as case-based reasoning, appear each year in the journals of many fields.

The Darwinian inspiration is not accidental. Biological evolution is the most creative process that we know. Since the 1950s Donald Campbell (e.g., 1974) had argued that all creative gains, all inductive achievements, result from Darwinian processes of blind (undirected) variation plus selective retention (BVSR). Luck at the micro-level is pervasive in creative activities. Among the adherents of this universal Darwinism, in its various guises, are Richard Dawkins, David Hull, and Daniel Dennett. Their claim is not that all creative processes are directly analogous to biological mechanisms, rather that Darwin was first to discover the secret of creativity by opening the door to the vast space of BVSR mechanisms.

At present, with the possible exception of complexity theory (self-organizing systems), we have no serious competitor to the BVSR account of creativity (versions of which have been controversially applied to cultural evolution in the form of memetics or meme theory). Here the discussion is analogous to that of the evolution–development ("evo–devo") debate. The question is whether the self-organization exhibited by complex systems is itself an independent source of creative form or design, perhaps one that provides the conditions under which BVSR processes become possible; or whether, on the contrary, it falls within the scope of BVSR processes.

When Campbell advanced his BVSR thesis, he considered it a *reductio ad absurdum* of methodology of discovery, since the BVSR process is just a ramped-up form of trial-and-error. After all, the old method of hypothesis is basically a Darwinian process reduced to a tiny trickle of one or a few hypotheses at a time (provided that cumulative redesign occurs); and selection of blindly produced variants invites an application of the two-context distinction. However, today's evolutionary computation demonstrates that precisely this scaling-up allows the process to be methodized – and with built-in hypothesis generators to boot. If universal Darwinism is correct, then we may have, in nascent form, a quite general method of problem-solving after all. Ironically, we can reply to the Darwinian Campbell in the same way as to the naysayers who still liken the Darwinian process to a bunch of monkeys at typewriters: until recently the problem has been – not enough monkeys! (Of course, the right sort of cumulative selection–retention mechanisms also need to be in place, and these can be exceedingly difficult to find.) On this Darwinian view of scientific innovation, the methodologies of the seventeenth century and the "scientific method" as taught in schools amount to a kind of secularized *intelligent design* theory of science, with intelligent Method playing God.

Turning now to causal networks, we also find a computer-based scaling-up producing a revolutionary transformation. Working at the intersection of statistics, experimental design, computer science, and philosophy of discovery, Clark Glymour and his associates in Pittsburgh are not content to study discovery methods from a philosophical or historical distance. They are helping to produce a battery of methods that can replace defective data-analysis methods to provide more powerful and reliable ways in which to mine data-bases (Glymour and Cooper 1999; Spirtes et al. 2000). Their methods have already been applied to a wide range of theoretical and practical problems, including gene regulation, satellite imaging technologies, child development, learning theory generally, and lead poisoning in children. Their approach recaptures something of the old dream of distilling knowledge from ignorance in that it often permits reliable inferences to underlying causal structures, even when many of the probabilistic dependences are initially unknown. And, like evolutionary computation, it revives the idea that there can be reliable methods of discovery of considerable generality.

The basic idea does not depend on a precise philosophical analysis of causation. Correlation is not causation, but a network of correlations among variables imposes constraints on the possible causal structures. The structures can be represented as directed graphs in which the variables are vertices or nodes, and the edges, arcs, or arrows between them are causal relations. There are various methods of searching through the vast space of possible causal structures in order to zero-in on the best one, or a sufficiently good one, given the (sometimes radically incomplete) observational data, relevant background knowledge, and some plausibility assumptions. The computational problem explodes with the size of the network and the density of its causal relations, but in a wide range of cases probabilistic independence permits the discovery of fast algorithms that keep the search manageable. Bayesian methods have become especially popular (*Bayesian causal nets*). Given a problem with spotty data-sets, the Bayesian assigns prior probability values to the corresponding variables, and calculates the posterior probability of each candidate's causal model over each possible situation. The causal model in the search space that gets the highest (statistically averaged) score wins.

Not only can these network methods work on radically incomplete data-sets but they can also treat descriptive, observational data in a causal or quasi-causal manner, thus doing what traditional experimental designers declared to be impossible – reliably finding causal structure without intervention in nature – without randomized experiments! Obviously, this technique greatly expands the reach of scientific investigation by moving the boundary of *correlational* approaches more deeply into theoretical–causal territory, thereby making claims for scientific realism in those domains more plausible.

Conclusion: goodbye to the global, two-context distinction

While we still need to make context distinctions, it is a mistake to lump them all into one, global discovery–justification distinction (Schickore and Steinle 2006). Scientific practices do not neatly separate out in this manner, either logically or temporally. Search-and-discover operations are ubiquitous in research, from problem formulation to predictive testing. For example, writing and evaluating research proposals requires heuristic appraisal – evaluation of the future promise of fertility of problems, approaches, models, techniques, pieces of apparatus, etc. Although normative, this exercise often involves constructing what might be called "discovery sketches" – plausible lines of development and application – and it differs from epistemic appraisal of truth based on the past empirical track record. We also meet *discovery* issues at the meta-level. After all, the nineteenth-century methodological inversion in theory of justification occurred largely for *heuristic* reasons! As William Wimsatt likes to say, "science is heuristics all the way down." And how a normative practice itself originates or emerges and gets constituted is an intriguing meta-level *discovery* problem distinct from normative questions about how specific products of that practice are justified within the practice.

For the logical empiricists and the Popperians, context of discovery, epistemically speaking, was just noise, something external to philosophy of science. Thus, ironically, their view cut itself off from the sources of innovation, the very thing that is supposed to drive inquiry. Philosophy of science left itself without the resources with which to address what was supposed to be its central epistemological problem: how knowledge grows. Stated in economic lingo, the received view-ers made scientific innovation exogenous. At bottom the problem is Plato's *Meno* paradox, a how-possibly problem (Nickles 2003). How is successful inquiry possible? How is it possible to push back the frontier of knowledge, to come to know what we previously could not even imagine? And insofar as it is possible, how far can our methodological tools improve on blind luck in order to accelerate inquiry (again, a problem with similarities to biological evolution)? If a central task of epistemology and philosophy of science is to solve those problems, including that of understanding how science works; and if another task is to contribute to the better working of science, then those philosophers who simply ceded context of discovery to historiography, psychology, and sociology threw out the baby with the bathwater.

See also Critical rationalism; Experiment; The historical turn in the philosophy of science; Logical empiricism; The role of logic in philosophy of science; Scientific method.

References

Brannigan, A. (1981) *The Social Basis of Scientific Discovery*, Cambridge: Cambridge University Press.

Campbell, D. T. (1974) "Evolutionary Epistemology," in P. A. Schilpp (ed.) *The Philosophy of Karl R. Popper*, LaSalle, IL: Open Court, pp. 413–63.

Darden, L. (2006) *Reasoning in Biological Discoveries: Essays on Mechanisms, Interfield Relations and Anomaly Resolution*, Cambridge: Cambridge University Press.

Glymour, C. and Cooper, G. (eds) (1999) *Computation, Causation, and Discovery*, Cambridge, MA: MIT Press.

Hintikka, J. (2004) *Inquiry as Inquiry: A Logic of Scientific Discovery* (selected papers), Dordrecht: Springer.

Kuhn, T. S. (1970 [1962]) *The Structure of Scientific Revolutions*, 2nd edn with Postscript, Chicago: University of Chicago Press.

Kelly, K. T. (1996) *The Logic of Reliable Inquiry*, New York: Oxford University Press.

Koza, J. (1992) *Genetic Programming: On the Programming of Computers by Natural Selection*, Cambridge, MA: MIT Press.

Langley, P., Simon, H. A., Bradshaw, G., and Zytkow, J. (eds) (1987) *Scientific Discovery: Computational Explorations of the Creative Process*, Cambridge, MA: MIT Press.

Laudan, L. (1981) *Science and Hypothesis*, Dordrecht: Reidel.

Nickles, T. (2003) "Evolutionary Models of Innovation and the Meno Problem," in L. Shavinina (ed.) *International Handbook on Innovation*, Amsterdam: Elsevier Scientific Publications, pp. 54–78.

Popper, K. R. (1959), *The Logic of Scientific Discovery*, London: Hutchinson (expanded translation of his *Logik der Forschung* of 1934).

Schaffer, S. (1994) "Making Up Discovery," in M. Boden (ed.) *Dimensions of Creativity*, Cambridge, MA: MIT Press, pp. 13–51.

Schickore, J. and F. Steinle (eds) (2006) *Revisiting Discovery and Justification: Historical and Philosophical Perspectives on the Context Distinction*, Dordrecht: Springer.

Simon, H. A. (1977) *Models of Discovery*, Dordrecht: Reidel.

Snyder, Laura (2006) *Reforming Philosophy: A Victorian Debate on Science and Society*, Chicago: University of Chicago Press.

Spirtes, P., Glymour, C., and Scheines, R. (2000) *Causation, Prediction, and Search*, 2nd edn, Cambridge, MA: MIT Press.

Thagard, P. (1992) *Conceptual Revolutions*, Princeton, NJ: Princeton University Press.

Wolpert, D., and Macready, W. (1997) "No Free Lunch Theorems for Optimization," *IEEE Transactions on Evolutionary Computation* 1: 67–82 (condensed version of 1995 Santa Fe Institute Technical Report, SFI TR 95–02–010, "No Free Lunch Theorems for Search").

Further reading

For the state of play as viewed by many philosophers and historians around 1980, at a Reno conference, see T. Nickles (ed.) *Scientific Discovery, Logic, and Rationality* and *Scientific Discovery: Case Studies* (both Dordrecht: Reidel, 1980). For papers from a similar conference in Ghent, twenty years later, see issues 3 and 4 of *Foundations of Science* 4 (1999); and J. Meheus and T. Nickles (eds) *Models of Discovery and Creativity* (forthcoming). For an entry into model-based reasoning, consult L. Magnani and N. J. Nersessian (eds) *Model-Based Reasoning in Scientific Discovery* (Dordrecht: Springer, 2001). Koza (1992) is an intuitive introduction to genetic algorithms. Later volumes extend his approach to more difficult problems. Among the many publications from computer science, see books by Judea Pearl and the Springer series of conference volumes, *Discovery Science*. Space limitations prevented discussion of other important approaches to discovery and problem-solving, e.g., the resolution method in the Turing tradition described by Donald Gillies in *Artificial Intelligence and Scientific Method* (Oxford: Oxford University Press, 1996). In *The Logic of Discovery: A Theory of the Rationality of Scientific Research* (Dordrecht: Kluwer, 1993), Scott Kleiner applies Hintikka's interrogative model of inquiry. Aharon Kantorovich, *Scientific Discovery: Logic and Tinkering* (Albany, NY: SUNY Press, 1993) defends an evolutionary epistemological approach similar to Campbell's. Theodore Arabatzis foregrounds realism and representation problems in *Representing Electrons* (Chicago: University of Chicago Press, 2006).

43

SPACE AND TIME

Oliver Pooley

Introduction

The question that has dominated discussion of space and time in the philosophy of science concerns their *ontological status*. Newton, famously, claimed that space was an entity in its own right (1999 [1687]: 408). His *substantivalist* position was lambasted by Leibniz, who argued for the *relationalist* view that space is nothing "besides the order of bodies among themselves" (Leibniz 1956 [1716]: 26). Both views attracted adherents in the two centuries that followed, before the context was radically transformed by Einstein's theories of relativity.

In the first half of the twentieth century, philosophical consensus judged that general relativity vindicated Leibniz's relationalism (Reichenbach 1959). With the demise of logical empiricism, opinion changed. Newton was portrayed as making a respectable inference to the best explanation, from inertial effects to the existence of absolute motion and thus to absolute space. This inference (suitably modified) was thought to remain legitimate in general relativity. Recent historical and philosophical work reveals this to be a badly misleading caricature of Newton's arguments (Rynasiewicz 1995). But arguably this recent scholarship casts Newton, and his realism about spacetime structure, in even better light.

Another question concerns the *explanatory role* of space and time. The idea that Newton advanced an inference from inertial effects to the existence of space suggests a picture in which space exerts something like a causal influence on its material contents. Some think that this gets the order of explanation exactly the wrong way round: it is not that, for example, rods and clocks are constrained to behave as they do by the geometric structure of the spacetime in which they are immersed. Rather, goes the claim, it is the correlated lawlike behavior of rods and clocks that underwrites spacetime's geometric structure.

Two important topics are not discussed further below. The first is *conventionalism*: to what extent is our attribution of a particular geometry to physical space and time a stipulative convention? The second is the so-called "arrow of time" and in particular how the time asymmetry of thermodynamics is related to supposedly time-symmetric fundamental physics. Those interested in pursuing these topics are referred to the suggestions for further reading at the end of this chapter.

Space and time in classical mechanics

Newton was the progenitor of what we now recognize as physics, but he built on the work of a number of near contemporaries. In particular, he was indebted to Descartes for his first law of motion, the *principle of inertia*, which states that every body continues in its state of rest or uniform motion unless its state is changed by an applied force. This law plays a foundational role in Newtonian mechanics. Exaggerating slightly, the whole business of mechanics is to account for observed deviations from the inertial motions specified by the first law, in terms of the second law and particular force laws.

The principle of inertia also occupies a central place in Descartes's physics and yet he elaborated a philosophical account of motion hopelessly incompatible with it (Descartes 1985 [1644]). Descartes claimed that a body's motion, as ordinarily understood, is its change of position with respect to some arbitrarily chosen reference bodies, taken to be at rest. In addition, he identified a body's *true motion* with its motion from the vicinity of those bodies in immediate contact with it that are regarded as at rest.

Newton subjected Descartes's views to devastating criticism in a manuscript, known as "De Gravitatione," not published until the 1960s (Newton 1962). Newton details at length what he saw as absurd and self-contradictory aspects of Descartes's position. His most telling criticism, as Stein (1967) emphasizes, is the following.

According to both of Descartes's definitions, no body has a determinate velocity, and there is no definite trajectory it follows. For consider motion in the ordinary sense. This consists in change of position with respect to arbitrarily chosen bodies regarded as at rest. But which bodies can be regarded as at rest? Descartes cannot appeal to the sun or the fixed stars, for these are all in relative motion (both according to Descartes's vortex theory – as Newton painstakingly points out – and according to the mechanics Newton was to develop). What of motion in the strict sense? Here the matter is even worse. A body's motion is defined with respect to those bodies in immediate contact with it, which (for any body "truly moving") are continually changing. Nothing in either picture allows us to identify at some time the exact places through which a body has traveled, and so *a fortiori* nothing can tell us whether those places constitute a straight line which the body has traversed at a uniform rate. Descartes's account of motion cannot be combined with the principle of inertia, which requires that there be a fact of the matter about whether a body is moving uniformly.

Differential geometry and the notion of spacetime provide an illuminating framework in which we can clearly state which spacetime structures Descartes acknowledges, and which additional structures the principle of inertia requires. Figure 43.1 is a spacetime diagram depicting aspects of Descartes's universe. There is an objective fact about how spacetime divides into instantaneous states of the world ("simultaneity surfaces"), the geometry of each of which is Euclidean. There are facts of the matter about the relative temporal intervals (T_{AB} and T_{BC}) between instants. At each instant, the world is a plenum of only one kind of stuff, whose only attribute is extension. There must be facts of the matter about the identity over time of the parts of the plenum (such as *a* and *b* in the diagram) for there to be facts about the relative motions of such parts.

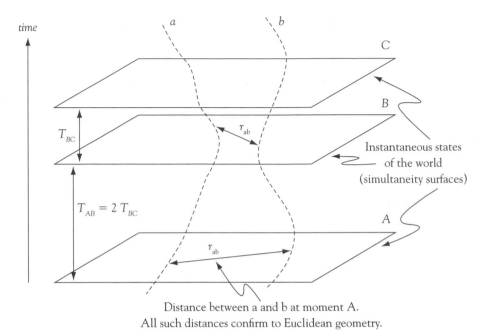

Figure 43.1 Descartes's spacetime

But, crucially, these cross-time identities between the parts of the material world are the only links between instants.

Without some additional structure, no determinate motion can be assigned to body *a*. Newton's solution was to postulate the existence of "absolute places": things truly distinct from bodies whose relative positions remain constant. This additional structure is depicted in Figure 43.2: point *q* at B represents the same point of absolute space as point *p* at A. There is therefore a determinate fact of the matter that *a* moves (changes its absolute place) between A and B. There being a fact of the matter about the relative temporal intervals between instants (i.e., a temporal metric) is also essential in securing a fact of the matter about the uniformity of such motion.

Newton's absolute space successfully grounds the distinctions that his laws require, but it underwrites some unneeded, physically undetectable distinctions too. A *frame of reference* is a standard of rest, simultaneity, and time with respect to which determinate motions can be assigned to bodies. Now imagine judging motion relative to a frame of reference moving uniformly relative to Newton's absolute space but otherwise matching Newton's framework from instant to instant. This frame agrees with Newton's on whether bodies are moving uniformly and, crucially, on the magnitude of their accelerations and hence on the forces to which they must be subject. In other words, Newton's laws do not pick out a unique standard of rest. Instead a whole family of frames of reference (the *inertial frames*) suffice to ground the distinctions that the laws require. Although a body's acceleration is empirically determinable, its velocity with respect to absolute space is not. The *relativity principle* is the statement of this equivalence among the inertial frames.

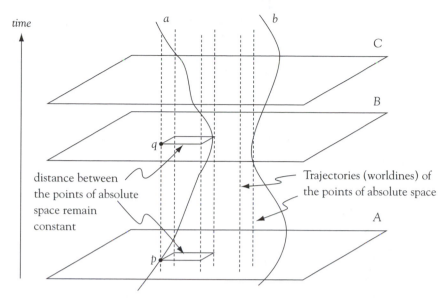

Figure 43.2 Newtonian spacetime

In the context of the dispute over the reality of space, the situation presents something of a dilemma. On the one hand, to make sense of the successful laws of mechanics we have to acknowledge more spacetime structure than Descartes and Leibniz were prepared to countenance. On the other hand, Newton's manner of securing a sufficiently rich structure introduces more than is required. Is there a third way?

Substantivalism, relationalism, and Mach's principle

Newtonian mechanics is formulated in terms of the simultaneity structure, instantaneous Euclidean geometry, and temporal metric common to Descartes's and Newton's spacetimes. It additionally requires some extra *transtemporal* structure. Geometrically, the additional structure required is a standard of *straightness* (for paths in spacetime), provided in differential geometry by a mathematical object called a *connection*. The possible trajectories of ideal force-free bodies correspond to straight lines in spacetime that do not lie within surfaces of simultaneity. These straight lines fall into families of non-intersecting lines that fill spacetime. Each family of lines forms the trajectories of the points of the "space" of some inertial frame. Newton's laws can be recast in a coordinate-free manner that makes explicit reference to this geometrical structure.

Now one interpretation of this structure reifies, not Newton's absolute space, but *spacetime*. One conceives of spacetime as a genuine entity literally endowed with the geometric structure that the connection, among other things, encodes. In general there are two relationalist strategies to resist such *spacetime substantivalism*:

(1) Replace Newtonian physics with an alternative theory that transparently makes do only with Cartesian spacetime structure (or an even weaker structure).

(2) Provide a relationalist interpretation of standard Newtonian mechanics.

Either way, one must provide a reduction of the empirically identifiable inertial frames.

The first strategy is famously associated with Ernst Mach. Newton claimed that the surface of water in a bucket suspended from a wound cord and then released becomes concave because it is rotating with respect to absolute space. Mach noted that one might instead attribute the effect to the water's rotation with respect to the fixed stars. This points towards the possibility that detectable local inertial structure is determined by distant masses. Inertial effects might result from bodies' non-uniform motion with respect to the average mass of the universe.

One theory along these lines was repeatedly rediscovered during the twentieth century. Although it recovers various welcome Newtonian features, it also predicts a mass anisotropy effect of a size ruled out by experiment. In the 1980s, however, Barbour and Bertotti discovered a new way to formulate a form of Machian mechanics (for references, see Barbour 1994).

One standard formulation of Newtonian dynamics involves a system's *configuration space*, Q. For a system of N massive point-particles, each point of its $3N$-dimensional configuration space corresponds to a specification of the positions of each particle in absolute space. As the system evolves, the point in configuration space representing the system's instantaneous state traces out a continuous curve. In the Lagrangian formulation of mechanics, one considers curves representing possible histories for the system in the product space formed from Q and a one-dimensional space T representing time. The physically possible history between two instantaneous states is the one for which a particular function of such histories (the *action*) takes a minimum (or, in general, an extremal) value.

Barbour and Bertotti reject Q in favor of the *relative configuration space* (Q_{RCS}), the points of which represent only the relative distances between particles. Their theory involves a metric defined on Q_{RCS} through a process Barbour calls "best matching." Imagine rigidly shifting infinitesimally differing relative configurations with respect to one another so as to extremize a trial "distance" function between them. The relative placement of the two configurations that extremizes the function is their "best matched" position, and the distance function so defined provides a metric on Q_{RCS}. Shortest paths (with respect to this metric) between two points of Q_{RCS} then represent the physically possible sequences of relative configurations for the system.

Note four features of Barbour and Bertotti's theory. First, it is clearly relational; the only spacetime structures involved in the theory are the simultaneity surfaces and the Euclidean nature of the distances between material points with respect to such surfaces. Second, although the temporal metric and inertial structure of Newtonian mechanics do not feature in the foundations of the theory, they do emerge from the dynamics. The best matching process described in the previous paragraph yields a preferred way of identifying the points of space from instant to instant (the identification provided by the "best-matched" relative positioning). The temporal metric is recovered as a simplifying parameter. Third, the sequences of relative configurations predicted by the theory exactly match those of a subset of the solutions of standard Newtonian theory, namely Newtonian solutions with zero overall angular momentum. In Popperian terms this makes Barbour and Bertotti's the better theory: it is more falsifiable. The relative standing of the two theories becomes particularly interesting when one notes that our universe appears to have no overall rotation. The Machian theory then looks superior both because it saves the phenomena with less postulated theoretical structure and because it predicts and explains a striking feature of our universe, namely its non-rotation. Finally, the theory generalizes to relativity. A particular formulation of general relativity itself conforms to a natural extension of the framework. This suggests a novel interpretation of general relativity, as well as new ways in which general relativity might be generalized in the search for new theories.

While Machians offer a *dynamical* reduction of inertial structure, the alternative anti-substantivalist strategy allows that inertial structure may feature in a theory's formulation but seeks an interpretation of the familiar equations that offers a *metaphysical* reduction. One suggestion is that relationalists are simply entitled to claim that, as a matter of physical necessity, the evolution of the relative distances between bodies is constrained so that they obey Newton's laws with respect to some sets of coordinate systems on space and time. Relationalists are not thereby committed to the independent reality of the spacetime structure encoded in these coordinate systems. This gives rise to questions of explanatory priority. The view involves the claim that it is the lawlike behavior of bodies that grounds spacetime's having the inertial structure that it has. It is not the independent existence of this structure, together with the way the laws of nature constrain bodies to conform to it, that explains the behavior of bodies.

Huggett (2006) has pursued a related approach within the Mill–Ramsey–Lewis framework for laws of nature. He suggests that, in a Newtonian context, the relation-alist can take the total history of the relative distances between all the particles in the universe, together with facts about their masses and other intrinsic properties, to exhaust the fundamental facts about the world. If the pattern of relative distances is such that, relative to some spacetime coordinate systems, the particles obey Newton's laws together with simple force laws, then such equations will clearly constitute the description of the universe that best combines simplicity and strength. In this way, Huggett claims, a relationalist ontology can underwrite Newton's privileged inertial frames. It is not clear whether the strategy successfully extends to relativity.

Special relativity

In the nineteenth century, electric and magnetic phenomena were unified by Maxwell's equations for the electric and magnetic fields. Light was recognized to be a type of electromagnetic radiation: a propagating wavelike disturbance in electric and magnetic field values. Such electromagnetic waves were thought to be disturbances of a substantival entity, the ether. Just as the speed of sound in air is independent of the speed of its source, so this picture accounted for the fact that the speed of light is independent of the speed of its source and (in the ether's rest frame) isotropic.

At one level, this picture is no more in conflict with the physical equivalence of inertial frames than the fact that some particular body of air is at rest in some particular inertial frame. But the picture does privilege the rest frame of the all-pervading ether. It also suggests that we should be able to determine our velocity with respect to this privileged frame by observing an anisotropy in the velocity of light. Famously, experiments performed by Michelson and Morley failed to detect any anisotropy. But of equal importance for Einstein was that the conceptual difference between rest and uniform motion relative to the ether appeared to have as little empirical reality as Newton's distinction between rest and uniform motion with respect to absolute space. Maxwell's equations predict that a relative motion between a conductor and a magnetic will induce an electric current in the conductor. From the pre-relativistic perspective, the explanation of this effect is very different depending on whether the magnet or the conductor is at rest in the ether. But since the effect is the same in either case, this looks like a difference without a difference. Einstein's genius was to see how to restore the strict equivalence of inertial frames consistently with the isotropy and the source-independence of the speed of light.

In 1905 Einstein derived the *Lorentz transformations*; coordinate transformations between inertial frames that are consistent with both the relativity principle and the constancy of the speed of light. A key step was his recognition that two frames in uniform relative motion can disagree about which sets of events are simultaneous. Suppose that in the inertial frame of reference in which I am at rest I measure the two-way speed of light to be isotropic. This suggests that light signals are a sensible way for me to synchronize distant clocks. I fire a light pulse at a distant mirror and record when I receive its reflection. If I regard the reflection event as occurring at a time half way between the original emission event and the reception event, I will also judge the one-way speed of light to be isotropic. But now suppose you are moving uniformly with respect to me. If the relativity principle is true, our rest frames are strictly physically equivalent, and such a synchronization method must be equally legitimate for you. As is shown in Figure 43.3, by their both encoding this method of synchrony, the two frames will disagree about which sets of event are simultaneous.

The Lorentz transformations predict that moving rods contract and that moving clocks run slow. For consider: I measure the speed of light to be $c = 3 \times 10^8$ ms^{-1}, but so does someone moving relative to me at $c/2$. If I am to predict that they also measure the velocity of light to be c, I must judge that their measuring rods and clocks are contracted and dilated relative to mine. (The situation is entirely symmetrical: consistently with the relativity principle, they judge my rods and clocks to be contracted and dilated by the same amount. Our disagreement about which events are simultaneous is an essential element in what makes this symmetry possible.) In this way the spatial and temporal intervals between any two events becomes a frame-relative matter. But the *spacetime interval*, $\Delta s^2 = \Delta t^2 - \Delta x^2$ (in units where the speed of light is 1), is a frame-invariant quantity.

As Minkowski showed, this fact finds natural expression in terms of the attribution to spacetime of an elegant geometric structure. Spacetime is thought of as a (pseudo-)

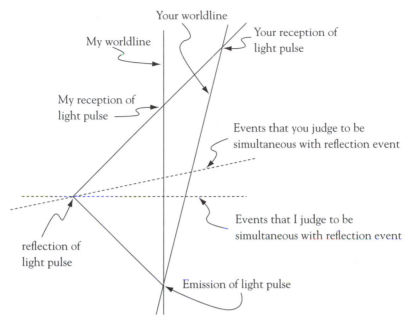

Figure 43.3 The relativity of simultaneity

metric space: there is an objective fact about the spacetime *distance* between any two spacetime points. With respect to any point p of spacetime, points in the rest of spacetime fall into three classes: (i) points that are *spacelike* related to p (points for which $\Delta s^2 < 0$; they cannot be connected to p by any signal); (ii) points that are *timelike* related to p (points for which $\Delta s^2 > 0$; they are points that can be connected to p by signals traveling at less than the speed of light); and (iii) points that are *lightlike* related to p (points for which $\Delta s^2 = 0$ and which are connectable to p by signals traveling at the speed of light). The lightcone at p (the set of points *lightlike* related to p) separates points spacelike related to p from the two sets of points timelike related to p in its past and future (see Figure 43.4). Even the privileged inertial trajectories receive an interpretation in terms of the spatiotemporal metrical structure: they are paths of greatest temporal length between any two timelike related points. The inertial connection thus no longer needs to be postulated as an independent element.

The geometric structure of Minkowski spacetime features in the formulation of any specially relativistic theory. This is transparent in generally covariant, coordinate-free formulations of the equations, where the Minkowski metric structure is explicit. But it is equally true of the "standard" formulations of the equations, which hold true only relative to privileged inertial coordinate systems related by Lorentz transformations. These coordinate systems are the spacetime analogues of Cartesian coordinates on Euclidean space: the coordinate intervals encode the spacetime distances. Minkowski geometry is thus implicit in the standard formulation of the laws. Recall the spacetime substantivalist interpretation of Newtonian mechanics: spacetime itself is regarded as a genuine entity literally possessing the geometric structure in terms of which

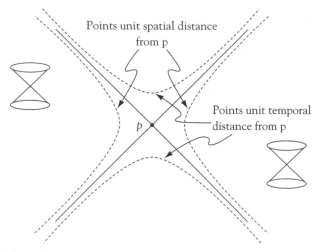

Figure 43.4 Minkowski spacetime

Newtonian mechanics is formulated. The elegant, unified nature of the geometric structure of Minkowski spacetime is even more suggestive of this view.

Substantivalists typically hold that certain phenomena can be explained by appeal to the geometry of spacetime. Such substantivalist explanations do not involve simplistic appeals to geometry. Consider the "twin-paradox" scenario. Of two initially synchronized clocks, one remains on earth while the other performs a round trip at near the speed of light. On its return the traveling clock has ticked away less time than the stay-at-home clock. The geometrical facts behind this phenomenon are straightforward: the inertial trajectory of the stay-at-home clock is simply a longer timelike path than the trajectory of the traveling clock. The substantivalist, however, does not offer as a brute assertion the claim that a clock's ticks must match the spacetime distance along its trajectory. Clocks are complicated systems the parts of which obey various (relativistic) laws. One should look to these laws for a proper understanding of why the ticks of such a system will indeed correspond to equal temporal intervals of the system's trajectory. But since, for the substantivalist, those laws make (implicit or explicit) reference to an independently real geometric structure, an explanation that appeals to the details of the laws will, in part, be an explanation in terms of the postulated geometric structure.

As in the case of Newtonian mechanics, there is an alternative, relationalist point of view. Rather than interpreting the equations as expressing the lawlike ways in which the material content of spacetime is constrained to be adapted to independently real spacetime structure, one might view the lawlike constraints on the behavior of material systems, and in particular the Lorentz symmetries inherent in those laws, as underwriting the geometric structure of spacetime. The latter point of view has been pursued by Brown and Pooley (see, in particular, Brown 2005). To reduce things to slogans, the issue is whether rods and clocks do what they do because spacetime has the geometrical structure that it has (and the laws constrain them to be adapted to this structure in ways that can be made perfectly explicit and perspicuous), or whether spacetime has the geometric structure that it has because rods and clocks (are constrained by Lorentz-invariant laws to) do what they do.

A full defense of the second view arguably requires further articulation of the relevant notion of laws and, in particular, how the symmetries of such laws should be understood independently of spacetime's geometric structure. But there is one reason why one might be tempted to pursue this anti-substantivalist program. The geometrical structures of the spacetimes of classical mechanics and special relativity place constraints on the evolution of the material content of spacetime. In at least this sense, spacetime *acts* on matter. But matter has no effect on spacetime's geometric structure. This violation of the *action–reaction principle* lies behind the anti-realist attitude that some hold towards the spacetime structures of these theories. As we shall see, this asymmetry is abolished in general relativity.

Special relativity and the philosophy of time

Three debates dominate the philosophy of time. First there is the debate between eternalists and their opponents. Just as distant places are standardly taken to be no less real than our immediate spatial locality, *eternalists* regard past and future times as no less real than the present moment. They are opposed by *presentists*, who think that only the ever-changing present moment exists, and by those who endorse a "growing block" model of the universe in which the past and present, but not the future, exist.

The second debate is between *tensers* and *detensers*. Tensers believe that tensed language is ineliminable in any metaphysically adequate account of reality. They believe in observer-independent tensed facts. Detensers, in contrast, view tense as an indexical device, and believe that tensed language can be given tenseless truth-conditions, just as truth-conditions for sentences involving "here" and "there" can be stated in language that presupposes no particular spatial location.

The third debate concerns how ordinary objects persist through time. *Perdurantists* hold that an object's existence at more than one moment is analogous to a spatially extended object's (partial) existence in more than one place. Objects extend through space in virtue of being composed of distinct parts wholly and exactly located at distinct spatial locations. Perdurantists claim that objects persist in virtue of having numerically distinct *temporal parts* exactly located at the different times at which they exist. Perdurantists are opposed by *endurantists*, who deny that persisting objects are made up of momentary temporal parts.

The first two debates are closely related to another question: is there real *becoming* and temporal passage. Critics of the combination of eternalism and detenserism charge that it depicts a static world devoid of real change. Defenders respond that change is simply a matter of objects exemplifying different properties at different times. The felt

461

passage of time involves nothing more than experiencing subjects enjoying a sequence of different perspectives on reality at the different times at which they exist. The idea of an objective flow of time over and above these appearances is, eternalist detensers claim, incoherent.

Eternalism, detenserism, and perdurantism all involve the claim that time is, in particular ways, like space. The views therefore find a natural home in relativistic spacetime, in which a distinction between spacelike and timelike relations is drawn but space and time themselves do not feature. But while perdurance is natural from the point of view of relativity, persistence by endurance is not obviously incompatible with Minkowski spacetime. In contrast, relativity favors an eternalist detenser view much more strongly.

The trouble with the alternatives is that their formulation requires something like a *present moment*, either to be the literal extent of reality or to be the boundary between what has objectively become and what is yet to occur. Properly relativistic spacetime simply admits no such thing. Pre-relativistic spacetimes also do not include a privileged moment. But they do offer a privileged family of simultaneity surfaces, each of which can be understood as representing the present moment as time passes (in whatever sense is required).

The tenser can choose to regard the relativistic picture of the world as incomplete. While this view is logically compatible with relativity, it prompts an immediate question: are the extra-relativistic facts observable? For anyone who believes that in principle no experiential phenomena fall outside the domain of (relativistic) physics, including phenomena associated with our idea that time passes, the tenser's postulated additional metaphysical facts lack motivation. They are unobservable to the extent that even the nature of our temporal experience fails to constitute evidence for them.

The best-known explicit argument to the effect that relativity rules out a tensed view of time was given by Putnam (1967). He was roundly criticized by Stein (see, especially, Stein 1991), but ultimately it is not clear that the two should be seen as disagreeing (Saunders 2002). Stein criticizes Putnam for using concepts that are inappropriate in relativity. But Putnam's argument is easily reformulated without those concepts (just as the definitions of eternalism and detenserism above can be made relativistically acceptable by replacing reference to "times" with reference to appropriate spacetime notions). On the other side, Stein's definition of "that which has become as of some spacetime point" (in terms of the past lightcone of the point) seems entirely congenial to the eternalist, who is surely obliged to give an account of temporal passage, at least as experienced. Stein's point-relative definition makes sense in such a context, but it cannot ground a more robust ontological distinction without relativizing what is real to spacetime points.

General relativity

Special relativity restored the full equivalence of inertial frames. Einstein next sought both a relativistic theory of gravity and a theory that generalized the relativity principle to frames of reference in arbitrary relative motion. A key step on the way to general relativity was the *equivalence principle*. In Newtonian theory the gravitational force on a body depends linearly on its mass. As a result the rate at which bodies accelerate in a gravitational field is independent of their mass and constitution. Bodies subject to a homogeneous gravitational field will describe the same trajectories with respect to an inertial frame as those described by force-free bodies with respect to an appropriately accelerated frame. Einstein generalized this, postulating a full equivalence between physics in the presence of a uniform gravitational field and in a uniformly accelerated frame.

Another key idea was that the theory should be *generally covariant*: its equations should hold true in coordinate systems related by smooth but otherwise arbitrary transformations. The group of these transformations contains as a proper sub-group transformations between frames of reference in arbitrary states of motion. Hence any generally covariant theory would seem to embody a generalized relativity principle. Einstein's equations of 1915 are indeed generally covariant, but the modern understanding of the principles that led Einstein to their discovery could not be further from Einstein's original view.

As Kretschmann noted in 1917, general covariance appears to be a constraint only on a theory's formulation and not its empirical content. Newtonian and specially relativistic theories were subsequently formulated generally covariantly. General covariance thus cannot implement a generalized relativity principle for these theories involve only restricted relativity principles involving the equivalence of frames adapted to the theories' spacetime structures. It is the existence of non-trivial symmetries of these structures that leads to a plurality of equivalent frames. *Arbitrary* frames of reference in such theories are not physically equivalent.

The points of comparison between a specially relativistic theory and its generally relativistic analogue are instructive. Both theories involve a (pseudo-)metrical spacetime structure of the kind discussed under "Special relativity." The generally covariant equations that determine locally how material fields in spacetime must be adapted to this structure are also identical. The *sole* difference is that the spacetime structure of the specially relativistic theory is stipulated to be *flat*, while that of the generally relativistic theory is curved. Einstein's field equations relate the curvature of spacetime to the stress–energy properties of its material content, and thus matter finally *acts back* on spacetime.

Spacetime's variable curvature means that, in general, extended privileged coordinate systems adapted to spacetime's geometrical structure do not exist. However, for each point in spacetime, there are privileged *local* coordinate systems centered around the point. In such coordinate systems the equations governing matter reduce to their "standard" special relativistic form at that point. This requirement is what is nowadays known as the *equivalence principle*.

The equivalence of an accelerated frame and an inertial frame containing a uniform gravitational field is secured by denying the existence of the latter. What were previously thought to be such things (for example, to a good approximation, short-lived, spatially restricted frames comoving with the surface of the earth) turn out to be non-inertial, accelerated frames. The true inertial frames are the (infinitesimal) "freely falling" frames. In general relativity there is no force of gravity. Phenomena previously attributed to the action of a force are either to be recognized as artifacts of describing things with respect to accelerated frames or as manifestations of spacetime curvature.

In the picture just sketched, substantivalism is vindicated. Previously immutable spacetime structures are now dynamical players, on all fours with the contents of spacetime. There would seem to be little hope of a relationalist eliminative reduction of spacetime structure along the lines of Brown's dynamical approach to special relativity. Brown himself is a realist about the metric field, but does not regard himself as a substantivalist. He views the metric field as just another dynamical field that only merits a geometric interpretation in virtue of the special way it interacts with other fields. At this point it is not clear how much of substance remains in dispute. All sides think the metric field represents something genuinely physical. The substantivalist stresses the continuities between its role in general relativity and the role of the analogous structures in pre-relativistic theories (structures universally regarded as representing properties of spacetime). Brown stresses that the field connects to the physical geometry exemplified by material systems only through the unique way in which it couples to other fields. But this is also true of the analogous fields in pre-relativistic theories.

There remains the Machian route. In the standard formulation of general relativity, the field encoding the *four*-dimensional geometry of spacetime is taken as one of the basic variables. But the equations can be recast so as to describe the evolution of the geometric structure of *three*-dimensional space. This decomposition is well known and is central to one of the main approaches to quantum gravity. What Barbour's Machian perspective stresses is that this decomposition can be understood in genuinely three-dimensional terms. According to the Machian, four-dimensional spacetime structure, in particular distances along timelike curves and the privileged inertial trajectories, emerges from the relational dynamics of three-dimensional space.

In one sense the picture is substantivalist: the theory's basic entity is (instantaneous) space itself. But in another sense relationalists are vindicated because the transtemporal structure that led Newton to postulate absolute space is seen as redundant. The interesting interpretative question is no longer whether spacetime structure is reducible to properties of the material contents of spacetime, but whether three-dimensional or four-dimensional structure is fundamental.

The hole argument

Some reject the substantivalist interpretation of general relativity because of the *hole argument*. The argument, originally due to Einstein and revived in the 1980s by Stachel, was cast as an explicitly anti-substantivalist argument by Earman and Norton (1987). It revives one of Leibniz's objections to Newton's absolute space, which I rehearse briefly.

According to Leibniz, defenders of absolute space are committed to the following violation of the *principle of the identity of indiscernibles*. Absolute space is homogeneous and isotropic: no point of space differs qualitatively from any other in its purely spatial characteristics. But since the parts of space are supposed to be real individuals, we have to recognize as a possible world distinct from the actual world a universe in which the entire material content of the universe occupies (at each moment) a location 5 feet to the North, say, of the position it actually occupies (at that moment). Such a universe is in every way identical to the actual world except for facts about where things are in space.

Unobservable global location differences might look suspicious, but many modern substantivalists were happy to bite the bullet. The twist provided by the hole argument is that, for generally covariant theories, such differences lead to a generic and radical breakdown in determinism.

Let (M, g_i, φ_i) be a model of a possible spacetime. M is a four-dimensional manifold of points intended to represent the points of spacetime. Defined on it are various fields: the g_i represent the geometric structure of spacetime and the φ_i represent its material content. A non-trivial diffeomorphism of the manifold, $d: M \rightarrow M$, is a differentiable bijective mapping of the manifold onto itself. It can be used to define a new model, $(M, d^*g_i, d^*\varphi_i)$, involving new fields that are defined in terms of the old by the map induced by the diffeomorphism. The two models are isomorphic: they differ solely over *where* on the manifold structurally identical sets of fields are placed. If (M, g_i, φ_i) is a model of a generally convariant theory, T, $(M, d^*g_i, d^*\varphi_i)$ is also a model of T, no matter what diffeomorphism is used to generate it. In particular, d might be a *hole diffeomorphism*: a map that is non-trivial only in a restricted region (the so-called "hole"), for example, all of M to the future of some three-dimensional spacelike "slice."

Various manifold points common to (M, g_i, φ_i) and $(M, d^*g_i, d^*\varphi_i)$ are mapped to different field values in each model. This suggests that certain spacetime points are represented as having different properties by each model and therefore that the substantivalist should interpret the two models as representing distinct possible worlds. But when d is a hole diffeomorphism, (M, g_i, φ_i) and $(M, d^*g_i, d^*\varphi_i)$ represent spacetimes that are identical up to some time but that then differ – a clear violation of determinism.

The models (M, g_i, φ_i) and $(M, d^*g_i, d^*\varphi_i)$ differ only over *which* points of M are assigned the various properties common to both models. One way to deny that T is indeterministic is thus to deny the existence of spacetime points. It is less clear whether those who believe that the points of M represent real, concrete spacetime points must accept that (M, g_i, φ_i) and $(M, d^*g_i, d^*\varphi_i)$ represent distinct yet genuinely possible worlds. In the wake of Earman and Norton's hole argument, most philosophers concluded they do not.

One route to this conclusion returns to Leibniz. Leibniz mounted an exactly parallel argument against the existence of atoms. Suppose that the actual world contains two intrinsically identical atoms, a and b. Leibniz argued that anyone committed to the existence of such things must admit as a genuinely distinct possible world a universe that differs from the actual world solely in the switching of a and b. The two worlds differ solely over which objects (a and b) have the various sets of relational characteristics common to both worlds. But many philosophers are skeptical of such *haecceitistic* distinctions, and believe that they can be given up without giving up the fundamental reality of the individuals involved, whether material atoms or spacetime points.

Earman himself believes that this response leaves philosophical discussion of general covariance irrelevant to the concerns of physicists grappling with the project of unifying quantum mechanics and gravity. Some workers in this field do draw from the hole argument the conclusion that general relativity breaks decisively from previous theories precisely in embodying a relational conception of space and time. But it is unclear that terms such as "relational" are being used to map out exactly the same notions by physicists and philosophers. In seeking to identify the conceptually novel elements in general relativity, physicists have recently focused on its *background independence*. As mentioned, in classical and specially relativistic theories, spacetime structure constrains the evolution of the material content of spacetime but is not acted back upon by matter. It is thus a background against which the dynamics is defined; it is not itself a dynamical player. In general relativity this asymmetry is abolished. But this notion of background independence would seem to have little to do with the hole argument.

See also Explanation; Logical empiricism; Physics; Realism/anti-realism; Symmetry; Underdetermination.

References

Barbour, J. B. (1994) "The Timelessness of Quantum Gravity: I. The Evidence from the Classical Theory," *Classical and Quantum Gravity* 11: 2853–73.

Brown, H. R. (2005) *Physical Relativity: Space–Time Structure from a Dynamical Perspective*, Oxford: Oxford University Press.

Descartes, R. (1985 [1644]) "Principia Philosophiae," *The Philosophical Writings of Descartes*, Volume 1, trans. and ed. J. Cottingham, R. Stoothoff, and D. Murdoch, Cambridge: Cambridge University Press.

Earman, J. and Norton, J. (1987) "What Price Spacetime Substantivalism? The Hole Story," *British Journal for the Philosophy of Science* 38: 515–25.

Huggett, N. (2006) "The Regularity Account of Relational Spacetime," *Mind* 115: 41–73.

Leibniz, G. W. (1956 [1716]) "Mr. Leibnitz's Third Paper," in H. G. Alexander (ed.) *The Leibniz–Clarke Correspondence*, Manchester: Manchester University Press.

Newton, I. (1962) "De Gravitatione et Aequipondio Fluidorum," in A. R. Hall and M. B. Hall (eds) *Unpublished Scientific Papers of Isaac Newton*, Cambridge: Cambridge University Press.

—— (1999 [1687]) *The Principia: Mathematical Principles of Natural Philosophy*, Berkeley: University of California Press.

Putnam, H. (1967) "Time and Physical Geometry," *Journal of Philosophy* 64: 240–7.

Reichenbach, H. (1959) "The Theory of Motion According to Newton, Leibniz and Huyghens," in M. Reichenbach (ed.) *Modern Philosophy of Science: Selected Essays*, London: Routledge & Kegan Paul.

Rynasiewicz, R. A. (1995) "'By Their Properties, Causes, and Effects': Newton's Scholium on Time, Space, Place, and Motion – I The Text," *Studies in History and Philosophy of Science* 26: 133–53.

Saunders, S. W. (2002) "How Relativity Contradicts Presentism," in C. Callender (ed.) *Time, Reality and Experience*, Cambridge: Cambridge University Press.

Stein, H. (1967) "Newtonian Space–Time," *Texas Quarterly* 10: 174–200. Reprinted in Robert Palter (ed.) *The Annus Mirabilis of Sir Isaac Newton 1666–1966*, Cambridge, MA: MIT Press, 1970.

—— (1991) "On Relativity Theory and Openness of the Future," *Philosophy of Science* 58: 147–67.

Further reading

Both Larry Sklar's *Space, Time, and Spacetime* (Berkeley: University of California Press, 1974) and Barry Dainton's *Time and Space* (Montreal and Kingston: McGill–Queen's University Press: 2001) are accessible and wide-ranging, covering conventionalism, the direction of time, and the substantivalist–relationalist debate. Roberto Torretti's *Relativity and Geometry* (Oxford: Pergamon Press, 1983; New York: Dover, 1996) is a masterful, historically sensitive philosophical study of Einstein's theories of relativity. John Earman's *World Enough and Space–Time: Absolute versus Relational Theories of Space and Time* (Cambridge, MA: MIT Press, 1989) is an incisive study of the substantivalist–relationalist dispute from its historical origins up to the immediate responses to his and Norton's Hole Argument. Norton's "The Hole Argument," in Edward N. Zalta (ed.) *Stanford Encyclopedia of Philosophy* (http://plato.stanford.edu/entries/spacetime-holearg) gives references to more recent discussion. For a non-technical debate about the relevance of some of these issues to conceptual problems in quantum gravity, see Earman's "Thoroughly Modern McTaggart: Or, What McTaggart Would Have Said If He Had Read the General Theory of Relativity," *Philosophers' Imprint* 2 (2002) (http://www.philosophersimprint.org/002003); and Tim Maudlin's reply in the same issue. Robert DiSalle's *Understanding Spacetime* (Cambridge: Cambridge University Press, 2006) focuses on issues orthogonal to the substantivalist–relationalist debate, emphasizing how conceptual analysis of the concepts of space and time implicit in scientific practice has been crucial to theoretical progress. Chapters 3 and 4 contain a sympathetic but critical discussion of conventionalism. For a version of the logical positivists' conventionalism, see Hans Reichenbach's *The Philosophy of Space and Time*, trans. Maria Reichenbach (New York: Dover, 1957). Independently of general theses concerning conventionalism, there is the question whether *simultaneity* is conventional in relativity. Central to this debate is a uniqueness result proved by David Malament in "Causal Theories of Time and the Conventionality of Simultaneity," *Noûs* 11 (1977): 293–300. Robert Rynasiewicz's "Is Simultaneity Conventional Despite Malament's Result?" *Philosophy of Science* 68 (2001) (Supplement): S345–S357, provides a way into this literature. Huw Price's *Time's Arrow and Archimedes' Point* (Oxford: Oxford University Press, 1996) and David Albert's *Time and Chance* (Cambridge, MA: Harvard University Press, 2000) are two recent books devoted to the problem of the direction of time. A central topic is the so-called "past hypothesis": that the state of the early universe was a state of very low entropy, and in particular whether these initial conditions stand in need of explanation. In "Measures, Explanation and the Past: Should 'Special' Initial Conditions Be Explained?" *British Journal for the Philosophy of Science* 55 (2004): 195–217, Craig Callender argues that it does not. In "The 'Past Hypothesis': Not Even False," *Studies in History and Philosophy of Modern Physics* 37 (2006): 399–430 (an issue of the journal devoted to the arrow of time), Earman argues that the hypothesis cannot do the work its defenders claim. In "Bluff Your Way in the Second Law of Thermodynamics," *Studies in History and Philosophy of Modern Physics* 32 (2001): 305–94, Jos Uffink examines the status of time asymmetry in thermodynamics itself. Those interested in the compatibility of relativity and an objective passage of time should start with Howard Stein (1991). The Supplement to *Philosophy of Science* 67 (2000) contains symposium papers on the topic by Savitt, Hinchliff, Callender, and Saunders. A number of recent papers are also found in Dennis Dieks (ed.) *The Ontology of Spacetime* (Amsterdam: Elsevier, 2006). The nature of persistence in relativity has attracted attention only recently. For an overview and references, see Ian Gibson and Oliver Pooley, "Relativistic Persistence," *Philosophical Perspectives* 20 (2006): 157–98.

44
SYMMETRY
Margaret Morrison

The basics

When we talk at an intuitive level about "symmetries of nature" we usually have in mind objects that have perfectly symmetrical shapes; for example, the geometric symmetry of crystals or the spherical shapes and motions of the planets. Those symmetries supposedly reflect the inner simplicity and harmony of the universe. The history of the concept of symmetry starts with the ancient Greeks and has developed in various ways to include the notions of beauty, harmony, and unity. One of the best examples of the power of symmetry arguments in the history of science comes from Kepler's *Mysterium Cosmographicum* (1596). Because he believed that God created the solar system according to a mathematical pattern, Kepler attempted to correlate the distances of the planets from the sun with the radii of spherical shells that were inscribed within and circumscribed around a nest of solids. The goal was to find an agreement between the observed ratios of the radii of the planets and the ratios calculated from the geometry of the nested solids. Although the latter ratios disagreed with empirical data he went on to search for deeper mathematical harmonies in the solar system and succeeded in formulating his three laws of planetary motion; a corrected version of which later formed the foundation of Newtonian mechanics. But this is not just a historical peculiarity: belief in the mathematical harmony of the universe still holds a prominent place in various branches of physics. However, as Herman Weyl (1952) remarked "we no longer seek this harmony in static forms like regular solids, but in dynamic laws." The statement expressed a shifting away from thinking about symmetry in terms of objects or phenomena to focus instead on the symmetry of *laws*. So, what exactly is the connection between symmetries and laws?

Symmetry in physics involves the notion of *invariance*. If something remains unchanged (invariant) under a particular operation or transformation, we say that it is symmetric under that operation. For example, a cylinder is invariant under rotations about its axis, and a sphere, which has a greater degree of symmetry, is invariant under rotations about any axis through its centre. The two examples also exhibit a reflection symmetry, meaning that they look the same in a mirror. When we speak about laws, however, what is important is that they behave in the same way with respect to a variety of possible reference frames. Einstein's principle of relativity is an example of this. It states that the laws of physics (and the behavior of light) must be the same for any two observers moving with a constant velocity relative to one another. This equivalence of different points of view was extended in his theory of general relativity to incorporate all possible observers including those that are rotating and accelerating. What this means, in physical terms, is that the inertial effects of acceleration or rotation (e.g., the forces an astronaut feels during blast off) can be attributed to either your own motion or the presence of different gravitational forces. This conclusion, expressed more formally in Einstein's principle of equivalence, states that the laws of gravity are such that the apparent forces due to any kind of motion are indistinguishable from gravitational forces. In that sense we can see how symmetries are related to the *dynamical* properties of physical systems; in other words the symmetries describe how systems or phenomena react to forces.

The connection between symmetries and dynamics helps to reveal the connection between symmetries of laws and symmetries of objects. If we think of our example of the sphere, the rotation under which it remained invariant can be described by the mathematical equation that governs the sphere. Because the equation does not depend in any way on the angles of rotation, we say that both the equation and the sphere are invariant under rotation. In order to fully investigate the physical consequences of symmetry it is necessary to learn about the specific transformations or sets of transformations that leave a particular object or function invariant. The theory that deals with this is called "group theory" where a group is defined as a mathematical structure or set of elements that can be transformed into each other by means of certain operations. The set of all transformations that leaves an object or law invariant forms the *symmetry group* of that object. We can then make the connection between laws and objects more specific by saying that a physical object/phenomenon obeys a certain symmetry if its laws are invariant under any transformation of the corresponding symmetry group. For example, space is symmetric under translations – no point in space is privileged over any other – and, consequently, that invariance under spatial translation means that the laws of physics are the same in London as in Toronto. Similarly, if physical laws are independent of time (time-invariance) then experimental results will be the same regardless of when the experiment is performed.

A further way in which laws and symmetries are connected involves the link between invariance under a symmetry operation and the existence of conservation laws in physics, laws stating that the total amount of some quantity is constant and does not change with time. A well-known example is the conservation of energy, which says that energy cannot be created or destroyed but only transformed from one form to another. A theorem first proved by Emmy Noether in 1918 states that for every symmetry of the laws of physics there is a corresponding conservation law. (The reverse is also true although that wasn't part of her original theorem.) What this means is that for any invariance in a particular symmetry group there is a corresponding physical quantity that is conserved under the applicable transformation. For example, the conservation of energy and momentum is associated with the impossibility of measuring an absolute position in time and space, respectively, which is in turn associated with the homogeneity of time and space; in other words, every moment in time and every point in space is as good as any other. Put slightly differently, because of time-invariance the laws of physics predict the same evolution of identical processes regardless of when they occur, which in turn implies that the conservation of energy is built into the laws describing the process. Invariance under spatial rotations implies conservation of angular momentum, which is the product of the mass, velocity, and position of a particle.

The link between symmetry and conserved quantities points to a slightly more precise definition of Noether's theorem: for every symmetry of the equations of motion of a system there is a quantity that is conserved by its dynamics. However, when we say that equations or *laws* of a theory are unchanged under specific transformations, we say that they are "covariant." The technically precise use of the term "invariance" involves reference to specific *objects* or things that remain unchanged under certain transformations. And, in the case of conservation laws, the thing that remains invariant is the conserved quantity. The notion of symmetrical laws or equations becomes important in the discussion of hidden and local symmetries; so now let us turn our attention to some of the different kinds of symmetries in order to give us a better understanding of the way symmetry functions in modern physics.

The symmetries important for physics can be divided into the following categories: *global* and *local*, *continuous* and *discrete*, as well as *geometrical* and *internal*. Global symmetries deal with transformations that are not affected by position in space and time. They can be either geometrical, reflecting the homogeneity of space and time or internal which refers to the intrinsic nature of particles (like the conservation of various charges) rather than their position or motion. The symmetries mentioned above (translation through space, translation through time, as well as rotation about an axis) are all geometrical symmetries. But, we can also have global internal symmetries which involve the transformation of several field components into one another in such a way that the physical situation remains unchanged; that is, each component is rotated to the same degree, with the total field energy remaining constant. In the case of local internal symmetries the rotation of field components varies from point to point so that a rotation at one position does not necessarily correspond to a rotation at another. An example of a continuous symmetry is the rotation of a circle; it is a continuous operation describable by groups that possess an infinite number of elements.

In contrast to continuous symmetries there are also discrete symmetries, instances of which include the rotations of a square or a triangle. Spatial reflections (things looking the same in a mirror) are also discrete symmetries where the associated transformation group contains only two elements, reflection of spatial coordinates and identity. Discrete internal symmetries involve invariance under charge conjugation where there is an exchange of particles with their anti-particles. Continuous internal symmetries govern specific properties of particles and the continuous transformation of quantized fields. This is an extension of the ordinary geometrical symmetries; so, for example, the $U(1)$ group governs the continuous rotations of a circle and also describes the symmetry of a single field.

Symmetry and scientific theories

Since the 1960s the relation between symmetry and the laws of physics has become a fundamental feature of theory construction. All interactions are now thought to be caused by a special kind of field, called a "gauge field," whose structure and behavior are dictated by the requirement of local symmetry. And, for every gauge field there is a corresponding symmetry group of that field. The origins of gauge invariance go back to Hermann Weyl's work in 1918. Weyl aimed to draw attention to the requirement that the laws of physics should remain the same if the scale of all length measurements were to be changed by a constant factor. His hypothesis, that this was a local symmetry of general relativity and electromagnetism, proved unsuccessful; however, the idea was resurrected in 1927 by Fritz London who showed the proper symmetry for electric charge was *phase* rather than *scale* invariance. What this means is that the electromagnetic field allowed for an arbitrary variation in the phase factor from point to point in space–time. Even though this has nothing to do with the notion of a *gauge*, the term was retained because Weyl was also associated with the new formulation.

In general a theory that is globally invariant will not be invariant under locally varying transformations. But, by introducing new force fields (gauge fields) that transform in certain ways and interact with the particles postulated by the theory (e.g., the photon in electromagnetism), local invariance can be restored. In the case of local symmetries the forces that arise are due to the gauge fields interacting with conserved quantities. Recall that the laws of physics show a local symmetry if their equivalence from different frames of reference remains even when we choose a different point of view at every single point in space and at every possible time. An application of Noether's theorem in this context shows that the conserved quantity that corresponds to the symmetry is just that thing which interacts with the gauge field. For example, it is possible to show (with a rather complicated derivation) that from the conservation of electric charge one can, on the basis of Noether's theorem, assume the existence of a symmetry, and the requirement that it be local forces us to introduce a gauge field, which is just the electromagnetic field. In other words, the electromagnetic field is necessary for the preservation of local symmetry. The structure of the field is dictated by symmetry constraints which, in turn, determine, almost uniquely, the form that the electromagnetic interaction will have. The particles that carry the forces are known as "gauge bosons," with the photon being the gauge boson for electromagnetic interaction. We can see, then, that there is an intimate relationship between continuous symmetries, conservation laws, and the fundamental forces of nature.

The unification of electromagnetism with the weak force (which governs the decay of long-lived elementary particles like beta decay and kaon decay) to produce the *electroweak theory* also involves a symmetry that governs changes in our point of view regarding the identity of different kinds of elementary particles rather than points in space and time. Just as in quantum mechanics, where it is possible for a particle to have no definite position or momentum until it is measured, it is also possible for a particle to be in a state that is neither an electron nor a neutrino until some property, like electric charge, is measured that would distinguish the two. What this implies is that in the electroweak theory the form of the laws of nature is unchanged if, in the equations, we replace electrons and neutrinos with mixed states that are neither electrons nor neutrinos.

The symmetry that connects the electromagnetic force with the weak force is an example of a local internal symmetry. It is *internal* because it governs the intrinsic nature of particles and it is *local* because the rotation of a particle at one point in space or at one moment in time has no effect on what happens at other times or positions. In other words, the symmetry operation involves an independent rotation at each point, with the laws of nature not affected by those position-dependent and time-dependent transformations. As we saw above, this symmetry is possible only if there are gauge fields, and so just as the existence of local symmetries makes the gravitational field necessary, the local symmetry between electrons and neutrinos makes the weak W and Z fields necessary. Another local symmetry associated with quarks is known as "color" and is used to distinguish three different kinds of quarks such that the force between each pair is the same. And, as with other local symmetries, the laws of nature take the same form if we replace any of the three different kinds of quarks with mixtures of the three, even when those mixtures vary from place to place and from time to time. This replacement also requires the introduction of a family of gauge fields that interact with the quarks, as described by the standard model.

We can see, then, how symmetry plays a central role in the way we understand the forces and elementary particles of nature. Although we can understand physical laws as expressions of these symmetries, some, including Nobel Laureate Steven Weinberg (1993), would go even further, claiming that in the fusion of relativity with quantum mechanics matter has lost its central role, a role that has been "usurped by principles of symmetry." With this radical shift in our understanding come a number of interpretive problems concerning not only the ontological status of symmetries as fundamental features of the physical world, but also what exactly symmetry arguments provide in the way of justification for physical theories and hypotheses. In other words, what is the connection between symmetries, understood mathematically in terms of group theory, and the physical dynamics that are *derived* from symmetry principles. The issues are further complicated by the fact that our understanding of many different types of physical systems are based on the notion of *broken symmetry*. So, in order to address those interpretive issues, we first need to look at how broken symmetry functions as a dynamical principle.

Spontaneous symmetry-breaking: between symmetry and asymmetry

"Symmetry-breaking" is a generic term describing the deviation from exact symmetry exhibited by the kinds of physical systems described above. It can occur explicitly or spontaneously, with distinct observable consequences characterizing each of the two cases. In the *explicit* case the system is *not quite* the same for two configurations related by an exact symmetry. For example, if we have a bicycle wheel with the valve stem sticking out, it is almost symmetric with respect to rotations about the bicycle axis, but the symmetry is broken by the stem. In physics, the energy equation (Hamiltonian) describing electrons inside a spherical cavity is symmetric with respect to rotations; but if a magnetic field is applied the electron spin will react with the field and the energy will be different, according to whether the spin is up or down, hence breaking the rotational symmetry. As a result, the Hamiltonian describing this situation will be *almost* symmetric. In the case of symmetry that is *spontaneously* broken (SSB) the Hamiltonian always displays an exact symmetry, but the state of lowest energy of the system itself does not share that symmetry; in other words, the solutions to the equations of motion (the physical states) will have less symmetry than the equations themselves. Because the equations remain symmetrical, this is sometimes referred to as "hidden" symmetry; so while the empirical evidence points to asymmetrical physical states, the equations indicate a deeper symmetrical reality. Once again Steven Weinberg aptly describes the situation in the following observation: "Broken symmetry is a very Platonic notion: the reality we observe in our laboratories is only an imperfect reflection of a deeper and more beautiful reality, the reality of the equations that display all the symmetries of the theory" (1993: 195).

An intuitive example of a spontaneously broken symmetry is a spinning roulette-wheel settling into a state with a ball in one slot; another is the permanent magnet. The equations governing iron atoms and the magnetic field in a magnet are perfectly symmetrical with respect to spatial direction. But, when a piece of iron is cooled below $770\,°C$, it spontaneously develops a magnetic field that points in a specific direction, effectively breaking the symmetry among the different directions. The electroweak theory mentioned above also has a broken symmetry which manifests itself in the difference between the particles that carry the electromagnetic force, the massless photon, and the heavy, massive particles that carry the weak force. The challenge has been how to explain the breakdown of symmetry while maintaining perfectly symmetrical equations. The current explanation involves the postulation of an additional particle, called the "Higgs particle," and its accompanying field; but no experimental verification of the Higgs particle has yet been found (Morrison 2000). This symmetry-breaking is important not only for the electroweak theory itself but for describing different phases of physical systems, such as the superconducting phases of conductors, liquid helium, and many other effects. In the next section I mention some of the interpretive difficulties that arise in connection with SSB; but before looking at them, let us consider some of the more general philosophical issues relating to symmetries, issues that arise mainly from questions concerning the relation of mathematics to the world.

In the discussion above, I mentioned group theory as the area of mathematics that deals with symmetry transformations. Each group is characterized by a set of mathematical rules that are independent of what is being transformed, and it is those groups of continuous transformations ("Lie groups") that govern not only rotations in space but the mixing of electrons and neutrinos. One particular Lie group, the $SU(3)$, was found to be a very powerful tool for imposing a structure on the large number of elementary particles that were discovered experimentally. This symmetry classification scheme, known as the "eightfold way," led to the successful prediction of the Ω-particle simply on the basis of gaps in the structure (Gell-Mann and Ne'eman

1964). Because mathematics provides the language in which our physical theories are expressed, it is perhaps not surprising that symmetry, understood as a mathematical notion, has proved enormously successful in theory construction.

We can view symmetry as a mathematical tool, but it is also thought to be a fundamental aspect of the physical world in virtue of the kinds of applications described above. But, how should we understand the relation between these two notions? Certainly symmetry has tremendous heuristic value, and its methodological role and predictive success in contemporary physics has been nothing short of remarkable. The physicist Eugene Wigner (1967) noted this when he spoke about the unreasonable effectiveness of mathematics in the quantum description of the world. Group theory and other mathematical concepts, like Hilbert space, complex numbers, etc., were developed in the context of mathematical investigation because they fostered beautiful – aesthetically pleasing – theorems, not because they had any applicability to physics. Hence, it is extraordinary that they have played such a successful role in describing the empirical world.

The simple answer to Wigner's puzzle is, of course, that the world itself is structured in symmetrical ways, and the convergence between physics and mathematics simply reflects the underlying order and mathematical harmony present in the empirical world. So, we can understand the heuristic, methodological role played by symmetries as evidence for an ontological claim concerning their place as fundamental features of the physical world. This is a classic case of what is known in the philosophical literature as *inference to the best explanation*. Simply put: postulating the existence of symmetries in nature is the best explanation of the success of symmetry principles and arguments in physics. And, that explanatory success is evidence for their existence. Because this method of inference has come under severe criticism in the philosophy of science literature (Cartwright 1983; van Fraassen 1989; Morrison 1990), we need a stronger justification for the existence of symmetries, specifically some form of direct empirical evidence. The question then is whether that is possible and if so what that evidence consists in.

Interpretive issues: between mathematics and physics

Earlier we saw that Noether's theorem establishes a direct connection between certain continuous symmetries of the Lagrangian and conserved quantities. One way of thinking about the connection is to say that conservation laws/conserved quantities provide the empirical manifestation of symmetries (Morrison 1995); but that does little to establish an empirical basis for symmetries themselves since the link fails to guarantee the reality of the symmetries present in the Lagrangian. The other relevant issue is the distinction between symmetries of laws and symmetries of objects. One could claim that the symmetries present in the Euler–Lagrange equations have to do with the mathematical form of the equations themselves, and, as such, need not imply anything about symmetries as physical features of the world. However, since much of the debate about symmetries concerns symmetries of laws, I leave aside the laws–object problem and assume for the sake of argument that symmetries of laws do say something about the world; so the question then is whether the symmetries present in those laws can be directly observed.

Brading and Brown (2004) answer the question by distinguishing different kinds of symmetries and considering whether the evidence for each of them is direct or indirect. They highlight two conditions required for a symmetry to have direct empirical significance: first, the transformation with respect to a reference system must yield an empirically distinguishable scenario; and, second, the internal evolution of the transformed and untransformed systems must be empirically indistinguishable. Brading and Brown claim that even when a conservation law is connected to a symmetry, the connection does not exhaust the empirical manifestation of the symmetry. For example, invariance of the dynamical laws under spatial translation is directly manifested by the insensitivity of the dynamical evolution of systems to their location. Another instance where a symmetry transformation is directly observable and physically implementable is the Galileo ship example (Galileo 1967; Budden 1997). This involves comparing the ship at rest and in uniform motion with respect to the shore; the symmetry is observed by noticing that relative to the cabin of the ship the phenomena inside do not allow us to distinguish between the two scenarios. However, as Brading and Brown point out, in order for symmetries to have direct empirical significance, it must be possible to isolate the relevant sub-systems that are to be directly transformed. That is not always a straightforward affair, but they claim it should suffice that the comparison of the two distinct scenarios is theoretically possible.

The analysis above turns on the distinction between *directly observing* the symmetry itself and concluding that a particular observed event or phenomenon is the *effect* of a symmetry. Even if we were to accept Brading and Brown's claim that we can directly observe the kinds of global continuous symmetries described above, the situation alters dramatically when we consider the case of local internal symmetries. They conclude that local symmetries, such as gauge invariance, have only indirect empirical significance because the kind of transformation required to assess two different systems is simply not possible in those cases; unlike the Galileo experiment, the symmetry transformations here have no observable consequences. This indirect empirical significance refers to the properties that the laws of physics have as a *consequence* of their connection with a particular symmetry. Despite any intuitive appeal these kinds of arguments might have, they are by no means uncontroversial. The argument for direct empirical significance relies on a notion of direct access that itself depends on conditions requiring isolation, transformations, and interactions which may be definable only theoretically. Moreover, the claim that a symmetry such as local gauge invariance has even indirect empirical significance assumes, to some extent, that symmetries are part of the physical furniture of the universe, and the question is just whether we have direct or indirect access; but it is exactly that physical status which is at issue.

Hidden symmetries give rise to similar concerns. As we have seen, these cases involve symmetrical equations of motion (Lagrangian) whose solutions are *asymmetrical*; in other words the physical system does not display the symmetry of the laws that describe it. Many physical phenomena are thought to result from the phenomenon of spontaneously broken symmetry – superconductivity, ferromagnetism, and super-fluidity as well as the electroweak theory which describes the unification of the weak and electromagnetic forces. In each of those cases the symmetry-breaking needs to be identified with some physical phenomenon or process. In the electroweak case, the mechanism responsible is thought to be the Higgs particle/field, although experimental confirmation has not been forthcoming. Clearly, our belief in hidden symmetry will be, to a great extent, bound up with the legitimacy of the physical theory that explains the symmetry-breaking. In the case of the Higgs mechanism, there are several theoretical and philosophical issues that render the case somewhat problematic; issues that are different in kind from and extend well beyond the absence of its experimental confirmation (Morrison 2003).

Although we frequently think of symmetries as mathematical entities, all the symmetries discussed above share a common feature: namely, their association with or connection to certain physical effects or phenomena. Despite the different strategies employed for evaluating their physical status, we also saw that those kinds of strategies by no means furnish unequivocal answers to the question of whether the symmetries inherent in our physical theories/laws are fundamental features of the empirical world. The latter question is similar to the metaphysical question regarding the relation between mathematics and the world; a question that has a long history in both philosophy and science. Leibniz, for example, thought that the role of symmetry in physical theory was as a mirror of God's design in the world. However, we need not engage in metaphysics in order to make sense of the place of symmetry in physics. We can account for the significance of symmetry by understanding it as illuminating the structure of models and theories (van Fraassen 1989) or as structural constraints on generating theories and physical laws (Morrison 1995). In this latter case symmetries can be seen as meta-laws that dictate what the laws of nature must be like (e.g., the covariance associated with space–time symmetries). Speculation about the deep and fundamental symmetries of the universe is where the distinction between empirical science and metaphysics breaks down. The existence of the Higgs particle as a manifestation of broken symmetry is an empirical question, whereas the existence of hidden symmetry itself is a metaphysical one. One of the important tasks of philosophy of science is learning how to differentiate the two.

See also Inference to the best explanation; Laws of nature; Physics; Space and time; Unification.

References

Brading, K. and Brown, H. (2004) "Are Gauge Symmetry Transformations Observable?" *British Journal for the Philosophy of Science* 55: 645–67.

Brading, K. and Castellani, E. (eds) (2003) *Symmetries in Physics: Philosophical Reflections*, Cambridge: Cambridge University Press.

Budden, T. (1997) "Galileo's Ship and Spacetime Symmetry," *British Journal for the Philosophy of Science* 48: 483–516.

Cartwright, N. (1983) *How the Laws of Physics Lie*, Oxford: Oxford University Press.

Galileo, G. (1967) *Dialogue Concerning the Two Chief World Systems*, trans. Stillman Drake, Berkeley: University of California Press.

Gell-Mann, M. and Ne'eman, Y. (1964) *The Eightfold Way*, New York: Benjamin.

Noether, E. (1918) "Invarante Variationsprobleme," *Königliche Gesellschaft der Wissenschaften zu Göttingen. Mathematisch–Physikalische Klasse. Nachrichten*, trans. M. A. Tavel as "Noether's Theorem," *Transport Theory and Statistical Physics* 1 (1971): 183–207.

Morrison, M. (1990) "Reduction, Realism and Inference," *British Journal for the Philosophy of Science* 41: 305–32.

—— (1995) "The New Aspect: Symmetries as Meta-Laws – Structural Metaphysics," in F. Weinert (ed.) *Laws of Nature: Essays on the Philosophical, Scientific, and Historical Dimensions*, New York: de Gruyter, pp. 157–88.

—— (2000) *Unifying Scientific Theories*, Cambridge: Cambridge University Press.

—— (2003) "Spontaneous Symmetry Breaking: Theoretical Arguments and Philosophical Problems," in Brading and Castellani (eds) (2003), pp. 347–63.

Van Fraassen, B. (1989) *Laws and Symmetries*, Oxford: Oxford University Press.

Weinberg, S. (1993) *Dreams of a Final Theory*, New York: Pantheon.

Weyl, H. (1918) "Gravitation und Elektrizität," translated as "Gravitation and Electricity," in L. Ó Raifeartaigh (1997) *The Dawning of Gauge Theory*, Princeton, NJ: Princeton University Press, pp. 24–37.

—— (1952) *Symmetry*, Princeton, NJ: Princeton University Press.

Wigner, E. (1967) *Symmetries and Reflections*, Bloomington: University of Indiana Press.

Further reading

Many of the primary sources on symmetry that are most often cited in the literature are included in the references above. However, because symmetry is a topic with many different facets there are several different levels from which one can approach the subject. Two semi-popular accounts of the relation between symmetries and laws can be found in J. Barrow, *Theories of Everything* (Oxford University Press, 1990) and Heinz Pagels, *Perfect Symmetry: The Search for the Beginning of Time* (New York: Simon & Shuster, 1986). A reasonably elementary but still rather technical treatment of some of the important issues can be found in Weyl (1952), who discusses also symmetry in art and its relation to symmetry in science. *The Force of Symmetry* by Vincent Icke (Cambridge University Press, 1995) discusses virtually all the aspects of symmetry in a scientifically rigorous way, but without complicated mathematics; written in a lively and entertaining style, the exposition is extremely clear and comprehensive. A more technical account of the history of the notion of symmetry in physics can be found in a collection of papers edited by M. G. Doncel, A. Hermann, L. Michel, and A. Pais: *Symmetries in Physics: 1600–1890* (Barcelona: Servei di Publicacions). Finally, a mathematical treatment is given in I. J. R. Aitchinson, *An Informal Introduction to Gauge Field Theories* (Cambridge: Cambridge University Press, 1982).

45

TRUTHLIKENESS

Graham Oddie

An inquiry is a search for the truth of some matter. A person may embark on an inquiry for all manner of reasons: to relieve boredom, to satisfy a client, to help make gadgets, to win the Nobel Prize, to get a raise, or to impress his friends. Still an inquiry *qua* inquiry is a search for truth, and success is determined by the extent to which the inquiry reveals that truth. Scientific inquiry may be special in various ways, but it shares with inquiry in general this constitutive goal of revealing truth.

On the face of it, scientific inquiry has been an astonishingly successful enterprise. There is scarcely an aspect of contemporary life that, for good or for ill, is not pervasively and deeply penetrated by the discoveries of the scientific enterprise. Paradoxically, its most dramatic successes have often been initially promising theories subsequently shown to be false. How can the apparent success of scientific inquiry be reconciled with its embarrassingly regular failure to realize the constitutive goal of truth? One might – in a spirit of conceptual vandalism – drop *truth* and reframe success in terms of empirical adequacy, the discovery of useful theoretical tools, or the production of handy technology. Alternatively, one could respect truth as the goal and entertain the concept of *truthlikeness*, or *verisimilitude*. For if some false propositions are closer than others to the truth, progress towards the goal of truth through a succession of false, or even falsified, theories is entirely possible.

At a purely common-sense level some propositions do seem closer than others to the truth. Assume that there are just eight planets (Pluto having been recently stripped of full planetary status). Then the falsehood that there are 7 planets seems closer to the truth than the ancient hypothesis, also false, that there are 5. Some truths seem closer to the whole truth than other truths: the truth that there are between 7 and 9 planets seems closer to the whole truth than the weaker truth that there are between 1 and 100 planets. And some falsehoods seem closer to the truth than some truths: the falsehood that there are seven planets seems closer to the truth than the tautology – that there is some number or other of planets. So the familiar dichotomy of propositions into truths and falsehoods is compatible with a more fine-grained partition, one that reflects *degrees of truthlikeness*.

The logical problem of truthlikeness is to provide an account of the concept and to explore its logical properties. However, the concept would be practically useless if we had no epistemic handle on its application, and it would be theoretically uninteresting unless we could grasp the value of truthlikeness. So the logical problem intersects with problems in both epistemology and value theory. A solution to any one of these problems of truthlikeness will have ramifications for the others.

While the concept of truth has been a focus of philosophical scrutiny for millennia, the concept of truthlikeness has come under the spotlight only relatively recently, and it is still rare for philosophers to devote much attention to it. This "latecomer" status is not hard to explain. The problem becomes urgent for a particular combination of realism, fallibilism, and optimism, which is itself of relatively recent vintage.

Epistemology since Descartes has been a reluctant and fitful retreat from the ideal of infallible knowledge. It is replete with attempts to establish a solid beachhead against skeptical assaults, but sadly these have failed to guarantee certain knowledge of anything terribly interesting. Further, the history of science is a parade of promising theories eventually shown to be false. (Consider theories of the motions of the planets, from Ptolemy to Newton.) So, for both philosophical and historical reasons, we are all fallibilists now.

Fallibilism would not by itself compel us to tackle the problem of truthlikeness. One could, instead, abandon realism. Radical anti-realists (postmodernists, say) would have little use for the concept; and subtler, more reasonable, anti-realists might simply sidestep the problem. Suppose truth is taken to be whatever scientific inquiry will yield in the limit. A long preamble of false theories wouldn't be so troubling, since we could know *a priori* (by semantic fiat) that scientific inquiry will reveal the truth in the long run. The problem is pressing only if we yoke fallibilism to a robust realism – that there is a verification-transcendent truth of the matter, and we cannot be certain that, even in the limit, scientific inquiry will reveal it.

This is still insufficient to force us to tackle the problem, for we could simply abandon the pretension that the scientific enterprise can make progress. So we need, in addition, a certain optimism: an affirmation of the promise of progress. These three necessary conditions for the problem are also jointly sufficient. The logical problem of truthlikeness should be on the agenda of every realist who is also a fallibilist and an optimist.

The content approach

It is unsurprising that Karl Popper – among the first philosophers to embrace consciously this combination of realism, fallibilism and optimism – was the first to tackle the problem. Popper, arguing from the logical asymmetry of verification and falsification, repudiated verifiability and embraced falsifiability as both demarcation criterion for science and key to the problem of induction. For Popper, the primary virtue of a scientific theory is its falsifiability, and a secondary virtue is its lack of actual falsifications. High degree of falsifiability correlates with both strong logical content and low probability. Scientific inquiry is the pursuit of truth, of course, but not just any old truth. Scientists are after highly falsifiable, highly improbable, highly *contentful* truth. The content approach can be broadly characterized thus: truthlikeness is a function of just two variables, truth-value and content (where content is a decreasing function of logical probability).

The disentangling of epistemic probability and truthlikeness is possibly Popper's most important contribution to philosophy, standing even if everything else about falsificationism falls. A proposition has high epistemic probability if it *seems* true. A proposition has high degree of verisimilitude if it is *similar* to the truth. Seeming truth concerns the subjective appearances while similarity to truth concerns an objective relation to facts. The truism that there is some number of planets has maximal probability, but it isn't close to the truth. The false proposition that there are seven planets has minimal epistemic probability (it has been falsified) but it is very close to the truth. The examples also strongly suggest the characteristic Popperian thesis that, *ceteris paribus*, the greater the content, the closer to the truth.

Divide the set of consequences of a proposition into truths (its *truth content*) and falsehoods (its *falsity content*). According to Popper, A is closer to the truth than B just in case: A's truth content contains B's truth content, B's falsity content contains A's falsity content, and one of these containments is proper (Popper 1963).

Popper's account has some appealing features. The strongest true theory, aptly dubbed "the truth," is closer to the truth than any other proposition. If A and B are true, A is closer to the truth than B just in case A entails B and B does not entail A (call this the *content principle for truths*). If A is false then the truth content of A is closer to the truth than A itself.

There are also some less than happy features. The account rules out any falsehood being closer to the whole truth than any truth. (So Newton's theory is no closer than is a tautology to the truth about motion.) The content principle for truths has limited application to actual rival theories, since actual rivals are rarely true or even compatible. Finally, on this account all falsehoods are incommensurable for truth-likeness, for the simple reason that one cannot increase the truth content of a false proposition without increasing its falsity content (Miller 1974; Tichý 1974).

In response to this incommensurability result, suppose we drop the clause pertaining to falsity content, and measure truthlikeness by truth content alone: A is as close to the truth as B if A entails the truth content of B, and is closer if in addition B does not entail the truth content of A. This yields the content principle for truths, but also a parallel (and disastrous) *content principle for falsehoods*: that the *stronger* of two false theories is the closer to the truth (cf. Miller 1978 and Kuipers 1987). So given a known falsehood (e.g., the number of planets is less than eight) you can ensure progress towards the truth simply by conjoining to it any other false proposition you like (e.g., that the number of planets is less than one).

There are other straightforward implementations of the content approach, but they are even less plausible. Truthlikeness might be a decreasing function of content for false propositions and an increasing function for true propositions. But then, by continuity, the tautology would be sandwiched in the middle, and so no falsehood could be more truthlike than any truth. Or truthlikeness might be a decreasing function of content for both true and false theories. But that would render the tautology more truthlike than the whole truth.

Clearly, what we need are more resources to discriminate among both truths and falsehoods.

The likeness approach

It is standard now to contrast the content approach with the *likeness* approach (see Oddie 1986; Zwart 2001). A proposition allows a range of possible worlds – all those compatible with its being true – and rules out the rest. On the content approach possible worlds are classified crudely as either actual or non-actual, leaving us with just two parameters to juggle – truth (whether the *actual* world lies within the range) and content (*how many* worlds lie within the range). Suppose, however, that non-actual worlds are ordered according to their varying closeness or likeness to the actual world. Then the closeness of a proposition to the truth, or to the actual world, could be sensitive to the closeness to the actual world of the worlds in its range. The kernel of the likeness approach (Tichý 1974; Hilpinen 1976) can be characterized thus: truthlikeness is a function of the closeness of the worlds in the range to the actual world, together with some logical weighting function (perhaps derived from logical probability).

We could utilize either a qualitative ordering by similarity of worlds (Hilpinen 1976), or a numerical measure of similarity–distance (Tichý 1974). A qualitative ordering suggests two potentially relevant indicators: the *minimum* and the *maximum* distance of the worlds in the range from the actual world. A numerical measure suggests in addition: the average of the minimum and the maximum; the overall average distance from the actual world; the expected distance from the actual world; the sum of the distances from the actual world, and so on. To evaluate different proposals involving those indicators we could use some concrete cases – straightforward cases, of course, framed in simple logical spaces.

Consider a weather space with three basic states: hot, rainy, and windy. Assuming that the truth is that it is hot (h), rainy (r) and windy (w), the following complete propositions are ranked in order from least to most truthlike:

$\sim h \& \sim r \& \sim w$
$h \& \sim r \& \sim w$
$h \& r \& \sim w$
$h \& r \& w$.

The following incomplete propositions are also ranked in order from least to most truthlike:

$\sim h \& \sim r \& \sim w$
$\sim h \& \sim r$
$\sim h$
$h \vee \sim h$
$h \vee r$
h
$h \& r$
$h \& r \& w$.

Judgments such as these can be used fairly unproblematically to test theories. For example, all these judgments are compatible with the content principle for truths, but the ranking of the first three in the second list violates the content principle for falsehoods.

A first step in developing a similarity account is to define a plausible ordering on the worlds of such simple frameworks. A *finite propositional space* is generated by distributions of truth-values over a finite number of logically independent basic states. The *symmetric difference* of two worlds is the set of basic states to which they assign different truth-values. The larger the symmetric difference, the larger the distance between the worlds. A qualitative ordering by distance is yielded by the subset relation on symmetric differences. A numerical ordering is yielded by the number of states in the symmetric difference (perhaps weighted according to significance).

The closeness of a complete proposition to the truth is adequately measured by the closeness of its sole member to the actual world, but what about incomplete propositions? $min(A)$ (respectively: $max(A)$) is the distance of worlds in A closest to (respectively: farthest from) the actual world. A is true simpliciter if $min(A)$ is zero, and it is close to being true if $min(A)$ is small. $min(A)$ is thus a reasonable measure of *closeness to being true*, but, in failing to distinguish the truthlikeness of the tautology from that of the whole truth, it falls well short of closeness to the truth. $max(A)$ is, for true propositions, a crude measure of the spread of worlds in A. *Ceteris paribus*, the further from the actual world are A's furthest worlds, the less truthlike A is. $max(A)$ does distinguish between the tautology and the whole truth, but not between the tautology and that disastrously false theory which contains all and only worlds farthest from the actual world. Hilpinen (1976) proposed that *min* be taken as the "truth factor" and *max* as the "content factor" and, following Popper, suggested that an increase in truthlikeness comes with an improvement in one or other factor. Combined with the qualitative symmetric difference ordering, the *min–max* proposal captures all the above judgments except one: it ranks $h \vee r$ and h equally truthlike, violating the content principle for truths.

Tichý (1974) employed the numerical symmetric difference measure for worlds, together with the overall average function. This measure captures all the above judgments, as do a number of others (see Zwart 2001).

So much for examples drawn from such simple spaces – finite propositional spaces. The content program can be easily applied to any framework at all. Can the likeness program also handle more realistic frameworks – for example, those generated by polyadic first-order properties and relations, continuous magnitudes, or higher-order properties, relations, and magnitudes, together with infinite domains? The piecemeal likeness approach (e.g., Niiniluoto 1987) takes the appropriate measure of distance to be a function of the specific features that define a particular cognitive problem. The advantage of this is that results are readily accessible and generally accord with pre-theoretic intuitions. The disadvantage is a certain ad hocness in the selection of the measure. The unified likeness approach (e.g., Oddie 1986) assumes that any interesting framework can be modeled either in first-order or higher-order logic. A distance function can be derived by generalizing the numerical symmetric difference measure, by using the structural features of first-order distributive normal forms or of higher-order permutative normal forms. The advantage of this approach is theoretical unity; the disadvantage, that deriving results for realistic cases faces prohibitive computational complexities.

Which of the various content principles are compatible with the likeness approach? The *min* factor of a falsehood can be improved by weakening – adding a non-actual world that is closer than the others in its range. The *min–max* measure thus rightly repudiates the content principle for falsehoods, as does the *overall average* measure, since one can improve the overall average distance by adding worlds that are closer to the actual world. The *min–max* measure, although violating the content principle for truths, does deliver a weaker consequence of it: viz. that the stronger of two truths is never further from the truth. But since, quite generally, average closeness increases by adding any world to the range whose distance from the actual world is less than the existing average, the average closeness of both true and false propositions can be increased by weakening. So the *overall average* violates all the Content Principles, including the weak version for Truths implied by *min–max*.

The question arises whether there is some natural hybrid account that combines commonsense intuitions about likeness with the commitment to content embodied in the full content principle for truths.

Hybrid approaches

The *min–max* proposal is typically located within the similarity program as characterized above, but interestingly Hilpinen himself thought of *min–max* as a superior articulation of the content program, departing from the pure content approach only by incorporating distance into the truth and content factors. A defect of *min–max* is that no falsehood is deemed closer to the truth than any truth. This can be remedied by assuming quantitative distances, and letting A's distance from the truth be some weighted average of *min* and *max*. *min–max–average* renders all propositions comparable for truthlikeness, and some falsehoods are deemed more truthlike than some truths. But while *min–max–average* falls within the scope of likeness approaches as defined, it is not totally satisfactory from either content or likeness perspectives. Let A be a true proposition with a number of worlds tightly clustered around the actual world α. Let Z be a false proposition with a number of worlds tightly clustered around a world ω maximally distant from actuality. A is highly truthlike, and Z highly untruthlike, and *min–max–average* agrees. But now let Z+ be Z plus α, and A+, A plus ω. Considerations of both continuity and likeness suggest that A+ is much more truthlike than Z+, but they are deemed equally truthlike by *min–max–average*. Further, *min–max–average* deems both A+ and Z+ equal in truthlikeness to the tautology, violating the content principle for truths.

Part of the problem, from the content perspective, is that *max* is, as noted above, a crude measure of content. Niiniluoto suggests a different content measure: the (normalized) *sum* of the distances of worlds in A from the actual world . Formally, *sum* is a probability measure, and hence a measure of a kind of logical weakness. But *sum* is also a content–likeness hybrid, rendering a proposition more contentful the closer its worlds are to actuality. Being genuinely sensitive to size, *sum* is clearly a better measure of lack of content than *max*, and *min–sum–average* ranks the tautology, Z+ and A+ in that order.

According to *min–sum–average*: all propositions are commensurable for truthlikeness; the full content principle for truths holds provided the content factor gets non-zero weight; the truth has greater truthlikeness than any other proposition provided all non-actual worlds are some distance from the actual world; some false propositions are closer to the truth than others; the content principle for falsehoods is violated provided the *min* factor gets some weight; if A is false, the truth content of A is more truthlike than A itself, again provided the *min* factor gets some weight. *min–sum–average* thus seems like a happy compromise between content and likeness approaches.

Much of the work on truthlikeness has been conducted in a somewhat ad hoc way, with proposals being evaluated against particular cases selected by protagonists for the purpose of supporting a favored theory against rivals. There have been surprisingly few general results derived about, for example, the logical relations between the content and likeness approaches. An attempt to remedy this has been made recently by Zwart and Franssen (2007), arguing that Arrow's *impossibility theorem* in social choice theory can be applied to obtain a surprising general result: that there is a precise sense in which there can be no genuine compromise between qualitative versions of the content and likeness approaches, that any apparent compromise capitulates to one paradigm or the other. This theorem represents a genuine advance in methodology, but it is dependent on contestable characterizations of the two approaches. There is, after all, a sense in which the numerical measure, *min–sum–average*, seems like a genuine compromise between the two approaches. To see this, assume (with the pure content theorists) that there is effectively no differentiation amongst non-actual worlds – they are all the same distance from actuality. Then *min–sum–average* collapses into a pure content account, delivering both Content Principles, for falsehoods as well as truths. The repudiation of the content principle for falsehoods is achieved by employing a non-trivial likeness function, but *min–sum–average* preserves the content theorist's predilection for strength among truths.

Frame dependence

One desideratum on a theory of truthlikeness is that truthlikeness, like truth, should be *invariant under equivalence*.

Aronson (1990) and Psillos (1999) argue that the combination of symmetric difference and *overall-average* violates this desideratum, because the degree of truthlikeness of a proposition depends on the number of other basic states generating the space in which it is framed. Where n is the number of basic states, the truthlikeness of a true atomic proposition is $(n+1)/2n$ and the truthlikeness of a false atomic proposition is $(n-1)/2n$. So in our little weather frame, h has truthlikeness 2/3 and $\sim h$ has truthlikeness 1/3. Embedded in a frame of ten basic states, however, h drops to

11/20 and ~h rises to 9/20. Both approach the truthlikeness of a tautology (1/2) as n increases. Niiniluoto notes that truthlikeness *should* be dependent on the context of the cognitive problem at issue, since the target proposition (the truth) may change. As the truth is enlarged, the proportion of the truth that h captures shrinks. While that response is certainly cogent, another is also possible. The invariance at issue is an artifact of normalization, and can be simply eliminated. Take the closeness of two worlds to be given by the number of agreements on basic states minus the number disagreements. Then, taking truthlikeness to be given by the average closeness of worlds, this yields the same ordering as the normalized measure, while absolute closeness of a proposition to the truth is independent of the number of atomic states. For example, the truthlikeness of any conjunction of t true and f false atomic proposi- tions is simply $(t-f)$, whatever n is.

Another invariance problem involves reversal of orderings of apparently equivalent propositions (Miller 1974). Miller's argument resembles the grue-bleen problem of induction. Take the three weather states and define two new states in terms of them: Minnesotan (= hot if and only if rainy) and Arizonan (= hot if and only if windy). h&r&w is then equivalent to h&m&a; ~h&r&w to ~h&~m&~a; and ~h&~r&~w to ~h&m&a. If we take as basic the states, hot, Minnesotan and Arizonan, then distances, according to the symmetric difference measure, are reversed.

As in the grue-bleen debate it is tempting to say that Minnesotan and Arizonan are "gerrymandered" conditions because their specification involves reference to two different states. But, as with grue-bleen, the situation is symmetrical. Taking Minnesotan and Arizonan as basic we can specify rainy and windy thus: rainy = hot if and only if Minnesotan; windy = hot if and only if Arizonan.

Despite this formal symmetry, one might still maintain that rainy is a more *natural* condition than Minnesotan, so that the situation is not perfectly symmetrical after all. Conditions like rainy, unlike Minnesotan, "carve reality and the joints." What makes a condition a genuine property, an appropriate primitive? Either it would be a necessary and presumably *a priori* matter which conditions are genuine properties, or a contingent and presumably *a posteriori* matter, perhaps to be determined by mature science. Either way, some conditions are more fundamental, more basic, than others, and it is the basic properties and relations, not gerrymandered conditions, which determine relations of similarity between worlds

A more radical challenge to frame-dependence is to concede that nothing in the world privileges one class of conditions over another, but deny that the two frames yield genuine equivalences. Rather, they involve distinct possibilities and so generate distinct non-equivalent propositions. This radical position is not without support, but it leaves the realist with an unpalatable incommensurability of frameworks.

In the light of apparent radical frame-dependence, some philosophers despair of giving a coherent account of truthlikeness (e.g., Urbach 1983; Smith 1998; Teller 2001), and suggest various proxies for truthlikeness to account for the differing accuracy of falsehoods. In fact most of the suggested proxies traffic in some notion of similarity or closeness – either between models (i.e., proxies for worlds) or between theories, or between theories and models. Since any proposal that depends on similarity is subject to some version of Miller's frame-dependence objection, those proposals cannot so easily sidestep the problem.

Truthlikeness and value theory

As noted, a striking feature of the investigation of truthlikeness is that much of it has taken place in a piecemeal, even ad hoc manner – testing this or that proposal against this or that putative intuition about cases. There have been relatively few attempts to derive general constraints on the logical structure of the concept through the formulation of simple, plausible principles. Contrast this with the concepts of *goodness* and *betterness*. Economists, measurement theorists and value theorists have done interesting work on the logical structure of value, articulating, for example, concepts of *separability* and *additivity*, and exploring their logical connections. Furthermore, since truthlikeness is supposed to be valuable (that's the whole point of it) the connection between the value of one proposition and others should not be a random affair. This suggests that we should be able to learn something about the logical structure of truthlikeness from the logical structure of value generally, and possibly vice versa.

Here is one connection. Several theorists assume that intuitions about distances between worlds can be captured by an essentially *additive* measure. Under what conditions is an intuitively given ordering of worlds representable by an additive measure? It turns out that there is an interesting qualitative condition which is necessary and sufficient for the existence of an additive representation: the principle of *recombinant values* (Oddie 2001b). The idea is simple enough: if you decompose a bunch of worlds into their basic states and reassemble them in some other way, then the overall value of the new set of worlds is equivalent to the overall value of the old set. That is a purely qualitative articulation of the idea that the values of the individual components of a world are independent of surrounding factors. So, applied to truth, the cognitive value of a piece of true information (like the proposition that it is hot) does not depend on whatever else happens to be true (for example, whether it happens to be rainy or dry, windy or still).

Of course, there might be some good reason to reject this strong independence of value of true bits of information, just as there might be reason to reject the additivity of value. According to Kant, for example, it is better that a saint be happy than miserable, but it is also better that a villain be miserable than happy. So, value is not additive – happiness adds value to virtue, but subtracts value from vice. Interestingly, we can reframe Kant's ordering in terms of virtue and desert (Oddie 2001a). Someone gets his deserts just in case he is happy if virtuous, and unhappy if vicious. That is to say, desert = virtuous if and only if happy. Given Kant's preferred ordering, both virtue and desert now add value regardless. So is value additive or not? It depends. "Regardless" is frame-dependent. It means "holding the other basic factor(s) constant." But what the other basic factors are depends on the choice of factors. Whether Kant's value ordering is additive thus depends on what we take to be the basic *axiological factors* or *axiological atoms* (Oddie 2001a). The fact that virtue and desert render Kant's ordering additive is evidence that virtue and desert (rather than virtue and happiness) are the fundamental (Kantian) values.

In that light, Miller's result can be framed differently. Suppose we are given an ordering of propositions (whatever the vocabulary used to express them) according to truthlikeness. Likeness depends on the identification of basic states, in terms of which the likenesses are reckoned. We might be wrong in assuming that the basic states are encoded in the primitive vocabulary, but we can cast about for a set of primitives which renders the value of information, as given by that ordering, additive. That is to say, we can *identify* the basic states by means of the ordering itself, and assign cognitive value to those in such a way both that the value of a complex is the sum of the values of its basic constituents, and the ordering is preserved. It turns out that, subject to very weak constraints, there is not an additive frame for every ordering – some orderings are intrinsically non-additive. But just as in the general value case, we can use the additivity of truthlikeness as a kind of regulative ideal. If an intuitively given ordering is rendered additive by a certain choice of primitives, then that is a point in favor of that choice. An intuitively acceptable ordering can enable us to identify the states in terms of which likeness should be reckoned and cognitive value measured.

Concluding remarks

Four decades of work on the concept of truthlikeness have not yielded enormous theoretical consensus, leading Psillos (1999) to suggest that we forego analysis and rest content with settled intuitive judgments on particular cases. After all, not every concept can be analyzed, and the paucity of uncontested philosophical analyses suggests rather that none can be given a successful philosophical analysis! Since any account of the concept will give some, probably considerable, weight to intuitive judgments, there can be no decisive objection to Psillos's proposal that is not also an objection to theorizing. (Further, a moratorium on truthlikeness analysis would hardly render redundant a large number of philosophers – unlike closing down the knowledge-analysis factory, say.) But for good or for ill there is a resilience to the analytical spirit which such prudent counsel is unlikely to sway. And even if we have not yet lighted upon the demonstrably correct account, at least we now know of several proposals that they are inadequate, and of others that they have weaknesses as well as strengths – evidence that we have made some progress.

See also Confirmation; Critical rationalism; Probability; Realism/anti-realism; Scientific method.

References

Aronson, J. L. (1990) "Verisimilitude and Type Hierarchies," *Philosophical Topics* 18: 5–28.
Aronson, J., Harré, R., and Way, E. C. (1995) *Realism Rescued: How Scientific Progress Is Possible*, Chicago: Open Court.
Hilpinen, R. (1976) "Approximate Truth and Truthlikeness," in M. Przelecki, K. Szaniawski, and R. Wójcicki (eds) *Formal Methods in the Methodology of the Empirical Sciences*, Dordrecht: Reidel, pp. 19–42.
Kuipers, T. (1987) "A Structuralist Approach to Truthlikeness," in T. Kuipers (ed.) *What Is Closer-to-the-Truth? A Parade of Approaches to Truthlikeness*, Amsterdam: Rodopi, pp. 79–99.

Miller, D. (1974) "Popper's Qualitative Theory of Verisimilitude," *British Journal for the Philosophy of Science* 25: 166–77.

—— (1978) "Distance from the Truth as a True Distance," in J. Hintikka, I. Niiniluoto, and E. Saarinen (eds) *Essays on Mathematical and Philosophical Logic*, Dordrecht: Reidel, pp. 15–26.

Niiniluoto, I. (1987) *Truthlikeness*, Dordrecht: Reidel.

—— (1998) "Verisimilitude: The Third Period," *British Journal for the Philosophy of Science* 49: 1–29.

Oddie, G. (1986) *Likeness to Truth*, Dordrecht: Reidel.

—— (2001a) "Axiological Atomism," *Australasian Journal of Philosophy* 79: 313–32.

—— (2001b) "Recombinant Values," *Philosophical Studies* 106: 259–92.

Popper, K. (1963) *Conjectures and Refutations*, London: Routledge.

Psillos, S. (1999) *Scientific Realism: How Science Tracks Truth*, London: Routledge.

Smith, P. (1998) "Approximate Truth for Minimalists," *Philosophical Papers* 27: 119–28.

Teller, P. (2001) "The Twilight of the Perfect Model Model," *Erkenntnis* 55: 393–415.

Tichý, P. (1974) "On Popper's Definitions of Verisimilitude," *British Journal for the Philosophy of Science* 25: 155–60.

Urbach, P. (1983) "Intimations of Similarity: The Shaky Basis of Verisimilitude," *British Journal for the Philosophy of Science* 34: 166–75.

Zwart, S. D. (2001) *Refined Verisimilitude*, Dordrecht: Kluwer.

Zwart, S. D. and Franssen, M. (2007) "An Impossibility Theorem for Verisimilitude," *Synthese* 158: 75–92.

Further reading

For Popper's early work on truthlikeness see his 1963 *Conjectures and Refutations*, and also *Objective Knowledge* (Oxford: Clarendon Press, 1972). Surveys of the debate in the 1970s and early 1980s can be found in Niiniluoto's extremely detailed and comprehensive *Truthlikeness* (1987). Kuipers's 1987 book *What Is Closer-to-the-Truth?* gave antagonists in the debate an opportunity to state the latest versions of their accounts and argue for them. Both Niiniluoto (1998) and Zwart (2001) contain surveys and critical commentary on the significant developments of the 1990s, and are particularly strong in their detailed accounts of a range of hybrid approaches.

46

UNIFICATION

Todd Jones

Introduction

Throughout the history of science, indeed throughout the history of knowledge, unification has been touted as a central aim of intellectual inquiry. We have always wanted to discover as many facts about the universe as possible; but, at the same time, we have wanted to understand how such facts are linked and interrelated. Much time and effort have been spent trying to show that diverse arrays of things can be seen as different manifestations of some common underlying entities or properties. Thales is said to have originated philosophy and science with his declaration that everything was, at base, a form of water. Plato's theory of the forms was thought to be a magnificent accomplishment because it gave a unified solution to the separate problems of the relation between knowledge and belief, the grounding of objective values, and how continuity is possible amid change. Pasteur made numerous medical advancements possible by demonstrating the interconnection between micro-organisms and human disease symptoms. Many technological advances were aided by Maxwell's showing that light is a kind of electromagnetic radiation. The attempt to unify the various known forces is often referred to as "the holy grail" of physics. Some philosophers have even suggested that providing explanations is itself a sort of unification. The idea of unifying our knowledge through science has sometimes taken on social, cultural, and political overtones as well. The logical positivists believed that a unified scientific approach to knowledge could help save people from a multitude of local irrationalities. The notion that unity has political or cultural overtones has also been part of the thinking of recent advocates for the *dis*unity of science, who believe that pressures for unity can smother scientific creativity, stifle dissenting views, and prevent us from noticing important diversities.

But while "unification" (like "simplicity") has often been hailed as central to science, the meaning of the term is not altogether clear. Scientists often do not specify what, precisely, they mean by unification. And in cases where what they mean *is* clear, different thinkers plainly mean *different* things by the term. What are the various senses of "unification" and why has unification been such an important aim in the history of inquiry?

What is unification?

There is certainly a bewildering variety of things called "unification." The types of unification accomplished by Plato and Pasteur, for example, certainly seem to be vastly different. Is there any systematic way in which to think about this diversity? In my view, we should begin by recognizing two main families of unification: one might be called "subtype and similarity" (SS) unification; the other might be called "conjunction and coordination" (CC) unification. SS unification involves showing that things which seem different really share some or other dimension of similarity. CC unification involves showing that different items (which may or may not be similar) connect with one another in some way. Within these families, there are kinds and degrees of similarity, and kinds and degrees of connection.

A type of weak CC unification is achieved when we group together, under a single term, a set of things connected by being *next to* each other in space or time, such as when someone describes a large set of adjacent mountains as "the Appalachians" or a series of battles as "the Hundred Years War." We have very strong CC unification, on the other hand, when we group together items that mutually causally influence each other and work together to produce effects in an integrated functional system. We can now talk, for example, about the workings of the hypothalamus, pituitary, adrenal glands, and the hormones ACTH and cortisol, in one breath by talking about an "endocrine alarm clock" that wakes us. In between these are the sorts of moderately CC unified pictures that come into being when people discover that previously-thought-to-be unrelated things have a cause and effect relationship – for example, carbon dioxide emissions and the melting of polar ice-caps. Since we have some type of unification whenever we uncover a relationship between entities or properties (including between dissimilar ones), then there is going to be an enormous number and variety of scientific discoveries that can be thought of as effecting a unification of a CC sort.

The other family of unification, the SS family, involves showing that a group of seemingly different entities or properties belongs to a common general type. The most maximal, thoroughgoing type of unification in this family is reductive identification. Maxwell's work showing that light is not just *related to* electromagnetism, but actually *is* a form of electromagnetic radiation, is perhaps the best-known example of this sort of unification by ontological simplification via identity. By contrast, a weak type of SS unification involves showing that different things are each *members of* a broader category of things sharing some properties. The recent claim that both the pattern of energy of atoms in gases at thermal equilibrium and the distribution of people's income levels in developed countries follow an exponential distribution pattern (Hogan 2005) is an example of this more minimal type of SS unification. So is the claim that both dolphins and pigs are mammals. Some scholars (e.g., Morrison 2000) have pointed out the importance of feature-sharing unification and how it differs from the fully reductive kind. (A lesser number have pointed out how this type also differs from CC unification.) An even weaker type of SS unification is claiming that different things are members of the same broader class – not necessarily because each member shares a common set of properties with other members, but because each member is linked via some or other similarity to a central prototype. The class *fish* seems to unify things in this minimal way (see Gould 1983).

There are numerous different ways for scientists to accomplish SS unifications because there are many ways in which two things can be judged to be similar. The term "vertebrate" unifies all those animals that are thought to be similar by virtue of the *internal* property of having a backbone. The things unified by "gene," by contrast, need not share particular internal properties. Being a particular gene is defined largely in terms of having the *external* property of producing certain effects on developing organisms. Being a gene is one of many multiply realized properties, defined by similarities in their external functional role, rather than similarities in their internal structure. Another kind of similarity is having a shared holistic structure, rather than having shared particular internal features. The Hardy–Weinberg equation, for example, talks about overall population growth in highly diverse reproducing species. Things can also be classed as similar, not because they share *particular* properties, but because they share particular *amounts* or proportions of a property. So, one might give a unifying description of a stage of growth in different plants by talking about a common reduced amount of chlorophyll at that stage. Things sharing *large numbers* of properties (but not necessarily one common one) can also be classed as a similar type. Marketing research might isolate groups of people who have a certain family resemblance about which one can make specific economic generalizations. Things could also be classed as similar because they *lack* certain things, even if they are quite varied in other ways. So a mentally retarded child and a Ph.D. chemist might both be described as autistics who lack an empathetic understanding of others. There are as many ways to unify as there are ways of finding similarity-based classes about which one can make generalizations. It is not surprising, then, that various scholars describe lots of different kinds of scientific achievements as accomplishing a unification.

It is not uncommon for scholars to be engaged in finding conjunction and coordination and similarity and subtype unification at the same time. For example, understanding a concept that unifies various elements in a CC manner (sodium atoms can become linked to chlorine atoms through ionic bonding) quite often also involves making a unifying SS *identification* between the low-level coordinating parts and the high-level concept (sodium chloride = salt). Explaining something by bringing together theories from different domains also often involves making both SS and CC unifications. Why is the sky blue? We combine optics, chemistry, meteorology, and biology when we say that, at certain times of the day, light goes through a certain amount of atmosphere, hitting small nitrogen and oxygen particles; the light bouncing off these particles has a wavelength of 0.390–0.492 microns, which is the blue and violet spectrum, and our eyes are especially sensitive to blue light. Describing how the various distinct elements interact to produce a certain result combines them into a CC unified story. But such combining often requires to first make SS unifications which allow us to identify high-level concepts (like atmosphere) with low-level comprising details (like nitrogen and oxygen particles) so we know more about what to connect with items in other theories. There are not only different types of unification, then, but different types happen simultaneously. It is no wonder that it is difficult to explain exactly what scientific unification is.

We should note that up until now I have been speaking mostly about what might be called "metaphysical" unification – finding ways to think about existing things in the world in a unified way. But scholars have also been interested in *epistemic* and *normative* unification. Epistemic unification involves bringing together different methods of investigating and reasoning about the world (e.g., Popper's idea that science revolved around falsification). Normative unification involves bringing together diverse aims and goals of inquiry (e.g., van Fraassen's attempts to convince people that the central aim of science should be developing empirically adequate models). I believe that epistemic and normative unification can each be divided into SS and CC types as well. SS *epistemic* unification aims at showing that different investigative tools are actually quite *similar* in one way or another. CC *epistemic* unification aims at showing that different methods of investigating *work well together* to produce certain kinds of information. SS *normative* unification, meanwhile, tries to show that different scientific endeavors really have similar goals, while CC *normative* unification aims to show that different scientific goals can be highly complementary.

We see, then, why so many very different kinds of activities can all be thought of as providing us with a kind of unification. But why is coming up with such unifications thought to be such an *important* activity? One underlying feature that makes unification such an important virtue is surprisingly little discussed (though it was central to Mach's (1960 [1893]) conception of science), but is, nevertheless, quite straightforward. Unification provides agents with a way of saving precious cognitive resources. It saves resources with regard to both the information that individual agents can possess, and the collective knowledge held by groups in libraries or computer banks. When various things are linked in a CC unification, the people who learn these unified theories come to have associative networks in their minds which provide efficient search engines for numerous facts. With a unified picture, the fact of what happens, say, after two carbon atoms are oxidized in the Krebs cycle, can be located very quickly, without having to search blindly through a myriad of items in memory. Memory *space* is saved by CC unification as well. When we make CC unifications by tying together items that are strongly correlated, this allows us to *infer* the presence of various features, rather than having to explicitly store them. If we know that X correlates with Y in a certain way, we need only store (or perceive) that X has a certain value, and the value of Y is automatically accessible to us. (E.g., we do not have to independently discover and store the presence of certain antibodies and the presence of the HIV virus.)

SS unification also saves memory space. Classifying all variants of a certain arrangement of electrons, protons, and neutrons as belonging to a single unified kind – say *carbon atom* – enables us to store information about carbon atoms in a single place in memory. That information can be referred back to continually, instead of having to have a space-hogging representation of a complex arrangement of electrons, protons, and neutrons for each place where carbon is present. SS unification can save time as well, for memory is far more efficiently searched if things are categorized as subtypes of subtypes of subtypes, rather than as independent facts (see Jones 2004 for a detailed discussion). The time and space resource-saving that unification provides gives us access to far more information about the world than we could possess if we had to memorize facts about the world in a non-unified way. The more information we have access to, the better epistemic agents we are and the easier we can meet our various goals. What is more, the more unification we have, the fewer facts we must regard as brutely unexplainable ones that are derivable neither from being an instance of a more general fact nor from a knowledge of causal antecedents. Presumably, we prefer that there be few facts we must regard as brute. Reducing their number is made possible by unification.

Unification and explanation

Most scholars consider unification a highly desirable virtue in science. But there have been scholars (notably Huxley, Friedman, and Kitcher) who hold that it is *more* than just a desirable virtue. For some, it is through unification that we really *explain* things with science. The most well-developed version of this view has been put forward in a couple of papers by Kitcher (1981, 1989). On Kitcher's view, explanations are deductive derivations which conclude with a statement of the fact to be explained. But whether an account is really an explanation cannot be determined by looking at that account alone. To qualify as an explanation, an account first must be a particular instance of a general schematic "derivation pattern" whose concrete instances are used to generate lots of different conclusions. And that derivation pattern must itself belong to a particular *set* of derivation patterns that together constitute something called the "explanatory store." The explanatory store is composed of the *smallest set* of derivation patterns that together can be used to generate the *largest amount* of our total knowledge of the universe. (Kitcher's theory also has a requirement that the derivations be maximally stringent, preventing derivations from relying on overly vague terms.) By deriving conclusions from a sparse store of patterns, we show how numerous different facts about the world can be derived using the same patterns over and over again. We *understand* the world when we produce the most systematic, most unified, representation of it that we can. We *explain* particular facts when we show how they fit into and can be derived from that best understanding of the world.

As one might expect, there have been numerous objections to the view that explanation is a type of unification. Among scholars most dubious about the unification theory are those who believe that the essence of explanation is revealing the underlying mechanisms (usually causal) that make an event happen. This view has been termed the "ontic" conception of explanation (see Coffa 1977; Railton 1980; Salmon 1989). The unification view, by contrast, is an example of an "epistemic" conception in which explanation is a matter of finding the generalizations that tell us that a certain type of event is the one we should *expect*. For enthusiasts of the ontic approach, epistemic approaches just do not capture what we ordinarily mean by "explanation." This can be readily seen, according to enthusiasts of ontic approaches, by looking at the problems that things like *asymmetry* pose for epistemic conceptions.

The most well-worked out epistemic approach to explanation has been Hempel's deductive–nomological (D–N) model. Yet explanatory asymmetry poses severe problems for this view. Bromberger (1963) pointed out that describing the height of a tower and the angle of elevation of the sun together provide a D–N explanation of the length of the corresponding shadow; but a similar derivation using the length of the shadow and the angle of the sun to calculate the height of the tower does not intuitively explain the tower's height. A good theory of explanation must show why only certain kinds of derivations count as explanatory. There are various possible ways of doing this. But many theorists believe that counting only descriptions that mention uni-directional causal mechanisms to be explanatory is our best way of accounting for asymmetry.

Theorists holding the epistemic conception of explanation tend to be more skeptically inclined toward underlying mechanisms. They believe we must be cautious about asserting the existence of underlying mechanisms that are usually invisible and to which we rarely have any direct epistemic access. We hypothesize that certain invisible mechanisms or laws exist because we reason that if these existed then they could be responsible for our observations. But it is often the case that numerous *different* postulated combinations of mechanisms or laws could logically be responsible for our observations. Which ones best explain them? Ontic conceptions of explanation cannot really tell us, say epistemic conception proponents. The unification theory, on the other hand, counsels us to pick, out of the many possible derivations, the account that best helps systematize and unify our knowledge. Meanwhile, there are *additional* worries about how to find underlying *causal* mechanisms. Epistemic conception theories point to the fact that no one has yet given a fully satisfactory answer to Hume's worries about showing what a causal connection is. How can locating causes be what explaining is all about, when we do not really know what it is to locate a cause?

Unification theorists also believe that the asymmetry problem is not really a problem for their particular type of epistemic approach. While we can derive the height of a tower from information about the angle of the sun and the length of the shadow, the unification theory provides us with criteria for ruling out such derivations as *non-explanatory* ones. The explanatory derivations, according to the unification theory, are the ones that can be used to derive the largest set of facts about the world from the smallest set of derivation patterns. We *can* derive the dimensions of some objects, using a pattern based on the length of their shadows. But we cannot derive the dimensions of transparent objects, luminescent objects, huge objects, or tiny objects, which do not cast shadows this way. We can derive the dimensions of almost any structure, on the other hand, using a general schema that might be called the "origin and development" derivation pattern. Since that pattern schema allows us to derive *more facts* than the shadow-based one, it is part of the preferred explanatory set. Deriving the height of the tower from knowing the intentions of the designer at the time it was built and any subsequent alterations made to the structure since that time is an instance of this schema. It is therefore the derivation of the tower's height that should be deemed explanatory, not a shadow-based one (Kitcher 1989: 485).

Unificationists have replied to other proposed asymmetry cases as well. Eric Barnes (1992) discusses a case in which we can derive the fact that a dinosaur of a certain skeletal type existed, based on finding a fossil skeleton. But it might be the case that current paleontologists are in no position to tell us why skeletal structure S rather than others came to exist. Since there are no competing ways to derive the skeletal structure other than using an "evidentiary" derivation, says Barnes, the unification theory is forced to label this intuitively non-explanatory account as explanatory. In "How the Unification Theory of Explanation Escapes Asymmetry" (Jones 1995), I responded that unificationists need not prefer the fossil-based derivation to other accounts. In our store of commonly used explanations of organism morphologies, there is a pattern that can be termed the "Darwinian evolution of skeletal structure" pattern. A Darwinian argument pattern would have us look at the predecessor skeletal forms and at the various selection pressures that could lead these forms to be modified. The problem with using this pattern is *not* that we could not fill in the pattern with detailed information about past conditions to generate the skeletal structure conclusion. Rather, the problem is that we really do not have enough access to the past to have complete confidence in the accuracy of the premises used in this derivation. But in that situation, we could still give a *speculative* account in which one generates the detailed conclusion using premises whose truth is, to varying degrees, less than certain. Alternatively, we could give a *partial* explanation using the Darwinian pattern, where we derive a less detailed conclusion using only premises that are well accepted. There is no reason that unification theory advocates would have to prefer, as more unifying, a more detail-yielding derivation based on a *larger* store of derivation patters to a partial or speculative derivation that comes from a *smaller* set that can generate a wider variety of conclusions. Unification theorists, then, believe that the asymmetry problem can be solved without having to reintroduce age-old problems regarding underdetermination and causation.

But even if one is not committed to an ontic conception of explanation, there are other problems that unificationists must overcome if they are to convince people that an explanation is the account that is the most unifying. Chief among them is the fact that unificationists have never spelled out in any detail how to choose between accounts that are unifying in different ways. One way that we could better unify our knowledge is by accounting for far more facts, even if that means increasing the number of patterns of derivation we must use. Another way is to use far fewer patterns to account for a high number of facts derived, while perhaps being able to derive fewer facts. A third way is to increase derived facts and reduce the number of patterns by playing with the stringency requirement. Most likely, we could increase our "unification score" best by doing some combination of the three. There are, however, a theoretically infinite number of ways that one could add scores on the number of conclusions, paucity of patterns, and stringency to get a higher unification score than the best previous systematization (e.g., $5 + 5 + 5 = 15$, so does $5 + 6 + 4$, so does $5 + 5.0001 + 4.9999$, and so on). Current formulations of the unification account say little about how to choose between perhaps radically different systematizations that are *tied* with respect to their unifying power.

This is not automatically a problem. Scientists often give quite different explanations of the same phenomena. The idea that different accounts can be unifying in different ways may be why they do so. Indeed, the fact that the unification theory allows different kinds of accounts to be thought of as explanatory might be considered a special *virtue*, not a liability. Ultimately, however, it can be a virtue only if different ways of unifying do not *also* end up counting various intuitively *non-explanatory* derivations as unifying explanations. At this point, when a scholar proposes that an intuitively non-explanatory account can count as part of the best systematization of our knowledge, unificationists respond by showing there is a *more unifying* systematization that produces an intuitively explanatory account. Kitcher (1989) has expressed optimism that in actual scientific practice (as opposed to the world of logical possibility), we do not find intuitively non-explanatory accounts that stem from systematizations that are more unifying than others. Neither the optimism of unification proponents nor a few case-by-case demonstrations is sufficient to convince skeptics that there are *no* non-explanatory systematizations that unify our knowledge as well as the systematizations that produce intuitively explanatory accounts. To satisfy their critics, unificationists need to find ways of showing that no intuitively non-explanatory accounts could be part of our most unifying knowledge systematizations. They might do this (a) by explicating *additional principles* that further limit which unifying knowledge systematizations are more unifying than others, and/or (b) via *additional arguments* showing why current principles or augmented ones will *generally* rule out systematizations that yield intuitively non-explanatory derivations. Without these, discussions of how celebrated scientific explanations have unified our knowledge cannot convince those who doubt that explanation is a form of unification.

In summary, unification is undeniably important in science. There appear to be many different types of unification. There also appear to be important links between the different types. Whether unification is at the heart of science, enabling us to give and identify explanations, remains an important issue for debate.

See also Causation; Explanation; Logical empiricism; The historical turn in the philosophy of science; Mechanisms; Scientific method; The virtues of a good theory.

References

Barnes, E. (1992) "Explanatory Unification and the Problem of Asymmetry," *Philosophy of Science* 59: 558–71.

Bromberger, S. (1963) "A Theory about the Theory of Theory and about the Theory of Theories," in W. Reese (ed.) *Philosophy of Science: The Delaware Seminar*, New York: John Wiley.

Coffa, J. A. (1977) "Probabilities: Reasonable or True?" *Philosophy of Science* 44: 186–98.

Hogan, J (2005) "Why it Is Hard to Share the Wealth," *New Scientist* (12 March) 2490: 6.

Jones, T. (1995) "How the Unification Theory of Explanation Escapes Asymmetry," *Erkenntnis* 43: 229–40.

—— (2004) "Reduction and Anti-Reduction: Rights and Wrongs," *Metaphilosophy* 25: 614–47.

Kitcher, P. (1981) "Explanatory Unification," *Philosophy of Science* 48: 505–31.

—— (1989) "Explanatory Unification and the Causal Structure of the World," in W. C. Salmon and P. Kitcher (eds) *Minnesota Studies in the Philosophy of Science*, Volume 13: *Scientific Explanation*, Minneapolis: University of Minnesota Press.

Mach, E. (1960 [1893]) *The Science of Mechanics*, trans. T. J. McCormack, 6th edn, La Salle, IL: Open Court Publishing.

Morrison, M. (2000) *Unifying Scientific Theories*, Oxford: Oxford University Press.

Railton, P. (1980) "Explaining Probability," Ph.D dissertation, Princeton University.

Salmon, W. C. (1989) "Four Decades of Scientific Explanation," in W. C. Salmon and P. Kitcher (eds) *Minnesota Studies in the Philosophy of Science*, Volume 13: *Scientific Explanation*, Minneapolis: University of Minnesota Press.

Further reading

An early modern discussion of the importance of unification in science was given by Mach (1960 [1893]). The Vienna Circle followers of Mach, O. Neurath, R. Carnap, C. Morris, who went on to create *The International Encyclopedia of Unified Science* (later *Foundations of the Unity of Science* (Chicago: University of Chicago Press, 1955) gave many defenses of different conceptions of unity in those volumes. P. Oppenheim and H. Putnam's "Unity of Science as a Working Hypothesis," in H. Feigl, M. Scriven, and G. Maxwell (eds) *Minnesota Studies in the Philosophy of Science*, Volume 2: *Concepts, Theories, and the Mind–Body Problem* (Minneapolis: University of Minnesota Press, 1958) was a somewhat later articulation of a widely shared consensus on scientific unity. An important early criticism of this view was given in J. Fodor's "The Disunity of Science as Working Hypothesis," *Synthese* 28 (1975): 97–115. P. Galison and D. Stump's volume *The Disunity of Science* (Stanford, CA: Stanford University Press, 1996) is a good collection of various kinds of dissent from seeing unification as an ideal. M. Friedman's "Explanation and Scientific Understanding," *Journal of Philosophy* 71 (1974): 5–19, and the works by P. Kitcher cited above are the main explications of the notion of explanation as unification. I have given some defenses and refinements of this view in the two essays of mine cited above, and also in my "Unification, Reduction, and Non-Ideal Explanations," *Synthese* 112 (1997): 75–96. Important criticisms of explanation as unification can be found in Barnes (1994) and in I. Halonen, and J. Hintikka's "Unification: It's Magnificent but Is it Explanation?" *Synthese* 120 (1999): 27–47. W. C. Salmon in *Four Decades of Scientific Explanation* (Minneapolis: University of Minnesota Press, 1990) gives an interesting attempt to unite unification and non-unification approaches to explanation, as does M. Strevens in "The Causal and Unification Approaches to Explanation Unified – Causally," *Noûs* 38 (2004): 154–76.

47

THE VIRTUES OF A GOOD THEORY

Ernan McMullin

Scientists are constantly involved in the work of assessing the quality of observation reports, of generalizations drawn from a set of such reports, or of theories purporting to explain why such generalizations hold. What qualities are looked for in theory assessment, the last and most complex of these? It sounds like a simple question; but, like so many simple-sounding questions in the philosophy of science, it evokes instant disagreement. Before addressing it directly, it may be best to recall something of its history.

A little history

As astronomy developed in the West, the question arose: how was one to account for the irregular motions of the celestial bodies of most interest, the planets? One sort of response was to construct elaborate mathematical formalisms that would describe and, as far as possible, predict the observed motions. The other was to go on from description to explain how those motions might be brought about. It was not easy to harmonize the two very different approaches. Aristotle proposed a complex structure of fifty-five concentric carrier-spheres that gave a plausible account of how the planets were moved. But as time went on, it was seen to account for the phenomena less and less well. On the other hand, more observationally and mathematically inclined viewers of the heavens, Ptolemy the most successful among them, constructed formalisms that were more and more complex, but also more and more difficult to interpret in terms of causal mechanisms.

Which quality, then, was one to prefer in astronomy: the explanatory facility of Aristotle's account or the predictive merits of Ptolemy's? The debate was to continue throughout the Middle Ages, the commonest response being to take explanatory virtue to testify to the truth of the Aristotelian nested spheres, while the Ptolemaic model would be favored if predictive accuracy were to be the goal. To some philosophers, Averroes and Aquinas among them, the situation seemed far from satisfactory: ideally the two criteria ought to yield the same answer (McMullin 1984).

Copernicus attempted to bring the two into closer alignment. His system had all the predictive merit of the Ptolemaic one but could in addition explain (make sense of) several features of the planetary motions, like their retrograde features, left unexplained by Ptolemy. Kepler carried this line of argument farther. Recognizing the approximate equivalence of the two systems in empirical terms, he called on an additional criterion to settle the issue between them: "False hypotheses, which together yield the truth by chance, do not ... retain the habit of yielding the truth but betray themselves" (*Apologia pro Tychone*, 1600, quoted in Jardine 1984: 140). One sure sign of this failure, he notes, is the introduction of ad hoc modifications to save the theory from refutation.

But Kepler had not forgotten about the virtue that Aristotelians had long claimed as their own. In his *Astronomia Nova* (1609), he set out to construct a physics to go with the heliocentric model, postulating an imaginative combination of attraction with swirling agencies emitted from the sun, to explain the newly discovered elliptical shape of the planetary motions. The theory was highly speculative, and he kept modifying it. But he could now claim to have harmonized two theory virtues long sundered – *predictive accuracy* and *explanatory appeal* – and to have suggested a third that could, in the long run, render a decisive verdict, separating the true from the false.

In his *Two New Sciences* (1638), Galileo did not inquire into the cause of falling motion; his two laws of motion remained at the level of (admittedly somewhat idealized) observable regularity. Descartes, on the other hand, set out to explain not only motion but the constitution of material bodies in terms of invisible corpuscles and ether vortices. He appealed very little to empirically established regularities, basing his physics rather on a combination of metaphysical principle and explanatory plausibility. Two different components were gradually beginning to separate in the new sciences: one of them specified regularities, observed or idealized, which were coming to be called "laws"; the other explained the regularities of observation and measurement by appealing, rather more tentatively, to unobserved causal structures of one kind or another, which were coming to be called "theories." The distinction is not as sharp, for a number of reasons, as this might make it appear. But it is sharp enough to allow us to maintain the distinction when discussing the topic of *theory* assessment, enabling us to set aside the very different issue of the virtues that are prized in evaluation of lawlike claims, whether empirical generalizations or idealizations.

As the seventeenth century wore on, the proponents of the "mechanical philosophy" took note of the increasingly hypothetical direction in which their science, with its imperceptibly small corpuscles, was tending and hence the need to make explicit what Boyle would call "the requisites of a good hypothesis." He himself enumerated 10 of these theory virtues, 6 of them for a "good" hypothesis and 4 for an "excellent" one. Among them were internal consistency, coherence with other parts of physics, absence of ad hoc features, and simplicity (McMullin 1990). Huygens likewise described the features one should expect in a good theory, among them the variety and the novelty of the predictions it could generate. By the latter part of the century, theory became an accepted part of the mechanical philosophy, inspiring Locke to speculate about the epistemic change this would bring about in the status of natural science itself. Despite the empiricist emphasis of the time, it was clear that empirical fit alone could not suffice in theory assessment; other virtues had to be taken into account if the epistemic goals of science were to be achieved.

Concern about the mix of factors involved in theory assessment is not as recent a development in philosophy of science, then, as one might be tempted to assume from surveying the current literature. The pioneers of modern science were, for the most part, aware that the shift to explanatory theory entailed a new and more sophisticated approach to assessment, one that would not reduce either to logical rule or to a simple saving of the phenomena at hand. That insight would frequently tend to be obscured by the forms which empiricism took in the ages that followed, as well as by some of the specifics of Newtonian theory (McMullin 2001). It was the reaction to logical positivism that launched the recent revival of interest in the issue.

Kuhn and the multiplicity of theory virtues

Its label implies that the twin pillars of logical positivism were the primacy it accorded to logic in the matter of epistemic assessment and to observation-statements as the foundation on which that assessment rested. It was the measure of support that those observation statements, and they alone, offered to the *laws* of which science was assumed to consist that constituted confirmation. Explanation was law-related, "nomothetic," in character. Theory was secondary, and somewhat problematic because of its invocation of entities not themselves directly empirically testable. Theory could be legitimate but primarily on pragmatic grounds, as auxiliary to the establishment of lawlikeness. The only virtue other than empirical fit that occasionally gained mention was *simplicity*; it was easy, after all, to dismiss its evidential force, characterizing simplicity instead in pragmatic or aesthetic terms.

Almost from the beginning, logical positivism was changing, thanks as much to pressures from within as to criticisms from without. The anomalous status of theory in the positivist scheme of things became ever more evident. The idea that confirmation in the sciences could be reduced to a rule-governed logic of any sort appeared increasingly far-fetched, not least because of the obvious, and salutary, prevalence of controversy in science at all levels. It was clear that assessment both of observation reports and of theories was far more complex, far more open to difference, than positivism had allowed.

In his far-reaching re-evaluation of the philosophy of science, Kuhn dwelt on this last point with particular vigor. Theory assessment was not to be construed in terms of rules; rather, it was to be understood as trying simultaneously to maximize a set of disparate values (Kuhn 1977). Values do not function in assessment as rules do. Rules are meant to be decisive and to be understood in the same way by all who use them. Value judgment can be much more tentative. It involves the prior experience of the person judging as well as that person's understanding of what the value in question amounts to. The potential for disagreement is evident (Buchdahl 1970).

In *The Structure of Scientific Revolutions*, Kuhn noted the way in which the values governing assessment change over the course of time:

> When paradigms change, there are usually significant shifts in the criteria determining the legitimacy both of problems and of proposed solutions... [That is] why the choice between competing paradigms regularly raised questions that cannot be resolved by the criteria of normal science... In the partially circular arguments that regularly result, each paradigm will be shown to satisfy more or less the criteria that it dictates for itself and to fall short of a few of those dictated by an opponent. (Kuhn 1970: 109–10)

Construing assessment in this way, so different from that favored in logical positivism, was a major factor in leading Kuhn to insist on the epistemically problematic character of paradigm-change. Under pressure from critics who accused him of compromising the rationality of science, however, he later altered course significantly:

> I have implicitly assumed that, whatever their initial source, the criteria or values deployed in theory-choice are fixed once and for all, unaffected by their transition from one theory to another. Roughly speaking, but only roughly speaking, I take that to be the case. If the list of relevant values be kept short (I have mentioned five, not all independent) and if their specification be left vague, then such values as accuracy, scope, and fruitfulness are permanent attributes of science. (Kuhn 1977: 335)

Instead of the values involved in theory choice being only partially shared between the proponents of rival paradigms, thus leading to intractable disagreement between them, Kuhn now makes the very different claim that the sought-after theory virtues are "permanent attributes of science" that persist as guideposts through paradigm change, thus making rational change possible. And he persisted in this view. In his late retrospective, "Afterwords," he adds simplicity and consistency to the three virtues mentioned above and adds that these criteria are "necessarily permanent, for abandoning them would be abandoning science altogether" (Kuhn 1993: 331–2).

It is time now to turn to these confirmatory values themselves to investigate how they might be catalogued and what their epistemic significance is. Calling them "virtues" rather than "values" draws attention to their status as attributes at once objective and desirable. The assessment of theory is a form of inference quite different from induction over a set of observation reports resulting in a lawlike generalization. Since it takes the form of inferring backwards from effect to cause, following Peirce it may conveniently be called "retroduction." Our inquiry here is, in the first instance, into the confirmatory virtues that guide retroductive inference.

Empirical fit and explanatory power

Empirical fit might be called the primary theory virtue. Since the first requirement of theory is to account for data already in hand, the extent to which it does so is obviously a significant measure of its success. However, departures from empirical fit can be tolerated, especially in the early stages of theory development. As time passes, however, such departures may turn into troublesome anomalies and have to be taken seriously. Coping with them quite often leads to fruitful modification of the theory rather than to abandonment.

Empirical fit should be distinguished from *empirical adequacy*, as this is defined in van Fraassen's constructive empiricism. Empirical adequacy refers to *all* of the consequences of a theory, regardless of whether they have ever actually been drawn or checked against observation. It cannot, therefore, be employed in theory assessment as a criterion. Attributing empirical adequacy to a theory is a promissory claim; it cannot be definitively made good. Empirical adequacy is a goal of theory, of course, and as such could qualify as a theory virtue but not one itself relevant to the task of assessment (McMullin 2003).

A more comprehensive theory virtue might be *explanatory power*. A formalism that merely saves the phenomena without attempting further explanation does not qualify as a theory, as that term is used here. All of the other virtues, empirical fit included, contribute to the theory's success as an explanation. If a theory lacks in any one of them, it is to that extent deficient as an explanation. In this general sense, then, explanatory power ought not be listed as a separate virtue, as though it could be separately applied in assessment. When it makes its appearance in tentative lists of theory virtues, as it occasionally does, it is likely to refer to the persuasiveness in general of the underlying causal structure postulated by the theory, to how well it fits into our causal notions generally. In that sense it is likely to reduce to one or to a combination of the other virtues still to be listed.

I argue for the relevance of a whole series of confirmatory virtues that complement the central virtue of empirical fit, transforming natural science from a mere saving of the phenomena to a genuinely explanatory and ontologically expansive enterprise. These are best described as *complementary* virtues; the labels sometimes attached to them, "superempirical" and "non-empirical," do not quite fit. There is no agreed taxonomy of these virtues but one way of classifying them is to divide them first into three easily distinguished categories: internal, contextual, and diachronic.

Internal virtues

One might look first at theory as a logical construction in its own right, abstracting from its relations to such external factors as other theories. The crucial virtue here is, of course, *internal consistency*. Though a formally inconsistent theory might in some circumstances serve as a successful short-term means of prediction, it would fail as explanation and would leave open the possibility of aberrant predictions later. Inconsistency can take less obvious forms: an unacknowledged premise might be smuggled in or the conclusion arrived at might not be the one originally announced.

A less obvious internal virtue is *internal coherence*, the absence of ad hoc features. The Ptolemaic system, as we saw, had many ad hoc features that counted against it. Each planet had associated with it, for example, a precise yearly period, either in its deferent or in its epicyclic orbital motion, yet the planetary motions were not linked in any physical way to one another. A coincidence? Ptolemy could factor it into his model in order to achieve empirical fit. But was this all that mattered? Kepler did not think so. Attaching the one-year period to the earth eliminated the coincidence, explained it away. According to the empiricist this sort of feature ought not count; one must be willing to tolerate coincidence in the interest of empiricist principle. In Kepler's eyes, it *did* count.

The internal virtue most often cited, yet also the most controverted, is *simplicity*. Some would rank it as a primary theory virtue (Swinburne 1997). Others would classify it, rather, as an indication of falsity (Cartwright 1983). Simplicity is clearly context-dependent; a theoretical physicist might be more likely to speak in its favor than would a biochemist. The practical advantages of simplicity in regard to ease of testing or of application would, of course, be generally acknowledged. And the aesthetic attraction of simplicity can undoubtedly play a role in favoring certain sorts of theories.

Admitting simplicity to epistemic status as a complementary virtue in its own right, however, runs into two immediate difficulties. First, it seems to take many different forms, Dirac for example equating it with beauty. Some of these forms, at least, are reducible to one or the other of the more easily defined complementary virtues. More seriously, the question arises: Why *is* a simple theory more likely to be true than a less simple one? On balance, it seems best not to insist on including simplicity in our list of internal virtues that play an acknowledged and distinct role in scientific theory assessment generally.

Contextual virtues

Theories are not isolated constructs; they are embedded in a wider cognitive context that must therefore be taken into consideration in evaluating the theories themselves. The first major contextual virtue is *external consistency*. Consistency with the wider theoretical context takes on a greater or lesser significance depending on the epistemic authority of that segment of the context and the degree of its involvement with the theory. This virtue, then, may be called *consonance*. Like internal consistency it draws attention to itself mainly by its absence, by a dissonance between the theory and some part of its intellectual context. But it is a positive virtue as well. A theory will almost inevitably depend in part on other related theories; the stronger their warrant, the better its own case. And its success in its own sphere will reflect well on those from which it draws support. This sort of complex relationship suggests the metaphors of harmony and consonance.

How far out does this sort of interdependence stretch? Some distinctions might help at this point.

First-level consonance would involve other parts of the sciences, as a chemical theory might make use of well-supported parts of physics. (Assessing their degree of support is a complication I have to pass over.) Dissonance at this level is rare but it does sometimes arise, as when steady-state cosmology appeared to set aside the principle of conservation of energy. The expectation is that this sort of dissonance must be taken seriously and must ultimately be resolved. Consonance at this level is for the most part taken for granted but is nonetheless significant.

Second-level consonance involves broader metaphysical principles bearing on the natural order – the principle of contact action or the principle of causality, for example, both of which have played a significant role in physics through the ages. But those two principles themselves illustrate the possibility of dissonance, the first in Newton's physics, the second in quantum theory. Principles of conservation of one kind or another are seminal in contemporary physics. Do they have some sort of independent warrant? There are complex issues here, but enough has been said to suggest that consonance at this level continues to influence theory choice.

Third-level consonance extends to broader social, political, and moral issues and convictions, and is obviously much more disputable in general. The tradition in the natural sciences has been to regard influences of this sort as "idols," as Bacon called them, potentially distortive in epistemic terms. But in recent years, the issue has become a highly charged one. The issue is not whether such factors influence scientific work in all sorts of ways – of course they do. Rather, it is whether that influence can, in some circumstances at least, be beneficial to science *as* science.

Making the point that theory is ordinarily underdetermined by the data brought in its support, some argue that there is space here in the decision process for factors judged to be worthy causes in their own right. Others urge the broader theme of science as a form of social construction and challenge the propriety of drawing any sort of principled distinction between epistemic and non-epistemic factors in the first place. The issue can only be hinted at here, but it is at least clear that it hinges on the acceptability of various forms of third-level consonance and the theory virtues that would accompany them.

The other major contextual virtue of a good theory may be called *optimality*. Scientists are obviously concerned to know whether a theory affords the best explanation available. This lies outside the bounds of retroduction, which is concerned only with the intrinsic explanatory worth of a theory, regardless of the merits of its rivals. The contingent issue of whether there *are*, in fact, any rivals and how they compare does not affect the worth of the original theory as an explanation. It seems desirable, therefore, in this (and only in this) case to go beyond retroduction when listing the confirmatory virtues of a "good" theory. Determining that the theory is, in addition, the *best* theory available has recently come to be called "inference to best explanation," a more complex form explicitly involving two separate sorts of assessment, one retroductive and the other comparative. Optimality is thus a partially extrinsic virtue, but is none the less real for that.

Diachronic virtues

The most disputed of the complementary virtues are the diachronic ones, those that manifest themselves only over the course of time, as the career of the theory unfolds. They are the virtues that one would expect a theory to display over time if the underlying explanatory structure it postulates – that which constitutes the theory as a theory – approximates to the real or, equivalently, if the theory is approximately true. These are the virtues then that reveal the merits of the theory precisely as a theory. Putting it this way immediately signals why instrumentalists and empiricists generally are likely to challenge their significance. There is no agreed list here, but three such virtues seem to stand out and may conveniently be labeled *fertility, consilience,* and *durability*.

The fertility in question is *proven* fertility, fertility already displayed, to be distinguished from the fertility one might look for in a research program, pointing to promising lines of research as yet unexplored (McMullin 1976). Fertility can show itself in a variety of ways. The one that has always excited most attention is the successful prediction of "novel" results. How exactly novelty is to be understood here has given rise to much debate, particularly in the context of Lakatos's *methodology of scientific research programs*, where novelty played a central role. The emphasis on novelty here should not be taken to imply, as it did for many in the falsificationist tradition, that without successful novel prediction, the original empirical fit can be discounted entirely as evidence, as "fudging." Provided that it was accompanied by an explanatory hypothesis, it could already claim some degree of evidential support.

What one wishes to evaluate here is the possibility that the original theory *was*, in fact, nothing more than an ingenious way of saving the phenomena at hand, the postulated explanatory structure amounting to nothing more than useful fiction. In the light of this, a "novel" prediction may be defined as one whose success would count as unexpected were the postulated structure indeed to be a fiction, unexpected because the novel result lies to some degree outside the scope of the data originally accommodated by the theory. The farther outside, the more unexpected it would be and the stronger the confirmation it would offer for the theory's ontological grounding. So, for example, the discovery in 1965 of the cosmic background microwave radiation supported the Big Bang theory much more strongly than if that datum had been part of the quite different sort of evidence around which the theory had been originally constructed. Assessing the theory here in epistemic terms amounts to choosing between just two alternatives: the postulated explanatory structure approximates to some degree to the real or it does not. Which of them is the more likely to account for the novel result and hence to be supported by it? There is an extensive literature on this issue; the argument above is a shorthand version of the realist position (McMullin 1996).

Fertility can take other forms. What is the theory's capacity to meet anomaly when it arises? Does it have the resources to suggest possible modifications, possible avenues to explore? Think, for example, of the transition to plate tectonics suggested by the theory of continental drift in geology. Or, again, recall the path from Bohr's *planetary theory* of the atom to the notion of electron *spin*. The theory in this case serves somewhat as a metaphor can in literature, pointing in directions no longer restricted to strict logical consequence. Only a theory which has a measure of truth is likely to function in that manner.

One further manifestation of fertility is the way in which a theory's causal structure is gradually filled in and elaborated on. The original atom was a featureless ball; then it was differentiated into a nucleus and orbital electrons; then nucleic structure was further developed. And the same could be said of the cell in biology or of the DNA molecule in biochemistry. What about the discontinuities that mark the history of science, of which so much has been made? There are difficult issues here, too difficult for elaboration in limited space. But it is simply a fact that there has been a steady development of detailed structures in the major natural sciences in modern times. (The most general physical science, mechanics, is untypical in that regard.) The structures in these cases are physical and not just mathematical. There are few instances where a long-elaborated structure was abandoned. The discontinuities, important as they are, for the most part lie elsewhere. Once again it was the measure of truth in the original theory that made possible the further elaboration of structure.

For a second diachronic virtue we can employ Whewell's term *consilience*, though restricting its range rather more than he did. A good theory will often display remarkable powers of unification, making different classes of phenomena "leap together" over the course of time. Domains previously thought to be disparate now become one, the textbook example, of course, being Maxwell's unification of magnetism, electricity, and light. Examples abound in recent science, a particularly striking one being the development of the plate-tectonic model in geology. Assuming that this unifying power manifests itself over time, it testifies to the epistemic resources of the original theory and hence to that theory's having been more than mere accommodation. If the unification was achieved by the original theory, however, the virtue involved would no longer be diachronic. It could still count as a virtue, now an internal one that Lipton calls "variety," if one assumes that "heterogeneous evidence provides more support than the same amount of very similar evidence" (Lipton 2004: 168). Thagard describes this distinction as one between static consilience and dynamic consilience (1978: 82–4).

Over the course of time, a theory is tested by challenges of all sorts. Survival testifies to a virtue that we may call *durability*. Popper was hesitant to allow positive epistemic merit to such survival. The more prolonged the challenge, however, the more severe the tests, the more confidence the theory inspires and the easier it is, once more, to choose between the only two alternatives: the explanatory structure constituting the theory as a theory has an entirely contingent relationship with real structure or it approximates to some degree with the real. The precise degree of that approximation cannot, however, be determined.

The diachronic dividend

This discussion of theory virtues exposes a fault-line in philosophy of science that goes all the way back to Hume. It separates two very different visions of what the natural sciences are all about. According to one, they simply provide a set of formalisms that harmonize in a lawlike format the regularities of observation and experiment so as to make possible accurate prediction and technical control. According to the other, the sciences make use of these regularities as a retroductive bridge to worlds beyond the reach of direct human observation. On one side have been anti-realists of various persuasions: instrumentalists, logical positivists, and most recently many social constructivists. On the other side are diverse realists, including, it should be said, most scientists. Two special cases may be mentioned: Kuhn, whose emphasis on the role of the theory virtues consorts poorly with his dogged anti-realism; and van Fraassen, whose brand of empiricism admits a measure of realism: it allows theory to reach out to the unobserved, though not the unobservable (McMullin 2003).

Though the members of the first group extol empirical fit as the only genuinely evidential virtue, they might allow some weight on pragmatic grounds to the internal and the contextual virtues, considered as pre-conditions. Where the two sides sharply disagree is in regard to the diachronic virtues, as is brought out by their relative roles in the debate about whether to accord extra epistemic weight to novel predictions. It is now easy to see why this debate remains unresolved, since it usually masks a deeper difference about the epistemic function of theory itself. For those who deny any sort of realist ontological status to the explanatory structures that constitute theory as theory, it is plausible to maintain that the diachronic difference between novel data and data originally in hand is irrelevant as evidence. And so it may easily seem, if what is being evaluated is no more than an instrumentally useful formalism.

For the realist, successful novel prediction strengthens the epistemic claim of a theory, its claim to respectable ontological status for the underlying causal structures it postulates. That, in turn, could improve its all-round standing even as a means of prediction. This accords with the nearly universal belief in the significance of novel predictions on the part of scientists generally. Philosophers who have challenged that significance, from J. S. Mill onwards, would be likely to find themselves also challenging the realist preconceptions of those same scientists, not perhaps realizing the link on both sides of the debate between the two strands in their philosophy of science.

Should the theory virtues outlined above be regarded, in Kuhn's phrase, as permanent attributes of science? On balance, yes, though they may well be articulated differently over time. Their efficacy in certifying the fruitful directions that science has taken in revealing the hidden structures of the large, the small, and the long past, has long since been proven, though no doubt the last word has not been said in their regard. The most important discovery in the history of science to date has been the manner in which that activity itself should be carried on and what expectations should guide it. The expectations I have called "theory virtues" have helped to shape it well.

See also Empiricism; Inference to the best explanation; Prediction; Realism/anti-realism; Social studies of science; Theory-change in science; Underdetermination; Unification.

References

Buchdahl, G. (1970) "History of Science and Criteria of Choice," in R. H. Stuewer (ed.) *Minnesota Studies in the Philosophy of Science*, Volume 5: *Historical and Philosophical Perspectives of Science*, Minneapolis: University of Minnesota Press, pp. 204–30.

Cartwright, N. (1983) *How the Laws of Physics Lie*, Oxford: Clarendon Press.

Churchland, P. (1985) "The Ontological Status of Observables: In Praise of the Superempirical Virtues," in P. M. Churchland and C. A. Hooker (eds) *Images of Science*, Chicago: University of Chicago Press, pp. 35–47.

Jardine, N. (1984) *The Birth of History and Philosophy of Science*, Cambridge: Cambridge University Press.

Kuhn, T. (1970) *The Structure of Scientific Revolutions*, 2nd edn, Chicago: University of Chicago Press.

—— (1977) "Objectivity, Value Judgment, and Theory Choice," in T. S. Kuhn, *The Essential Tension*, Chicago: University of Chicago Press, pp. 320–39.

—— (1993) "Afterwords," in P. Horwich (ed.) *World Changes: Thomas Kuhn and the Nature of Science*, Cambridge, MA: MIT Press.

Lipton, P. (2004) *Inference to Best Explanation*, London: Routledge.

McMullin, E. (1976) "The Fertility of Theory and the Unit for Appraisal in Science," *Boston Studies in the Philosophy of Science* 39: 395–432.

—— (1984) "The Goals of Natural Science," *Proceedings of the American Philosophical Association* 58: 37–64.

—— (1990) "Conceptions of Science in the Scientific Revolution," in D. Lindberg and R. Westman (eds) *Reappraisals of the Scientific Revolution*, Cambridge: Cambridge University Press, pp. 27–92.

—— (1996) "Epistemic Virtue and Theory-Appraisal," in I. Douven and L. Horsten (eds) *Realism and the Sciences*, Leuven: University of Leuven Press, pp. 13–34.

—— (2001) "The Impact of Newton's *Principia* on the Philosophy of Science," *Philosophy of Science* 68: 279–310.

—— (2003) "Van Fraassen's Unappreciated Realism," *Philosophy of Science* 70: 458–78.

Swinburne, R. (1997) *Simplicity as Evidence of Truth*, Milwaukee, WI: Marquette University Press.

Thagard, P. (1978) "The Best Explanation: Criteria for Theory-Choice," *Journal of Philosophy* 75: 76–92.

Further reading

The success of Newton's *Principia* seemed to many to deny a place, in science proper, to hypothetical inference to unobserved causal structure (McMullin 2001). No need, then, to appeal to complementary virtues! It was only with the work of Herschel and especially Whewell (*Philosophy of the Inductive Sciences*, 1847) that the discussion resumed. The decline of logical positivism led to a new revival, prompted in part by the heavy emphasis that Lakatos laid on novelty as the prime virtue of a research program: see M. Gardner, "Predicting Novel Facts," *British Journal for the Philosophy of Science* 33 (1982): 1–15. Friedman promotes instead the virtue of unifying power: "Explanation and Scientific Understanding," *Journal of Philosophy* 91 (1974): 5–19. Van Fraassen argues that invoking *any* complementary epistemic virtue leads inevitably to incoherence: *Laws and Symmetry* (Oxford: Clarendon Press, 1989). Critics respond that the charge of incoherence can be more properly laid instead against the refusal to allow an epistemic role to complementary virtue: A. Kukla, "Non-Empirical Theoretical Virtues and the Argument from Underdetermination," *Erkenntnis* 41 (1994): 157–76; S. Psillos, *Scientific Realism: How Science Tracks Ttruth* (London: Routledge, 1999). Postmodern and especially feminist philosophers tend to enlarge the scope of complementary virtues while questioning the distinction between epistemic and non-epistemic that underlies much of the discussion: see, e.g., H. Longino, *Science as Social Knowledge* (Princeton, NJ: Princeton University Press, 1990).

Part IV

INDIVIDUAL SCIENCES

48

BIOLOGY

Alexander Rosenberg

It is only since the 1950s that philosophers of science began to pay serious attention to biology. Initially philosophers used biological examples to test the claims about science that logical positivists and logical empiricists had drawn from their studies of physics. Over the same time the revolution in biological theorizing – both evolutionary and molecular – gave rise to a number of abstract questions that have jointly interested biologists and philosophers with no independent interest in assessing positivism or the post-positivist picture of science that succeeded it (Monod 1971; Wilson 1975; Dawkins 1976). Nonetheless, this work was done with enough knowledge of the details of the biological revolution and developments in philosophy of science to draw conclusions about the adequacy or failure of post-positivist accounts of laws, theories, explanations, reduction, and scientific method. This essay examines the main issues that interest contemporary philosophers of biology, issues that clearly show the relevance of biology not only for philosophy of science but for philosophy in general.

Darwin refutes Kant

Some philosophers date the emergence of biology as a separate science from no earlier than 1859, when Darwin published *On the Origin of Species*. Darwin appreciated that his work would have important ramifications for philosophy. He wrote in his notebook as early as 1837: "Origin of man now proved.... He who understands baboon would do more towards metaphysics than Locke." Darwin's other works, especially *The Descent of Man* and *The Expression of the Emotions in Man and Animals*, are full of insights subsequently taken up by social and behavioral scientists and philosophers, among them sexual selection, group selection, moral norms, and evolutionary psychology. Naturalistic philosophers of psychology (especially teleosemanticists such as Fred Dretske, Ruth Millikan, and Karen Neander), students of meta-ethics (J. L. Mackie and Allan Gibbard), a long tradition of epistemologists (Donald T. Campbell, Karl Popper), and even students of the metaphysics of natural kinds (W. V. Quine) have vindicated Darwin's prescient observations.

Darwin's theory of random, or blind, variation and natural selection, or rather environmental filtration, provides the first purely causal account of phenomena in nature that appear purposive and that had hitherto seemed to require a teleological science, all the way from Aristotle to Kant. It was the latter who famously held, twenty years before Darwin's birth, that "there will never be a Newton for the blade of grass," meaning that teleology – immanent or eminent (i.e., God-imposed design) – will always be with us. By showing how adaptations could arise through a purely causal process Darwin either made real purposes safe for natural science or banished them as mere appearances – overlays that we place on nature. Asked at various times by defenders of purpose and opponents of it whether one or the other of these was his accomplishment, Darwin diplomatically but inconsistently agreed separately with each of his mutually opposed interlocutors – Asa Gray and Thomas Huxley – that he had done both. The matter has not been settled, though once biologists had a causal account of the appearance of design, not only could they reconcile biology with physical science, but they could employ with equanimity expressions such as "design problem" and "solution," as well as "function" in both description and explanation as well as the even more anthropomorphic vocabulary of molecular biology – recognition, information, proof-reading, signal, messenger, etc. – free of the charge of anthropomorphism. That is, biology could do so if it could vindicate the scientific status of the theory of natural selection.

Doubts about the theory of natural selection have been raised repeatedly since the nineteenth century, largely owing to the difficulty of defining the key explanatory term, "fitness," in ways that do not render tautological the version of the theory targeted by its critics. For example, one version of the theory makes the principle of natural selection (PNS) a central empirical law by construing PNS as the claim that for two populations x and y, if x is fitter than y, then x will probably leave more descendants than y (Brandon 1990). But if fitness is defined in terms of differential reproductive rates, the PNS is an evident tautology (if x has more descendants than y, then x has more descendants than y) and is therefore deprived, on well understood empiricist grounds, of explanatory power. Accordingly there have been many attempts either to define fitness in ways that circumvent this problem or to provide an account of the theory which does not require the PNS. The most popular ploy has been to define fitness as a probabilistic propensity to have more offspring, and so sever the definitional connection between fitness and actual reproduction. This account is defeated by the fact that some organisms of lesser fitness have a greater probability of producing more offspring in the short term, while the fitter have a greater probability of producing more in the long term, where the short and the long term cannot easily be specified. Sometimes variance in reproductive rates is relevant to fitness, and would need to be added to the definition, and sometimes it is not, and would need to be subtracted. Many philosophers of biology were first introduced to the subject through this debate about the meaning of "fitness."

Biological laws

Charges that the theory of natural selection did not embody clear cases of scientific laws – exceptionless, universal, contingent, explanatory generalizations that support counterfactuals – led many philosophers to search for nomological generalizations elsewhere in the discipline. Candidate laws seemed easy to identify among the mathematical models of genetics, population biology, island biogeography, molecular biology, and phylogenetics. Alas, in each case, the generalizations fall foul of one or another objection. The *Hardy–Weinberg model* and *Fischer's sex-ratio model* were stigmatized as necessary mathematical truths. Ecological generalizations like the *competitive exclusion principle* were shown to be derived theorems of the theory of natural selection and, therefore, tautological if it was. Generalizations from molecular biology like the central dogma – the direction of information transfer is always from DNA to RNA to protein – turned out to have exceptions (RNA viruses, prions). Phylogenetic principles of classification and their consequences (e.g., the robin's egg is blue) employed non-qualitative predicates such as species-names, and can be undermined by arms-race competitions (if its egg being blue comes to subject robins to predation, its color will change or the robin will go extinct). Of course, each of the arguments against these candidates provoked a series of counterarguments which has made the existence of distinctively biological laws a matter of continuing interest among philosophers. Additionally, it has led philosophers interested in biology (among them Philip Kitcher, Sandra Mitchell, and James Woodward) to suggest important revisions to the account of laws and their explanatory role that was derived from physics and which standard generalizations in biology do not satisfy.

Functional attributions and explanations

Of equal and related interest to philosophers of biology has been whether biological explanation is *distinctive*, owing either to the allegedly non-nomological nature of the theory of natural selection or to the reliance of biologists on functional attributions in description and explanation. Biology's taxonomy is thoroughly functional: concepts like wing, heart, cell, gene, are all characterized by the *purposes* they serve for the biological systems that contain them; and explanations of biological processes and structures often proceed by citing the purpose, goal, or end which the process or structure serves. Ever since Harvey in the seventeenth century it has been accepted that the heart beats in order to circulate the blood. That explanation is still deemed largely correct, yet it explains a prior event – the beating – by a subsequent one – the movement of quantities of blood. As Spinoza said, such an explanation reverses the order of nature. Following the overthrow of Aristotelian teleology in favor of mechanical, efficient causation in the scientific revolution of the seventeenth century, such attributions and explanations have been a problem. Moreover, the attempt to force obvious explanatory generalizations such as "animals have hearts in order to circulate the blood" into the deductive–nomological model of explanation also faced the problem that the generalization might not be a law; additionally, hearts are neither necessary nor sufficient for beating, and adding *ceteris paribus* clauses to the explanation makes it even less testable.

Many important philosophers of science have tackled the problems raised by functional attribution and functional explanation, and there is widespread agreement that, following Larry Wright, such implicitly purposeful descriptions can be cashed in for Darwinian variation/selection scenarios. It is evident that this move puts further pressure on the vindication of the nomological status of the components of the Darwinian theory. Moreover, dissident voices have persisted in claiming that functional attributions are not always or even ever implicitly teleological and have provided alternative analyses of them. In particular, dissidents have endorsed an account of function in terms of causal roles advanced originally for functional psychological concepts by Robert Cummins. On his view, to accord an item a function is simply to identify how its capacities contribute to the capacities of systems that contain it. In advancing this view Cummins was not disturbed by the fact that, on his analysis, many non-biological items nested in larger systems would have a function for the larger system by contributing to its capacities quite accidentally. For example, Cummins's account implies that the rocks in a stream have a function for it if they contribute to its turbulence.

One attractive feature of Cummins's account is that its freedom from Darwinian adaptationalist assumptions enables biologists to identify biological structures without presupposing that they are evolutionary adaptations, instead of constraints, by-products or accidents. Claims by biologists and philosophers about the nature and inevitability of functional description and explanation in biology also provoke careful studies of how adaptation (which explains the emergence of functional traits) is related to random drift in the theory of natural selection, and this in turn made the nature of evolutionary probabilities a vexed question. The importance of the issue is hard to exaggerate, as the whole interpretation of natural selection as the evolutionary trajectory of particular lineages (as opposed to central statistical tendencies) hinges on the nature of drift.

By implicitly according any functionally characterized item an adaptational Darwinian etiology in the past, the account of such concepts derived from Wright strongly encouraged adaptational approaches across the philosophies of biology and the social sciences. Even more important, the power of adaptational thinking in evolutionary biology was increasingly manifest in the last quarter of the twentieth century by exponents of sociobiology and evolutionary psychology who sought to explain many socially significant traits by the evolutionary design problems they were alleged to solve, as we shall see below. But the initial appearance of the program of sociobiology provoked a strong response by two of the biologists most influential in philosophy, Stephen Jay Gould and Richard Lewontin. Their 1979 paper "The Spandrels of San Marco and the Panglossian Paradigm" became a lightning rod for subsequent discussion of many of these issues, including the existence of biological laws, the role of drift, selection, and physical constraint on the course of evolution, and the testability of evolutionary claims about particular terrestrial phenomena. As such, the challenge they mounted required responses from exponents of the selected effects/adaptational analysis of biological taxonomy and explanation. (See Dennett 1995 for such responses.)

Reduction of functional to molecular biology

One issue that initially appeared independent of questions about Darwinism and natural selection was whether the rest of biology was reducible to molecular biology and, via that reduction, eventually to be grounded in physical science, as some of the most prominent of twentieth-century biologists (Monod 1971) had hoped and predicted. At first, philosophers approached this problem by employing the post-positivist account of reduction and the derivation of narrower theories from broader ones, and tried to show in particular that generalizations in Mendelian genetics could be derived from generalizations in molecular biology once "gene" came to be characterized as referring to the polynucleotide sequences that realize particular genes.

Besides the many problems advanced against derivational reduction in physical science, it soon became apparent that many of the other apparently independent issues in the philosophy of biology really do bear heavily on this reductionist thesis. Among them, there is the doubt about whether there are distinctive laws in biology, whether molecular or non-molecular; if there are none, then there is nothing to reduce by derivation and nothing to which it may be reduced. Moreover, it was evident early on that molecular biology is shot through with functional attribution and explanation (e.g. "DNA contains thymine in order to discharge its function in high-fidelity information transmission"). Such attribution made any reduction of the rest of biology to it moot as evidence of reduction of biology to physical science; for functional claims in molecular biology cannot be reduced to non-functional claims in organic chemistry. Most importantly, for subsequent discussion of reductionism in biology (as well as for all the behavioral and social sciences), it was shown that multiple realizability characterizes the supervenience bases of each level of organization in biology and that this multiple realizability was due to the blindness to structural differences of natural selection for functionally equivalent biological systems. For example, a biological process such as flight can be and is discharged by forty or more different physical structures, and even so fundamental a biological function as oxygen transport is undertaken by hemoglobin molecules that differ widely in their amino acid sequences, and other physical properties. Since each different structure works equally well in oxygen transport, natural selection has been blind to those differences in selecting oxygen-transport systems. In general, the structures that accomplish almost any biologically significant function, from the level of the cellular organelle to the level of the whole social group, will be heterogeneous and so make the identification between structurally characterized and functionally characterized systems unwieldy at best and impossible at worst. All this, plus the failure to identify indisputably biological laws anywhere in the discipline, has meant that an informative debate about the prospects for the reduction of biology to physical science must turn on a complete reconfiguration of the concept of *reduction* in the life sciences. Instead of being construed as a thesis about derivation of narrower theories and laws from broader, more fundamental ones, reductionism must be viewed as a thesis about *explanations*. Since all biological explanations explicitly or implicitly invoke Darwinian natural selection, the reductionist must show how Darwin's theory can be grounded in physical science. Failure satisfactorily to do so will ensure the sort of autonomy of biology from physical science that must refute reductionism as an explanatory doctrine (see Rosenberg 2006).

Levels and units of selection

A great deal of interest in the philosophy of biology on the part of biologists and social scientists was first whetted by the debate about group selection – the suggestion that groups of individuals might have evolutionary trajectories shaped by the operation of natural selection over random variation of traits of the group as a whole and not of any of its members. This notion, repeatedly raised in the twentieth century, was the target of a number of influential biologists (G. C. Williams and, for a time, W. D. Hamilton) who sought to foreclose it with *a priori* arguments and novel evolutionary theorizing. Naturally enough, those arguments attracted the attention of philosophers, who following Elliott Sober (1984) and William Wimsatt especially, undertook to analyze the notions of *levels* and *units of selection*, to evaluate the arguments from considerations of simplicity and economy, as well as the empirical and factual arguments for and against these claims. By the end of the twentieth century, work by Sober, especially with the biologist D. S. Wilson (Sober and Wilson 1998), as well as by Wimsatt, Brandon, and Okasha (2006), had vindicated *group selection* as a significant evolutionary possibility, largely by exploiting and developing important ideas of George Price developed by W. D. Hamilton. (But see Sterelny and Kitcher 1988 for an influential dissent.) The result opens a number of sub-disciplines in the social and behavioral sciences to important Darwinian theories, theories like that of Sterelny (2003), which make random variation and natural selection – operating at the level of the group and, sometimes, without an underlying genetical mechanism of hereditary transmission – the source of important social adaptations. The group selection debate also revived interest among philosophers of biology in debates about the emergence of sexual reproduction, macroevolution and the so-called major transitions in the history of life on earth, occasions when organisms at one level of selection suddenly find themselves packaged together into large units in which the reproductive interests of the original individual organisms are sacrificed to that of the package, a phenomenon that Darwinian theory demands we explain (Maynard Smith and Szathmáry 1997).

Biology and the human sciences

All of these issues come together in the philosophical assessment of the biologization of large swathes of the social and behavioral sciences that accelerated at the end of the twentieth and beginning of the twenty-first century. From the time of E. O. Wilson's 1975 magisterial treatment of *social behavior* among infrahuman species from the insect to the primate, and his extrapolation of it to human affairs, philosophers like Rosenberg (2006) and Kitcher (1985) have been arguing for and against that prospect, employing all the tools honed in the several philosophical disputes described above. Thus, for example, some arguments against the genetic determination of socially significant traits such as gender roles, or intelligence, or incest avoidance, or alcoholism, etc., turn on allegations that the very concept of a *gene for* X is unintelligible, and indeed on even more basic claims in the reductionism debate that genes do not carry information of any kind, let alone information about, say, IQ or sexual orientation (Griffiths and Gray 1994).

On the other hand, alternative philosophical arguments against the very possibility of cultural natural selection turn on the denial that there is anything that could function in cultural evolution in the way the gene does in biological evolution. This debate is often framed in terms of whether there are "memes" on the model of *genes* and sometimes framed in terms of whether Darwinizing cultural evolution really requires any such a thing (Dawkins 1976; Dennett 1995). This is evidently an issue about the fundamental structure of the theory of natural selection and its implications for any theory of trait transmission. On a widely influential expression of Darwinian theory, it requires replicators and interactors, where the former bear three essential traits: fertility in replication; longevity in evolution; and, most of all, fidelity in transmission. If cultural change is to be a case of Darwinian natural selection, as it is sometimes held to be, then there must be some replicator in culture with these three features. Since it seems plausible that memes are not transmitted with sufficient fidelity or longevity, cultural change cannot literally be a Darwinian selection of memes. Some defenders of a literal application of Darwin's theory to explain cultural change reject both the assumption that their view requires replicators with exactly the properties of genes and the attribution to their account of having any truck with memes (Richerson and Boyd 2004).

The role of group selection in human evolution has also been a controversial subject among biologists and social scientists, so all of the debate the matter has raised among philosophers is relevant here as well. Philosophers and social scientists have been debating the nature–nurture question at least since Descartes, and in the twentieth century many psychologists have taken unintended Darwinian inspiration from Chomsky's arguments for the innateness of language from the impoverishment of the stimulus to which children are exposed and the rapidity with which they learn language nevertheless. The research program these evolutionary psychologists have spawned, together with an independent Darwinian approach to the analysis of intentionality by philosophers like Fred Dretske, Ruth Millikan, and Karen Neander (all following out ideas initially advanced independently by Bennett 1976) eventually made it clear to philosophers of biology and of psychology that their agenda of basic problems were substantially overlapping if not largely identical.

Biology, ethics, and meta-ethics

Even since before Darwin, some thinkers have sought to ground the normative in the biological. The most egregious of these thinkers was Herbert Spencer whose moral philosophy, which made whatever survived the good, quite wrongly gained circulation under the name *social Darwinism*. Independently of this normative claim, a Darwinian approach to culture holds out the prospect of providing a metathical account that begins with an explanation of moral norms and especially those of cooperation, by the employment of mechanisms of group selection, the emergence of the moral emotions, and their harnessing to norms of strategic interaction that capitalize on the individual fitness benefits of cooperation (Hodge and Radick 2003). The first stage in this program is the appropriation of results from evolutionary game theory to show that cooperation, and norms of equality and fairness, are individually fitness maximizing in iterated cases of strategic non-cooperative games such as the prisoner's dilemma, cut the cake, and the ultimatum game. Subsequent work by moral philosophers such as Gibbard on the coordination of emotions of guilt, anger, shame and disdain to maintain these cooperative norms, together with research by social scientists (e.g., Robert Frank) following Darwin on the universality of such emotion harnessed by such norms, has done much to ground cross-cultural moral agreement on biological foundations. Adding in mechanisms such as punishment strongly sustains a group-selection model for the emergence of human morality (Sober and Wilson 1998).

The more one explores the ramifications of the scientific revolution that Darwin began and the implications of the Darwinian paradigm (in Kuhn's sense) for every area of human life and thought, the more obvious it becomes that a close study of biology by the philosopher of science must have payoffs across the entire field.

See also Explanation; Function; Laws of nature; Logical empiricism; Reduction.

References

Bennett, Jonathan (1976) *Linguistic Behaviour*, Cambridge, Cambridge University Press.

Brandon, Robert (1990) *Adaptation and Environment*, Princeton, NJ: Princeton University Press.

Darwin, Charles (1859) *On the Origin of Species*, 1st edn reprint, ed. W. J. Burrow, Harmondsworth: Penguin, 1968.

Dawkins, Richard (1989) *The Selfish Gene*, 2nd edn, Oxford: Oxford University Press.

Dennett, Daniel (1995) *Darwin's Dangerous Idea: Evolution and the Meanings of Life*, Harmondsworth: Penguin.

Gould, Stephen Jay and Lewontin, Richard (1979) "The Spandrels of San Marco and the Panglossian Paradigm: A Critique of the Adaptationist Programme," *Proceedings of the Royal Society of London* B205: 581–98.

Griffiths, Paul and Gray, Russell (1994) "Developmental Systems and Evolutionary Explanation," *Journal of Philosophy* 91: 277–304.

Hodge, Jonathan, and Radick, Gregory (eds) (2003) *Cambridge Companion to Darwin*, Cambridge: Cambridge University Press.

Kitcher, Philip (1985) *Vaulting Ambition*, Cambridge, MA: MIT Press,

Maynard Smith, John and Szathmáry, Eörs (1997), *The Major Transitions in Evolution*, 2nd edn, Oxford: Oxford University Press.

Monod, Jacques (1971) *Chance and Necessity*, London: Fontana.

Okasha, Samir (2006) *Evolution and the Levels of Selection*, New York: Oxford University Press.

Richerson, Peter J. and Boyd, Robert (2004) *Not by Genes Alone: How Culture Transformed Human Evolution*, Chicago: University of Chicago Press.

Rosenberg, Alex (2006) *Darwinian Reductionism*, Chicago: University of Chicago Press.

Sober, Elliott (1984) *The Nature of Selection*, Cambridge, MA: MIT Press.

—— and Wilson, David Sloan (1998) *Unto Others*, Cambridge, MA: Harvard University Press.

Sterelny, Kim (2003) *Thought in a Hostile World*, Oxford: Blackwell.

—— and Kitcher, Philip (1988) "The Return of the Gene," *Journal of Philosophy* 85: 339–61.

Wilson, Edward O. (1975) *Sociobiology*, Cambridge, MA: Belknap Press of Harvard University Press.

Further reading

Besides the works cited above, many important papers appear in Elliott Sober (ed.) *Conceptual Issues in Evolutionary Biology*, 3rd edn (Cambridge, MA: MIT Press, 2006). For the main alternatives in the debate over the definition of fitness see Frederic Bouchard and Alex Rosenberg,"Fitness," in Edward N. Zalta (ed.) *The Stanford Encyclopedia of Philosophy* (Winter 2002 edition); available: http://plato.stanford.edu/archives/win2002/entries/fitness. Teleosemantics is elaborated by Ruth Millikan *Language, Thought and Other Biological Categories* (Cambridge, MA: MIT Press, 1984) and Fred Dretske *Explaining Behavior* (Cambridge, MA: MIT Press, 1998). Other papers on the subject are reprinted in Valerie Hardcastle (ed.) *Where Biology Meets Psychology* (Cambridge, MA: MIT Press, 1999). Most of the important papers in the controversy about functional attributions and explanations can be found in Mark Bekoff and Colin Allen *Nature's Purposes* (Cambridge, MA: MIT Press, 1998). Besides Darwin, there is no more influential evolutionary biologist than W. D. Hamilton. In *Narrow Roads of Gene Land*, Volume 1: *Evolution of Social Behaviour* (Oxford: Oxford University Press, 1996), Hamilton discusses the work on group selection of George Price "Extension of Covariance Selection Mathematics," *Annals of Human Genetics* 35 (1972): 485–90. These and related views are treated in Sterelny and Kitcher (1988), George C. Williams *Adaptation and Natural Selection* (Princeton, NJ: Princeton University Press, 1966), and William Wimsatt "Reductionist Research Strategies and Their Biases in the Units of Selection Controversy," in Thomas Nickles (ed.) *Scientific Discovery: Case Studies* (Dordrecht: Reidel, 1980), pp. 213–59. Monod (1971) is an early defense of reductionism by a Nobel Prize winning molecular biologist. Kitcher (1985) is a vigorous attack on early sociobiology while Sterelny (2003) offers an important Darwinian but not genetic account of cultural and cognitive human evolution. Daniel McShea and Alex Rosenberg *Philosophy of Biology: A Contemporary Introduction* (London: Routledge, 2007) provides a comprehensive introduction to the philosophy of biology.

49
CHEMISTRY
Robin Findlay Hendry

Chemistry attempts to understand transformations between substances. Central to this endeavor is the concept of an *element*. Elements are the building-blocks of chemistry: they survive chemical change, and chemical explanations track them from one composite substance to another, thereby explaining both the direction of chemical change and the properties of the substances they compose. The hypothesis that each element is characterized by a distinct kind of atom was controversial for most of the nineteenth century, but was broadly accepted in the twentieth century. During the same period, organic chemists developed structural formulae for chemical substances, although it was again controversial how seriously they were to be taken as representing the real arrangement of atoms in space connected by bonds. In the twentieth century there was a much closer interaction between chemistry and physics, with the application of quantum mechanics and experimental methods such as spectroscopy and X-ray crystallography, allowing deeper theoretical and empirical investigations of the molecular structures of substances. These chemical categories – *element*, *substance*, *structure* – remain indispensable to chemical explanation, and are central topics in the philosophical study of chemistry.

Chemical kinds

In the 1970s, Saul Kripke and Hilary Putnam developed a causal theory of the reference of natural-kind terms, central to which were two chemical examples: water and gold. Kripke and Putnam assumed that chemical-kind terms tracked microstructural properties, the extensions of element names being determined by sameness of nuclear charge (gold is the element with atomic number 79); and those of compound substances determined by their *chemical structure* (water is H_2O). Central to this view is semantic externalism, the thesis that the extension of a *kind* term can be determined by properties of which users of the term may be ignorant. Thus "gold" referred to stuff with atomic number 79 long before atomic number was thought of, and the twentieth-century identification of gold as the element with atomic number 79 constituted an *empirical discovery*, rather than a refinement or revision of its definition. This is not the place to rehearse Kripke's and Putnam's arguments for their view. Instead I will concentrate on the claim that the extensions of the names of chemical substances are determined by microstructural properties, beginning with a survey of different chemical kinds.

Kinds of chemical kinds, with examples

Chemists study both substances and microscopic species. They group together higher kinds of substances like the metals, groups of elements like the halogens, and classes of compounds that share either an elemental component (e.g., hydrides), a microstructural feature (carboxylic acids), or merely a pattern of chemical behavior (acids). Chemical formulae are typically ambiguous, naming both substances and microscopic species. In one sense, "H_2O" names a molecular species: an oxygen atom bonded to two hydrogen atoms. In another sense it names a *substance* composed of hydrogen and oxygen in the molar ratio 2:1. Not every microscopic species, however, has a corresponding substance: some, like H_3O^+ or NH_4^+ correspond only to (possibly notional) parts of substances. Others, like He_2, are too short-lived to characterize a stable substance, although some unstable species are explanatorily important. Carbonium ions, for instance, are positively charged organic ions formed as intermediates in organic reactions, whose structures and relative stabilities are important in explaining the mechanisms and product structures of additions to alkenes. Conversely, not every chemical substance corresponds to a single microscopic species. Common salt, for instance, contains sodium (Na^+) and chloride (Cl^-) ions arranged in a lattice, but no single microscopic species characterizes the substance.

Substances may be *elements*, *compounds*, or *mixtures*, although the distinction between compounds and mixtures may well be vague. The elements come first, since they are the components of every other chemical substance. As F. A. Paneth notes (1962: section 5), the names of the elements are used in two distinct ways. In one sense ("*free* element" or simple substance), they apply only when the element is chemically combined with no other, for instance when we say that sodium is a reactive metal and chlorine is a poisonous green gas. In the other sense ("element" or basic substance), element names apply to any state of combination: "chlorine" in this sense applies to the common component of the green gas, sodium chloride, carbon tetrachloride, and so on. The latter notion is the more general: free metallic sodium falls within the extension of "sodium," understood as the element, along with the sodium combined in common salt. It is the elements rather than the free elements that populate the periodic table and are central to chemistry. Dmitri Mendeleev constructed the periodic table by appealing to properties of compounds, not just of free elements. Paneth notes that free elements do not persist in their compounds, and so cannot explain their properties. In 1923, the International Union of Pure and Applied Chemistry (IUPAC) defined elements as populations of atoms with the same nuclear charge (i.e., atomic number), allowing that atoms of the same element may have different masses, overthrowing the nineteenth-century assumption that atoms of the same element are identical in that respect.

Microstructuralism

Microstructuralism is the thesis that the extensions of the names of chemical substances are determined by microstructural properties, and is presumably the basis of more robustly metaphysical claims that chemical substances have microstructural essences. Paul Needham (2000) and Jaap van Brakel (2000: Chs 3 and 4) argue that Kripke's and Putnam's microstructuralism is vague and poorly motivated, whether by their own account of reference or by the chemical facts. Microstructuralism surely is independent of the Kripke–Putnam account of reference. Needham (2000: 16–17) has suggested that thermodynamics provides a macroscopic criterion of difference between substances: any two different substances, however alike, exhibit a positive entropy change on mixing. So the *absence* of entropy change on isothermal mixing provides a criterion of *sameness of kind*. There is no reason why this sameness-of-kind relation may not be adopted by the causal theory of reference: "Gold is the substance that bears the no-entropy-of-mixing relation to *this*." Hence even if the Kripke–Putnam view of reference is accepted, microstructuralism requires an argument grounded, presumably, in chemistry and its classificatory practices and interests.

Consider the elements first: Kripke and Putnam took the necessity of "Krypton has atomic number 36" to establish that having atomic number 36 is what makes something krypton. However, as van Brakel points out (2000: section 4.2), krypton bears many properties with necessity: its ground-state electronic structure and its chemical and spectroscopic behavior, for instance. How, then, does the necessity of krypton having atomic number 36 entail that it is what makes something krypton? There are several problems here. One concerns the inference from necessity to essence (a more general issue that I set aside), along with the question of whether semantic intuitions are capable of establishing necessity. A more specific problem is why, among all the properties that krypton bears with necessity, atomic number should be thought to have some special status. The answer must lie in the classificatory interests of chemistry itself, as revealed in the 1923 IUPAC decision. Remember that element names apply regardless of the state of chemical combination: whatever earns something membership of the extension of "krypton" must be a property that can survive chemical change and, therefore, the gain and loss of electrons. Hence it must be a nuclear property. The two obvious candidates are nuclear charge (i.e., atomic number) and nuclear mass. Isotopes (like carbon-12 and carbon-14) have the same nuclear charge (6, in the case of carbon), but differ in nuclear mass because the nuclei contain different numbers of neutrons. There are chemical differences between isotopes, but in general they are subtle and quantitative rather than gross and qualitative. Broadly, isotopes undergo the same reactions, but at different rates, though the differences can be striking: pure heavy water (deuterium oxide, ^2D_2O) is mildly toxic because, compared with protium oxide (^1H_2O), it slows down metabolic processes by a factor of 6 or 7, which is enough to kill fish placed in it. The kinetic differences between hydrogen's isotopes are far more marked than those for other elements, however, because isotope variations are marginal effects, determined by percentage differences between their atomic weights: adding a neutron to a heavier nucleus makes a smaller proportional difference to its mass. In fact, isotope effects diminish rapidly as atomic weight increases. Reactions involving ^{37}Cl are slowed down only by a modest factor of 1.01 or so with respect to ^{35}Cl. So the isotope effect in hydrogen is an extreme case. In general, nuclear charge is the overwhelming determinant of an element's chemical behavior, while nuclear mass is a negligible factor. Returning to van Brakel's challenge, given relevant laws of nature (quantum mechanics, the exclusion principle) nuclear charge determines and explains electronic structure and spectroscopic behavior, but not vice versa. Hence the IUPAC choice of nuclear charge as defining the elements seems overwhelmingly natural, given that chemists wish to understand chemical change.

If elemental composition were sufficient to determine the identity of compound substances, extending microstructuralism to compounds would be simple. However, isomerism makes elemental composition insufficient. Isomers are distinct compounds with distinct chemical and physical properties that contain the same elements in the same proportions. For instance ethanol (CH_3CH_2OH), the active ingredient of whisky, boils at 78.4°C. Dimethyl ether (CH_3OCH_3) is sometimes used as an aerosol propellant, and boils at -24.9°C. Clearly the distinctness of these substances must lie in their different molecular structures, but the appeal to structure is vague and problematic in a number of ways. Firstly, sameness of molecular structure is a vague relation because structure is determined by continuously varying quantities like bond lengths and bond angles. That vagueness will be inherited by any criterion of sameness of substance that depends on it. Molecular species and compound substances would then correspond to overlapping (rather than disjoint) regions in a space of molecular structures. Secondly, it is not clear how molecular structure is realized in quantum mechanics (see below under "Chemistry and physics"). Thirdly, compound substances are sometimes heterogeneous at the molecular level: even when pure they are complex mixtures of different microscopic species. Water is a well-known case in point.

The slogan "Water is H_2O" might tempt one to think that bodies of water are mere assemblages of H_2O molecules, as Putnam implied in saying that the extension of "water" is "the set of all wholes consisting of H_2O molecules" (1975: 224). Needham (2000) challenges that identification however, arguing that real water is far from homogeneous at the molecular level. Firstly, in any body of pure water some H_2O molecules disassociate:

$$2H_2O \rightleftharpoons H_3O^+ + OH^-.$$

Secondly, undissociated H_2O molecules are polar, with partial charges centered on the hydrogen and oxygen nuclei. Strong interactions between these charges greatly increase the melting- and boiling-points of water, and give rise to oligomolecular species, chains of H_2O molecules linked by hydrogen bonds between centers of opposite charge, which are similar in structure to ice. In short, macroscopic bodies of water are complex and dynamic congeries of different molecular species, in which there is a constant dissociation of individual molecules, re-association of ions, and formation, growth and disassociation of oligomers.

One might still identify bodies of water with assemblages of H_2O molecules by regarding the ions and oligomers as something other than water, natural impurities that arise from chemical interactions between H_2O molecules. However, the oligomers affect water's physical properties, like its viscosity, right up to its boiling-point. Both the oligomers and the ions are involved in the mechanism of electrical conduction in water, so if they are impurities then chemists are mistaken in thinking that the electrical conductivity as measured is a property of *water*, rather than of an aqueous solution of its ionic disassociation products. The proposal that bodies of water are mere assemblages of H_2O molecules looks to be a wholesale revision of scientific usage. But what then are they?

In response to the molecular complexity issue, Needham and van Brakel see a body of water as a macroscopic object with a microstructure that can be investigated empirically, and which can be explanatorily important. But Needham and van Brakel deny that the microstructure is what makes it water. Substance identity and difference should be determined instead by macroscopic similarities and differences. One possibility is entropy of mixing, but changes in entropy accompany isotopic mixing, so the entropic criterion distinguishes substances more finely than the IUPAC definition of "element." If the IUPAC criterion preserves the extensions of element names in the usage of historical scientists like Lavoisier and Mendeleev (Hendry 2008: Chs 2–4), then it is unclear that the entropy criterion fits chemical classificatory interests. An alternative macroscopic view (see van Brakel 2000: section 3.1) takes chemistry to be a "science of stuffs," which, by manipulating and transforming macroscopic samples of particular substances, investigates their place in a "chemical space" the coordinates of which are dispositional chemical properties. On any macroscopic view, however, it would seem that individual H_2O molecules fail to count as water, because they cannot bear macroscopic chemical or thermodynamic properties. This motivates another look at microstructuralism, and how it may accommodate molecular complexity.

Suppose the microstructuralist accepts that macroscopic quantities of water can be complex and dynamic entities, heterogeneous at the molecular level, and relatively independent of the molecules they contain. This means that not every body of water can be regarded as a mere assemblage of H_2O molecules, although assemblages of H_2O molecules should still count as quantities of water, along with individual H_2O molecules. Being water should then be understood as *composition* by H_2O molecules, with "composition" understood so as to encompass both simple aggregation and the interactions in which some of the H_2O molecules disappear. After all, how else can water be made, except by creating, or bringing together, some H_2O molecules? If they do count as water, individual H_2O molecules are the smallest items that can qualify as water on their own account. Hydroxyl ions and protons, in contrast, qualify as water only as part of a larger body. (See Hendry 2008: Ch. 4 for further development of this proposal.)

Unlike biology, chemistry seems to be unified in respect of its classificatory practices and interests. The case for microstructuralism about the elements seems strong, but there is no similarly general argument for microstructuralism about compound substances, of which I considered only the one case, water. Other molecular substances are more homogeneous than water at the molecular level, and so present fewer puzzles. Yet other substances are non-molecular, and microstructuralism needs to be filled out in quite different ways. The discussion has also been discipline-specific, emphasizing the classificatory interests of chemists. The extensions of substance names in other disciplines, or in ordinary language, may be quite independent of microstructural properties. For instance the extensions of "wood," "wool," and "silk" might be picked out by causal origin rather than microstructure, allowing for a microstructural duplicate of silk (artificial silk) that is not silk. This need not undermine microstructuralism about *chemical* substances, however, because usage and classificatory interests may well vary. To take a well-known example, the term "jade" applies to two microstructurally distinct substances, jadeite, and nephrite. But even if jewelers count both jadeite and nephrite as jade, chemists will attend to the difference between them.

Chemistry and physics

The central issue in discussing the relationship between chemistry and physics is *reduction*. Although chemistry is distinct from physics from the point of view of its practice and history, the relationship has often been viewed as the clearest example of a true interdisciplinary reduction. Ernest Nagel contended: "The reduction of various parts of chemistry to the quantum theory of atomic structure now seems to be making slow if steady headway" (1961: 365). Oppenheim and Putnam (1958: 417–18) fitted chemistry into the hierarchical structure of science just above atomic physics, and they interpreted the twentieth-century unification of chemical and physical theories of molecular reality accordingly as a micro-reduction. Now chemistry studies both macroscopic and microscopic kinds, so there are two layers to the reduction issue: between macroscopic substances and their characteristic microscopic species, and between chemical microspecies like molecules and their physical bases. One may also address these candidate reductions in quite different ways, emphasizing either *intertheoretic* or *ontological* relationships. I address these in turn.

Intertheoretic reduction

Quantum chemistry is the interdisciplinary field that uses quantum mechanics to explain the structure and bonding of atoms and molecules. For any isolated atom or molecule, its non-relativistic Schrödinger equation is determined by enumerating the electrons and nuclei in the system, and the forces by which they interact. Of the 4 fundamental physical forces, 3 (gravitational, weak, and strong nuclear) can be neglected in calculating the quantum-mechanical states governing molecular structure. Intertheoretic reduction, then, requires a derivation of the properties of atoms and molecules from the quantum mechanics of systems of electrons and nuclei interacting via electrostatic forces, by solving relevant Schrödinger equations. There is an exact analytical solution to the non-relativistic Schrödinger equation for the hydrogen atom and other one-electron systems, but these cases are special owing to their simplicity and symmetry properties. Caution is required in drawing any consequences for how quantum mechanics applies to chemical systems more generally. The Schrödinger equation for the next simplest atom, helium, cannot be solved analytically, and to solve the Schrödinger equations for more complex atoms, or for any molecule, quantum chemists apply a battery of approximate methods and models which have become very accurate with the development of powerful digital computing.

Whether they address the electronic structure of atoms or the structure and bonding of molecules, many explanatory models are calibrated by an array of theoretical assumptions drawn from chemistry itself. Commentators therefore argue that explanations in quantum chemistry do not meet the strict demands of classical reduction, because the models of molecules they employ bear only a loose relationship to exact atomic and molecular Schrödinger equations (for references see the suggested readings). In the case of atomic calculations, quantum-mechanical calculations assign electrons to one-electron orbitals that, to a first approximation, ignore interactions between electrons. Scerri (2007: Chs 8 and 9) argues that although the orbitals are artefacts of an approximation scheme, they seem to play an important role in explaining the structure of atomic electron shells, and the order in which they are filled is determined by chemical information rather than fundamental theory. In the case of molecular calculations, the nuclei are constrained within empirically calibrated semi-classical structures, with the electrons moving in the resultant field. Only the electrons are assumed to move quantum-mechanically, and the molecular structure is *imposed* rather than explained.

Reductionists can make two responses here. The first is that the models are just ad hoc, but since these models provide much of the evidence for the explanatory success of quantum mechanics in chemistry, the response would seem to undermine the motivation for reductionism. The second response is that inexact models are common in computationally complex parts of physics, and do not signal any deep explanatory failure. There is something of worth in this response, but it requires that atomic and molecular models that are used in explanations are justifiable as approximations to solutions of exact Schrödinger equations, and stand in for them in explanations of molecular properties (hence call this the "proxy defense" of inexact models). This is a more stringent condition than it may sound, requiring that the inexact models attribute no explanatorily relevant features to atoms or molecules that cannot be justified in the exact treatments. The Born–Oppenheimer, or "clamped nucleus," approximation seems to offer a justification for the assumed semi-classical molecular structures because the masses of atomic nuclei are thousands of times greater than those of electrons, and so move much more slowly. Fixing the positions of the nuclei makes little difference to the calculated energy, so in calculating the electronic motions the nuclei may be considered to be approximately at rest.

However, chemical physicist R. G. Woolley argues that Born–Oppenheimer clamping of nuclei cannot be regarded as an approximation to exact quantum mechanics in this way. One problem concerns isomerism. As noted previously, ethanol (CH_3CH_2OH) and dimethyl ether (CH_3OCH_3) are different compounds with distinct molecular structures, but contain the same nuclei and electrons. If the Schrödinger equation is determined only by the nuclei and electrons present, then the alcohol and the ether share the same Schrödinger equation, and it is difficult to see how their structures could be recovered from it (see Woolley 1998). Symmetry properties pose a deeper problem. Arbitrary solutions to exact Coulombic Schrödinger equations should be spherically symmetrical, but the Born–Oppenheimer models simply replace this higher symmetry with structures of lower symmetry (see Woolley and Sutcliffe

2005). Therefore the Born–Oppenheimer clamping of nuclei cannot be regarded as an approximation, because although it makes only a small difference to the calculated energy of a molecule, it makes a big difference to its symmetry properties.

To give an example, chirality is a form of molecular asymmetry in which, for instance, a carbon atom is bonded to four different groups of atoms arranged at the corners of a tetrahedron, and is not superimposable on its mirror image. Hence chirality gives rise to a form of isomerism (the different forms are called "enantiomers"), and it has been known since the nineteenth century that in some cases the two enantiomers will rotate plane-polarized light in opposite directions, but by the same angle. Within the Born–Oppenheimer approximation, in which nuclear positions are fixed, it is possible to calculate the observed optical rotation angles. Exact solutions to the isolated molecule Hamiltonian, in contrast, ought to yield an optical rotation angle of zero. The symmetry problem is not specific to optical activity: asymmetries in molecular structures are essential to all kinds of explanation at the molecular level. Hence the "proxy defense" of the Born–Oppenheimer models seems to fail, because they do seem to attribute explanatorily relevant features to molecules that cannot be justified by exact quantum mechanics.

It is worth emphasizing that Woolley's symmetry problem has nothing to do with either the insolubility of Schrödinger equations for molecules or the computational complexity of numerical methods for solving them. The problem is not that molecular structure is difficult to recover from the exact quantum mechanics, but that it is not there to begin with. It arises from the mathematical properties of electrostatic Schrödinger equations for isolated molecules, suggesting that molecular structure might ultimately be explained through (i) non-electrostatic forces or (ii) a molecule's interactions with its environment. On the latter option, molecular structure would turn out to be an oddly relational feature of molecules. In advance of further investigation of those options, however, molecular structure seems to be an unexplained explainer in quantum chemistry.

Ontological reducibility

The confidence of classical reductionists like Nagel, Oppenheim, and Putnam was far from naive. They were aware that massive computational complexity blocked simple deductive relationships between physical and chemical theories. They were aware also that the explanatory relationship between chemistry and physics is a function of the available theories (see for instance Nagel 1961: 365). Even if reduction fails at one point in the development of science, the situation may well change, either because physics provides new theories that are more successful in this respect or because chemistry eliminates the explanatory concepts that resisted reduction, providing alternative explanations for the phenomena those concepts were used to explain. One can, however, distinguish two broad kinds of reason why chemistry might be *permanently* irreducible to physics.

The first kind of reason arises from the ways in which chemists and physicists represent, or think about, their subject matters. There might, for instance, be concepts or explanatory practices that do not fit on to or match those of physics, yet are ineliminable from chemistry, for instance because they are constitutive of ways of thinking that characterize the science. By analogy with Davidson's account of the mental, this invites a *non-realist* interpretation of the non-reducible chemical concepts, although it is a further question whether there is one *global* ontology, and whether it is physical. According to Primas (1983: Ch. 5), molecular structure is something that chemistry reads into the surface patterns of a fundamentally quantum-mechanical world. On the other hand van Brakel is ontologically pluralistic (2000: Ch. 8), seeing physics and chemistry as only two among many different levels of discourse, none of which is ontologically privileged.

The second kind of reason for the irreducibility of the chemical is more congenial to scientific realism, and concerns the ontological relationship between the subject matters of the two sciences, that is, their entities, properties, and laws. Assuming a clear distinction between a theory and its subject matter, one might describe the issue as follows: whether or not the chemically important properties of molecules are deducible from current or future physical theory, is chemistry's subject matter *nothing but* that of physics? A's being *nothing but* B is here understood to be an ontological relationship, quite distinct from any explanatory relationships that might exist between theories about A and B. Let us pursue the issue of ontological reducibility directly.

Chemical entities like molecules and substances are clearly composed of more basic physical entities. If the microstructural account of chemical kinds is broadly correct, chemical-kind membership must also supervene on micro-physical properties: there can be no change in chemical-kind membership without micro-physical change. Neither composition nor supervenience amounts to reducibility, however. Composition establishes only a weak ontological dependence that is compatible with non-reducibility. Supervenience is not an ontological relationship, being just modally robust property co-variance, and is also compatible with both reducibility and emergence (see, e.g., Kim 1998: Ch. 1). Robin Le Poidevin (2005) distinguishes intertheoretic (or as he calls it, "epistemological") reduction from ontological reducibility, arguing, rightly, that the unfeasibility of intertheoretic reduction does not settle the issue of ontological reducibility. He attempts to identify just what could count as an argument for ontological reducibility of the chemical to the physical: chemical properties, he argues, are more than merely correlated with microphysical properties; they are *exhausted* by them. All *possible* instances of chemical properties are constituted by combinations of discretely varying physical properties. It is just not possible that there is an element between (say) helium and lithium. There are two lines of objection to an argument of the kind Le Poidevin envisages (see Hendry and Needham 2007). Firstly, it applies only to properties that vary discretely, like the elements. The elements do not exhaust the whole of chemistry, however, because as we have seen, isomers are distinct substances that are identical in respect of their elemental composition, yet differ in respect of their molecular structure. Furthermore molecular structure is not discrete but defined in terms of continuously varying quantities like bond lengths and bond angles. Secondly, it is not clear just why the exhaustion of chemical properties by combinations of physical properties would establish the ontological reducibility of the chemical. Here's why not. In recent philosophy of mind, ontological reducibility has been understood in terms of causal powers: A is ontologically reducible to B just in case the causal powers conferred by possession of A-properties are exhausted by those conferred by possession of B-properties (see Kim 1998: Ch. 4). On this formulation neither Le Poidevin's combinatorial determination nor micro-structuralist supervenience is sufficient for ontological reduction, for the A-properties may confer *additional* causal powers. If, for each cluster of B-properties corresponding to an A-property, there is a *sui generis* law of nature conferring distinct causal powers that are not conferred by more fundamental laws governing the B-properties, then the A-properties are irreducible to the B-properties in a robustly ontological sense.

Is this more than a mere logical possibility? The symmetry problem discussed earlier would seem to indicate that it is. For over a century, chemical explanations of the causal powers of molecules, and of the substances they compose, have appealed to molecular structures attributed on the basis of chemical and physical evidence. Yet the existence of such structures does not seem to have an explanation in exact quantum mechanics. To be an ontological reductionist is to think that molecular structures are determined by more fundamental laws, and that the required explanation must in some sense exist, even if it is unfinished business for physics. The *emergentist* interpretation of the situation is that for each molecular structure there is a *sui generis* law of nature that can be expressed in the language of quantum mechanics, but is an instance of no deeper physical law. The issue of ontological reduction is not settled by the existence of quantum-mechanical explanations of molecular structure and bonding. Both reductionism and emergence are compatible with there being such explanations, differing over their structure and the degree to which the laws that appear in them are unified. To address the issue of the ontological reduction of chemistry is to assess the relative plausibility of those two interpretations (see McLaughlin 1992 and Hendry 2008: Chs 9 and 10 for differing views).

Apart from physics itself, chemistry is unique in the way that detailed applications of fundamental physical theories have deepened and extended its explanations. This is significant beyond the philosophy of chemistry: in philosophy of mind, arguments for the causal exclusion of the mental assume that there is evidence from science itself that the physical is causally closed, yet only rarely is the science considered in any detail. Quantum chemistry is a unique source of such evidence.

Although it is a central issue, reduction is not the only foundational problem involved in quantum chemistry. Nineteenth-century chemists attributed detailed structures to organic molecules on chemical evidence alone, decades before there was any detailed interaction with physics. Many such structures continue to play important explanatory roles in modern chemistry: with its allied notion of the chemical bond, molecular structure seems here to stay in modern science. Yet as we have seen, it is far from clear how either molecular structure or the chemical bond are realized in quantum-mechanical states.

See also Essentialism and natural kinds; Explanation; Laws of nature; Models; Philosophy of language; Physics; Reduction.

References

Hendry, Robin Findlay (2008) *The Metaphysics of Chemistry*, New York: Oxford University Press.

Hendry, Robin Findlay and Needham, Paul (2007) "Le Poidevin on the Reduction of Chemistry," *British Journal for the Philosophy of Science* 58: 339–53.

Kim, Jaegwon (1998) *Mind in a Physical World*, Cambridge, MA: MIT Press.

Le Poidevin, Robin (2005) "Missing Elements and Missing Premises: A Combinatorial Argument for the Ontological Reduction of Chemistry," *British Journal for the Philosophy of Science* 56: 117–34.

McLaughlin, Brian (1992) "The Rise and Fall of British Emergentism," in A. Beckermann, H. Flohr, and J. Kim (eds) *Emergence or Reduction? Essays on the Prospects for Non-Reductive Physicalism*, Berlin: Walter de Gruyter, pp. 49–93.

Nagel, Ernest (1961) *The Structure of Science*, London: Routledge and Kegan Paul.

Needham, Paul (2000) "What is Water?" *Analysis* 60: 13–21.

Oppenheim, Paul and Putnam, Hilary (1958) "Unity of Science as a Working Hypothesis," in H. Feigl, M. Scriven, and G. Maxwell (eds), *Minnesota Studies in the Philosophy of Science*, Volume 2: *Concepts, Theories, and the Mind–Body Problem*, Minneapolis: University of Minnesota Press, pp. 3–36. Page numbers refer to the 1991 reprint in R. Boyd, P. Gasper, and J. D. Trout (eds) *The Philosophy of Science*, Cambridge, MA: MIT Press, pp. 405–27.

Paneth, F. A. (1962) "The Epistemological Status of the Chemical Concept of Element," *British Journal for the Philosophy of Science* 13: 1–14; 144–60.

Primas, Hans (1983) *Chemistry, Quantum Mechanics and Reductionism*, 2nd edn, Berlin: Springer-Verlag.

Putnam, Hilary (1975) "The Meaning of 'Meaning'," in *Mind, Language and Reality*, Cambridge: Cambridge University Press, pp. 215–71.

Scerri, Eric (2007) *The Periodic Table: Its Story and its Significance*, Oxford: Oxford University Press.

Woolley, R. G. (1998) "Is There a Quantum Definition of a Molecule?" *Journal of Mathematical Chemistry* 23: 3–12.

Woolley, R. G. and Sutcliffe, B. T. (2005) "Molecular Structure Calculations Without Clamping the Nuclei," *Physical Chemistry, Chemical Physics* 7: 3664–76.

Van Brakel, Jaap (2000) *Philosophy of Chemistry*, Leuven: Leuven University Press.

Further reading

Two journals are devoted to the philosophy of chemistry, *Foundations of Chemistry* and *Hyle*. Two recent collections of articles covering a range of issues in the philosophy of chemistry are: N. Bhushan and S. Rosenfeld (eds) *Of Minds and Molecules: New Philosophical Perspectives on Chemistry* (Oxford: Oxford University Press, 2000) and D. Baird, E. Scerri, and L. McIntyre (eds) *Philosophy of Chemistry: Synthesis of a New Discipline* (Dordrecht: Springer, 2006). For the historical background to the identification of the elements in terms of nuclear charge, see Helge Kragh, "Conceptual Changes in Chemistry: The Notion of a Chemical Element, ca. 1900–1925," *Studies in History and Philosophy of Modern Physics* 31B (2000): 435–50. On the question of whether it was discovered that water is H_2O, see Joseph LaPorte, *Natural Kinds and Conceptual Change* (Cambridge: Cambridge University Press, 2004) and Paul Needham, "The Discovery that Water Is H_2O," *International Studies in the Philosophy of Science* 16 (2002): 205–26. On reductionism and models see: Paul Bogaard "The Limitations of Physics as a Chemical Reducing Agent," in *PSA 1978* (East Lansing, MI: Philosophy of Science Association, 1981), Volume 2, pp. 345–56; Mario Bunge "Is Chemistry a Branch of Physics?" *Zeitschrift für Allgemeine Wissenschaftstheorie* 13 (1982): 209–23; and James Hofmann "How the Models of Chemistry Vie," in *PSA 1990* (East Lansing, MI: Philosophy of Science Association, 1990), Volume 1, pp. 405–19. On the status of molecular structure in quantum mechanics, see Jeffry Ramsey, "Realism, Essentialism and Intrinsic Properties: The Case of Molecular Shape," in Bhushan and Rosenfeld (eds) *Of Minds and Molecules*, pp. 118–28.

50
COGNITIVE SCIENCE
Paul Thagard

Introduction

Cognitive science is the interdisciplinary investigation of mind and intelligence, embracing psychology, neuroscience, anthropology, artificial intelligence, and philosophy. There are many important philosophical questions related to this investigation, but this short essay focuses on the following three.

- What is the nature of the explanations and theories developed in cognitive science?
- What are the relations among the five disciplines that comprise cognitive science?
- What are the implications of cognitive science research for general issues in the philosophy of science?

I argue that cognitive theories and explanations depend on representations of mechanisms and that the relations among the five disciplines, especially psychology and neuroscience, depend on relations between kinds of mechanisms. Those conclusions have implications for such central problems in general philosophy of science as the nature of theories, explanations, and reduction between theories at different levels.

Theories and explanations: mechanisms

The primary goal of cognitive science is to explain the operations of the human mind, but what is an *explanation*? In general philosophy of science, explanations have often been discussed as deductions from general laws or, sometimes, as schematic patterns that unify diverse phenomena. It is becoming increasingly clear, however, that explanations in cognitive science employ representations of mechanisms that provide causal accounts of such mental phenomena as perception, memory, problem-solving, and learning. Theories are sets of hypotheses about the constituents of the explanatory mechanisms. Numerous philosophers of science have defended the mechanistic account of explanations in various fields (see Bechtel and Abrahamsen 2005). I now describe how explanations of human thinking involve mechanisms.

Cognitive science began in the mid-1950s when psychologists, linguists, and researchers in the nascent enterprise of artificial intelligence realized that ideas from the emerging field of computer science could be used to explain how minds work. The first operational computational model of mind was Newell, Shaw, and Simon's *logic theorist*, which simulated how people do proofs in deductive logic. That model and many later ones worked with what became the fundamental analogy of cognitive science: just as computer programs run by applying algorithms to data structures, so the human mind works by applying computational procedures to mental representations.

Many competing proposals have been made about what are the most important mental representations in human thinking, ranging from rules to concepts to images to analogies to neural networks. And for each kind of mental representation there are different kinds of computational procedure; for example, rules are IF–THEN structures that work by matching the IF part and then applying the THEN part. But all of those approaches assume that thinking is like computation, in that it applies algorithmic procedures to structured representations.

Explanations that employ computational ideas are clearly *mechanistic*. A mechanism is a system of objects related to one another in various ways including part–whole and spatial contiguity, such that the properties of the parts and the relations between them produce regular changes in the system. For example, a bicycle is a mechanism consisting of parts (e.g., the frame, wheels, and pedals) that are related to one another so that the bicycle moves when force is applied to the pedals. Similarly, according to the computational hypothesis of cognitive science, the mind is a mechanism whose parts are mental representations of various sorts, organized such that there are computational procedures which operate on them to produce new representations. No one would disagree that computers are mechanisms built out of hardware and software that enable them to perform complex tasks, and the computer–mind analogy made it possible for the first time to see how highly complex thinking could be performed mechanically. Prior to the emergence of cognitive science in the 1950s, many mental mechanisms had been proposed, ranging from clockwork to association of ideas to telephone switchboards to stimulus–response connections. But only with the development of advanced hardware and software did it become possible to understand how the most sophisticated kinds of human problem-solving, learning, and language could operate mechanistically.

Of course, not everyone in the constituent fields of cognitive science has been attracted to the computational approach to explaining mental phenomena. In philosophy there are still *dualists* who think that consciousness is not explicable in terms of physical mechanisms, but their arguments consist of thought-experiments that merely serve to reinforce their own prejudices (see Churchland 2002 for an accessible review). More usefully, a host of cognitive scientists have pointed out that we should not explain thinking solely in terms of the internal operations of the mind, but should take into account also ways in which humans have bodies that enable them to interact causally with the world. But robots can also have bodies that enable them to interact with the world and form meaningful representations of it, so the claims that cognition is embodied and situated are extensions to the computational view of mind, not replacements for it.

If cognitive explanations consist of showing how mental mechanisms can produce psychological phenomena, then psychological theories are representations of such mechanisms. Representations of mechanisms can be *verbal*, as when I described a bicycle in terms of its parts and their relations. But they can also be *visual*, as, for example, when a bicycle is portrayed using a diagram or, even better, using a movie that shows it in operation. Similarly, psychological theories are usually presented via a combination of verbal and visual representations. For example, theories of concepts are often presented by a combination of verbal descriptions, mathematical equations that describe such procedures as spreading activation, and diagrams that portray how different concepts are related to each other. Similarly, theories about how neural networks produce psychological phenomena are presented using a combination of verbal, mathematical, and visual representations. These multimodal representations of theories may seem puzzling from the traditional view in philosophy of science that theories are universal statements in a formal language, but they make complete sense if explanation is understood not as deduction in a formal system but as application of mechanisms. From that perspective, the primary purpose of theories is to depict mechanisms, and visual representations are often more effective means of representing the part–whole and spatial relations of objects in a mechanism than purely verbal representations. Later in this essay I argue that most scientific theories, not just cognitive ones, can be understood as representations of mechanisms.

Thus far, I have been discussing computational mechanisms of the sort that dominated cognitive theorizing in the second half of the twentieth century. But rapid increases in knowledge about how brains work have led increasingly to psychological explanations that are based on neural mechanisms rather than abstract computational ones. In the 1980s, there was a revival of interest in computational models that employ artificial neural networks, but until recently these were so artificial that they are more aptly classified as abstract computational models rather than as neurological ones. What were called "connectionist" or "parallel distributed processing" models are giving way to more biologically realistic ones.

Neurocognitive theories are now being proposed that have three key properties that differentiate them from their much simpler predecessors. First, their main components are *artificial neurons* that are much more biologically realistic than connectionist neurons, which typically possess an activation value that represents their rate of firing. The new wave of neurocognitive models takes into account that neurons not only have firing *rates* – how often they fire in a given stretch of time – but also firing *patterns*. Two neurons may each fire twenty times a second, but have very different patterns when they are firing and when they are resting, and there are psychological and computational reasons to believe that such patterns are important. Second, whereas connectionist models typically used *small* numbers (often less than 100) of artificial neurons to model psychological phenomena, more biologically realistic neurocognitive models usually have *thousands* of less artificial neurons interacting with each other. Such models are still puny compared to the billions of neurons operating in the brain, but they have greater capacity to capture the representational and computational power of brains. Third, and probably most importantly, the new wave of neurocognitive models takes *brain anatomy* seriously, organizing groups of artificial neurons in correspondence to actual brain areas. The brain is not just one big neural network, but is highly organized into functional areas that accomplish particular tasks, such as vision, motor control, language, and reasoning. The different areas are highly interconnected, so that there are not isolated modules operating independently, but the interconnections within a particular brain area are much denser than the connections with other brain areas. Accordingly, neurocognitive models increasingly have dedicated groups of neurons representing particular brain areas, such as parts of the prefrontal cortex, the hippocampus, and the amygdala. For examples of neurocognitive models that use more biologically realistic neurons and neural organization, see Eliasmith and Anderson (2003).

It should be evident that the more biologically realistic neurocognitive models are still mechanistic and computational. They are mechanistic in that they consist of objects – neurons – organized via part–whole and spatial relations. Neurons are parts of neuronal groups that are parts of brain areas such as the prefrontal cortex. Neurons are related to one another not just by spatial contiguity, but more importantly by *axons* and *dendrites* that connect them physically via *synapses*, making them capable of exciting or inhibiting the firing of other neurons. Hence changes in the firing patterns of individual neurons lead to changes in the activity of entire brain areas and, ultimately, to changes in behavior. Thus the complexes of neurons postulated by neurocognitive models are clearly mechanisms and theories of neural functioning are well understood as representations of mechanisms. Perusal of textbooks in neuroscience and cognitive psychology will confirm that such representations are usually multimodal, involving a combination of verbal description, mathematical equations that describe neural behavior, and diagrams that indicate spatial and temporal relations.

But are biologically realistic models still computational? The cognitive models discussed earlier are "computational" in a dual sense, in that they not only use computers to do the complex calculations required for modeling, but also postulate that minds are actually performing a kind of computation. Contrast computer models in fields such as physics, chemistry, and weather-forecasting, where no one thinks that the systems being modeled are actually doing computations. Neurocognitive models are also computational in the dual sense, in that it is reasonable to postulate that brains are actually computing by encoding, decoding, and transforming information. Hence they do not involve rejection of the fundamental analogy of cognitive science that thinking is computing, only a substantial enrichment of it in terms of more biologically realistic neural processes.

Computational and neural mechanisms are not the only ones relevant to explaining human thinking. Humans are social animals, and much thinking takes place in interaction with other people. Decision-making, for example, is often not just one person deciding alone, but groups of people interacting to work things out together. Social groups can also be understood as mechanisms, in which the parts are people and sub-groups and the relations are interpersonal ones such as communication. As indicated by the inclusion of anthropology as one of the disciplines of cognitive science, the field is open to the inclusion of the social dimension of thinking, so that attention to *social mechanisms* is a natural part of cognitive science.

Similarly, cognitive science should be amenable to moving down levels of organization as well as up. Neuroscience is increasingly paying attention to *molecular mechanisms* that explain how neurons work. That molecular biology is mechanistic is evident from explanations of the functions and behavior of cells based on the chemical reactions of their constituents, such as proteins. Explanations in molecular biology are not alternatives to psychological explanations, but complement them just as social explanations do. In the next section, I describe how such complementation works in terms of *interactions of mechanisms at different levels*.

Disciplinary interrelations

Consider the highly interesting phenomenon of falling in love, as, for example, when it was experienced by Shakespeare's Romeo and Juliet. A full understanding of this phenomenon needs to pay attention to at least *four* levels of explanation: social, psychological, neurological, and molecular. The star-crossed lovers meet at a *social* event, a party at Juliet's house; this social interaction occurs in the larger context of a feud between her family and Romeo's. Once they begin to interact, they have many thoughts about each other, for example when Romeo likens Juliet to the sun. Such thoughts must be understand in terms of various *psychological* processes, including perception, analogy, and language production and comprehension. Unknown to Shakespeare, those psychological processes have corresponding *neurological* processes, for instance the firing of neuronal groups in cognitive brain areas such as the prefrontal cortex and in emotional brain areas such as the nucleus accumbens. Presumably Romeo and Juliet experienced high levels of activity in the latter brain area as they anticipated seeing each other with intense pleasure. Finally, there is evidence that such neurotransmitters as dopamine are highly relevant to explaining what happens when people fall in love, so that the *molecular* level of explanation must also be taken into account. What are the relations among the social, psychological, neurological, and molecular explanations of falling in love?

Philosophical answers to this question are usually either *reductionist*, claiming that each higher level reduces to the next lower level, or *anti-reductionist*, claiming that higher levels are largely independent of lower levels. The most ruthlessly reductionist position would claim that ultimately everything must be explained in terms of the fundamental constituents of matter identified by sub-atomic physics, but it is hard to see how anything about quarks or strings is relevant to understanding how Romeo and Juliet fell in love. Similarly, although the fact that Romeo's dopamine levels spiked when he first saw Juliet is certainly relevant to understanding his falling in love with her, the molecular occurrences in his and Juliet's brains tell only part of the story about what was going on when they met at the party. Hence a reductionism claiming that there is a fundamental level of explanation is implausible in cognitive science.

But anti-reductionism is implausible also, as it would be folly to try to give a purely sociological account of Romeo and Juliet falling in love without also paying attention to their thoughts about each other, for example their mental representations of each other and each other's families. Hence the *social* explanation needs the *psychological* one, and there is abundant evidence from recent work in cognitive science that psychological explanations can be enriched by *neurological* ones that identify the brain areas and kinds of neural activity responsible for perception, inference, and emotion. Those neurological explanations in turn employ *molecular* processes, such as cascades of dopamine activity in the nucleus accumbens and other brain areas. So if both reductionism and anti-reductionism are implausible as accounts of the multi-layered explanation of falling in love, how can philosophers of science give a plausible account of the relations among different levels of explanation?

The ideas about mechanism described under "Theories and explanations" are very useful for describing the relations between different levels of explanation. Table 50.1 schematizes some of the mechanisms operating at the various levels.

At each level, there are components consisting of objects with relations to each other, whose interactions produce changes in the whole system. The components form a part–whole hierarchy, as when the Montague family includes Romeo, and Romeo has a mind with many representations and procedures, and his body includes a brain with numerous neuronal groups, and his neurons are cells made up of various molecules, such as proteins. The hierarchy supports a kind of ontological reductionism, according to which the higher-level entities are nothing more than the kinds of things that make them up, for example, that families are constituted by the people who make them up. But it does not support an epistemological reductionism concerned with how explanations are actually carried out. A full-blown reductionism of the kind would require that the changes at each level would have to be explained by the changes at the subordinate level, with all changes ultimately being explained at some lower level. But there are at least two reasons why an understanding of mechanisms would not work that way.

First, we often have a good understanding of how a mechanism works without being able to say how it arises from subordinate mechanisms. For example, there are many social mechanisms, verbal and non-verbal communication for instance, that can be described in detail without knowing all the psychological mechanisms that make them

Mechanisms	Components	Relations	Interactions	Changes
Social	Persons and social groups	Association, membership	Communication	Influence, group decisions
Psychological	Mental representations such as concepts	Constituents, associations, implication	Computational processes	Inferences
Neural	Neurons, neural groups	Synaptic connections	Excitation, inhibition	Brain activity
Molecular	Molecules such as neurotransmitters and proteins	Constituents, physical connection	Biochemical reactions	Transformation of molecules

Table 50.1 Constituents of mental mechanisms

possible. Similarly, there are currently good computational theories of inference and problem-solving that work well at the psychological level even though the specific neural mechanisms that support them are little understood. Given the enormous complexity of social, psychological, and neural mechanisms, it is unlikely that we will ever be able to fill them out fully at the molecular level, let alone the subatomic physics level.

Second, the interactions between levels are not always upward, from molecular to neural to psychological to social. For example, the best explanation of why Romeo has molecules of cortisol circulating in his bloodstream at a particular time may not operate purely at the molecular level, but should also take into account the social fact that Romeo has encountered members of the opposing clan, the psychological fact that he believes them to be hostile, the neural fact that his amygdala has neurons firing rapidly in a fear response, as well as the molecular fact that amygdala activity had activated his glands to pump out more cortisol, a hormone influenced by stress. Hence a social mechanism – interaction of conflicting groups – is a key part of the explanation of what happens to the molecular mechanism of cortisol production. Intervening between these two levels are the other two, because the social interaction produces mental representations comprised by neural activity that causes changes in cortisol levels. Hence explanation of why Romeo and Juliet fell in love operates best at multiple, linked levels, invoking all the relevant mechanisms.

These two reasons show why we should not expect there to be a purely neuro-chemical theory of falling in love. The neurochemistry should not be ignored, as dopamine activity in the brain's reward areas is undoubtedly part of the process by which two people become romantically attached to each other. But all the other levels are highly relevant as well, including the *social* level concerning the kinds of group-based interactions that Romeo and Juliet had, the *psychological* level concerning the mental representations that they have of each other and their situation, and the *neural* level concerning how their brains process information about each other. We are unlikely ever to have enough knowledge of all the relevant mechanisms to be able to reduce the social to the molecular, and even if we did we would have to appreciate that the explanations do not all proceed from lower to higher levels. For example, to understand why both Romeo and Juliet have high dopamine levels we would have to cite the relevant *social* fact that they are gazing into each other's eyes, the relevant *psychological* fact that they have mental representations about each other, and the relevant *neural* fact that neurons are spiking rapidly in their brains' reward areas.

Figure 50.1 illustrates a multilevel, multidisciplinary explanation of why Romeo fell in love with Juliet, including social, psychological, neurological, and molecular factors.

Table 50.1 provided a more specific view of what the components, interactions, and changes are at each level. The resulting picture is partly reductionist in that it shows how components at each level can be constituted by components at the lower level, for example, when social groups are understood to consist of individual thinkers. It is reductionist, also, in that the interactions at each level are to be understood, at least in part, in terms of interactions at lower levels, for example, when people communicate

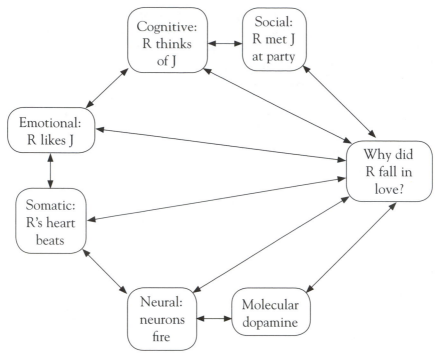

Figure 50.1 Sketch of a multilevel mechanistic explanation of why Romeo fell in love. A full causal picture would have more arrows.

with one another by virtue of psychological processes of language production and comprehension. But it is emphatically *not* reductionist in that the characterization of components, interactions, and changes at each level does not have to be fully specified in lower-level terms. Moreover, the bi-directional arrows allow changes at a higher level to causally produce changes at the lower levels, as in my examples of social conflict increasing cortisol and lovers' gazes increasing dopamine.

Thus the relations among different disciplines in cognitive science involve representations of mechanisms operating at different levels. Anthropology, psychology, and neuroscience illustrate interactions among the social, psychological, neural, and molecular levels of explanation. Linguistics cuts across these levels, as the use of language is clearly a social and a psychological phenomenon that is carried out in specifiable brain areas governed by molecular processes such as genetics. Because cognitive science supports the materialist view that mental changes can be wholly explained naturalistically in physical terms, the philosophical position defended here can be called "multilevel mechanistic materialism."

Where does philosophy fit in cognitive science? Some philosophers see themselves as standing above the sciences, using *a priori* reflection to critique the conceptual confusions that arise there. Others see philosophy as providing under-laborers to clear away some of the rubbish that lies in the way of the development of scientific knowledge. My own view is that the interconnection between science and philosophy is much tighter than either of these more common views reflects. Philosophy of mind and cognitive science are tightly intertwined, with philosophical reflections ideally going hand in hand with scientific developments in fields such as anthropology, psychology, neuroscience, and molecular biology. Philosophy differs from the sciences in two main ways: in its concerns with very general matters and with normative issues.

Philosophy has greater generality than particular sciences that concern themselves with a narrower range of phenomena, as psychologists, for example, seek explanations of processes such as perception, memory, and problem-solving. Such topics are of great philosophical interest, but they are only part of a more general concern with the nature of knowledge and existence. The generality of philosophy makes it of great importance to an interdisciplinary field such as cognitive science, because philosophy can attend to the full range of phenomena concerning the mind studied by people in different fields, and help to provide some of the theoretical glue that holds them all together.

The second way that philosophy differs from specific cognitive sciences is that it is concerned not only with how thinking works but also with how it can work better. Epistemology and ethics are both fields that are essentially normative, the former concerned with how people ought to think if their thinking is to constitute knowledge, and the latter concerned with how people ought to treat each other. Theories about how people ought to think and how they ought to act should be connected with scientific theories about how people *do* think and act, but the connections are not so simple that the normative concerns of epistemology and ethics can be dispensed with in favor of purely descriptive matters. For description of how the normative issues of philosophy can cohere with empirical matters, see Thagard (2000).

That completes my picture of how the different disciplines of cognitive science are related to each other. Philosophical reflection on the nature of theories, explanations, and mechanisms provides a way of seeing how disparate disciplines can cooperate to promote understanding of the nature of mind and intelligence. Now I describe how this view of the nature of scientific activity has important implications for philosophy of science in general.

General philosophical implications

Cognitive science is not only a subject for discussion in the philosophy of science, like other special sciences; it is also a source of new ways of thinking about the structure and growth of scientific knowledge, with implications for general questions about the nature of theories, explanations, justification, and discovery. This section reviews some of the general contributions that cognitive science can make to the philosophy of science.

Much of twentieth-century philosophy of science was dominated by the philosophical views of the logical positivists, who understood scientific theories as formalized statements in logical systems and explanations as deductions in such systems. Many problems were identified with logical analyses of scientific theories and explanations, but it was difficult to see what might be an alternative to giving a rigorous and insightful account of scientific knowledge. Some philosophers turned to other formal methods, such as set theory and probability theory, to attempt to provide richer accounts of scientific practice, but mapping them onto actual scientific theories and reasoning has been problematic. Other philosophers of science have taken a more historical approach, but have had to resort to vague notions, like the paradigms of Thomas Kuhn and the research programs of Imre Lakatos, to describe the structure and development of scientific knowledge.

Cognitive science provides a whole new set of intellectual tools for addressing issues in the philosophy of science, and cognitive accounts have been proposed by such philosophers as Lindley Darden (2006), Ronald Giere (2002), Nancy Nersessian (2002), and myself (1992, 1999). On my version of the cognitive approach, we should think of a scientific theory as a complex mental representation, a structure in human brains that contributes to various mental processes. The nature of these mental representations varies with different sciences, and not all sciences seem to work with theories that are mental representations of mechanisms of the sort I discussed above as appropriate for theories in cognitive science. Some do: biological theories such as genetics and evolution by natural selection can naturally be understood as representations of mechanisms, and so can many theories in chemistry and many areas of physics. But mathematical theories at the quantum level or qualitative theories in sociology may need to be understood as representations of a different sort.

If theories are mental representations, then explanations are mental processes that apply the theories to mental representations of phenomena to be explained. How this works is best understood by means of computer programs such as the one described in Thagard (1988). It is possible to develop computational models of scientific thinking that have just as much rigor as models relying on formal logic, set theory, and probability theory, but with much greater applicability to actual scientific theories and their uses. The mental representations that constitute theories are usually verbal and mathematical, but they can also be visual, as we saw with the representations of mechanisms discussed earlier.

Many philosophers, such as Frege, have thought that the sort of naturalistic, psychologistic account of reasoning that cognitive science offers is incompatible with rationality and objectivity. On the contrary, an approach to the theory of knowledge based on cognitive science can avoid the sheer irrelevance that models based on formal logic and probability theory have to actual scientific practice. Computational models of scientific reasoning can be intended not merely as descriptive of how scientists think but as normative of scientific thinking at its best. For example, my theory of explanatory coherence, which has been used to model many important episodes of scientific reasoning, including major scientific revolutions, is both descriptive and normative (Thagard 1992, 1999, 2000). It enables us to see how theory evaluation is both a process that occurs in actual human minds and a process that can be thoroughly rational when done right. Because the theory has a direct connection with human psychology, it can also tie in with explanations of cases where rationality fails, for example, where personal motivations lead scientists to ignore evidence and alternative theories in ways that make their coherence-based inferences less than rational (Thagard 2006).

Within logic-based approaches to the philosophy of science, it is difficult to say much about the nature of discovery, one of the most exciting aspects of scientific practice. But if theories are mental representations, then their construction can be explained by specifying mental processes that generate new hypotheses, such as analogy and abductive inference. Claims about processes that are supposed to be sufficient to generate discoveries can be evaluated by building computer programs to see if the processes are computationally feasible and sufficiently powerful to produce the desired discoveries. For example, cognitive scientists have developed computational models of how analogies can be used to generate scientific discoveries.

Hence, just as computational modeling has provided a powerful set of tools for understanding psychological and neurological processes; it can be used also to address central issues in the philosophy of science concerning epistemological processes. Philosophers do not typically have these tools, but they can be acquired by developing familiarity with the relevant theories and methods from cognitive psychology, neuroscience, and artificial intelligence. A new direction for work in philosophy of science from a cognitive science perspective will develop models of how the brains of human scientists function to understand complex phenomena. For example, Thagard and Litt (forthcoming) have developed a computational model of how thousands of neurons can operate to generate explanations of surprising phenomena. Another promising area of general philosophical research might be to apply the mechanism-based account of interdisciplinary relations that I gave for cognitive science to other combinations of fields, producing a more general theory of reductionism and its limits.

See also Biology; Explanation; Mechanism; Psychology; Reduction; Representation in science; Scientific discovery; The role of logic in philosophy of science; Social sciences.

References

Bechtel, William and Abrahamsen, A. A. (2005) "Explanation: A Mechanistic Alternative," *Studies in History and Philosophy of Biology and Biomedical Sciences* 36: 421–41.

Churchland, P. S. (2002) *Brain-Wise: Studies in Neurophilosophy*, Cambridge, MA: MIT Press.

Darden, Lindley (2006) *Reasoning in Biological Discoveries*, Cambridge: Cambridge University Press.

Eliasmith, Chris and Anderson, Charles (2003) *Neural Engineering: Computation, Representation, and Dynamics in Neurobiological Systems*, Cambridge, MA: MIT Press.

Giere, Ronald (2002) "Scientific Cognition as Distributed Cognition," in P. Carruthers, S. Stich, and M. Seigal (eds) *The Cognitive Basis of Science*, Cambridge: Cambridge University Press, pp. 285–99.

Nersessian, Nancy (2002) "The Cognitive Basis of Model-Based Reasoning in Science," in P. Carruthers, S. Stich, and M. Siegal (eds) *The Cognitive Basis of Science*, Cambridge: Cambridge University Press, pp. 133–53.

Thagard, Paul (1988) *Computational Philosophy of Science*, Cambridge, MA: MIT Press–Bradford Books.

—— (1992) *Conceptual Revolutions*, Princeton, NJ: Princeton University Press.

—— (1999) *How Scientists Explain Disease*, Princeton, NJ: Princeton University Press.

—— (2000) *Coherence in Thought and Action*, Cambridge, MA: MIT Press.

—— (2006) *Hot Thought: Mechanisms and Applications of Emotional Cognition*, Cambridge, MA: MIT Press.

Thagard, Paul and Litt, Abninder (forthcoming) "Models of Scientific Explanation," in R. Sun (ed.) *The Cambridge Handbook of Computational Cognitive Modelling*, Cambridge: Cambridge University Press.

Further reading

For an accessible interdisciplinary introduction to cognitive science, see P. Thagard, *Mind: Introduction to Cognitive Science*, 2nd edn (Cambridge, MA: MIT Press, 2005). An account of the history of cognitive science is M. Boden's *Mind as Machine: A History of Cognitive Science*, 2 vols (Oxford: Oxford University Press, 2006). On the philosophy of cognitive science, introductions include A. I. Goldman's *Philosophical Applications of Cognitive Science* (Boulder, CO: Westview Press, 1993) and A. Clark's *Mindware: An Introduction to the Philosophy of Cognitive Science* (New York: Oxford University Press, 2001). For an excellent discussion of explanation and mechanisms in neuroscience, see C. F. Craver, *Explaining the Brain* (New York: Oxford University Press, 2007).

51

ECONOMICS

Uskali Mäki

Economists about economics

Economics is a controversial discipline: the highly successful "queen of the social sciences" as well as the miserable "dismal science." No wonder there is ongoing philosophical debate around issues of justification.

From Nassau Senior and John Stuart Mill in the 1830s to Lionel Robbins in the 1930s, there was a dominant conception among practicing economists about the structure and justification of economic theory. One idea was that the premises or postulates (later to be called "assumptions") of economic theory were by and large true: they capture the key causal factors that are in operation in producing economic phenomena – such as the selfish pursuit of maximum wealth by agents and of diminishing returns in agriculture. While these were confirmed by ordinary experience, the predictions of economic theory are not typically well confirmed by evidence. The reason is that the theory is incomplete: it captures only a limited portion of the multiplicity of the causes that jointly influence the actual economic outcomes. The accuracy of predictions is thus not a reliable indicator of its truth. As Mill says, a theory may be true in the abstract – in the absence of disturbing causes – without being true in the concrete – when the disturbing causes are allowed to make their contribution. Another way was to say that a theory describes tendencies towards those outcomes rather than regularities among them or between them and their causes.

Confirmation of economic theory thus rested on the assurance that the premises are correct rather than on checking the predictive implications against evidence. Testing by implications as in the hypothetico-deductive view does not work in economics. One starts rather by isolating component causes and making well-supported claims about them, and then, in applying the theory, proceeds to add them to one another as in vector addition. The method is that of decomposition and composition, analysis and synthesis, or isolation and de-isolation. This method was often justified by appeal to a special characteristic of economics: we have relatively easy access to the key causes of economic phenomena by way of ordinary experience, thus there is no need for conjecture and lengthy inference about hidden unobservables as in the natural sciences.

Up to the present day, there have been critical voices insisting on a different approach. These included many German and British historicists (in the nineteenth century) and North American institutionalists (in the early twentieth century). Their objection was that conventional theory has taken the decomposition of causes too far: the causes interact and constitute larger wholes, the parts of which cannot be isolated from one another without distorting important facts about social reality. Economics should have a broader scope and be flexible about its disciplinary boundaries. The critics also argued that the claims made about those component parts, especially about self-interested maximizing, were evidently incorrect descriptions of human behavior. Those charges remain common today. Many of the critics also insisted that economists should start their investigations by collecting lots of empirical data and only gradually generalize the regularities discovered therein.

From a Millian point of view, this is wrong. Empirical data manifest the functioning of multiple causes in irregular combinations and thus cannot provide a reliable basis for generalization (or testing). This was argued by Carl Menger (1883), who launched the famous *Methodenstreit* against the German historicists. He outlined a version of the Millian account with Aristotelian characteristics. Economic theory is about general *types* and *typical relations*. Of these, *exact laws* depict *de re* necessities that derive from individuals' economizing action; they are Aristotelian, second-order universals that connect first-order universals. Exact laws, such as the law of demand, do not permit exceptions, while empirically established regularities do. The historicist method was capable only of producing the latter. But exact laws are unable to yield reliable and accurate predictions of phenomena in the complex actual world: they are exceptionless only in the simple world of economic universals.

The discrepancy between what is predicted and what is observed has remained a chronic issue that shows no sign of going away. Nevertheless, the legend has it that the Millian tradition was left behind in the 1950s with Fritz Machlup's and Milton Friedman's contributions. The burden of justification was then put on the predictive implications rather than the assumptions of a theory. This can be seen as a strategic response to the challenges leveled against the neo-classical theory that they defended. In empirical studies carried out in the UK and the USA in the late 1930s and early 1940s, the profit-maximization assumption had been questioned. That gave rise to the "marginalist controversies" in which the issue was whether business managers maximize profits by producing quantities of goods that equate marginal cost and marginal revenue, and if they do not (and the empirical studies showed they indeed do not), whether this would undermine neo-classical theory. Machlup and Friedman put forward arguments suggesting that such assumptions do not need to be realistic in order for the theory to be just fine. All that matters is *predictive* performance. Methodological debate in economics in the 1950s and the 1960s was dominated by that theme, and it continues.

Testability and progress: Popper and Lakatos

Prior to the 1970s, philosophical and methodological reflection on economics was provided mostly by working economists. During that decade, the philosophy and methodology of economics started taking shape as a separate research field, prompted by changes in economics and in the philosophy of science. Themes and concepts adopted from Karl Popper and Imre Lakatos first became popular. This was largely due to authors who worked at the interface of the philosophy and history of economics and who were concerned that economists had accepted theories without sufficiently strong evidential warrant. Others looked for ways of discriminating between schools of economic thinking that again had started to proliferate. Popper and Lakatos seemed to offer appropriately stringent standards for assessing – and improving – a discipline that aspired to be an empirical science.

In 1938, Terence Hutchison had incorporated *falsificationist* elements in his otherwise logical positivist account of economic theory. Between years 1957 and 1963, Popper's falsificationism was more seriously entertained by the "M²T" group of economists and philosophers at the London School of Economics. They examined a variety of economic theories against falsificationist standards, and concluded that there is an irresolvable tension: economic theories are not strictly falsifiable. One of them had to go, and it was falsificationism that was to be sacrificed (see De Marchi 1988).

In the 1970s, falsificationism made a comeback, both in Popper's and in Lakatos's modified versions. It was again soon concluded that any simple version of falsificationism in economics would be descriptively inadequate and normatively utopian, thus in a sense itself falsified – even though commentators, like Mark Blaug (1992 [1980]), kept insisting that economists should just try harder to meet falsificationist standards. Others, like Larry Boland, have defended Popper's more general doctrine of critical rationalism.

Lakatos's *methodology of scientific research programs* (MSRP) has enjoyed a longer life. It was introduced to economics by Spiro Latsis, a student of Lakatos, soon to be adopted by others (Latsis 1976). Fifteen years later, it was almost unanimously dropped (De Marchi and Blaug 1991). Meanwhile, numerous applications and case studies were undertaken and employed in arguments either about economics or about Lakatosian methodology. Research programs were identified by formulating their hard cores, protective belts, and heuristics, and they were assessed in terms of progress (De Marchi and Blaug 1991).

The MSRP had obvious advantages. It helped see that the unit of assessment is larger than a single hypothesis or theory, and that not all parts of a theory are equally flexible when confronted with empirical evidence. It helped highlight the ongoing adjustment of theories in economics. The idea of predicting novel facts captured a notion held by many economists: predicting data that were not used in the construction of a model yields it greater support than predicting data that were so used.

When applied to economics, the MSRP suffered from obvious problems. The identification of research programs – choosing their scale and drawing their boundaries – turned out to be somewhat arbitrary, making it unclear how one can assess their relative performance in a sensible way. The hard cores of many candidate programs are not as hard as the MSRP would require. The MSRP lacks other resources needed for recognizing programs as rivals that can be reasonably compared; that would require pointing out their shared goals. This is made harder by further problems in reliably identifying cases of progress and degeneration. And, again, economists' actual decisions as to whether to accept or reject a program seemed to have little to do with their apparent progress or degeneration.

Popperian and Lakatosian frameworks were dropped also because they lacked the resources needed for addressing many core issues in the philosophical reflection on economics. Much has happened after (and parallel to) this episode, such as philosophical analyses of causation in macro-economics and econometrics, and of experimental economics, by specialists like Kevin Hoover and Francesco Guala (see Further reading). In what follows I select four other core themes: theoretical models; rhetoric of economics; use of economics in the socialization of the philosophy of science; and the interdisciplinary relations of economics.

Models and their assumptions

There are many kinds of models in economics, such as large-scale econometric forecasting models and small-scale theoretical models. Forecasting models have their own associated philosophical issues, but the focus of most of the philosophy of economics has been on *theoretical* models.

To make progress in investigating the issues of empirical testing, one needs to have an understanding of what exactly is being tested, and what kind of performance it is tested for. This is a precondition that has not been fully met by the Popperian–Lakatosian episode that can be seen as a detour that ignored the Millian heritage. That heritage has been upheld – but not in one choir – by Daniel Hausman (1992), Nancy Cartwright (1989), and myself (1992), of whom the last two have also been influenced by the work of the Poznan School on idealizations and the Aristotelian tradition.

The most central issue in the philosophy of economics derives from the popular complaint that economics employs imaginary models with highly unrealistic assumptions, therefore failing to offer true accounts of the real world. Economists often react by saying that all models are false anyway. Or they follow Milton Friedman's influential advice (1953): it does not matter even if the assumptions of a model are false, provided its predictions succeed. Those responses have inspired the conclusion that economists generally are inclined towards an *instrumentalist* conception of theory and model. Friedman's view is instrumentalist, and so are others appealing to Friedman's arguments. Among the premises of this interpretation are these two: the truth-value of a model is essentially dependent on the truth-values of its assumptions; and instrumentalism views models as false tools of inquiry.

Such conclusions have been hasty in that they are not based on any detailed examination of the structure of models and the various roles that assumptions play in those models. The first premise of the received view of economic instrumentalism must be rejected: the truth-value of a model cannot be derived from the truth-values of its assumptions. There are other ways of interpreting economic theory and model.

While some thinkers (such as Mary Morgan – see Further reading) have focused more on how models function in actual research practice, others have tried to analyze the structure of models from the point of view of the question of how they are – or fail to be – connected to the real world. In Hausman's 1992 account, a model as such contains no claims about the real world, it is rather a definition of a predicate given by the assumptions of the model, and such definitions are not truth-valued. Models as bundles of assumptions define predicates such as "... is a Keynesian system" and "... is a general equilibrium system," and economists examine the properties of such predicates in exercising *conceptual exploration*. On the other hand, *theoretical hypotheses* are truth-valued claims about the applicability of the models to real economic systems. "The Greek economy is a Walrasian system" is one such true-or-false hypothesis.

My worry about this account is that the original suspicions about utterly false economic models would remain intact. Theoretical hypotheses would not perform any better in truth acquisition than if models were directly considered as truth-bearers. They would turn out to be false just as often as models would. The source of this trouble is the same: models play a role in both approaches in their entirety, including all their unrealistic assumptions. "The Greek economy is a Walrasian system" is as false as the general equilibrium model described in terms of the usual, highly unrealistic, Walrasian assumptions if the model is indiscriminately taken as a unitary truth-bearer.

The alternative is to take the truth-bearer to be more limited and to be clear about the special roles played by false assumptions. The intended truth-claim when using a model is often about a real dependence relation or a powerful causal mechanism, its structure and characteristic way of functioning. The role of false assumptions is to help isolate that mechanism from other influences. This allows us to reject popular beliefs held by economists: "This model is based on false assumptions, therefore the model is false" is as false as the claim "No model can capture the whole complexity of the real world, therefore all models are false."

The key is to examine the roles that assumptions play within models. Their role is not one of assertion. No truth-claim, no belief in their truth is involved, not even a conjecture that they might be true. The function of many assumptions is to neutralize other factors the influence of which is not considered in the model – and thereby to isolate a limited set of factors for closer inspection. One makes idealizing assumptions about the absence, zero-strength, constancy, and normalcy of those other things. Such assumptions are believed to be (always or much of the time) false if considered as truth-claims.

On that account, theoretical models are analogous to ordinary experiments in which such isolations are based on causally effective material controls. In theoretical models, such controls are accomplished by idealizing assumptions. In both cases, the goal is to acquire truthful information about some major dependence relation or the operation of a causal mechanism (Mäki 1992). Employing this way of framing things, the received interpretation of Friedman (1953) as an instrumentalist statement can be questioned: he defended unrealistic assumptions from a realist point of view.

From another perspective, one can show that apparently false assumptions can often be paraphrased so as to turn them into candidates for true claims. Many assumptions appear falsely to assume that some quantity is zero (closed economy, zero transaction costs, time needed for adjustment). Some of them serve to remove from consideration factors that are supposed to be causally weak or otherwise irrelevant, in which case the assumption may be used to make the true assertion that such a factor is negligible for the purposes at hand (negligibility assumption: actual foreign trade makes a negligible impact on the outcome). In case such a factor is causally strong, the claim intended may be to suggest that it will be included later on by relaxing the false assumption (early-step assumption: the closed economy assumption is to be relaxed in later versions of the model); or else to use the assumption for fixing the domain of application of the model (applicability assumption: the model applies only to circumstances in which foreign trade has a negligibly small effect) (Musgrave 1981; Mäki 2000).

Consider then the very concept of model. Models can be viewed as representations in that they serve as representatives of what they represent – as surrogate or substitute systems of the target systems. One directly examines the model in order to acquire indirectly information about the target system. Animal subjects are examined to learn about human beings; miniature airplanes are examined in artificial wind-tunnels to learn about the prospective behavior of real airplanes in non-artificial conditions; systems of mathematical equations are studied in order to learn about the Big Bang; imagined simple $2 \times 2 \times 2$ worlds containing only two countries, two goods and two factors of production are studied to learn about the mechanisms of comparative advantage in international trade. Indeed, models are of a broad variety of kinds, and they can be described using a variety of media, such as mathematical equations, flowchart diagrams, and verbal stories. An implication of this account is that ordinary material experiments also count as models.

The long tradition of blaming economic models for being out of touch with the real world can be translated into the suspicion that models are treated as nothing but surrogate worlds, without the right kind of further connection with the real world. Accordingly, economists take the easy route of examining the properties of the model systems while not bothering themselves with the effort of determining how they are related to the properties of real systems. Economists would be missing another aspect of models as representations: *resemblance*. It is trivial that models do not resemble the target systems in all respects and in all details, hence the thought that all models are false. But a model has to resemble the target system in relevant respects and in sufficient details in order to serve as an adequate representative. As soon as one is clear about what exactly a model is intended to represent – such as one tiny mechanism among many others – the question about its truth can be raised. The whole truth is not the goal. One pursues only truths about partial aspects of a total situation. Models may in principle be true – nothing-but-true – about such partial aspects.

Robert Sugden's account of models as "credible worlds" (2002) fits in that framework. Models have to be such that the imaginary worlds they describe – such as segregated housing markets in Thomas Schelling's checkerboard models of cities – are factually possible worlds in that what causes those imaginary worlds to work the way they do is plausible, given our beliefs about their constituent elements and causes in the actual world. This enables an inductive move from model worlds to the actual world: by examining a number of closely related model worlds (e.g., checkerboard cities) one discovers the same mechanism producing the same outcome (thereby establishing its robustness) and infers to the conclusion that the mechanism is in operation also in the actual world (in real-world cities). If one wants to call this "testing," it is different from testing according to hypothetico-deductivism.

Rhetorical persuasion and truth

The frustrations with falsificationism in economic methodology not only gave a boost to a renewed interest in the Millian tradition and its elaborations, but they also encouraged the spread of emerging social constructivist trends: given that the fate of theories is not determined by incorrupt empirical evidence, there is ample room for social factors to play a role. An early start was made by the rhetoric of economics, on which the work by Deirdre McCloskey and Arjo Klamer (see Klamer, McCloskey, and Solow 1988) has become the subject of an extended debate. Their claim is that much, or almost all, of what scientists do is a matter of attempting to persuade their various audiences (colleagues, students, administrators, funding agencies, political decision-makers, lay audiences).

One of their contributions has been the identification of various *rhetorical ploys* and textual strategies used by economists, such as the use of attractive metaphors, and appeals to authority and mathematical brilliance. Another characteristic is a *conversational model* of rhetoric: persuasion takes place in a conversation that is very much akin to exchange in a marketplace. "Honest conversation" abides to the *Sprachethik*, and this is included in the very concept of rhetoric: "Don't lie; pay attention; don't sneer; cooperate; don't shout; let other people talk; be open-minded; explain yourself when asked; don't resort to violence or conspiracy in aid of your ideas." A third characteristic is an overt *anti-methodology*: no space for the traditional concern with methodological principles and rules. Good economics will be promoted just by raising the awareness among the practitioners about the rhetorical features of their conversations and by persuading them to adhere to the *Sprachethik*. Further "methodological intervention" would do nothing but harm.

In response, one may acknowledge the presence and power of rhetoric in science, as well as the importance of some ethical principles of research and communication, while insisting that the *Sprachethik* should not be included in the general concept of rhetoric – but will be fine as part of the idea of appropriate rhetoric – and that the awareness of the ploys used in the ongoing rhetorical persuasion cannot replace methodological principles.

The fourth feature of this project has been its outright anti-realism, variously self-identified as relativism, pragmatism, social constructivism, postmodernism. This is part of a larger current of rejecting the ideas of objective reality and objective truth. Whatever there is in the world, and whatever is true about it, are merely the results of persuasion. Truth is equated with persuasiveness, and thus truths are "made" rather than "discovered."

The alternative, realist, view is to take truth to be independent of any rhetorical efforts. A model is not made true (false) by being found persuasive (unpersuasive) by

549

a cohort of economists with a certain educational background and academic incentive structure. Background beliefs and institutional structure shape what is found persuasive and what is regarded as true at any given time – and even the likelihood of tracking truths about the world by a community of inquirers. The distinction is between what is true (or real) and what counts as true or is believed to be true (in some culture or group, or at a certain time). We do not have to think that the *reality* of the natural rate of unemployment or the *truth* of our theory of it is a function of rhetorical persuasion even if we think that our *belief* in its reality and in the truth of our theory of it can be influenced by rhetoric. The recognition that rhetoric is real and effective also in scientific communication is relatively neutral regarding its philosophical implications and presuppositions.

There is an extreme reading of the McCloskey–Klamer conception that would help resist the above charges. Economics as it is currently practiced is nothing but a rhetorical game of persuasion, perhaps one that chronically violates the *Sprachethik*. Being "nothing but rhetoric" would suggest that realism is unfit, since economics is presently not in the least interested in generating truthful information about the real world (perhaps it is preoccupied just with the study of the surrogate worlds of theoretical models). Even if this were true of some parts of current economics, it is unlikely to be true of all of it. And the natural remedy would be to preach not just rhetorical awareness and the *Sprachethik*, but to preach them *together with realism*.

Economics as a resource for the philosophy of science

In line with the larger currents in the social studies of science and social epistemology, economics is now customarily viewed as a form of social activity. The theoretical resources for highlighting the social aspects of economic inquiry are derived not just from rhetorical studies but also from sociology – and from economics itself. The contributors include Wade Hands, Philip Mirowski, Esther-Mirjam Sent, Roy Weintraub, and others. A special portion of this work suggests reversing the roles of economics and philosophy in their interactions.

Economics is playing an increasingly important role in the *naturalization* of the philosophy of science: philosophical accounts of various aspects of science are to be informed by the best scientific accounts of matters related to those aspects. Its social aspects call for *socializing* philosophy by appealing to social sciences. The question is how to choose the theoretical resources for this purpose given the variety of social science disciplines as well as the theoretical variety and disagreement within and between those disciplines.

The earlier, simplified, description of good science was in terms of disinterested scientists thrown in an institutional vacuum, and pursuing nothing but truthful (or otherwise epistemically virtuous) information about the world. Using economic concepts, philosophers such as Alvin Goldman, Philip Kitcher, and Jesus Zamora now portray scientists as being driven by self-seeking desires in a competitive market for ideas: scientists strategically seek to maximize their own fame and fortune, credibility and prestige, and other such non-cognitive social goals that enhance their personal utility. Scientists make investments and expect returns, suffer costs and enjoy benefits, acquire property rights and respond to incentives, and do these things within an "industrial organization" of scientific production governed by the rules of the game with a contractual structure.

Two philosophically interesting issues stand out. First, viewing science as an economy means transferring the familiar ideological and political issues from economics to science theory along the dimension of hands-off free market to hands-on regulation. The capacity of science to reach whatever epistemic or other goals depends on its industrial organization, market structure, regime of regulation, or governance structure. This has a theoretical aspect: which structure of academic institutions is the most conducive to epistemic success? And it has a policy aspect: how is that structure to be designed and implemented? Philosophy of science becomes more explicitly political.

Second, naturalizing science theory in terms of economics is taken by some to imply dispensing with traditional issues in scientific methodology, replacing it with a social science of science (see Hands 2001). I do not think that the traditional issues in the philosophy and methodology of science – or of economics – are dead at all, for two reasons. The first is that the familiar philosophical questions about *the target of science* remain as alive as ever. If we portray a science as an economy and scientists as economic agents seeking their own non-cognitive goals, it will be difficult to answer further questions, such as whether and how such an activity will be able to generate knowledge and cognitive progress, and what are the rational grounds of belief and settlement of disagreement in science. On such issues, economics offers theoretical resources that have been employed to alleviate emerging concerns: the market of science is in operation with the capacity to coordinate individual scientists' activities so as to transform them into epistemically virtuous outcomes as if by an invisible hand. But this requires a troublesome translation from economic theory to the philosophical vocabulary of knowledge and its growth.

The second reason why familiar philosophical issues will not go away is perhaps even more obvious. If we portray science in economic terms, we are employing a theoretical resource that is supposed to supply very demanding services. Not just any such possible resource or tool will do. Only the best and most reliable tools should be adopted in the service of purposes of such importance. Questions arise about *the credibility and reliability of economics itself* as such a candidate tool. Economics is unable to justify itself: a reflexivity test of that kind lacks the required power (Mäki 1999). And it will not do to appeal to the prestige of economics as a social science given that it is such a controversial discipline. Instead of replacing or eliminating familiar philosophical concerns, the reverse is true: the use of economics as a resource in the naturalization of our accounts of science only makes those concerns more pressing.

Explanatory expansionism and interdisciplinary relations

Economics is currently participating in interdisciplinary interactions in two ways: as an imperialist imposer; and as a humble learner. The first is a relatively new (post-1950s) trend, while the second means returning to the nineteenth-century ways of flexible or non-existent disciplinary boundaries, with intellectual traffic flowing freely. These appear to pull in different directions. The first is more conservative of the conventional contents of economic theory, while the second is reformist, even revolutionary. Such trends respond to traditional complaints about economics being closed-off from other disciplines. Borders are now being opened, in both directions.

One such direction is a version of the urge to explain as many kinds of economic phenomena as possible in terms of the same small set of causal factors or explanatory principles. This manifests itself in the *intra-disciplinary* unification of theories and fields (such as trade, growth, and location theories), and in the micro-foundationist project of reducing all economic phenomena to individual constrained maximization. Economics is no exception within the family of scientific disciplines: unification is a driving methodological ideal (see Mäki 2001). An *interdisciplinary* version of explanatory unificationism is economics imperialism, the aspiration of using economic concepts and explanatory principles in accounting for phenomena that traditionally belonged to the domain of disciplines other than economics (such as law, political science, sociology, anthropology, history, human geography, science studies). Almost all human behavior is now depicted as self-interested, rational choice in a market or market-like social setting — such as the marriage market and the market for votes, religions, and scientific ideas. The more controversial applications include explaining phenomena such as serial killing and drug addiction as informed self-regarding rational choice that balances the relevant utilities, harms, and the associated likelihoods (of one's own early death, for example). Emotions, morality, routines, and social norms are not supposed to play a role in such explanations if they cannot be redescribed in terms of self-regarding instrumental rationality.

Are we here witnessing empirically supported progress towards a more unified social science that succeeds in capturing the real unity of human action and social structure, thus establishing ontological unification of the variety of phenomena regardless of their previous disciplinary home domains? Or is it rather a matter of one limited discipline colonizing its neighbors by way of dubious maneuvering of flexibilities in testing, including the questionable redefinition of key concepts (such as *cost* and *market*) so as to enable only ontologically uncommitted derivational unification?

But interdisciplinary influences also travel in the other direction. Economics increasingly gives up its disciplinary autonomy and, under interdisciplinary pressure, modifies narrow conceptions of rational action and market adjustment. New branches of economics (such as institutional economics, behavioral economics, neuroeconomics, and evolutionary economics) are dependent on consulting other disciplines (such as sociology, experimental psychology, neuroscience, and evolutionary biology) for information and insight. They recognize the importance for economic action and outcomes of cognitive limitations, social norms, emotions, moral commitment. Next to rational deliberation, people are moved as much, if not more, by routine and affect, by considerations and feelings of fairness and reciprocity, shame and esteem, trustworthiness and retaliation, and they keep making systematic mistakes. This enriched folk psychology has neurobiological correlates, the investigation of which shows that the capacity of the human brain for rational choice is much weaker than economic theory or our ordinary introspective judgment would suggest.

Among the more radical conclusions that have been drawn is that standard rational choice remains an exceptional special case, thus should lose its dominance in economic modeling. On the other hand, those defending standard economics argue that its framework of rational choice is flexible enough to accommodate a broad range of mental dispositions and that it is not contradicted by neurosciences, due to differences in disciplinary domains and their constitutive explanatory questions. The debate will continue, and its analysis will require adopting and developing a rich range of philosophical tools as yet untried in the philosophy of economics.

See also Critical rationalism; Idealization; Mechanisms; Models; Realism/anti-realism; Relativism in science; Representation in science; Social science; Social studies of science; The structure of theories.

References

Blaug, M. (1992 [1980]) *The Methodology of Economics*, 2nd edn, Cambridge: Cambridge University Press.

Cartwright, N. (1989) *Nature's Capacities and Their Measurement*, Oxford: Oxford University Press.

De Marchi, N. (1988) "Popper and the LSE Economists," in N. de Marchi (ed.) *The Popperian Legacy in Economics*, Cambridge: Cambridge University Press, pp. 139–66.

De Marchi, N. and Blaug, M. (eds) (1991) *Appraising Economic Theories: Studies in the Methodology of Research Programmes*, Aldershot: Elgar.

Friedman, M. (1953) "Methodology of Positive Economics," in *Essays in Positive Economics*, Chicago: University of Chicago Press, pp. 3–43.

Hands, D. W. (2001) *Reflection Without Rules: Economic Methodology and Contemporary Science Theory*, Cambridge: Cambridge University Press.

Hausman, D. M. (1992) *The Inexact and Separate Science of Economics*, Cambridge: Cambridge University Press.

Klamer, A., McCloskey, D., and Solow, R. (eds) (1988) *The Consequences of Economic Rhetoric*, Cambridge: Cambridge University Press.

Latsis, S. (ed.) (1976) *Method and Appraisal in Economics*, Cambridge: Cambridge University Press.

Mäki, U. (1992) "On the Method of Isolation in Economics," *Poznan Studies in the Philosophy of the Sciences and the Humanities* 26 (special issue): 319–54.

—— (1999) "Science as a Free Market: A Reflexivity Test in an Economics of Economics," *Perspectives on Science* 7: 486–509.

—— (2000) "Kinds of Assumptions and Their Truth: Shaking an Untwisted F-Twist," *Kyklos* 53: 303–22.

—— (2001) "Explanatory Unification: Double and Doubtful," *Philosophy of the Social Sciences* 31, 488–506.

Menger, C. (1883) *Untersuchungen über die Methode der Socialwissenschaften und der Politischen Ökonomie Insbesondere*, Leipzig: Duncker & Humblot.

Musgrave, A. (1981) "'Unreal Assumptions' in Economic Theory: The F-Twist Untwisted," *Kyklos* 34: 377–87.

Sugden, R. (2002) "Credible Worlds: The Status of Theoretical Models in Economics," in U. Mäki (ed.) *Fact and Fiction in Economics: Models, Realism and Social Construction*, Cambridge: Cambridge University Press, pp. 107–36.

Further reading

The classic work in the Millian tradition that also defines economics as the (almost universally applicable) science of choice in conditions of scarcity is Lionel Robbins, *An Essay on the Nature and Significance of Economic Science* (London: Macmillan, 1935). An analysis of Menger's earlier version in the same tradition mentioned in the text is U. Mäki, "Universals and the *Methodenstreit*: A Reexamination of Carl Menger's Conception of Economics as an Exact Science," *Studies in History and Philosophy of Science* 28 (1997): 475–95. Logical positivist ideas have influenced T. Hutchison, *The Significance and Basic Postulates of Economic Theory* (London: Macmillan, 1938). On contributions and debates in the Popperian and Lakatosian traditions, one should consult D. W. Hands, *Testing, Rationality, and Progress: Essays on the Popperian Tradition in Economic Methodology* (Totowa, NJ: Rowman & Littlefield, 1993), and R. Backhouse, *Explorations in Economic Methodology* (London: Routledge, 1998). The philosophical analysis of economic models is now spreading in many directions. For Mary Morgan's important contributions, one may start with M. Morgan and M. Morrison (eds) *Models as Mediators: Perspectives on Natural and Social Sciences* (Cambridge: Cambridge University Press, 1999). An outline of my account is in U. Mäki, "Models Are Experiments, Experiments are Models," *Journal of Economic Methodology* 12 (2005): 303–15. The classic work on the rhetoric of economics is D. McCloskey, *The Rhetoric of Economics* (Madison: University of Wisconsin Press, 1985). My critique and alternative view are outlined in U. Mäki, "Diagnosing McCloskey," *Journal of Economic Literature* 33 (1995): 1300–18. For themes mentioned but not covered in the text, one should consult K. D. Hoover, *Causality in Macroeconomics* (Cambridge: Cambridge University Press, 2001) and F. Guala, *The Methodology of Experimental Economics* (Cambridge: Cambridge University Press, 2005). There are good collections of essays that provide accessible introductions to the philosophy and methodology of economics. They fall in three categories. Among handbooks, there are J. B. Davis, D. W. Hands, and U. Mäki (eds) *The Handbook of Economic Methodology* (Cheltenham: Edward Elgar, 1998); H. Kincaid and D. Ross (eds) *The Handbook of the Philosophy of Economics* (Oxford: Oxford University Press, 2007); and U. Mäki, *The Handbook of the Philosophy of Economics* (Amsterdam: Elsevier, 2007). The first of these contains numerous shorter entries, while the other two consist of fewer and longer essays. Anthologies of previously published representative papers include B. Caldwell (ed.) *The Philosophy and Methodology of Economics*, 3 vols (Cheltenham: Edward Elgar, 1993); J. B. Davis (ed.) *Recent Developments in Economic Methodology*, 3 vols (Cheltenham: Edward Elgar, 2006); and D. M. Hausman (ed.) *Philosophy of Economics: An Anthology* (Cambridge: Cambridge University Press, 2007). The third category includes edited volumes on more focused themes. R. Backhouse, D. M. Hausman, U. Mäki, and A. Salanti (eds) *Economics and Methodology: Crossing Boundaries* (London: Macmillan, 1998) is a collection of case studies that was designed to turn philosophy of economics in a more empirical direction. R. Backhouse and A. Salanti (eds) *Macroeconomics and the Real World*, 2 vols (Oxford: Oxford University Press, 2000) is devoted to methodological issues in macroeconomics. U. Mäki (ed.) *The Economic World View: Studies in the Ontology of Economics* (Cambridge: Cambridge University Press, 2001) collects work on economic ontology. U. Mäki (ed.) *Fact and Fiction in Economics: Realism, Models and Social Construction* (Cambridge: Cambridge University Press, 2002) approaches the core conundrum from a variety of angles, while U. Mäki (ed.) *The Methodology of Positive Economics: Milton Friedman's Essay Half a Century Later* (Cambridge: Cambridge University Press, 2007) does the same, focusing on Friedman's controversial and poorly understood essay.

52

MATHEMATICS

Peter Clark

Introduction

In the early years of the twenty-first century, one might well look back over the previous 100 years and come to the conclusion that the notion of human progress – intellectual, political, and moral – is at best ambiguous and equivocal. Indeed some philosophers (for example Thomas Kuhn, Paul Feyerabend, and Richard Rorty) have written in recent years as if no such notion could be made out and they have seriously challenged the idea that standards of rational scientific progress exist. However, there is one area of autonomous, human, scientific endeavor where the idea of, and achievement of, real progress, the discovery of ever deeper and more general theorems, is unambiguous and pellucidly clear, it is mathematics.

In 1900, in a famous address to the Second International Congress of mathematicians in Paris, David Hilbert listed some twenty-three open problems of then outstanding significance. In the intervening period many of those problems have been definitively solved, or shown to be insoluble, culminating most recently, in 1994, with the proof of Fermat's Last Theorem by Andrew Wiles. Along with enormous progress in the disciplines of pure and applied mathematics there has also come real insight into the methods of mathematics (both classical and constructive), and into the nature of proof and its relation to mathematical truth. Considerable progress has also been made in meta-mathematics (that is the mathematical study of such key notions as demonstrability, definability, predicativity, and truth), in areas just hinted at in the nineteenth century like computability and information theory, and in foundational issues with which this essay will be primarily concerned. One of the most notable foundational achievements has been the reduction of the corpus of mathematics to Zermelo–Fraenkel set theory (with the *Axiom of Choice*) and the proofs of the consistency of various branches of mathematics relative to it.

It is also remarkable how much interesting mathematics has actually been produced in the pursuit of philosophical claims about the objects of mathematics and the nature of mathematical truth. Witness *Frege's Theorem* (see below) on the one hand and the major results of intuitionistic analysis on the other, and how much philosophical insight has been gained by the interpretation of certain very deep theorems indeed of mathematics proper, the *Gödel Incompleteness Theorems* and the *Paris–Harrington*

Theorem, to give but one generic example. The Paris–Harrington Theorem is especially interesting in that it provides a clear example of a statement of obvious combinatorial arithmetic content (the *Modified Finite Ramsey Theorem*) which is independent of the first-order *Peano Axioms* for arithmetic. This is one of a number of results of clear arithmetic content used in everyday mathematics that have been shown to be independent of the Peano Axioms, thus adding to the purely meta-mathematical significance of Gödel's original theorem.

Frege's Constraint

In a relatively short essay on the subject of modern mathematics it is quite impossible to attempt a survey of even some of these very deep achievements. However in a companion devoted to the philosophy of science it is appropriate to pay particular attention to applied mathematics and the problem of how it is that the calculus of arithmetic and geometry apply to physical reality, for that is one salient fact about pure mathematics, that it can be and has been so successfully applied in all branches of natural science. In every branch of scientific knowledge, from fluid mechanics to computational ecology, the application of arithmetic and real and complex analysis to the problems posed in explaining the natural phenomena characterizing those fields has been highly successful. Indeed the overwhelming majority of concepts used in the description of nature cannot even be formulated without appeal to key pure mathematical concepts.

Interestingly it was Frege, a thoroughgoing Platonist, who put the application problem at the core of his now famous account of the nature of numbers and how we come to know them. Frege insisted that a proper account of the nature of natural number (and real number) must build the applications of arithmetic (and analysis) into the account that it gives of the statements of arithmetic as an essential part, and not as something requiring extra, additional, special premises (call this idea "Frege's Constraint"). Dummett (1991: 272) has put the point very well for both the Fregean account of natural number and of real number:

> A correct definition of the *natural numbers* must, on [Frege's] view, show how such a number can be used to say how many matches that there are in a box or books on a shelf. Yet number theory has nothing to do with matches or with books: its business in this regard is only to display what, in general, is involved in stating the cardinality of the objects, of whatever source, that fall under some concept, and how the natural numbers can be used for the purpose. In the same way, analysis has nothing to do with electric charge or mechanical work, with length or temporal duration; but it must display the general principle underlying the use of the real numbers to characterise the magnitude of quantities of these and other kinds.

Frege's account was an answer to the question posed at the opening of Section 62 of the *Grundlagen* (1884), viz.: "how then are numbers given to us, if we cannot have any ideas or intuitions of them?" It is founded on the answer, by explaining the senses of identity statements in which number words occur. This was to be done, at least in part, by appeal to what is now called "Hume's Principle," the claim that the cardinal numbers corresponding to two concepts are identical if, and only if, the two concepts are equinumerous. This is only an explanation in part of the sense of identity statements because, as Frege had noted in Section 56 of the *Grundlagen*, appeal to the principle could not explain the senses of identity statements which occur in the form "The number of Fs is q," where q is not given in the form "the number of Gs," for some G. (Frege called this the "Julius Caesar problem" since he noted Hume's Principle cannot decide the truth value of the sentence "The number of things which are not identical to themselves is Julius Caesar." We would assert that that sentence is false but Hume's Principle does not convey that.) He therefore adopted an explicit definition of "number" in terms of extensions or classes. That is that "the number of Fs" is "the class of all concepts G, such that G is equinumerous with F."

That definition, together with Frege's *Basic Law Five*, the principle which was intended to explain the senses of identity statements involving extensions – that the extensions of two concepts are identical when, and only when, everything falling under either one of the concepts falls under the other – entails Hume's Principle. With this apparatus in place Frege showed, informally in the *Grundlagen* and explicitly in the *Grundgesetze*, that axiomatic second-order logic together with Basic Law Five entails the second-order *Peano–Dedekind Axioms* for arithmetic. In fact, this is achieved in two steps, first by showing that Hume's Principle follows from Basic Law Five and the explicit definition of cardinal number, and then by showing that from Hume's Principle the Peano–Dedekind Axioms follow in second-order logic. This latter is a clear example of a theorem of genuine mathematical content flowing directly from a foundational philosophical program.

So, the truths of arithmetic could be seen to be analytic, that is, mere definitional extensions of second-order logic. Further, arithmetic could be seen as a body of truths about independently existing objects – the natural numbers – which were revealed as purely logical objects and the infinity of the natural number series given an explanation based purely on logical principles. Similarly our knowledge of arithmetic could be exhibited as *a priori* in Frege's sense (at least) that it could be shown to depend on principles neither in need of, nor admitting of, proof. Further and fundamentally, the problem of the application of arithmetic to reality was completely solved. The solution is that arithmetic is applicable to reality because the concepts, under which things fall, themselves fall under numerical concepts. So number does not apply to apples and chairs, but applies to the concepts "is an apple," "is a chair," which of course themselves apply to reality. The application of arithmetic is guaranteed by the fact that it is possible to prove in general in second-order logic that $\exists_n xFx$ – that is, there are exactly n Fs – if, and only if, the number of Fs *is n*.

Of course the serpent had already entered Eden. Basic Law Five says that:

$$(\forall F)(\forall G)(\text{Ext}(F) = \text{Ext}(G) \leftrightarrow (\forall x)(Fx \leftrightarrow Gx)),$$

that is, that there is a mapping from concepts to objects, in fact from the concept F to the object which is its extension $(\text{Ext}(F))$ and that when two concepts are identical (that is have the same objects falling under them), their corresponding extensions are identical. So Basic Law Five says that the mapping from concepts to objects is functional. However reading left to right it also asserts that this function is one-to-one, since when two extensions are identical, the two concepts whose extensions they are, are identical. So Basic Law Five asserts that there is a one-to-one function from concepts to objects.

Before we can reason with this law, we need to know what falls under the universal quantifiers at the left of the expression of Basic Law Five. In other words, we need to know what properties there are. The *Comprehension Principle* for second-order logic, which says that every condition formalizable in the vocabulary of second-order logic determines a property, answers this question. So there is a property corresponding to the condition $(\exists F)(\text{Ext}(F) = x \,\&\, {\sim}Fx)$. Russell's paradox immediately follows when this property falls in the range of the universal quantifier in Basic Law Five, which it must by the Comprehension Principle. Another way of seeing essentially the same point is to notice that Basic Law Five directly contradicts *Cantor's Theorem*, which says that there is *no* one-to-one correspondence from the collection of all subsets of a set to the members of that set. But each concept definable over a set determines a subset and Basic Law Five says that there is a one-to-one correspondence from concepts to objects, so from subsets to objects in the set and so from subsets to members. Contradiction. Is all lost including the explanation of the infinity of the number series and the applicability of arithmetic to reality? The answer according to a recent view is most certainly not.

Abstractionism

Let us formulate Hume's Principle as

$$(\forall F)(\forall G)(NxFx = NxGx \leftrightarrow \exists R(F \approx_R G))$$

where $Nx\ldots x$ is a term-forming operator acting on concepts to produce the object which is the number of that concept, and $\exists R(F \approx_R G)$ says that the concepts F and G stand in one-to-one correspondence by the relation R. In effect, like Basic Law Five, Hume's Principle asserts the existence of a function $Nx\ldots x$ from concepts to objects, but unlike Basic Law Five it asserts that merely non-equinumerous concepts (not non-coextensive concepts) can be mapped to distinct objects and this is possible provided that the domain is Dedekind infinite. (A set is Dedekind infinite if, and only if, it can be put into one-to-one correspondence with a proper subset of itself.) It cannot be satisfied in a finite domain. For a domain of k objects, there are $k+1$ non-equinumerous concepts definable over it. Since each application of the function $Nx\ldots x$ to a subset (concept definable over the domain) of the domain must yield an object in the domain, there must be at least $k+1$ objects in the domain, but there are only k. So no finite domain can satisfy Hume's Principle.

Unlike Basic Law Five Hume's Principle is consistent. Further, from Hume's Principle and second-order logic the Peano–Dedekind axioms for arithmetic with the full second-order *Induction Axiom* can be derived. This result needs to be stated carefully. Formally the central result is that *if* a formalization of the key "definition" (Hume's Principle) is added as an axiom to standard axiomatic second-order logic, second-order arithmetic (arithmetic with the full second-order Induction Axiom) can be interpreted in the resulting theory, often called "Frege Arithmetic." We thus have a reconstruction of our knowledge of arithmetic on this account, but that itself poses an interesting philosophical question as to the relationship between the practice so reconstructed and the arithmetic knowledge that fully informed practitioners actually possess.

Hale and Wright have argued at length (see particularly 2001) that this shows that it is, after all, still possible to accomplish Frege's central philosophical and mathematical aims, not just for the theory of natural numbers but for *real analysis* and more extensive mathematical domains as well.

Hume's Principle has the form of what are called "abstraction principles." Abstraction principles come in two types, *conceptual* abstractions and *objectual* ones, but all have the following form. There is a domain of entities, denoted say, by α, β, etc., and a relation R defined over them. Then an abstraction principle has the form

$$\Sigma(\alpha) = \Sigma(\beta) \leftrightarrow R(\alpha, \beta)$$

where $R(,)$ is an equivalence relation among the α and β's. An abstraction principle may be called a logical abstraction when the relation $R(,)$ is definable in purely logical vocabulary, e.g. equinumerosity among concepts or ordinal similarity among binary relations. Under the classical canonical interpretation $\Sigma(\alpha)$ is the equivalence class of α under the relation R and exists (where it does) in virtue of a set-existence axiom. That is, the existence and uniqueness of $\Sigma(\alpha)$ has in effect to be guaranteed by a separate principle of set or class existence. This is what the axioms of set theory do: they assert the existence of certain sets, and we use them to establish the existence of other sets. As an example, take the *Pair Set Axiom*. This says that, for any sets x and y the set $\{x, y\}$ exists. Given this axiom, we can prove that singleton sets exist, i.e., if x is a set, by the Pair Set Axiom, $\{x, x\}$ exists; that is $\{x\}$ exists. Similarly, we can prove the existence of ordered pairs, provided we have the Pair Set Axiom. If x is a set and y is a set, by Pair Set, we have the existence of $\{x, y\}$ and by pairing again, this time using x and $\{x, y\}$, we have $\{x, \{x, y\}\}$ which is the ordered pair, $<x, y>$.

A more interesting question is what set-existence principles are needed to develop Peano Arithmetic? They are: the *Axiom of Extensionality*, which says that if two sets have the same members they are identical; the *Adjunction Axiom*, which says that for any two sets x and y there is a set whose members are all the members of x and the set y itself; and the *Separation Principle*, which says for any set x and any condition A on the members of x there is a set whose members are exactly those members of x for which condition A holds. So canonically to reconstruct arithmetic we will need some set-theoretic existence axioms. Wright and Hale however argue that in certain cases logical abstraction principles (like Hume's Principle in the proof of Frege's Theorem) can play the role of *stipulations*; and if the relation on the right-hand side of the *if, and only if,* is ever satisfied, no further question concerning the existence of the $\Sigma(\alpha)$ need arise, no appeal need be made in these cases to existence axioms, set theoretic or otherwise.

Of course, Wright and Hale do not argue that it is always legitimate to introduce mathematical objects in this way. Two examples of conceptual logical abstraction principles which fail to introduce entities are Basic Law Five and what might be called "Ordinal Hume," which is the claim that

$$(\forall R)(\forall S)(\text{Ord } R = \text{Ord } S \leftrightarrow R \text{ is similar to } S).$$

This has the form of an abstraction principle, since similarity is an equivalence relation among binary relations. But Ordinal Hume leads directly to the *Burali–Forti Paradox,* viz., that the class of all ordinal numbers both has and has not an ordinal number associated with it. Wright has argued that there are general principles, which can be used to distinguish between good and bad abstraction principles and in any case there is no similar problem about Hume's Principle, since it is consistent.

Frege was concerned to extend his analysis to the real numbers, and here too an abstractionist account can be given but one which does not lie easily with Frege's Constraint. Shapiro (2000) has shown that using what he has called the "Cut Abstraction Principle" (to the effect that the cut of P is identical with the cut of Q if and only if P and Q share all their upper bounds in the rational numbers, and identifying the real numbers with the Cuts so introduced), the axioms of second-order real analysis can be derived from the Cut Principle just as the Peano–Dedekind Axioms for second-order arithmetic can be derived from Hume's Principle. But this reconstruction follows very much the approach to the "construction" of the real numbers employed by Dedekind. Dedekind is such a significant figure in the foundations of mathematics precisely because he discovered such important results for both the logicist and structuralist traditions.

In his masterpiece of 1888 *Was Sind und was Sollen die Zahlen?* Dedekind introduces the natural numbers in a mathematically very similar manner to Frege. But in the same work, his *Theorem 132* (viz., the categoricity result for second-order arithmetic, which says that arithmetic with the second-order Induction Axiom has only one model – the natural numbers – up to isomorphism), is the foundational theorem for the structural interpretation of arithmetic. However Dedekind's (1872) "construction" of the real numbers does not satisfy Frege's Constraint, as I have called it, for that construction in no way avers to the applications of the real numbers. This is completely at odds with Frege's proposed analysis of real number in the *Grundgesetze* where he seeks to explain the possibility of applications of the real numbers to quantitative domains and measures from the start. That this was essential was fundamental to his program. In Section 159 of the *Grundgesetze* Frege wrote:

> Our hope is thus neither to lose our grip on the applicability of [analysis] in specific areas of knowledge nor to contaminate it with the objects, concepts

and relations taken from those areas and so to threaten its peculiar nature and independence. The display of such possibilities of application is something one should have the right to expect from [analysis] notwithstanding that that application is not itself its subject matter.

Abandoning Frege's Constraint however invites a structuralist account of analysis and it is to structuralism in mathematics in general that we now turn.

Structuralism

In a clear sense, much of the foundational work in mathematics in the twentieth century can be thought of as revealing that mathematics is the science of structures since the objects of mathematics have all been shown to be set-theoretic structures. In a way, that is precisely what the great technical achievement of the reduction of the whole of the corpus of mathematics to set theory (in textbook cases usually Zermelo–Fraenkel set theory with Axiom of Choice) shows: it shows that mathematics is the study of set theoretic structures. But that, though a marvelous technical achievement, could hardly be philosophically satisfying, for though correct we are left entirely in the dark as to what sort of structures sets are. Why is it that some collections are sets, that is, they are genuine structures, while others (like the universe of sets or the collection of all ordinals) are *not* sets, are not genuine structures? They lead to paradox if we postulate that they are sets, but that brute fact is not an explanation of *why* they are not sets. Clearly, something more is needed than the mathematical fact that specific mathematical theories, for example the theory of a complete ordered field or the theory of groups, can be seen as talking about a specific type of set-theoretical structure.

What has come to be called "*ante rem* structuralism" seeks to supply the missing step. According to this view structures are abstract universals. As Benacerraf (1965) pointed out, the natural number series can be identified with many different sequences of sets. We can think of zero as the empty set ∅, one as {∅}, two as {∅, {∅}} etc. or we can think of zero as the empty set ∅, one as {∅}, two as {{∅}} etc. or indeed we can think of zero as the class of all classes with no elements, one as the class of all classes with one element, two as the class of all classes with two elements etc. (Again, of course, we shall have to assume certain set- or class-existence axioms to prove that those sets exist, as noted under "Abstractionism".) All those representations have in common the structure type of an ω-sequence (a sequence like that of the natural numbers with a first but no last member). According to *ante rem* structuralism that structure type is a universal whose existence is quite independent of any instantiation of it in a particular set theory. Here then is another form of abstractionism – this time abstracting over identity in structure. What structures in this sense exist? The answer according to *ante rem* structuralism is: any structure that satisfies a condition expressible in a second-order language, that of coherence (see particularly Shapiro 1997), where coherence is understood as a primitive notion corresponding very roughly to satisfiability.

In fact, the answer is very like that of Hilbert, or at least the Hilbert of legend, who characterized the existence of mathematical domains in terms of the consistency (satisfiability) of sets of sentences describing them. What then of mathematical objects like natural numbers and ordinal numbers? They turn out to be simply place-holders in a structure.

There is a second form of structuralism, which tries to avoid reference to abstract structures altogether, and that is *modal* structuralism. Modal structuralists do not assert the existence of anything abstract, such as universals, but assert merely the possibility of the existence of ω-sequences and further that as a matter of necessity any such sequence must satisfy the Dedekind–Peano Axioms. A similar reconstruction can be carried out for the real number system, for the complex numbers and for the sets of the cumulative hierarchy. The advantage of modal structuralism, it is argued, is that it sharply distinguishes mathematical existence from ordinary existence, and that there is no tendency within it to generate such non-structures as the universe of sets or the collection of all ordinals, for there is no postulate saying that there is (or possibly is) a collection of all things which might have existed (see particularly Hellman 1989).

Whatever the philosophical merits of structuralism, it cannot be denied that the history of mathematics in the twentieth century was indeed a structuralist triumph, the work of the Bourbaki School of French mathematics being a paradigm example of the structuralist method in mathematics proper. Nor, in the end, is Frege's Constraint totally ignored, for the application problem is very systematically treated in structuralist accounts of applied mathematics, though in a highly non-Fregean manner, by establishing key representation theorems. These theorems have considerable intrinsic mathematical interest and form the foundation of measurement theory. In the case, for example, of the measurement of mass, of length of rigid bodies or, indeed, of subjective probabilities, certain basic properties are identified as characteristic of such measurements; then certain algebraic structures are given which have just those properties; and then it is shown in the representation theorem that for every such structure there is a rational (real) valued function taking elements of the abstract algebraic structure as arguments which behaves as a measure function mirroring the basic properties of mass and length or degree of belief. Where such representation theorems are provable they form the foundations of the application of the real numbers. The account is very different from that envisioned by Frege; nevertheless it is a mathematically fully viable way of explaining the application of the real and complex numbers. It thus meets in a *mathematical* manner the requirement stressed by Dummett in the extract quoted at the beginning of this essay, that whatever account we give of the real numbers and their application "must display the general principle underlying the use of the real numbers to characterize the magnitude of quantities of these and other kinds."

However one construes these matters, following either Frege or Dedekind, one is left with abstract structures (actual or possible) and the apparently irreducible fact that mathematics, as practiced, is science about abstract objects or structures *par excellence*. But our knowledge of abstract objects is an extremely puzzling matter for causal theories of knowledge. This fact no doubt provides the central motivation for modern nominalism. If, as Quine and Putnam have argued (see particularly Putnam

1971; Quine 1981), it is the whole of the web of belief which acquires confirmation holistically from positive evidence, then, since mathematics and physics employ the objects and concepts of pure mathematics, perhaps the best evidence for the existence of such objects is the confirmation which the whole of mathematical physics receives from the evidence. There is no sharp partition then in epistemology between knowledge of the abstract and knowledge of the concrete, but rather a continuum of evidence ranging from that for birds, rabbits and footballs through that for electrons, positrons and neutrinos to that for groups, rings, fields, and sets. Since good physics gives us reason to believe in electrons and other elementary particles because of their successful explanatory role, surely it provides just as good evidence for the existence of sets, because of their key explanatory role.

Such is the Quine–Putnam indispensability argument and the key argument in the defense of naturalism in the philosophy of mathematics. But the argument is only as good as the strength of the explanatory role of sets and classes in physics. So the argument invites the question: What indeed is indispensable to the explanation of exactly what? The nominalist answer to the question is revealing. Let us find a nominalistically acceptable vocabulary which makes no reference to abstract objects and expresses the basic, well-confirmed, experimental results, of say, Newtonian mechanics. Can we find a theory whose consequences are all the nominalistically acceptable consequences of mechanics, which are expressible in purely nominalistically acceptable terms? Surprisingly we can – call it "synthetic" mechanics – and then we can, as Field (1980) showed, obtain the result that classical mechanics involving the full panoply of classical mathematical methods is conservative with respect to synthetic mechanics. In other words, any logical consequence of fully classical mechanics, which is expressible as a statement of synthetic mechanics, is a logical consequence of synthetic mechanics alone. Classical mechanics produces no new consequences in synthetic vocabulary. One has to be very careful as to how this result is expressed. The underlying logic deployed by Field is second-order logic; hence, the Completeness Principle no longer holds, so some proposition p may be a logical consequence of synthetic mechanics without being provable from it. Thus proving that p follows from synthetic mechanics may require the use of the full mathematical apparatus of the theory. The conservativeness result holds only for consequence, not for derivability, as was pointed out by Shapiro (1983). In so far as synthetic mechanics does express the fundamental explanatory successes of mechanics, the conservativeness result shows classical mathematics to be dispensable (in some sense of dispensable), contrary to the import of the indispensability argument.

Does this then undermine the naturalist position? Hardly directly, because of the problem which I have already alluded to in connection with the Fregean program: the problem of the reconstruction of practice. The problem at its most stark is just this. Suppose that one can reconstruct a practice, say, that of doing applied mathematics to the level of the best professional standards, so that practice can be seen as cohering with some acceptable philosophical standard, but one which nevertheless requires a reconstruction and reinterpretation of what the practitioners standardly think they are doing. What, then, does one think one has achieved, even when no violation of that practice is entailed? It does not simply follow from this that philosophical insight as to what is actually going on has been gained. If the philosophical account cannot reconstruct the practice, it is, in fact, proposing a *new* practice, which must be judged on professional, not philosophical, standards. If the account can reconstruct the practice, but only by radically reinterpreting the practice, it is very unclear as to what has been achieved by way of epistemological insight. It certainly does not achieve a knock-down blow for a particular philosophical view (the one espoused in the reconstruction) which is thereby vindicated, for the philosophical account has reinterpreted what the practitioners thought they were doing and there is, in a deep sense, no other authority than the practitioners as to what they think they do.

Applied mathematics and set theory

Whatever the outcome of nominalistic reconstructions, a question which naturally arises concerning applied mathematics is exactly how much by way of set existence we require in order to obtain what one might call the "core principles" of mathematical physics. This is a very difficult question in general, but it can be answered, at least in part, by one of the most interesting developments in mathematics proper in recent years – the program of "reverse" mathematics. The problem is to find the minimum postulates of set existence, telling us what sorts of sets have to exist, that are needed to obtain what might be called the "core theorems" of the practice of mathematical physics, for example those theorems which govern the existence and uniqueness of solution in the theory of ordinary differential equations. One might then be able to answer the question of whether they would be obtainable using purely predicative postulates, or of which constructivist principles of intuitionistic or computable analysis would be required to obtain them and of what relative strength. This program of reverse mathematics, which is a partial realization of Hilbert's program, has been systematically investigated by Harvey Friedman and by Stephen Simpson and his colleagues.

The basic idea of the program is to take a very weak number-theoretic system as a basis, essentially recursive arithmetic (RCA) and to find for a given mathematical theorem, say φ, a set-existence axiom (like the example of the Pair Set Axiom used in the section on abstractionism, above) π such that

$$\text{RCA} \vdash \pi \leftrightarrow \varphi.$$

Thus for example, if we take the classical *Bolzano–Weierstrass Theorem* (every bounded sequence of real numbers has a least convergent subsequence for φ, then it turns out that π tells us that we need not assume the existence of the full classical power set of all the subsets of the set of the natural numbers, but need only assume the existence of those subsets of the natural numbers which are described by formulas involving only existential quantification of formulas themselves involving only bounded number quantifiers. To take an example directly from physics, if we take φ to be the *Cauchy–Peano Existence Theorem* for the solutions of ordinary differential equations, then π is essentially a comprehension principle asserting the existence of an infinite path in any infinite binary tree.

Such examples suffice to illustrate that for doing ordinary mathematical physics (basic classical physics) the necessary axioms of set existence are extremely weak viewed from the canonical, classical standpoint, according to which the continuum or real line is thought of as the collection of all the subsets of N, i.e. where the full classical power set existence axiom is employed. Indeed this relative paucity of set theoretical apparatus is true of almost all mathematics familiar to the working mathematician, for it seems that all the set theory necessary for that can be found in the cumulative hierarchy of sets below $V_{\omega+\omega,}$ not requiring anything like the standard model of the Zermelo–Fraenkel set theory with Axiom of Choice (ZFC), with iteration up to the level of an inaccessible cardinal.

Conclusion

Frege determined to provide a decisive refutation of Kant's view of mathematics as based on the forms of pure intuition. He failed not because his system of logic was inadequate for exhibiting the validity of every valid mathematical inference – that it was – nor because he could not base arithmetic on propositions not needing or being capable of proof – Hume's Principle could well have been taken as such – but because he sought to found the principles of mathematics on the notion of *extension*, which he thought was plainly a logical notion. But the notion he employed was inconsistent and the adequate notion – that of set – is equally plainly non-logical in character. This then invites the thought, argued for long ago by Poincaré and Hilbert, that intuition plays a vital role in the foundations of mathematics as a form which guarantees, quasi-concretely, that certain iterative constructions in elementary arithmetic (the successor operation) and geometry (ruler and compass constructions) can be carried out. This further invites the thought that it is to a psychological, active capacity of the mind that appeal should be sought in understanding at least finitary elementary mathematics. The study of the psychogenetic origin of mathematical concepts, which has been so long neglected and which Poincaré so championed, may well be, after all, a direction of fruitful future research.

See also Measurement; Naturalism.

References

Benacerraf, Paul (1965) "What Numbers Could Not Be," *Philosophical Review* 74: 47–73; reprinted in P. Benacerraf and H. Putnam (eds) (1983) *Philosophy of Mathematics*, Cambridge: Cambridge University Press, pp. 272–94.

Dekekind, Richard (1872) *Stetigkeit und irrationale Zahlen*, Braunschweig: Viewig; trans. and ed. W. W. Beman (1963) as "Continuity and Irrational Numbers," in Richard Dedekind, *Essays on the Theory of Numbers*, Part 1, New York: Dover Publications.

Dummett, Michael (1991) *Frege: Philosophy of Mathematics*, London: Duckworth.

Field, Hartry (1980) *Science Without Numbers*, Princeton, NJ: Princeton University Press.

Frege, Gottlob (1884) *Die Grundlagen der Arithmetik: Eine logisch–mathematische Untersuchung über den Begriff der Zahl*, Breslau: Koebner, trans J. L. Austin (1953) as *The Foundations of Arithmetic: A Logico-Mathematical Enquiry into the Concept of Number*, Oxford: Basil Blackwell.

—— (1893/1902) *Grundgesetze der Arithmetik: Begriffsschriftlich abgeleitet*, vol. 1 (1893) and vol. 2 (1902), Jena: H. Pohle.

Hale, Bob and Wright, Crispin (2001) *The Reason's Proper Study: Essays towards a Neo-Fregean Philosophy of Mathematics*, Oxford: Oxford University Press.

Hellman, Geoffrey (1989) *Mathematics Without Numbers: Towards a Modal Structural Interpretation*, Oxford: Clarendon Press.

Putnam, Hilary (1971) *Philosophy of Logic*, New York: Harper Torchbooks.

Quine, W. V. (1981) *Theories and Things*, Cambridge, MA: Harvard University Press.

Shapiro, Stuart (1983) "Conservativeness and Incompleteness," *Journal of Philosophy* 80: 521–31.

—— (1997) *Philosophy of Mathematics: Structure and Ontology*, New York: Oxford University Press.

—— (2000) "Frege Meets Dedekind: A Neologicist Treatment of Real Analysis," *Notre Dame Journal of Formal Logic* 4: 335–64.

Further reading

There is an excellent account of Hilbert's problems and their solutions in Jeremy Gray, *The Hilbert Challenge: A Perspective on Twentieth-Century Mathematics* (Oxford: Oxford University Press, 2000). An account of the Paris–Harrington Theorem and related results can be found in S. G. Simpson (ed.) *Logic and Combinatorics: Contemporary Mathematics*, vol. 65 (Providence, RI: American Mathematical Society, 1987). An excellent source for articles on many of the topics discussed above is S. Shapiro (ed.) *The Oxford Handbook of Philosophy of Mathematics and Logic* (Oxford: Oxford University Press, 2005). The *locus classicus* for neo-logicism is Crispin Wright's *Frege's Conception of Numbers as Objects* (Aberdeen: Aberdeen University Press, 1983). George Boolos's excellent *Logic, Logic, and Logic* (Cambridge, MA: Harvard University Press, 1998) contains some classic articles on Fregean themes and the repair of Frege's system. The consistency strength of Hume's Principle and related abstraction principles is the subject of John Burgess, *Fixing Frege* (Princeton, NJ: Princeton University Press, 2005). A full treatment of the general theory of abstraction principles can be found in Kit Fine, *The Limits of Abstraction* (Oxford: Oxford University Press, 2000). The classic work on representations and measurement theory is D. H. Krantz, R. D. Luce, P. Suppes, and A. Tversky, *Foundations of Measurement*, 3 vols (New York: Academic Press, 1971, 1989, 1990). An important modal nominalist theory is developed in Charles Chihara, *Constructibility and Existence* (Oxford: Oxford University Press, 1990). Nominalist reconstructions of mathematics are fully discussed in J. P. Burgess and G. Rosen, *A Subject With No Object: Strategies for Nominalistic Interpretation of Mathematics* (Oxford: Oxford University Press, 1997). A helpful account of the results of reverse mathematics can be found in Solomon Feferman, *In the Light of Logic* (Oxford: Oxford University Press, 1998). No study of the philosophy of mathematics should be undertaken without reference to Charles Parson's work – see his *Mathematics in Philosophy: Selected Essays* (Ithaca, NY: Cornell University Press, 1983).

53
PHYSICS

Simon Saunders

"Physics, and physics alone, has complete coverage," according to Quine. Philosophers of physics will mostly agree. But there is less consensus among physicists, many of whom have a sneaking regard for philosophical questions, about, for example, the use of the word "reality."

Why be mealy-mouthed when it comes to what is real? The answer lies in *quantum mechanics*. Very little happens in physics these days without quantum mechanics having its say: never has a theory been so prolific in predicting new and astounding effects, with so vast a scope. But for all its uncanny fecundity, there is a certain difficulty. After a century of debate, there is very little agreement on how this difficulty should be resolved – indeed, what consensus there was on it has slowly evaporated. The crucial point of contention concerns the interface between macro and micro. Since experiments on the micro-world involve measurements, and measurements involve observable changes in the instrumentation, it is unsurprising how the difficulty found its name: "the problem of measurement." But really it is a problem of how, and whether, the theory describes any actual events. As Werner Heisenberg (1959: 121) put it, "it is the 'factual' character of an event describable in terms of the concepts of daily life which is not without further comment contained in the mathematical formalism of quantum theory."

The problem is so strange, so intractable, and so far-reaching, that, along with space-time philosophy, it has come to dominate the philosophy of physics. The philosophy of space-time is the subject of a separate chapter: no apology, then, is needed, for devoting this chapter to the *problem of measurement* alone.

Orthodoxy

Quantum mechanics was all but completed in 1926. But it only compounded – entrenched – a problem that had been obvious for years: *wave-particle duality*. For a simple example, consider Young's two-slit experiment, in which monochromatic light, incident on two narrow, parallel slits, subsequently produces an interference pattern on a distant screen (in this case, closely spaced bands of light and dark parallel to the slits). If either of the slits is closed, the pattern is lost. If one or other slit is closed sporadically and randomly, so that only one is open at any one time, the pattern is lost.

There is no difficulty in understanding this effect on the supposition that light consists of waves; but on careful examination of low-intensity light, the interference pattern is built up, *one spot after another* – as if light consists of particles (photons). The pattern slowly emerges even if only one photon is in the apparatus at any one time; and yet it is lost when only one slit is open at any one time. It appears, absurdly, as if the photon must pass through both slits and interfere with itself. As Richard Feynman (1963: 37) observed in his *Lectures on Physics*, this is "a phenomenon which is impossible, absolutely impossible, to explain in any classical way, and which has in it the heart of quantum mechanics. In reality, it contains the only mystery."

Albert Einstein, in 1905, was the first to argue for this dual nature to light; Niels Bohr, in 1924, was the last to accept it. For Einstein the equations discovered by Heisenberg and Erwin Schrödinger did nothing to make it more understandable. On this point, indeed, he and Bohr were in agreement (Bohr was interested in understanding experiments, rather than equations); but Bohr, unlike Einstein, was prepared to see in the wave-particle duality not a puzzle to be solved but a limitation to be lived with, forced upon us by the very existence of the "quantum of action" (resulting from Planck's constant h, defining in certain circumstances a minimal unit of action); what Bohr also called the quantum postulate. The implication, he thought, was that a certain "ideal of explanation" had to be given up, not that classical concepts were inadequate or incomplete or that new concepts were needed. This ideal was *the independence of a phenomenon of the means by which it is observed.*

With this ideal abandoned, the experimental context must enter into the very definition of a phenomenon. But that meant classical concepts enter essentially too, if only because the apparatus must be classically describable. In fact, Bohr held the more radical view that these were the *only* real concepts available (they were unrevisable; in his later writings, they were a condition on communicability, on the very use of ordinary language).

Less obviously, the quantum postulate also implied limitations on the "mutual definability" of classical concepts. But therein lay the key to what Bohr called the "generalization" of classical mechanics: certain classical concepts, like *space-time description, causation, particle, wave*, if given operational meaning in a given experimental context, excluded the use of others. Thus the momentum and position of a system could not both, in a single experimental context, be given a precise meaning: momentum in the range Δp and position in the range Δx must satisfy the inequality $\Delta p \Delta x \geqslant h$ (an example of the *Heisenberg uncertainty relations*).

As a result, phenomena were to be described and explained, in a given context, using only a subset of the total set of classical concepts normally available – and to neither require nor permit of any dovetailing with those in another, mutually exclusive, experimental context, using a different subset of concepts. That, in fact, is how genuine novelty was to arise, according to Bohr, despite the unrevisability of classical concepts: thus light behaved like a wave in one context, like a particle in another, without contradiction.

Concepts standing in this exclusionary relation he called "complementary." Bohr's great success was that he could show that indeed complementary concepts, at least those that could be codified in uncertainty relationships, could not be operationally defined in a single experimental context. Thus, in the case of the two-slit experiment, any attempt to determine which slit the photon passes through (say by measuring the recoil, hence the momentum, of the slit) leads to an uncertainty in its position sufficient to destroy the interference pattern. These were the highly publicized debates over foundations that Bohr held with Einstein, in the critical years just after the discovery of the new equations; Bohr won them all.

Bohr looked to the phenomena, not to the equations, surely a selling-point of his interpretation in the 1920s: the new formalism was after all mathematically challenging. When he first presented his philosophy of complementarity, at the Como lecture of 1927, he made clear that it was based on "the general trend of the development of the theory from its very beginning" (Bohr 1934: 52) – a reference to the so-called "old" quantum theory, rather than to the new formalism. The latter, he acknowledged, others in the audience understood much better than he.

It is in the equations that the problem of measurement is most starkly seen. The state ψ in non-relativistic quantum mechanics is a function on the *configuration space* of a system (or one isomorphic to it, like momentum space). A point in that space specifies the positions of all the particles comprising a system at each instant of time (respectively, their *momenta*). This function must be square-integrable, and is normalized so that its integral over configuration space (momentum space) is one. Its time development is determined by the *Schrödinger equation*, which is linear – meaning, if $\psi_1(t)$, $\psi_2(t)$ are solutions, then so is $c_1\psi_1(t)+c_2\psi_2(t)$, for arbitrary complex numbers c_1, c_2.

Now for the killer question. In many cases the linear (1:1 and norm-preserving, hence *unitary*) evolution of each state ψ_k admits of a perfectly respectable, deterministic, and indeed classical (or at least approximately classical) description, of a kind that can be verified and is largely uncontentious. Thus the system in state ψ_1, having passed through a semi-reflecting mirror, reliably triggers a detector. The system in state ψ_2, having been reflected by the mirror, reliably passes it by. But, by linearity, if ψ_1 and ψ_2 are solutions to the Schrödinger equation, so is $c_1\psi_1(t)+c_2\psi_2(t)$. What happens then?

The orthodox answer to that question is given by the *measurement postulate*: that in a situation like this, the state $c_1\psi_1(t)+c_2\psi_2(t)$ exists only prior to measurement. When the apparatus couples to the system, on measurement, the detector either fires or it does not, with probability $|c_1|^2$ and $|c_2|^2$ respectively. Indeed, as is often the case, when the measurement is *repeatable* – over sufficiently short times, the same measurement can be performed on the same system, yielding the same outcome – the state *must* have changed on the first experiment, from the initial superposition, $c_1\psi_1(t)+c_2\psi_2(t)$, to either the state ψ_1 or to the state ψ_2 (in which it thereafter persists on repeated measurements). That transition is in contradiction with the unitary evolution of the state, prior to measurement. It is *wave-packet reduction* (WPR).

What has that to do with the wave-particle duality? Just this: let the state of the photon as it is incident on the screen on the far side of the slits be written as the superposition $c_1\psi_1+c_2\psi_2+c_3\psi_3+\ldots+c_n\psi_n$, where ψ_k is the state in which the photon is localized in the kth region of the screen. Then, by the measurement postulate, and supposing it is *photon position* that is measured by exposing and processing a photographic emulsion, the photon is measured to be in region k with probability $|c_k|^2$. In this way the *wave* (the superposition, the wave extended over the whole screen) is converted to the *particle* (a localized spot on the screen). The appearance of a localized spot (and the disappearance of the wave everywhere else across the screen) is WPR.

Might WPR (and in particular the apparent conflict between it and the unitary evolution prior to measurement) be a consequence of the fact that the measurement apparatus has not itself been included in the dynamical description? Then model the apparatus explicitly, if only in the most schematic and idealized terms. Suppose, as before (as we require of a good measuring device), that the (unitary) dynamics is such that if the microscopic system is initially in the state ψ_k, then the state of the joint system (microscopic system together with the apparatus) after the measurement is reliably Ψ_k (with the apparatus showing "the kth-outcome recorded"). It now follows from linearity that if one has initially the superposition $c_1\psi_1+c_2\psi_2+\dots$, one obtains after measurement (by nothing but unitarity) the final state $c_1\Psi_1+c_2\Psi_2+\dots$, and nothing has been gained.

Should one then model the human observer as well? It is a fool's errand. The "chain of observation" has to stop somewhere – by applying the measurement postulate, not by modeling further details of the measuring process explicitly or the observers as physical systems themselves.

These observations were first made in detail, and with great rigor, by the mathematician John von Neumann in his *Mathematical Foundations of Quantum Mechanics* in 1932. They were also made informally by Erwin Schrödinger, by means of a well-known thought-experiment, in which a cat is treated as a physical system and modeled explicitly, as developing into a superposition of two macroscopic outcomes. It was upsetting (and not only to cat-lovers) to consider the situation when detection of ψ_1 reliably causes not only a Geiger-counter to fire but also the release of a poison that causes the *death* of the cat, described by Ψ_1. We, performing the experiment (if quantum mechanics is to believed), will produce a superposition of a live and dead cat of the form $c_1\Psi_1+c_2\Psi_2$. Is it only when we go on to *observe which it is* that we should apply the measurement postulate and conclude it is dead (with probability $|c_1|^2$ or alive (with probability $|c_2|^2$)? Or has the cat got there before us, and already settled the question? As Einstein inquired, "Is the moon there when nobody looks?" If so, then the state $c_1\Psi_1+c_2\Psi_2$ is simply a *wrong* or (at best) an *incomplete description* of the cat and the decaying atom, prior to observation.

The implication is obvious: why not look for a more detailed level of description? But von Neumann and Schrödinger hinted at the idea that a limitation like this was *inevitable*; that WPR was an expression of a certain limit to physical science; that it somehow brokered the link between the objective and the subjective aspects of science, between the object of knowledge, and the knowing subject; that ... Writings on this score trod a fine line between science and mysticism – or idealism.

Hence John Wheeler's summary (1983: 192), which reads like Berkeleyian idealism: "In today's words Bohr's point – and the central point of quantum theory – can be put into a single, simple sentence. 'No elementary phenomenon is a phenomenon until it is a registered (observed) phenomenon.'" And Heisenberg's: the "factual element" missing from the formalism "appears in the Copenhagen [orthodox] interpretation by the introduction of the observer." The term "the observer" was already ubiquitous in writings on relativity, but there it could be replaced by "inertial frame," meaning a concrete system of rods and clocks: no such easy translation was available in quantum mechanics.

Einstein had a simpler explanation. The quantum mechanical state is an *incomplete description*. WPR is purely *epistemic* – the consequence of learning something new. His argument (devised with Boris Podolsky and Nathan Rosen) was independent of micro–macro correlations, resting rather on correlations between *distant* systems: they too could be engineered so as to occur in a superposition. Thus Ψ_k might describe a particle A in state ψ_k correlated with particle B in state φ_k, where A and B are spatially remote from one another. In that case the observation that A is in state ψ_k would imply that B is in state φ_k – and one will learn this (with probability $|c_k|^2$) by applying the measurement postulate to the total system, as given by the state $c_1\Psi_1 + c_2\Psi_2$, on the basis only of measurements on A. How can B *acquire* a definite state (either φ_1 or φ_2) on the basis of the observation of the distant particle A? – and correspondingly, how can the probabilities of certain outcomes on measurements of B be changed? The implication, if there is to be no "spooky action-at-a-distance," is that B was *already* in one or the other states φ_1 or φ_2 – in which case the initial description of the composite system $c_1\Psi_1 + c_2\Psi_2$ was simply *wrong*, or at best *incomplete*. This is the famous *EPR argument*.

It was by investigating the statistical nature of such correlations in the 1960s and 1970s that foundational questions re-entered the mainstream of physics. They were posed by the physicist John Bell, in terms of a theory – any theory – that gives additional information about the systems A, B, over and above that defined by the quantum-mechanical state. He found that if such additional values to physical quantities ("hidden variables") are *local* – unchanged by remote experiments – then their averages (that one might hope will yield the quantum-mechanically predicted statistics) must satisfy a certain inequality. Schematically:

Hidden variables + Locality (+ background assumptions) ⇒ Bell inequality.

But experiment, and the quantum-mechanical predictions, went against the Bell inequality. Experiment thus went against Einstein: if there is to be a hidden level of description, not provided by the quantum-mechanical state, and satisfying very general background assumptions, it will have to be non-local.

But is that argument from non-locality, following on from Bell's work, really an argument against hidden variables? Not if quantum mechanics is *already* judged non-local, as it appears, assuming the completeness of the state, and making use of the measurement postulate. Bohr's reply to EPR in effect accepted this point: once the type of experiment performed remotely is changed, yielding some outcome, so too does the state for a local-event change; so too do the probabilities for local outcomes change. So, were single-case probabilities measurable, one would be able to signal superluminally (but of course neither they nor the state is directly measurable). Whether or not there are hidden variables, it seems, there is non-locality.

Pilot-wave theory

By the mid-1960s, the climate was altogether transformed. Not only had questions of realism and non-locality been subject to experimental tests, but it was realized – again, largely due to Bell's writings, newly anthologized as *Speakable and Unspeakable in Quantum Mechanics* – that something was amiss with Bohr's arguments for complementarity. For a detailed solution to the problem of measurement – incorporating, admittedly, a form of non-locality – was now clearly on the table, demonstrably equivalent to standard quantum mechanics.

That solution is the *pilot-wave theory* (also called "Bohmian mechanics"). It is explicitly dualistic: the wave function must satisfy Schrödinger's equation, as in the conventional theory, but it is taken as a physical field, albeit one that is defined on configuration space E^{3N} (where N is the number of particles); and in addition there is a unique trajectory in E^{3N} – specifying, instant by instant, the configuration of all the particles, as determined by the wave function.

Any complex-valued function ψ on a space can be written as $\psi = A \exp iS$, where A and S are real-valued functions on that space. In the simplest case of a single-particle ($N=1$) configuration, space is ordinary Euclidean space E^3. Let $\psi(x,t)$ satisfy the Schrödinger equation; the new postulate (the *guidance equation*) is that a particle of mass m at the point x at time t must have the velocity:

$$v(x,t) = (h/m)\nabla S(x,t).$$

If, furthermore, the probability density $\rho(x,t)$ on the configuration space of the particle at time t is given by the *Born rule*:

$$\rho(x,t) = A^2(x,t),$$

that is, if $\rho(x,t)\Delta V$ is the probability of finding the particle in volume ΔV about the point x at time t', then the probability of finding it in the region $\Delta V'$, to which ΔV is mapped by the guidance equation at time t', will be the same:

$$\rho'(x',t')\Delta V' = \rho(x,t)\Delta V.$$

What does "probability" really mean here? Never mind: that is a can of worms in any deterministic theory. Let us say it means whatever probability means in *classical* statistical mechanics, which is likewise deterministic. Thus conclude: the probability of a region of configuration space, as given by the Born rule, is preserved under the flow of the velocity field.

It is a humble enough claim, but it secures the empirical equivalence of the theory with the standard formalism, equipped with the measurement postulate, so long as particle positions are all that is directly measured. And it solves the measurement problem: nothing particularly special occurs on measurement. Rather, one simply discovers what is there – the particle positions at the instant they are observed.

The theory was in fact proposed very early, by Count Louis de Broglie, at the Fifth Solvay Conference, 1927. It found few supporters, and not even de Broglie was enthusiastic: it was a flat-footed version of what he was really after, a theory in which particles were singularities in fields. When it was rediscovered by David Bohm in 1952, the thought was likewise that it was a step to something more (a solution, perhaps, to the mathematical pathologies that plagued relativistic quantum theory). As such it languished: Bell was the first to present the theory for what it was, a complete solution to the problem of measurement in the non-relativistic arena.

Might orthodoxy have turned out to be different had de Broglie's ideas been championed more clearly or forcefully at Solvay and subsequently? Perhaps. But the window of opportunity was small. Paul Dirac and others, architects of the relativistic quantum theory, were rapidly led to a theory in which the particle number of a given species must dynamically change. This appeared forced by relativity theory, for reasons internal to the structure of the new mechanics. Since hugely successful, experimentally, by the mid-1930s there was a rather decisive reason to reject the pilot-wave theory: for no guidance equation could be found, then or subsequently, that described change in particle number. The empirical equivalence of the theory with standard quantum mechanics extended only to non-relativistic phenomena.

There was, however, another dimension to its neglect. For, if de Broglie's later writings are to be believed (de Broglie 1990: 178), what was never clear to him, even *following* Bohm's revival of the theory (and, we must infer, what was unclear to everyone else in this period), was how the pilot-wave theory accounted for WPR. It is that, in certain circumstances, the wave function can be written as a superposition of states, the vast majority of which at time t can, given a specific particle trajectory at time t, be *ignored*, both from the point of view of the guidance equation and for determining the probability measure over configuration space. This "dropping" – pragmatically ignoring – of components of the state amounts to WPR. It is an *effective* process, reflecting a computational convenience. The point is not difficult to grasp in simple cases – supposing the states superposed are completely non-overlapping, for example – but it was only implicit in Bohm's 1952 revival of the theory, and the generic understanding of this phenomenon, named "decoherence" in the 1970s by Dieter Zeh, was slow in coming. So too was an understanding of the true dimensions of the state. This is the conception that de Broglie had failed to grasp and that not even Bohm had made clear: that of the *wave-function of the universe*, a field on configuration space of vast dimensionality, subject to a continuous process of branching, corresponding to the countlessly large numbers of possible alternatives sanctioned by decoherence, including among them all possible experimental outcomes. It is because they decohere, with no interference, that you can ignore all the other branches save your own. This, the unitarily evolving universal state in pilot-wave theory, extends, as it must, to the entire universe. It is the same wave-function of the universe that one has in the Everett interpretation (see below).

State-reduction theories

The pilot-wave theory obviously has certain deficiencies, even setting to one side its failure in particle physics. Chief of them is the whiff of epiphenomenalism: the trajectories are controlled by the wave function, but the latter is the same whatever the trajectory. Relatedly, it is the wave function – the *effective* local part of it – that explains the dynamical properties and relations of quantum systems. Probability, meanwhile, remains the enigma that, classically, it has always been – but now tied to the Born rule, a rule presumably to be applied to that first configuration of particles which (together with the wave function) made up the initial conditions of the universe.

Subtlety is one thing, malice is another, as Einstein said: the Born probability measure, like the Liouville measure in classical statistical mechanics, *ought* to admit of exceptions – fluctuations away from equilibrium. The experimental implications of non-equilibrium pilot-wave theory are far-reaching; to suppose they will be forever concealed in perfect equilibrium smacks of conspiracy. They are so far-reaching, indeed, that they had better be confined to length-scales thus far unexplored: to the *Planck length*, for example, hence to the very early universe. Still, there may be signatures of hidden variables written in the heavens, and waiting to be found.

What if no such evidence of hidden variables is uncovered? What if no progress is made with relativistic guidance equations? De Broglie might have posed those questions in 1927, and probably did: eighty years later, dispiritingly, we are posing them again.

But the alternative is scarcely welcoming. Given that Bohr did not rely on any distinctively relativistic effects, the very existence of a fully realistic theory, involving additional equations to the standard formalism and dispensing with the measurement postulate, able to account for the appearance of WPR, and yielding the same probabilities as ordinary quantum mechanics, undermines Bohr's arguments for complementarity. Bohr argued for the *impossibility* of classical realism, not for its inferiority to idealism. If pilot-wave theory is such a realism, those arguments cannot stand.

Furthermore, Bohr's positive claims for complementarity now seem implausible. One of them, for the explanation of novelty even given the restriction to classical concepts, was supposed to apply whenever the use of some such concepts excluded, as a matter of principle, certain others. Bohr gave as examples the life sciences and psychology, but nothing came of either suggestion. And the restriction to classical concepts seems wrong, in the light of decoherence theory and the approach to the classical limit which that theory engenders. In terms of *theories*, it seems just the reverse. It is quantum theory that seems better able to mimic the classical, not the other way round.

It is against this backdrop that the advent of dynamical WPR theories should be assessed. The first WPR theory with a claim to genuinely foundational status is due to GianCarlo Ghirardi, Alberto Rimini, and Tullio Weber (1986). The GRW theory made explicit appeal to a *stochastic process* – in the simplest case, to a "hitting" process, under which the wave function ψ at random times t and at random points q is multiplied by a Gaussian ("bell-shaped") function well-localized about q. The result (for a single particle) is the transition

$$\psi(x,t) \rightarrow \psi_q(x,t) = K exp(-(1/(2d^2))(x-q)^2)\psi(x,t)$$

in which d is a new fundamental physical constant (with the dimensions of length), determining the degree of localization of the Gaussian, and K is a normalization constant. A further fundamental constant f determines the mean frequency with which this hitting occurs. Both are chosen so that for atomic systems the wave function is scarcely changed (the hits are infrequent, say with mean frequency 10^{-16} sec, and d is large, say 10^{-5}m, in comparison to atomic dimensions).

Two further key ideas are, first, that the probability of a hit at point q is determined by the norm of ψ_q (the integral of the modulus square of the RHS with respect to x) – this has the effect that a hit is more likely where the amplitude of the state prior to the hitting is large – and, second, that when two or more particles are present, each particle is subject to a hitting process. It follows that the state becomes well localized at q if the wave function of any one of the particles it describes is localized about q – that is to say, it is the sum of the probabilities of any one of its constituents becoming localized at q that matter. For very large numbers of particles (of the order of Avogadro's number, as comprise anything like a macroscopic, observable object), even with f as small as 10^{-16} sec, an individual atom is hit on average once in a hundred million years, so the wave function of a macroscopic system will become localized in a microsecond or less.

So much for the simplest model of this kind. There are various complications – for example, it turns out that one constant f is not enough (you need one constant for each species of particle, where the lighter the particle, the smaller the frequency) – and various sophistications – the *continuous state-reduction theory* of Ghirardi, Rimini, Weber, and Philip Pearle, which also accommodates particle indistinguishability and the concomitant symmetrization of the state. But on a number of points the key ideas are the same. There are, of course, no measurement postulates; the wave function, at any instant, is perfectly categorical – it is the distribution of "stuff" at that time. In conventional quantum mechanics (if we ask about position), only if the wave function vanishes outside ΔV is a particle really (with certainty) in ΔV: all that goes out of the window. The distribution of stuff determines the probabilities for subsequent "hits," but it is not itself probabilistic. This point tells against the criticism that Gaussians centered on any point q have "tails," suggesting that a particle thus localized at q is not really (not with probability one) at q.

Unless there is a genuine conceptual difficulty with the theory, the implication is this. With the *minimum* of philosophical complications – without introducing anything epiphenomenal, or a dualistic ontology, or things (trajectories) behaving in ways that have no operational meaning – *merely by changing the equations*, the measurement problem is solved. Therefore it cannot be a philosophical problem; genuinely philosophical problems are never like that.

But is it true that dynamical state-reduction theories are free of conceptual difficulties? Here is a *different* difficulty, concerning the tails. Consider, for example, the Schrödinger cat superposition $c_1\Psi_1 + c_2\Psi_2$. While the hitting mechanism will, in a microsecond or less, greatly reduce the amplitude of one term (say Ψ_1, describing the dead cat), in comparison to the other, it does not *eliminate* it – it is still there, as described by Ψ_1 (complete with grieving or outraged pet-lovers, etc.). All that structure is still there, encoded in the state. But the GRW theory simply denies that structure like this depicts anything – because its amplitude is so much less than that of the other component.

Whether or not you find this a serious problem will probably depend on your viewpoint on the Everett interpretation (see below). But unproblematically, uncontroversially, dynamical state reduction theories face an overwhelming difficulty: there is no relativistic GRW theory. Whether the problem is a principled one (whether dynamical WPR theories are in outright conflict with relativity) is debatable; that there is a theoretical problem is not: we are, it seems, to laboriously work out the equations of relativistic particle physics *all over again*.

The Everett interpretation

If this were all there was to say about the foundations of physics, the conclusion would be deeply troubling: the philosophy of physics would say of physics that it is seriously confused, in need of revision. From a naturalistic point of view, one might better conclude that it is the philosophy that is in trouble – specifically, that it is *realism* that is in trouble or, if not realism, then another fragment of our presuppositions.

Enter the *Everett interpretation*. Like GRW and pilot-wave theories, it involves wave-function realism, and like them it solves the measurement problem. Unlike them, it is *only* an interpretation. Crucially, it does not rely on any aspects of non-relativistic quantum mechanics not available in relativistic theory. So it applies smoothly to the latter. It demands no revisions.

With so much going for it, there had better be a terrible negative. It is that quantum mechanics under the Everett interpretation is *fantastic* – too fantastic, perhaps, to take seriously. For, in the face of the unitary development of a superposition of states which, in isolation, would each correspond to a distinct macroscopic state of affairs, it declares that *all* of them are real. It does not look for a mechanism to enhance the amplitude of one of them over all the others, or to otherwise put a marker on one rather than all the others. Welcome to the "many worlds interpretation."

Is the approach at all believable? But we should put that question to one side. (How believable, after all, is *classical* cosmology?) It was not, in any case, the usual question (however much it may have weighed privately); the usual question was whether the theory was even well defined. Here some more history is needed.

The achievement of Hugh Everett III, in his seminal 1957 paper, was to show how branching – the development of a single component of the wave function into a superposition – would as a consequence of the unitary evolution give rise to *registrations of sequences of states, as though punctuated by* WPR. To that end, he considered the unitary dynamical description of a recording instrument – a device with memory – and the question of what its memory would contain. What results after branching is a plurality of recording instruments, each with a record of a definite sequence of states (each of them the *relative state* of the state of the recording instrument at that time). The Born rule now defines a measure over this plurality, much as it did in the pilot-wave theory, thus recovering the usual predictions of quantum mechanics.

The approach, however, has a drawback. It hinted that *only* registration, or memory, or consciousness, need be involved in this notion of multiplicity; that, in fact, the theory was ultimately a theory of consciousness, and, to make good on its promise, that it had to explain why consciousness of branching was impossible.

There is further the objection: what are the probabilities *about*? In pilot-wave terms they were about the real trajectory of the universe in configuration space – of which is actual or real. Uncertainty about chance events always reflects ignorance, it might be thought. But if Everett is to be believed, all such trajectories come about. There is nothing to be ignorant of.

The interpretation was stillborn in another respect. Branching is basis-dependent, meaning that the quantum state can be represented as a superposition with respect to any orthogonal set of states. Which one (which basis) is to be used? Normally this is fixed by the measurement postulate: the states used represent the possible outcomes of the experiment. In pilot-wave and GRW theory the multiplicity is, roughly speaking, the possible particle configurations in E^{3N}. But here Everett made no comment. As framed by Bryce de Witt, in terms of a multiplicity of universes, the question is more urgent: what is this plurality, the "preferred basis," so called?

The three problems of *probability*, *consciousness*, and the *preferred basis* can all be linked. Thus, as conjectured by Michael Lockwood (1989), a theory of consciousness (or consciousness itself) might pick out a preferred basis, and even, according to David Albert and Barry Loewer (1988), a criterion of identity over time. The latter, Albert and Loewer insisted, was needed to make sense of probability, of what one is ignorant of (of what will happen *to me*). But if these are add-ons to the standard formalism, and idealistic to boot, they are self-defeating. The selling-point of the Everett interpretation is that it is a realist interpretation, based on physics *as is*. No wonder it languished in this period.

But with the concept of *decoherence*, in the early 1990s, came a different solution to the preferred-basis problem. The key to it is that branching and classicality concern only an *effective* dynamics, just as does WPR in the pilot-wave theory. Branching and the emergence of a quasi-classical dynamics go together FAPP ("for all practical purposes").

If branching reflects decoherence, and nothing else, no wonder there is no precise definition of the preferred basis; no wonder, either, that there is no precise classical limit to quantum mechanics (no limit of the form $h \to 0$), but only *effective* equations, FAPP, more or less approximate, depending on the regime of energy, mass, and scale concerned.

This philosophy is moreover continuous with now-standard methodology in the physical sciences. Thus Kenneth Wilson, winner of the 1982 Nobel Prize for Physics, showed how renormalization was best viewed as a demonstrably stable scheme of approximation, defined by a coarse-graining of an underlying physics that never needs to be explicitly known. It is the same in condensed-matter physics. In philosophy of science quite generally, there is wide consensus on this point: from nuclear physics to the solid state and biochemistry, the use of approximations and phenomenological equations is the norm. Who today would demand that there exist a precise and axiomatic theory of "molecules," for example, to legitimize the term?

But if the preferred-basis problem can be answered, the probability problem remains. Branch amplitudes had better be the quantity to which expectations should be tied, or we make nonsense of our reason for taking quantum mechanics seriously in the first place. Why should they be? Why the particular function of the amplitudes used in the Born rule? And the overriding question: what is the appropriate epistemic attitude to take in the face of branching? Does it make sense to speak of uncertainty? What are the probabilities probabilities of?

Defenders of Everett have answers to those questions. For example, to take the last, that they are the probabilities that things now are thus-and-so, given that they were such-and-such then. But whether that is enough to ground an objective notion of *uncertainty* is hard to say. If such a notion is available, they can also give reasons why it should take the quantitative form that it does, in terms of the Born rule. Thus Deutsch, following Bruno de Finetti's approach to probability, considered the constraints placed on rational agents by the axioms of decision theory. Let them fix their utilities on the outcomes of quantum experiments ("games") as they see fit; then, if subject to those constraints, their preferences among games implicitly define a probability measure over the outcomes of each game (as that which yields the same ordering in terms of the expected utilities of each game). Given quantum mechanics, the claim goes, then, whatever the choice of utilities, the only permitted measure is the Born rule.

Whither quantum mechanics?

And yet the Everett interpretation remains inherently fantastic. The prospects for a relativistic pilot-wave theory or state-reduction theory are discouraging. Bohr's doctrine of complementarity, as something forced by experiment, is no longer credible.

No wonder then that, in the circumstances, many look to the frontiers of physics, and especially to developments, whether theoretical or experimental, in quantum gravity. There, all are agreed, key concepts of relativity theory or quantum theory, or both, will have to give. Others look to frontiers in technology: whatever the deficiencies of experiments to date to discriminate between the realist solutions on offer, discriminate they eventually will (taking pilot-wave theory to include the concept of *quantum disequilibrium*) – whether at the ultra-microscopic level or at the boundary between micro and macro, experiment will ultimately decide.

That, in the final analysis, is what is wrong with Bohr's quietism today. Grant that there are realist alternatives, and it is reasonable to expect experiment eventually to decide between them. Bohr could not so much as acknowledge them as genuine alternatives. There are lessons for neo-Bohrians, today, who propose to view quantum mechanics as a generalization, not of classical mechanics, but of classical probability or of information theory: it is not enough to have as their intended outcome a form of quietism; they must show there are no realist alternatives. There is nothing in their arguments to date to so much as hint that they can.

See also Determinism; Measurement; Probability; Space and time.

References

Albert, D. Z. and Loewer, Barry (1988) "Interpreting the Many Worlds Interpretation," *Synthese* 77: 195–213.

Bohm, David (1952) "A Suggested Interpretation of the Quantum Theory in Terms of 'Hidden' Variables, I and II," *Physical Review* 85: 166–93.

Bohr, Niels (1934) *Atomic Theory and the Description of Nature*, Cambridge: Cambridge University Press (translation of *Atomtheorie und Naturbeschreibung*, Berlin: Springer, 1931).

de Broglie, Louis (1990) *Heisenberg's Uncertainties and the Probabilistic Interpretation of Wave Mechanics*, Dordrecht: Kluwer.

Everett, Hugh III (1957) "'Relative State' Formulation of Quantum Mechanics," *Reviews of Modern Physics* 29: 454–62.

Feynman, R. P. with Leighton, R. B., and Sands, M. (1963) *The Feynman Lectures on Physics*, Volume I, Reading, MA: Addison-Wesley.

Ghirardi, G. C., Rimini, A., and Weber, T. (1986) "Unified Dynamics for Microscopic and Macroscopic Systems," *Physical Review* D34: 470.

Heisenberg, Werner (1959) *Physics and Philosophy*, London: Allen & Unwin.

Lockwood, Michael (1989) *Mind, Brain and the Quantum*, Oxford: Blackwell.

Wheeler, J. A. (1983) "Law Without Law," in J. A. Wheeler and W. H. Zurek (eds) *Quantum Theory and Experiment*, Princeton, NJ: Princeton University Press.

Further reading

Apart from the text already cited, Bohr's most important writings on foundations is his "Can Quantum-Mechanical Description of Physical Reality Be Considered Complete?"(1935), and "Discussion with Einstein on Epistemological Problems in Atomic Physics" (1949), both reprinted in J. Wheeler and W. Zurek (eds) *The Quantum Theory of Measurement* (Princeton, NJ: Princeton University Press, 1983). This is a collection of nearly all the most important writings on the problem of measurement in the first half-century of quantum mechanics (but note that the order of pages 148 and 149 of Bohr's 1935 paper in Wheeler and Zurek should be reversed). For a commentary on the debates between Einstein and Bohr, with special attention to the EPR argument, see A. Fine, *The Shaky Game* (Chicago: University of Chicago Press, 1986). For the charge that orthodoxy in quantum mechanics amounted to "Copenhagen hegemony," see J. T. Cushing, *Quantum Mechanics* (Chicago: University of Chicago Press, 1994); for a contrasting view, see S. Saunders, "Complementarity and Scientific Rationality," *Foundations of Physics* 35 (2005): 347–72; available: http://arxiv.org/abs/quant-ph/0412195. For detailed commentaries and the proceedings of the Fifth Solvay Conference in English translation, including an extensive discussion of the pilot-wave theory, see A. Valentini and G. Bacciagaluppi, *Quantum Theory at the Crossroads: Reconsidering the 1927 Solvay Conference* (Cambridge: Cambridge University Press, 2007); available online at http://arxiv.org/abs/quant-ph/0609184. For examples of antirealist approaches today, see A. Zeilinger, "The message of the Quantum" *Nature* 438: 743 (2005), and J. Bub, "Quantum Mechanics Is About Quantum Information"; available: http://arxiv.org/abs/quant-ph/0408020v2. For an overview of the measurement problem and much else in physics as it stands today, see Ch. 29 of R. Penrose, *The Road to Reality* (London: Jonathan

Cape, 2004); for reasons to think that the decisive solution to the problem (or "paradox," as Penrose calls it) lies in the realm of quantum gravity, see Ch. 30. More introductory is A. Rae, *Quantum Physics: Illusion or Reality?* (Cambridge: Cambridge University Press, 1986), and, for mathematical beginners who yet seek rigor, R. Hughes, *The Structure and Interpretation of Quantum Mechanics* (Cambridge: Cambridge University Press, 1989). The first chapter of M. Redhead's *Incompleteness, Non-Locality and Realism* (Oxford: Oxford University Press, 1987) is a self-contained introduction to the formalism, but at a much faster pace. The rest of Redhead's book is a systematic study of the constraints on hidden variables posed by quantum mechanics, whether by violation of the Bell inequalities, or by other, algebraic constraints. Similar ground, but on a more general (geometric and logical) plane, is covered by I. Pitowsky's *Quantum Probability–Quantum Logic* (New York: Springer-Verlag, 1989). Neither Redhead nor Pitowsky discuss the pilot-wave theory (nor, indeed, special relativity) explicitly. For an investigation of quantum non-locality in those contexts, see T. Maudlin's *Quantum Non-Locality and Relativity*, 2nd edn (Oxford: Blackwell, 2002). See J. S. Bell's anthology *Speakable and Unspeakable in Quantum Mechanics* (Cambridge: Cambridge University Press, 1987) for the dozen or more papers on similar themes that so reinvigorated the debate over foundations in quantum mechanics. The penultimate chapter "Are There Quantum Jumps?" remains one of the clearest published outlines of the then just-discovered GRW theory. For a recent review of state reduction theory, see C. Ghirardi, in E. Zalta (ed.) "Collapse Theories," The Stanford Encyclopedia of Philosophy (spring 2002 edition); available: http://plato.stanford.edu/archives/spr2002/entries/qm-collapse. For pilot-wave theory, see S. Goldstein, "Bohmian Mechanics," in *ibid.*; available: http://plato.stanford.edu/entries/qm-bohm. For "non-equilibrium" pilot-wave theory, and the clear hope of an experimental verdict on the existence of hidden variables, see A. Valentini, "Black Holes, Information Loss, and Hidden Variables"; available: http://arxiv.org/abs/hep-th/0407032. For the decoherence-based Everett interpretation, see M. Gell-Mann and J. Hartle, "Quantum Mechanics in the Light of Quantum Cosmology," in W. Zurek (ed.) *Complexity, Entropy, and the Physics of Information* (Redwood City, CA: Addison Wesley, 1990). For elaborations, see S. Saunders, "Time, Quantum Mechanics, and Probability," *Synthese* 114 (1998): 405–44; available: http://arxiv.org/abs/quant-ph/0111047, and D. Wallace, "Everett and Structure," *Studies in the History and Philosophy of Modern Physics* 34 (2002): 87–105; available: http://arxiv.org/abs/quant-ph/0107144. For a review of decoherence theory that is non-committal on many worlds, see W. Zurek, "Decoherence and the Transition from Quantum to Classical," *Physics Today* 44 (1991): 36; available, with added commentary: http://arxiv.org/abs/quant-ph/0306072. For Deutsch's decision-theory argument, see "Quantum Theory of Probability and Decisions," in *Proceedings of the Royal Society of London* A455 (1999): 3129–37, available: http://arxiv.org/abs/quant-ph/9906015, and its subsequent strengthening by D. Wallace, "Quantum Probability from Subjective Likelihood: Improving on Deutsch's Proof of the Probability Rule," *Studies in the History and Philosophy of Modern Physics* 38 (2007) 311–32, available at: http://philsci-archive.pitt.edu. For criticism of the Everett interpretation on the ground of probability, see D. Lewis's "How Many Tails Has Schrödinger's Cat?" in F. Jackson and G. Priest (eds) *Lewisian Themes* (Oxford: Oxford University Press, 2004).

54

PSYCHOLOGY

Richard Samuels

Introduction

The philosophy of psychology is concerned with issues that span work in the philosophy of science, philosophy of mind, and empirical psychology. Psychology is not a unified field but a diverse confederation of subfields and research programs, any of which could form a focal point for philosophical attention; and indeed many have, including psychoanalysis, social psychology, and abnormal psychology. But it is *cognitive psychology* – and the field of cognitive science, of which it is a central part – that has dominated research in the philosophy of psychology; and it is this research that I focus on here.

Though cognitive scientists disagree on many issues, one widespread commitment is that the mind is a *mechanism* of some sort: roughly, a physical device decomposable into functionally specifiable subparts. On this assumption, a central task for psychology is to characterize the nature of that mechanism: its basic operations, component parts, and development. Much philosophy of psychology is concerned with the project; and in the following sections I aim to provide a flavor of the research by considering three prominent issues:

- Is the mind a *computer* of some sort?
- To what extent are minds *modular* in organization?
- To what extent is our mental structure *innately* specified?

Each issue combines in complex ways empirical and philosophical considerations; and collectively they identify many of the major faultlines that divide central positions in the philosophy of psychology and cognitive science.

Computationalism

If the mind is a machine, then what sort of machine might it be? One very influential answer is that the mind is a *computer*. According to this view, psychological processes such as perceiving, reasoning and remembering are – or, at any rate, depend on – computational processes. Although this general idea has dominated much philosophy of psychology and cognitive science, it has been elaborated in different ways; and among the most important and widely discussed distinctions is that between so-called *classical* and *connectionist* (or parallel distributed processing) versions.

Classical computationalism

Classicism is a view with deep historical roots, though it is perhaps the research of twentieth-century logicians, such as Alan Turing, that has exerted greatest influence on its conception of computation and, hence, of psychological processes. According to this view, the mind is a *symbol manipulation* device: an information-processing mechanism that operates on internally encoded bodies of information, called "data structures" or "symbols." Slightly more precisely, according to classicism:

(a) *Psychological processes employ mental symbols.* Such representations are language-like in that they possess both *semantic* properties – such as reference and meaning – and formal, or *syntactic*, properties: they are composed from constituents combined according to grammatical rules. For this reason classicists are sometimes said to advocate a "language of thought hypothesis" (Fodor 1975).

(b) *Psychological processes are sensitive to the syntactic structure of symbols.* Though symbols have semantic properties, cognitive processes are sensitive only to their *syntactic* or formal properties.

(c) *Psychological processes are algorithmic.* Roughly put, they can be characterized by sets of basic operations that are guaranteed to produce a determinate outcome in some finite number of steps. Those basic operations are sometimes said to be merely mechanical in the sense that no insight or ingenuity is required either to perform them or to determine what step to perform next.

Together these claims yield a general conception of psychological processes as algorithmically specifiable ones defined over the syntactic properties of mental symbols. For almost fifty years this proposal has been central to much work in cognitive science, where researchers have sought to specify the representations and algorithms on which such cognitive capacities as language, vision and reasoning depend. Moreover, it has played double duty as a metaphysics of mind. Minds, it is claimed, just are classical computers of the right sort; and having a thought (belief, desire, etc.) just is to bear an appropriate computational relation to some symbolic mental representation.

Virtues
Advocates of classical computationalism typically defend their view on explanatory grounds; for not only has it underwritten much productive empirical research, but it also helps explain some pervasive and fundamental aspects of cognition. Two are especially worthy of mention.

Rational causation

Many mental processes – most obviously reasoning – involve relations between mental states that are both causal and inferential (or rational). If I believe, for example, that all men are mortal and that I am a man, I may thereby come to believe I am mortal as well. In such a case, the earlier beliefs not only cause the latter, their meanings are also related in such a way as to provide premises from which to infer the latter. Historically, this phenomenon posed a serious explanatory challenge: a version of the notorious *homunculus regress*. To explain such rational-cum-causal relations, it seems that meanings themselves must be causally efficacious, which in turn appears to require some inner interpreter – an intelligent subsystem, or homunculus – for which thoughts have meanings. But then the same problem of coordinating semantic and causal relations recurs for the homunculus, resulting in a regress of interpreters.

Classicists seek to address the problem by rejecting the assumption that rational causation is explicable only if meanings are causally efficacious. Instead they invoke an idea familiar to logicians, that inferences can be characterized proof-theoretically in terms of formal rules. (*Modus ponens* is a simple example.) When applied to the task of understanding cognition, the idea is that mental processes are inferential not because of any unexplained sensitivity to meanings, but because they depend on formal rules which, though defined over the syntax of representations, are like logical rules in that they preserve semantic relations. Moreover, since by assumption cognitive processes are algorithmic, they are ultimately decomposable into combinations of operations the execution of which requires no intelligence at all. The threat of regress is thus blocked and the homunculi expelled.

Productivity and systematicity

A second, widely cited, virtue of classicism is that it explains the productivity and systematicity of thought (Fodor and Pylyshyn 1988). Human thought seems *productive* in at least the sense that at any particular time we are capable of entertaining a great many thoughts, many of which are novel to us. Further, human thought seems *systematic* in roughly the sense that if someone is capable of entertaining some thoughts, he or she is thereby capable of thinking others as well. So far as we know, for example, no one is capable of entertaining the thought that John loves Mary, yet incapable of entertaining the thought that Mary loves John.

Classicists purport to explain those phenomena by assuming that thought depends on a combinatorial system of representations. On this view, thought is productive because relatively simple representations – if you like, words in the language of thought – can be combined according to syntactic rules to produce more complex expressions, which can in turn be combined according to the very same rules to produce still more complex representations, and so on *ad infinitum*. Similarly, thought is systematic because given some set of mental representations – "MARY," "LOVES," and "JOHN," for example – the very same rules, being defined over the syntax of the representations, permit the generation of multiple complex expressions – in the present case, both "JOHN LOVES MARY" and "MARY LOVES JOHN." Classicism's ability to provide elegant explanations of systematicity and productivity is widely regarded as among its main virtues.

Objections

For all its apparent virtues classicism has been subject to a bewildering array of objections. Some are relatively *a priori* in character. In his notorious *Chinese Room argument*, for example, John Searle purports to show that performing the right computations is insufficient for understanding. The argument proceeds from a thought-experiment:

> A native English speaker who knows no Chinese [is] locked in a room full of boxes of Chinese symbols (a database) together with a book of instructions for manipulating the symbols (the program). Imagine that people outside the room send in other Chinese symbols which, unknown to the person in the room, are questions in Chinese (the input). And imagine that by following the instructions in the program the man in the room is able to pass out Chinese symbols which are correct answers to the questions (the output). (Searle 1999: 115)

From outside it seems that the system understands Chinese. But, according to Searle, no matter what program the man executes, he won't know what the symbols *mean*. Thus mastery of syntactic operations – of the program – is insufficient for semantics; and since understanding a sentence requires a grasp of what the sentence *means*, running a program is insufficient for understanding as well.

The critical discussion surrounding Searle's argument is too large to consider in detail here (see Preston and Bishop 2002). But one common response is that, as an objection to classicism, it misses the mark. Classicists do not claim that executing the right program is, by itself, sufficient for thought. That would require the acceptance of a claim which classicists routinely deny: that computational role – the way the program uses a representation – determines its meaning. Rather, what classicists maintain is that thinking is a computational process operating on semantically evaluable representations, while *leaving open* – indeed frequently *endorsing* – the option that semantic properties are determined by something other than computational role, such as causal relations to the environment. Thus, according to the objection, the conclusion of Searle's argument is wholly compatible with the truth of classicism.

Another, more empirically oriented, kind of objection to classicism seeks to draw conclusions from explanatory failures of cognitive science. One major class of difficulties, often subsumed under the heading of the "frame problem," concern the explanatory challenge posed by our ability to determine the information that is *relevant* to the tasks we perform (Ford and Pylyshyn 1996). In particular, when making plans or revising our beliefs, we somehow manage to identify the information that is relevant to the task at hand and ignore the rest. How is this *relevance sensitivity* to be explained in classical terms? It is implausible that we survey *all* our beliefs, since such a strategy would require more time and computational power than we possess. Some more computationally feasible process is required. Yet many doubt that such a process can be specified in classical terms. It has been suggested, for example, that relevance is unlikely to be explicable in classical terms because it is a *holistic* property of thought, in roughly the sense that the relevance of a given thought depends on a broad array of *surrounding conditions*, such as one's background beliefs and intentions.

Connectionism

Whether classicists can address this and other problems remains a point of considerable dispute. But many have taken such challenges as grounds for exploring alternative accounts of cognition, of which the most influential is *connectionism*. Though connectionist proposals vary considerably in detail, they share a basic, neurally inspired, conception of our cognitive machinery. Cognitive systems are, on this view, *multilayer* networks of *nodes* attached to one another by *weighted connections*. In prototypical networks, activation spreads from an input layer of nodes to an output layer – typically via *hidden* layers of units – and the weights of connecting nodes are adjusted by some sort of *learning algorithm*, such as back-propagation, so that the system can "learn" to perform various tasks. This general conception of cognitive systems has proven to be of considerable utility to psychologists and has been used with varying degrees of success to model many psychological processes and capacities, including vision, language acquisition, concept-learning, and motor control.

On some conceptions of connnectionism, there is no conflict with classicism. For example, one common view, known as "implementational connectionism," seeks not to replace classicism but merely to explain how classical systems are implemented or realized in the brain. But even those who seek to displace classical accounts – so-called "eliminative connectionists" – typically acknowledge many important commonalities. Specifically, they often share with classicists the assumptions that cognition is both representational and computational. It is representational because the nodes in a connectionist network – especially input and output nodes – are widely assumed to represent properties and objects; and they are computational both because learning rules are algorithmic and because the spread of activation from input to output nodes can be interpreted as computing a function.

Where, then, *do* the main differences reside? Perhaps the most widely cited difference is that connectionist representations are typically not *syntactically* structured. As a consequence, connectionists typically reject both the classical conception of mental representation and the attendant account of cognitive processes as defined over the syntactic properties of representations.

Virtues

Connectionist systems are often said to possess characteristics that make them apt for modeling cognition, including:

- *Speed*: because networks process information in parallel they can be fast.
- *"Graceful degradation"*: in contrast to classical computers, the performance of a neural network remains relatively unaffected by degradation in the input signal or by damage to the system.
- *Neural-realism*: networks are more brain-like than are classical computers.

- *Learning*: connectionist networks show an impressive ability to "learn from experience."
- *Multiple constraint satisfaction*: neural networks easily address problems that require the resolution of many conflicting constraints in parallel.

Critics respond that some of those virtues (e.g., speed and "graceful degradation") are not reasons for rejecting classicism, but at most reasons for adopting implementational connectionism. Other putative virtues, they claim, have been over-sold. For example, it has been argued that the resemblance to real brains is a very loose one; and that classical systems also learn and solve problems involving multiple constraints. An assessment of those claims remains a topic of ongoing debate.

Objections

It has also been argued that eliminative connectionism exhibits some serious deficiencies. Perhaps the most common complaint is that it fails to explain core aspects of our representational capacities. For instance, Fodor and Pylyshyn (1988) argue that connectionists lack a satisfactory explanation of the systematicity and productivity of thought. More recently, Gary Marcus (2001) has argued that connectionist networks of the normal sort fail to accommodate the fact that humans not only represent categories (such as the category of *cats*) but also individuals (e.g., Tiddles and Tom).

Another concern is that connectionism has done little to address the deepest problems encountered by classical approaches. For example, the frame problem arises most clearly in relation to flexible, knowledge-intensive, processes such as reasoning and planning. But connectionism has made relatively little progress in understanding such processes, let alone in providing any systematic account of how we successfully identify relevant information when engaged in reasoning or planning.

Hybrid views and radical alternatives

In recent years, theorists have become less inclined to view the *classicism–connectionism* debate as a dispute between two mutually exclusive versions of computationalism. One common proposal is that we need to posit *hybrid* models that combine both classical and connectionist components. It has been suggested, for example, that "higher" cognitive processes, such as planning and deliberative reasoning, depend on a classical architecture, while more associative processes, such as implicit learning, depend on connectionist mechanisms (Sloman 1996).

Another, more radical, development is the claim that both classicists and most connectionists are wrong to assume that the mind is a computer of *any* sort. Instead, it is claimed that we should think of the brain's neural networks and the connectionist systems used to model them as *dynamical systems* best described by the sorts of differential equations found in physics (Port and van Gelder 1995). Assessing this dynamical systems theory and other alternatives remains a central project for the philosophy of psychology.

Modularity

The classicism–connectionism debate is concerned largely with the mind's *micro-architecture*: the basic elements and operations on which mental activity depends. But there is widespread agreement that minds are also organized into larger *macro-architectural* units. Historically, these were called "faculties," though contemporary theorists tend to speak of "cognitive systems"; and in recent years much discussion of the nature of those systems has occurred in the context of debate over *modularity*.

To a first approximation, debates over modularity concern the extent to which minds are composed from autonomous systems dedicated to restricted information-processing tasks. Systems that are restricted in those ways tend to be referred to as "modules"; and those relatively free from such constraints are said to be "non-modular." At one extreme, for example, is the sort of radically *non-modular* view of minds as comprised of one (or perhaps a few) general-purpose computers that can process many different kinds of information, and thereby perform many different tasks. At the other extreme, is the sort of radical modularity on which minds are composed from thousands of highly specialized and entirely autonomous devices, each dedicated to a very specific task and capable of processing only a highly restricted range of information. In reality, neither position is taken seriously. Instead, the debate is concerned largely with articulating and assessing a range of intermediate positions.

Fodorian modularity

One well-known modularity hypothesis defended by Fodor (1983) and others is that the modular structure of the mind is restricted to *input* systems (those responsible for perception, including language perception) and *output* systems (those responsible for producing behavior). On this view, central systems – those responsible for reasoning and decision-making – are non-modular. Thus minds are modular only at the periphery.

Fodor's defense of this proposal goes hand-in-hand with an attempt to articulate an appropriate notion of modularity. Fodorian modules are characterized by a cluster of features that they tend to exhibit to some interesting degree. Specifically, modules are prototypically:

- *domain-specific*: they operate on a limited range of inputs, defined by some task domain like vision or language-processing;
- *informationally encapsulated*: they have limited access to information in other systems;
- *inaccessible*: other mental systems have only limited access to a module's computations;
- *shallow*: their outputs are not conceptually elaborated;
- *mandatory*: they respond automatically to input;
- *fast*: their operation is relatively fast;
- *neurally localized*;
- subject to *characteristic* and *specific breakdowns*; and
- their development exhibits a *characteristic pace* and *sequence*.

Not all of these characteristics are of equal theoretical importance. Domain specificity and informational encapsulation are the most central, while the others, in large measure, are empirical consequences of those more central characteristics. Fodor argues, on the basis of evidence from the study of vision and speech comprehension, that input systems are modular in the above sense. In contrast, he maintains, central systems are likely to be both domain-general and informationally unencapsulated. They are likely to be domain-general because the processes responsible for reasoning and decision-making function to combine inputs from different perceptual domains. And they are likely to be unencapsulated because there are few constraints on the sorts of information we can use in determining what to believe or what to do. For example, Fodor maintains that almost any of a person's beliefs can be relevant to the sort of reasoning characteristic of science – what is sometimes called "abductive" reasoning, or "inference to the best explanation."

Massive modularity

Though Fodor's view has been challenged from many directions, one of the most recent and intriguing responses comes from those who advocate a *massive modularity hypothesis* (MM). Advocates of MM accept that input and output systems are modular. But, *pace* Fodor, they maintain that central systems are largely or entirely modular as well. So, for example, it has been suggested that there are modules for such central processes as social reasoning, biological categorization, and probabilistic inference.

What should we make of that proposal? As one would expect, it will depend in large measure on an assessment of evidence for and against the existence of particular modules – evidence which at this time is inconclusive. But advocates of MM also defend their views on the basis of quite general considerations about the nature of cognition. Consider the following example:

> *Task Specificity Argument:* There are a great many cognitive tasks whose solutions impose quite different demands. So, for example, the demands on vision are distinct from those of speech recognition, probabilistic judgment, grammar induction, and so on. Moreover, since it is very hard to believe there could be a single general inference mechanism for all of them, for each such task we should postulate the existence of a distinct mechanism, whose internal processes are computationally specialized for processing different sorts of information in the way required to solve the task. (Carruthers 2006)

This argument is not intended as a deductive proof of MM, but only to render it plausible. Nonetheless, I doubt it shows even this much. If the only alternative to MM were a mind comprised of a single *general-purpose* mechanism treating all problems in the same way, then MM would be the more plausible option. But these are manifestly *not* the only options. First, denying MM is wholly compatible with the existence of many specialized mechanisms for perception and motor control. But even if we focus on central systems, positing multiple dedicated modules is not the only way of explaining our capacity to perform many different reasoning tasks. A familiar alternative is that relatively unspecialized inference mechanisms use different bodies of specialized information in solving different problems. A major difficulty with the present argument is that it fails to adjudicate between MM and this familiar alternative.

So, it is far from clear that the standard arguments for MM are satisfactory. It is also worth noting that MM, at least in radical form, struggles to accommodate some central aspects of human cognition. For example:

- *Conceptual integration*: we are capable of freely combining concepts across different subject matters or content domains. Not only can I have thoughts about colors, about numbers, about shapes, and so on, but I can have thoughts that concern *all* these things – for example, that I had two, roughly round, red steaks for lunch.
- *Generality of thought*: not only can we freely combine concepts, we can also deploy the resulting thoughts in our theoretical and practical deliberations – to assess their truth or plausibility, but also to assess their relevance to our plans and projects.
- *Inferential holism*: given surrounding conditions – especially background beliefs – the relevance of a representation to the theoretical or practical tasks in which one engages can change dramatically. Indeed, it would seem that given appropriate background assumptions, almost any belief can be relevant to the task in which one engages.

Although some maintain that those features can be accommodated within a wholly modular account of cognition, a more plausible approach is to posit some genuinely non-modular central systems. This does not require that all central systems be modular in the way Fodor appears to suppose. Another possibility is that central processes are subserved by both modular and non-modular systems (Stanovich 2004). According to its advocates, this *dual systems* account possesses the virtues of MM while better accommodating a host of phenomena, including those outlined above.

Nativism

Thus far I have discussed two general issues about the structure of the mind. A related issue concerns the *acquisition* of mental structure: To what extent is the mind's structure *innately specified*? Discussion of the question is often couched as a dispute between *nativism* and *non-nativism* of which empiricism is a central sort. In brief, nativists claim that the mind contains *lots* of innate structures: concepts, bodies of information, psychological mechanisms, and modules. In contrast, non-nativists maintain that the mind contains relatively little innate structure. For example, empiricists typically suggest that the mind comes equipped with little more than perceptual mechanisms and a few systems for domain-general learning, such as associative learning mechanisms (e.g., Pavlovian conditioning) and general-purpose, inductive, learning mechanisms.

Linguistic nativism

Disputes over innateness have emerged in connection with a broad array of psychological phenomena, including our intuitive understanding of the physical world, arithmetic, and concept acquisition. But it is in connection with language that the issues have been most extensively explored. Here, largely under Noam Chomsky's influence, nativist proposals have dominated research for almost half a century.

Researchers working on language tend to suppose that when acquiring a language one comes to possess an internal grammar – or an internal representation of a grammar – for that language. (This helps explain, among other things, the systematicity and productivity of language.) Clearly, it is implausible that the grammar possessed by a competent speaker – for instance, a grammar for English as opposed to French or Hindi – is innately specified since the grammar that one acquires depends on the linguistic environment that one inhabits. Nonetheless, in contrast to other organisms, all humans everywhere – save those suffering extreme pathology or environmental deprivation – reliably acquire competence in some natural language within the first few years of life. That suggests, with only a hint of idealization, that humans share some set of innate resources – some *initial state* – that permits the acquisition of a grammar for the language they speak. A central problem for any account of language acquisition is thus to characterize the initial state: those innate resources which reliably enable a grammar to be acquired on the basis of the available environmental information.

What are the options? One major distinction is that between linguistic *empiricism* and linguistic *nativism*. Empiricists claim that language acquisition depends on the same domain-general mechanisms that are responsible for cognitive development in other domains. In contrast, linguistic nativists claim that at least some of the innate resources on which language acquisition depends are specific to the domain of language. But even if one endorses some version of linguistic nativism, there is still plenty of room for disagreement over the nature and extent of our innate language-specific resources. For instance, Chomskians claim that we possess an innate *universal grammar*: a rich body of innately specified knowledge that specifies the properties shared by all natural languages (Chomsky 1980). But one may be a linguistic nativist without being a Chomskian. For example, one might think there is an innately specified, language-specific, learning mechanism or module, while denying that there is an innate universal grammar.

Arguments

The debate over linguistic nativism is a largely empirical one; and like other empirical debates, different proposals are assessed in terms of their overall ability to accommodate evidence in a simple, powerful, and conservative manner. Here, there are many sorts of evidence that are relevant, including: evidence for linguistic universals; evidence concerning the relative ease of language acquisition; evidence concerning the specific patterns of error that occur during language acquisition; evidence of selective impairment and genetic disorders; and evidence from computational modeling. But perhaps the most influential argument for linguistic nativism – and the one that has received most attention from philosophers – has come to be known as the *poverty of the stimulus argument* (PoSA).

The PoSA has been formulated in a number of different ways. But the rough idea is that some version of linguistic nativism must be correct because the information that children receive from the environment is too impoverished to permit an *empiricist learner* – one lacking any innate language-specific knowledge, mechanisms, or biases – to acquire the grammar for their language.

Though the PoSA has been widely accepted by linguists, it has also been subjected to sustained criticism. One major challenge concerns the issue of *what* environmentally derived information is available in the course of language acquisition. Nativists have tended, for example, to suppose that children are seldom provided with negative data – roughly, information about when an utterance is *not* grammatical. But recently that assumption has come under scrutiny; and researchers have argued that such data are both available to and used by children in the course of language development (Chouinard and Clark 2003).

Another major challenge concerns the nature of empiricist learners. Almost everyone agrees that traditional empiricist accounts of language-learning, such as those that have emerged from the behaviorist tradition, are inadequate. But in recent years there has been an explosion of research on statistical learning (Pereira 2000); and some have suggested that this research may form the basis for a satisfactory empiricist account of language acquisition. Though a systematic assessment of the methods is beyond the scope of the present chapter, it is far from clear that they undermine the PoSA for linguistic nativism. Recall: What the PoSA purports to show is merely that language acquisition requires some set of innate language-specific structures or biases. But the current state of research on statistical learning seems wholly compatible with this claim. Specifically, our most successful computational models of language-learning invariably assume language-specific constraints. For example, they assume some model (or representational scheme) relevant to the domain of language; and they presuppose constraints on the inputs that the learning system receives (e.g., sentences in the target language as opposed to the myriad other kinds of inputs that a learning device may receive). Though there is much more to say on the matter, it is far from clear that without an account of how such constraints are acquired by empiricist learning, those models vindicate empiricism as opposed to suggesting a variant on linguistic nativism: one which posits an innate language-specific, statistical, learning mechanism or module.

What is innateness?

Much debate over *innateness* in cognitive science proceeds under the assumption that the notion is clear enough to permit the framing of substantive empirical issues. But there are, in fact, considerable difficulties in understanding what innateness is; and some prominent theorists have even suggested that very concept is "fundamentally confused" (Griffiths 2002). If such a claim could be sustained, it would appear to have important implications for research in psychology. For not only would it undermine nativism in its various forms, but it would also threaten the main empiricist alternatives, since they too presuppose the coherence of the innateness concept.

One standard reason for claiming that innateness is a confused concept is that it is said to confound several properties under a single term: properties that are neither co-extensive nor, by themselves, adequate to characterize what we mean by "innate." For instance, it is sometimes claimed that innate traits are those that are *present at birth*, even though presence at birth is neither necessary nor sufficient for innateness. It is not sufficient, because prenatal learning is possible; and is it not necessary, because, as Descartes observed long ago, innate characteristics can be acquired quite late in development. (Illustration: pubic hair is plausibly innate but clearly not present at birth.) Similarly, it is sometimes said that innate traits are solely the products of internal (including genetic) causes, even though this is clearly not necessary for innateness, since, like all contemporary theorists, nativists wholeheartedly accept the banal thesis that cognitive traits are caused jointly by internal *and* environmental factors.

In view of the problems with standard claims about innateness, philosophers of psychology have responded in a variety of ways. One response is to conclude that innateness is a confused concept and map out the implications of this for future psychological research. Another response is to try to make systematic sense of the notion of innateness that figures in psychology and allied sciences. Though this is not the place to pursue the matter in detail, at least two proposals merit further consideration. The first is that innate traits are those that are environmentally *canalized*. Roughly put: a trait is innate on this view when it is relatively insensitive to the range of environmental conditions under which it emerges (Ariew 1999). The second suggestion is that an innate psychological trait is one that is *psychologically primitive*. Roughly: it is acquired in the normal course of events, though not by psychological processes, such as learning or perception (Cowie 1999; Samuels 2002). Like so many other issues in the philosophy of psychology, deciding which (if any) of these options to adopt remains a topic for active and ongoing debate.

See also Cognitive science; Observation.

References

Ariew, André (1999) "Innateness Is Canalization: A Defense of a Developmental Account of Innateness," in V. Hardcastle (ed.) *When Biology Meets Psychology*, Cambridge, MA: MIT Press.

Carruthers, Peter (2006) *The Architecture of the Mind: Massive Modularity and the Flexibility of Thought*, Oxford: Oxford University Press.

Chomsky, Noam (1980) *Rules and Representations*, New York: Columbia University Press.

Chouinard, M. M. and Clark, E. V. (2003) "Adult Reformulations of Child Errors as Negative Evidence," *Journal of Child Language* 30: 637–69.

Cowie, Fiona (1999) *What's Within? Nativism Reconsidered*, New York: Oxford University Press.

Fodor, J. A. (1975) *The Language of Thought*, New York: Thomas Crowell.

—— (1983) *The Modularity of Mind*, Cambridge, MA: MIT Press.

Fodor, J. and Pylyshyn, Z. (1988) "Connectionism and Cognitive Architecture: A Critical Analysis," *Cognition* 28: 3–71.

Ford, K. M. and Pylyshyn, Z. W. (eds) (1996) *The Robot's Dilemma Revisited: The Frame Problem in Artificial Intelligence*, Norwood, NJ: Ablex.

Griffiths, Paul (2002) "What Is Innateness?" *Monist* 85: 70–85.

Marcus, Gary F. (2001) *The Algebraic Mind*, Cambridge, MA: MIT Press.

Pereira, Fernando (2000) "Formal Grammar and Information Theory: Together Again?" in *Philosophical Transactions of the Royal Society* A358: 1239–53.

Port, R. and van Gelder, T. J. (1995) *Mind as Motion: Explorations in the Dynamics of Cognition*, Cambridge, MA: MIT Press.

Preston, John and Bishop, Michael (eds) (2002) *Views into the Chinese Room: New Essays on Searle and Artificial Intelligence*, New York: Oxford University Press.

Samuels, Richard (2002) "Nativism in Cognitive Science," *Mind and Language* 17: 233–65.

Searle, John (1999) "The Chinese Room," in R. A. Wilson and F. Keil (eds) *The MIT Encyclopedia of the Cognitive Sciences*, Cambridge, MA: MIT Press.

Sloman, S. A. (1996) "The Empirical Case for Two Systems of Reasoning," *Psychological Bulletin* 119: 3–22.

Stanovich, K. E. (2004) *The Robot's Rebellion: Finding Meaning in the Age of Darwin*, Chicago: University of Chicago Press.

Further reading

There are a number of good anthologies and introductory texts in the philosophy of psychology: José Luis Bermúdez, *Philosophy of Psychology: A Contemporary Introduction* (New York: Routledge, 2005); Andy Clark, *Mindware: An Introduction to the Philosophy of Cognitive Science* (Oxford: Oxford University Press, 2001); and George Botterill and Peter Carruthers, *The Philosophy of Psychology* (Cambridge University Press, 1999) all provide good, though quite different, introductions to the field. Denise Delarosa Cummins and Robert Cummins (eds) *Minds, Brains and Computers* (Oxford: Blackwell, 2000) contains many influential papers, especially on computational approaches to cognition; and the relative merits of classicism and connectionism are discussed at length in Cynthia Macdonald and Graham Macdonald (eds) *Connectionism: Debates on Psychological Explanation* (Oxford: Blackwell, 1995). For very different assessments of connectionist theory see: William Bechtel and Adele Abrahamson, *Connectionism and the Mind*, 2nd edn (Malden, MA: Blackwell, 2002); and Gary Marcus, *The Algebraic Mind* (Cambridge, MA: MIT Press, 2001). For discussion of various facets of debate over nativism, see Cowie (1999); and for differing treatments of modularity, see Steven Pinker, *How the Mind Works* (New York: W. W. Norton, 1997); Jerry Fodor, *The Mind Doesn't Work That Way* (Cambridge, MA: MIT Press, 2000). For an impressive range of papers on innateness and modularity, see Peter Carruthers, Stephen Laurence, and Stephen Stich's 3-volume *The Innate Mind* (New York: Oxford University Press, 2005, 2006, 2007). Finally, Rob Stainton (ed.) *Contemporary Debates in Cognitive Science* (Malden, MA: Blackwell, 2006) contains state-of-the-art discussions of many central topics in the philosophy of psychology.

55
SOCIAL SCIENCES
Harold Kincaid

Under the rubric of "the social sciences" falls an enormous and diverse body of topics, methods, and results. From this diverse body of work I have I chosen four topics with implications for the social sciences and philosophy of science in general: the role of idealized models, the place of individual behavior in social explanation, the status of teleological and evolutionary explanations, and the role of values.

Models and reality

One key issue in the philosophy of the social sciences concerns the use of models that make unrealistic or false assumptions. Such models are widespread and they give rise to several puzzles. How can a model using false assumptions explain the real world? How can we tell when these unrealistic models are supported by the evidence rather than being just fanciful stories?

It will be helpful to have some concrete examples to hand before turning to the issues. One standard result in micro-economic theory is that firms will produce that quantity of goods such that the marginal revenue – the price on the last unit sold – is equal to the price of the good. This result follows from a model that assumes, among other things, that firms maximize profits and that firms are price-*takers*, i.e. that no firm is large enough compared to the size of the market to influence price by its decisions. Those assumptions might not be true. Firms might have goals other than that of profit maximization. The number of firms might be small, sufficiently small that their decisions on how much to produce influences price. Governments might set mandatory production quotas in time of war. So the question arises whether firms in the real world will actually produce that amount which equates marginal revenue and price.

Note that there are two different kinds of unrealistic assumptions at work here – what we might call *idealizations* and *abstractions*. Idealizations assume that some factor in the model is approximately like the real world. So in a given real market, the firms might be small enough relative to the size of the market that they have very little influence on price. Abstractions are assumptions in a model that altogether omit certain factors: thus to assume no government interference is to engage in abstraction.

One response to such unrealistic aspects of social science models is to deny that they matter so long as the models employing them successfully predict, the view advocated by Nobel Prize winning economist Milton Friedman (1953). The response adopts the general position on the status of theories known as *instrumentalism* in the philosophy of science. Instrumentalism holds that the job of theories is not to explain but to predict – they are tools for saving the phenomena.

There are some fairly convincing objections to instrumentalism and these apply to any version of it in the social sciences. We want theories that explain *why* things happen, not just tell us what will happen. We want to know that past successful predictions will hold up in the future, and we want evidence that the model in question cites real underlying causes of the phenomena we observe.

Another route to justifying unrealistic models in the social sciences is in effect to deny that there are falsehoods involved. The general claims of the social sciences such as price equals marginal revenue are really generalizations with an implicit clause saying "assuming other things are equal." Thus the laws used to explain are not false but are qualified *ceteris paribus*. This view is sometimes supported by arguments that even in physics the fundamental laws are qualified *ceteris paribus* (see Cartwright 1983) – the force on a body due to gravity is equal to mass multiplied by acceleration *only assuming no other physical forces are present*.

Several objections have been raised against this defense (Earman and Roberts 1999; Earman, Roberts, and Smith 2002). There is the worry that treating social science claims as being qualified *ceteris paribus* renders them either non-falsifiable or else superfluous. Either we can specify what the "other things being equal" are or we cannot do so. If we cannot, then social claims qualified *ceteris paribus* seem unfalsifiable, for every failed prediction has an "out" – other things weren't equal. If in fact we can specify what those "other things" are and show that the model is accurate when they are present, then those conditions can just be added in and we do not need to think of social science claims as qualified *ceteris paribus* at all. Moreover, it is not clear that the basic laws of physics *are* qualified *ceteris paribus*. It is true that the fundamental laws describe different fundamental forces and that real explanations frequently have to combine those forces. However, in many cases it is possible to say how the forces combine.

Perhaps a more defensible version of the "other things being equal" strategy is to adopt what is called the *semantic view* of theories. Putting complexities aside, the semantic view denies that theories are set of statements that are either true or false of the world. Theories instead are definitions of abstract entities – possible models. Thus the theory of evolution is defining a possible entity, namely, a Darwinian system. That system is one in which there is heritable variation and selection. On the semantic view of theories it is a separate and further empirical question whether anything in the world corresponds to the abstract entity described by the theory.

Viewing social science theories from the semantic perspective certainly avoids the awkwardness of claiming that social science generalizations are true *ceteris paribus*. However, it may be that it does so simply by putting the problem elsewhere, for we still have the issue to address of which models actually describe the world and which do not – or, put differently, how does a model of possible reality explain the actual world if it makes assumptions not true of it?

Those questions are pursued by a sizable literature in general philosophy of science on the role of models which provides several alternative ways to tell whether a model is explanatory:

- It provides *insight* – an informal rationale common among social scientists as a defense of particular models.
- It *unifies*, i.e. shows how different phenomena might be captured by the same model (Morgan and Morrison 1999).
- It serves as an *instrument* – we can do things with it (*ibid.*).
- It is *isomorphic* to the phenomena of interest (Giere 1990).

No doubt there is something to each of those claims. Yet none of them by itself seems sufficient to help us tell the good–unrealistic models from the bad–unrealistic models. Insight threatens to be nothing more than a warm, fuzzy intellectual feeling – we need some kind of explanation of what insight is, how we tell when it is legitimate, and so on. Models that apply across diverse phenomena generally gain some kind of support from doing so. However, it is also possible to tell the same false story over and over again about different phenomena. Many have accused advocates of rational choice models with highly unrealistic assumptions (perfect foresight, etc) of doing just that. Likewise, it is surely right that models serve multiple functions, among them allowing manipulation of components to determine consequences. Still, we can manipulate an abstract model that applies to nothing at all. Under what circumstances does the manipulation of an abstract model show that it captures real processes rather than imaginary ones?

Without further detail, the idea that good models are those that stand in some kind of one-to-one relationship with things in the world is also insufficient, though it is more promising than the previous criteria. How do the idealizations of a model stand in a one-to-one relation to the world exactly? Do the agents with perfect foresight in the market economy model stand in such a relation to real world agents? We can posit a relation, but the question still seems to remain whether doing so explains anything. Moreover, when models are based on abstractions – on leaving out factors – there is presumably nothing in the model that represents them. How do I know that is not a problem?

One reasonable route around the problems cited above is to focus on finding *causes*. If we have evidence that a model with unrealistic assumptions is picking out the causes of certain effects, then we can to that extent use it to explain, despite the "irrealism." If I can show that my *insight* is that a particular causal process is operative, then I am doing more than reporting a warm feeling. If I can show that the same causal process is behind different phenomena, then *unification* is grounded in reality. If I can provide evidence that I use my model as an *instrument* because it allows me to describe real causes, I can have confidence in it. Finally, if I can show that the causes postulated in the model are operative in the world, I can begin to provide evidence that the model really *does* explain.

How is it possible to show that a model picks out real causes even though it is unrealistic? Social scientists adopt a number of strategies to do so. Sometimes it is possible to show that as an idealization is made more realistic, the model in question improves in its predictive power. Another strategy is doing what is known as a "sensitivity analysis." Various possible complicating factors can be modeled to see their influence on outcomes. If the predictions of a model hold up regardless of the complicating factors that are added in, we have some reason to think the model captures the causal processes, despite its idealizations or abstractions. There are a number of other such methods potentially available to social scientists. After all, the natural sciences use idealizations and abstractions with success on a regular basis, so there must be ways of dealing with them.

Mechanisms and individuals

Related but somewhat orthogonal to those issues are controversies over the mechanisms needed in social explanations, in particular mechanisms in terms of the actions of individuals. This is closely related to a longstanding debate over methodological individualism in the social sciences, which is roughly the view that all explanations in the social sciences should be in terms of individuals.

The idea that all social phenomena can be explained in terms of individuals can be taken as a reductionist thesis. A theory A reduces to a theory B when it can be shown that in principle everything explained by A can be explained by B. Since different theories use different vocabularies, there must be some way of connecting the categories of the two theories. Usually this is thought to require *bridge laws* – statements of the form "Category of theory A applies if and only if category of theory B applies." For example, the laws relating pressure and temperature of a gas have arguably been reduced to Newton's laws applied to molecules. Doing that required equating *temperature* – a category of the theory of gases that is to be reduced – with the *mean kinetic energy* of molecules, thus allowing explanations of temperature to be expressed in terms of molecules. Thus, to explain all social phenomena in individualist terms, we need bridge laws connecting social categories to descriptions of the behavior of individuals.

There are various potential obstacles to producing such reductions. The most frequently cited problem is that of *multiple realization*. Multiple realization occurs when a category from one kind of description can be brought about in indefinitely many ways when described with different categories from another kind of vocabulary. So, for example, "chairs" arguably have indefinitely many different physical realizations and thus physical descriptions. When one vocabulary is multiply realized in another, there will not be bridge laws relating the two – there is no statement of the form "The category chair applies only when such and such a physical description is true." In effect, the term "chair" does explanatory work for us that cannot be had at the level of physical detail. Of course, we could try to define "chair" by simply combining different kinds of chairs – rocking-chair, armchair, etc. Yet that would only be a disjointed list, not a description we would expect to hold up when designers create new kinds of chairs.

There are good reasons to think that the social sciences are irreducible to explanations in terms of individuals because social scientific categories do something similar for us – they identify patterns not capturable at the individual level. Thus there are numerous things we can say about business firms and their behavior, both in economics and other social sciences. Firms and their actions such as profit-maximization are arguably multiply realized in the behavior of individuals; there are indefinitely many collections of individual behaviors that can make up a firm and its actions. We can furthermore give a good reason why that should be so: the competitive process that determines which firms survive and which do not "cares" about firm profitability, not about the details of how it comes about.

Reductionism is a strong thesis. Claims that the social sciences need mechanisms and need them in terms of individuals might still be plausible even if reductionism is false. While this claim is popular, it is seldom explicitly stated what the thesis is and what the arguments for it are. At least the following distinctions need to be made:

- *Mechanisms as continuous causal processes and componential analysis*: Wesley Salmon advocated the former thesis, which is arguably a modern-day instantiation of the *mechanical philosophy* in physics which rejected action at a distance. Mechanism in the componential sense thinks that explanation proceeds in explaining a complex whole by invoking the elements comprising the whole and their interaction. Identifying continuous causal processes need not involve identifying element mechanisms.
- *Horizontal vs. vertical mechanisms*: a continuous causal process involves specifying the intervening steps between a given cause and its ultimate effect, a horizontal mechanism. Identifying the components of a complex whole is giving a vertical mechanism – explaining the behavior or causal capacities of a complex whole by identifying component elements and their relations.
- *Mechanisms as necessary for any successful explanation vs. mechanisms as necessary for complete explanation*: The notion of *complete explanation* is not without its ambiguities, but roughly one explanation is more complete than another when it answers more questions or cites more causes. If mechanisms are necessary, no questions are answered without them.
- *Mechanisms at different levels of detail*: the notion of *the mechanism* is incoherent, for we always have a causal process picked out under a description that can be at various levels of detail. What is the mechanism of inheritance, for example? We can describe it as genes without giving details about how genes work, or as DNA replication without giving the quantum mechanical details, etc.

A first question about the demand for individualist mechanisms is why must the mechanism be at the individual level? I might explain the mechanism connecting inflation and interest rates by citing other macro-economic variables connecting the two. I certainly can imagine that providing individual-level detail can sometimes be quite fruitful, but I see no argument that they are the only kinds of mechanisms that can be so.

A second question is whether the strong claim that mechanisms are *essential* can be upheld. A *reductio* argument is hard to ignore: if mechanisms at the finest level of detail are essential, then we have no well-confirmed explanations until we know all the quantum mechanical details, i.e. most of the sciences do not explain.

The reasonable conclusion seems to be that individualist mechanisms can be useful, but only that. Three of the key factors determining when individualist mechanisms seem to be important are:

1 Does a given social explanation involve very strong presuppositions about the behavior of individuals?
2 How confident are we about our knowledge at the social level?
3 How confident are we in our knowledge at the individual level? When a social theory makes strong assumptions about individuals in areas where we have good evidence about individual behavior and the social theories are speculative, mechanisms can be quite important. However, we are not always in that situation.

Evolution and function

From their inception in the nineteenth century, the social sciences have invoked evolutionary ideas and claimed that things in the social world – norms, institutions, etc. – have functions; in fact, Spencer's notions of *competition* and *selection* in the *social realm* were a major influence on Darwin. Two basic questions confront evolutionary notions in the social sciences since Darwin: how do their explanations relate to those of evolutionary biology? Can the social sciences provide a rational basis for teleology in the way that Darwin did in biology?

Some examples of where such questions arise will be useful background. The social sciences past and present regularly claim that various social practices exist *in order to* have some effect. So Marx thought that the state exists in order to protect the interests of the ruling class. Durkheim claimed that the division of labor exists in order to promote social solidarity. How are we to understand and evaluate these claims?

Some philosophers have approached the question of *teleology* in large part by attempting to explicate the idea that something has a *function*. The project here is to look for individually necessary and jointly sufficient conditions for use of the term "function" tested by our ordinary intuitions. While various useful things have come from this literature, I think its general goal is misguided. Many useful concepts do not have the strict boundaries that this project requires. And ordinary language intuitions, even those of scientists, may not do much to clarify the scientific issues involved.

One useful distinction that has arisen out of this literature concerns two different ways of understanding the idea that something has a function. In the philosophy of mind and cognitive psychology literature, component parts of our cognitive architecture have a function in that they have a specific causal role in systems. This idea of breaking complex systems into subsystems with specified interactions has a long history in the social sciences as well. This sense of "function" needs to be distinguished from the further, stronger claim that something exists in order to fulfill its function. Marx did not just believe that the state protects the interests of the ruling class, he also believed in some sense that it is there *because it does so*.

One way to understand such claims is as causal claims about specific feedback processes. If a practice, norm, institution at one instance has a certain causal effect and then persists thereafter because it has that effect, then "existing in order to" can be understood as a specific type of causal relation. Darwinian natural selection would then be one possible instance of this general causal pattern: a gene has specific effect and via differential survival and heritability of the trait, it persists in the population.

Genetic variation and natural selection are not the only ways of instantiating this causal pattern. For example, an area of sociology known as "organization ecology" studies the strategies of organizations in dealing with their environments, and provides evidence that there are differences in the survival and birth of organizations of different types according to which strategy works best in which environment. Here organizational strategies exist because they promote survival. There are numerous areas in the social sciences that make these types of causal claim. Boyd and Richerson (2005), for example, develop models and evidence for such processes in the transmission of culture.

The most general objection to evolutionary thinking in the social sciences is that it makes illicit biological analogies. For example, it is frequently argued that there are no "social genes" to serve as the unit of heritance and that social institutions do not reproduce. However, such criticisms miss the target if we take seriously the distinction made above between the general causal pattern of something existing because of the effects it has and standard Darwinian natural selection as one way of bringing about this general causal pattern. Literal copying of coded information is not required; nor is reproduction. Indeed, philosophers of biology (Godfrey-Smith 2000; Harms 2004) have noticed that there are important selectionist processes in biology that are not realized by literal copying and survival of genes.

So I would argue that there is nothing inherently suspicious about explaining the existence of social practices by their effects. But plenty of difficult issues are still open concerning exactly how those explanations are confirmed in practice.

Fact and value

There is a long held view that the social sciences, like any science, should be value free. However, the historical and sociological turn in science studies made most famous by Kuhn's *The Structure of Scientific Revolutions* has muddied the waters over the issue. The social sciences add further complications, because they are so intimately involved in studying value-laden phenomena and providing policy advice. Of particular interest are the basic categories that social scientists use to explain social phenomena – are they natural kinds like sodium or are they socially constructed and thus value-laden? Also lurking in the background are debates in meta-ethics about the objectivity of moral and political values. So this issue cuts across large swathes of philosophy of science and philosophy more generally.

Getting any traction on these issues requires some careful work upfront to distinguish the different issues involved (see Kincaid, Dupré, and Wylie 2007). We can separate the claim that social science is value-laden into four different dimensions: the kinds of values involved, how they are involved, where they are involved, and what effect their involvement has.

1 *Kinds of values* Social scientists may value truth, but that presumably is not what is meant by value freedom. So we need to distinguish epistemic values from moral and political ones.
2 *How they are involved* Certainly, some science has been motivated by moral and political values, but that may be evidence only of biased science. No one would deny that the social sciences could sometimes be biased in this way. Thus the more interesting claim is not that social science *can* be value-laden but that it *must* be. Another important distinction in the ways values might be involved concerns whether they are directly involved or involved by implication. For example, a social scientific finding that was devoid of values itself might have normative implications once made public.
3 *Where values are involved* Social scientists have personal goals like anyone else – promotion and tenure, grants, and public recognition being chief among them, alongside standard political and moral values. These things may certainly influence the questions social scientists ask. Yet that is still a relatively weak value-ladenness claim, for it is compatible with such values being absent from the evidence provided for the answers they give. There are many aspects of science; finding values in some does not preclude finding none in others.
4 *With what effect* Here the key question is whether the presence of values entails the absence of objectivity and truth.

With these distinctions in mind, let us look at some of the arguments that have been advanced.

Gunnar Myrdal (1970), a Swedish economist working on economic underdevelopment in the 1950s and 1960s, argued that the mainstream economics of his day was value-laden. Economists then, as now, developed models explaining growth that focused on the equilibrium states of their models – on the case where there are no forces for change away from the steady state. Myrdal believed that this emphasis inevitably meant that non-equilibrium phenomena were ignored, phenomena he thought crucial to underdevelopment. The emphasis on equilibrium among mainstream economists derived from, and reinforced, their trust in markets and dislike of government programs – in short, their social and political values.

What does this argument claim to establish and how? Like a great many authors who claim to find values present in science, Myrdal is not entirely explicit about this. I cannot see an argument for the conclusion that values are inevitably involved in the core practice of providing evidence. But there may be one for claiming that they are essentially involved in providing explanations. One way to construe what Myrdal is suggesting is by using recent work on the role of *context* in explanation. A fruitful way of thinking about explanations is that they are answers to questions. Work on the logic of answers and questions suggests that any specific question and the answer to it must be spelled out by contextual factors. If I ask "Why did Adam eat the apple?" I might be asking any one of several possible questions: Why did he eat the apple as opposed to throwing it, etc.? Why did Adam rather than Eve eat the apple? Why did Adam eat an apple rather than a mango, etc.? These are contrast classes and arguably they are made explicit only through knowledge of the audience and the speaker. Contextual factors might also be involved in the kind of answers that are relevant to the question even after the context is specified.

So Myrdal's argument might be that any explanation presumes contextual parameters, that the focus on equilibrium outcomes assumes a specific set of parameters, and that social and political values influence which parameters are assumed. I am not sure that this shows that values are inevitably involved (could the contextual issues be resolved solely on epistemic grounds?), but it does show a way that values can be, and perhaps frequently are, involved in a core activity of economics. What does that entail about objectivity? Once the question is fully specified, the correct answer could be a fully objective matter. The example thus illustrates what I take to be true in general: the question of whether social science is value-laden is really many different questions with no uniform answer or consequence.

Another route to value-ladenness makes use of views on the philosophy of language developed by Quine and others in 1960s. Concepts get their meanings, the argument goes, from their role in the total linguistic system. However, the argument goes on, that system inevitably has moral and political value-laden concepts as well scientific concepts. Therefore there is no prospect of a pristine, value-free language, and thus science is value-laden. Putnam (2004) has put forward some version of this argument about science in general.

I doubt that this argument works in general. Maybe, calling DNA the "master molecule" is an instance of where it works. Yet, surely, similar stories cannot be told about all parts of science. And it is also not clear what the implication is – is molecular biology in its description of the causal process leading from DNA to proteins dependent in its evidence on moral and political values? Can we really not spell this out without invoking gender roles?

However, if the argument does not work in general, there might nonetheless be specific things about the social sciences that make it more compelling there. Root (1993) and Dupré (2007) have made some interesting arguments for saying that it is. One argument is this. Social science is interested essentially in things of importance to human beings. Describing and categorizing those things inevitably involves using "thick" terms with moral connotations. Take, for instance, "spousal abuse." Social scientists study spousal abuse, counting up the number of cases and looking for causes that explain them. Yet, calling something "spousal abuse" is surely to make a value-judgment. One can try to eliminate the value-judgment by searching for "thinner" concepts, for instance, talking of "physical assault." In response, Root and Dupré will doubt that these so-called thinner concepts are entirely bereft of value-judgments and will argue that the thinner a concept gets, the less likely is it to get at what we are interested in.

I am not sure these arguments show that social science inevitably involves moral and political values everywhere and always. Nonetheless, it is interesting to consider what they imply about the objectivity of the social sciences when they are applicable. The standard worry is that moral and political values are subjective and thus that their presence makes the social science that makes use of them subjective as well. This is, of course, a big issue in meta-ethics, one that I cannot address here. Yet, even if moral values are subjective it is not clear that this would make the social sciences inevitably so. Moral assumptions can be made explicit and results can be relativized to those assumptions. So scientists studying spousal abuse might admit upfront their moral assumptions about such abuse – what they count as an instance of it and why. Research results could then be evaluated with those assumptions in mind and alternative results, based on alternative assumptions, could be explored. I see no reason why the results themselves would be subjective.

See also Biology; Explanation; Function; The historical turn in the philosophy of science; Idealization; Laws of nature; Mechanism; Reduction; The structure of theories.

References

Boyd, Robert and Richerson, Peter J. (2005) *The Origin and Evolution of Cultures*, Oxford: Oxford University Press.

Cartwright, Nancy (1983) *How the Laws of Physics Lie*, Oxford: Oxford University Press.

Dupré, John (2007) "Fact and Value," in Kincaid, Dupré, and Wylie (2007).

Earman, John and Roberts, John (1999) "*Ceteris Paribus*, There Are No Provisos," *Synthese* 118: 439–78.

Earman, John, Roberts, John and Smith, Sheldon (2002) "*Ceteris Paribus* Lost," *Erkenntnis* 57: 281–301.

Friedman, Milton (1953) "The Methodology of Positive Economics," in *Essays in Positive Economics*, Chicago: University of Chicago Press.

Giere, Ronald (1990) *Explaining Science*, Chicago: University of Chicago Press.

Godfrey-Smith, Peter (2000) "The Replicator in Retrospect," *Biology and Philosophy* 15: 403–23.

Harms, William F. (2004) *Information and Meaning in Evolutionary Processes*, Cambridge: Cambridge University Press.

Kincaid, Harold, Dupré, John, and Wylie, Alison (eds) (2007) *Value-Free Science: Ideal or Illusion?* Oxford: Oxford University Press.

Morgan, Mary and Morrison, Margaret (eds) (1999) *Models as Mediators*, Cambridge: Cambridge University Press.

Myrdal, Gunnar (1970) *The Challenge of World Poverty: A World Anti-Poverty Program in Outline*, New York: Pantheon.

Putnam, Hilary (2004) *The Fact–Value Distinction and Other Essays*, Cambridge, MA: Harvard University Press.

Root, Michael (1993) *Philosophy of Social Sciences*, Oxford: Blackwell.

Further reading

Friedman (1953) is a classic discussion of the use of unrealistic models. Julian Reiss's "Mechanisms in Social Explanation," *Philosophy of the Social Sciences* (forthcoming) provides a clear survey of the issues involved in providing mechanisms in the social sciences. Dan Hausman's *The Inexact and Separate Science of Economics* (Cambridge: Cambridge University Press, 1992) provides an important early discussion of the *ceteris paribus* problem. C. Hallpike's *Principles of Social Evolution* (New York: Oxford University Press, 1986) develops a sustained critique of functional explanations in the social sciences. Kincaid's *Philosophical Foundations of the Social Sciences* (Cambridge: Cambridge University Press, 1996) discusses those concerns in detail, as well as the many different issues associated with methodological individualism. Carl Hempel's "Science and Human Values," in his *Aspects of Scientific Explanation* (New York: Free Press, 1965) is a classic and insightful early discussion of values in science.

INDEX